Through the Eye of Katrina

Through the Eye of Katrina

Social Justice in the United States

Second Edition

Edited by

Kristin A. Bates
Richelle S. Swan

CAROLINA ACADEMIC PRESS
Durham, North Carolina

Library of Congress Cataloging-in-Publication Data

Through the eye of Katrina : social justice in the United States / [edited by]
Kristin A. Bates, Richelle S. Swan. -- 2nd ed.
    p. cm.
Includes bibliographical references and index.
ISBN 978-1-59460-735-6 (alk. paper)
 1. Hurricane Katrina, 2005--Social aspects. 2. Social justice--United States.
3. Disaster relief--Social aspects--Louisiana--New Orleans. 4. Marginality,
Social--Louisiana--New Orleans. 5. Poor--Government policy--United States.
6. New Orleans (La.)--Race relations. 7. United States--Race relations. I.
Bates, Kristin Ann. II. Swan, Richelle S. III. Title.

 HV636 2005 .N4 T47 2010
 976.3'35064--dc22

                                        2009050356

CAROLINA ACADEMIC PRESS
700 Kent Street
Durham, North Carolina 27701
Telephone (919) 489-7486
Fax (919) 493-5668
www.cap-press.com

*This book is for the victims of Hurricane Katrina
and the victims of social injustice everywhere,
and to those dedicated to the struggle
for social justice and social change.*

Contents

Preface

The struggle for social justice and the study of social justice are not confined to a single discipline. This book is an example of the multidisciplinary nature of this struggle. The chapters of this book represent a vast array of disciplines: Communication, Criminology, Critical Studies, Education, Ethnic Studies, Geography, History, Justice Studies, Law, Political Science, Sociology, Urban Planning, and Women's Studies. It is our hope that those who read this volume will recognize the importance of multiple perspectives in the study of and fight for social justice.

Acknowledgments

A project like this, to be successful, requires a lot of committed people. We would like to thank the authors for their dedication to social justice and their topics; Jill Watts, CSUSM History professor, for her help with the proposal; the faculty, staff, and students in the Department of Sociology at CSUSM for their understanding and support; Rachel Gragg, Federal Policy Director of the Workforce Alliance, for her helpful discussions on poverty public policy; Allison Carr, CSUSM librarian, for her invaluable research help; Jeff Henson for his help with the photographs, and Clayton Bower, Raeven Chandler, Mandi Contreras, Heather Donoho, and especially, Garrett Herr, for assisting in the first round of editing tasks. In addition, we would like to thank the staff at Carolina Academic Press—Beth Hall for answering all those crazy questions throughout the creation of both volumes (and for encouraging a second edition), Karen Clayton for the hours she spent helping us finalize both editions, and Tim Colton for his artistic eye. A special thank you to those who embraced the first edition and gave us such wonderful encouragement and feedback—we appreciate the opportunity to engage in this social justice dialogue.

Finally, projects like these can rarely be undertaken without the commitment and sacrifices of those close to us. Kristin would like to thank her husband, Jeff, and her sons, William and Christopher, for reminding her to spend some time in the land of bad sci-fi movies and dinosaurs; and Richelle, her "daytime partner" for making her a better scholar. Richelle would like to thank Kristin for being such an inspiring collaborator, Chendo for his encouragement throughout the creation of both editions of this book, and her family, friends, and students for all of their support.

Thank you!

Through the Eye of Katrina

Chapter 1

A Dangerous Equation:
Social Injustice = Social Disaster

Richelle S. Swan and Kristin A. Bates

The danger is that the disaster's most far-reaching lessons will be quickly forgotten, as the voices of the city's exiles grow quiet and fresh crises and issues dominate the news.... We can change that by helping our fellow citizens wrestle with the legacy of the disaster while it remains strong in common memory—to give it its due as one of those iconic moments with the power to transform political life and individual hearts and souls. For now America is still wrestling with what happened and why, with what it will mean for those now exiled, with how the disaster affects our common future.... But like the post-9/11 reflection, this newfound concern won't continue automatically. It needs a context in which to bloom. Some of this is already being created, as we weave lessons from the disaster into arguments we're already making on issues from global warming to the war in Iraq, to the dangers of selling America's every institution to the highest bidder. But the tragedy also calls for specific responses.... Suppose every college or high school made New Orleans a focus over the coming year, working, from the perspective of every possible discipline, to explore the interconnected roots and lessons of the disaster.

—Paul Loeb in *Mother Jones*, October 31, 2005

The idea for this book came out of a conversation between colleagues and friends, in some ways a million miles from the devastation of Hurricane Katrina and in other ways right at its back door. As professors teaching in a fledgling new major, criminology and justice studies, we were struggling with ways to facilitate discussion in the classroom about issues of social justice. We wanted this discussion to be multidisciplinary in order to help students get a sense of the breadth and depth of the field of justice studies and to show them how the concept of social justice is wrestled with across disciplines. In addition, we wanted it to be relevant to the world the students were experiencing.

Our fall semester of 2005 had just begun in late August, simultaneous with the development and landfall of the hurricanes that struck the Gulf Coast region. We introduced the topic of Hurricane Katrina in several classroom discussions in the hopes of using student responses to the hurricane and its aftermath as jumping-off points for social justice analyses, and quickly found that student responses ranged from those who saw the relationship between historical, pre-existing structural inequities and the immense devastation of the event to those who had a strong tendency to see social problems as individual-level dilemmas. It became clear to us then and there that as instructors we would benefit from a compilation of scholarly sources that documented and analyzed the intersection of social (in)justice and social disasters. We decided to create a volume of analyses that would bring life to social justice concepts through a case study of Hurricane Katrina—a volume that would embody the ongoing and interdisciplinary examination suggested by Paul Loeb in his quote above.

In order to reach a wide cross-section of scholars, we posted a call for papers on every disciplinary listserv we could think of requesting submissions from social justice scholars. The response was overwhelming and what ultimately transpired has been one of the most rewarding experiences of our professional lives. It has been a privilege to work with the activists and scholars in this volume, as we crafted a multidisciplinary examination of social justice in the United States through the eye of Katrina.

Ever since Hurricane Katrina hit New Orleans and surrounding areas in August 2005, two things have become unmistakable: the physical devastation created by the disaster was enormous and the social divisions that were exposed and then rocked American society in the aftermath of the disaster were equally powerful. The events surrounding Hurricane Katrina offer a remarkable case study of the continuing social divide in the United States. Hurricane Katrina and its aftermath constitute what is probably the most visible, devastating set of events that a community has experienced in some time. The victims of these events—the hurricane and our collective response to it—continue to work to put their lives back together long after the spotlight has dimmed. What these victims know and the rest of us must learn from these events is that this devastation should not have been a surprise—it has been built upon centuries of inequity and bad faith.

As we prepare the second edition of this book in early 2010, we are heartened by the fact that many scholars, activists, and community members have embraced the analysis of Hurricane Katrina as a social justice issue in the years following the disaster. The implications of this case study, although related to a series of interlocking factors that created a disaster, are not limited to the field of disaster studies, but instead, can be applied to general analyses of race, class, gender, and ethnicity in the 21st century United States. What becomes clear as we step back from the analyses in the book, is that social injustice often results in social disaster.

The Birth of the Project:
In/Justice Talk after the Disaster

After Hurricane Katrina struck, popular discussions about justice shifted to include a more frequent, if not more informed, consideration of social justice matters. It has served as a case in which some media outlets generated a dialogue about current issues of race and class in the United States. As professors who teach classes in sociology and justice studies, we were heartened to notice the occasional critical analysis being forwarded amidst the other more superficial analyses, and yet we were eventually dismayed to find that such analyses were all too rare. When they were presented in the media they were often met with vehement opposition and a refusal to acknowledge structural inequality. This held true in the local and national media as well as in our classrooms. We had hoped that analysis of the disaster would allow students to readily make the connections between the concepts of class, race, ethnicity, gender, and the material consequences of the hurricane. Somewhat surprisingly, given the egregious examples of social injustice that were plastered all over national newscasts, we found that student responses to the events were heavily skewed toward those that denied the role of social forces in the tragedy that was unfolding.

Indeed, when our students were asked to engage in an online dialogue about the aftermath of Katrina subsequent to reading an article about displaced residents' views of race and the hurricane, their responses were typically written in the following vein:

> Instead of sitting around and pointing fingers, why don't they jump in and help? All that energy that they are using to complain, they could be more productive and help out the aid workers. This incident down in the South is tragic, but we cannot blame anyone for this disaster, it was a natural disaster, not a man-made disaster. I believe that the injustice that has occurred here is that instead of trying to figure a way out of this mess, people want to do nothing but complain.
>
> (Anonymous undergraduate student, 2005)

The students' discussion, which took place at the very beginning of the semester before any analysis of the hurricane had taken place in the classroom, included frequent references to U.S. Secretary of State Condoleeza Rice's claim that she did not believe that racism and discrimination were at the core of the lackluster federal relief effort because, "No American wants to see another American suffer ..." (as cited in Democracy Now, 2005, n.p.). Her words and the words of other government officials were taken as sufficient evidence for the position that the government's response to the crisis was justifiable and that its form, although inadequate, could be fully attributed to the powerlessness of well-meaning humans in the face of nature's wrath, although ample evidence existed to the contrary.

It became painfully clear that the students would benefit from being exposed to other sources of information on which they could base their positions, such as existing findings from scholarly research that elucidate broad stratification issues and those from emergent research that consider these issues in light of the specifics of the hurricane crisis. This edited volume was created in an effort to incorporate both types of information in one resource and to frame the analyses as ones related directly to the field of justice studies and rooted in the concept of social disaster.

Social Disaster as an In/Justice Concept

What does it mean for a society to be just? Although this question is one that has inspired countless great thinkers, it is one that is typically given very little attention by those outside of activist and academic circles in the United States today. Over the last three decades, popular discussions of justice in this country have come to be dominated by talk of retribution (a "paying back" of specific offenders) and deterrence (prevention of future offending) as the language of crime control has eclipsed all other ways of communicating about justice. This level of discussion privileges an emphasis on individuals—individual wrongs and individual rights—and detracts from serious consideration of group concerns and social justice. The connections between human beings and their social location are often deemed irrelevant, while discussions about race, ethnicity, class, gender, and sexuality, as well as other topics, are dismissed as useless exercises in political correctness.

Those of us who have been inspired to study and teach about social justice issues, issues related to group rights, opportunities, and resources (Barry, 2005), often find ourselves up against a figurative wall when it comes to making the analysis of social in/justice real for our students, family, friends, or other target audiences. Although the exaggerated emphasis on individualism that is part of our cultural training and the media perpetuation of this ideology are clearly powerful influences, we are often surprised at the ease by which others dismiss social justice concerns in spite of their own lived experiences. The resistance to nuanced social analysis at the collective level became more apparent than ever in the aftermath of Hurricane Katrina. This disaster and the subsequent response to it provide an illustration of the ways in which social justice concerns are often denied, minimized and/or ignored, to tragic effect. The Hurricane Katrina event signifies much more than an environmental crisis, but instead epitomizes what we call a *social disaster: a disaster predicated upon and exacerbated by structural inequality and human decision-making.* A social disaster can be triggered by a force of nature, such as a hurricane, but ultimately it is rooted in the choices that society's members make and the prioritization of some lives over others. Social disasters reproduce and reinforce social injustices.

The conceptualization of the events around Hurricane Katrina as a social disaster is one that is in keeping with a branch of disaster studies that situates disasters as social events (see Perry, 2007). Social structure has long been theorized to be both affected by and the cause of disaster (Kreps, 1984, 1985; Quarantelli & Dynes, 1977; Quarantelli, 1998). The redefinition of a disaster from one that is simply generated by natural forces to one that is related to social action is one that has been has been resisted by the public and by some disaster scholars, yet has been gaining in popularity (Stallings, 2002). What is largely absent from definitions of disaster in the traditional disaster studies field is an explicit consideration of the social injustices to which they are related.

As we see it, the role of society must be central to any definitions of disaster, and by extension, such definitions should include an acknowledgment of the injustices that both predate and follow any disaster. Structural injustice is central to this understanding, and has been defined by political philosopher Iris Young (2006a) as:

> ... exist[ing] when social processes put large categories of persons under a systematic threat of domination or deprivation of the means to develop and exercise their capabilities, at the same time these processes enable others to dominate or have a wide range of opportunities for developing or exercising their capacities.... All of the persons who participate by their actions in the ongoing schemes of cooperation that constitute these structures are responsible for them, in the sense that they are part of the process that causes them. (p. 114)

In a social disaster, structural injustices in the form of racism, classism, and a faulty infrastructure, come to bear on the situation and as Young (2006b) commented upon the aftermath of Katrina, "Responsibility has to be spread across a large number of actors, some of whom may not be aware of their contributions, and most of whom act according to rules and practices that we typically regard as normal" (p. 42).

Young's vision of justice as social responsibility, a broad vision of justice that counters popular notions of justice, helps ground the consideration of social disaster and its aftermath. As we continue to contemplate the rebuilding of the Gulf Coast region affected by Hurricane Katrina years after the event, the social responsibility model can help us reimagine society. We can see that it is important that the institutions that we have created, and that individuals continue to collectively re-create daily, must be ones that are accountable to all members of society. Under a global responsibility model, the structural factors that led to faulty decision-making on the part of many individuals in power prior to and after Hurricane Katrina must be acknowledged as affecting the social disaster that emerged if we are interested in creating a just society. The interconnectedness assumed by such a model allows us to change the focus of our analysis of disaster and to envision what a society that is "civil," or embodies civility, looks like. To do so makes it clear that the recovery efforts related to a social disaster cannot be relegated to non-profit agencies or private charities, but instead, must be addressed directly by our most powerful governmental bodies. In a country in which neoliberalism and individualism reign, it is a challenge to forward such a model of justice, but it is all the more crucial in order to stop the reproduction of social injustices through our responses to disasters.

Looking at Hurricane Katrina through Multiple Lenses

In order to begin to understand the human role in the particular impact that the disaster had in the hurricane-stricken areas, and construction of the reaction to the disaster, it is necessary to traverse the boundaries of any one discipline and to utilize the contributions of multiple disciplines. This approach is keeping in line with the field of justice studies, which calls for interdisciplinary and multidisciplinary examination of justice-related issues. This volume includes scholarly articles examining the continued struggle for social justice from the perspectives of communication, criminology, education, ethnic studies, history, justice studies, law, political science, and sociology. This multidisciplinary case study approach is a highly effective way of helping readers understand contemporary debates about justice including the roles of historically persistent structural inequality, racism and classism, media portrayals of life-changing events, government reactions and responsibilities in the face of crises, and the role of public policy and activism in response to social injustices.

This collection of articles is divided into three sections representing the causes of, consequences of, and responses to social injustice as illustrated through Hurricane Katrina. The first section, *Images from the Past: Social Justice and Hurricane Katrina in Context* examines the structural inequality and cultural divisions in the United States that make a just response to disaster difficult. The second section, *Images of the Disaster: Reactions to Hurricane Katrina*, offers analyses of the continuing struggle for social justice in the face of an event of the magnitude of Hurricane Katrina. The third section, *Images of the Future: Policy, Activism, and Justice*, focuses on public policy and activist responses that are potential avenues to a more just society.

Images from the Past: Social Justice and Hurricane Katrina in Context

The first section of this book includes five articles devoted to a discussion of conditions in New Orleans and the United States leading up to Hurricane Katrina. These chapters examine conditions in the United States that exacerbated the fate of victims of Hurricane Katrina in the aftermath of the storm. In Chapter 2, "Setting the Stage: Roots of Social Inequality and the Human Tragedy of Hurricane Katrina," Miller and Rivera reveal the historical underpinnings of the social disaster that followed one of the worst hurricanes to hit the U.S. soil. While the physical damage of this hurricane cannot be denied, Miller and Rivera examine the historical responses to the many hurricanes and floods that had occurred in the South, specifically the Mississippi Valley and New Orleans, and contend that given the region's long history of racial conflict and oppression, the experiences of victims after Hurricane Katrina looks remarkably similar to the experiences of those who lived through earlier devastations.

Chapter 3, "'Revolutions May Go Backwards': The Persistence of Voter Disenfranchisement in the United States," by Inderbitzin, Fawcett, Uggen, and Bates examines the use of voter disenfranchisement to silence marginalized communities in the United States. They argue that while most forms of voter disenfranchisement have been found illegal in this country, disenfranchisement is nonetheless used as a way to control racial and ethnic minority communities. This control, leading to less civic engagement and less political capital, they argue, was used in the months right after the hurricane to limit the ability of victims of the storm to vote in primary and mayoral elections.

In Chapter 4, "Locked and Loaded: The Prison Industrial Complex and the Response to Hurricane Katrina," Agid examines perhaps the most overt form of social control, the prison industrial complex, and its effect on the ability of communities to respond in a just manner to the plight of the victims of the storm. Using the state response to Hurricane Katrina as the example, Agid argues that the growth of the prison industrial complex since the late 1960s has made anything but a "law-and-order" response to community disasters nearly impossible. Swan, in Chapter 5, "Social Justice Movements: Education Disregarded, Lessons Ignored," analyzes the major lessons of three of the country's most important social justice movements: the civil rights movement, the labor movement, and the environmental justice movement, and demonstrates that these movements have long pointed out social facts that have traditionally fallen on unresponsive ears. Those who have been involved in the movements, or have paid heed to their lessons, were quite aware of the social realities that subsequently colored the disaster that followed in Katrina's wake, thus explaining the chasm between those people shocked by Katrina's aftermath and those who were saddened and/or outraged, but basically unsurprised. Finally, in Chapter 6, "Reminders of Poverty,

Soon Forgotten," Keyssar offers an historical analysis of poverty policy in the United States, and suggests that the U.S. is a country that has never offered a sound policy devoted to reducing poverty, and one that has regressed in this respect since the last comprehensive attempts to do so in the 1930s and 1960s. As with the prior chapters, Keyssar's analysis establishes a context for the disaster and demonstrates that the response to the hurricane was an extension of pre-existing responses to social injustice.

Images of the Disaster: Reactions to Hurricane Katrina

The second section of the book contains eight articles examining the days, weeks, and months directly following the hurricane. The first two articles analyze current racial discourse in the United States, using the media and societal reactions to Hurricane Katrina and its victims to argue that racist ideologies are an unsurprising, even routine response in U.S. culture. Using media discourse, Doane, in Chapter 7, "New Song, Same Old Tune: Racial Discourse in the Aftermath of Hurricane Katrina," argues that Hurricane Katrina was a racial event that illustrates the continuing racial divisions in the United States. Moon and Hurst, in Chapter 8, "'Reasonable Racism': The 'New' White Supremacy and Hurricane Katrina," also examine this racial discourse by showing that the same themes that can be found in white supremacist discussions on the web can also be found in the general discourse of race through the media and in everyday discussions that invoke race and ethnicity. The authors of both chapters reveal that the institutionalization of racism poses formidable challenges to the notion that racial and ethnic equity has emerged during the time period following the heyday of the civil rights era.

The next two chapters in this section examine the "invisible" experience of racial and ethnic minorities beyond the construction of the black/white divide. Illustrating the experiences of Latino/as and Vietnamese Americans, Trujillo-Pagán, in Chapter 9, "Katrina's Latinos: What Natural Events Tell Us About Social Disasters Among New Orleans' Latinos," and Leong, Airriess, Chen, Keith, Li, Wang, and Adams, in Chapter 10, "From Invisibility to Hypervisibility: The Complexity of Race, Survival, and Resiliency for the Vietnamese American Community in Eastern New Orleans," argue that many racial and ethnic minority communities were ignored altogether in favor of simplified conversations about race and ethnicity that often used them as scapegoats. Each of these articles documents the experience of racial and ethnic minority communities that were left out of media analyses and are much needed additions to an ongoing discussion about contemporary race matters in the United States.

Chapters 11 and 12 examine media responses before and after the hurricane closely, suggesting that the responses that were forthcoming were ineffectual and misguided. In Chapter 11, "Disaster Pornography: Hurricane Katrina,

Voyeurism, and the Television Viewer," Bates and Ahmed examine the media coverage of the events immediately following the hurricane and illustrate that the response from the media and television viewer dehumanized the victims of this disaster, allowing the television viewer to think of these victims as objects rather than human beings. They claim that ultimately the coverage was tantamount to a form of disaster pornography and back up their claim by drawing upon feminist work on and legal considerations of sexual pornography. Lachlan, Spence, and Eith, in Chapter 12, "Access to Mediated Emergency Messages: Differences in Crisis Knowledge Across Age, Race, and Socioeconomic Status," argue that individuals do not receive important emergency information in the same manner and that emergency messages that are too general, inadequate, and that do not target specific communities, will in the end miss their intended targets. The findings of this article support the findings of the earlier chapters of Trujillo-Pagán and Leong et al. that demonstrate that emergency information about the oncoming hurricane was not adequately relayed to either the Latino or Vietnamese American communities.

Finally, the last two chapters of this section examine the societal perceptions of victims of the hurricane and how these perceptions affected the likelihood that victims were received as "deserving" of help. Haubert Weil, in Chapter 13, "Discrimination, Segregation, and the Racialized Search for Housing Post-Katrina," documents her experiences searching for housing after being displaced by the hurricane, and the racialized nature of the help being offered to victims. She finds that racial segregation was perpetuated during the months after Hurricane Katrina as a subset of those offering to help victims of the disaster extended an offer of help to "whites only"—some actually using the reasoning that existing segregation and racism made continued segregation and racism necessary. And in Chapter 14, "The Voices of Katrina: Ethos, Race, and Congressional Testimonials," Check examines the reception that black victims of Hurricane Katrina received in a Congressional hearing designed to address the claims of racism made by witnesses to the aftermath of the hurricane. Check shows that the experiences of these witnesses who testified fairly mirrored the experiences they had had while in New Orleans—they were discounted and dismissed.

Images of the Future: Policy, Activism, and Justice

The final section of the book examines the local, state, and federal government responses to Hurricane Katrina as well as activist responses to the social disaster. In a number of chapters, suggestions for supporting social justice through changes in public policy and increased efforts in social activism are also raised.

In Chapter 15, "George Bush Does Not Care About Black People: Hip-Hop and the Struggle for Katrina Justice," Leonard examines the role of hip-hop music as a tool for activism. Leonard argues that while hip-hop has been demonized (and consequently, those who are associated with it—black and brown youth and the urban poor), there is a strong subset of hip-hop artists (perhaps most notably illustrated by the very public pronouncement of Kanye West) and hip-hop music that advocate for social change and a more just society. Chapter 21, a new chapter written for this edition of the book, also examines the issue of social activism. In his chapter, "Redistributions of Responsibility: Gendered Divisions of Labor and the Politics of Post-Disaster Cleanup Projects," David examines the effect of the gendered work of volunteering on the creation of socially just responses to disaster. He does this by means of a case study of Katrina Krewe, a women-led community organization that engaged in clean-up efforts after the hurricane. David analyzes the resiliency exemplified by the women in this group, and questions the effect of their gendered activism on conceptualizations of responsibility and the societal division of labor post-disasters.

Arena, in Chapter 20, "Whose City Is It? Public Housing, Public Sociology, and the Struggle for Social Justice in New Orleans Before and After Katrina," documents the very public struggle for housing rights pre- and post-Katrina. Arena advocates for the use of public sociology, the intersection of sociology and activism, to address social ills, and documents his struggle in the New Orleans public housing movement. In the same vein, Foster, in Chapter 16, "Ordinary Struggle and the 'Public Good': Navigating Vernacular Voices, State Power, and the Public Sphere in Quests for Social Justice," discusses the importance of including the "ordinary" voices of the general public when addressing social problems and advocating for social change. She does this through an analysis that juxtaposes media coverage of the Katrina aftermath with that of coverage of public housing closures resulting from federal welfare law changes and demonstrates that the inclusion of vernacular voices increases the likelihood of a socially just outcome.

Chapters 17 and 19 focus on the federal government's response to Hurricane Katrina and disaster scenarios in general and posit that the federal government needs to take more responsibility for the well-being of their citizens in times of crisis. Travis, in Chapter 17, "Human Rights in Disaster Policy: Improving the Federal Response to Natural Disasters, Disease Pandemics, and Terrorist Attacks," claims that the federal government needs to prioritize housing and health care, disparities in access to essential services, and deficiencies in disaster preparedness information—concentrating on those with the least power, racial and ethnic minorities, the urban poor, single mothers and their children, and seniors on fixed incomes. In his article, Travis focuses not only on the poor responses to Hurricane Katrina, but also upon the problems generated by disaster planning prior to 9/11, and several predicted future disasters—such as another terrorist attack or a flu pandemic. Stillman and Villmoare, in Chapter 19, "Social Justice after Katrina: The Need for a Revitalized Public Sphere," also make the argument that the government needs to become more responsible during these times of crisis. In their article, they trace the history of disaster relief efforts, focusing specifically on FEMA as the federal agency theoretically responsible for managing disaster relief in the United States, and claim that a strengthened, more accountable public sphere is vital to successful social justice efforts and is easily justified. Chapter 22, "The Disappearing Neighborhood: An Urban Planner's Tour of New Orleans," by Knowles-Yánez, offers a planner's perspective of the recovery effort nearly two years after Hurricane Katrina hit New Orleans. In her article, Knowles-Yánez argues that with the disappearance of grocery stores, housing, and schools, post-Katrina New Orleans neighborhoods are likely to disappear, too. As with Chapters 17 and 19, Knowles-Yánez points to the problems with the federal and local government responses to the disaster as adding to the likelihood of the disappearing neighborhood in New Orleans.

Chapter 18, "Hurricane Katrina and the Nation's Obligation to Black Colleges," by Gasman and Drezner advocates for a concerted awareness of the importance of black colleges to the social justice movement. Gasman and Drezner trace the history of black colleges in and around New Orleans, their success in offering education to black individuals, many who may not have the opportunity for a quality education elsewhere, the importance this has for the nation as a whole, and the impact that Hurricane Katrina had on their ability to continue this work. The authors state that while concerted, systematic federal help is needed, individuals can make a difference by donating to black colleges in New Orleans and around the nation. Another new chapter for this edition, Chapter 23, "Social Justice, Planning, and Opportunity Post-Katrina" by Knowles-Yánez, considers the theory and practice behind socially just urban planning. Her article looks at the challenges and opportunities that emerged in New Orleans after Hurricane Katrina as planners, urban planning students, and community members worked together to on rebuilding projects. Ultimately, she finds that although structural injustice constrains socially just planning, positive developments are occurring in the discipline and on the ground. Our final chapter, Chapter 24, "You CAN Get There from Here, but the Road is Long and Hard: The Role of Public, Private, and Activist Organizations in the Search for Social Justice" brings the volume full circle by examining the relationship between various forms of social institutions, their responses (or lack thereof) to the social disaster that was Hurricane Katrina, and recommendations related to the creation of a more socially just society.

Although this volume as a whole sheds light upon the various obstacles that make the road to justice a bumpy one, it also reveals some exciting possibilities for social change and concrete methods that are currently being utilized in order to make this country a more just one. It is in this spirit that we have chosen to conclude the volume, in the hopes that the reader will be inspired to learn more about social justice and to act in its name.

References

Barry, Brian. (2005). *Why social justice matters.* Cambridge, UK: Polity Press.

Democracy Now. (2005, Sept. 7). Three displaced New Orleans residents discuss race and Hurricane Katrina. *Democracy Now online.* Retrieved September 10, 2005 from http://www.democracynow.org/article.pl?sid=05/09/07/1415225.

Kreps, G.A. (1984). Sociological inquiry and disaster research. *Annual Review of Sociology,* 10, 309–330.

———. (1985). Disaster and the social order. *Sociological Theory,* 3(1), 49–64.

Loeb, P. (2005, October 31). Hard questions about the big easy. *Mother Jones.* Retrieved December 13, 2005 from http://www.motherjones.com/commentary/columns/2005/10/hard_questions.html.

Perry, R.W. (2007). What is a disaster? pp. 1–15 in H. Rodríguez, E.L. Quarantelli, and R.R. Dynes (Eds.) *Handbook of Disaster Research.* New York: Springer.

Quarantelli, E. L. (1998). What is a disaster? Perspectives on the question. New York: Routledge.

Quarantelli, E. L. & Dynes, R. R. (1977). "Response to Social Crisis and Disaster." *Annual Review of Sociology,* 3, 23–49.

Stallings, R. A. (2002). Weberian political sociology and sociological disaster studies. *Sociological Forum,* 17(2), 281–305.

Young, I.M. (2006a). Katrina: Too much blame, not enough responsibility. *Dissent,* pp. 41–46.

———. (2006b). Responsibility and global justice: A social connection model. *Social Philosophy and Policy,* 102–130.

Images from the Past: Social Justice and Hurricane Katrina in Context

Chapter 2

Setting the Stage: Roots of Social Inequity and the Human Tragedy of Hurricane Katrina

DeMond Shondell Miller and Jason David Rivera

In the aftermath of Hurricane Katrina, inhabitants of the United States experienced a collective shock as millions of their fellow citizens' cries for help initially went unheard. The poorest residents of New Orleans seemed to be the most vulnerable to the ill-crafted policies of the past that today spawn high levels of social distress, unemployment, rampant alienation, neglect of communities, and practical isolation. Atkins and Moy (2005) argued that this human tragedy may seem to be an anomaly, but it is part of past and present social inequities.

The Hurricane Everyone Feared

The National Weather Service records indicate that on August 23, 2005, Hurricane Katrina initially developed as a tropical depression 175 miles southeast of Nassau, Bahamas, and on August 24 was upgraded to a tropical storm. The storm moved on a northwesterly and then westerly track through the Bahamas, strengthening to a Category 1 hurricane by the time it reached landfall between Hallandale Beach and North Miami Beach, Florida, on August 25. Katrina then moved southwesterly across Florida, dropping over a foot of rain, ripping down trees and power lines, and damaging homes and businesses. On August 28, after crossing Florida, Katrina entered the Gulf of Mexico, about 250 miles south-southeast of the mouth of the Mississippi River, by which time Katrina had strengthened into a Category 5 hurricane. When Katrina's winds reached a peak of 175 miles per hour, the hurricane turned northwest and then north making its second landfall on August 29 in Plaquemines Parish, Louisiana, where it sustained winds of 140 miles per hour. Katrina continued north and made landfall again along the Louisiana/Mississippi border with wind speeds near 125 miles per hour, lowering its status to a Category 3. Katrina eventually became a tropical depression as it neared Clarksville, Tennessee, on August 30, and by the end of the month the remnants of Katrina moved east-northeast toward Binghamton, New York.[1]

The chaotic and unpredictable winds of the hurricane were no match for the whirlwind of chaos that touched the lives of its victims. The amount of human suffering inflicted upon the United States by Hurricane Katrina has been greater than any other hurricane to strike the nation in several generations (Knabb, Rhome & Brown, 2005). Although the initial estimation of ten thousand deaths was "over[ly]-pessimistic" (al-Khudhairy et al., 2005), as of September 16, 2005, the death toll reached 1,336—which included deaths related to Katrina in five[2] southern states (Knabb et al., 2005). In the early morning hours of August 29, while the hurricane bore down on New Orleans, local residents and police sought some sort of shelter; yet, tourists who were not familiar with the city remained where they were in hotels and bars (Reagan et al., 2005). Those residents who could escape Katrina were on their way north while those that could not were scattered between hotels, hospitals, shelters, and the Superdome in the search for shelter (Reagan et al., 2005). Additionally, the levees[3] that had been in place to hold back the flood waters ruptured and caused water to enter the city (see Figure 2.1). In the submerged parts of the city, the water continued to rise without any help from the levees and pumps in place to divert such an occurrence (Reagan et al., 2005). Later that day, reporters began to hear stories about bodies floating in flood water and police officers incapable of reaching rescue boats to begin search and rescue missions. Also, reports of the rising water trapping people in their homes and forcing some residents into their attics and on top of their roofs (Reagan et al., 2005) began to circulate throughout the media. The city had become what one journalist had predicted early in May 2005, "a festering stew of sewage, gasoline, refinery chemicals and debris" (Mooney, 2005, as cited in Dyson, 2006, pp. 79–80).

The decision to begin evacuating the 23,000 people from the overcrowded Superdome to the Astrodome in Houston, Texas was not made until the fourth

---

1. Information pertaining to the development and tracking of Hurricane Katrina was provided by The National Weather Service (2005) and The National Climate Data Center (2005).

2. By September 16th the death toll had reached 1090 fatalities in Louisiana, 228 in Mississippi, 14 in Florida, 2 in Georgia and 2 in Alabama (Knabb et al., 2005).

3. The use of levees to contain the Mississippi River was adopted in 1885. According to Rivera and Miller (2006), "The theory behind the policy was that by containing the river with levees, the force of the high water would scour out the bottom of the river, deepening the channel to carry any flood water straight out to sea" (p. 7).

Figure 2.1 The destruction of the levee caused a barge to float from the banks of the Industrial Street Canal. Photo by DeMond Miller.

day of the disaster (Reagan et al., 2005). On September 1, a second wave of problems manifested themselves when a Chinook helicopter used to transport evacuees out of the Superdome was fired upon, causing evacuations to be temporarily suspended (Reagan et al., 2005). The suspension of air transport slowed evacuation to buses only, allowing only 10,000 people to be evacuated (Reagan et al., 2005). Moreover, by September 2, approximately 50,000 survivors remained on rooftops and in an assortment of other places (Reagan et al., 2005). At this time, there was no comprehensive plan to offer residents of the region full-scale assistance. By September 4, 30,000 people had been evacuated out of the Superdome and another 20,000 people had been evacuated from the Convention Center (Reagan et al., 2005). These evacuations were often met with overt resistance, as members of openly racist communities refused to allow evacuees access (Dyson, 2006; Powell, 2005).

Social Conditions Prior to Katrina

The social injustices and gross civil rights violations that took place in New Orleans during Hurricane Katrina gained international attention. Although many observers were shocked and outraged at the events that unfolded, a close examination of the social conditions of the city prior to the disaster makes it clear that the injustices were very much in keeping with the history of the re-

Most states use counties to denote political governing units. However, Louisiana utilizes 64 parishes in lieu of counties, as a means of designating political governing units. This practice extends back to the Louisianan colonial period when both the French and Spanish officially designated Louisiana as a Roman Catholic region and thus used ecclesiastical governing units. Out of the 64 parishes in Louisiana, eight were affected by Hurricane Katrina including: Orleans, Jefferson, Plaquemines, St. Bernard, St. Charles, St. James, St. John the Baptist, and St. Tammany. Approximately 650,000 people lived in these most heavily damaged parishes (Logan, 2006). In the parishes of St. Bernard and Orleans, more than 70 percent of the populations lived in damaged zones (Logan, 2006).

When one examines the racial and class composition of the parishes prior to the hurricane, it becomes clear that within all of these parishes there are varying degrees of poverty in addition to racial composition. *Table 2.1* illustrates the racial and class compositions between the affected and surrounding parishes:

Table 2.1 Louisianan Parish Demographics

Parish Name	Total Population	White Population	Black/ African American Population	Asian Population	Latino Population	Percentage of Population Below the Poverty Line
Ascension	76,627	59,304	15,539	258	1,883	12.95
Assumption	23,388	15,710	7,371	<100	<100	21.83
E. Baton Rouge	412,852	231,886	165,526	8,585	7,363	17.87
Iberia	73,266	47,682	22,574	1,414	1,101	23.55
Iberville	33,320	16,412	16,560	<100	343	23.11
Jefferson**	455,466	318,002	104,121	14,065	32,418	13.65
Lafourche	89,974	74,544	11,349	599	1,284	16.53
Livingston	91,814	86,625	3,874	<100	1,017	11.37
Orleans**	484,674	135,956	325,947	10,972	14,826	27.94
Plaquemines**	26,757	18,668	6,258	700	433	18.03
St. Bernard**	67,229	59,356	5,122	889	3,425	13.11
St. Charles**	48,072	34,803	12,130	265	1,346	11.40
St. Helena	10,525	4,897	5,517	<100	<100	26.83
St. James**	21,216	10,606	10,476	10	130	20.69
St. John the Baptist**	43,044	22,633	19,268	229	1,230	16.72
St. Martin	48,583	32,040	15,535	449	405	21.55
St. Mary	53,500	33,591	17,009	877	1,152	23.61
St. Tammany**	191,268	166,458	18,929	1,420	4,737	9.72
Tangipahoa	100,588	70,175	28,519	<100	1,536	22.69
Terrebonne	104,503	77,401	18,594	845	1,631	19.09
Washington	43,926	29,614	13,851	<100	<100	24.69

All data used in this table were taken from the U.S. Census of 2000
** Parishes significantly affected by Hurricane Katrina

Figure 2.2 Louisiana Parish Map. U.S. Census Bureau, n.d.

gion. In 2004, 19 percent of all Louisianans were considered to be poor—a statistic far above the national poverty rate of 13 percent and the second highest poverty rate in the entire nation (Sherman & Shapiro, 2005).[4] The city of New Orleans, considered one of the country's 245 largest cities, was ranked as the sixth poorest city in the 2000 census with 28 percent of the city's residents living below the poverty line (Sherman & Shapiro, 2005). Moreover, between 2003 and 2004 the poverty rate rose to 23.2 percent for the entire city (Fronczek, 2005, as cited in Berube & Katz, 2005). Poverty and unemployment were concentrated mainly within the African American population, which composed 67 percent of the city's population—and 84 percent of this group was found to live below the poverty line (Berube & Katz, 2005; Brookings Institute, 2005).

---

4. The only state with a higher poverty rate was Mississippi with a poverty rate of 21.6 percent (Sherman & Shapiro, 2005).

Racial inequality was also part and parcel of the housing and transportation conditions in New Orleans prior to Hurricane Katrina. Residential neighborhoods were historically visibly divided between whites and blacks, with blacks comprising the majority of New Orleans residents living in the poorest areas. Between 1980 and 2000, segregation between blacks and whites grew causing the isolation of poor households in poor neighborhoods (Berube & Katz, 2005). Most of these predominantly poor black communities were centered in the downtown area and the city's economically struggling eastern half (Berube & Katz, 2005; Brookings Institute, 2005). A large number of the African Americans in the city did not own a car. In fact, thirty-five percent of all black households lacked a vehicle, and fifty-nine percent of all *poor* black households lacked a vehicle (Sherman & Shapiro, 2005). The lack of transportation available to this segment of the population contributed to the group's inability to escape the hurricane as it made its approach into the city.

Immediately following Katrina, speculation surrounding the racial dynamics of the federal government's response to the disaster garnered attention. Allegations that the government's slow and inadequate response was due to the lack of interest in aiding African Americans made the topic center stage in national debates. Although Hurricane Katrina destroyed property and life indiscriminately, the vulnerability of the black population within the city of New Orleans, due to its lack of transportation and poor housing conditions, made its members more susceptible to loss. An intersection of racially based social stratification, socioeconomic healthcare disparities, and political disfranchisement present during and immediately after Hurricane Katrina was not a culmination of recent social trends in population composition, but an extension of a history of racial, economic, and social injustice that has been perpetuated throughout the history of Louisiana, and more specifically New Orleans, since its colonial founding.

Following the hurricane, an argument was forwarded that the African American population of New Orleans was a socially vulnerable group. Social vulnerability can be defined as:

> ... the susceptibility of social groups to the impacts of hazards, as well as their resiliency, or ability to adequately recover from them. This susceptibility is not only a function of the demographic characteristics of the population (age, gender, wealth, etc.), but also the more complex constructs such as health care provision, social capital, and access to lifelines (e.g., emergency response personnel, goods, services). (Cutter & Emrich, 2006, p. 103)

Given that social vulnerability is a product of social inequities (Cutter, 2005; Cutter et al., 2003; Miller & Rivera, 2006), arguments of this position are rooted not in the "vulnerable" population's situation prior to the disaster, but its situation after the disaster. According to Kates (1977, as cited in Cutter &

Emrich, 2006), "Disasters magnify the existing social and economic trends in places; they do not fundamentally change them" (p. 104).

Katrina and Environmental Justice Concerns

Pastor et al. (2006) explain that Hurricane Katrina swept away the "traditional belief" that natural disasters are equally devastating on populations and do not discriminate in terms of whom and what is destroyed. This was a result of the government's relief response to the hurricane and its inefficacy in helping the resident population most affected—poor blacks. Environmental justice requires that individuals have a clean and safe environment in which to live; however, this is not the case for everyone and, "environmental inequities by race and often by income seem to be an established part of the American urban landscape—Katrina simply tore back the cover on this unfortunate fact" (Pastor et al., 2006, p. 1). The woefully inadequate relief response prolonged the time that residents were exposed to environmental hazards and was a continuation of the series of environmentally related harms that residents were exposed to prior to the hurricane. For example, for some time prior to the hurricane New Orleanians had been experiencing environmental health problems related to lead poisoning as well as high rates of asthma and other respiratory diseases (Pastor et al., 2006; Wright, 2005). These experiences of New Orleans residents reflected a larger pattern of social injustice in which blacks in the southern United States as a whole have suffered the brunt of environmental degradation more seriously than other residents of the country (Pastor et al., 2006).

The flooding that ensued after Katrina exposed a number of other environmental injustices. Many of the risk reduction measures that were in place to aid in flood control provided location-specific benefits to the people that lived in protected areas. Thus, individuals with the resources to live and invest in specified areas were protected while others were not (Pastor et al., 2006). Furthermore, policies and plans in place to alleviate public distress, evacuate citizens, and provide shelter in time of disaster were insubstantial if they existed at all, leaving many New Orleans residents to fend for themselves. "A Times-Picayune reporter, Bruce Nolan, summed up the emergency transportation place eloquently: 'City, state and federal emergency officials are preparing to give the poorest of New Orleans' poor a historically blunt message: In the event of a major hurricane, you're on your own'" (Nolan, 2005, as cited in Pastor et al., 2006, p. 3). This failure to address issues of social justice in a manner in which all community stakeholders could mutually benefit from the local environment is a message the marginalized of New Orleans had heard before.

The History of Flooding in the Mississippi Valley

As noted previously, there has long been a history of racial segregation in New Orleans neighborhoods. This segregation made black communities physically vulnerable to natural disasters and even worse, government neglect. One example of governmental neglect of black communities in New Orleans occurred during the Mississippi Flood of 1927. During this massive flood, black communities in New Orleans were left to fend for themselves (Associated Press, 2005; Barry, 1997; Miller & Rivera, 2006). The Mississippi River swelled to 100 miles wide in some areas, while moving at a speed of nine miles per hour and flooding an area of 27,000 square miles (WGBH Educational Foundation, 2001). Moreover, the water of the Mississippi rose so high that one of its tributaries, the Arkansas River, flowed backwards (WGBH Educational Foundation, 2001). Similar to the situation that occurred with Hurricane Katrina, authorities in New Orleans did not believe that the flood would be as severe as it eventually became, nor did they believe that the flood would breach the levees above the city (Barry, 1997).

According to Barry (1997), the weakest levees in Louisiana lay thirty miles up-river from New Orleans, and any breaching of these levees would flood the city from the rear as it had during the last major flood of the region in 1849. When New Orleans eventually flooded, racial discrimination quickly surfaced. Evacuations and relief supplies were first distributed to whites and then only after whites had taken what they wanted of the supplies or of the boats needed to evacuate did blacks have the opportunity to take what was left (WGBH Educational Foundation, 2001). The evacuation of blacks (see Figure 2.3) from the area was such a low priority that in some instances animals held priority over people:

> A letter from a black Republican activist read: "It is said that many relief boats have hauled whites only, have gone to imperiled districts and taken all whites out and left the Negroes; it is also said that planters in some instances hold their labor at the point of gun for fear they would get away and not return. In other instances, it is said that mules have been given preference on boats to Negroes."
>
> (Redmond, 1927, as cited in Barry, 1997, p. 320)

Moreover, in an effort to possibly divert the flood waters from New Orleans, engineers destroyed a levee, allowing water to flood the marshlands below the city, displacing 10,000 people (National Geographic, 2005), most of whom were black (see Figure 2.4). The destruction of levees by rivaling state populations was a constant fear during the flood. Levees that protected Alabama and Mississippi were under constant guard by authorities so that neither popula-

Figure 2.3 When blacks were evacuated, they were usually placed on the
levees to ensure that they would not leave the region completely.
© National Geographic, 2005, p. 73, photo by Clifton Adams.

tion from either state would intentionally destroy the levees in order to wash
away unwanted segments of the other states' residents (WGBH Educational
Foundation, 2001). Survival problems were exacerbated in the black communities by flawed drainage systems and a lack of political interest in aiding black
communities on the part of the white population (Rivera & Miller, 2006).

Figure 2.4 The destruction of the levee in 1927.
© National Geographic, 2005, p. 73, photo by Clifton Adams.

Therefore, when the levee was destroyed in 1927, there was little concern about the welfare of the black population residing in the floodplain.

The same sentiment could be observed in New Orleans in 2005 and was an expression of centuries of social manipulation and racial classifications that have been detrimental to the black community's evolution. The experience the United States knows as the tragedy of Hurricane Katrina began more than two centuries ago.

Historical, Social, and Environmental Factors

Colonialism

In British North American colonies (1607–1776) the distinctions between people were simplistic. Most notably, a clear distinction existed in the belief of the superiority of whites over people of color, and there was a belief that blacks were brought into creation for the expressed purpose of slavery (see Duvallon, 1806). To most Protestant colonials in North America during Louisiana's colonial period, the slightest amount of "Negro" blood was enough to make an individual fully black. This idea of "part black, fully black" was a concept that was unique to the British colonies; this ideology was not present in French and Spanish colonization that occurred.

For the purposes of this chapter, colonialism is the act of a mother-nation assuming political and/or economic control over another, whereby the mother-nation defines the colony's laws and general administration in addition to acquiring a significant portion of the colony's generated revenues. The Louisiana area was colonized by the French, the Spanish, and finally the United States as a result of the Louisiana Purchase.[5] Each of these colonizing forces brought with them its own definitions and understandings of race and ethnicity. Thus, the status of people of color in this region varied depending upon the colonizing government. The classification *gens de couleur libre* was used by the French colonizing forces in New Orleans between the years 1718 and 1768 to describe those people of color who were legally free, and its use effectively created a tripartite racial categorization schema (Dominguez, 1986).[6] In addition, the term *creole* began to be applied in different ways within the colony of New Orleans. Initially, the term was used to describe anyone born in

---

5. The United States purchased the Louisiana Territory from the French on December 20, 1803, who had reacquired it from the Spanish thirty days earlier.

6. Dominguez (1986) explained that the term *gens de couleur libre* was a legal distinction within the French colonies that rested on the application of two criteria: the possession or lack of possession of legal freedom and descent or lack of descent from Africans.

the New World; however, years later when a large number of immigrants from St. Dominigue (present day Haiti) arrived in New Orleans, the meaning of the term *creole* morphed into one that referred to individuals of European descent (Dominguez, 1977). International racial ideology contributed to the shift in application of the word[7] because the presence of African blood became associated with inferiority and the incapability of self rule.

When Louisiana fell under the administration of the Spanish in 1768, the new governing administration's laws further perpetuated racial distinctions. The issue of racial purity became more of a concern to the elite white population when some people of African descent began to pass as whites in society (Dominguez, 1986). Subsequently, there was an explicit effort to privilege whiteness and to create additional racial categories that denigrated people based upon their degree of African ancestry. Racial distinctions within the black community were created by means of language that referred to people in terms of their assumed percentage of African blood. This generated a hierarchical racial structure[8] within the black population (Kephart, 1948).

After the Louisiana Purchase of 1803, a shift in social identification and social status within New Orleans society transpired. Moreover, old residents of the colony felt at odds with the new administration's social culture and resisted U.S. assimilation up until the Civil War (Brooks, 1998). Although an obvious separation between U.S. and *creole* culture within the newly acquired territory and specifically in New Orleans[9] could be seen, the major social change occurred with respect to blacks within the mainstream society. During the American administration of Louisiana prior to the Civil War, the white elite, both French-Creoles and Anglo-Americans, consolidated their political and economic power, making them impervious to black or colored challenge (Tregle, 1992). In this new social order, it was not only important to be free, but also to

---

7. Hall (1992) explained that in the French and Spanish Colonies during the eighteenth century, "the term *creole* was used to distinguish U.S.-born from African-born slaves; all first-generation slaves born in the U.S. and their descendants were designated creoles" (p. 60).

8. Kephart (1948) explained the distinctions made between blacks with different percentages of African blood. He broke down the distinctions between the castes as follows: (1) Pure Black—"Negro," (2) 3/4 Black—"Sambo" or "Mangro," (3) 1/2 Black—"Mulatto," (4) 1/4 Black—"Quadroon" and (5) Less than 1/4 Black—"Octoroon," "Mustifee" or "Pass for White."

9. According to Hirsch & Logsdon (1992) the Americans adopted a Parisian model of city government in which the city of New Orleans was divided into three separate municipalities. Each of the municipalities was almost entirely autonomous and was segregated between one uptown municipality for Anglo-Americans and two downtown municipalities for French-Creoles. Each of the municipalities conducted official business in its own language and each attempted to perpetuate its own culture through its own public school system.

be totally devoid of African blood. For blacks in New Orleans prior to the Civil War the only avenue to social mobility open to *gens de couleur libre* was *passe-blanc*,[10] which necessitated a total break with African ancestry for an acceptance of a white culture not necessarily their own (Kaslow, 1981).

While free blacks and other people of color were contending with the changing rules of racial categorization during this time period, other individuals from Africa or of African descent were living under the tyranny of slavery. Ethnocentric European cultures enslaved those whom they thought to be sub-human or uncivilized peoples who lived within the areas that they colonized in an effort to create a labor force for colonial development. These slaves were used to generate a labor force that would aid in the further development of what was deemed the "New World." Between 1803 and 1840 a population explosion occurred in the South, with an ever-increasing slave population utilized to maintain the cotton economy (Kaslow, 1981). Institutionally the practice of slavery was not officially banned until the end of the Civil War in 1865.

Reconstruction

With the close of the Civil War, New Orleans faced the obstacle of Reconstruction. Beginning in 1866, federal troops had occupied the city of New Orleans to instill military and economic control over the region. One of the more prevalent concerns of leaders during the first few years of federal occupation was the stream of blacks immigrating into the city from the surrounding plantations (Kaslow, 1981). Due to the large concentration of blacks now residing within the city in such close proximity to whites (Somers, 1974), racial conflicts arose and federal troops attempted to address them by organizing blacks into labor camps (Kaslow, 1981). However, militarization was extremely ineffectual in combating racial strife considering the overwhelmingly pervasive white supremacist sentiments that fueled the policy.

Although an apparent animosity existed between the two races within the city of New Orleans, blacks and whites resided in the same communities with minimum friction (Somers, 1974).[11] In the countryside on the other hand, blacks were reintegrated back into the plantation system as wage slaves or semi-feudal tenant farmers (Kaslow, 1981), further motivating blacks to immi-

---

10. "Passing for white."

11. Somers (1974) explained that in the city of New Orleans blacks and whites were capable of living side-by-side one another in relative harmony because urban whites did not insist upon the complete subjugation of blacks. Although racial violence did occur from time to time, the ability of blacks to have better social standing in the urban setting was reflective of the decline in white population and a doubling of the black population between 1860 and 1870.

grate into urban areas to find alternative means of work. When arriving in the city, however, the former plantation workers were faced with the problem of competing for work with skilled freedmen as well as whites. Kaslow (1981) explains that the black community was discriminated against on the basis of race, making it exceedingly difficult for any black worker, skilled or unskilled, to find a job when competing with white workers. However, there were class distinctions in the black community, for example, creoles, usually those who had been educated abroad during the 1850s, were more successful than their less educated counterparts and often went on to become part of the political leadership of the community.[12]

Despite a strong presence of white supremacy, the belief in white superiority, and the labor discrimination practices of the immediate post-war period, black elites began to pursue political rights such as voting rights and access to public facilities. According to Somers (1974), in 1868 the Louisiana constitution was written by black and white "radicals" and granted full rights to all citizens (including the vote), prohibited segregation in public schools, and opened public facilities "to the accommodation and patronage of all persons, without distinction or discrimination on account of race or color" (State Constitutional Convention of the State of Louisiana, 1868, as cited in Somers, 1974, pp. 23–24). Moreover, by 1876, legislators outlawed discrimination in state institutions, legalized interracial marriages, and passed bills establishing racially integrated public schools throughout the entire state (Somers, 1974). Black children entered several of New Orleans' previously white institutions only two years after the constitution of 1868. Although school integration ended in 1877, about a third of the city's schools had opened their doors to both black and white children (Somers, 1974).

Reconstruction efforts, when left to the state, began to curtail the rights and privileges of the black population.

> Several terrorist organizations sprang up in Louisiana during the Reconstruction era. They primarily aimed to intimidate Republican voters and officeholders of both races, obstruct implementation of Radical Republican policies, and restore Louisiana to rule by native whites. The main instruments of white terror in Louisiana were the Knights of the White Camellia, formed in 1868, and their successor group, the White League, which had spread across the state by 1874. The earliest of white supremacy groups was the Ku Klux Klan, formed in Tennessee in 1866; the White League and the Klan created conditions worse than slavery. Whites, many of them Democrats, joined these terrorist or-

---

12. The leadership of the black community was left to the city's freeborn blacks who were sometimes called "colored creoles," and included merchants, men of property, lawyers, doctors, journalists, musicians, artists, and skilled workmen (Somers, 1974).

ganizations when they began losing power to Radical Republicans, both white and black.

(Louisiana State Museum, 2006, p. 11)

The immediate goal of these groups was to keep those wishing to institute reforms away from polling places through violent tactics targeted at black leaders, which led to a strong white supremacist movement in Louisiana.

The Creation of Redeemer Governments and Segregation

The flirtation with equal rights and school integration was severely curtailed at the end of the Reconstruction Era, specifically when federal troops ended their occupation of New Orleans in 1877. Although blacks continued to pursue equality, the adoption of the Redeemer Constitution of 1879[13] and a series of unfavorable U.S. Supreme Court decisions greatly limited the ability of black leaders to single-handedly push for the exercise of equal rights for all citizens (Somers, 1974).

As Rutherford B. Hayes was elected President of the United States, three Southern states (Florida, South Carolina and Louisiana) remained occupied with Northern military troops after the Civil War. Hayes allowed the remaining states to complete the process of Reconstruction with little Northern interference. In Louisiana, a group of powerful Democrats, under the leadership of Governor Nicholls, wrote the Redeemer Constitution while "… Republican[s] maintained a shadow government until the end of April 1877. A mostly Democratic convention wrote a new constitution that voters ratified in 1879, returning Louisiana to 'home rule,' with white supremacist Democrats controlling most of the state, parish, and municipal institutions" (Louisiana State Museum, 2006, p. 11). While the new state government implemented the 1879 Constitution, during the 1880s and 1890s, blacks migrated from the countryside into the city. The expanding black population of New Orleans at the end of the nineteenth century did little to advance racial equality among the population because whites in New Orleans, as in other places, became committed to white supremacy and a caste system that came to be associated with the southern way of life (Somers, 1974). The exit of blacks from politics and the concomitant lack of racial equality were illustrated by the words of the New Orleans city mayor Martin Behrman, "After all is said and done, it must be admitted that the Convention of 1898 made good with the people. We promised to put the Negro out of politics and keep him out" (Kemp, 1977 as cited in Kaslow, 1981, p. 51).

---

13. The Redeemer Constitution of 1879 repealed all equal rights provisions established by the Constitution of 1868.

In addition to isolating blacks from politics, Jim Crow laws segregated them from the rest of society as well. No longer was it possible for blacks to pursue any type of equality along political lines, and, therefore, isolation within their own communities was the result. Kaslow (1981) contended that after Emancipation, blacks were confined to living in areas with poor drainage, scarce transportation, and practically no public facilities. According to Frymer, Strolovitch, and Warren (2005), even legislation enacted by the federal government to help ease social and economic strife in the early twentieth century promoted racial segregation and poverty, because although their semantics were generalized to the public, the government was more obliged to economically aid whites rather than blacks.[14]

Civil Rights Movement

During the civil rights movement, blacks in New Orleans were again attempting to regain the civil liberties they had once enjoyed almost a hundred years before during Reconstruction. During the 1960s, there was an advancement of black civil liberties, but the political benefits of the movement were not significantly enjoyed by a majority of the black community due to residual supremacist sentiments. Moreover, any political advancements were not accompanied by corresponding socio-economic success (Kaslow, 1981). During the same time that the community made political strides, the community remained economically and spatially segregated. From the 1960s on, predominantly black and white neighborhoods persisted and served as evidence that there was widespread resistance to true social and economic integration. Over the years, the effects of this segregation were compounded by the occurrence of "white flight" that continually increased the black-to-white ratio of the city (Kaslow, 1981). Ironically, the end of white supremacist rule in New Orleans resulted not in integration but in intransigent racial polarization,

> Racism permeates every facet of institutional life in New Orleans, from lending policies by banks, to school enrollment in public education, to demographic shifts in housing, employment opportunities, and to police harassment and criminal justice.
>
> (Kaslow, 1981, pp. 59–60)

With such a system in place, it comes with no surprise that when disaster struck New Orleans, the black communities were structurally ill-prepared to

---

14. The Wagner Act and the Social Security Act did not include occupations in which African Americans were a majority of the workers. These acts that excluded African Americans from receiving benefits were directly responsible for the disproportionate number of poor African Americans in New Orleans (Frymer et al., 2005; Miller & Rivera, 2006).

deal with the devastation inflicted by Hurricane Katrina. In essence, these communities were neglected long before Katrina made landfall.

Conclusion

The interaction of variables including policy, poverty, and race in the aftermath of Hurricane Katrina has exposed an ugly underside of the experience lived daily by millions of Americans. The technological disaster (i.e., levee breaches in New Orleans) forever changed the physical, social, economic, and political environment of New Orleans. As Atkins and Moy (2005) stated, "Live images of uncollected corpses and families clinging to rooftops made vivid what decades of statistics could not: that being poor in America, and especially being poor and black in a poor southern state, is still hazardous to your health" (p. 916). The reality-style cable news television coverage of the disaster, which aired on a twenty-four-hour, seven-days-a-week basis, made it clear, "... that the U.S. has not resolved fundamental domestic disparities and inadequacies. Katrina did not create these inequities; it simply added an important reminder that they are deeply embedded and constitutive of American political, economic, and social life" (Frymer et al., 2005, p. 1). These scenes and "scripts of horror" viewed around the world were centuries in the making.

Fundamentally, future challenges lie in the creation, implementation, and support of public policies that do not reinforce the patterns of concentrated poverty. In essence, policy makers must consider broader social contexts when developing policy. The persisting problems of infrastructure disinvestment, poverty, and racial inequity are all part of the existing landscape that serves to deepen the ongoing tragedy caused by geographic displacement following the hurricane. The improvement of the centuries-long disparities in social conditions brought to light by the natural disaster has to be on the agenda in the same way that securing the levees and rebuilding the business infrastructure are. Still months after the disaster, it appears that little has been done to alleviate the problems in New Orleans (see Figure 2.5). Failing to address the social conditions in the Gulf Coast region will set the stage for another human tragedy (Miller, 2006).

> The simple reality is that [a socially just] democratic government works better in every way when it is one element in a vibrant network of communities, associations, and families; when its citizens care what it does, [have] reasonable faith in its leaders, and participate actively in politics and policy making. That kind of essential citizen involvement and public trust to drive it are often absent from contemporary government in America.
>
> (Panel on Civil Trust and Citizen Responsibility, 1999, p. 2)

Figure 2.5 The destruction of a home in the Lower Ninth Ward,
New Orleans. Photo by Vanessa St. Eleine.

In post-Katrina New Orleans, distrust in elected and public officials reached a tipping point when help did not arrive in a timely manner[15]—when a massive flood and hurricane combined to wreak similar damage—begging an answer to the same question that was asked more than three-quarters of a century ago: "[h]ow they could have been left behind so egregiously in a disaster foreseen for decades?" (Associated Press, 2005, p. 1). In addition, distrust has been further perpetuated because "good faith" efforts to effectively organize and administer timely assistance have not occurred even several months after the tragedy. The nature of such catastrophes is not new to the city and region. This is the *third time* flood waters have devastated the region and black communities were left to fend for themselves in New Orleans.[16] It would seem that by the third flood, government agencies, at all levels, would have been better prepared and better policies would have been put in place to faster alleviate the

15. However, Barry (1997, p. 407) contended that after the Mississippi River flood of 1927, responsibility for the Mississippi River "vastly expanded federal involvement in local affairs," and that it set a precedent that reflected that the federal government had a proper role and obligation to attempt to prevent mass devastation caused by natural forces.

16. According to the Associated Press (2005, p. 1), blacks were "intentionally left behind—to suffer, to starve, to drown" in New Orleans' Lower Ninth Ward from the destruction caused by Hurricane Betsy in 1965 in order to save the "whiter parts of the city." (In sum, the first time the flood region flooded the region and left black communities to fend for themselves was the Flood of 1927, the second time was during Hurricane Betsy, and the third time was Hurricane Katrina.)

effects of the damage. The distrust on the behalf of the black population is so high post-Katrina that there are people who believe that the Industrial Canal levee was deliberately damaged in 1927 during the Mississippi River flood and during Katrina in order to flood the "[h]eavily impoverished Lower Ninth Ward and save the whiter parts of the city" (Associated Press, 2005, p. 2).

Being left behind is not new, it is evidence of a larger constellation of concerns that stem from earlier times and remain present in American society today. When a group is viewed as inferior, the proverbial flood gates open to unleash a host of other insidious forms of social injustices—including white privilege and racial superiority. These ideas manifest themselves in the racial discourse of this country in public policy arenas and are at the heart of American values as we understand our obligations to a city, a state, a region, and a people.

References

al-Khudhairy, D., Annunziato, C., Best, M., Bettio, I., Caravaggi, R., Confalonieri, M., Christou, D., Ehrlich, M., Ketselidis, C., Louvrier, J.C., Martinez, P., Russ, W., Schrimf, A.S. & Vollmer, G. (2005). Katrina event information report. European Commission Joint Research Centre.

Associated Press. (2005, October 24). Deep distrust over New Orleans rebuilding: Many Black residents don't believe promise of city officials. Retrieved November 13, 2005 from http://www.msnbc.mns.com/id/9796942/.

Atkins, D. & Moy, E. M. (2005). Left behind: The legacy of Hurricane Katrina: Hurricane Katrina puts the health effects of poverty and race in plain view. *British Medical Journal, 331*, 916–918.

Barry, J.M. (1997). *Rising tide: The Great Mississippi Flood of 1927 and how it changed:America.* New York, NY: Simon & Schuster.

Berube, A. & Katz, B. (2005). Katrina's window: Confronting concentrated poverty across America. *Special analysis in metropolitan policy.* Washington, DC: The Brookings Institution. Brookings Metropolitan Policy Program. (2005). *New Orleans after the storm: Lessons from the past, a plan for the future.* Washington, DC: The Brookings Institution.

Brooks, K. (1998). Alice Dunbar-Nelson's local colors of ethnicity, class and place. *MELUS, 23*(2), 3–26.

Cutter, S.L. (2005, September 23). The geography of social vulnerability: Race, class, and catastrophe. *Social Science Research Council.* Retrieved November 5, 2005 from http://understandingkatrina.ssrc.org/Cutter.

Cutter, S.L., Boruff, B. J., & Shirley, W.L. (2003). Social vulnerability to environmental hazards. *Social Science Quarterly, 84*(1), 242–261.

Cutter, S.L. & Emrich, C. (2006). Moral hazard, social catastrophe: The changing face of vulnerability along the hurricane coasts. *The Annals of the American Academy of Political and Social Science, 604*(1), 102–112.

Dominguez, V.R. (1977). Social classification in Creole Louisiana. *American Ethnologist,* 589–602.

————. (1986). *White By definition: Social classification in Creole Louisiana.* New Brunswick, New Jersey: Rutgers University Press.

Duvallon, B. (1806). *Travels in Louisiana and the Floridas, in the year, 1802: Giving a correct picture of those countries.* (Trans. John Davis). New York: I Riley and Company.

Dyson, M.E. (2006). *Come hell or high water: Hurricane Katrina and the color of disaster.* New York, NY: Basic Civitas Books.

Fronczek, P. (2005). *Income, earnings, and poverty from the 2004 American Community Survey. Report ACS-01.* Washington, DC: U.S. Census Bureau.

Frymer, P., Strolovitch, D.Z. & Warren, D. T. (2005, September 28). *Katrina's political roots and divisions: Race, class, and federalism in American politics.* Social Science Research Council. Retrieved November 5, 2005 from http://understandingkatrina.ssrc.org/FrymerStrolovitchWarren.

Hall, G.M. (1992). The formation of Afro-Creole culture. In A.R. Hirsch & J. Logsdon (Eds.), *Creole New Orleans: Race and Americanization* (pp. 58–87). Baton Rouge, LA: Louisiana State University Press.

Hirsch, A. (1992). Simply a matter of black and white: The transformation of race and politics in twentieth-century New Orleans. In A.R. Hirsch & J. Logsdon (Eds.), *Creole New Orleans: Race and Americanization* (pp. 262–320). Baton Rouge, LA: Louisiana State University Press.

Hirsch, A. & Logsdon, J. (1992) Introduction to Part II: American challenge. In A.R. Hirsch & J. Logsdon (Eds.), *Creole New Orleans: Race and Americanization* (pp. 91–100). Baton Rouge, LA: Louisiana State University Press.

Kaslow, A.J. (1981) *Oppression and adaptation: The social organization and expressive culture of an Afro-American community in New Orleans, Louisiana.* Unpublished Ph.D. dissertation. New York: Columbia University.

Kates, R.W. (1977). Major insights: A summary and recommendation. In J.E. Hass, R.W. Kates, and M.J. Bowden (Eds.), *Reconstruction following disaster* (pp. 261–293). Cambridge, MA: MIT Press.

Kephart, W.M. (1948). Is the American Negro becoming lighter? An analysis of the sociological and biological trends. *American Sociological Review, 13*(3), 437–443.

Kemp, J.S. (1977). *Martin Behrman of New Orleans: Memoirs of a city boss.* Baton Rouge, LA: Louisiana State University Press.

Knabb, R. D, Rhome, J. R., & Brown, D. P. (2005). Tropical cyclone report Hurricane Katrina 23–30 August 2005. National Hurricane Center. Retrieved January 2, 2006 from http://www.nhc.noaa.gov/pdf/TCR-AL122005_Katrina.pdf.

Logan, J. R. (2006). *The impact of Katrina: Race and class in storm-damaged neighborhoods.* Retrieved June 2, 2006 from http://www.s4.brown.edu/ Katrina/ report.pdf.

Louisiana State Museum (2006). *Reconstruction: A divided state.* The Cabildo: The Louisiana State Museum. Retrieved September 28, 2006 from http:// lsm.crt.state.la.us/ cabildo/cab11.htm.

Miller, D. S. (2006) Visualizing the corrosive community: Looting in the aftermath of Hurricane Katrina. *Space and Culture, 9*(1), 71–73.

Miller, D. S. & Rivera, J. D. (2006). Guiding principles: Rebuilding trust in government and public policy in the aftermath of Hurricane Katrina, *Journal of Public Management & Social Policy, 12*(1), 37–47.

Mooney, C. (2005, May 23). Thinking big about hurricanes: It's time to get serious about saving New Orleans. *The American Protest.* Retrieved December 30, 2005 from http://www. prospect.org web/page.ww?section=root& name=ViewWeb&articleId=9754.

NAOO/National Climatic Data Center. (2005, December 29). Climate of 2005 summary of Hurricane Katrina. Retrieved December 30, 2005 from http://lwf.ncdc.noaa.gov/oa/climate/research/2005/katrina.html.

NAOO/National Weather Service. (2005, Sept. 1). Monthly tropical weather summary. Retrieved December 30, 2005 from http://www.nhc.noaa.gov/ archive/2005/tws/MIATWSATaug.shtml.

National Geographic. (2005, December 26). The past comes back. Katrina. Why it became a man-made disaster—where it could happen next, pp. 70–75.

NOCA/National Flood Commission.(1927). See undated report from late January 1927 to February 1927.

Nolan, B. (2005, July 24). In storm, N.O. wants no one left behind [Electronic version]. *The Times-Picayune.* Retrieved February 9, 2006 from http:// www.nola.com/ printer/printer.ssf?/base/news-10/1122184560198030.xml.

Panel on Civic Trust and Citizen Responsibility. (1999). *A government to trust and respect: Rebuilding citizen-government relations for the 21st century.* Washington, DC: National Academy of Public Administration.

Pastor, M., Bullard, R.D., Boyce, J.K., Fothergill, A., Morello-Frosch, R. & Wright, B. (2006). *In the wake of the storm: Environment, disaster, and race after Katrina.* New York, NY: The Russell Sage Foundation.

Powell, L. N. (September 2005). New Orleans: An American Pompeii? Paper in authors' possession.

Reagan, M., Webb, G., Harkleroad, C., Brown, Reagan, L. & Murphy, D. (2005). *Katrina state of emergency.* Kansas City, MO: Lionheart Books.

Redmond, S. (1927, April 27). *Sidney Redmond to Coolidge.* Coolidge Papers, LC.

Reed, G. (1965). Race legislation in Louisiana, 1964–1920, *Louisiana History,* 6, 382.

Rivera, J. D. & Miller, D. S. (2006). A brief history of the evolution of United States' natural disaster policy. *Journal of Public Management & Social Policy, 12*(1), 5–14.

Sabine, G. (1952). The two democratic traditions. *The Philosophical Review, 61,* 471.

Sherman, A. & Shapiro, I. (2005). Essential facts about the victims of Hurricane Katrina. *Center on Budget and Policy Priorities.* Retrieved February 6, 2006 from http://www.cbpp.org.

Somers, D. (1974). Black and white in New Orleans: A study in urban race relations, 1865–1900. *The Journal of Southern History, 40*(1), 19–42.

State Constitution of the State of Louisiana, March 7, 1868. (1868). New Orleans.

Tregle, J. G., Jr. (1992). Creoles and Americans. In A.R. Hirsch & J. Logsdon (Eds.), *Creole New Orleans: Race and Americanization* (pp. 131–185). Baton Rouge, LA: Louisiana State University Press.

U.S. Census. (2000). *Selected counties in Hurricane Katrina affected area: 2000.* Census 2000 Summary File 1, Tables P1, P8, P17 P33, H1 & H4 and Census Summary File 3, Tables P21, P26, P36, P37, P53, P82, P88, H24, H30, H35, H41, H44, H63 & H76.

———. (n.d.). *Louisiana county selection map.* U.S. Census Bureau, State & County QuickFacts. Retrieved July 25, 2006 from http://quickfacts.census.gov/qfd/maps/louisiana_map.html.

WGBH Educational Foundation. (2001). *Fatal flood.* Public Broadcasting Service.

Wright, B. (2005). Living and dying in Louisiana's Cancer Alley. In R.D. Bullard (Ed.), *The quest for environmental justice: Human rights and the political of pollution* (pp. 87–107). San Francisco, CA: Sierra Club Books.

Chapter 3

"Revolutions May Go Backwards": The Persistence of Voter Disenfranchisement in the United States

Michelle Inderbitzin, Kelly Fawcett,
Christopher Uggen, and Kristin A. Bates

New Orleans has long been pivotal in the struggle for black voting rights. During the Civil War, free blacks there demanded suffrage; their efforts resulted in Lincoln's first call for voting rights for some blacks in the final speech of his life. Once these rights were won, New Orleans blacks took an active part in politics, leading to the establishment of the South's only integrated public school system. But rights once gained aren't necessarily secure; after Reconstruction, blacks in New Orleans lost the right to vote. As Thomas Wentworth Higginson wrote at the time of the Civil War, "revolutions may go backwards."

—*The Nation*, May 1, 2006, n.p.

From its inception, the United States' political and legal processes have been vulnerable to the race, gender, and social class of its citizens. These characteristics have played a pivotal role in determining whose perspective and voice will be heard in national and community level decisions; most visibly, race, gender, and social class have been primary considerations in who has been deemed eligible to vote. Although many Americans take the right to vote for granted, this chapter considers two cases in which blocks to political participation have persisted on a large scale. We first take up the issue of felon disenfranchisement, which today bars more than five million U.S. citizens from the ballot box. The history and contemporary impact of felon voting restrictions represent a powerful and instructive exception to the principle and practice of universal suffrage in the United States. We then consider how Hurricane Katrina dramatically reshaped the New Orleans electorate, decisively shifting the balance of political power. In both cases, the burden of disenfranchisement is borne disproportionately by blacks and the poor. Yet the laws and practices are facially neutral with regard to race and class. To help explain this paradox, we turn to a body of theory that considers law through the lens of racial inequality.

Critical Race Theory

Critical Race theory first came to prominence through the writings of legal scholars in the 1970s. These scholars were interested in explaining why the civil rights movement of the 1960s had stalled and why the advances in the 1960s had come under attack (Crenshaw, Gotanda, Peller, & Thomas, 1995). Often through the use of storytelling and narration, these scholars offered a counter-story to the dominant, mainstream accounts of the events of the civil rights movement and the use of law as a tool of equality. According to Cornell West (1995) "Critical Race theory ... compels us to confront critically the most explosive issue in American civilization: the historical centrality and complicity of law in upholding white supremacy ..." (p. xi).

While the theory first began to coalesce among legal scholars, today it is used in the areas of communication, education, and sociology by an array of race scholars who are unified by two goals:

> The first is to understand how a of regime of white supremacy and its subordination of people of color have been created and maintained in America, and, in particular, to examine the relationship between that social structure and professed ideals such as "the rule of law" and "equal protection." The second is a desire not merely to understand the vexed bond between law and racial power but to *change* it.
>
> (Crenshaw et al., 1995, p. xiii)

Challenging this idea of white supremacy and thus the belief that the white experience is the normative standard by which all other experiences are measured, Critical Race theorists argue that to understand law and racial exclusion we must understand the experiences of people of color under this legal system. These scholars insist "that the social and experiential context of racial oppression is crucial for understanding racial dynamics, particularly the way that current inequalities are connected to earlier, more overt, practices of racial exclusion" (Taylor, 1998, p. 122). Critical Race theory, then, can be used to examine the historical use of voter disenfranchisement in the United States to silence the voices of people of color, women, and the poor.

The law, scholars argue, is not "neutral" or "objective" in its creation or application and, instead, has been used, overtly, when possible, and covertly, when necessary to subordinate people of color (Crenshaw et al., 1995). Even in such arenas as affirmative action, a policy from the civil rights era designed to help people of color, the law has been used, in the end, to mute this goal (Aguirre, 2000; Crenshaw et al., 1995).

At its very foundation, Critical Race theory offers a unique position in the forum of legal critique by proposing that racism is an intricate and enduring pattern in the fabric of American life, woven into the social structure and social institutions of modern day (Crenshaw et al., 1995). This is in direct contrast to even most liberal legal and social scholars who argue that racism and discrimination, in general, are sociopathic, anomalous acts that not only can be explained by individual, evil behavior, but can be fixed through accepted legal practices (Fan, 1997). As Crenshaw et al. (1995) note:

> From its inception mainstream legal thinking in the U.S. has been characterized by a curiously constricted understanding of race and power. Within this cramped conception of racial domination, the evil of racism exists when—and only when—one can point to specific, discrete acts of racial discrimination, which is in turn narrowly defined as decision-making based on the irrational and irrelevant attribute of race. (p. xx)

One of the most important tenets of Critical Race theory may be its supposition that racial domination is at the center of much of today's legal and social decision making—and that this domination is so routine it is accepted as both legally and morally legitimate.

It is with this understanding that we examine the historical use of voter disenfranchisement. It is not surprising, that voter disenfranchisement still exists in the United States practiced, overtly, through felon disenfranchisement (Manza & Uggen, 2006), and covertly through polarizing election tactics (Overton, 2006).

Race and the History of Voter Disenfranchisement

After Hurricane Katrina left a major city in the United States in disarray, the mayoral elections in New Orleans brought renewed attention to inequality and discriminatory practices at the polls. This is far from a new issue, however, as the South has been plagued with a lurid history of both openly violent and more subterranean efforts to keep blacks out of the political process. A brief overview of this history helps to situate voting practices after Hurricane Katrina within an ongoing battle between the ideals of democracy and the reality of unequal access to and ownership of the full rights of citizenship (Keyssar, 2000).

Voting and the civic life of any community are played out against the backdrop of struggles to attain and to hold onto power. As the majority population, historically whites in the South went to great lengths to keep their stronghold on the labor market, social scene, and the political process. As Behrens, Uggen, and Manza (2003) point out, "the prospective enfranchising of racial minorities during the Reconstruction period (with the adoption of the Fourteen and Fifteenth amendments in 1868 and 1870) threatened to shift the balance of power among racial groups in the United States, engendering a particularly strong backlash" (p. 560).

Universal suffrage was hotly contended for decades in the South. "The U.S. Constitution of 1787 neither granted nor denied anyone the right to vote" (Behrens et al., 2003, p. 561). It was not until the 1860s that the "Reconstruction Acts," which allowed former Confederate states representation in Congress, required Southern states to grant broad and race neutral access to the ballot. Blacks were not considered legal citizens of the United States until 1868 when the Fourteenth Amendment extended the definition of American citizenship to include all persons born in the United States (Keyssar, 2000).

In 1870, the Fifteenth Amendment explicitly eliminated states' ability to deny the right to vote based on race (Uggen et al., 2003). As such, the right to vote was extended to black men. Black women, along with women of all races and ethnicities, were still denied the vote. They would not be allowed to vote until the 1920 passage of the Nineteenth Amendment. The United States Army enforced the law while occupying the former confederacy, thus there was initially a large impact on black suffrage (Chin, 2004). During that time, blacks were allowed to vote, hold public office, and even to mix with whites to a limited degree (Wacquant, 2002). Yet, there remained violent opposition to universal suffrage and weak federal enforcement to ensure that black men were allowed access to the ballot.

The Louisiana Constitution of 1898 invented the grandfather clause, exempting from educational and property tests, those who were entitled to vote on or before January 1, 1867, or the son or grandson of such a person. Louisiana's Lieutenant Governor explained the goal of the clause in no uncertain terms: "every white man shall vote, because he is white, and no black man shall vote, because he is black" (as cited in Chin, 2004, p. 1592).

Disenfranchisement, or legally denying populations the right to vote, occurred first in Mississippi, South Carolina, and Louisiana, jurisdictions with black majorities. Again, this was an issue of power: "Where African-Americans were small minorities, disenfranchisement was unnecessary to render them powerless" (Chin, 2004, p. 1605). Behrens et al. (2003) offer a compelling example of this idea of racial threat when they quote from the opening address of the Alabama Constitutional Convention of 1901:

> The justification for whatever manipulation of the ballot that has occurred in this State has been the *menace of negro domination* ... These provisions are justified in law and in morals, because it is said that the

negro is not discriminated against on account of his race, but on account of his intellectual and moral condition (p. 571).

In response to this perceived threat, Southern states enacted Jim Crow laws, "social and legal codes that prescribed the complete separation of the 'races' and sharply circumscribed the life chances of African-Americans" (Wacquant, 2002, p. 46).

While blacks formally earned the right to vote after the Civil War, poll taxes and literacy tests kept blacks informally disenfranchised well after (Behrens et al., 2003). Essentially, blacks were "deprived of the right to vote in the self-appointed cradle of democracy" (Wacquant, 2002, p. 44) until the 1960s. Wacquant (2002) further argues that the Jim Crow system was a "race making" institution, which helped to create the divisions between blacks and whites:

> The highly particular conception of "race" that America has invented, virtually unique in the world for its rigidity and consequentiality, is a direct outcome of the momentous collision between slavery and democracy … The Jim Crow regime reworked the racialized boundary between slave and free into a rigid caste separation between "whites" and "Negros"—comprising all persons of known African ancestry, no matter how minimal—that infected every crevice of the postbellum social system in the South. (pp. 54–55)

The Voting Rights Act of 1965 brought significant change to the South by mandating that blacks be given entry to the political process. It specifically guaranteed blacks the right to register to vote and outlawed literacy tests and all other measures serving as obstacles (Joubert & Crouch, 1977). The Voting Rights Act of 1965 differed from the Fifteenth Amendment because it also provided federal examiners to enforce the mandate, finally giving blacks access to collective political power. Substantial increases in black registration subsequently allowed for the election of black officials in the 1970s (Joubert & Crouch, 1977; Knickrehm & Bent, 1988).

With these changes, fear and racial threat again came into play. While voting turnout was historically low among southerners, white southerners increased participation and used their votes to resist black demands. As Hammond (1977) argues, "changes in behavior of white southerners must be understood as a response to changes in the position of blacks" (p. 14).

A report entitled *The Long Shadow of Jim Crow: Voter Intimidation and Suppression in America Today,* written by People for the American Way and the National Association for the Advancement of Colored People (NAACP) claims:

> In every national American election since Reconstruction, every election since the Voting Rights Act passed in 1965, voters—particularly African American voter and other minorities—have faced calculated and determined efforts at intimidation and suppression. The bloody days of violence and retribution following the Civil War and Recon-

struction are gone. The poll taxes, literacy tests and physical violence of the Jim Crow era have disappeared. Today, more subtle, cynical and creative tactics have taken their place. (p. 1)

The report goes on to document decades of nonviolent, subtle, and often clever tactics used to try to suppress the minority vote. As one example, in Louisiana in 2002, flyers were distributed in black communities urging voters to go to the polls three days after a Senate runoff election was actually held. The 2000 Florida elections offered an example of negligence rather than outright coercion, but still resulted in suppression of minority votes as counties with large minority populations were more likely to have outdated and faulty voting machines and to have their ballots rejected (Hines, 2002, p. 72).

After weighing the evidence, Wacquant (2002) makes a strong claim concerning the relevance of racial threat: "Race or, to be more precise, *blackness—* for, since the origins, it is the presence of dishonoured dark-skinned persons brought in chains from Africa that has necessitated the (re)invention and perpetuation of racial vision and division—is properly understood as America's *primeval civic felony*" (p. 136).

Race and Felon Disenfranchisement

Felon disenfranchisement, then, is a fundamental example of continued voter suppression. While the Voting Rights Act of 1965 eliminated most disenfranchising practices, felon disenfranchisement remains an accepted practice. Felon disenfranchisement, the act of denying the vote to those in prison, or often, on parole, probation, or of ex-felon status has existed in the U.S. for over 300 years. There is evidence that as early as the colonial era, offenders were disenfranchised (Manza & Uggen, 2006). Felon disenfranchisement laws are state based, meaning that all 50 states have different, although often overlapping laws concerning a felon or ex-felon's right to vote. According to Manza and Uggen (2006) states adopted these laws in two waves. The first wave came in the northeast after changes in state suffrage rules expanded the right to vote. The second wave occurred in the south after the Civil War and the adoption of the Fifteenth Amendment which extended the right to vote specifically to black men.

Currently, 48 states deny the right to vote to felons—as of 2006, only Maine and Vermont allowed inmates in state prisons to vote (Sentencing Project, 2006). Thirty-five states deny felony parolees the right to vote and 30 states deny felony probationers the right to vote. Finally, three states deny ex-felons the right to vote, while nine other states deny ex-felons the right to vote for a waiting period and/or permanently deny voting rights for certain offenses (Sentencing Project, 2006).

There has been a movement to reform felon disenfranchisement laws in the past 30 years (King, 2006), but even with this movement an increasing number of individuals have lost the right to vote. As of October 2006, 5.3 million Americans could not vote because of prior criminal behavior (Manza & Uggen, 2006). In fact, while the crime rate in the U.S. has declined between 1991 and 2005, the incarceration rate during this same period increased by 50 percent (Sentencing Project, 2005). This percentage illustrates a 33-year increase in incarceration rates in the United States and has a significant effect on felon voter disenfranchisement even as reform in this country is in progress.

Of utmost importance is that these policies disproportionately impact blacks in the U.S., with 1 in 12 blacks ineligible to vote in 2004 due to felony convictions—which is almost five times higher than non-black rates (King, 2006). It is hard not to question the reason for such policies when one sees the impact on individuals and communities of color. It is even more difficult when the basis for the earliest policies is examined.

One of the best examples of the intersection of race and felon disenfranchisement is the discourse of the Mississippi Supreme Court in 1896 justifying the Mississippi disenfranchisement law (as cited in Behrens et al., 2003).

> The [constitutional] convention swept the circle of expedients to obstruct the exercise of the franchise by the negro race. By reason of its previous condition of servitude and dependence, this race had acquired or accentuated certain peculiarities of habit, of temperament and of character, which clearly distinguish it, as a race, from that of the whites—a patient and docile people, but careless, landless, and migratory within narrow limits, without aforethought, and its criminal members given rather to furtive offenses than to the robust crimes of the whites. Restrained by the federal constitution from discriminating against the negro race, the convention discriminated against its characteristics and the offenses to which its weaker member were prone. (p. 570)

Given the above characterization and reasoning, crimes in Mississippi such as theft and burglary were disqualifications for voting, while crimes in which violence was a principle component were not (Kennedy, 1997).

Behrens et al. (2003) argue while overt discourse such as the justification by the Mississippi Supreme Court certainly shows a racist basis for disenfranchisement policy, the covert discourse of recent policy discussions should be considered no less racist as they are built on these first policies. In fact, when viewed through the lens of racial threat theories, felon disenfranchisement laws have served to dilute the voting strength of groups perceived to be a threat to the majority population. Analyses of such laws and the voting strength of racial and economic minorities, specifically blacks, show this dilution (Behrens et al., 2003) and add support to the theory. This same covert racist reasoning, or what Bobo and Smith (1998) refer to as "laissez-faire racism," can be seen in the experiences of victims of Hurricane Katrina and their pursuit to vote in the aftermath of the hurricane.

Race and Voter Disenfranchisement after Katrina

Issues of voter disenfranchisement again came to the forefront in New Orleans in the wake of Hurricane Katrina. The hurricane and its aftermath disrupted voting practices in a way that dramatically disadvantaged blacks and the poor. Moreover, attempts to gain greater inclusiveness were ignored and sometimes met with outright resistance.

After Hurricane Katrina ravaged the south, thousands of residents were forced from their homes; studies estimate that approximately 60 percent of New Orleans' original population had not yet returned by the 2006 mayoral election (Harden, 2006). The 2006 mayoral elections, which took place in April and May, were the first elections held since the disaster. Because thousands of residents from Louisiana were forced to seek refuge in areas across the United States, many argued that the large number of displaced voters created an unfair election (Krupa, 2006a). While extra amendments to voting policies were made to help boost voter turnout, civil rights activists suggested that those who were able and informed enough to vote were still divided across racial lines (Varney, 2006).

Elections in Louisiana—with the exception of U.S. presidential elections—follow a variation of the open primary system. In the 2006 New Orleans mayoral elections, all of the candidates were listed on one ballot, regardless of party affiliation, and therefore, voters did not need to limit themselves to the candidates of one party. By Louisiana law, unless one candidate takes more than 50 percent of the votes in the first round, a runoff election is held between the top two candidates. In the primaries which took place on April 22, no candidate took 50 percent of the votes, and a run-off election between the top two candidates—incumbent mayor Ray Nagin and Louisiana Lieutenant Governor Mitch Landrieu—took place on May 22.

The primary election was initially scheduled to be held on February 4 and the runoff on March 4, but the election was postponed due to the devastation in the aftermath of Hurricane Katrina (Donze & Russell, 2006). Even then, the date chosen for the new election raised concern over issues of fairness and race for civil rights advocates. Some business and political leaders urged that the election be held as early as possible to keep the incumbents' terms from being extended without voter approval (Whoriskey, 2006). Alternatively, activists argued that the election should be delayed to give evacuees, the majority of whom were black, more time to move back to the city (Whoriskey, 2006).

Civil rights advocates and community groups argued that the changing demographics of New Orleans would have a significant impact on voter turnout. While the population of the city was once two-thirds black, the figures were reversed after Hurricane Katrina as the majority of those who were able to move back to New Orleans were white (Eggler, 2006a; Harden, 2006). Some black leaders suggested the mayoral election was a ploy by the city's white power structure to "take back City Hall" which since 1978 had been occupied by a black mayor (Donze & Russell, 2006; Eggler, 2006a). Of the 22 mayoral candidates that ran in the primaries, only three of them were black, including incumbent mayor Nagin (Eggler, 2006a). Bruce Gordon, president of the NAACP (National Coalition for the Advancement of Colored People), was quoted as saying, "I'm not here to tell you this is all about racism, but we know race is an issue here" (Varney, 2006, p. 1).

Hundreds of thousands of black New Orleanians were still living away from the city at the time of the election; the black evacuees tended to be considerably poorer and therefore were often relocated further away from the city than white evacuees, making it more difficult for them to cast a ballot (Eggler, 2006a). The correlation between poverty and education also played a role in the election as impoverished individuals are generally less likely to be registered to vote or to understand how the voting process works (Thevenot, 2006). Also, citizens relocated away from New Orleans were less likely to have access to information on the candidates and the details of the election (Thevenot & Williams, 2006; Varney, 2006).

The Reverend Jesse Jackson expressed grave concern over the mayoral election, contending, "… the election is fundamentally unfair because of the number of citizens who are disenfranchised by lack of equal access and therefore lack of equal opportunity" (Krupa, 2006a). Because civil rights activists rallied for amendments to voting policies and threatened to challenge the election results with lawsuits, the 2006 mayoral elections in New Orleans have been hailed as "the most scrutinized election in American history" (Thevenot, 2006, p. 1).

Louisiana Secretary of State Al Ater was appointed to the task of ensuring a fair election, and new policies and strategies were adopted in an effort to boost voter turnout (Thevenot, 2006). Voting laws prior to Hurricane Katrina mandated that only those who were registered to vote and living in New Orleans could participate in the election; those who were outside of New Orleans at the time of an election could register to vote by mail with an absentee ballot (Eggler, 2006a). First-time voters were not eligible for absentee ballots, however, because the original law stated that first-time voters must cast ballots in-person at least once before voting by absentee ballot (Anderson, 2006a; Thevenot, 2006).

The state legislature approved a proposal that allowed absentee ballots and limited in-state satellite voting and got it approved by the Justice Department. This was seen as the most cost-effective way to encourage voting; new provisions passed in February allowed those who registered to vote between October 5, 2004 and September 24, 2005 to mail or fax in absentee request forms, rather than having to vote in person the first time (Anderson, 2006a; Thevenot, 2006).

New policy was also approved that created ten satellite polling locations in cities across Louisiana (Brazile, 2006). The locations were determined by urbanity, and cities with over 100,000 residents hosted a satellite polling station (Eggler, 2006a). The satellite polling stations allowed people to cast early ballots across Louisiana in person on April 10–13 and April 15 for the primary, and also allowed new voters who did not register to vote between October 5, 2004 and September 24, 2005 to request absentee ballots (Brazile, 2006). While the stations did relieve voters of driving all of the way to New Orleans to cast ballots, civil rights activists argued that many displaced residents were outside of Louisiana. Those still in or near the state who made the effort to vote may have had to spend hard-earned money to arrange transportation to the nearest satellite polling station, which for some was still hundreds of miles away (Eggler, 2006a; Filosa & Nolan, 2006).

Civil rights advocates and grassroots organizations pushed for several other amendments, including satellite polling stations outside of Louisiana where there were a large number of evacuees, particularly in cities like Houston, Atlanta, and Jackson, Mississippi (Anderson, 2006b; Varney, 2006). This bill was rejected on the grounds that organizing polling stations outside of Louisiana would further delay the election and be expensive to implement (Eggler, 2006a). Secretary of State Ater contended that the improvements in absentee voting would be sufficient to reach those who were outside of New Orleans (Anderson, 2006a). Advocates also proposed a bill that would have required state election officials to provide political candidates a list of voters who had been displaced because of the hurricane (Whoriskey, 2006). This bill was also rejected on the grounds of protecting the privacy rights of FEMA aid recipients; the list of evacuees—which was never converted to a list of eligible registered voters—was held as confidential by Ater (Anderson, 2006a; Whoriskey, 2006). Finally, advocates proposed a measure that would require election officials to send out absentee ballots and candidate information to known evacuees in a time of disaster (Anderson, 2006a). This bill gained support, but ultimately did not have time to be implemented before the primary ballots were due (Anderson, 2006b).

Louisiana's refusal to set up out-of-state polling locations sparked a protest march over the Mississippi River Bridge in New Orleans on April 1, which was organized by the Reverend Jesse Jackson and his Rainbow/Push Coalition (Donze & Filosa, 2006; Thevenot, 2006). Thousands of primarily black citizens, including members of ACORN (Associations of Community Organizations for Reform Now) and the NAACP (National Coalition for the Advancement of Colored People), called for the postponement of the elections until equal access to the candidates, information about the election, and actual voting places could be guaranteed to all residents (Black, 2006; Donze & Filosa, 2006). In particular, the activists attacked the Bush Administration for setting up satellite polling for Iraqi, Bosnian, and Mexican citizens in the U.S. during elections for those countries, but refusing to allow this for the thousands of displaced New Orleans residents (Anderson, 2006b; Black, 2006). Many protesters also compared the absence of polling stations outside of Louisiana to the poll taxes and Jim Crow Laws that historically prevented blacks from voting in the early 20th century (Black, 2006).

Groups found creative solutions to transportation challenges by setting up bussing systems to transport evacuees to the nearest polling stations in Louisiana (Filosa & Nolan, 2006). ACORN, the largest community organization of low income families in the United States, organized busses from Dallas, Houston, and Little Rock, which helped hundreds who may not have otherwise been able to vote to cast ballots in the primaries (Donze & Russell, 2006; Krupa, 2006a).

While absentee ballots did allow those who were outside of New Orleans to vote in the mayoral election, many black voters still felt deep distrust in the absentee and satellite polling system (Donze & Russell, 2006; Filosa & Nolan, 2006; Thevenot & Williams, 2006). One native of New Orleans who was forced to relocate in Houston explained, "I'm not even sure my vote was counted" (Filosa & Nolan, 2006, p. 12).

Defense lawyers argued that the absentee system was cumbersome, confusing, and that those who were most likely to have difficulty navigating through official paperwork were the impoverished minorities who were disproportionately forced to flee New Orleans (Eggler, 2006b; Thevenot, 2006). Theodore Shaw, president of the NAACP Legal Defense Fund, which joined with other groups to protest the rejection of out-of-state polls, contended that Louisiana's absentee system created "high tech disenfranchisement on a massive scale" (Thevenot, 2006, p. 1). Further, civil rights advocates argued that having to mail in absentee requests and to receive the official ballot by mail caused citizens to depend twice on a potentially faulty mail system (Anderson, 2006b). Some absentee ballots were reported to have been mailed to former New Orleans addresses or to not have come in time to be cast for the primary and runoff election dates (Anderson, 2006b).

Advocates also argued that the provisions that allowed those who had registered to vote between October 5, 2004 and September 24, 2005 to mail in absentee request forms only helped 1,800 out of 15,000 potential first-time voters, 72 percent of whom were black (Eggler, 2006b; Thevenot, 2006). Also, the satellite polling that allowed voters to cast early ballots throughout Louisiana only applied for those who had registered to vote prior to September 24, 2005, although registration for the election did not close until the week of March 26, 2006 (Eggler, 2006b).

Other signs of disenfranchisement were evidenced in statements from former residents outside of Louisiana who claimed that they were not adequately informed about the election (Thevenot, 2006). One woman in Houston said that there was no information in the papers about where or how to vote, or even who the candidates were in the primaries (Thevenot, 2006). Others became confused about resident status; many had taken jobs and enrolled their children in schools in other cities and were unclear on where they could claim voting rights (Thevenot & Williams, 2006).

While observers had speculated that the political strength of displaced voters could be a major factor in the election, the results showed that only about 22,500 absentee and satellite votes were cast in the primaries, and about 25,000 were cast in the runoff (Filosa & Nolan, 2006; Krupa, 2006b). Researchers speculated that approximately 200,000 registered voters were still displaced from New Orleans; as such, participation in the election was much lower than advocates had hoped for (Donze & Russell, 2006; Krupa, 2006b). Secretary of State Ater reported that there were about 20,000 requests for absentee ballots during the primary election, but it seemed that either these requests were not adequately met, or that voters failed to trust the system and chose not to send in their ballots.

Estimates from the primaries showed that about 31 percent of eligible blacks voted, compared with 45 percent in the 2002 primary (Roberts, 2006). The percentage of white voters remained unchanged from both elections, with 50 percent voter turnout (Roberts, 2006). The evidence is clear that those who were hardest hit by Hurricane Katrina were the least likely to vote in the mayoral election, and those that were hit the hardest were disproportionately black (Donze & Russell, 2006; Harden, 2006; Roberts, 2006). One news analysis reported that the voting turnout from natives to the Lower Ninth Ward of New Orleans—a predominantly impoverished black neighborhood that was devastated by Katrina—fell nearly 50 percent compared to the 2002 mayoral election (Harden, 2006). By comparison, voter turnout in Lakeview, a white, affluent neighborhood across town, only fell 6 percent (Harden, 2006).

While many civil rights activists feared that the disproportionately large number of white voters would create a white City Hall, the black incumbent mayor Ray Nagin won the runoff against white candidate Mitch Landrieu on May 20 by a 4 percent margin. The election was seen as especially important for the people of New Orleans as it determined who would lead the re-building of the city (Filosa & Nolan, 2006). This, combined with the issues of race and voter disenfranchisement, caused the election to catch the public's eye on a national scale more than any other mayoral election in U.S. history.

While many civil rights groups challenged the procedures used in this election with lawsuits claiming the election was unfair due to the high percentage of displaced voters, those appeals have not held up in the courts. The Justice Department ruled that the election, with the addition of the absentee and satellite polling amendments, complied with the terms of the 1965 Voting Rights Act and did not discriminate against black voters or significantly reduce black electoral strength (Donze & Russell, 2006; Grace, 2006). Despite this, civil rights advocates still contend that much more could have been done to "get the vote out," especially surrounding the issue of out-of-state satellite polling and displaced voters' ability to obtain information about the candidates and the election (Krupa, 2006a).

Controlling Race through Disenfranchisement

As we have shown, the United States has a long history of legally validated voter disenfranchisement. What explains the unlikely persistence of felon disenfranchisement and the dramatic political inequalities following Hurricane Katrina? Consistent with the arguments of Critical Race theory, both cases point to the fundamental role of racial considerations in shaping legal decision making and political outcomes.

Critical Race theory examines the use of law, especially the discourse of law as a neutral, objective arbitrator, to discourage racial equality and encourage a system of white supremacy. The experiences of victims of Hurricane Katrina as they tried to navigate the primary election and subsequent runoff election for mayor of New Orleans serves as an example of the use of law to legitimate inequality.

From the beginning, the policies put in place to facilitate these elections focused on issues of "cost-effectiveness" and "efficiency," not on maximizing the number of evacuees given the chance to vote. For example, satellite voting sites were only created in Louisiana, even though over 150,000 people were evacuated to Houston, Texas alone. While civil rights activists proposed policies designed to enfranchise as many displaced New Orleans residents as possible, going so far as to rent buses to bus individuals to the nearest polling sites, the Justice Department ruled that the provisions that had been put in place by the federal government complied with the 1965 Voting Rights Act, thus suggesting that these provisions offered an equal opportunity for those displaced.

Probably most troubling is that proposals to organize the voting process and make the elections accessible to the most evacuees possible, thus ensuring the right to vote, were actually rejected, not only on the grounds that they would delay the process and be too expensive to implement, but that they would violate the right to privacy. While the right to privacy is clearly important, it is troubling that this argument was used to stop the process of enfranchising as many individuals as possible. A federal government that does not see the importance of preserving the right to vote especially in times of crisis, is not doing all it can to preserve the civil rights of its citizens. This is especially troubling given that during this exact same time period the federal government was also advocating for the right to engage in warrantless wiretapping by arguing that this program *did not* violate the right to privacy.

These rulings underscore the use of law and the political system to strengthen the rights of the federal government at the cost of individual civil rights. The 1965 Voting Rights Act was used in this instance to legitimate a process that contributed to the disenfranchisement of individuals, the majority of which were the poor and people of color—thus becoming another example of a law once designed to decrease inequality instead supporting the continued propagation of white privilege.

References

Aguirre, Jr., A. (2000). Academic storytelling: A critical race theory story of affirmative action. *Sociological Perspectives, 43*(2), 319–339.

Anderson, E. (2006b, March 30). Panel sinks out-of-state vote bill: OKs automatic ballot mailing. *The Times-Picayune.* Retrieved January 30, 2007 from LexisNexis database.

———. (2006a, April 6). Panel OKs release of displaced voters list: Whether state would go along is unclear. *The Times-Picayune.* Retrieved January 30, 2007 from LexisNexis database.

Behrens, A., Uggen, C., & Manza, J. (2003). Ballot manipulation and the "menace of Negro domination": Racial threat and felon disenfranchisement in the United States, 1850–2002. *American Journal of Sociology, 109*, 559–605.

Black, M. B. (2006, April 3). Universal human rights: Public challenges impending New Orleans elections & human rights. *New Orleans Indymedia.* Retrieved January 30, 2007 from http://neworleans.indymedia.org/news/2006/04/7429.php.

Bobo, L. & Smith, R. (1998). From Jim Crow racism to laissez-faire racism: The transformation of racial attitudes. In W. F. Katkin, N. Landsman & A. Tyree (Eds.), *Beyond pluralism: The conception of groups and group identities in America* (pp. 182–220). Chicago: University of Illinois Press.

Brazile, K. T. (2006, March 19). Morial adds his voice to election protests: Outcome likely to be contested, he says. *The Times-Picayune*. Retrieved January 30, 2007 from LexisNexis database.

Chin, G. J. (2004). The "Voting Rights Act of 1867": The constitutionality of federal regulation of suffrage during reconstruction. *North Carolina Law Review, 82,* 1581–1608.

Crenshaw, K., Gotanda, N., Peller, G. & Thomas, K. (1995). Introduction. In K. Crenshaw, N. Gotanda, G. Peller & K. Thomas (Eds.), *Critical Race Theory: The Key Writings that Formed the Movement* (pp. xiii–xxii). New York: New Press.

Donze, F., & Filosa, G. (2006, April 2). Bridge march hails justice, voter rights: Thousands join Jesse Jackson in crossing river. *The Times-Picayune*. Retrieved January 30, 2007 from LexisNexis database.

Donze, F., & Russell, G. (2006, April 23). Nagin vs. Landrieu: Forman runs distant 3rd, runoff set for May 20. *The Times-Picayune*. Retrieved January 30, 2007 from LexisNexis database.

Eggler, B. (2006a, February 25). Evacuees can vote absentee or in Louisiana: Judge rules against out-of-state polling. *The Times-Picayune*. Retrieved January 30, 2007 from LexisNexis database.

———. (2006b, March 25). Judge to rehear poll complaints: N.O. plan is called unfair to black voters. *The Times-Picayune*. Retrieved January 30, 2007 from LexisNexis database.

Fan, S. (1997). Immigration law and the promise of critical race theory: Opening the academy to the voices of aliens and immigrants. Columbia Law Review, *97*(4), 1202–1240.

Filosa, G., & Nolan, B. (2006, May 21). Voters determined to take a stand: Many drive in to make sure voices get heard. *The Times-Picayune*. Retrieved January 30, 2007 from LexisNexis database.

Grace, S. (2006, March 30). A vote for closure. *The Times-Picayune*. Retrieved January 30, 2007 from LexisNexis database.

Hammond, J. L. (1977). Race and electoral mobilization: White southerners, 1952–1968. *The Public Opinion Quarterly, 41,* 13–27.

Harden, B. (2006, May 18). New Orleans: A tale of two cities. *The Seattle Times*. Retrieved January 30, 2007 from http://archives.seattletimes.nw source.com/.

Hines, R. I. (2002). The silent voices: 2000 presidential election and the minority vote in Florida. *The Western Journal of Black Studies, 26,* 71–74.

Joubert, P. E. & Crouch, B. M. (1977). Mississippi Blacks and the Voting Rights Act of 1965. *The Journal of Negro Education, 46,* 157–167.

Kennedy, R. (1997). *Race, crime, and the law.* New York: Vintage Books.

Keyssar, A. (2000). *The right to vote: The contested history of democracy in the United States.* New York: Basic Books.

King, R. (2006). *A decade of reform: Felony disenfranchisement policy in the United States.* The Sentencing Project. Retrieved December 18, 2006 from http://www.sentencingproject.org/pdfs/FVR_Decade_Reform.pdf.

Knickrehm, K. M., & Bent, D. (1988). Voting rights, voter turnout, and realignment: The impact of the 1965 Voting Rights Act. *Journal of Black Studies, 18,* 283–296.

Krupa, M. (2006a, April 25). New challenges of election vowed. *The Times-Picayune.* Retrieved January 30, 2007 from LexisNexis database.

———. (2006b, May 21). Candidates shrink travel plans, displaced voters not a high priority. *The Times-Picayune.* Retrieved January 30, 2007 from http://www.nola.com/newslogs/topnews/index.ssf?/mtlogs/nola_topnews/archives/2006_05_10.html.

Manza, J., & Uggen, C. (2006). *Locked out: Felon disenfranchisement and American democracy.* New York: Oxford University Press, Inc.

Overton, S. (2006). *Stealing democracy: The new politics of voter suppression.* New York: W. W. Norton & Company.

Roberts, M. (2006, May, 6). NO's 1st post-Katrina vote drew fewer black voters. *Houston Chronicle.* Retrieved January, 30, 2007 from http://www.chron.com.

Suppressing the N.O. vote. (2006, May 1). Retrieved September 16, 2006 from http://www.thenation.com/doc/20060501/editors.

The Sentencing Project. (2005). *New incarceration figures: Thirty-three years of consecutive growth.* Retrieved December 18, 2006 from http://www.sentencingproject.org/pdfs/1044.pdf.

———. (2006). *Felony disenfranchisement laws in the United States.* Retrieved December 18, 2006 from http://www.sentencingproject.org/pdfs/1046.pdf.

Taylor, E. (1998). A primer on critical race theory. *The Journal of Blacks in Higher Education, 19,* 122–124.

Thevenot, B. (2006, April 3). Absentee voters' interest is brisk; but how many cast ballot is big question. *The Times-Picayune.* Retrieved January 30, 2007 from LexisNexis database.

Thevenot, B. & Williams, L. (2006, April, 11). 2,190 cast early ballots in New Orleans elections: Some displaced voters bused to satellite polls. *The Times-Picayune.* Retrieved January 30, 2007 from http://www.nola.com/frontpage/t-p/index.ssf?/base/news-5/114473818311400.xml.

Uggen, C., Manza, J., & Behrens, A. (2003). Felony voting rights and the disenfranchisement of African Americans. *Souls, 5,* 48–57.

Varney, J. (2006, March 14). NAACP warns of challenge to next month's elections: Group fears too few will be able to vote. *The Times-Picayune*. Retrieved January 30, 2007 from LexisNexis database.

Wacquant, L. (2002). From slavery to mass incarceration: Rethinking the "race question" in the U.S. *New Left Review, 13,* 41–60.

———. (2005). Race as civic felony. *International Social Science Journal, 57,* 127–142.

West, C. (1995). Forward. In K. Crenshaw, N. Gotanda, G. Peller, & K. Thomas (Eds.), *Critical Race Theory: The Key Writings that Formed the Movement* (pp. xi–xii). New York: New Press.

Whoriskey, P. (2006, March 6). A mayoral free-for-all in changed New Orleans: Incumbent Nagin now counts on absentee voters for win. *The Washington Post*. Retrieved January 30, 2007 from http://www.washington post.com/wpyn/content/article/2006/03/05/AR2006030500884_pf.htm.

Chapter 4

Locked and Loaded: The Prison Industrial Complex and the Response to Hurricane Katrina

Shana Agid

"[The troops] brought a sense of order and peace, and it was a beautiful sight to see that we're ramping up. We are seeing a show of force. It's putting confidence back in our hearts and in the minds of our people. We're going to make it through."

— Louisiana Governor Kathleen Babineaux Blanco,
September 4, 2005

"You can't have reconstruction until you have law and order, and you can't have law and order without a jail … So we have a jail. Without the vision to have a jail, you can't have reconstruction. So it's a wonderful thing."

— Angola prison warden, Burl Cain

"Increased coercive control within jurisdictions is, as we have seen in the U.S. context, one way to manage the effects of organized abandonment."

— Scholar and activist, Ruth Wilson Gilmore[1]

Within days of Hurricane Katrina's historic and devastating landfall on the Gulf Coast of the United States, New Orleans already had a new jail. Fashioned from the empty hulk of the bus depot, "Camp Greyhound," as it came to be called, was set to lock over 700 people in rapidly erected cages surrounded by cyclone-fencing. In its first days the jail saw nearly 250 people move through its

---

1. Gov. Blanco as quoted in McFadden (2005, p. 30); Cain as quoted in CNN broadcasts included in Hunt (2006) documentary, *I Won't Drown on this Levee and you ain't gonna break my back;* and Gilmore quote is from Gilmore (2002, p. 272).

doors. Many were black men arrested for "looting" in the wake of the most destructive storm in recent memory that, paired with lagging government response, left basic survival resources scarce and transportation to drier, safer land nearly impossible to find. On September 2, 2005, Burl Cain, warden of the infamous Louisiana State Prison, better known as Angola, volunteered to come down to New Orleans to run what came to be called Camp Greyhound. It was, he said, a "real start" to rebuilding the city (Berenson, 2005, n.p.).

As survivors struggled to live with limited supplies of food and water, many turning increasingly to taking what they needed (and sometimes more) from the shuttered stores around them, politicians and media sources lambasted them, calling New Orleans "lawless" and calling survivors—mostly black and poor people who could not afford to leave before the storm and who had not been helped since—"looters," "thugs," and "hoodlums." And while survivors sat waiting for information, medical care, and resources four days after the storm passed, President George W. Bush said there would be "'zero tolerance' for law-breakers" (Bode & Siemasko, 2005, n.p.) and Governor Kathleen Babineaux Blanco said National Guard members coming to New Orleans from Arkansas to, as the *New York Times* put it, "reclaim the city" had "M-16's and they are locked and loaded" (Treaster & Sontag, 2005, n.p.). The following day, the Governor reiterated: "I have one message for these hoodlums. These troops know how to shoot and kill, and they are more than willing to do so if necessary" (Dao & Kleinfeld, 2005, n.p.).

Why, in the face of the worst natural disaster ever to hit the United States, was the primary response to put "law and order" first? The mobilization of massive numbers of police, prison guards, military, and private security in the relief effort immediately following Hurricane Katrina highlights the increasingly central role of *control* in the face of social and economic crises. Just two days after the hurricane hit and thousands of people awaited rescue, New Orleans Mayor Ray Nagin ordered all 1,500 local police to cease search and rescue operations and focus instead on arresting "looters" (McFadden & Blumenthal, 2005). By September 3rd, five days after the levees broke and covered 80 percent of the city in water, federal troops were finally given a shoot-to-kill order (Siemasko, 2005). As hundreds of people trying to survive the disaster were criminalized for their actions, thousands of prisoners already under state control were stranded in the city's largest jail, Orleans Parish Prison, after the Sheriff chose not to evacuate and many deputies deserted their posts. As water line rose to eight feet, buildings flooded, power was lost, and some prisoners were left locked into cells with scant food and water for days (American Civil Liberties Union, 2006).

If building a jail was, in fact, going to be considered the first step in rebuilding the city of New Orleans, it would be a step with far-reaching historical implications, brought on in large part by the ideologies and technologies of the contemporary punishment industry. This chapter examines the aftermath of Hurricane Katrina through the lens of a 30-year build-up of the reliance on

prisons, policing, and control to address social, economic, and political problems—what many have come to call the prison industrial complex.

Context for Disaster:
The Prison Industrial Complex

The idea that prisons are a standard tool for punishment and the creation of
public safety is overwhelmingly familiar—prisons and jails are constantly
imagined in television, news media, and film representations. And for many
people, especially those in poor and working-class communities, as well as in
communities of color, they are experienced as a feature of the contemporary
landscape. However, prisons, and the policing and surveillance techniques
used in conjunction with confinement, are far from natural. Rather, the imposition of the policies and techniques of caging and controlling people are socially, politically, and historically contingent, reflecting geographer and activist
Ruth Wilson Gilmore's (2002) crucial insight that "prison-building is state-
building at its least contested" (p. 272).

Since the 1980s, the U.S. has seen not only a rapid rise in prison construction, matched just after it began by an explosion in the number of prisoners
confined in U.S. prisons and jails, but the formation of a network of government and private interests that emphasizes the use of policing, surveillance,
imprisonment, and social control to address social and economic problems.
This is what many activists and scholars now call the prison industrial complex. The PIC gains its power both from the military might of its police and
immigration control forces and from its acceptance as a necessary form of
"crime" control, focused on communities of color, even after three decades of
decreasing crime rates and well-documented policing and prison abuse, troubled courts, and false convictions. The PIC is constituted of not only prisons
themselves, but the systems that funnel people, usually poor people and people
of color, into cages; the news and entertainment media that help to make prisons, policing, and machinations of so-called criminal justice systems common
sense; the increasingly lucrative markets produced by prisons and law enforcement; and the restructuring of economies that produces surplus labor. Historically, its origins and justifications can be traced to crises of the racial and capitalist state (Gilmore, 1999, 2002).

Following Gilmore's trajectory, this contemporary state-building project
began to gather steam with the law and order platform that propelled Richard
Nixon's 1968 presidential campaign. She explains that the strategy of enforcement and punishment grew out of multiple political and social conditions, including a state reaction to the political organizing and activism of people of
color, anti-imperialist groups, and other radical formations in that era of eco-

nomic crisis and shifting U.S. and global politics. Gilmore (2002) notes that the moral panic about "crime," central to the law-and-order platform Nixon and other Republicans used to define their campaigns, was, in fact, rooted in an idea of *disorder*, personified in images of youth and people of color, often acting in opposition to state practices. She writes:

> Mid-1960s radical activism—both spontaneous and organized—had successfully produced widespread disorder throughout society. The ascendant right used the fact of disorder to persuade voters that the incumbents failed to govern. The claim accurately described objective conditions. But in order to exploit the evidence for political gain, the right had to interpret the turmoil as something they could contain, if elected, using already-existing capacities: the power to defend the nation against enemies foreign and domestic. And so the *contemporary* U.S. crime problem was born … The disorder that became "crime" had particular urban and racial qualities, and the collective characteristics of activists—whose relative visibility as enemies inversely reflected their structural powerlessness—defined the face of the individual criminal. (p. 267)

Through the 1980s, the "criminal" in question became the corporeal backbone of a massively bursting prison system, assisted by an ever-expanding police force throughout the nation's cities and border regions, in particular. By the time prison expansion was on the rise, crime rates were declining (as they have continued to decline overall since the mid-1970s), but the *utility* of the ever-increasing network of cages to the state, both economically and politically, was just beginning. At the time of Gilmore's 1998 writing, she explained that "the statistical inversion, by race, of those arrested (70 percent white) to those put in cages (70 percent persons of color) quantitatively indicates that the system punishes different kinds of people differently" (p. 174).

In addition to the law and order remedies implemented by the state and the construction of the "criminal" in racial, economic, gendered, and political terms, the prison boom—and by association the rapid growth of the PIC—also unfolded during a period of deindustrialization and economic restructuring. This moment, Gilmore (2002) explains, produced surpluses of labor, capital, land, and state capacity and prisons presented "a geographical solution to socio-economic problems" (p. 268). Throughout the 1980s and 1990s, the state also came to rely on rhetorics of policing, enforcement, punishment, and safety as a means of incorporating demands for ending violence against women, people of color, and lesbian, gay, bisexual, and ultimately transgender people into state-building projects. In response both to a shifting national focus that pressed politicians and government to demonstrate non-racist, non-sexist, and sometimes non-homophobic commitments, and to the policy advocacy of some mainstream organizations, the '80s and '90s witnessed a turn toward an idea of justice as a law-enforcement/criminal approach to addressing claims and demands of political and social activists of the 1960s and 1970s.[2]

Thus, the PIC, its capacity to control and contain and to produce what would pass as reasonable justifications for these actions—the fear of "crime" and the promise of "safety"—became a tool for addressing the political, social, and economic problems raised by the loss of jobs and job prospects, the closing of farms and factories, and the neoconservative (and popular) push to end welfare and other social services (Gilmore, 2002). The PIC was additionally bolstered by its invocation as a protector of civil and human rights, and the state's claims of "inclusion" in the post-civil rights era (Agid, 2005).

Now, the U.S. lays claim to the largest prison system in the world. By the end of 2004 there were 2,135,901 people locked up in U.S. jails and prisons, even after a drop in the rate of incarceration from previous periods. If we include people on probation and parole that number grows to nearly 7 million. The majority of those under the state's control are people of color: by the end of 2004, white people made up 34.3 percent of state and federal prisoners, black people accounted for 40.7 percent, Hispanics [sic] 19.2 percent, people identifying as "two or more races," 2.9 percent, and people classified as "other," including Asians, Pacific Islanders, and Native Americans, accounted for 2.9 percent (Bureau of Justice Statistics (BJS), 2005). Black men were seven times as likely to be serving time sentenced to a year or more than white men, while black women, who are the fastest growing group of prisoners in the U.S. (Bohrman & Murakawa, 2005), were four times as likely as white women to be doing a year or more in state or federal prisons. Latino/as, incarcerated at lower rates than black people, were still overrepresented inside as compared to their population in the U.S., with Latino men two and half times more likely than white men to be locked up, and Latina women almost twice as likely to be in prison than white women (BJS, 2005). Numbers of incarcerated people, however, do not in any way reflect a boiling-down of numbers of people doing activities classified as illegal, nor do they echo arrest rates, as noted above. For instance, returning to Gilmore's assertion that the PIC "punishes different kinds of people differently," African Americans make up 13 percent of the U.S. population, and about 13 percent of drug users, but account for 35 percent of those arrested for drug-related offences, 55 percent of those convicted, and fully 71 percent of all those actually sentenced to punishment (Bohrman & Murakawa, 2005).

---

2. Thanks to Emily Thuma for conversations highlighting this aspect of the solidification of the PIC in the '80s and '90s, specifically in terms of domestic violence and other anti-violence funding and policy making. For more on this idea in relationship to hate crime rhetorics and media discourse, see S. Agid (2005), *"Fags Doom Nations" and Other Parables of Hate: Representations of "Hate Crime" and Constructions of U.S. National Identity,* article-excerpt from an unpublished thesis available at http://sites.cca.edu/sightlines/2005/sagid_thesis.html.

Couched in the rhetoric of public safety, the contemporary PIC is a manifestation not only of racist policies and practices in the current moment, but an outgrowth of the techniques of racial management intrinsic to the U.S. racial state—a state organized by and through racialized access to power and resources—from the outset (Omi & Winant, 1986). Scholar, activist, and former prisoner Angela Y. Davis has shown, for example, that there are ideological and practical links between the U.S. slave economy and socio-political structure and the contemporary prison industrial complex. Noting that these connections were established during the "earliest period of U.S. history," Davis (2003) explains that "... race has always played a central role in constructing presumptions of criminality," (p. 28) including the revision of the Slave Codes—laws that regulated the status, behavior, and punishment of slaves before the abolition of slavery—into the Black Codes, enacted in many former slave states after the Civil War. The Black Codes, responsible for the incarceration of large numbers of free black people who were then often forced into unpaid labor as a part of their punishment, "proscribed a range of actions—such as vagrancy, absence from work, breach of job contracts, the possession of firearms, and insulting gestures or acts—that were criminalized only when the person charged was black" (p. 28). As Davis notes, the development of the punishment system especially in southern states after slavery sought specifically to restrict the freedom of large numbers of recently released slaves. This is one example of the ways in which prisons, and the lawmaking, policing, and surveillance practices used to fill and sustain them are, in fact, rooted in racist conglomerations of power to control bodies for the maintenance of white supremacy and financial gain in moments of major economic and political change.

How, then, is this legacy of penal control reiterated or remixed in a contemporary context? As Gilmore's analysis suggests, the political will to control anti-racist and other radical activism in the 1960s and 1970s through legal means (and sometimes extralegal means carried out by police and other state agents) paired with the upheaval that accompanied deindustrialization and shifts in local and global economic structures made way for a rapid and unprecedented expansion of technologies of control and confinement. But how did the exponentially growing number of prisons get so full? How did we get to 2 million and more? And how does this period of punishment expansion manifest *outside* the prison walls?

In the 30-plus years since the rise of law and order politics, the terrain of lawmaking, law enforcement, and sentencing has shifted forcefully toward not only mass incarceration, but the incorporation of policing and surveillance into the everyday lives of especially poor people and people of color in the U.S. This growth has taken shape in part through the declaration of multiple "wars" enacted on domestic and international fronts—the war on crime, the war on drugs, and now the war on terror—that have facilitated new categories of crime and harsher punishments, the collusion of police and military forces, and a pervasive culture of fear. Political scientists Rebecca Bohrman and Naomi Murakawa (2005) refer to this period as a fortification of the disciplinary state during which federal spending on law enforcement initiatives, "including immigration control, crime control, and drug enforcement ... has grown almost every year ... with an average yearly increase of 10 percent" (p. 110). Like Gilmore, Bohrman and Murakawa link the dismantling of welfare and other social projects and federal social service spending to the considerable disciplinary state-building project implemented through a national focus on enforcement and punishment. They note that federal spending on "justice administration" has more than tripled since 1960, as spending on unemployment, housing, and food and nutrition assistance has decreased since 1975. Federal employment also reveals disciplinary priorities:

> Even though federal employment is at its lowest level since 1960, law enforcement employment is at its highest level ever. Over the last twenty years the biggest increases in federal employment have been within immigration and crime control agencies. By 2002, the number of federal law enforcement workers surpassed the number of service provision workers. (p. 110)

The federal "wars" on drugs and crime, initiated by Richard Nixon in the 1970s and carried out in various forms especially during the Reagan, G. H. W. Bush, Clinton, G.W. Bush administrations not only resulted in these kinds of resource shifts, but in state and federal legislative trends toward harsher sentences for all categories of crime. This was especially true in the area of drug possession and sales, in the criminalization of formerly non-criminal acts, and in the treatment of once minor infractions as major violations (Gilmore, 2002). As Gilmore (2002) notes, changes in what counted as crime and in the punishments meted out upon conviction impacted poor people and people of color most intensively, with Native American people and people of African descent most severely criminalized, but with far-reaching consequences for Latino/a people and Asians and Pacific Islanders, as well. Changes in immigration law, like the 1996 passage of the Illegal Immigration Reform and Immigrant Responsibility Act (IIRAIRA), also extended laws regarding deportation and detention of immigrants and established new hyper-punitive requirements for lock-up and removal of even legal resident immigrants with criminal convictions from years before. Prior to IIRAIRA, the detention of migrants based solely on their national origin, and some perceived link to political or health threats, was already a contested but regular U.S. government practice. In 1986, the country's then-largest immigration detention center opened just months before the rededication ceremony for the Statue of Liberty (Rand, 2005). With the war on drugs came new sentencing and punishment policies such as state and federal mandatory minimum sentences for drug possession, carrying sentences of up to 25 years to life for relatively minor quantities of illegal drugs and mandatory deportation of non-citizens for felony drug convictions, even for those who have lived in the U.S. most of their lives.

Gilmore (2002) explains that the flurry of lawmaking and prison building did not reflect a growing "crime problem." In fact, she writes, "the best estimate for crime as a driving force of prison expansion shows it to account for little more than 10 percent of the increase" (p. 270). According to one study, mass incarceration may even drive up crime rates in areas where a "tipping point" of more than one to one and a half percent of a community is locked up (Justice Policy Institute, 2003). Instead, it was the state's move in this era toward more punitive policies and enforcement—plus the idea that prisons could be economic drivers in industry-starved rural towns[3]—that fed massively expanding prison populations and the resulting perception of an increase in crime, a concern to which we will return below.

As the tactics of control took hold, resources used to propel the wars on drugs and crime converged in increasingly militaristic police forces and increasingly localized military forces. In urban policing, the development of SWAT (Special Weapons and Tactics) units, the incorporation of military helicopters and other equipment brought a distinctly military strategy to police work. Angela Davis notes that when military defense contracts were on the wane in the early 1990s, the companies making military equipment courted law enforcement and the punishment industry to sell their wares as they "retool[ed] their defense technology for America's streets," as one story in the *Wall Street Journal* put it (as cited in, Davis, 2003, p. 87). The U.S. military became increasingly involved in both border patrol and drug enforcement throughout the 1980s and 1990s, and agents of the former Immigration and Naturalization Service were deputized to enforce narcotics and contraband laws, allowing them to seize drugs and property and make drug-related arrests of immigrants (Bohrman & Murakawa, 2005). (The INS was folded into the Department of Homeland Security after its creation by G.W. Bush, where the immigration control agency's focus became even more enforcement-oriented.)

The alignment of the goals, operations, and tactics of these enforcement/warfare agencies, and their consistent presence in neighborhoods of color, poor neighborhoods, and border areas, were, and still are, further rationalized by the continued panic over a perceived crime epidemic and an intrinsic, if inaccurate, belief that more enforcement and more confinement cre-

---

3. Incidentally, prisons are often failures as economic drivers. Offered as a recession-proof industry in towns that have usually lost other forms of major industry or agriculture, prisons tend not to lessen unemployment, often create environmental and land-use problems, and pave the way for big "box" stores that put smaller local business owners out of work. For more, see R.W. Gilmore and C. Gilmore (2004) and the work of the California Prison Moratorium Project.

ate more safety. But if the prison and policing booms largely *followed* decreasing crime rates, and the overall result of this expansion of the policing and punishment industries affects poor people and people of color in overwhelmingly disproportionate ways, we are left wondering what kind of safety is being prioritized and for whom? Conditions created by growing structural economic inequalities (Scott & Leonhardt, 2005),[4] and the distribution of resources according to race, class, gender, citizen status, sexuality, etc., arguably produce distinctly *unsafe* living conditions for precisely the people most targeted by the PIC in its safety-making efforts. These same conditions—poverty, racism, lack of job or educational opportunity, for example—render those most likely to end up in the system most vulnerable to it.

Rather than actually producing marked differences in people's real safety, the PIC is propelled by ideological support for its work, which in turn is driven by images of both panic-worthy dangers and those that reinforce the idea that only police and prisons can create what gets called "safety," an idea itself that is abstracted through political positioning and media construction. Since the 1970s, Democratic and Republican politicians and hopefuls have relied on tough on crime rhetoric to demonstrate their commitment to public safety. Bill Clinton famously traveled back to Arkansas, where he was governor, during his 1992 campaign for the presidency to preside over the execution of a mentally disabled man. In 2005, Arnold Schwarzenegger, governor of California, denied clemency or reprieve to Stanley "Tookie" Williams, co-founder of the Crips gang who had dedicated his later life to ending gang violence and working with black and poor urban youth. In the same year he was executed, Williams was nominated for a Nobel Peace Prize. This tough on crime tactic has resulted in broad legislative and gubernatorial support for many of the sentencing changes discussed above, most notably the imposition of three strikes laws, which carry sentences of 25 years to life for people who are convicted of three felonies, no matter the character of the charge, and mandatory minimum sentences for drug possession, like those created in 1973 by governor Nelson Rockefeller in New York, which are notoriously punitive, especially toward drug users and low-level couriers, who are often women of color (Sudbury, 2005). This rhetoric has also figured prominently in unwritten (and possibly illegal) policies in major prisons states like California and New York to deny all parole, in particular for those convicted of felonies classified as violent, regardless of a prisoner's history or likeliness to commit other harms.

---

4. The authors note, "The after-tax income of the top 1 percent of American households jumped 139 percent, to more than $700,000, from 1979 to 2001, according to the Congressional Budget Office, which adjusted its numbers to account for inflation. The income of the middle fifth rose by just 17 percent, to $43,700, and the income of the poorest fifth rose only 9 percent" (p. 1).

Public support for these criminal justice policies is propelled by representations of crime, criminality, and enforcement in the media—print, television news, and entertainment. Not only do viewers who have never experienced prison, courts, arrest, or even "crime," have access every day on television and in movies to myriad depictions of the systems that make up the PIC—the *CSI* and *Law & Order* franchises alone air six different shows during primetime—but the news media exaggerates the prevalence of crime, especially violence, in the U.S. In the period between 1990 and 1998, for example, homicide rates fell by more than half their previous levels across the country, but stories about homicide increased fourfold on major television networks (Beiser, 2001). A 2002 study noted that a major local news network in Northern California's Bay Area featured stories about youth and crime nearly two-thirds of the time young people were covered at all, and mentioned only once in the same period that the actual rate of youth crime had been steadily declining. The researchers put these numbers in context:

> Seventy-six percent of the public say they form their opinions about social issues like crime from what they read and watch in the news. And despite a 33 percent decline in juvenile crime since 1993, two-thirds of the American public still believe crime is rising. From 1990 to 1998, the national crime rate dropped by 20 percent, but news coverage of crime increased by 83 percent.
>
> (We Interrupt This Message, 2002, p. 5)

Not only do the media help to shape, and exaggerate, ideas about how much crime there is, the images and language used to tell these stories both reflect and construct public perceptions about *who* does crime. These images are, as Gilmore and Davis point out, historically constructed as black and brown people, poor people, and, increasingly, immigrants. And while images of the "criminal" circulate widely through the media, these sources do not create ideas of who is to be considered dangerous or worthy of lock-up alone, nor do they project them in a vacuum. Davis (2002) puts it this way:

> We ... think about imprisonment as a fate reserved for others, a fate reserved for the "evildoers," to use a term recently popularized by George W. Bush. Because of the persistent power of racism, "criminals" and "evildoers" are, in the collective imagination, fantasized as people of color. The prison therefore functions ideologically as an abstract site into which undesirables are deposited, relieving us of the responsibility of thinking about the real issues affecting those communities from which prisoners are drawn in such disproportionate numbers. This is the ideological work that the prison performs—it relieves us of the responsibility of seriously engaging with problems of our society, especially those produced by racism and, increasingly, global capitalism. (p. 16)

Despite failing to achieve greater measures of safety in most public spheres, thirty-plus years of the expanding prison industrial complex and its justifications have made contemporary policing and imprisonment practices common sense in the U.S. (although there are growing movements to challenge the PIC and call for its abolition[5]). It is this legacy, and this context, into which the mostly poor and black survivors of Hurricane Katrina were thrown, both free and imprisoned, in the frenzy and abandonment that descended on New Orleans after August 29th, 2005.

Before the Storm: New Orleans, Louisiana, and the PIC in Brief

In June 2005, just before Katrina hit, Louisiana had the highest incarceration rate of any state in the nation. Of every 100,000 people living in Louisiana, 1,138—more than 1 percent of the state's total population—were in prison or jail. Louisiana locked up its residents at nearly one and a half times the rate of the United States overall, which holds the dubious distinction of having the highest incarceration rate in the world (BJS, 2005). A 2003 study of prison expansion in the southern U.S. noted that Louisiana held more people in prisons and jails than some countries, including Canada and Argentina (JPI, 2003). The state is also home to Angola, the largest prison in the U.S. where more aging prisoners die behind its walls than walk out of them. In the past five years, conditions in two notoriously brutal youth prisons, Jena and Tallulah, came to light in successful campaigns, led by local organizations and parents' groups, to shut them down.

People of color are strikingly over-represented in Louisiana's prisons, reflecting the national patterns discussed above. A 2002 report used Department of Justice statistics along with U.S. Census numbers to determine incarceration rates in U.S. states by race and ethnicity. This study found that the incarceration rate for black Louisiana residents, at 2,475, was almost 6 times higher than the rate for white residents, at 421 per 100,000. Similar disparities existed for Latino residents, with an incarceration rate of 1,736 per 100,000. While black people made up just over 32 percent of the state's population, they made up 72 percent of the prison population (Human Rights Watch, 2002).

As jail and prison populations boomed, and racial disparities in Louisiana's criminal justice system meant that this affected primarily poor black and

---

5. For more information see: Critical Resistance (criticalresistance.org), Justice Now (jnow.org), All of Us or None (allofusornone.org), Prison Activist Resource Center (prisonactivist.org), INCITE! Women of Color Against Violence (incite-national.org). Recent books by Angela Davis, *Are Prisons Obsolete?* (2003) and *Abolition Democracy* (2005), also take this question up in detail.

Latino communities, the state simultaneously radically increased funding for prisons and policing while decreasing support for social services and education. Mirroring the phenomena Bohrman and Murakawa noted in the growing power of the U.S. disciplinary state, between 1980 and 2000 Louisiana turned its energy and funds toward control and punishment. With total increases in state employment topping out at 244 percent growth over that 20-year period, employment in policing and corrections increased a full 413 percent. In sharp contrast, state job growth in higher education saw only a 93 percent increase and public welfare jobs only grew by 44 percent (JPI, 2003). The growth of Louisiana's disciplinary state function, with a focus on addressing social problems and concerns through policing and confinement functions, clearly outpaced state emphasis on addressing concerns like poverty, educational opportunity, and other social welfare issues, constituting "safety" as a matter of control.

In addition to state job growth, the focus on incarceration can be seen in increases in prison spending in Louisiana. According to a 2005 Justice Policy Institute report, spending on corrections reached 729 million dollars in 2004, 619 million of which came from general funds, the same place from which dollars for education and public welfare services are often drawn. And while state spending on higher education stands a bit higher, at 15 percent of general fund allocations, Louisiana's prison and punishment system accounts for 9.5 percent of general fund spending and has grown over the past twenty years at twice the rate of funding for higher education (JPI, 2003). Despite this massive increase in spending and confinement, however, there is ample evidence that it had minimal impact on reported crime. In fact, a number of states with remarkably smaller increases in incarceration rates saw a larger drop in reported crime rates (JPI, 2003, 2005).

The growth and scope of the prison industrial complex in Louisiana is, not surprisingly, reflected in the city of New Orleans itself. Even before Katrina, the city was rife with police brutality and scandal[6] and host to one of the largest local jails in the country, Orleans Parish Prison, which on any given day before the storm held upwards of 6500 people, many of whom were pre-trial

---

6. A 1998 Human Rights Watch report on police abuse in the United States remarked that the NOPD had "accomplished the rare feat of leading nationally in" brutality, corruption, and ineptitude. They note stand-out cases, like the NOPD officer who hired a hit man to kill a woman who had lodged a complaint against him, or those accused of robbing a Vietnamese restaurant and shooting its owners and an off-duty cop working private security there. But HRW also explains that the NOPD had the "highest ranking of citizen complaints of police brutality in 1991 and that after the department implemented "quality of life" policing (made popular by the NYPD), complaints rose by 27 percent between 1996 and 97. For the full report, go to: http://www.hrw.org/reports98/police/uspo92.htm#P2446_622387.

detainees (ACLU, 2006). New Orleans also incarcerated its residents at the highest rate of any large city in the country, locking up 1,480 of every 100,000. Prior to Katrina, OPP was notorious for its poor conditions, lack of services and programs, exploitative hiring out of prisoner labor, and for deaths due to negligence and guard violence. In each of the three months before Katrina, a prisoner died at OPP (Gerharz & Hong, 2006). The jail, and the state's prisons, are fed in part by rampant arrests and incarceration on charges for which people could be issued tickets instead. Police attention and arrests target people of color, and mostly black residents. Prior to Katrina, Orleans Parish was 66.6 percent black, but fully 90 percent of those locked up in OPP were black (ACLU, 2006). Once in the system, New Orleans residents who need or qualify for a public defender—nearly 90 percent of those charged—have to rely on an indigent defense system that is funded almost entirely through traffic violation fines and is funded per case approximately three times lower than prosecutors (Gerharz & Hong, 2006; Landry, 2006).

Leading up to Katrina's impact, both the primacy of "law and order" techniques and ideologies in Louisiana and New Orleans and the entrenchment of government resource allocation to law enforcement and incarceration paved the way for storm responses that relied on policing and control and disregarded the lives of people already locked away in OPP. In keeping with national trends, and what would become the national focus on "lawlessness" and "anarchy" in New Orleans after Katrina, the decades-long buildup to post-storm priorities helps clarify the place of surveillance, policing, and control in an analysis of the character and tactics of disaster relief in the era of the prison industrial complex.

When the Storm Hit: "Law and Order" in a Flooded New Orleans

By Wednesday, August 31, national press painted a picture of New Orleans as a city not only in storm-related chaos, but one under siege. For the next week, daily reports from the flood ravaged city highlighted "looting" and rumors of violence in the streets and at the Superdome and Convention Center, where thousands of people took shelter and waited for help. Even as U.S. news outlets uncharacteristically raised concerns about the possibility that the U.S. government response to Katrina's aftermath, or lack of preparation prior to the storm, were racist, these same sources circulated images and ideas of those left in New Orleans as "out-of-control," "wild" and "brazen," "thugs" and "criminals." By and large, these descriptions were applied to the mostly black residents of New Orleans who survived the storm, many who lacked the resources to evacuate when Mayor Nagin issued a mandatory order to do so. In one well-publicized instance, Internet bloggers picked up on two similar photographs of people wading through chest-deep water with items taken from stores that had been featured on a *Yahoo! News* page. The caption of one photograph, of two white or light-skinned people, said the pair had "found" the items. The other, attached to an image of a black person, said he had "looted" them. Even after one of the images was removed from *Yahoo!*, debate raged about the intention and implications of the captions. In another incident, armed police forces blocked the Crescent City Connection to Gretna, a majority white town across the Mississippi River and stopped people from New Orleans, many of whom were black, from entering even as New Orleans continued to flood (Riccardi, 2005; Sharockman, 2005). For many, these were clear signs that black New Orleanians were being criminalized and contained in the days following the storm.

In the aftermath of Katrina's landfall and the flooding caused by New Orleans' broken levees, law and order emerged quickly as a central part of the relief effort. Beginning August 28, Louisiana National Guard was mobilized in large numbers to provide security at the Superdome, considered a shelter of last resort before the storm hit. Over the course of the day, 586 soldiers from at least four divisions arrived: the Special Reaction Team, "a unit highly trained in Law Enforcement missions" began with "Law and Order/Area Security missions"; the 527th Ready Reaction Force came with the "principle mission [of] crowd control"; the 225th Engineer Group to "assist with security operations"; and the 159th Fighter Wing to provide more security. Joining the 586 soldiers, also from the Louisiana National Guard, was a total of just 71 medical personnel (United States Executive Office of the President, 2006). In the week following landfall, active duty military and additional National Guard were called up, both from Louisiana and other states. On August 31 there were 9,700 National Guard soldiers in New Orleans (Select Bipartisan Committee to Investigate the Preparation for and Response to Hurricane Katrina, 2006). In addition, by September 1, there were 3,000 active duty soldiers in the city. Four days later, there were 14,232 (United States Executive Office of the President, 2006). As troops arrived Governor Blanco issued her well-reported warning that they were coming to New Orleans "locked and loaded."

Eventually 50,000 National Guard members would be deployed along the Gulf Coast, in New Orleans, many of them serving in a law enforcement capacity (United States Executive Office of the President, 2006). Unlike active duty military, who cannot enforce local laws, National Guard are deputized and can function essentially as additional police, making these forces the go-to military units activated in the event not just of natural disaster, but of urban uprisings and domestic unrest, as often happened in the highly charged political upheavals of the 1960s and 1970s, and after the Rodney King verdict in Los Angeles in 1992. As the New Orleans Police Department (NOPD) numbers dwindled—numerous NOPD officers did not report to work after the storm—National Guard troops and police from other parts of the country who came to New Orleans through the Emergency Management Assistance Compact (EMAC) fulfilled multiple functions. For example, the Louisiana National Guard "conducted roving patrols, manned checkpoints, and supported the NOPD in the parishes" (Select Bipartisan Committee to Investigate the Preparation for and Response to Hurricane Katrina, 2006, p. 207). As mentioned earlier, those NOPD officers who remained in New Orleans were redirected from search and rescue work shortly after the storm to focus on so-called looting instead. In addition, federal law enforcement from fourteen different departments and agencies went to New Orleans in the week following the storm, including 1,444 officers from the Department of Homeland Security (DHS) and 566 from the Department of Justice (DOJ) (Select Bipartisan Committee to Investigate the Preparation for and Response to Hurricane Katrina, 2006; United States Executive Office of the President, 2006). By mid-September, reports emerged that military and federal and local law enforcement had been joined by mercenaries from private companies like Blackwater Security—whose agents usually work in war zones and have been active in Iraq and Afghanistan—under contract with the Federal Emergency Management Agency (FEMA), adding another force of armed personnel to New Orleans' streets (Scahill & Crespo, 2005). This remarkable law enforcement/military deployment was considered central to the recovery and relief efforts by both the media and myriad figures in local, state, and federal government.[7] Thus, control and, ultimately, confinement—whether in the new jail at Camp Greyhound or the shelters in and outside the city—became a primary feature of the disaster response.

While the people left in New Orleans became "thugs" and "hoodlums," those already in its massive jail when the storm hit were effectively abandoned with little or no preparation for Katrina's effects. When Mayor Nagin issued his mandatory evacuation order for Orleans Parish on August 28, people locked up at Orleans Parish Prison and the staff of the Sheriff's Office who ran it were exempted. Despite offers of assistance in evacuating the prisoners, Sheriff Gusman declined, saying, "… We're going to keep our prisoners where they belong" (ACLU, 2006, p. 20). The result: the over 6,000 people in OPP, plus additional prisoners, including young people, who had been brought to OPP to ride out the storm were trapped in the jail's multiple buildings, with limited food and water, no electricity, and no information, some on ground floors where by late Monday the water reached their chests (ACLU, 2006). Prisoners' phones were turned off on August 26, three days before the storm hit, cutting them off from

---

7. Ironically, there were a number of concerns articulated in liberal and progressive anti-war circles that the deployment of National Guard to Iraq (and to a lesser extent Afghanistan) reduced the number in the U.S. to respond to Katrina, despite their role in the U.S. in some instances as an invading police/military force.

family and friends as people began to evacuate. Before landfall, the jail was locked down, all those who resided in cells were locked in and those confined in dorm-like rooms were locked into the dorms (ACLU, 2006, pp. 29–30). When the levees broke, water flooded the jail's buildings, shorting out electrical systems. Eventually generators also failed. In some buildings, food and medical supplies in first-floor rooms were destroyed or unreachable. Without electricity, OPP went dark and air-conditioning in closed buildings turned off. Prisoners reported being left in locked cells with water rising, having to drink contaminated flood water, and going without food for several days.

Evacuation of OPP didn't begin until late August 30 or 31 and was not complete until September 1 or 2, five days after Katrina hit. When OPP's prisoners were finally evacuated, they reported having to stand for hours in chest-high water waiting for a boat to take them to a highway overpass. There, many asserted that conditions got worse as they waited, often with no water, in 90-plus degree heat. Prisoners were pepper-sprayed for asking for water, and standing to stretch or urinate. Many spent several days there before being transferred by bus to prisons around the state. At some of those prisons, conditions continued to worsen. Prisoners were subjected to degrading and methodical violence (e.g., one man was forced to lick his own blood off the floor after having been beaten by guards), repeated racial slurs, and in some cases little food or water (ACLU, 2006).

Many of those in OPP at the time of the storm were being held pending court dates, and over 100 had just been arrested in the two days prior to Katrina's landfall even as evacuation orders were being made (ACLU, 2006). These prisoners and others with approaching release dates ended up being held, far from home, for sometimes weeks and more often months without recourse. While the Sheriff maintains still that no one died in OPP after the storm, several eyewitness accounts from both prisoners and guards suggest otherwise. It is certain that some people died as a result of injuries or medical problems sustained or exacerbated during the evacuation. When confronted with accounts of prisoners in OPP, Sheriff Gusman denied their claims altogether and demonstrated total disregard for the people themselves, saying, "Don't rely on crackheads, cowards, and criminals to say what the story is" (ACLU, 2006. p. 71).[8]

The mobilization of tens of thousands of military and law enforcement personnel in the wake of Katrina and the abandonment, then systematic abuse, of prisoners from New Orleans highlights practices and presumptions that are neither abnormal nor extreme. Rather, they represent the terrifyingly logical

---

8. For more and more detailed information about the treatment of prisoners from OPP during and after the storm, see *Abandoned and Abused: Orleans Parish Prisoners in the Wake of Hurricane Katrina*, published by the ACLU in August 2006. It is available at http://www.aclu.org/prison/ conditions/26198res20060809.html.

outcomes of the prison industrial complex and its justifications, even in the face of (ostensibly) natural disaster.

Conclusion

Along Rampart Street between Dumaine and Canal Streets, in the center median, there is a long line of lampposts stretching high above the road. Embedded in the posts are four plaques, each documenting the spans of different controlling powers in New Orleans—French, Spanish, Confederate, and, finally: "American Domination. 1803–1861. 1865 to date."[9] Since most of the troops and out-of-state police have left the city, the NOPD have taken over again, and have already been sited for brutality (e.g., some officers were featured on national television news beating a man in the French Quarter) and excessive targeting of poor and people of color residents (Gerharz & Hong, 2006). In June 2006, amid concerns about theft and violence in a city with few opportunities, expensive housing, and little assistance in recovery of basic functions, the state called in the National Guard again, 300-strong, to patrol the city (PBS NewsHour, 2006). OPP reopened some buildings shortly after the storm, despite a lack of necessary clean-up from toxic flood waters. By May 2006, as many as 150 people were being newly committed there each day (ACLU, 2006). Immigrant workers, many drawn to the Gulf Coast and New Orleans with promises of work, have faced not only terrible working conditions and haphazard pay, but have been targeted by Immigration and Customs Enforcement (ICE) sweeps, assisted by the NOPD (Crow & Cruz, 2006). Meanwhile, displaced residents of New Orleans face discrimination and criminalization in many of the areas to which they've relocated, and community-based organizations are working hard to assert a right to return for over 300,000 people from southern Louisiana scattered around the country.

A little over a year has passed since the hurricane as of this writing. Two government reports, one requested by President Bush and one authored by Congress, make considerable recommendations for the further integration of military and policing responses to similar disasters in the future. Since the events of September 11, 2001, all moments of physical disaster, regardless of their instigation by human or nature's forces, are addressed by the post-9/11 mega-agency, the Department of Homeland Security. Critiques of the efficacy of this plan abound, and problems in the DHS and FEMA responses to this storm—lack of organization, lack of planning, lack of preparedness for anything other than a "terrorist attack," to name a few—offer some of the clearest examples. But the primary concern in this analysis is, rather, the simple way in

---

9. Thanks to RWG and RMH for a trip to see these in another context.

which addressing human suffering and safety in preparations for or response to any catastrophic event has become a matter of law enforcement and control.

Widespread criticism in relationship to Hurricane Katrina and its aftermath correctly focuses on structural racism and class antagonism as a cause of local, state, and federal government neglect and failure. In addition, it is important that we understand the massive and taken-for-granted presence of armed and deputized enforcers intrinsic to the relief effort—in short, the militarized policing centerpiece of the Katrina response—as another expression of the racism and class conflict at play in the hurricane's effects and the government's response at all levels. Further, it is crucial to maintain the link between this moment and this response, and the dominating common sense of the prison industrial complex. In other words, the occupation of New Orleans must be fully historically situated. The disregard for the lives of those in OPP and the patterns of threat, enforcement, and confinement carried out largely on the bodies of poor people of color trying to survive their abandonment remind us that the logic of the PIC permeates contemporary political decision-making and media representations, even and especially in moments of crisis.

References

Agid, S. (2005). *"Fags doom nations" and other parables of hate: Representations of "hate crime" and constructions of U.S. national identity.* Excerpt from an unpublished thesis retrieved on November 6, 2006 from http://sites.cca.edu/sightlines/2005/sagid_thesis.html.

American Civil Liberties Union. (2006). *Abandoned and abused: Orleans Parish Prison in the wake of Hurricane Katrina.* Washington, D.C.: American Civil Liberties Union.

Beiser, V. (2001, July 10). How we got to two million. *MotherJones.com Special Report.* Retrieved October 11, 2006 from http://www.motherjones.com/news/special_reports/ prisons/overview.html.

Berenson, A. (2005, September 7). With jails flooded, bus station fills the void. *The New York Times*, p. A20.

Bode, N. & Siemaszko, C. (2005, September 2). Trapped In a watery hell. *The Daily News*, p. 2.

Bohrman, R. & Murakawa, N. (2005). Remaking big government: Immigration and crime control in the United States. In J. Sudbury (Ed.), *Global Lockdown: Race, gender, and the Prison Industrial Complex* (pp. 109–126). New York: Routledge.

Bureau of Justice Statistics. (2005). *Prison and jail inmates at mid-year 2005* (NCJ 213133). Washington, D.C.: Department of Justice.

Crow, M. & Cruz, R. (2006) ICE steps up raids in Gulf Coast. *Immigrants' Rights Update,* 20(2). Retrieved October 15, 2006 from www.nilc.org/ disaster_assistance/da003.htm.

Dao, J. & Kleinfield, R. (2005, September 3). More troops and aid reach New Orleans; Bush visits area; Chaotic exodus continues. *The New York Times,* pp. A1, A18.

Dao, J., Treaster, J. & Barringer, F. (2005, September 2). New Orleans is awaiting deliverance. *The New York Times,* pp. A15, A20.

Davis, A.Y. (2005). *Abolition democracy.* New York: Seven Stories Press.

Davis, A.Y. (2003). *Are prisons obsolete?* New York: Seven Stories Press.

Gendar, A. & Moore, F. (2005, September 3). Finest and 100 buses to help out. *The Daily News,* p. 10.

Gerharz, B. & Hong, S. (2006) Down By Law: Orleans Parish Prison before and after Katrina. *Dollars & Sense, March/April 2006.* Retrieved October 11, 2006 from www.dollarsandsense.org /archives/2006/0306gerharzhong. html.

Gilmore, R.W. (2002). Race and Globalization. In R.J. Johnson, P. Taylor, & M. Watts (Eds.), *Geographies of Global Change: Remapping the World, 2nd Edition*(pp. 261–274). Malden, MA: Blackwell.

————. (1999). Globalization and U.S. Prison Growth: from Military Keynesianism to post-Keynesian militarism. *Race & Class, 40*(2/3), 171–188.

Gilmore, R.W. & Gilmore, C. (2004). The other California. In D. Solnit (Ed.), *Globalize Liberation* (pp. 381–396). San Francisco: City Lights Publishers.

Gonzalez, D. (2005, September 2). From margins of society to center of the tragedy. *The New York Times,* pp. A1, A21.

Human Rights Watch. (2002). *Race and incarceration in the United States.* Washington, D.C.: Human Rights Watch.

Hunt, A. [Director] (2006). *I won't drown on this levee and you ain't gonna break my back* [DVD]. Los Angeles, CA: the Corrections Documentary Project.

Justice Policy Institute. (2005). *Louisiana Leads the Nation and the World in Lock Up; Prisons and Jails: Expensive — Not Keeping Communities Safer.* Washington, D.C.: JPI. Retrieved October 12, 2006 from www.crititcal resistance.org/katrina/louisianaleads.html.

————. (2003). *Deep impact: Quantifying the effect of prison expansion in the South.* Washington, D.C.: JPI. Retrieved October 6, 2006 from http://www.justicepolicy.org/ article.php?id=124.

Kronenwetter, M. (1997). Drug war. In M. Kronenwetter (Ed.), *Encyclopedia of modern American social issues* (pp. 96–99). Santa Barbara: ABC-CLIO, Inc.

Landry, V. (2006). Defenseless. *The Gambit Weekly, 9/5/06*. Retrieved October 12, 2006 from www.bestofneworleans.com/dispatch/2006-09-05/cover_story.php.

Lipton, E. & Schmitt, E. (2005, August 31). Navy ships and maritime rescue teams are sent to region. *The New York Times*, p. A14.

McFadden, R. (2005, September 4). Bush pledges more troops as the evacuation grows; Guard patrols New Orleans after days of despair. *The New York Times*, pp. A1, A30.

McFadden, R. & Blumenthal, R. (2005, September 1). Bush sees long recovery effort for New Orleans; 30,000 troops in largest U.S. relief effort. *The New York Times*, pp. A1, A17.

Omi, M. & Howard Winant. (1986). *Racial formation in the United States*. New York: Routledge.

PBS NewsHour. Crime increases in New Orleans as the city recovers from Hurricane Katrina. (2006, June 26). *PBS NewsHour*. [Television News Program]. Retrieved October 11, 2006 from www.pbs.org/newshour/bb/social_issues/jan-june06/neworleans_06-26.htm.

Rand, E. (2005). *The Ellis Island snow globe*. Durham: Duke University Press.

Riccardi, N. (2005, September 18). Katrina's aftermath; Blocked evacuation route; Police decision to close bridge justified, city says; Some call move racist; Gretna blames violence at mall for blockade. *The Houston Chronicle*, p. 25. Retrieved October 14, 2006 from Custom Newspapers, Thomson Gale, Brooklyn Public Library—Central Library.

Scahill, J. & Crespo, D. (2005). Overkill: Feared Blackwater mercenaries deploy in New Orleans. *DemocracyNow.org*. Retrieved October 12, 2006 from http://www.democracynow.org/static/Overkill.shtml.

Scott, J. & Leonhardt, D. (2005, May 15). Shadowy lines that still divide: Class matters. *The New York Times*, p. 1.

Select Bipartisan Committee to Investigate the Preparation for and Response to Hurricane Katrina. (2006). *A Failure of Initiative*. Washington, D.C.: U.S. Government Printing Office.

Sharockman, A. (2005 September 17). Neighboring town denied evacuees. *The St. Petersburg Times*, p. 1A.

Siemaszko, C. (2005, September 3). Help reaches frenzied city; Troops met by victims angry over long delay. *The Daily News*, pp. 2–3.

Sisk, R. & Siemaszko, C. (2005, August 31). The lost city. *The Daily News*, p. 3.

Sudbury, J. (2005). Introduction: Feminist critiques, transnational landscapes, abolitionist visions. In J. Sudbury (Ed.), *Global lockdown: Race, gender, and the Prison Industrial Complex* (pp. xi–xxviii). New York: Routledge.

Treaster, J. & Sontag, D. (2005, September 2). Despair and lawlessness grip New Orleans as thousands remain stranded in squalor. *The New York Times*, pp. A1, A20.

United States Executive Office of the President. (2006). *The federal response to Hurricane Katrina: Lessons Learned.* Washington, D.C.: U.S. Government Printing Office.

We Interrupt This Message. (2002). *Speaking for ourselves.* San Francisco: We Interrupt This Message.

Chapter 5

Social Justice Movements: Education Disregarded, Lessons Ignored

Richelle S. Swan

Introduction

The impact of Hurricane Katrina on communities in the Gulf region has served as an example of the way in which the "natural" world and the social world can interact and create situations of such magnitude that their mutual influence can no longer be ignored by the masses. During the days following Katrina, the news media made the tragedy of the event real to those outside of the region through gripping visuals and conversations with residents of the impacted regions. The collective dismay expressed in the wake of the hurricane by the general public was, on the whole, heartfelt and deep. In many cases, people unaffected directly by the tragedy expressed a sense of horror and surprise that such a disaster could occur in the United States today. In other cases, however, people were similarly horrified by the tragedy, but not entirely surprised at the way that human choices shaped the outcome of the events. In fact, very little about the social aspects of the disaster or the wreckage generated in its wake was shocking to observers cognizant of the historical roots of injustice in the United States.

One powerful way that people have become aware about issues of justice is by means of the various social movements that have become part of the U.S. landscape since its founding. Over the centuries, innumerable people have joined forces in an attempt to eliminate, or at a minimum to mitigate, injustices that they have observed in the world around them. Yet, the efforts of social movement activists to educate the public about injustices, no matter how blatant those injustices might be, sometimes only are acknowledged by those who suffer their consequences. Those who are not frequently required to confront these injustices in a material way are less apt to recognize their origins, even when exposed to them through the activities of a social movement.

In contemplating the reasons why Hurricane Katrina impacted the least privileged of our society in the most severe way, it is helpful to turn to the efforts of some of the social justice movements of recent times and to reconsider their histories and their lessons, which have in many cases been forgotten or ignored. In this chapter I will provide a brief overview of three social movements that are particularly relevant to the tragedy surrounding the hurricane: the civil rights movement, the labor movement, and the environmental justice movement. Because it is impossible to fully analyze social movements that other scholars have dedicated volumes of research to in a single chapter, I have chosen to simply highlight the trajectories of the movements and the basic claims they forward. Taken as a whole, such an overview conveys a clear sense of the why the post-Katrina disaster took the shape that it did.

Defining Social Movements

Before delving into an examination of the aforementioned social movements, it is important to understand what a social movement is and what it can teach the interested observer. A social movement can be defined as a, "sustained and self-conscious challenge to authorities or cultural codes by a field of actors—organizations and advocacy networks—some which employ extra-institutional means of influence" (Gamson & Wolsfeld, 1993, p. 115) or similarly as, "a collectivity acting with some degree of organization and continuity outside of institutional channels for the purpose of promoting or resisting change in the group, society, or world order of which it is a part" (McAdam & Snow, 1997, p. xviii). Both of these definitions convey a sense of what Lofland (1996), building upon Goffman's work, stated is the fundamental quality of a social movement: the presentation of insurgent realities or "collective challenges to mainstream conceptions of how society ought to be conceptualized and how people ought to live" (p. 1). Social movements, especially those that take on some momentum, are indicative of the social climate of a given time, as they highlight the major concerns of groups of people.

A social movement that persists over decades is one that often speaks to deeply rooted concerns that are characterized as injustices. The construction of a movement around a master frame whose central attribute is its identification of injustice that has occurred or that is occurring is a popular movement tactic (Gamson, 1992; Gamson, Fireman, & Rytina, 1982). Once an injustice has been identified, concerned individuals can work to mobilize resources and support in the name of their cause with an eye towards the "opportunity structure" of the day—the way that the political and social climate either facilitates or hinders activism around a given cause (Mueller, 1992; Zald, 1992). Injustices may be related to material concerns, such as the inadequate or unfair distributions of resources, and/or may be conceived of in terms of ideological or symbolic terms, such as concern over the ways in which one's identity as part of a given group is maligned or denigrated by others outside of the group (see Davis, 2002; Larana, Johnston, & Gusfield, 1994; Polletta & Jasper, 2001). It is often the case that symbolic and material grievances are intermeshed and that social movement participants hope to draw attention to both dimensions of their cause in the hopes of generating meaningful change.

The social movements that I will highlight in the remainder of this chapter are movements that can claim varying degrees of success in generating such change. It is undeniable that the civil rights movement and the labor movement, for example, are movements that have contributed to many important legal and policy changes in our society and that the environmental justice movement has also begun to make a significant impact. Yet, it is also clear, given the disparate impact of Katrina on communities of color and the poor and working class, that many of the most crucial lessons of these movements are still disregarded by those in power and the more privileged members of the general population. By reviewing the basics of these social movements and examining some of their prominent claims of injustice, we can be reminded of the social realities that must be addressed in any grounded analysis of Katrina-related events.

The Civil Rights Movement

The civil rights movement is one of best-known social movements in U.S. history and one that has had a marked impact on discussions about justice in society as well as on concrete changes in the political and social realms (Andrews, 2002; Morris, 1984). It is difficult to place a definitive date on its beginnings, as varied people over the centuries have struggled in the name of civil rights, but popular references to the movement usually cite the 1940s as the decade when it truly began to gain momentum. At its core, the movement attempted to establish legal equality and social equity for all people in the United States. The civil rights movement laid the groundwork for today's discussions about decency and what we should be able to expect out of our government and out of one another. And, most importantly, it has demonstrated that formal legal equality is no guarantee of social justice.

Lawyers, activists, scholars, ministers, and laypeople began the early civil rights movement with the goal of getting law on the books to reflect the values of equality and justice that were so often lauded as American values, yet were clearly absent from the existing legal and social practices of the land. Beginning in the 1940s, there was an emphasis on the development of legal cases as a means of challenging Jim Crow laws and the violence and segregation that re-sulted in the years following the end of slavery. The best known outcome of this legal campaign was the groundbreaking decision in *Brown v. Board of Education* (1954), which stated that public accommodations that separated black people from people of other races and ethnicities were not legally acceptable under the 14th Amendment. Following this decision, civil rights advocates continued working towards a dismantling of laws that sanctioned institutional-ized racism.

The social justice work undertaken in the early years of the civil rights movement utilized multiple forms of activism. The "equal rights" concept or frame was a social organizing tool that was promoted by means of lunch counter sit-ins, the Freedom Rides, boycotts, and peace marches in its name. The movement gained momentum as individuals became involved through family and friend networks, through their ties to community institutions, and through less direct means such as media exposure to the movement and mail-ings (Platt & Fraser, 1998). Black churches in the South played an important part in promulgating the equal rights frame and they were energized by the re-sponse of the power structure of which they were lamenting. As Tarrow (1991) explains,

> In this transformation of the culture of the black southern churches, the white power structure was an unwitting collaborator, for it responded to nonviolence with violence, answered the message of love with the rheto-ric of hatred, turned the dogs of war on the messengers of people. The more violent and unchristian the behavior of their antagonists—as un-derstood and amplified by the media—the more the moral superiority of the peaceful disobedience tactic was brought home to Blacks in the South and prospective allies in Washington and the North. Out of struggle, blacks invented a new collective action frame. (p. 191)

The equal rights frame established by the civil rights activists in the years immediately following the *Brown* decision utilized integrationist messages in the 1950s and 1960s as a means of appealing to the establishment and as a log-ical outgrowth of a tradition rooted in Gandhian activism. The use of this frame was effective for a time, particularly in terms of its ability to generate the groundbreaking legal changes related to civil rights in the two decades follow-ing *Brown*. Most notably, collective movement activity utilizing the frame cul-minated in the landmark passage of the Civil Rights Act of 1964, a measure that stated that discrimination based upon race, class, gender, religion, and nationality were illegal in the public realm. The act was a formal acknowledge-ment of the equal rights concept and its passage made Jim Crow laws and seg-regation legally prohibited in the United States. This was swiftly followed by the passage of the Voting Rights Act of 1965, legislation that made the voting restrictions placed on blacks in the South illegal. These changes were significant breakthroughs that set the scene for future legal developments related to busing, integration, and fair housing policies.

In spite of changes to the law that can be attributed in part to civil rights activism over the decades, scholars and other observers have bemoaned the lack of follow-through needed to translate those laws into just social practices and arrangements. This is one of the important lessons that has emerged in the aftermath of legal victories, formal legal equality—the existence of laws that treat everyone on paper as equals—does not necessarily have the desired consequence of equity for structurally oppressed groups of people (Bell, 1987; Guinier, 1998; Omi and Winant, 1994). On contemplating the legacy of the civil rights movement from the vantage point of the mid-1980s, critical legal scholar Derrick Bell (1987, p. 5) proclaimed that, "the task of equal justice advocates has not become easier simply because neither slavery's chains, nor the lyncher's rope, nor humiliating Jim Crow signs are no longer the main means of holding black people in subordinate status." Lani Guinier (1998), a civil rights advocate and law professor, explained that subordination has been maintained as a type of approach that many presidential administrations have supported. This approach was rooted in the Reagan era and it,

> … denied the existence of disadvantaged groups who by virtue of historical, social, and economic circumstances were structurally positioned at the bottom, unable to take advantage of formal neutrality. Indeed, it transformed the reality of group oppression into individual pathology and bad character, and in its more virulent form, bad genes. Moreover, it co-opted the rhetoric of formal equality to a principle of inaction. If we simply declared everyone equal, then that assertion stood for itself. We had absolved society, and particularly its governmental agencies, from acting to remedy anything but isolated acts of contemptible racial animus directed at single individuals. By limiting civil rights to discrimination against honorable victims, they individualized a systemic problem and justified doing nothing to help either black Americans or white working-class Americans as a group or class. (pp. 85–86)

Bonilla-Silva (2001, 2003) similarly explained that racism and discrimination have been rearticulated rather than eliminated during the years following the passage of the Civil Rights Act—a period he labels the "post-civil rights era." He claimed a more subtle, colorblind racism has taken hold in the decades following the 1960s. Thus, although the resistance of those in the civil rights movement has helped improve the life chances of many people in this country, it is important to acknowledge the new contours of the oppression the movement grapples with today.

In recent years, disillusionment with the entrenchment of hierarchical power relations in the U.S. in spite of civil rights advancements on paper, has led some in the black community to endorse a reparations movement (Oliver & Shapiro, 1997). Reparations advocates claim that black community should be repaid for the harms that were inflicted both during the days of slavery and the inequities that were then cemented into the social structure of the United States (see Robinson, 2000; Winbush, 2003). This discussion about reparations for slavery preceded the beginning of the civil rights era, yet over the years has often been dismissed or relegated to the margins of popular discourse (Winbush, 2003). Since the 1990s, these discussions have garnered more attention as folks have recognized the economic and ideological roots of the inequities that are seemingly intransigent,

> During the 1990s over one-half of all of black children continued to live in poverty. A black baby was over twice as likely as a white baby to die before its first birthday. More black men in their twenties were in prison, or on parole or on probation than attended college. The average black family earned only 56–60 percent of the income enjoyed by their white counterparts. A black man was six times more likely to be murdered than a white man.
>
> (Verney, 2000, p. 117)

The civil rights movement lives on because its claims of injustice have not been fully heeded. Today the movement is involved with a variety of causes, including those related to a lack of affirmative action in remedying injustices and immigrant rights. The relevance of the contemporary civil rights movement to the Katrina crisis, a crisis that has been said to be "less about rain and wind than it is race and class" (Equal Justice Society, 2005), is especially apparent. The lessons of another social movement, the labor movement, are intimately tied to those of the civil rights movement (Vargas, 2005).

The Labor Movement

> The workers share a common struggle. They may have come to New Orleans in different ships, but they are now in the same boat.
>
> (Browne-Dinanis, Lai, Hincapie & Soni, 2006, p. 11).

The labor movement in the United States has long drawn attention to the socioeconomic disparities that are perpetuated by the labor market. For over two centuries, activists have highlighted the socio-structural dynamics that create society's "haves" and "have-nots" and the often objectionable ways that the bottom line and the desire for profit affect workers. Given that a surplus labor force is necessitated by a capitalist economy (Marx, 1992), the interests of workers and people looking for work, are countered in numerous ways. As a result, working-class people have joined together in an effort to gain power through numbers as a means of challenging the establishment and voicing discontent with the status quo.

One of the key lessons of the labor movement is that class inequities are built into the economic system of the United States and such inequities must be acknowledged and mitigated for economic and social justice to prevail in a democratic society. The Social Darwinist view of the poor or working class as a group of wholly lazy and/ or deficient humans is inaccurate, yet rears its ugly head repeatedly in discussions about resource distribution in this country. The labor movement has challenged this stereotype over the years and is currently contending with it in light of a global economy that makes individuals' working lives less and less secure (Babson, 1999). Once the intersection of class dynamics with racial and gender dynamics are taken into account, it becomes evident that some people's lives are even more precariously positioned than others'. Taken as a whole, the accomplishments and lessons of the movement offer insight into the mechanisms that reproduce poverty of the sort many in the Gulf Coast region experienced before and after the hurricane.

The labor movement has had a long and varied history of efforts to improve the lives of workers and to make working conditions on the whole more humane. The movement is best known for its accomplishments at the beginning of the 20th century—those related to the passage of child labor and maximum working hour laws, as well as those related to the need for worker benefits and safe working conditions. The passage of the National Labor Relations Act of 1935, federal legislation that gave workers the right to form and join unions and collectively bargain, and the creation of the Equal Employment Opportunity Commission (EEOC) as mandated by Title VII of the Civil Rights Act in 1964, both resulted in part as a result of labor organizing. The trade and professional unions that exist today were developed after years of toil on the part of labor activists. Although there has been much talk in recent years about the death of the unionism and labor organizing as a means of fighting economic injustice, as Babson (1999) explained, the original impetus behind the labor movement still has force today,

> After all, the modern labor movement took form in reaction to the unwanted state of dependency that industrial capitalism forced upon workers, and that state of dependency remains with us. The vast majority of people are still compelled by their relative lack of wealth to work for a wage or salary, and usually not under terms of their choosing. When this fundamental dependency compels them to work for corporate and government bureaucracies that dwarf the individual, then collective action—in some form—suggests itself as the means for securing individual prosperity on a socially equitable basis. (p. xiv)

The economic gains that were expected to accompany the formal legal changes brought about in the mid-to-late 20th century as a result of both labor organizing and civil rights organizing allowed some folks to enter the middle class, but on the whole, did not substantially change the socioeconomic position of those who were poor (Piven & Cloward, 1979). As was the case with the creation of civil rights laws, the formal changes that labor was successful in generating over the years were lauded as important breakthroughs. Yet, when new mechanisms were instituted to create change but essentially had no backbone to them, that is, no way of enforcing those very changes, they became less than effective. As Honey (1999) explained in his oral history of black workers,

> The National Labor Relations Board, the Equal Employment Opportunities Commission, and the perception of other governmental support for labor and civil rights had once given black workers means and encouragement to win employment disputes. But the federal government itself increasingly sabotaged the enforcement mechanisms the laws had set up and understaffed and underfunded both the EEOC and the NRLB so they could not effectively operate. In place of federal enforcement came assertions that equality had largely been attained and avowals of an almost religious belief in the "free market," which undermined all sense of community or government responsibility for workers. (p. 366)

The consequence of this gap between the law on the books and the law in action is a perpetuation of a series of social inequities that have impeded many people of color in the United States from obtaining wealth or ownership of assets. This impediment has been especially evident in the lives of black individuals. As Oliver & Shapiro (1997) explained, "... the cumulative effects of the past have seemingly cemented blacks to the bottom of society's economic hierarchy. A history of low wages, poor schooling and segregation affected not one or two generations of blacks but practically all African Americans well into the middle of the twentieth century" (p. 5). The economic marginalization of blacks can be attributed to the same social structure that has facilitated the transfer of assets and accumulation of wealth over the generations in white families.

The labor movement has faced an uphill battle because, as is predicted by conflict theory, grievances on the part of potential workers and workers have been misdirected from the powers that be to inter-group conflicts between workers themselves. This misdirection has weakened the movement over the years. With the advent of a global economy, it has become increasingly difficult for working-class individuals to pinpoint exactly to whom their grievances about reduced hours, reduced benefits or elimination of jobs should be addressed. In addition, in some states collective bargaining is not permitted and in most private workforces workers are too intimidated to organize (Carty, 2006). Typically, women and people of color are the most negatively impacted by cost-cutting decisions. Thus, in these times, as in times previous, misplaced aggression about economic injustice is often racialized and people of color face conflict from both above and within their ranks as workers.

Although all workers are affected by the quest for profit in a capitalist economy, labor organizing efforts themselves have not always fully represented all of the workers' varied needs and have oftentimes been hampered by racism, sexism, and ethnic conflict (Zamudio, 2002). The worth of black workers as a group in the movement is often devalued (Honey, 1999) and the needs of immigrant laborers and women are often ignored. History has shown that white workers in the labor movement have often been easily convinced by their bosses not to join in struggle with black workers (Babson, 1999; Honey, 1999), and in the event that such coalitions have formed, harassment and racism have been prevalent (Babson, 1999). Another ongoing tension that characterizes the labor movement today is one between low-paid resident workers and immigrant or migrant workers, both documented and undocumented. With massive closures affecting the manufacturing sector and the growth of the low-paid and temporary service sector, good-paying jobs are hard to come by for those without an advanced education. The face of the service economy is increasingly that of the immigrant woman (Zamudio, 2002) and the labor movement is currently attempting not only to speak to the needs of this vulnerable population, but also to other poor and working-class people searching for meaningful jobs.

The hostility that is currently being directed toward the immigrant workforce is often countered with a discussion of its willingness to take jobs nobody else will take. In turn, this is often met with disagreement by other segments of the labor force, as well as the unemployed or underemployed, who believe the argument is a false one that de-emphasizes the role of worker exploitation and the structural nature of the problem. The situation of workers in the Gulf region post-Katrina is certainly one that must be assessed with these pre-existing tensions in mind. With the temporary obliteration of the tourist economy that kept many financially afloat, especially in New Orleans, and the utilization of low-paid migrant workers in lieu of available black workers, labor grievances are running high. Yet as the authors of *Injustice for All: Workers' Lives in the Reconstruction of New Orleans* (Browne-Dianis et al., 2006, p. 8) stated, the differences being emphasized by the media just detract from the fact that, "In reality, low-wage workers of color are all losers in a 'race to the bottom.'" Although that characterization may appear to be harshly pessimistic, it encapsulates the frustrating state of affairs that many workers face today.

The Environmental Justice Movement

In New Orleans, three Superfund sites were affected by the storm and flood waters. One was the Agricultural Street Landfill, a 94-acre site that included a predominantly black, low-income community housing project and elementary school built on a municipal landfill containing liquid hazardous waste. EPA chose to excavate and treat less than two-thirds of the site, instead placing two feet of dirt on top of much of the hazardous waste. So concerned were the residents that they had filed a lawsuit seeking relocation, a suit pending at the time Katrina hit. In addition to the obvious question—why one would cap a contaminated site located in an area prone to hurricanes and flooding?—we must also ask whether the cleanup remedies for the New Orleans sites fit this national pattern of unequal treatment, and consequently made environmental conditions worse. (Gauna, 2005, n.p.)

Although a much younger social movement than the civil rights and labor rights movements, the environmental justice movement and its claims are no less vital to an understanding of why a hurricane, or any sort of disaster, tends to affect low-income communities of color more negatively than other communities. The chief lesson of the environmental justice movement as it relates to the other two movements analyzed in this chapter is that policies generated on the basis of race, ethnicity, and class distinctions have long perpetuated environmental racism and classism. When assessing the aftermath of the 2005 Gulf Coast hurricanes, it is important to recognize that injustices related to resource distribution and lack of access to prime physical locations have mediated the impact that the disaster had on those affected by it. People of color and the poor often reside in sub-prime neighborhoods and face a lack of responsiveness in times of need—times that are not limited to situations officially deemed emergencies by the government.

The environmentalist movement is a broad-based movement that includes a number of different groups who share varied concerns related to the conservation of the environment as a goal in itself, as well as the preservation of the environment for future generations of humans to enjoy (Pepper, 1993; Weisheit & Morn, 2004). The 1968 publication of Rachel Carson's *Silent Spring,* a book on the dangers of pesticides, is often considered the event that spawned the modern-day environmentalist movement (Frumkin, 2005; Vertovec, 2003). Numerous social movement organizations were developed after its publication as individuals became inspired to mobilize in the name of addressing problems of pollution, deforestation, global warming, whaling and toxic waste. In the early years of environmentalist activity the majority of these organizations were dominated by white, middle-class individuals, but in the early 1980s the movement broadened to include people of color and working-class people (Bullard, 1994, 2000). These folks began bringing the language of civil rights and the civil rights movement's tactics to the table as they spread the word about the environmental *justice* movement.

The environmental justice movement began by framing its cause in the tradition of the civil rights movement and forwarding claims that access to a healthy environment as well as protection from an unhealthy environment are *rights,* not merely privileges (Bullard & Johnson, 2000). The pivotal event that was central to the genesis of the movement also borrowed from the techniques of the civil rights movement; in 1982, civil disobedience was utilized as a means of demonstrating resistance to a plan to site a PCB (polychlorinated biphenyls) landfill in a predominately black and rural Warren County, North Carolina. More than 500 people were arrested and jailed because of their involvement in the protest and they were ultimately effective at getting more people in the civil rights community to pay attention to the seriousness and prevalence of environmental injustice (Bullard, 1994). This event was followed the next year by the dissemination of the U.S. General Accounting Office's finding that toxic waste landfills were disproportionately placed in black communities in eight Southern states (Bullard, 1994). The egregious nature of the problems facing communities of color as a result of such land use decisions drove the creation of a movement that spoke to those problems specifically and that drew activists directly from those communities. The first major event meeting of the movement was 1991's First National People of Color Environmental Leadership Summit. In the years to follow, similar events of differing scales have been organized as a means of facilitating the movement, including conferences of the Coalition Against Environmental Racism and events hosted by the Environmental Justice Resource Center.

The environmental justice movement forwards claims about injustice that reflect the race and class-based concerns of the civil rights and labor movements. Its advocates have noted that environmental racism is simply a continuation of longstanding discriminatory practices against people of color, or "old wine in a new bottle" (see Robinson, 2000). Robert Bullard (1994), the preeminent scholar of environmental racism explained that,

> The signs [of segregation] are gone, but the residuals of Jim Crow housing and unfair industrial and land use policies are still with us. African Americans and other people of color are burdened with more than their share of toxic waste dumps, landfills, incinerators, lead smelters, dirty air and drinking water, and other forms of pollution that threaten their health in their homes and in the workplace. (p. vii)

Robinson (2000, n.p.) further elucidated the challenges that the environmental justice movement faces in the 21st century,

> In the United States, the victims of environmental racism are African Americans, Latinos, Native Americans, Asians, and Pacific Islanders, who are more likely than Whites to live in environmentally hazardous conditions. Three out of five African Americans live in communities with uncontrolled toxic waste sites. Native American lands and sacred places are home to extensive mining operations and radioactive waste sites. Three of the five largest commercial hazardous waste landfills are located in predominantly African American and Latino communi-

ties. As a consequence, the residents of these communities suffer shorter life spans, higher infant and adult mortality, poor health, poverty, diminished economic opportunities, substandard housing, and an overall degraded quality of life.

The environmental justice movement also works to draw attention to environmental classism, the process by which planning decisions target low-income communities to bear the brunt of environmental hazards, disregard the communities' needs, and lower their residents' general quality of life. Advocates note that oftentimes, due to an intersection of race/ethnicity and class status, environmental racism and environmental classism are acting within the same communities. In order to counter these inequities, the environmental justice movement, like the civil rights and labor movements, emphasizes a fair enforcement of existing laws that are on the books as a first step to benefit communities with little political power. Movement advocates strongly encourage the Environmental Protection Agency, the federal agency that was established in 1970 to address environmental concerns, to take a leading role in this effort, as would befit it given its mandate (Bullard & Johnson, 2000).

In addition to the environmental justice movement's basic lesson about the persistence of environmental racism and classism, it also has highlighted the regional dynamics that formed the backdrop of the Hurricane Katrina crisis. The research arm of the environmental justice movement has been working since the 1980s to examine regional differences in land use and environmental policies. Researchers have demonstrated that the deep south of the United States has been found to be particularly vulnerable to policymaking that endangers the less privileged. Essentially, the region has been used as the primary dumping ground for the nation's waste. In turn, environmental protection policies have rarely been enforced, and corporate polluters have been rewarded with tax breaks (Bullard & Johnson, 2000).

The plight of Louisiana was already of concern to environmental justice advocates prior to Katrina because it had long been one of the worst states in the union in terms of environmental health. Its infamous "Cancer Alley," an 85-mile long region along the Mississippi River that includes over 100 petrochemical companies, motivated residents who were concerned about the toxic waste that is infiltrating the land, the groundwater, and the air to organize in the name of environmental justice (Wright, Bryant & Bullard, 1994). Their collective endeavors have forwarded claims related to the risks that communities with little political capital face as the result of the pollutants created by nearby factories producing products plastics, gasoline, paint, and fertilizers (Bullard & Johnson, 2000). In spite of the vitality of the environmental justice movement in the South prior to Hurricanes Katrina and Rita, its lessons were largely disregarded by governmental agencies in their planning for any emergencies that might stir up the already present environmental hazards. *Social* problems were treated instead as individual problems and the planning decisions were thus individualistic rather than community oriented; for example, in New Orleans the use of private transportation was to be encouraged in a time of crisis instead of the use of public transportation (Guana, 2005). Such a plan ignored the fact that a substantial segment of the population did not have access to such private resources and thus, they were unjustly burdened by a requirement that they contend with the elements on their own. As a result, the most vulnerable members of the population became even more vulnerable to environmental hazards during and after the disaster, and environmental inequities were reproduced on a dangerous scale.

The environmental justice movement continues to highlight the dangers of official inattentiveness to the needs of poor communities and communities of color as well as the inequities involved in public planning decisions. The major emphasis of this struggle is material—on the betterment of the daily lives of the least privileged in our society. The other aspect of this struggle is symbolic—a quest for recognition on the part of government officials and public planners that all lives are equally valuable and in need of protection.

Conclusion

News related to the controversial unfolding of the aftermath of Hurricane Katrina and the rebuilding of affected regions has broken daily in the period since it touched down in the autumn of 2005. These developments continue to demonstrate that particular *groups* of people have been systematically disadvantaged by the hurricane, and that the disaster is but one catastrophic piece of an ongoing pattern of structural disadvantage. The social movements that have been discussed in this chapter have been addressing the various mechanisms by which this disadvantage gets perpetuated for decades, yet their claims often go unacknowledged.

It is clear from a cursory introduction to the civil rights, labor, and environmental justice movements that participants in the movements have traditionally framed their causes in terms of equal rights, but have discovered that although formal legal equality is essential to justice, it is not sufficient in and of itself. For true social justice to exist, proper enforcement of the law is necessary. On both the substantive and procedural fronts—that is, those related to the content of law and its enforcement—commitment to social justice must be a priority. This has proven to be challenging as both laws and the people who enforce them have traditionally been influenced in the direction of the status quo.

Moreover, the movements themselves continue to grapple with the social complexities of the subjects around which they have organized. Although in this day and age it is easy for people to profess a commitment to equal rights, a true commitment to them requires frank examination of the varied ways racism, classism, and other injustices intersect and manifest themselves in today's world. In the cases of the civil rights and labor movements, a quick review of their long trajectories demonstrates that movement advocates have had to reconsider their aims in light of the deeply rooted problems they are attempting to address and the ways in which those very problems influence their own interactions. The environmental justice movement, because of its relative youth and narrow scope, has not yet had to negotiate those issues in the same manner.

Guinier (1998) claimed that the most important accomplishment of the civil rights movement is that it has inspired many people who have traditionally been silenced to be given voice. Indeed, all social justice movements enjoy some success in this regard. In the aftermath and reconstruction of New Orleans and the Gulf Coast region, it is crucial that we give similar voice to the victims of Katrina, and just as importantly, to listen to their words. It becomes quickly apparent when one does that their concerns parallel those that have been concerns of social movement activists for decades. It is time now for us to heed their lessons.

References

Andrews, K. (2002). Creating social change: Lessons from the civil rights movement. In D. Meyer, N. Whittier & B. Robnett (Eds.), *Social movements: Identity, culture, and the state* (pp. 105–117). Oxford: Oxford University Press.

Babson, S. (1999). *The unfinished struggle: Turning points in American labor, 1877–present.* Lanham, MD: Rowman & Littlefield Publishers.

Bell, D. (1987). *And we are not saved: The elusive quest for racial justice.* U.S.A.: Basic Books.

Bonilla-Silva, E. (2001). *White supremacy & racism in the post-civil rights era.* Boulder, CO: Lynne Rienner Publishers.

———. (2003.) *Racism without racists: Color-blind racism and the persistence of inequality in the U.S.* Landham, MD: Rowman & Littlefield Publishers.

Browne-Dinanis, J., Lai, J., Hincapie, M. & Soni, S. (2006). *And Injustice for All: Workers Lives in the Reconstruction of New Orleans.* Retrieved October 16, 2006 from http://www.advancementproject.org/reports/workersreport.pdf.

Bullard, R.D. (Ed.) (1994). *Unequal protection: environmental justice and communities of color.* San Francisco: Sierra Club Books.

———. (2000). *Dumping in Dixie: Race, class and environmental quality.* Boulder, CO: Westview Press.

Bullard, R.D. & Johnson, G.S. (2000) Environmental justice: Grassroots activism and its impact on public policy decision making. *Journal of Social Issues, 56*(3), 555–578.

Carty, V. (2006). Labor struggles, new social movements, and America's favorite pastime: New York workers take on New Era Cap Company. *Social Problems, 49*(2), 239–259.

Davis, J. (Ed.) (2002). *Stories of change: Narrative and social movements.* Albany: State University of New York Press.

Equal Justice Society. (2005, Dec.13). Class action lawsuit prompts judge to stop FEMA from forcing Katrina victims out of hotels. Retrieved Oct. 16, 2006 from http://www.equaljusticesociety.org/petition.

Frumkin, H. (2005). Health, equity & the built environment. *Environmental Health Perspectives, 113*(5), A290–A291.

Gamson, W. (1992). The social psychology of collective action. In A. Morris & C. Mueller (Eds.), *Frontiers in Social Movement Theory* (pp. 53–76). New Haven, CT: Yale University Press.

Gamson, W., Fireman, B. & Rytina, S. (1982). *Encounters with unjust authority.* Homewood, IL: Dorsey.

Gamson, W. & Wolfsfeld, G. (1993). Movements and media as interacting systems. *Annuals of the Academy of Political and Social Science, 528*, 114–125.

Guana, E. (2005, Oct. 10). Katrina and environmental justice. Retrieved Oct.16, 2006 from http://jurist.law.pitt.edu/forumy/2005/10/katrina-and-environmental-injustice.php.

Guinier, L. (1998). *Lift every voice: Turning a civil rights setback into a strong new vision of social justice.* New York: Simon & Schuster.

Honey, M. K. (1999). *Black workers remember: An oral history of segregation, unionism, and the freedom struggle.* Berkeley: University of California Press.

Johnston, H., Larana, E. & Gusfield, J. (1994). Identities, grievances, and new social movements. In E. Larana, H. Johnston & J. Gusfield (Eds.), *New social movements: From ideology to Identity*(pp. 3–35). Philadelphia: Temple University Press.

Lofland, J. (1996). *Social movement organizations.* New York: Aldine de Gruyter.

Marx, K. (1992). *Capital: Volume 1: A Critique of Political Economy*(B. Fowkes, Trans.). Penguin U.S.: Penguin Classics. Original work published in 1867.

McAdam, D. & Snow, D. (1997). Introduction. Social movements: Conceptual and theoretical issues. In D. McAdam & D. Snow (Eds.), *Social movements: Readings on their emergence, mobilization, and dynamics* (p. xvii–xxv). Los Angeles: Roxbury Publishing.

Morris, A. (1984). *The origins of the civil rights movement: Black communities organizing for change.* New York: Free Press.

Mueller, C.M. (1992). Building social movement theory. In A. Morris & C. Mueller (Eds.), *Frontiers in social movement theory* (p. 3–26). New Haven, CT: Yale University Press.

Oliver, M. & Shapiro, T.M. (1997) *Black wealth/White wealth: A new perspective on racial inequality.* New York: Routledge.

Omi, M. & Winant, H. (1994). *Racial formation in the United States*(2nd ed.). New York: Routledge.

Pepper, D. (1993). *Eco-socialism: From deep ecology to social justice.* London: Routledge.

Piven, F.F. & Cloward, R. (1979). *Poor people's movements: Why they succeed, how they fail.* New York: Vintage Books.

Platt, G. & Fraser, M. (1998). Race and gender discourses: Creating solidarity and framing the civil rights movement. *Social Problems, 45*(2), 160–179.

Polletta, F. & Jasper, J. (2001). Collective identity and social movements. *Annual Review of Sociology* (Annual), 283–305.

Robinson, D. (2000) Environmental racism, old wine in a new bottle. Retrieved Sept. 1, 2006 from http://www.wcc-coe.org/wcc/what/jpc/echoes/echoes-17-02.html.

Robinson, R. (2000). *The debt: What America owes to Blacks.* New York: Plume.

Tarrow, S. (1992). Mentalities, political cultures, and collective action frames: Constructing meanings through action.

Vargas, Z. (2005). *Labor rights are civil rights.* Princeton: Princeton University Press.

Verney, K. (2000). *Black civil rights in America.* London: Routledge.

Vertovec, S. (2003). Introduction. In S. Vertovec & D. Posey (Eds.), *Globalization, globalism, environments, and environmentalism* (pp. 1–7). Oxford: Oxford University Press.

Weisheit, R. & Morn, F. (2004). *Pursuing justice.* Belmont, CA: Wadsworth/Thomson Learning.

Winbush, R. (Ed.) (2003). *Should America pay? Slavery and the raging debate on reparations.* New York: Harper Collins.

Wright, B., Bryant, P. & Bullard, R.D. (1994). Coping with poisons in Cancer Alley. In R. Bullard (Ed.), *Unequal protection: Environmental justice and communities of color* (pp. 110–129). San Francisco: Sierra Club Books.

Zald, M.N. (1992). Looking forward to look backward: Reflections on the past and future of the resource mobilization research program. In A. Morris &

C. Mueller (Eds.), *Frontiers in social movement theory* (pp. 326–348). New Haven, CT: Yale University Press.

Zamudio, M. (2002). Segmentation, conflict, community, and coalitions: Lessons from the new labor movement. In C. Velez-Ibáñez & A. Sampaio (Eds.), *Transnational Latina/o communities: Politics, processes, and cultures* (pp. 205–224). Lanham, MD: Rowman & Littlefield Publishers.

Chapter 6

Reminders of Poverty, Soon Forgotten

Alexander Keyssar

For many Americans, Hurricane Katrina kicked up the hope that the United States might try once again to seriously address the problem of poverty. If we had forgotten that poor people still lived in the land of SUV's and hedge funds, we could no longer ignore that reality—not with the powerful news footage coming out of New Orleans. There they were, on our television screens, the storm's most desperate victims—disproportionately poor and black, wading through muddy water, carrying children and plastic bags containing a few meager possessions. An entire city was devastated, but some neighborhoods and some people were clearly hit far worse than others. One thing that being poor meant was that you didn't have the capacity to get out of the way of floodwaters when they came pouring down your street.

It took nearly a week, but the news media grabbed onto the issue, rediscovering poverty even while it was pounding the Federal Emergency Management Agency for its inept response to the storm. Major news magazines and television programs rushed to describe what the hurricane's aftermath revealed: Newsweek, for example, ran a cover emblazoned "Poverty, Race & Katrina: Lessons of a National Shame," containing a stunning blend of statistics and powerful photographs. We all learned that the charming, hedonistic city on the lower Mississippi had one of the highest poverty rates in the nation and that most of its poor were African-American. The New York Times apologetically acknowledged that, over the past decade, it had paid far more attention to New Orleans's restaurants than to the abject conditions in which many of its residents lived.

Hurricane Katrina seemed to be a wake-up call, a reminder to a prosperous nation that it still had domestic business to attend to. The cold fact that the fruits of recent economic growth had gone overwhelmingly to our richest citizens meant that millions of people continued to live in substandard housing, attend dysfunctional schools, travel slowly on broken-down public transportation systems, and die in overcrowded hospitals. While taxes were cut, public infrastructure—like the levees—was eroding, and an already frayed safety net was disintegrating. The poverty of many of Katrina's victims was an ugly and intolerable sight, and it seemed clear that we needed to do something about it.

That view, of course, was neither universal nor unalloyed by less benign portrayals of the men and women who were cast adrift by Katrina. From the beginning, there were reports of looting, of "thugs" seizing control of neighborhoods, of rapes and other violent crimes at sites where refugees had congregated; such reports—now known to have been exaggerated and distorted—made the victims seem less like our fellow citizens and more like denizens of another culture. Complaints were voiced that the people trapped in New Orleans had only themselves to blame, since they hadn't heeded the order to evacuate. (It turns out that a third of the city's African-American households did not own cars.) One reporter I spoke to said that when she interviewed middle-class escapees from the Gulf Coast, they criticized the government and the news media for giving too much attention and money to poor African-Americans in New Orleans.

Indeed, the early outbursts of indignation and hope—not about the wretched relief effort but about the exposure of poverty in Louisiana and Mississippi began to fade as one week bled into the next. News stories about poverty slowed to a trickle, while reporters dashed to Texas to cover Hurricane Rita. Michael D. Brown resigned, and then blamed local officials for the chaos, while large, well-connected corporations signed no-bid contracts to rebuild swaths of Louisiana and Mississippi. Then the spotlight of national news attention began to shift altogether, away from the Gulf and toward Harriet Miers, the vote on the Iraqi constitution, the devastating earthquake in Pakistan, and the World Series.

Serious discussions of poverty policy can still be heard on NPR, and activists in Louisiana are determined not to let the issue disappear from view. The new head of FEMA has announced that he is revisiting the issue of no-bid contracts, while considerable quantities of relief are actually reaching the people of the Gulf Coast. But there is no crescendo of national public opinion about the presence of millions of poor people in our midst, and President Bush has not announced the creation of a national task force to combat poverty. Some conservatives in Congress, meanwhile, seem determined to pay for the costs of Katrina by cutting other programs that, directly or indirectly, help the poor.

As a historian—and one who has taught and written about the history of poverty in the United States—I should not have been surprised by that quick reversion to "normalcy" (although I was). With the immediate crisis over, and many of the victims of Katrina and Rita scattered around the region and beyond, it was entirely foreseeable that the spotlight of public attention would shift to other issues and locales. Those whose homes and jobs disappeared inevitably become absorbed in the tedious, slow, painful task of rebuilding their lives, while elsewhere men and women of good will—however moved by the initial events, and perhaps after writing a check or two—go about their business.

But the problem runs deeper. Disasters and crises in American history have, in fact, rarely produced any fundamental changes in economic or social policy. Natural disasters, like hurricanes, floods, earthquakes, and fire, are invariably local events, leaving too much of the nation unscathed to generate any broad gauged shift in understanding or ideology. Moreover, the most readily adopted policy changes have involved technical issues, like the approval or revision of fire codes, the earthquake-proofing of new buildings, and the raising of the height of levees. The most far-reaching policy decision after the San Francisco earthquake of 1906 was to flood the beautiful Hetch Hetchy Valley to guarantee San Francisco a more reliable source of water.

Poverty, however, is not a technical issue, but a deep, structural problem that implicates our values, our economic institutions, and our conception of the proper role of the state. There are fixes, but no quick fixes—and no fixes that will not cost something to at least some other members of our society. Understandably, thus, there has always been resistance to government actions, such as increasing the minimum wage, that might aid the poor; and that resistance has long been grounded both in self-interest and in willful blindness of a type that does not succumb to relatively brief crises.

Nowhere is that more evident—or more relevant—than in the history of responses to the panics and depressions that have been a prominent feature of American economic life for almost two centuries. (We called them "panics" until the early 20th century, when widespread recognition that capitalist economies had business cycles led to the use of more reassuring words like "depression," "downturn," and, still later, "recession.")

As American society grew more industrial and urban in the 19th century, and as markets increasingly shaped the ability of its populace to earn a living, the impact of business-cycle downturns broadened and deepened. The long post-Civil War downturn of the 1870s, for example, toppled millions of people into destitution or near-destitution; arguably the first depression of the industrial era, it created widespread distress that prompted pioneering efforts to count the unemployed, while also contributing to outbursts of working-class violence in 1877. Less than a decade later (1884–86), the country lived through another downturn, followed in the 1890s by the most severe depression of the 19th century. The Panic of 1893 (which lasted until 1897) sharply lowered wages, while making jobs exceedingly scarce in many industries. It also prompted the first major protest march on Washington, a national movement of the unemployed led by Ohio's populist leader Jacob S. Coxey.

Yet many, if not most, Americans resisted the notion that millions of their fellow citizens were genuinely in need of aid. New York's distinguished Protestant cleric Henry Ward Beecher famously commented in 1877 that a man could easily support a family of eight on a dollar a day: "Is not a dollar a day enough to buy bread with? Water costs nothing; and a man who cannot live on bread is not fit to live." In the spring of 1894, after the dreadful winter that sparked the formation of Coxey's Army, Daniel B. Wesson, of Smith and Wesson, observed that "I don't think there was much suffering last winter." Others insisted that if men and women were destitute, it was because they were improvident or they drank: "Keep the people sober that ask for relief, and you will have no relief asked for," said Henry Faxon, a businessman from Quincy, Mass. Even Carroll D. Wright, who supervised the first count of the unemployed in American history in 1878 (and a few years later became the first head of the U.S. Bureau of Labor Statistics), expressed the view that most of the men who lacked jobs did not "really want employment."

Private charities, as well as what were called "overseers of the poor" (overseers? the language itself is telling), did, of course, provide some relief to the victims of economic crisis. Yet they did so grudgingly and warily, often insisting that recipients perform physical labor in return for food and fuel, while also (particularly with women) conducting home interviews to verify that applicants for aid were of good moral character. In many states, the sole legislative response to the depressions of the late 19th century was the passage of "anti-tramp" laws that made it illegal for poor workers to travel from place to place in search of work.

Over time, to be sure, the recurrence of panics, coupled with the learning gradually acquired by charity officials and dedicated antipoverty activists like settlement-house workers, did contribute to more-hospitable attitudes toward the poor. They also gave birth to new policy ideas (like unemployment insurance) that might help alleviate the problem of poverty. Such ideas, which began to gain a bit of traction in the early 20th century, were grounded in the supposition that American society had a responsibility to help not only the destitute, but also the poor: the millions of men and women who worked hard, and as steadily as they could, but lived in substandard conditions, a short distance from dire, material need.

Resistance to such proposals, however, did not vanish overnight: Suspicions that the poor were "unworthy" persisted, as did a reluctance to expand the role of government. Of equal importance, crisis conditions (as business-cycle theorists pointed out) did come to an end, lessening the visible urgency of the problem. That was particularly true during the first three, sharp depressions of the 20th century, in 1907–8, 1913–14, and 1920–22. The second of those led to the drafting of unemployment-insurance bills in several states, but by the time the bills were ready for legislative action, the economy was picking up, and interest had ebbed. In 1921 a charming, eccentric organizer named Urbain Ledoux put together sensational anti-unemployment demonstrations in both New York City and Boston, including mock auctions of unemployed "slaves" on the Boston Common. He garnered enough front-page attention to earn a meeting with President Warren G. Harding and an invitation to attend the President's Conference on Unemployment—which turned out to be a bureaucratic vehicle that effectively delayed action long enough for the economic crisis to come to an end, with no new policies put into place.

The Great Depression and the New Deal, of course, constitute the most dramatic and far-reaching exception to the pattern of a crisis causing (and revealing) poverty while yielding no basic changes in policy. As always, the exception sheds some light on the dynamics that produce the rule. The Great Depression gave rise to significant shifts in policy not just because the downturn was severe but also—and more important—because of its unprecedented length. There were few innovations in public responses to poverty and unemployment during the early years of the 1930s (no one, after all, knew that this depression would turn out to be the Great Depression), and the era's most durable, systematic legislation came more than two years after Franklin D. Roosevelt took office in 1933. The Social Security Act (with its provisions for unemployment and old-age insurance) and the Wagner Act (which strengthened the right of workers to join unions) were passed only in 1935, the same year that the pioneering work-relief programs of the Works Progress Administration were launched; the Fair Labor Standards Act, mandating a federal minimum wage, was not enacted until 1938, nearly a decade after the stock-market crash.

The greatest economic crisis in American history, thus, did not produce a quick turnaround in antipoverty policy, even though the ideas eventually put into effect had been circulating among progressives for decades. The recognition that millions of people were suffering (inescapable as early as 1931) was not enough to produce action. What was also needed was time for political movements to build and to generate a leadership with the political will to take action.

That involved not just the election of Roosevelt in 1932 (which was primarily a repudiation of Herbert Hoover) but also the Share-the-Wealth movement of Louisiana's own Huey P. Long, the election of many left-leaning Democrats to Congress in 1934, and Roosevelt's overwhelming re-election in 1936. It was at his second inaugural, in January 1937, that Roosevelt famously referred to "one-third of a nation ill-housed, ill-clad, ill-nourished" and committed his administration to dealing with the "tens of millions" of citizens "who at this very moment are denied the greater part of what the very lowest standards of today call the necessities of life." In language eerily resonant today (aimed at an audience with vivid memories of the deadly Labor Day Hurricane that struck Florida in 1935), Roosevelt also announced that his administration "refused to leave the problems of our common welfare to be solved by the winds of chance and the hurricanes of disaster."

The New Deal was a turning point not just because of the specific, permanent programs that the federal government adopted, but also because it expressed a new, dominant consensus about social justice and the role of government. The poverty of millions of Americans was viewed as a collective responsibility rather than an assembly of individual misfortunes or failures; and it became the responsibility of government to actively combat that poverty. The political will that Roosevelt voiced was precisely the will to embrace collective responsibility, which, as he himself observed, reflected a "change in the moral climate of America."

That same "moral climate" and political will also undergirded Lyndon B. Johnson's declaration of an "unconditional war on poverty" in 1964. Notably, the war on poverty did not originate in an economic crisis or a natural disaster: It was launched in a period of prosperity and linked directly to a middle-class recognition—akin to the "Katrina experience"—that poverty still existed within the plenty of post-World War II America. (The famous emblem of that recognition was John F. Kennedy reading Michael Harrington's The Other America.) Yet viewed from the perspective of 2005, what seems most remarkable about the war on poverty was neither the recognition that poverty still existed nor the mixed success of individual programs. Rather, it was the optimism of the "war" itself. In the mid-1960s, much of the political leadership of our nation actually believed that poverty could be eliminated from the richest nation on earth.

That optimism has eroded substantially over the last 40 years. The erosion has occurred, in part, because the war on poverty did not register the quick victory foreseen by officials like Sargent Shriver, the head of the Office of Economic Opportunity, who predicted in 1966 that the United States "virtually could eliminate" poverty. Although government programs did contribute to a decline in the poverty rate in the late 1960s and early 1970s (the official figure dropped from 22 percent to 11 percent between 1959 and 1973), progress stalled in the more uncertain and sluggish economic conditions of the 1970s and 1980s. Since the mid-1970s, in fact, the official rate has ranged up and down between 11 percent and 15 percent, roughly tracking the business cycle. The lack of decisive improvement after 1973 made possible Ronald Reagan's oft-quoted quip that the United States had conducted a war on poverty, and "poverty won." Americans like to keep their wars short.

Other factors also played a role. By the mid-1970s, social-welfare programs were becoming increasingly expensive, and, with the economy sputtering, public support for what appeared to be income redistribution began to sag. At the same time, critics of the war on poverty helped to resuscitate longstanding negative images of the poor as lazy and unworthy: For example, Russell Long, the influential Louisiana senator, insisted that the welfare system was being "abused by malingerers, cheaters, and outright frauds." Conservative intellectuals joined the fray with studies arguing that government programs had either failed to reduce poverty or made things worse. And in the 1980s public perceptions of poverty became increasingly linked to the image of a largely African-

American "underclass" that was rife with crime and unresponsive to the benign ministrations of mainstream American society.

Accompanying all those developments, of course, were the ideological attacks on government itself that became ascendant with the election of Reagan and that still stymie efforts to mobilize the political will to combat poverty. For more than 25 years, it has been Republican orthodoxy that government is the problem, not the solution. If there is a solution to the issues facing the poor, it lies in the magic of the free market, in letting private enterprise generate jobs and growth. Republicans, moreover, have no monopoly on such views: The centrist Democrats who rose to power in the 1990s have embraced much of the market-centered orthodoxy, undeterred by the historical fact that economic growth alone has never solved the problem of poverty anywhere. It was, after all, the Democrat Bill Clinton who declared that the "era of big government" was over. Most Democratic leaders today seem, indeed, to lack the convictions of their New Deal and Great Society predecessors, convictions that made it possible to translate outrage and empathy into policy initiatives. While President Bush promotes market-friendly responses to the crisis in the Gulf Coast, Democrats remain on the sidelines, fearful of being associated with either "big government" or economic redistribution.

As Hurricane Katrina pulled back the veil on American poverty, many news commentators openly wondered whether the scenes we were witnessing would revive the war on poverty of the 1960s. Two months later it is clear that no such revival will happen. The long history of crises and natural disasters in the United States suggests that they rarely provide auspicious moments for major policy initiatives—unless the political will for such initiatives is pre-existing or can readily be mobilized. That surely is not the case today. Billions of dollars will be spent in the Gulf states, and New Orleans and Biloxi will be rebuilt. But there will be no new national programs to aid the poor, and precious little in the way of targeted antipoverty programs in the Gulf. Perhaps the most disturbing fact that Hurricane Katrina has placed before our eyes is our society's loss of faith in its ability to truly help the people whose faces we glimpsed in September.

Section Two

Images from the Disaster:
Reactions to Hurricane Katrina

Chapter 7

New Song, Same Old Tune: Racial Discourse in the Aftermath of Hurricane Katrina

Ashley ("Woody") Doane

The natural disaster that was Hurricane Katrina exposed the social disasters of racism and poverty in the United States. As is the case with most disasters and social problems, from hurricanes to the sinking of the *Titanic*, from recession to war, the bulk of the burden was borne by the poorest members of society. In New Orleans, it was the poor who lived in the lowest areas, who had no means to evacuate, who had the fewest resources for coping with the storm, and who suffered the longest in its aftermath. And as was evident from television coverage, the face of poverty and despair in the wake of Hurricane Katrina was overwhelmingly African-American. These images again underscored the truth of Lani Guinier and Gerald Torres' (2003) characterization of African Americans as the "miner's canary" that makes visible the social ills and inequalities of American society.

In the aftermath of Hurricane Katrina, the claim was frequently made that this was a potential turning point in the social understanding of race and poverty in the United States. For example, the front cover headline on the September 19, 2005, issue of *Newsweek* was "Poverty, Race & Katrina: Lessons of a National Shame" and the popular weekly newsmagazine included a lengthy article (Alter, 2005) that used the New Orleans disaster to discuss the relationship between race and poverty. In an op-ed article in *Newsday*, Ed Gordon (2005) stated that, "it took Hurricane Katrina, a natural disaster of biblical proportions, but finally this country is talking about race" (p. A41). For the next few months, newspaper headlines around the United States announced the emergence of a new perspective on race: The *San Francisco Chronicle* asserted "Katrina Thrusts Race and Poverty onto National Stage" (Sandalow, 2005, p. A13); The *Boston Globe* proclaimed "Katrina as a Teaching Moment" (DeMarco, 2005, p. A32); and the *Omaha World-Herald* came forth with "Continuing the Discussion: Dialogue on Race has Potential to Trump Prejudice" (Continuing the Discussion, 2005, p. 6B). Based upon these and other headlines, an observer might conclude that a new and promising era of race relations was rising from the destruction wrought by the hurricane.

Hurricane Katrina was what I (Doane, 2006, 2007) have termed a "racial event;" that is, an occurrence whose character triggers extensive national or local public discussion of issues of race and racism in the United States. Such racial events as the Rodney King beating and its aftermath, the murder of James Byrd in Jasper, Texas, the verdict in the O.J. Simpson trial, and the recent University of Michigan affirmative action cases, as well as local hate crimes and cases of racial profiling or racially-based police brutality, have all led to extensive public debates of issues of race. I argue that racial events such as Hurricane Katrina illuminate racial fault lines and bring conflicting racial ideologies to the fore. More significantly, the debates following racial events have the potential to reshape racial ideologies and racial politics.

In this chapter, I use data from various written and electronic sources to analyze the racial discourse that took place in the months following Hurricane Katrina. I demonstrate that the Katrina disaster was a racial event that laid bare the "racial divide" in the United States and illustrated the continuing significance of race. At the same time, I argue that the major themes in the discourse in the weeks and months following Hurricane Katrina were *not* new, but that they instead reflected the major general racial ideologies in the United States in the twenty-first century. In other words, I assert that while the aftermath of Hurricane Katrina may have seemed to set a new direction for racial dialogue, what transpired is ultimately best understood within the "same old tune" of existing racial ideologies. I conclude with an assessment of the implications of post-Katrina racial discourse for racial politics and the movement for racial justice in the United States.

Racial Ideologies and Racial Politics

In societies where race plays a significant role in social life, *racial ideologies* or belief systems serve to explain social practices and social conditions (Bonilla-Silva, 2006). Shared ideologies also provide the context in which individuals interpret events. Historically, racial ideologies have played an important role in the United States, as individuals and groups have justified or contested such practices as enslavement, conquest, exclusion, and segregation. Dominant racial ideologies legitimize and reproduce the position of the dominant group by marginalizing the claims of oppressed groups and asserting that the dominant group world view should be normative for the larger society (Doane, 1997). In contrast, non-dominant ideologies, including those espoused by dissident factions within the dominant group, challenge the existing racial order and promote alternative social and political agendas. The social space where competing ideologies clash constitutes the *racial politics* of society.

The dominant racial ideology in the United States at the beginning of the twenty-first century is "color-blind" racial ideology (Bonilla-Silva, 2001, 2006; Brown et al., 2003; Carr, 1997; Doane, 2003). Summarized briefly, color-blind racial ideology is grounded upon the claim that in the post-civil rights era race no longer "matters" in American society. To say that race does not matter is not the same as saying that race does not exist (indeed, color-blindness is compatible with a kind of "designer diversity" that uses superficial differences to claim that race is not significant); it is to say that race does not play a significant role in the distribution of resources and that racism is essentially a thing of the past. From the color-blind perspective, the only racism that does persist involves prejudice or isolated hate crimes committed by individuals—who may be of any race. Such persons are—or should be—condemned by the overwhelming majority of Americans. In essence, color-blind ideology asserts that the United States is close to realizing Martin Luther King Jr.'s "dream" of a society where people are judged "not by the color of their skin but by the content of their character" (King, 1992 [1963], p. 104).

The pervasiveness of color-blind racial ideology has several important implications for racial politics in the United States. If race does not matter and everyone has equal opportunities, then persistent racial segregation and economic inequality can be attributed to coincidence, the natural choices of individuals, or dysfunctional and socially pathological behavior on the part of minority individuals and communities. Claims of discrimination can be dismissed as "whining" in the face of personal shortcomings or "playing the race card" for personal or political gain (Doane, 2006). Race-based policies such as affirmative action can be condemned as "reverse discrimination" against white Americans and as violations of core democratic principles of equal treatment. The ultimate conclusion of color-blind racial ideology is that nothing needs to be done about racism—other than educating the next generation that everyone is equal—because racism is no longer a significant social force.

While color-blindness is the dominant racial ideology in the United States in the twenty-first century, it is certainly not the only framework for explaining race relations. Perhaps the major non-dominant racial ideology is what I have elsewhere described (Doane, 2006, 2007) as *systemic racism* ideology. In contrast to color-blindness, systemic racism incorporates the claim that racism, both individual and structural, is widespread in American society and that grassroots social movements and substantial institutional and social change are necessary in order to move towards a racially just society. From this vantage point, color-blind ideology is criticized as a political project that defends the social and economic advantages that whites enjoy in the United States—as "racism without racists" (Bonilla-Silva, 2001, 2006). Proponents of systemic racism ideology are evident in academic writing on race (e.g., Bell, 1992; Brown et al., 2003; Carmichael & Hamilton, 1967; Feagin, 2000), in some (generally non-mainstream media outlets), and among antiracist organizations. In addition, color-blindness is opposed by white supremacist ideologies (cf. Berbrier, 1998; Daniels, 1997; Ferber, 1998) that assert the preeminence of white culture and the cultural and/or biological inferiority of racial minorities. White supremacists seek to defend white society against the threats of minority immigration and criminality and government policies that favor minorities and threaten white dominance. While the general tendency under color-blind racial ideology is to condemn white supremacy, a number of analysts (e.g., Daniels, 1997; Gabriel, 1998; Omi & Winant, 1986) have claimed that white supremacy provides political cover for less overt institutionalized white dominance by deflecting much of the media attention devoted to racial issues.

New Song: Hurricane Katrina and the Racial Divide

In the immediate aftermath of the disaster, one could not have been faulted for concluding that Hurricane Katrina was a racial event that would reconfigure how Americans talked and thought about race. The starkness of the racial divide seemingly clearly contradicted the color-blind claim that race no longer matters in the United States. Nowhere was the racial divide more evident than in assessment of the response of the federal government in the first days following the hurricane. As thousands waited on rooftops, overpasses, and in the Louisiana Superdome, entertainer Kanye West (as cited in Brick, 2005) stated during a nationally televised concert to raise funds for victims of the storm that "George Bush doesn't care about black people" (p. B7). Similar, albeit less personal, comments were made by other observers (Tizon, 2005). National survey data underscored the racial fault line. A Pew Research Center (2005, p. 2) poll found that 68 percent of African Americans felt that the response of the federal government would have been faster had the overwhelming majority of the victims been white; while 77 percent of white respondents believed that the response would have been the same. This result was echoed in other national surveys (Sandalow, 2005). Clearly, race mattered when it came to explaining the slow response of the federal government in providing relief to the residents of New Orleans.

Racial divisions were equally striking in terms of perceptions of people trapped in New Orleans. The Pew Research Center poll (2005, p. 5) also found that white respondents were twice as likely to say that those who were left in New Orleans wanted to stay. In the wake of the storm, pictures of destruction and suffering were overshadowed by apocryphal stories of mass lawlessness: rapes, freezers stacked with bodies of murder victims, and even a seven-year-old with her throat cut. The reality, which surfaced days later, was that there was limited violence in the two sites—the New Orleans Convention Center and the Louisiana Superdome—where thousands sought shelter and of the few who died, only one had apparently been slain (Gold, 2005; Thevenot & Russell, 2005). The uncritical readiness of so many to accept these stories at face value was reminiscent of the willingness to believe the (later proven to be false) allegations of a black male assailant in the Charles Stuart and Susan Smith murder cases in the 1990s. At the same time, a story circulating within the African-American community questioned whether the levees protecting New Orleans had been deliberately sabotaged to protect white areas and to remove poorer and black neighborhoods from the city (Satran, 2005; Witt, 2005)—a perception grounded in the legacy of generations of oppression. How people explained the causes and consequences of the disaster fell along a racial divide.

Racial differences were also evident in other areas. Media attention on lawlessness in the first few days also focused upon widespread reports of looting, which was used as another example of the breakdown of order among persons trapped in New Orleans. Interestingly, race also was related to interpretations of this behavior on the part of survivors. According to the Pew Research Center survey (2005, p. 5), 57 percent of blacks but only 38 percent of whites said that people who took things from homes and businesses in New Orleans were "ordinary people trying to survive." This debate carried over into the media, where much discussion centered on an Internet site that juxtaposed two pictures: one of a young black man after "looting" a grocery store, the other of a white couple after "finding" bread and soda at a grocery store (McDaniel, 2005). Others bristled at the use of the word "refugees" to describe people evacuated from New Orleans—with the implication that storm victims were somehow not part of American society (Hunter, 2005; McDaniel, 2005). These issues and the claim that the media overemphasized looting and violence were cited by many observers as prima facie evidence of the continuing significance of race.

The Katrina disaster also evoked expressions of overt racism. In an incident that had strong racial overtones, groups of mostly African-American evacuees attempting to leave New Orleans across the Mississippi River Bridge were turned back at gunpoint by police from the town of Gretna (Brown, 2005; Hamilton, 2006). This later spawned both a protest march and a federal lawsuit. White supremacist groups responded by cheering casualties and applauding the "ethnic cleansing" of New Orleans (Anti-Defamation League, 2005a). Others spoke apprehensively of a "black tsunami" of evacuees and promoted "whites only" relief efforts (Anti-Defamation League, 2005b). Jared Taylor, publisher of the racist *American Renaissance* magazine, was quoted (Anti-Defamation League, 2005b, n.p.; also circulated anonymously via e-mail) as claiming that,

to be sure, the story of Hurricane Katrina does have a moral for anyone not deliberately blind. The races are different. Blacks and whites
are different. When blacks are left entirely to their own devices, Western Civilization—any kind of civilization—disappears. And in a crisis, civilization disappears overnight.

For white supremacists, the aftermath of the hurricane served to reinforce
racist perspectives.

One final area where the events in New Orleans highlighted the racial divide
was in conclusions that were drawn regarding the significance of the disaster
for understanding race relations in the United States. Another finding of the
Pew Research Center survey (2005, p. 2) was that while 38 percent of respondents agreed that Hurricane Katrina showed that racial inequality remains a
major problem, this response split along racial lines, with 71 percent of blacks
and 22 percent of whites agreeing with the statement. As noted earlier,
Newsweek devoted a special report (Alter, 2005) to the relationship between
race and poverty. U.S. Congressman John Lewis (2005, p. 52) described the
situation as "a national disgrace." Other commentators spoke of persistent
racial inequality nationally, in New Orleans, and in other cities (Duke and
Wiltz, 2005; Jacklin, 2005; Sandalow, 2005). The scope of the disaster also provided fodder for advocates of the systemic racism perspective. For example, Ira
Katznelson (2005) described how Southern poverty was grounded in the racial
distortion of New Deal policies. Paul Krugman (2005) argued that American
reluctance to helping those in need was linked to the connection between race
and poverty. Liberal/progressive publications such as the *Nation* produced a
series of articles commenting upon the continuing significance of race in the
United States. In sum, this was perhaps the most concentrated assault on
color-blindness since the 1992 Rodney King verdict and the Los Angeles riots.

Same Old Tune: Color-Blindness and the Denial of Racism

Less than a week had passed after Hurricane Katrina before proponents of
color-blindness were claiming that race had nothing to do with the disaster.
Ward Connerly (as cited in Tizon, 2005) asserted that the discussion of race
was a "needless distraction," that it was "simply coincidence" that the hurricane
"happened to hit New Orleans, which happens to be predominantly black and
poor" (p. A11). George Will (2005) commented that "America's always fast-
flowing river of race-obsessing has overflowed its banks" (p. A13). Others expressed anger at "phony race-baiters in the media" and the "race card" played
by both "cowardly whites and racist blacks" (Geary, 2005; Grosso, 2005). One
citizen (as quoted in Badie, 2005) stated that she "would like to hear from

some black leaders who are not trying to gain politically from this" (p. 3JJ). Columnist Jeff Jacoby (2005) decried the "slimy and toxic accusation that help didn't reach the victims of Hurricane Katrina quickly enough because they are black." He concluded that the color-blind nature of the response ("Americans of every color are helping Americans of every color") proved that "racism is dead as a force in mainstream American life"(p. A15).

In addition to the claim that the relief effort illustrated that race no longer matters, another theme in the responses was to put forth alternative explanations. Several authors claimed that the slow initial response was a matter of "incompetence, not racism" (Cohen, 2005; Dukes, 2005). Others suggested that the problem was not race, but poverty. An editorial in the *Omaha World-Herald* (Katrina's Revelation, 2005) observed that the issues were "not black and white, but a puzzling gray" (p. 8B). The editorial writer called upon all Americans to "get past the predictable tendency to bicker, call names and wallow in the muck" and instead focus upon helping the poor—while at the same time noting that "poverty and race are often intertwined in a strange little dance." Syndicated columnist Leonard Pitts (2005), in an op-ed piece titled "Poor is Poor, and Colorblind," criticized Kanye West for charging President Bush with racism and stated that "at the end of the day poor is poor, color notwithstanding" (p. B7). Pitts also tempered his statement by saying that "the poor are disproportionately black," but did not pursue this line of analysis. In both cases, we are left with racial inequality without racism.

A third thread of discourse laid the blame for the problems at the feet of poor blacks. Rush Limbaugh (as cited in Pitts, 2005) argued that suffering in the wake of Katrina was due to a "welfare state mentality" that led blacks to "wait for government help instead of saving themselves" (p. B7). George Will (2005) inferred that a high percentage of African-American births in New Orleans were to unmarried women and concluded that this "translates into a large and constantly renewed cohort of lightly parented adolescent males, and that translates into chaos, in neighborhoods and schools, come rain or come shine" (p. A13). Cal Thomas (2005) asserted that the real problems in black America were not the result of racism, but stemmed from single parent families and indolence. He also cited approvingly a minister who stated that "it was blacks' moral poverty—not their material poverty—that cost them dearly in New Orleans" (p. 17A). For each of these commentators, the Katrina disaster did not highlight America's racial divide, but rather the pathologies of the black community.

The discourse described above closely fits existing descriptions of color-blind racial ideology. In his book *Racism Without Racists*, Eduardo Bonilla-Silva (2006) outlines the central frames or interpretive paths of color-blind racial ideology. These include the minimization or denial of racism (including the attempt to use "anything but racism"—e.g., incompetence or class), naturalization (the claim that phenomena such as racial segregation and inequality "just happen"), and cultural racism (the claim that minorities' negative values and behavior are the central cause of racial inequality and social problems). Elsewhere, I (Doane, 1996, 2006) have described some additional tactics of color-blindness, including dismissing claims of racism as name-calling, divisive, or "playing the race card" for personal or political gain. All of these are evident in the quotations in the preceding paragraphs.

One particularly interesting development occurred in December of 2005 when two analyses (Riccardi, Smith, & Zucchino, 2005; Simerman, Ott & Mellnik, 2005) concluded that the death toll from Katrina reflected the demography of New Orleans—that fatalities were not disproportionately poor and black. While the analysis was problematic—it excluded deaths with missing bodies or unknown locations and it deduced the income of victims from the census tract where their body was found—several media sources used this to argue that Hurricane Katrina was, after all, not about race. The *Columbus Dispatch* (Rush to Misjudgment, 2006) produced an editorial discussing these findings titled "Rush to Misjudgment." The *Hartford Courant* (Katrina by the Numbers, 2006) claimed that Hurricane Katrina was an "equal opportunity storm." A column in the *Boston Globe* (Young, 2006) used the study to decry "Katrina's racial paranoia." What is noteworthy about these claims is that they use mortality data (however incomplete) to reach conclusions about the overall impact of the disaster—although one editorial (Rush to Misjudgment, 2006) did note (in the next-to-last sentence) the reality that "deaths from the storm are only part of its impact" (p. 8A)—as these findings do not address issues of dislocation and economic loss. The move at the end of the year to disavow race as a factor in the disaster was in many ways as striking as the claims in the immediate wake of the storm that Katrina was opening a new dialogue on race.

Katrina and Racial Discourse: And the Beat Goes On …

As the months passed and a new year began, Katrina-related discourse continued—albeit at a lower level. One focal issue that persisted involved continuing racial differences in post disaster experiences. Analyses of evacuees found that poor African Americans were most likely to be far from home (Tizon & Smith, 2005). Others documented evidence of racial bias in housing, with whites being offered more housing and amenities, lower rents and security deposits, and "whites only" web postings (Filosa, 2006; Korosec, 2005b). In New Orleans, neighborhood opposition to placement of temporary FEMA trailers led to allegations of racial stereotyping (Nelson & Varney, 2005). A February survey of New Orleans residents found that black respondents were significantly more likely to report greater losses and more difficulty in having services restored (Page & Risser, 2006). Clearly, the racial divide persisted long after the initial impact of the disaster.

Perhaps the most controversial issue, and the one with the greatest potential to rekindle a debate on race, involved the rebuilding of New Orleans, especially the politically (and racially) charged questions of which neighborhoods would be rebuilt first and which would be rebuilt later—if at all. While the early stages of the discussion in the fall of 2005 focused upon the technical aspects of rebuilding (e.g., Romano, 2005), attention quickly shifted to the geography of rebuilding. By October, some experts and officials were suggesting that the predominantly black Ninth Ward and other areas below sea level should be converted to green space, marshland, or even a golf course (MacQuarrie, 2005; Schwartz & Revkin, 2005). Others advocated keeping neighborhoods intact and criticized redevelopment plans as designed to create a white, middle class theme park or tourist destination (Kelman, 2006; Klein, 2005; Korosec, 2005a). Observers noted how the forces of segregation and racism had given rise to a concentration of African Americans in the lowest-lying areas (DeBerry, 2006; Kelman, 2006).

This issue came to a head at the beginning of 2006 when the Urban Land Institute produced a report (2005) that advocated concentrating initial rebuilding efforts in areas that had not been flooded—and which also happened to be primarily white (Burdeau, 2006; Texeira, 2006). Shortly thereafter, the city's "Bring New Orleans Back" plan recommended that neighborhoods that could not demonstrate a "critical mass" (1/2 of population) would not be permitted to rebuild and would be "bought out" (Bustillo, 2006). Reaction was strong, with reference to "Katrina cleansing" and extinguishing New Orleans' African-American population and culture (Bustillo, 2006; Roig-Franza, 2006). In many cases, media headlines and articles depicted a clear racial divide, while proponents of the plans insisted that they were grounded in economics and science and that race had no influence on the proposals (Texeira, 2006). This scenario was repeated later in the year with subsequent panel reports.

The rebuilding debate in turn triggered the next racial event. New Orleans mayor Ray Nagin, who was running for re-election, sought to reassure the black community by saying in a Martin Luther King Day speech (as cited in Pope, 2006) that "This city will be chocolate at the end of the day. This city will be a majority African-American city. It's the way God wants it to be. You can't have New Orleans no other way" (p. 1). The racial directness of Nagin's remarks—the violation of "color blindness"—evoked a firestorm of criticism for being "divisive," "racist," offensive and harmful (Elie, 2006; Pope, 2006; Varney, 2006). Despite a subsequent apology, Nagin continued to be condemned for being "crazy," for injecting "racism" into the debate, and for widening the racial chasm (Gill, 2006; *Tone it Down,* 2006; Wooten, 2006). Others in turn defended Nagin, criticizing white outrage as "hypocritical" in light of efforts to keep blacks from returning to the city (Moline, 2006; O'Neil, 2006). In many ways, this was a prelude to the spring mayoral primary and election (postponed from February) where Nagin, who had previously garnered more support among white voters, sought and won re-election with significantly greater support in the black community (Gold, 2006; Nossiter, 2006b). Nevertheless, after the initial media flurry in January, much less national attention was paid to the city elections.

As 2006 progressed, another racialized issue involved the changing racial demography of New Orleans. Given the destruction of black neighborhoods and the greater dispersion of residents, it was not surprising that New Orleans began the year as a different city. This in turn continued to evoke sporadic discussion of racial issues. News articles observed that New Orleans' Carnival parties and its signature Mardi Gras celebration were "smaller and whiter" (Cass, 2006; Nossiter, 2006a; Usborne, 2006). Prior to the mayoral election, activists pushed for voting participation for displaced New Orleans residents. The racial impact of this issue was captured in an April march led by Jesse Jackson in which he compared the struggle for satellite voting sites with the 1965 Selma Campaign that helped bring about the 1965 Voting Rights Act (Donze & Filosa, 2006). The change in New Orleans became evident as data were collected. In June, the Census Bureau estimated that metropolitan New Orleans (including the city and its suburbs) had gone from 32 percent to 22 percent black (Data: Storms Prompted Population Shift, 2006, p. A6). Data from the summer indicated that New Orleans was less than half its pre-Katrina size and that residents who were poor, black, and who lived in female-headed households were disproportionately less likely to have returned (National Public Radio, 2006, n.p.).

This change in New Orleans was viewed differently across the racial divide. For African Americans, the changing demographics meant destruction of neighborhoods and loss of political power (Dao, 2006; Moline, 2006; Usborne, 2006). For some whites, although stated less openly, the population shift meant an opportunity to take back a city that had become majority black after decades of white flight (Nossiter, 2006b; Webster, 2006). An early summer 2006 poll by the Louisiana Redevelopment Authority (Collective Strength, 2006, p. 12) found a majority of white respondents taking the position that it was not important to them that New Orleans returns to its "pre-hurricane racial mix" as a majority black city (in contrast, 63 percent of African Americans said that this was extremely important). The reason why was articulated by at least one Louisiana resident (Zegar, 2006), who stated that "New Orleans' population was about 450,000 before Katrina and it's about 135,000 now—a much more manageable level. We've managed to 'export' vast numbers of criminals, healthy 20- to 60-year-old non-workers and others throughout the United States to spread the cost of education, health care and so forth to other states" (p. A17).

Despite the sporadic emergence of racialized issues and occasional updates on rebuilding, the media eye clearly began to turn elsewhere during 2006. If there was a more widespread dialogue, it was confined to New Orleans and not the national stage. Indeed by spring 2006, observers began to speak of "Katrina fatigue" and the failure of the disaster to produce a lasting dialogue on race and class in the United States (Deggans, 2006; Kurtz, 2006). As the one-year anniversary of Hurricane Katrina approached, commentators continued this theme. Cynthia Tucker (2006) wrote that "the hour for reflection on America's racial tensions—a brief period brought about by Hurricane Katrina—has passed" (p. 13A). Judy Hill (2006) lamented that the "opportunity to put the issues of race and class on the table … was an opportunity lost" (p. 1). Others (Hutchinson, 2006; Ward, 2006) noted that the racial divide persisted. More detailed analyses from the systemic racism perspective (e.g., *The Nation* devoted an issue, September 18, 2006, to "Katrina, One Year After") or from an overtly racist position (cf. Tracinski's—2006—discussion of the welfare state, black pathology, and black racism) appeared in non-mainstream publications or in the blogosphere. Subsequent articles have focused upon the lingering effects of the disaster, the failure to rebuild infrastructure and housing, and the continuing devastation of many neighborhoods (Herbert, 2006), as well as the repopulation of New Orleans at less than half the pre-hurricane population, with change viewed as inevitable—or even beneficial (Gordon, 2006; Nossiter, 2007).

The passage of additional years (2007–2009) has brought a continuation of the pattern of diminished attention paid to the Katrina disaster and related racial issues. Mainstream media coverage was reduced to occasional updates on a range of issues such as FEMA's readiness for the next disaster, the state of New Orleans' levees, rising insurance premiums, and the state of the recovery (Chu, 2007; Fox News, 2008; Heath, 2007; *USA Today*, 2008). Periodic commentaries lamented the slow pace of rebuilding, both during the Bush and Obama administrations (Kunzelman, 2009; Lardner, 2008). August of each year brought a spate of articles on the anniversary of the disaster; otherwise, coverage was increasingly sporadic. On the third anniversary (August 2008), reflections were overshadowed by the threat to New Orleans posed by Hurricane Gustav, which for a brief period threatened to repeat the devastation of Katrina. Much of the focus of coverage was on the irony of the Republican convention being held at the same time—which in turn led to commentaries recalling the failure of the original response of the Bush administration and attempts by the Republican party and its nominee Senator John McCain to move past the issue (Lightman, 2008). Ultimately, the dwindling interest in the ongoing problems stemming from Hurricane Katrina is probably not surprising, as the general pattern of social response to problems as disparate as the 2004 tsunami, famine, and homelessness is a brief period of engagement before attention turns elsewhere. Like so many other issues, the Katrina disaster became yet another example of the life cycle of social problems. Where Katrina has entered into popular culture is as a metric for comparing the impact of other disasters (hurricanes, California wildfires, Midwest flooding, the Greensburg, Kansas tornado) and the effectiveness of the response by government (see, for example, Stolberg, 2007). This may ensure the legacy of Katrina, but it does little to address the ongoing struggles of the city of New Orleans and its current and former citizens.

The diminishing attention paid to Katrina and its victims does not mean that issues of race have completely disappeared from the radar. *Time* published an article on the second anniversary of the disaster titled "Healing Katrina's Racial Wounds" (McCulley, 2007) which included discussion of conflict, racialized discussions of crime ("pimps and gangbangers"), black distrust and anger over a greater degree of suffering, and white denial of race as a factor. On the other hand, the article did not engage in any analysis of racial issues beyond attitudes and conflict. Other articles have continued to focus upon the demographics of New Orleans: the declining percentage of African-Americans from 70% to 55% of the population and the increasing percentage of Latinos from 3% to 15% (Gonzales, 2007, 2008). One article around the time of the third anniversary re-examined the Gretna bridge closure: no criminal charges were filed but civil suits are still progressing through the courts (Witt, 2008). Interestingly, the only other significant mention of race was in conjunction with research studies: "Katrina Evacuees Plagued by Stereotypes" (Turner, 2007) or "Katrina Hit Blacks Harder than Whites" (Whoriskey, 2007). This suggests that research, when disseminated to the media, perhaps does have some impact on public discourse. Overall, however, any meaningful discussion of issues of race has been in the non-mainstream media. The beat—of attention paid to issues of race, class and poverty—goes on, but with the volume dramatically reduced.

A Final Note: Hurricane Katrina and Racial Justice

What can we conclude about the impact of the Hurricane Katrina racial event on racial discourse and race relations in the United States? I find myself in agreement with several of the commentators cited above: the aftermath of disaster, despite its potential, has failed to kindle any persistent and meaningful dialogue on issues of race and poverty. In essence, the post-hurricane discourse fit comfortably into existing ideological frameworks. White supremacists saw pathologies in the African-American community, adherents of the systemic racism perspective engaged with the persistence of racism in social institutions, and proponents of color-blindness interpreted issues in terms of anything but race and decried those who suggested that race still mattered. If

Americans are talking about race now, it is with respect to new "racial events"—the presidency of Barack Obama, the nomination of Judge Sonia Sotomayor to the Supreme Court, the controversy around the police treatment of noted African-American scholar Henry Louis Gates, and ongoing affirmative action cases in the courts—and not the aftermath of Hurricane Katrina.

Perhaps the perfect metaphor for the national response to Hurricane Katrina came from President George W. Bush. Speaking at a National Cathedral prayer service two weeks after the storm, Bush promised aid to the victims of the disaster and noted that the relationship between poverty and race was a "legacy of inequality" that was grounded in "generations of segregation and discrimination" (Herman, 2005, p. 8A). At first glance, this statement suggested that the Bush Administration was seemingly prepared to engage the issues of race and poverty that had been exposed by Hurricane Katrina. Yet Bush's statement never specified any structural connection between the past and the present; that is, how past oppression created present circumstances and there was no further engagement with the issue. Like the President and his administration, the majority of American society has moved on to other issues.

In some ways, Hurricane Katrina may have widened the racial divide. For African Americans, the slow response, the non-rebuilding of many neighborhoods, and the feeling of abandonment may produce an increased sense of alienation from the rest of American society. For white Americans, images of victims, stories of looting, and the later discredited tales of violence may reinforce stereotypical images of poor blacks. While this was clearly evident in the white supremacist responses, it was also evident in more subtle ways. One study of how racial cues influenced willingness to support aid to hurricane victims (Iyengar & Morin, 2006) found that respondents recommended shorter periods of assistance for a hypothetical African-American victim and lower levels and shorter periods of assistance for hypothetical African-American respondents with a darkened skin color. That this occurred among a sample that included a disproportionate number of highly educated and politically liberal respondents suggests that racial stereotypes remain deeply ingrained in the psyche of many Americans.

Ultimately, I fear the persistence of colorblind racial ideology. Apparently, it survived Hurricane Katrina in much better condition than the city of New Orleans. If we argue that race has no place in the discussion, then it becomes possible to rebuild New Orleans without many of its black neighborhoods by making the argument that "market decisions" rather than deliberate decisions about housing, infrastructure, and relocation assistance shaped the process. If African Americans do not return to New Orleans, the color-blind conclusion is that this is a matter of "choice"—thus echoing Barbara Bush's comment that evacuees in the Houston Astrodome were better off than the life that they had in New Orleans (Sheehy, 2005). This also makes it possible to assert that if evacuees have not re-established themselves in the years after the hurricane, then it is their own fault for not taking advantage of the opportunities available in American society (Madkour, 2007). If this is the ultimate response to Hurricane Katrina, which illuminated issues of race and poverty in such stark terms, then how likely is it that American society will address the confluence of race and poverty in other parts of the United States—a situation that I described in the weeks after the storm as "New Orleans without the hurricane" (Doane, 2005, n.p.).

Yet there are still openings for progressive work towards racial justice. National attention has faded from New Orleans, but the Katrina disaster—like other racial events—can still be used as evidence of the continuing significance of race in the United States. Works such as those by Michael Eric Dyson (2006), Hartman and Squires (2006), and Reed (2006), as well as this collection, will ensure that Katrina-related issues will remain part of the national discourse. Researchers and journalists should continue to pay attention to the rebuilding of New Orleans and to the situations of both New Orleans residents and the Katrina diaspora. It is important to examine how the costs and benefits of evacuation and rebuilding follow lines of race and class. It is important to tell the ongoing stories of hurricane survivors in order to give a human face to our understanding of the long-term effects of the disaster. Scholars, teachers, and public intellectuals should continue to interpret the social forces that shaped the Katrina disaster and subsequent events. It is essential to remind the nation that the scope of the disaster, the failed response and the racially disparate impact did not just "happen," but that they were the natural outcome of the social dynamics that create and reproduce racism and poverty in American society. Perhaps then the Katrina disaster may yet contribute to the movement for social justice.

References

Alter, J. (2005, September 19). The other America. *Newsweek*, pp. 42–48.

Anti-Defamation League. (2005a). Bigots gloat over hurricane victims; spew racist and anti Semitic hate online. *Anti-Defamation League*. Retrieved October 3, 2005 from http://www.adl.org/PresRele/Internet_75/4786_41.htm.

Anti-Defamation League. (2005b). Racists blame Jews, seek to help whites only in hurricane's aftermath. *Anti-Defamation League*. Retrieved October 3, 2005 from http://www.adl.org/main_Extremism/Hurricane_katrina.htm.

Badie, R. (2005, September 18). Relief efforts don't reflect racial divide. *Atlanta Journal-Constitution*, p. 3JJ.

Bell, D. (1992). *Faces at the bottom of the well: The permanence of racism*. New York: Basic.

Berbrier, M. (1998). Half the battle: Cultural resonance, framing processes, and ethnic affectations in contemporary white separatist rhetoric. *Social Problems*, 45, 431–450.

Bonilla-Silva, E. (2001). *White supremacy & racism in the post-civil rights era*. Boulder, CO: Lynne Reinner.

———. E. (2006). *Racism without racists*. 2nd ed. Lanham, MD: Rowman & Littlefield.

Brick, M. (2005, September 16). Cultural divisions stretch to relief concerts. *New York Times*, p. B7.

Brown, M. (2005, November 8). Marchers protest blockade of evacuees after Katrina; activist: "The world needs to know what happened." *New Orleans Times-Picayune*, p. 1.

Brown, M., Carnoy, M., Currie, E., Duster, T., Oppenheimer, D., Shultz, M., & Wellman, D. (2003). *Whitewashing race: The myth of a color-blind society*. Berkeley, CA: University of California Press.

Burdeau, C. (2006, January 11). New Orleans rebuilding dreams are big, not easy. *Hartford Courant*, p. A9.

Bustillo, M. (2006, January 12). New Orleans revival plan provokes criticism. *Hartford Courant*, p. A3.

Carmichael, S., & Hamilton, C. (1967). *Black power: The politics of liberation in America*. New York: Vintage.

Carr, L. (1997). *Color-blind racism*. Thousand Oaks, CA: Sage.

Cass, J. (2006, February 25). Notable Mardi Gras absences reflect loss of black middle class. *Washington Post*, p. A1.

Chu, K. (2007, April 2). Insurance costs become 3rd storm. *USA Today*. Retrieved July 7, 2009 from http://www.usatoday.com/money/perfi/insurance/2007-04-02-gulf-recovery-usat_N.htm.

Cohen, R. (2005, September 20). Incompetence, not racism. *Washington Post*, p. A23.

Collective Strength. 2006. 2006 South Louisiana recovery survey: Citizen and civic leader research, summary of findings. Retrieved February 8, 2007 from http://lra.louisiana.gov/assets/junemeeting/2006RecoveryResearch Final 061506.pdf.

Continuing the discussion. (2005, October 21). Continuing the discussion: Dialogue on race has potential to trump prejudice. *Omaha World-Herald*, p. 6B.

Daniels, J. (1997). *White lies: Race, class, gender, and sexuality in white supremacist discourse*. New York: Routledge.

Dao, J. (2006, January 22). In New Orleans, smaller may mean whiter. *New York Times*, p. 1.

Data: Storms Prompted Population Shift. (2006, June 7). Data: Storms prompted population shift. *Hartford Courant*, p. A6.

DeBerry, J. (2006, January 31). Built by racism, areas became home. *New Orleans Times-Picayune*, p. 5.

Deggans, E. (2006, March 1). Katrina has failed to kindle dialogue on race and class. *St. Petersburg Times*, p. 1A.

DeMarco, P. (2005, October 23). Katrina as a teaching moment. *Boston Globe*, p. A32.

Doane, A. (1996). Contested terrain: Negotiating racial understandings in public discourse. *Humanity & Society, 20*(4), 32–51.

———. (1997). Dominant group ethnic identity in the United States: The role of "hidden" ethnicity in intergroup relations. *The Sociological Quarterly*, 38, 375–397.

———. (2003). Rethinking whiteness studies. In A.W. Doane, Jr. & E. Bonilla-Silva (Eds.), *White out: The continuing significance of racism* (pp. 3–18). New York: Routledge.

———. (2005). Now you see it, now you don't: Racism in the 21st century. Public lecture given at Christ Church Cathedral (sponsored by the Episcopal Diocese of Connecticut), Hartford, CT, September 30, 2005.

———. (2006). What is racism? Racial discourse and the politics of race. *Critical Sociology*, 32, 255–274.

———. (2007). The changing politics of color-blind racism. *Research in Race and Ethnic Relations*, 14, 181–197.

Donze, F., & Filosa, G. (2006, April 2). Bridge march hails justice, voter rights; thousands join Jesse Jackson in crossing river. *New Orleans Times-Picayune*, p. 1.

Duke, L., & Wiltz, T. (2005, September 4). A nation's castaways; Katrina blew in, and tossed up reminders of a tattered racial legacy. *Washington Post*, p. D1.

Dukes. M. (2005, September 15). Incompetence, not racism. *USA Today*, p. 12A.

Dyson, M. (2006). *Come hell or high water: Hurricane Katrina and the color of disaster*. New York: Basic Civitas.

Elie, L. (2006, January 18). Mayor misses the mark with speech. *New Orleans Times-Picayune*, p. 1.

Feagin, J. (2000). *Racist America: Roots, current realities and future reparations*. New York: Routledge.

Ferber, A. (1998). *White man falling: Race, gender, and white supremacy*. Boulder, CO: Rowman & Littlefield.

Filosa, G. (2006, January 3). Housing discrimination hits the Web; post-Katrina ads cited in federal complaints. *New Orleans Times-Picayune*, p. 1.

Fox News (2008, May 21). Leaky New Orleans flood levee worries experts. Retrieved July 20, 2009 from http://www.foxnews.com/story/0,2933,357043,00.html.

Gabriel, J. (1998). *Whitewash: Racialized politics and the media*. London: Routledge.

Geary, B. (2005, September 6). Some stayed out of choice. *The Oregonian*, p. B6.

Gill, J. (2006, January 18). We've survived crazy politicians before. *New Orleans Times-Picayune*, p. 99.

Gold, S. (2005, September 3). Katrina's aftermath; met by despair, not violence; as they begin to patrol the chaotic city, troops are surprised by what they don't find. *Los Angeles Times*, p. A1.

———. (2006, March 12). The nation; New Orleans mayor sees support shift; some white former backers hope to elect a new leader April 22, but many blacks see C. Ray Nagin as their candidate for the first time. *Los Angeles Times*, A20.

Gonzales, J. (2007, September 12). New Orleans keeps narrow black majority. *The Washington Post*.

———. (2008, December 23). Immigrants reshape post-disaster New Orleans. Retrieved on July 20, 2009 from http://www.foxnews.com/wires/2008Dec23/0,4670,NuevoOrleans,00.html.

Gordon, E. (2005, September 21). Let Katrina calm the waters of racism; our leaders—and the rest of us—have to talk abut the race issues stirred up by the storm. *Newsday*, p A41.

Gordon, M. (2006, November 29). N.O. population hits 200,000, new data show; city nearing 40 percent of pre-Katrina size. *New Orleans Times-Picayune*, p. 1.

Grosso, A. (2005, September 6). Don't play the race card. *The Oregonian*, p. B6.

Guinier, L., & Torres, G. (2003). *The miner's canary: Enlisting race, resisting power, transforming democracy*. Cambridge, MA: Harvard University Press.

Hamilton, B. (2006, January 4). Bridge standoff still under scope; Gretna faces lawsuit for stopping evacuees. *New Orleans Times-Picayune*, p. 1.

Hartman, C., & Squires, G. (Eds.). (2006).*There is no such thing as a natural disaster: Race, class, and Hurricane Katrina*. New York: Routledge.

Heath, B. (2008, December 13). Katrina's wrath lingers for New Orleans' poor. Retrieved July 20, 2009 from http://www.usatoday.com/news/nation/2007-12-13-katrinapoor_N.htm.

Herbert, B. (2006, December 21). America's open wound. *New York Times,* p. A39.

Herman, K. (2005, September 17). Race hot issue for Bush in storm's wake. *Atlanta Journal-Constitution,* p. 8A.

Hill, J. (2006, August 31). Katrina dialogue drifts away from race, class. *Tampa Tribune,* p. 1.

Hunter, K. (2005, September 11). Race and "refugees" add up to touchy topic. *Hartford. Courant,* p. C3.

Hutchinson, E. (2006, August 22). One year later, Katrina didn't close the racial divide. *Alternet.* Retrieved February 8, 2007 from http://www.alternet.org/ story/40701/.

Iyengar, S., & Morin, R. (2006, June 8). Natural disasters in black and white. *Washington Post.* Retrieved on February 11, 2007 from http://www.washingtonpost.com/wp-dyn/content/article/2006/06/07/AR2006 06071177_pf.html

Jacklin, M. (2005, September 14). Water rising for Hartford's underclass. *Hartford Courant,* p. A11.

Jacoby, J. (2005, September 14). Katrina's colorblind relief. *Boston Globe,* p. A15.

Katrina by the Numbers. (2006, January 5). Katrina by the numbers. *Hartford Courant,* p. A10.

Katrina's Revelation. (2005, September 18). Katrina's revelation: The hurricane exposed issues of poverty and race. It's not black and white, but a puzzling gray. *Omaha World-Herald,* p. 8B.

Katznelson, I. (2005, September 27). New Deal, raw deal; how aid became affirmative action for whites. *Washington Post,* p. A23.

Kelman, A. (2006, January 2). In the shadow of disaster. *The Nation,* pp. 13–15.

King, M. L. (1992 [1963]). *I have a dream: Writings and speeches that changed the world.* Edited by J. M. Washington. New York: Harper.

Klein, N. (2005, September 26). Needed: A people's reconstruction. *The Nation,* p. 12.

Korosec, T. (2005a, October 24). Katrina's aftermath; flooded 9th ward to evolve or vanish. *Houston Chronicle,* p. A1.

———. T. (2005b, December 27). Hurricane aftermath; survey finds bias in evacuee housing; 66 percent of white callers got better deals in Houston and 16 other cities. *Houston Chronicle,* p. B1.

Krugman, P. (2005, September 19). Tragedy in black and white. *New York Times,* p. A25.

Kunzelman, M. (2009, March 5). Pace of Katrina rebuilding disturbs Obama officials. *Houston Chronicle*. Retrieved July 7, 2009 from http://www.chron.com/disp/story.mpl/hurricane/ike/6295742.html.

Kurtz, H. (2006, May 14). The media's Katrina fatigue. *Hartford Courant*, p. C6.

Lardner, R. (2008, August 19). Bush: New Orleans still struggling after Katrina. Retrieved July 20, 2009 from http://www.foxnews.com/wires/2008 Aug19/0,4670,BushKatrina,00.html.

Lewis, J. (2005, September 12). This is a national disgrace. *Newsweek*, p. 52.

Lightman, D. (2008, August 31). McCain heads to Gulf as GOP hopes to bury Katrina images. Retrieved July 20, 2009 from http://www.star-telegram.com/804/story/874282.html.

MacQuarrie, B. (2005, October 2). A battle to rebuild looms in New Orleans; officials compete to have say in plan. *Boston Globe*, p. A1.

Madkour, R. (2007, May 30). Many Katrina evacuees are still jobless. Retrieved July 20, 2009 from http://sfgate.com/cgi-bin/article.cgi?f=/n/a/2007/05/30/national/a105810D28.DTL.

McCulley, D. (2007, August 27). Healing Katrina's racial wounds. Retrieved July 20, 2009 from http://www.time.com/time/nation/article/0,8599,1656 660,00.html.

McDaniel, M. (2005, September 19). Katrina's aftermath; racial bias comes to the forefront; terms, pictures used by the media prompt debate. *Houston Chronicle*, p. 1.

Moline, Z. (2006, January 23). White outrage over Nagin speech is hypocritical. *New Orleans Times-Picayune*, p. 4.

National Public Radio. (2006). New Orleans by the numbers. Retrieved February 8, 2007 from http://www.npr.org/news/specials/Katrina/oneyearlater/demographics/graphic.html.

Nelson, R., & Varney, J. (2005, December 26). "Not in my back yard" cry holding up FEMA trailers; emotional tone of opposition hints at role of stereotypes of race, class. *New Orleans Times-Picayune*, p. 1.

Nossiter, A. (2006a, February 25). Amid revelry, evidence of city's cruel transformation. *New York Times*, p. A8.

———. (2006b, April 4). New Orleans election hinges on race and not rebuilding. *New York Times*, p. A16.

———. (2007, January 21). New Orleans of future may stay half its old size. *New York Times*, p. 1.

Omi, M., & Winant, H. (1986). *Racial formation in the United States*. New York: Routledge.

O'Neill, L. (2006, January 19). Mayor may have had a point. *New Orleans Times-Picayune*, p. 6.

Page, S., & Risser, W. (2006, February 28). In New Orleans 4 out of 5 want to stay there; blacks report being hit harder by storm than whites. *USA Today*, p. 1A.

Pew Research Center. (2005, September 8). *Huge racial divide over Katrina and its consequences*. Washington, DC: author.

Pitts, L. (2005, September 23). Poor is poor, and colorblind. *Pittsburgh Post-Gazette*, p. B7.

Pope, J., (2006, January 17). Evoking King, Nagin calls N.O. "chocolate" city; speech addresses fear of losing black culture. *New Orleans Times-Picayune*, p. 1.

Reed, B. (ed.). (2006). *Unnatural disaster: The Nation on Hurricane Katrina*. New York: Nation Books.

Riccardi, N., Smith, D., & Zucchino, D. (2005, December 18). Katrina killed across class lines. *Los Angeles Times*, p. A1.

Roig-Franza, M. (2006, January 12). Hostility greets Katrina recovery plan; residents assail eminent domain and other facets of New Orleans proposal. *Washington Post*, A3.

Romano, A. (2005, September 19). Digging out. *Newsweek*, pp. 34–35).

Rush to Misjudgment. (2006, January 4). Rush to misjudgment; "conventional wisdom" that blacks were hurt most by Katrina might not prove true. *Columbus Dispatch*, p. 8A.

Sandalow, M. (2005, September 23). Katrina thrusts race and poverty onto national stage; Bush and Congress under pressure to act. *San Francisco Chronicle*, p. A13.

Satran, R. (2005, October 20). Reality of Katrina. *The Advertiser*, p. 57.

Schwartz, J., & Revkin, A. (2005, September 30). Levee reconstruction will restore, but not improve, defenses in New Orleans. *New York Times*, p. A22.

Sheehy, K. (2005, September 6). Barbara: Houston shelter is "working very well" for poor. *New York Post*, p. 6.

Simerman, J., Ott, D., & Mellnik, T. (2005, December 30). A look at Katrina's dead. *Hartford Courant*, pp. A1, A4.

Stolberg, S. (2007, October 24). With Katrina fresh, Bush moves briskly. *New York Times*. Retrieved July 10, 2009 from http://www.nytimes.com/2007/10/24/washington/24bush.html.

Texeira, E. (2006, January 8). Response in New Orleans angers many blacks. *Hartford Courant*, p. A7.

Thevenot, B., & Russell, G. (2005, September 26). Rumors of deaths greatly exaggerated [electronic version]. *New Orleans Times-Picayune*.

Thomas, C. (2005, October 19). Black "leaders" on wrong path. *Baltimore Sun*, p. 17A.

Tizon, T. (2005, September 3). Katrina's aftermath; images of the victims spark a racial debate. *Los Angeles Times*, p. A11.

Tizon, T., & Smith, D. (2005, December 12). Evacuees of Hurricane Katrina resettle along a racial divide. *Los Angeles Times*, p. A1.

Tone it Down. (2006, January 19). Tone it down; keep racism out of debate on serious issues. *San Diego Union-Tribune*, p. B-12.

Tracinski, R. (2006). The unlearned lesson of Katrina. *Real Clear Politics*. Retrieved on February 8, 2007 from http://www.realclearpolitics.com/articles/woo6/09/the_lesson_of_katrina_what_the.html

Tucker, C. (2006, August 9). America refuses to see that it isn't colorblind. *Atlanta Journal-Constitution*, p. 13A.

Turner, D. (2007, October 17). Study: Katrina evacuees plagued by stereotypes of laziness. Retrieved July 20, 2009 from http://www.chron.com/disp/story.mpl/nation/5220877.html.

Urban Land Institute. (2005). *New Orleans, Louisiana: A strategy for rebuilding*. Washington, DC: Urban Land Institute.

Usborne, D. (2006, January 2). Year ahead is smaller and whiter for New Orleans parties. *The Independent*, p. 19.

USA Today. (2008, April 2). Report: FEMA not ready for next Katrina. http://www.usatoday.com/news/washington/2008-04-02-fema-response_n.htm.

Varney, J. (2006, January 18). Nagin backpedals, apologizes; Katrina's wrath not God's will, he says. *New Orleans Times-Picayune*, p. 1.

Ward, A. (2006, August 23). Katrina rhetoric does little to calm growing storm among poor blacks. *Financial Times*, p. 7.

Webster, R. (2006, August 14). Experts: New Orleans race relations crumble under post-Katrina [electronic version]. *New Orleans City Business*. Retrieved February 11, 2007 from http://www.neworleanscitybusiness.com/viewStory.cfm?recID=16411.

Whoriskey, P. (2007, May 10). Katrina hit blacks harder than whites, study finds. *Washington Post*, p. A02.

Will, G. (2005, September 13). Assessing liberalism's post-Katrina ignorance. *Hartford Courant*, p. A13.

Witt, H. (2005, December 27). New Orleans flooding fuels suspicions. *Hartford Courant*, p. A10.

———. (2008, September 4). Katrina aftermath still roils Gretna. *Chicago Tribune*. Retrieved July 20, 2009 from http://www.calendarlive.com/chi-gretna_wittsep04,0,4857423.story.

Wooten, J. (2006, January 22). Public figures' rants widen racial chasm. *Atlanta Journal-Constitution*, p. 6B.

Young, C. (2006, January 16). Katrina's racial paranoia. *Boston Globe*, p. A13.

Zegar, S. (2006, May 20). New Orleans must rise again. *Hartford Courant*, p. A17.

Chapter 8

"Reasonable Racism": The "New" White Supremacy and Hurricane Katrina

Dreama G. Moon and Anthony Hurst

As the sixth largest storm ever recorded and possibly the largest hurricane in strength to approach the United States, Hurricane Katrina was a common media event on televisions across America as it churned toward the delta region. Satellite imagery of the storm looked like a monstrous, circular saw hurled across the Gulf of Mexico by a mischievous god. In the aftermath, Katrina reigns as arguably one of the most destructive and costly storms in recorded history, and the most deadly natural disaster since the 1928 Okeechobee Hurricane (Weather Underground, 2006). As if this were not enough, Katrina also precipitated one of the most disturbing public conversations on race and racism in the United States that we have seen in this "equality-reigns, color-blind, post-racist" era in which folks like Bush, D'Sousa, and Horowitz like to tell us that we are living. The destruction from Katrina laid bare to many (some for the first time) the depths of racism and the stranglehold that it seems to have on our social institutions and everyday life. For others, the storm served to reinforce beliefs of social and behavioral *difference* between races.

As observers of this conversation, we were taken aback by the manner in which Katrina victims were often criminalized, demonized, and demeaned in many media portrayals. We paid attention to past natural disasters and their aftermaths and could not remember an occasion in which victims were treated with less sympathy or more disdain. While this attitude also could be found in the mainstream media, it was widespread and furious on the so-called *hate sites*. In fact, shortly after Katrina impacted New Orleans, the Anti-Defamation League published an article on their webpage (ADL, 2005) documenting many of the conversations being held on the Internet on sites such as the *American Renaissance*. We became fascinated with this discourse and noticed how it seemed to echo things we were hearing and seeing in the mainstream media.

Our analysis begins with an examination of conversations about Katrina published on one such prominent "hate site." You may be surprised to learn that hate is an extremely popular online topic. In his publication of the *Hate Directory*, Raymond Franklin lists 144 pages of online hate groups (Franklin, 2006). He cites hundreds of racist groups, games, chats, and blogs readily available to those seriously seeking or simply browsing the Web.

You may find our interest in online "hate speech" peculiar or unimportant. Indeed, many have asked, "How seriously should we take white supremacists? Are they a real threat or are they part of a lunatic fringe, that if ignored, will go away?" (Daniels, 1997, p. 3). The idea that white supremacist rhetoric (or hate speech) is extremist and crazy is common, and reflects part of the denial that we as a country are enmeshed in when it comes to race and racism (Williamson, 2002). Even when scholars do study "hate sites" and "hate speech," their analyses almost always imply that this sort of speech is somehow out of the ordinary, contrary to how most Americans typically talk or think about race (Duffy, 2003; Ezekiel, 2002; Williamson, 2002).

Rather than finding racist discourse extreme or exceptional, we find that racism is a staple of the American discursive diet, as American as baseball or apple pie (Bertazzoni & Judson, 2000). Racism takes a variety of forms—from racial jokes to lynching—some being more overt than others, but all of the same cloth. We argue that these various forms of expression (i.e., jokes, representations) work together and reinforce one another to create a tightly woven ideological belief system about whites and the "Other" that naturalizes and normalizes white superiority and black inferiority, white worthiness and black unworthiness (Solin, 2004; Voithofer, 2006). Becker, Byers & Jipson (2000) suggest that "Hate speech tells us ... about the ways of life in a culture...." (p. 36), and it is our interest in understanding more about these cultural ways of life that propelled us toward the examination of so-called hate sites.

This project examines discourses of white supremacy. These discourses are often under-represented in scholarly work, possibly because they seem extreme and thus somehow not worthy of analytical attention. We will show that discourses of white supremacy are not confined to a few obscure websites. As we will show, white supremacist sentiments can be observed in everyday white attitudes as captured by national social survey research, media representations of minorities, and political discourses. The ubiquity and repetition of messages can lead to the appearance of truth.

In the aftermath of Hurricane Katrina a media spectacle unfolded, stirring citizens around the globe who were part of the audience. The stories and images in the wake of the storm illustrate that discourses of white supremacy have a symbiotic relationship with "mainstream" or legitimated public discourses; they rely on one another for their continued existence. If efforts toward racial justice are to succeed at all, we must be clear about the various manifestations of racism and their intersections and inter-linkages. As communication scholars committed to social justice, we believe that it is important to pay attention to the ways in which a tragedy like Katrina is interpreted through a world-view that proclaims white supremacy and the effects of such interpretations in the reproduction of injustice (Papa, Papa, Kandath, Worrell & Muthuswamy, 2005). In view of this interest, we decided to examine white supremacist discourse on so-called hate sites prior to, during and immediately after Katrina made landfall in the Gulf region.

Choosing a Hate Site to Analyze

In determining which sites to examine, we first turned for guidance to the Anti-Defamation League (http://www.adl.org/combating_hate/) and the Southern Poverty Law Center (http://www.splcenter.org/intel/intpro.jsp), organizations that routinely monitor and catalogue hate groups. An overwhelming number of hate groups currently operate both within the U.S. and abroad. We decided to focus on actively maintained websites that engage in dialogue rather than simply post information, that evidenced a discussion about Katrina and her aftermath, and that represented different spectrums of hate groups in the U.S. Sites that seemed reflective of the so-called *post-racism* era. Sites primarily comprised of trash-talking were excluded because we wanted to examine sites that gave the appearance of attempting to reason about race and its relationship to Katrina. This narrowing led us to *The American Renaissance* (AR), a popular and relatively new "middle of the road" site that positions its posters as "white racialists" or "racial realists" rather than white supremacists. We describe the site below.

American Renaissance

A product of the New Century Foundation, founded by Samuel Jared Taylor in 1990, *The American Renaissance* is an online magazine published monthly by Taylor and his associates. On the site, you can read interviews that Taylor has given to other media, selected news articles that support the site's point of view, or purchase materials on race sold by the organization. In addition, the magazine is distributed in electronic or print form to subscribers for an annual fee.

Glancing at the home page of the *American Renaissance*(AR) (http://www. amren.com/index.html), the organization at first strikes one as fairly reasoned and reasonable. The site lists AR's beliefs about race in these terms:

> Race is an important aspect of individual and group identity. Of all the fault lines that divide society—language, religion, class, ideology—it is the most prominent and divisive. Race and racial conflict are at the heart of the most serious challenges the western world

faces in the 21st century. The problems of race cannot be solved without adequate understanding. Attempts to gloss over the significance of race or even to deny its reality only make problems worse. Progress requires the study of all aspects of race, whether historical, cultural, or biological.

("What we believe," n.d., n.p.)

No one who has lived through the Civil Rights Movement or read about the long and painful history of race and racism in the United States could disagree with this. Race has long been divisive, and in fact was *intended* to be such.

The veneer of reason that the site occasionally achieves is attributable to its founder, Samuel Jared Taylor. Taylor is of a new breed of white supremacists, one diametrically opposed to stereotypical ideas of racists as redneck, uneducated, and ignorant. Reared in Japan by missionary parents, Taylor is well educated with degrees from Yale and the Paris Institute of Political Studies ("New Century Foundation," n.d., n.p.). The veneer of reason and "objectivity" swiftly fall apart, however, once one begins to examine AR discourse more closely. AR aims to create "a literate, undeceived journal of race, immigration and the decline of civility," and holds that "for a nation to be a nation—and not just a crowd—it must consist of people that share the same culture, language, history and aspirations." Under Taylor's stewardship, its authors use quasi-scientific, sociological and philosophical arguments to make a case for the purported superiority of the white race and the threat non-white minorities pose to American society ("New Century Foundation," n.d.). In the following section, we draw on the notion of racial fictions to help us analyze the comments posted on the AR website.

White Fictions and Racial "Realism"

Feagin (2001) uses the idea of *sincere fiction* as it operates in the lives of whites in relation to their understandings of race and racism in the U. S. In his view, these fictions refer to "images of white merit and moral superiority that shape, usually unconsciously, the views and attitudes of many white Americans who profess color blindness toward people of other racial and cultural groups, particularly African Americans" (Bell, 2002, p. 237). We suggest that a large part of being white in U.S. America entails being socialized into and then living daily in a fictional and fictionalized world in which colorblindness and equal opportunity are staple principles, i.e., "we don't see color" and "everyone has an equal chance to make it in America." These fictions are part of an "optimistic tale of continuous progress and social reform that bolsters images of white decency and goodness" (Bell, 2002, p. 237).

For some whites, these fictions are "sincere" in that those who espouse them honestly believe themselves to be "color blind people who do not discriminate against others" (Bell, 2002, p. 237). For others, these fictions are "insincere," or more strongly, "white lies" (Daniels, 1997) in that they work as a "self-deceptive screen that protects a status quo from which Whites as a group benefit" (Bell, 2002, p. 237). These sorts of sincere fictions obscure the reality of racism and enable "Whites to resolve the dissonance between beliefs in equality and participation in a racist society" (Spencer, 2004, p. 119).

If such sincere fictions were simply individual belief systems, then perhaps they would not be too much of a problem. Unfortunately these sincere fictions are supported by a social structure that perpetuates and reinforces white dominance while simultaneously giving lip service to a commitment to equality and opportunity (Bell, 2002). This makes the disruption of such fictions—pulling back the curtain on them as Dorothy did to the Wizard in *The Wizard of Oz*—an important strategy to achieve social justice. To this end, we examine white fictions in the context of AR discourse in terms of how they protect the racial status quo and simultaneously reveal the stories that whites must tell about themselves in order to believe that such protection is necessary, right, and inevitable.

Shortly after Katrina roared through the delta region, Jared Taylor posted the essay "Africa in our midst: Lessons from Katrina" to the AR website (Taylor, 2005). We analyzed 353 responses to the article posted to the site over September and October 2005, in the heat of the Katrina tragedy. In the essay, Taylor focuses almost exclusively on looting, murder, rape, and other forms of violence, or what he termed as the "barbaric behavior of the people of New Orleans" (Taylor, 2005, n.p.). There is no mention of the experience of Katrina victims who were black, no human-interest stories of heroic behavior by New Orleans citizens who were black, and certainly no empathy toward the plight of those whose lives were so dramatically changed by the storm. Given that he offers no evidence in the form of citing the sources from which he obtained this information, his version of the story is suspect at best. But in the fictional world of whiteness, truth is relative. The lessons to be learned from Katrina, according to Taylor, are that black people did not leave New Orleans (they couldn't, or they stayed to loot) and that black people engaged in horrid and violent behavior while whites would have acted differently if placed in the same situation. Taylor's conclusion gives you a good grasp of his overall message: "To be sure, the story of Hurricane Katrina does have a moral for anyone not deliberately blind. The races are different. Blacks and whites are different. When blacks are left entirely to their own devices, Western Civilization—any kind of civilization—disappears. And in a crisis, civilization disappears overnight" (Taylor, 2005, n.p.).

The above theme of "civilization" runs through the majority of the posts made in response to Taylor's essay, particularly in relationship to whites and blacks. The story of civilization as written by those who posted comments to this essay is a drama in which whites are superior in every way possible to blacks. As we read the postings, we were struck by the story of whiteness being constructed. In our analysis of the data, we identified three main themes that seem to form the foundation of this white narrative: (1) *Civilized White/Uncivilizable Black*; (2) *No Bridge Across*; and (3) *White Man's Burden*. In the next section, we elaborate each theme and provide examples that best illustrate the general trend in the posts under each theme. Being aware that many students of color and progressive whites will read this chapter, we have consciously chosen to limit the number of examples offered and to not reproduce the most heinous examples in order to minimize the amount of psychic violence we commit on these pages. In the interest of accuracy, all posts are presented in their original forms.

Civilized White/Uncivilizable Black

The first theme encompasses the notion that whites are the most civilized group who has ever lived on Planet Earth and that no matter what whites do on their behalf, blacks (and sometimes Mexicans) are "savages" for whom civilization efforts are a lost cause. Or as Boethius (2005, September 6) puts it, "As Grandma used to say, "You can dress them up, but you can't take them to town" (n.p.). In this theme, difference is conceived in terms of white "superiority" and goodness juxtaposed to black "inferiority" and inherent badness. In this fiction, whites are positioned as highly civilized (i.e., well behaved, creative, intelligent and so forth), well-intentioned, and superior to blacks and other people of color. In short, according to these posters, whites think better, do better, and at some foundational level, ARE better. For example, another poster notes, "No one is suggesting that whites cannot behave as savages or that individual blacks cannot behave in a civilised manner. The point is that on average through history white societies have attained and maintained higher standards of civilisation than black societies (notwithstanding Hitler and Lenin and Stalin)" (Keith, 2005, September 6, n.p.).

Within the context of discussion of this theme, posters almost always emphasized superior white intellect and inherent black criminality. Both of these emphases were generally intertwined with posters' proposed explanations for why some black Katrina victims did not leave the city once warned of danger. For instance, a poster notes, "One reason why so many blacks refused to evacuate has not been mentioned: They simply cannot trust other blacks not to loot their possessions in their absence" (Kenelm Digby, 2005, September 6, n.p.).

The focus on criminality was particularly widespread, drawing from selective mainstream media coverage and wild rumors circulating during the first few days after the levees broke. Black criminality is a favorite topic on the AR website and in fact, their sister organization, the New Century Foundation, publishes *The Color of Crime* which AR offers for sale in print copies, or which visitors can download for free. *The Color of Crime* misuses Uniform Crime Report data quite creatively to support arguments that blacks, Asians, and Mexicans are inherently more violent than whites and present a threat to the safety and well-being of whites. Peter (2005, September 6) notes that,

> Whites are the ones who built this great civilization and black Americans want to see it destroyed. That message is reiterated in their music, their culture and their belief systems, over and over and over again. This lesson we should al learn from Katrina is Whites need to protect themselves from black society because given the chance they will immediately rape, kill and steal everything they can. (n.p.)

Another poster adds,

> I'm not really that surprised by the events that unfolded in New Orleans after Katrina. In fact, by what I've seen and read in recent times and in the past with blacks in Africa and the U.S., the looting mentality is quite obvious and not really that new. It appears to be a cultural thing with a majority of blacks. This culture is destructive in nature and will only lead to things like murder, rape, tyrannical dictators, corruption, etc. This is in stark contrast to the chivalry code of the knights. Once again, there's nothing new under the sun with the way blacks behaved during this crisis.
>
> (Brad, 2005, September 25, n.p.)

The poster's historical reading of looting behavior after a natural disaster contradicts the work of Quarentelli & Dynes (1970), who note in their essay on looting norms that, "In civil disorders looting is very widespread whereas in natural disasters actual looting incidents are quite rare" (p. 173). More recently, Walker (2005) suggests that "When looting does follow a disaster, most of it is done covertly by individuals or small groups, rather than by mobs acting openly" (p. 27). Factors that can alter this include a person's basic needs (food and water) not being met, a disaster area characterized by widespread poverty, and a poorly managed response to the disaster (Walker, 2005). All of these horrendous conditions existed during and after Katrina, and in the year following the storm, many of the reported accounts of violent criminal behavior proved false (Welch, 2005). This is not to say that serious crimes were not committed, but rather to suggest that the crisis spawned many stories that were later refuted.

No Bridge Across

The second theme we noted in the posts is *No Bridge Across*, which is closely related to the first, and more specifically focuses on the idea of racial difference. The posters repetitively assert the idea that whites and blacks are *fundamentally* different, generally due to biology and genetics, but explained culturally as well. This notion of insurmountable difference does not bode well for difficult conversations around race yet to be had in the U.S. this century. It is interesting that posters generally explained the panicked behavior of disaster victims who lost everything they had, people that they loved, their lives as they knew them, and who were without basic human necessities like food, water, and safety, and for whom help was slow in coming in terms of innate racial difference. As one poster frames it, "The behavior demonstrated by the blacks in the "Big Easy" is innate. Period. No one with any sense, no one grounded in realism should be surprised at what we have seen so far" (Livin' in S. CA, 2005, September 7, n.p.). Another describes the usefulness of Katrina as a lesson about race: "Contrast Black New Orleans with the plight of poor white Mississippians, who braved devastation with typical White restraint and self-organizational skills. Glaring evidence of real racial differences" (Bethany, 2005, September 6, n.p.).

Some saw the aftermath of Katrina as a demonstration of genetic truth, "Genetics is truth. White people would have acted differently, as history shows they do…." (White woman, 2005, September 6, n.p.). Rosalyn, a self-identified Christian, elaborates: "Why must we be ashamed for speaking the truth? It is so frustrating! While I do have black people I am friendly with and that I care about, I am not fooled into thinking that they are like me. They are not only from a completely foreign culture but genetically we are very different" (Rosalyn, 2005, September 6, n.p.). Some saw Katrina as a valuable lesson: "The citizens of this country have been made to believe that blacks and whites are no different and the only thing keeping blacks down is white racism. Well now it's plain to see for all the world that Africans that reside here are just as savage and barbaric as their kinfolk in Africa" (Anonymous, 2005, September 5, n.p.). Mike (2005, September 30) sums up this theme when he says, "I think this debate is rather simple. We are dealing here with combination of genetic inferiority, lower evolutionary development and degenerate culture" (n.p.).

The next section examines the third theme, white benevolence and white frustration with trying to help Others. This claim functions to liberate whites from white responsibility for the creation, maintenance, and potential resolution for white supremacy.

White Man's Burden

An important staple in white fiction is the claim of white innocence and benevolence. In this narrative, whites are positioned as empathic and long-suffering people who go unappreciated in their continuous efforts to help blacks and other minorities. Nelly (2005, September 14) observes: "I can only really remember one thing when I see a problem like this. I recall a British statesman saying many, many, years ago that, 'black people are white man's burden'. New Orleans seems to bear this out completely" (n.p.).

The discourse is rife with paternalism, i.e., *I know what is good for you better than you possibly could*, and within that arrogant attitude, *I am going to help you do what I think you need to do*. For example, one poster notes,

> Because we are by nature compassionate and empathetic, whites tend to focus on seeing only the good in blacks and attempt to help the best black people live the best lives possible. And to make that easy on themselves, they ignore the statistics and the racial realities. Most white people I know are not fooled by the media's lies and distortions, but they are so determined not to hurt the feelings of that nice old black lady they know, or that poor truly nice orphaned black girl, or that sincerely Christian young black man, that they will keep their mouths shut and hope for the best. Their hearts are in the right place, but their tender-heartedness is ultimately destructive not merely of their own families and communities, which are necessary to help the minority of worthwhile black people, but to the very blacks that they wish to help."
>
> (abhorred hillbilly, 2005, September 6, n.p.)

Another poster expressed his anger over blacks' lack of appreciation for white aid:

> Every black in America should fall on his or her knees and thank providence that his ancestors were captured and put on a slave ship headed for America. If not, every day for you would be New Orleans in the aftermath of Hurricane Katrina! Blacks who can manage to live parasitically in a majority-white nation are the most fortunate of their breed—especially in America, where we kow-tow to them like royalty.… This is what you get when you insist on electing your own kind to govern you—stop looking for the white man to bail you out!
>
> (Bronco Billy, 2005, September 6, n.p.)

And yet another poster self-assuredly predicts the black response to white beneficence toward black Katrina victims: "The only ones that will benefit from this whole thing is the black community and they will still be ungrateful … as always" (more of the same, 2005, September 6, n.p.).

The white anger evident among the posters is captured in the following comment:

> Well Whitey, it ain't enough that you shelter, feed, school (thru college), and employ (okay, this is optional) blacks. It is also your responsibility to ride to their rescue when natural disaster strikes, to save them from nature as well as themselves. And you'd better be quick about it lest you be called "racist". Isn't this a kind of "White Man's Burden" redux? I mean, when things go bad for blacks, like in New Orleans or with AIDS in Africa, who's supposed to ride to their rescue? Why, that's you,

Whitey. We've become the servants of the blacks; and I don't think that's what Kipling had in mind.

(Crimethinker, 2005, September 6, n.p.)

Racial "Realism" and Common White Racial Attitudes

After reading the posted comments to AR, you might feel slightly ill and secretly relieved that sentiments like this are expressed in a tiny piece of cyberspace by a few of what Daniels (1997) referred to as the "lunatic fringe." The idea that white supremacist ideas are representative of only a few white Americans is a comforting idea. Unfortunately, it is also dangerously erroneous, reflective of the denial that we as a country tend to wallow in when it comes to racism. The sentiments expressed by posters to AR are commonly echoed by a healthy minority of "everyday" white U. S. Americans as indicated decade after decade by General Social Survey (GSS) findings. The GSS is a project of the National Opinion Research Center (NORC) at the University of Chicago Started in 1974, the GSS is administered each year and asks a standard core of demographic and attitudinal questions, plus topics of special interest. According to the NORC (2006) website, "The basic purposes of the GSS are to gather data on contemporary American society in order to monitor and explain trends and constants in attitudes, behaviors, and attributes; to examine the structure and functioning of society in general as well as the role played by relevant subgroups, to compare the United States to other societies in order to place American society in comparative perspective and develop cross-national models of human society; and to make high-quality data easily accessible to scholars, students, policy makers, and others, with minimal cost and waiting" (Except for the U. S. Census, "the GSS is the most frequently used source of information analyzed in the social sciences," n.p.).

For our purposes, we looked to the GSS as a source of white attitudes about race and people of color. We chose to examine those items that most closely corresponded to the themes that we identified in the AR posts: *Civilized White/Uncivilizable Black, No Bridge Across, and White Man's Burden.* Specifically, white attitudes about blacks were examined for 2000, and when available for, 2004.

As you recall, the first theme, *Civilized White/Uncivilizable Black,* captures the idea that black people are inherently uncivilized—criminal, violent, unintelligent and so forth. The survey asks respondents a series of questions regarding various racial groups, to which they respond on a 7-point Likert scale, with "1" indicating the negative belief toward the group (i.e., unintelligent or lazy) and "7" indicating the most positive belief (i.e., intelligent or hard-working). We took the sum of the two lowest negative scale ratings ("1" and "2") to provide what we believe is a fair rendering of negative white attitudes.

The three questions that we examined asked white respondents what they thought about blacks' propensity to violence, intelligence, and work ethic, and the data show that white attitudes toward blacks have remained fairly consistent since 1990. Just over 19 percent reported that they believe blacks are violence-prone, 6.6 percent reported that they believe blacks are unintelligent, and over 14 percent reported that they believe blacks tend to be lazy.

The second theme, *No Bridge Across,* asserts that blacks are fundamentally different from whites, due to either genetics or culture. As many of the posters saw it, the genetic truth about blacks is one of innate inferiority. For this theme, we looked at GSS questions that asked respondents to explain or account for observable social differences between whites and blacks. The prompt for the question reads, "On the average, Negroes/blacks/African Americans have worse jobs, income, and housing than white people. Do you think these differences are ____?" Respondents can give their opinions as to whether or not they think that these differences are attributable to external barriers such as lack of access to education and discrimination, or internal barriers such as lack of willpower or motivation and less inborn ability to learn. Not surprisingly, whites tend to believe that the differences between white and black material realities are best attributable to black internal lack of one sort or the other. For example, almost 60 percent of whites rejected lack of access to education as a factor in black difficulty in rising out of poverty, and 70 percent did NOT believe that discrimination was a main factor in accounting for black social problems. Conversely, a little over 50 percent of whites believed that the differences between black and white material circumstances are attributable to black lack of will power and motivation, and over 6.5 percent believe that black circumstances are due to their lack of inborn ability to learn.

The third theme, *White Man's Burden,* addresses the often expressed white point of view that whites have done enough to help blacks, and no matter how much whites do for blacks, it is never enough nor is it appreciated by black people. For this theme, we examined two questions regarding how white respondents rated public spending on social problems. We chose to include the question on welfare as many whites mistakenly assume that the overwhelming majority of welfare recipients are black. The question prompt is as follows: "We are faced with many problems in this country, none of which can be solved easily or inexpensively. I'm going to name some of these problems, and for each one I'd like you to tell me whether you think we're spending too much money on it, too little money, or bout the right amount." Then respondents are asked the question in regards to welfare spending and money spent to improve the conditions of black people. To this question, 44 percent of whites believe that we are spending too much money on welfare and over 18 percent believe that we are spending too much money on improving the conditions of blacks.

To put these numbers into perspective, according to the 2000 U.S. Census, about 75 percent or 211.5 million people reported their race as white only. Extrapolating the GSS findings outlined above to the Census numbers, we see that about 1 in 5 whites (or over 4.5 million) believe that blacks are prone to violence; 1 in 2, or 105 million whites, believe that differences between white and black material circumstances are due to black lack of willpower or motivation to change them; and almost 1 in 5 whites (well over 100 million) believe that we are spending too much money on improving the conditions of blacks. When viewed in this light, the "extreme" points of view expressed by AR and its posters do not seem so extraordinary at all, but instead, fairly routine among white Americans. In the next section, we examine one more piece of evidence to support our argument that white supremacist discourse is commonplace in U.S. society.

Connecting the Dots: White Supremacist Discourse and the Everyday Expressions of White Supremacy

These white folks have newspapers, magazines, radio, spokesmen to get their ideas across. If they want to tell the world a lie, they can tell it so well that it becomes the truth....

—Dr. Bledsoe to the hero in Ralph Ellison's *Invisible Man*[1]

At the beginning of this chapter, we argued that racist discourse is a staple in U.S. American life, rather than an anomaly, and that expressions of racism and white supremacy occur in forms ranging from racial humor to public outbursts of white rage (e.g., the Michael Richards[2] incident); from racial profiling to murder. As we see it, these various forms of expression work together and reinforce one another to support a persistent ideological belief system about whites and the "Other" that naturalizes and normalizes white superiority. These bits of "social information" about whites and others work together across a wide range of venue. Solin (2004) uses the notion of intertextual chains to describe how "claims produced in one domain are taken up in other domains" (p. 267). Here, we are interested in the ways in which claims across social discourses, or social facts "chain" or link together in ways that reinforce white supremacy. Thus far we have examined two specific texts: white su-

---

1. Ellison, R. (1990). *Invisible man.* NY: Vintage Books.

2. On November 17, 2006, Michael Richards, an actor famous for his role in the television show *Seinfeld*, shouted out a series of racist epithets at some of the black and Latino audience members during his comedy routine at a club in Los Angeles. He was taped doing so on an audience member's cellphone and the incident was widely publicized.

premacist discourse online and national social survey findings regarding white racial attitudes toward blacks. Next we turn to examples in the mainstream media.

As we look toward media, it is all too easy to locate mediated discourses that repeat the themes that we observed in AR posts and social survey data. When we contemplate the theme of *Civilized White/Uncivilizable Black*, for example, we can quickly see how this racial script is continuously played out in the media in the form of the hyper-criminalization of men of color, especially black men. In our analysis of AR posts, the "Uncivilizable Black" motif reiterated the belief that blacks are inherently dangerous over and over.

Repetitive consumption of media images (e.g., stereotypical stories about a particular group of people) conditions or frames our social attributions towards those groups. Daniels (1997) notes, "the widespread appearance of many white supremacist motifs in popular culture ... suggests that such themes resonate effectively beyond the audience of avowed white supremacists" (p. 135). In his study of white supremacist rhetoric, Daniels also observes that, "The fact that this discourse shares much in common with mainstream political discourse and popular culture representations has serious implications. For instance, the rise of the Third Reich was built on just such imagery" (p. 135).

The scholarly literature clearly supports this. For example, studies show that the racial script of white victim/black (or brown) perpetrator is told and retold on television news daily across the nation (Chiricos & Eschholz, 2002; Dixon & Azocar, 2006; Dixon, Azocar, & Casas et al., 2003; Dixon & Linz, 2000). This resonates with much of the rhetoric of AR writers and their readers. What this means is that on a daily basis, viewers are subjected to a subtle racial lesson about black and Latino men as violent and dangerous, disproportionate to their real numbers.

Historically within white supremacist rhetoric, black men have been framed as beasts that are by nature always on the verge of rape and mayhem (Daniels, 1997). Barnett (2003) concludes in research on visual biases in television that "Visual portrayals of the accused in television news do indeed affect perceptions of the people featured" (p. 39). As Barlow (1998) has observed in discourse about crime, "it is unnecessary to speak directly of race because, talking about crime *is* talk about race" (as quoted in Szkowny, 1994, p. 9). This attitude is illustrated by Bill O'Reilly, who states that about 10 percent of the population are "so chaotic for whatever reason that they're never, ever going to be able to fend for themselves and make a living" (Media Matters, 2005, September 15, n.p.). What has this to do with Katrina victims? O'Reilly tells his audience of this lack of civility of the New Orleans population:

> Many, many, many of the poor in New Orleans are in that condition. They weren't going to leave no matter what you did. They were drug-

addicted. They weren't going to get turned off from their source. They were thugs, whatever.

(Media Matters, 2005, September 15, n.p.)

Scholars believe that the "new racism" (covert expressions of racial superiority or inferiority) facilitates this linking of blacks and crime (Entman, 1990, 1992). As with white supremacy in general, however, the social reality regarding crime is far off the mark. As Hacker (1992) observes, although whites complain most loudly about crime and express more fear of becoming victims (especially of men of color), in fact, it is blacks who have a much greater likelihood of becoming victims of violent crime.

No Bridge Across

In the AR data, we identified a second theme, *No Bridge Across*, which positions blacks (and other people of color) as quintessentially different from whites. As we observed earlier, the sort of discourse locates blacks and whites as almost different "breeds" of humans. We see this sort of sentiment recently expressed in Californian Governor Arnold Schwarzenegger's observations about Cubans and Puerto Ricans during a speechwriting session: "They are all very hot," the governor says on the recording. "They have the, you know, part of the black blood in them and part of the Latino blood in them that together makes it" (Blood, 2006, n.p.). In the same article, another politician claims that this kind of discourse is routine: "This is usual political banter. We do this all the time.... In this case, it just happened to be taped." (Blood, 2006, n.p.). Schwarzenegger's comments have serious implications in a state where 35 percent of the population is of Hispanic origin (U.S. Census Bureau, 2005).

This type of "othering" is extremely dangerous and has been a common ploy in racist discourse throughout history. For example, in Nazi discourse, Jews were positioned as "vermin" and in slavery people of African descent were bought and sold like cattle. Clearly, once human beings have been de-humanized, it is much easier to enslave, abuse, and murder them. Today, this sort of "othering" is often more subtle. For example, more recently we saw this sort of white "othering" of people of color during a recent campaign rally by United States Senator George Allen. At the rally in his home state of Virginia, Senator Allen singled out an Indian American and asked the crowd to "... give a welcome to Macaca here. Welcome to America and the real world of Virginia" (Lewis, 2006, n.p.). The young man was an American citizen, born in Virginia. The term "Macaca" is the name of a genus of monkey.

William Bennett suggested in an oddly chosen hypothesis on his radio talk show shortly after Hurricane Katrina that aborting black babies would be an effective way to lower the crime rate (Wickham, 2005). Mr. Bennett was chagrined that critics took his hypothetical example out of its on-the-air context, but his choice of example is less than a stone's-throw away from the thoughts of posters on white supremacist websites who also suggest that lower crime rates will accompany destruction of areas where blacks live.

White Man's Burden

The last theme we identified in the AR data, *White Man's Burden*, addressed the idea that whites have done enough for black people and that black people ought to be more grateful and appreciative for all that whites have done for them over the years. When reading the mainstream media, this sentiment is often couched in terms of the government and government spending, affirmative action, and other social race remedy initiatives. For example, columnist Ann Coulter suggested that Maxine Waters' (a black legislator) campaign against Senator Joe Lieberman in the 2006 election was motivated by his publicly stated reservations about affirmative action "without which she [Waters] would not have a job that didn't involve wearing a paper hat" (Media Matters, 2006b, August 10, n.p.). Although whites often accuse blacks of being too lazy to work, when blacks like Waters succeed despite the many social barriers put in their way, whites attribute their success to white efforts (i.e., affirmative action). Recently, Mexican immigrants have been the frequent target of such sentiment. For example, last May the leader of Mothers Against Illegal Aliens spoke of the burden of having Mexican women immigrants in the United States as "their children's job is to dumb down the American children and overpopulate our schools" (Media Matters, 2006a, May 19, n.p.).

During the post-Katrina media frenzy, Bill O'Reilly hectored storm victims to avoid expecting the government to fix their problems:

First, the huge, bureaucratic government will never be able to protect you. If you rely on government for anything, anything, you're going to be disappointed, no matter who the president is.... if you don't get educated, if you don't develop a skill and force yourself to work hard, you'll most likely be poor. And sooner or later, you'll be standing on a symbolic rooftop waiting for help.

(Finke, 2005, September 8, n.p.)

Urging people to better their lot through hard work is not a racist idea, but O'Reilly implies that the victims are responsible for their plight because they aren't self-sufficient. His assumption is that victims of the storm, symbolic and otherwise, are responsible for their plights because they expect too much from others.

A more subtle example of this is in the form of rhetoric against "others" who dilute national purity through immigrating to the United States. For example, Mariscal (2003) describes the anti-Mexican rhetoric used by conservative politicians, not all of whom are considered on the fringes of public discourse (e.g., Bill O'Reilly, Ann Coulter). In one version of this rhetoric, the southwest United States is in danger of becoming a Mexican republic. Pat

Buchanan, conservative political commentator, argues that mixing ethnic populations destroys countries. He suggests that Mexican immigrants in the southwestern United States and Muslim immigration in Europe are problematic because these groups fail to assimilate. One of his solutions is to build a wall to keep Mexicans out (Levins, 2006). In this version of the theme, the failure of immigrants to relinquish their ethnicity is a threat to the existing racial climate in the United States. That is, immigrants *take* from the bounty of the U.S., but *give* nothing but problems in return.

These are just some recent examples of what we see as the overlap of white supremacist themes in public discourse, often by public officials. When racist expression is seen as an everyday behavior, extreme versions as located in AR do not seem so extraordinary, but only different in terms of degree.

On a Closing Note

Despite claims to the contrary, Katrina didn't blow the lid off anything other than the Superdome. The mediated images of storm victims were (and probably will continue to be) fodder for people seeking to advance positions of white supremacy. In short, our examination of *AR*, GSS data, and mainstream media examples demonstrate that overt and covert forms of racism exist and work together to maintain white supremacy. As Daniels (1997) notes, "What is most alarming about the white supremacist discourse produced by extremists is that it shares much in common with the white supremacist discourse produced by elected officials, Madison Avenue, mainstream political debate, academic intellectuals, and popular culture representations" (p. 2). What this means for social justice is that it is insufficient to develop hate crimes legislation, hate group monitoring systems, and teach multiculturalism when every day in the United States, Americans are conditioned to the "truth" about blacks and other people of color in white supremacist mainstream media. How do we begin to foster social justice in a society that is unwilling or perhaps unable to relinquish a fundamental form of racism perpetuation, its mainstream media?

References

abhorred hillbilly (2005, September 6). Africa in our midst: Lessons from Katrina. *American Renaissance*. Comment posted to http://www.amren.com/mtnews/archives/2005/09/africa_in_our_m.php.

ADL (2005, September 9). Racists blame Jews, seek to help whites only in hurricane aftermath. Retrieved October 11, 2006, from http://www.adl.org/main_Extremism/Hurricane_katrina.htm.

Anonymous (2005, September 11). Africa in our midst: Lessons from Katrina. *American Renaissance.* Comment posted to http://www.amren.com/mt news/archives/2005/09/africa_in_our_m.php.

Barnett, B. (2003). Guilty and threatening: Visual bias in television news crime stories. *Journalism & Communication Monographs,* 5(3), 103–155.

Becker, P. J., Byers, B., & Jipson, A. (2000). The contentious American debate: The First Amendment and Internet-based hate speech. *International Review of Law Computers & Technology,* 14(1), 33–41.

Bell, L. A. (2002). Sincere fictions: The pedagogical challenges for preparing white teachers for multicultural classrooms. *Equity and Excellence in Education,* 35(3), 236–244.

Bertazzoni, D. & Judson, J. (2000). The incendiary internet: Hate speech and the public good. In D. A. Schultz (Ed.), *It's show time! Media, politics, and popular culture* (pp. 229–243). NY: Peter Lang.

Bethany (2005, September 6). Africa in our midst: Lessons from Katrina. *American Renaissance.* Comment posted to http://www.amren.com/mt news/archives/2005/09/africa_in_our_m.php.

Blood, M.R. (2006, September 9). Schwarzenegger's hot-blooded ethnic remarks draw mixed reaction. *Monterey County Herald.* Retrieved September 10, 2006, from http://www.montereyherald.com/mld/montereyherald/15474644. htm.

Boethius (2005, September 6). Africa in our midst: Lessons from Katrina. *American Renaissance.* Comment posted to http://www.amren.co/mtnews/ archives/2005/09/africainourm.php.

Brad (2005, September 25). Africa in our midst: Lessons from Katrina. *American Renaissance.* Comment posted to http://www.amren.com/mt news/archives/2005/09/africa_in_our_m.php.

Bronco Billy (2005, September 6). Africa in our midst: Lessons from Katrina. *American Renaissance.* Comment posted to http://www.amren.com/mt news/archives/2005/09/africa_in_our_m.php.

Chiricos, T. & Eschholz, S. (2002). The racial and ethnic typification of crime and the criminal typification of race and ethnicity in local television news. *Journal of Research in Crime and Delinquency,* 39(4), 400–420.

Crimethinker (2005, September 6). Africa in our midst: Lessons from Katrina. *American Renaissance.* Comment posted to http://www.amren. com/mt news/archives/2005/09/africa_in_our_m.php.

Daniels, J. (1997). *White lies: Race, class, gender, and sexuality in white supremacist discourse.* NY: Routledge.

Dixon, T. L. & Azocar, C. L. (2006). The representation of juvenile offenders by race on Los Angeles area television news. *The Howard Journal of Communication*, 17, 143–161.

Dixon, T. L. & Linz, D. (2000). Race and the misrepresentation of victimization on local television news. *Communication Research*, 27(5), 547–573.

Dixon, T. L., Azocar, C. L., & Casas, M. (2003). The portrayal of race and crime on television network news. *Journal of Broadcasting & Electronic Media*, 47(4), 498–523.

Duffy, M. E. (2003). Web of hate: A fantasy theme analysis of the rhetorical vision of hate groups online. *Journal of Communication Inquiry*, 27(3), 291–312.

Ellison, R. (1990). *Invisible man*. NY: Vintage Books.

Entman, R. M. (1990). Modern racism and the images of Blacks in local television news. *Critical Studies in Mass Communication*, 7, 332–345.

Entman, R. M. (1992). Blacks in the news: Television, modern racism, and cultural change. *Journalism Quarterly*, 69, 101–113.

Ezekiel, R. S. (2002). An ethnographer looks at neo-Nazi and Klan groups. *American Behavioral Scientist*, 46(1), 51–71.

Feagin, J. R. (2001). Racist America: Roots, current realities, and future reparations. NY: Routledge.

Finke, N. (2005, September 8). They shoot news anchors, don't they? *LA Weekly*. Retrieved February 6, 2007 from http://www.laweekly.com/general/deadline-hollywood/they-shoot-news-anchors-dont-they/8165/.

Franklin, R. A. (2006). *The hate directory*. Retrieved September 21, 2006 from Baltimore County Public Library Web Site http://www.bcpl.net/~rfrankli/hatedir.pdf.

Hacker, A. (1992). *Two nations: Separate, hostile and unequal*. New York: Scribners.

Keith (2005, September 6). Africa in our midst: Lessons from Katrina. *American Renaissance*. Comment posted to http://www.amren.com/mtnews/archives/2005/09/africa_in_our_m.php.

Kenelm Digby (2005, September 6). Africa in our midst: Lessons from Katrina. *American Renaissance*. Comment posted to http://www.amren.com/mtnews/archives/2005/09/africa_in_our_m.php.

Levins, H. (2006, August 27). Emergency? Buchanan predicts takeover of America by burgeoning Hispanic population [review of the book *State of emergency: The third world invasion and conquest of America*]. *St. Louis Post-Dispatch*. Retrieved September 10, 2006 from LexisNexis Academic database.

Lewis, B. (2006, August 23). "Macaca" comment clouds Virginia senator's White House hopes. *The Associated Press*. Retrieved September 10, 2006 from LexisNexis Academic database.

Livin' in S. CA (2005, September 7). Africa in our midst: Lessons from Katrina. *American Renaissance.* Comment posted to http://www.amren.com/ mtnews/archives/2005/09/africa_in_our_m.php.

Mariscal, J. (2003, August 30). The smearing of Bustamante: The far right and Anti-Mexican racism. Retrieved September 8, 2006 from http://www. counterpunch.org/mariscal08302003.html.

Media Matters for America (2005, September 15). O'Reilly: "Many, many, many" hurricane victims who failed to evacuate New Orleans are "drug-addicted … thugs." Retrieved December 10, 2006 from http://www. mediamatters.org/ items/200509150001.

———. (2006a, May 19). Mothers against Illegal Aliens' founder: Job of illegal immigrants' children is "to dumb down the American children and over-populate our schools." Retrieved December 13, 2006 from http://media matters.org/items/200605190012.

———. (2006b, August 10). Coulter: Without affirmative action, Rep. Waters couldn't get a job "that didn't involve wearing a paper hat." Retrieved December 13, 2006 from http://mediamatters.org/items/200608100001.

Mike (2005, September 30). Africa in our midst: Lessons from Katrina. *American Renaissance.* Comment posted to http://www.amren.com/mtnews/ archives/2005/09/africa_in_our_m.php.

National Opinion Research Center (2006). *General Social Survey.* Retrieved November 26, 2006 from http://www.norc.uchicago.edu/projects/gensoc1. asp.

Nelly (2005, September 14). Africa in our midst: Lessons from Katrina. *American Renaissance.* Comment posted to http://www.amren.com/mtnews/ archives/2005/09/africa_in_our_m.php.

New Century Foundation (n.d.). Retrieved September 28, 2006, from http://www.adl.org/learn/ext_us/amren.asp?LEARN_Cat=Extremism& LEARN_SubCat=Extremism_in_America&xpicked=3&item=amren.

Papa, W. H., Papa, M. J., Kandath, K. P., Worrell, T., & Muthuswamy, N. (2005). Dialectic of unity and fragmentation in feeding the homeless: Promoting social justice through a communication. *Atlantic Journal of Communication,* 13(4), 242–271.

Peter (2005, September 6). Africa in our midst: Lessons from Katrina. *American Renaissance.* Comment posted to http://www.amren.com/mtnews/ archives/2005/09/africa_in_our_m.php.

Quarantelli, E.L., & Dynes, R.R. (1970). Property norms and looting: Their patterns in community crises. *Phylon,* 31, 168–182.

Rosalyn (2005, September 6). Africa in our midst: Lessons from Katrina. *American Renaissance.* Comment posted to http://www.amren.com/mt news/archives/2005/09/africa_in_our_m.php.

Solin, A. (2004). Intertextuality as mediation: On the analysis of intertextual relations in public discourse. *Text*, 24(2), 267–296.

Spencer, N. E. (2004). Sister act VI: Venus and Serena Williams at Indian Wells: "Sincere fictions" and white racism. *Journal of Sport and Social Issues*, 28(2), 115–135.

Szkowny, R. (1994). No justice, no peace: An interview with Jerome Miller. *The Humanist*, January/February, 9–19.

Taylor, J. (2005, September 5). Africa in our midst: Lessons from Katrina. Retrieved September 28, 2006 from http://www.amren.com/mtnews/archives/2005/09/africa_in_our_m.php.

U.S. Census Bureau (n.d.). State and county quickfacts. Retrieved February 6, 2007 from http://quickfacts.census.gov/gfd/index.html.

Voithofer, R. (2006). Studying intertextuality, discourse, and narratives to conceptualize online learning environments. *International Journal of Qualitative Studies in Education*, 19(2), 201–219.

Walker, J. (2005, December). Nightmare in New Orleans. *Reason*, 37, 26–29.

Weather Underground, Inc. (2006, September 22). *Deadliest U.S. hurricanes.* Retrieved on September 22, 2006 from http://www.wunderground.com/hurricane/usdeadly.asp.

Welch, M. (2005). They shoot helicopters, don't they? How journalists spread rumors during Katrina [electronic version]. *Reasononline*. Retrieved February 6, 2007 from http://www.reason.com/news/show/36327.html.

What we believe. (n.d.). Retrieved September 28, 2006 from http://www.amren.com/siteinfo/information.htm.

White woman (2005, September 6). Africa in our midst: Lessons from Katrina. *American Renaissance.* Comment posted to http://www.amren.com/ mtnews/archives/2005/09/africa_in_our_m.php.

Wickham, D. (2005, October 4). Bill Bennett's thesis: Racist? Maybe. Wrong? Absolutely. *USA Today*, p. 15A. Retrieved September 14, 2006 from Lexis-Nexis database.

Williamson, L. A. (2002). Racism, tolerance, and perfected redemption: A rhetorical critique of the dragging trial. *Southern Communication Journal*, 67(3), 245–258.

Chapter 9

Katrina's Latinos: Vulnerability and Disasters in Relief and Recovery[1]

Nicole Trujillo-Pagán

In its coverage of events surrounding Hurricane Katrina, the media addressed the influx of "imported [Latino] workers" but misrecognized earlier Latino migrants who resided in the city. When they did consider Latinos who had settled in New Orleans prior to Hurricane Katrina, the media cast them in brief individual narratives or as part of a vague group of immigrants who did not have a role or stake in the broader racial dynamics characterizing the disaster. The media was important because they reproduced a perception that Latino evacuees' experience of the disaster did not matter to the story of Hurricane Katrina and its aftermath.

Exploring Latinos' experience of the disaster is important because it refracts an important part of the Katrina story. Latinos' experience of the disaster demonstrates that they were part of what Giroux (2006) referred to as the vulnerable and "disposable" populations. This paper argues that, although the salience of race in New Orleans seems obvious to many observers, the broader refusal to consider Latinos' location within the city's racialized structures contributed to Latinos' experience of Hurricane Katrina as a racial/ethnic minority. For instance, many commentators, disaster response officials, and relief agencies argued that their ability to conduct systematic research on Latino evacuees was limited by the population's small size. This argument ignores the fact that the Latino population was stratified at the local level and could have been located outside of public view and easily ignored by others. Many Latino evacuees congregated in restaurants and churches outside New Orleans. Latinos avoided shelters because many lacked legal status, which prompted many

---

1. I wish to thank Jasmine James, Research Associate, GIS Clearinghouse Cooperative, for her support in creating the flood-depth map used in this article.

to fear possible arrest and deportation. Latinos' varied legal status positions put them at a unique disadvantage in relation to state and local welfare policies, which demonstrated how communities are stratified by policies that limit full citizenship for racial/ethnic minorities. The pre-Katrina Latino population experienced Hurricane Katrina as a racial/ethnic minority because they were often assumed to be post-Katrina migrants, ineligible for relief aid, and ignored by relief agencies.

By writing Latinos out of their coverage of Katrina, the media sidestepped the messy questions surrounding immigration, civil rights, and the entitlement Latino evacuees had to relief aid. In this way, the media ignored the complexity of the city's racial stratification and supported a broader denial that Latinos were made vulnerable by the economic and political structures operating in New Orleans.

Latinos' inability to access aid demonstrates the unintended consequences of political decisions. On the one hand, inadequate aid limited Latinos' ability to resettle in communities outside New Orleans. On the other hand, inadequate aid pushed some Latinos into hazardous jobs in recovery efforts. Many Latino evacuees that I spoke with in October 2005 explained that they still hadn't received any relief monies from either the Red Cross or the Federal Emergency Management Agency (FEMA). Not surprisingly, these workers hoped working at recovery jobs would help them make money that would enable them to reestablish themselves in the Greater New Orleans area. Some explained that they had evacuated to areas as far as Gonzalez, Louisiana but had been afraid to travel further because they believed there were "checkpoints" where they could be detained or deported. The ways in which the local, state, and federal governments denied responsibility for Latino evacuees reflect trends that may follow throughout other cities that do not recognize their Latino population and especially throughout the southern United States as a whole.

Latino evacuees experiences also reflected the significance of social networks for managing their experience of the disaster. When they met recruiters at local stores or restaurants, men left their wives and children behind at hotels outside of the impacted area while they worked in New Orleans. Some of these families relied on each other so that mothers could also take on jobs in recovery (i.e., demolition). These evacuees shared their worksites with a newer wave of Latino migrants that had come to the area for jobs in recovery. The population was estimated to be such an important part of recovery efforts that journalists started discussing "A New Spice in the Gumbo," (Campo-Flores, 2005), "The Changing Face of the Gulf Coast Work Force," (Rozemberg, 2006) and, "The Latinization of the New New Orleans" (Lovato, 2005).

Method

In addition to considering how media coverage framed the Latino population in New Orleans, I used a mixed-methods approach to collecting data. I analyzed reports developed after the hurricanes by government agencies and advocacy organizations, as well as sociological scholarship on disasters as it pertains to Latino populations. Drawing cautiously from the 2000 U.S. Census and the American Community Survey for the years from 2001–2005, I used current demographic data on the pre-Katrina New Orleans Latino population. Finally, I draw upon exploratory research I conducted in October 2005 within the Greater New Orleans area.

In the weeks following Hurricanes Katrina and Rita, media coverage of Latino evacuees was limited. Nonetheless, this coverage suggested that they were experiencing significant difficulties. For instance, one article in the Mexican newspaper *El Pais* discussed the case of three Mexican nationals who were afraid to leave their trailer and died of carbon monoxide poisoning. Other articles discussed Latino evacuees' fear of approaching relief agencies and shelters because they might be deported. Soon after this coverage, newspaper and online media coverage addressed detention and deportation proceedings against Latino evacuees.

Based on these events, I grew concerned about Latinos' recovery and their future in the city. I began contacting and speaking with government agency officials about their recent field experiences in New Orleans. I also spoke with community leaders, including the pastor of a Spanish-language church that housed many Latino evacuees. He explained that most Latino evacuees had left the church's shelter by mid- to late-September because they had been almost immediately recruited for work in New Orleans. The pastor invited me to stay at the church, which allowed me to talk with the several evacuees who remained and others who returned to the church searching for comfort and familiar faces. These evacuees confirmed that many of their friends and neighbors had already found jobs in recovery work.

I collected preliminary demographic data in the frantic weeks following the hurricanes. Based on the 2000 U.S. Census, Latinos represented 17 percent of the population within a neighborhood in Mid-City. This area corresponds with U.S. Census tract 65 (see Figure 9.1). Its location near the highway and several major streets often acted like borders that defined the boundaries of the neighborhood and somewhat insulated its residents from other areas. Thirty-eight percent (38%) of the "Hispanic" residents' income in this area fell below the poverty level, which was greater than the city's 28 percent overall poverty rate.[2] Census tract 65 was not the area with the greatest number of Latinos in

---

2. Based on "Income in 1999 below poverty level: Hispanic or Latino population for whom poverty status is determined" in Census tract 65 (U.S. Census, 2000).

New Orleans. The 2000 U.S. Census found that neighboring Census tract 50 had a population that was 19 percent "Hispanic or Latino." I decided to focus on Census tract 65 based upon my belief that more evacuees would be available in a relatively larger Census tract. The 2000 U.S. Census found that Census tract 65 contained 3,312 persons while Census tract 50 had 1,666 persons (U.S. Census, 2000).

When I first arrived in the neighborhood, I was surprised by the silence. Chalky-white cars, boats, glass, and telephone cables lined the street like solemn ghosts and, despite the solitude, I opted to walk amidst the debris. As I walked, I spoke to family members who stood awkwardly on the street as their mothers, daughters, and sons refused to part with their wet and moldy belongings. Gus wasn't able to discuss much beyond repeating his disbelief at the damage. Jimena pulled me into her small, wooden, and now crooked house that I was certain was about to crumble. She sobbed and tried to explain that her "American" daughter-in-law, who was white, only spoke English. Jimena was worried she wouldn't be able to reestablish her independent lifestyle. Unlike other areas of the city where charity vehicles patrolled the streets distributing snacks and beverages, Mid-City seemed shrouded and abandoned.

Once I left Mid-City to go to the neighboring Metairie, the streets were alive with workers and people seeking supplies. Parking lots were filled with cars and people who talked about where they had gone, where they were living and, if they were Latinos, where they worked. Pickup trucks filled with workers and contractors created rush-hour traffic jams. In Latino restaurants, exhausted crews talked about their jobs as waitresses busily moved among the full tables and waiting lines. In the newness of rapid construction, Metairie was vibrant and filled with movement.

In my conversations with workers, homeowners, and renters, people seemed eager to reconnect. Many explained that they still hadn't been able to contact all their neighbors. Some found housing with their employers and spent most of their time with their coworkers. Others returned to the church where I stayed to reconstruct some familiarity amidst the rapidly changing environment. In these conversations, Latino evacuees hoped they could regain what they lost in recovery. Some hoped insurance monies or FEMA would come through with financial support that would enable them to establish another home or return to Honduras. Others hoped they would benefit through work in what seemed to be a huge open labor market.

The story of Latinos' place in Mid-City seemed to reflect a larger story about their subordinate role in development. Latinos had created "place" in the area that seemed quickly displaced by the hurricanes. Those who stayed worked at dangerous jobs to create spaces for others. Whatever the storms hadn't washed away was eroded by the neglect of state policies in the form of inadequate recovery aid and a lack of labor policy enforcement.

Latinos and New Orleans

A basic perception that influenced how disaster responders, politicians, and the broader public responded to the Latino population in New Orleans was that it was small in size. Both the 2000 U.S. Census and the 2005 American Community Survey confirmed this perception because they estimated Latinos represented only 3.1 percent of the overall New Orleans population, which equated to fewer than 15,000 persons in both surveys. What this perception ignored was the potential for residential concentration and a significant undercount of recent and/or undocumented Latino immigrants.

Contrasting U.S. Census and American Community Survey figures, Latin American consulates and community advocates claimed the Latino population in New Orleans was much larger. For instance, the media reported Honduran Consulate estimates that ranged from 40,000 to 150,000 Hondurans living in the greater New Orleans area (Cevallos, 2005; Ciria-Cruz, 2005). They also reported similar ranges, based on Mexican government estimates, of 40,000 to 145,000 Mexicans in affected areas, but vacillated on whether the population was concentrated in New Orleans or in rural communities throughout the Gulf Coast (Miyashita, 2005; Associated Press, 2005). Maricel García of the National Alliance of Latin American and Caribbean Communities (NALACC) claimed there were 300,000 Latino evacuees, which may have included those living in Mississippi (Cevallos, 2005). Similarly, although the Mississippi Immigrant Rights Alliance (MIRA) recognized that 2000 Census figures estimated the Latino population in their state at 40,000 persons, they claimed the population had increased and "over 100,000 Latino immigrants were living in Mississippi, with 30,000 concentrated in the six Gulf Coast counties that host the casino and service industries" (Chandler & Gamboa, 2005, p. 2).

The difference between these estimates and Census figures has two probable explanations. First, this difference may have resulted from many Latinos' recent arrivals in the area. Brenda Muñiz (2006) of the National Council of La Raza (NCLR) claimed the Honduran population in the Greater New Orleans area had increased after 1998 as a result of Hurricane Mitch and several of my respondents had arrived after the last U.S. Census was conducted in 2000. Second, the difference between Census figures and local estimates had been recognized since the 1970s, when it was attributed to Census-taking methods and the population's transience. In discussing how these factors influenced estimates of Latino population size in New Orleans, one author found that "the U.S. Census figures state that there are only 44,430 persons of Spanish language in New Orleans.... the average of the figures provided by the Consulates, WJMR Radio Station, and *La Prensa*, place the Latin American population for Metropolitan New Orleans at 89,931. This is very close to the 80,000 figure claimed by the Social Security Administration Office in New Orleans … the Latin American community now comprises 15.5 percent of the population of the City of New Orleans" (uncited author in Stein, 1976, Appendix, p. 3). Official perceptions of the population's size minimized the potential for a significant undercount and overlooked the Latino population, thereby reproducing its limited visibility.

The issue of undercounting Latinos on the U.S. Census raises important problems for understanding the pre-Katrina population that lived in New Orleans and its surrounding areas. On the one hand, the Census provides valuable information that can help us understand how social structures promoted Latino vulnerability. On the other hand, the extent of the undercount suggests that Census figures should be approached with caution. Despite the possible undercount of Latino residents in the Greater New Orleans area, the Census does confirm trends that indicate how Latinos were structurally vulnerable before Hurricane Katrina.

The perception that Latinos were a small population ignored how their numbers had grown within the Greater New Orleans Metropolitan area. On the one hand, the number of Latinos in Orleans Parish decreased but they remained a steady part of the Orleans Parish population. Latinos consistently represented 3 percent of the Orleans Parish population from 2000 through 2005 (American Community Survey, 2000–2005). On the other hand, in adjoining areas within Jefferson Parish, the number and relative population of Latinos increased.

Latino migration to Jefferson Parish continued to increase after 2000 but was concentrated within specific areas. According to the American Community Survey, Latino representation in Jefferson Parish had grown from 7.2 percent in 2000 to 8.1 percent in 2005. In places like Kenner, however, the 2000 U.S. Census found that Latinos represented 13.6 percent of its overall population. Latinos in Kenner formed an ethnic community that included varied and numerous businesses and organizations centered in that area (Raices Inc., 2003). The number of Latinos also grew within other areas such as Metairie, Gretna, and Terrytown, where the existence of inexpensive Latino restaurants suggests pre-Katrina settlement.

Citizenship, Vulnerability, and the Right to Aid

Asking the seemingly simple question, "Were Latinos entitled to relief as evacuees?" involves highly politicized debates surrounding citizenship, immigration, race/ethnicity, and the right to relief aid. Despite Latinos' contributions to New Orleans and their presence in the city before and during the hurricane, they were often assumed to be "illegal" and therefore unworthy of legitimate access or entitlement to relief aid and services. This experience contrasted with the experiences of Latinos after other disasters, such as in New

York after the World Trade Center disaster; after that disaster *all* affected victims were assumed to be deserving of aid. Latinos were denied relief in New Orleans because they were, or were assumed to be, undocumented immigrants or post-Katrina migrant laborers.

Public perceptions of who Latinos are and what they represent in a city's race relations are important because they play a significant role in how relief services are allocated, particularly at a local level. As a result, the moment of Katrina affords an opportunity to question the consequences of policies designed to manage disasters. Specifically, the case of Latino residents demonstrates that legal definitions of citizenship and difference continue to inform the ways in which racial inequality is structured and reproduced within New Orleans.

Race and ethnicity play roles in the construction of legal and social citizenship. In particular, the post-Katrina moment was marked by activities comparable to public debates involved in nation building. For instance, New Orleanians protested when the media portrayed their city as indistinguishable from war-torn Africa or when they characterized the consequences of Hurricane Katrina as "Third World devastation in a First World country" (Deggans, 2005). Black New Orleanians protested the implied separation between city and state when they were called "refugees" in the media and their citizenship (and the rights they deserved) seemed undermined. Indeed, their concern was evidenced in the 2005 Racial Attitudes and Katrina Disaster Study that confirmed that media coverage and the word "refugee" influenced whites' perceptions of evacuees' citizenship and support for government spending on recovery because they involved ideas of deservedness (Dawson, 2006; Huddy & Feldman, 2006).

The case of Latinos demonstrates how social and political frameworks create disasters in human experience. Disaster sociologists argue that disasters are products of social and economic vulnerability, political decisions, and human action (see Bolin, 1999; Kleinenberg, 2003; Stallings, 2002). These structures were explicitly recognized and debated in the days and weeks following Hurricane Katrina's impact as U.S. audiences criticized local, state, and federal responses. More often, however, recognition of how these structures produce disasters is less obvious. For instance, U.S. audiences eventually associated federal relief efforts with a broader discourse on welfare when the Government Accountability Office found evidence of fraud in assistance payments. Although the GAO emphasized FEMA's role in facilitating fraud through multiple payments and a lack of instructions on FEMA-issued debit card use, newspapers and blogs quickly blamed evacuees for misspending assistance payments (Kutz, 2006).[3] Similarly, relief workers assumed that the Latinos they

---

3. The GAO also reported that "in isolated instances, a few debit cards were used to pay for items or services that, on their face, do not seem essential to satisfy disaster related needs. For example, these debit cards were used in part to purchase adult entertainment,

served were recent migrant workers rather than legitimate evacuees (Muñiz, 2006). Both cases, and the media coverage that followed, rested on public opinion and implicit questions of deservedness.

Concepts of citizenship, vulnerability, deservedness, and entitlement characterize both blacks' and Latinos' relationship to the disaster in similar ways. Both blacks and Latinos have been disproportionately impacted by cuts in social assistance spending and the racialization of welfare (Glenn, 2000). For instance, the 2000 U.S. Census demonstrated that, in New Orleans city, blacks and Latinos were more likely than Asians and non-Hispanic whites to be renters, which in turn was linked to greater degrees of difficulty in recovery amidst inadequate insurance coverage and limited housing options. Historically, blacks and Latinos have experienced direct discrimination in disaster relief assistance (Bolin & Stanford, 1991). Both blacks and Latinos who lived in New Orleans were discriminated against by many who worked with government relief and charity organizations. Both blacks and Latinos faced inadequate access to full citizenship and were alienated from our "imagined nation" as "refugees" and "undocumented immigrants." Ultimately, although many commentators recognized that blacks disproportionately experienced the Hurricane Katrina disaster as a racial/ethnic minority, it is important to recognize that Latinos had a comparable experience, but were excluded from a similar analysis.

Relief Assistance and Federal Welfare Policy

Katrina disaster management and relief included federal, state, and local government relief efforts as well as private, charitable assistance. The Department of Homeland Security oversees the Federal Emergency Management Agency (FEMA), which is in turn responsible for coordinating relief efforts among both government agencies and non-governmental organizations. The variety of federal agencies that supported disaster management and relief activities included the Immigration and Customs Enforcement (ICE). After Hurricane Katrina, FEMA quickly became associated with reports of immigration law enforcement and deportation. For instance, many organizations serving the Latino population expressed their frustration that they were receiving mixed messages about Latinos' entitlements to relief. On the one hand, they claimed President Bush, DHS, and FEMA had assured them all victims would receive aid (Cevallos, 2005; Miyashita, 2005). On the other hand, several evacuees were placed in deportation proceedings after seeking relief. In particular,

---

a .45 caliber hand gun, jewelry, bail bond services, and to pay for prior traffic violations" (Kutz, 2006, n.p.). See, for instance, a *Times-Picayune* article ironically titled "Most Relief Money Still Unspent" (Walsh, 2006) that implicitly blamed evacuees for FEMA's "wasted" spending.

Brenda Muñiz (2006) criticized federal agencies, "primarily FEMA and DHS," for being "rigid and inconsistent in interpreting and modifying community policy" (p. 3).

Bolin and Stanford (1999) argued that a "politics of fear" explains why many Latinos avoid relief agencies and assistance. More specifically, Bolin and Stanford argued that the history of places, political culture, and social policies can produce "a climate of fear and concern about non-residents" (p. 119). In turn, this climate renders Latino disaster victims political vulnerable. For instance, Bolin and Stanford demonstrated how both legal and illegal Latino victims of the Northridge earthquake disaster avoided federal programs. Legal immigrants were afraid of jeopardizing their residency status and illegal immigrants feared deportation. This argument is used by both scholars and activists to promote a change in political culture and/or cultural sensitivity for relief workers. Nonetheless, recognition of the cultural factors that may influence application for aid, should not deflect attention from government's role in reproducing structural vulnerability, exclusion, and discrimination. For instance, Latinos who lived in the Greater New Orleans area were systematically excluded from many relief services because they were, or were presumed to be, undocumented persons or "nonqualified aliens." This example of a lack of governmental accountability and lack of equity among evacuees was mirrored in the experiences of Latinos after the Northridge earthquake. Bolin and Stanford (1999) found that undocumented Latinos experienced structural disadvantages and that,

> ... the second tier of protection offered by CBOs (community-based organizations), NGOs (non-governmental organizations), and social service agencies, did provide additional resources. However, undocumented immigrants, intentionally disadvantaged by federal policy, were necessarily limited in their ability even to use this second level, remaining largely invisible and uncounted. (p. 170)

Federal welfare law set the broader context for Latino immigrants' structural vulnerability. Following the passage of the Personal Responsibility and Work Opportunity Reconciliation Act in 1996, Fix and Tumlin (1997) warned that the law could have "far-reaching effects on immigrants, on the nation's immigrant policy, or on the new role state and local governments will play in shaping the policies that govern immigrant integration" (p. 1). Also known as the "Welfare Reform Act," the PRWORA reduced immigrants' access to public assistance programs. Scholars like Sainsbury (2006) found that immigrants "bore a disproportionate burden due to cut-backs and the economic downturn in the 1980s and 1990s" (p. 229). Similarly, comparing six welfare regimes, Morissens and Sainsbury (2005) found that legal migrant residents were more likely to be in poverty than citizens. More important, they demonstrated that migrants' social rights were not based solely on legality or legal residence. They found that the disparity in poverty between citizens and legal migrants was particularly evident within the United States and that "Compared with citizens, migrants and ethnic minority migrants are less likely to enjoy a socially acceptable standard of living ..." (p. 654). Morissens and Sainsbury's findings drew attention to how social policies and racial/ethnic minority status influence Latino immigrants' economic vulnerability, which is compounded by disaster management officials. Similarly, Bolin and Stanford (1998) found that "the administrative requirements of federal bureaucracies are often at odds with the realities of day-to-day life for those who have been marginalized by poverty and discrimination" (p. 227).

Federal welfare law guided decisions about disaster relief spending and determinations of evacuees' eligibility for relief aid (Siskin, 2002). Nonetheless, federal policies on disaster relief undermined Latino immigrants' well-being because the exclusion of many classes of immigrants and the different legal statuses within a Latino family meant that evacuees were "penalized twice—once for being an immigrant and twice for being a victim of disaster" (Muñiz, 2006). Muñiz (2006) noted that many legal immigrants, including those with Temporary Protected Status (TPS) and H-2A work visas, were excluded from "cash assistance and other federal programs, such as food stamps, housing assistance, Social Security benefits, and unemployment insurance, among others" (p. 6). This exclusion was particularly consequential in the Greater New Orleans area, which boasts a large Central American population that has TPS status.

Despite the structural constraints Latinos experienced in relation to both public assistance and relief aid, eligibility was also influenced by public perceptions. Moore (1999) underscored this relationship when she discussed public perceptions and the Welfare Reform Act. "Fueled by the *perception* that increasing numbers of legal immigrants were receiving such [public] benefits, and by the belief that generous benefits provide an incentive to illegal immigration, Congress took action to restrict immigrants' eligibility for those benefits" (p. 22). These perceptions were also critical to the ways that disaster management agencies responded to the Latino population. For instance, in her report for Congress on "Hurricane Katrina-Related Immigration Issues and Legislation," Wasem (2005) reaffirmed the use of the Personal Responsibility and Work Opportunity Reconciliation Act of 1996 to interpret noncitizens' entitlement to relief. She stipulated that,

> ... noncitizens—regardless of their immigration status—are not barred from short-term, in-kind emergency disaster relief and services or assistance that deliver in-kind services at the community level, provide assistance without individual determinations of each recipient's needs, and are necessary for the protection of life and safety. (p. 6)

Ironically, Wasem also noted that "many of the victims of Hurricane Katrina lack personal identification documents as a result of being evacuated from their homes, loss or damage to personal items and records, and ongoing displacement in shelters and temporary housing" (p. 2). How then were undocumented evacuees distinguished?

As a matter of practice, perceptions of who Latinos were in New Orleans were consequential and influenced the ways in which relief was actually delivered. For instance, the perception that undocumented immigrants feared encounters with U.S. officials deflected attention from inequities in relief assistance. In Wasem's initial September 19th report, she wrote: "media accounts of aliens who are fearful of seeking emergency assistance following Hurricane Katrina infer that the *reported reluctance is due more to the risk of deportation than restricted access to benefits*" (p. 7, emphasis added). Wasem quoted DHS spokesperson Joanna Gonzalez saying "no one should be afraid to accept our offers to provide safety" (p. 7). Wasem's report indirectly blamed evacuees, and specifically "aliens," for inadequate emergency assistance delivery. She suggested that evacuees' fears of deportation were implausible and unfounded. One month later, in her October 18th updated report, Wasem quoted Gonzalez again, who this time noted that, "… as we move forward with the response, we can't turn a blind eye to the law" (2005b, p. 7). The shift in DHS policy that led to at least five deportation orders reflected an explicit political decision to distinguish evacuees who were legitimately entitled to relief from many Latinos who were now excluded from public relief, support, and protection.

The shift in DHS policy toward undocumented evacuees *who were Latinos* demonstrated that perceptions played a significant role in how Latino evacuees were treated. For instance, media coverage of an ICE round-up in Mississippi quoted one evacuee as saying, "I was singled out because of my skin" (Terhune & Pérez, 2005, p. B1). In New Orleans, a Latina evacuee related her experience that police officers and firefighters only saved whites and left blacks and Latinos to die (Contreras, 2005). The conflicting perceptions of Latinos as public charges and Latinos as workers were poignantly summarized by a Honduran evacuee who had been discussing rumors of recent immigration raids at a local hotel. She explained to me that, "I don't worry about *la migra* at work. They work next to me. Once I leave here [the worksite] … I don't know." Despite their experience of racial subordination in the context of Hurricane Katrina, Latinos were not recognized as legitimate evacuees and were often assumed to be ineligible for public assistance.

As a result of perceptions regarding the absence of any Latino evacuees, disaster management agencies discriminated against Latinos in relief allocation. For instance, Simmons (2005) reported that Latinos residing in Redwood Park Apartments in Kenner, Louisiana were assumed to be undocumented and were denied housing assistance. Muñiz (2006) found that "upon further investigation … many of the residents … were determined to be legal immigrants and, consequently, many of them would have been eligible for FEMA housing assistance" (p. 4). The Department of Homeland Security also confirmed that undocumented persons who were evacuees had no immunity from deportation.

In some cases, Latinos who sought shelter were required to provide Social Security numbers in order to apply for aid from FEMA.

Although federal welfare law set the broader context for immigrants' structural vulnerability, there is significant research on the positive role that CBOs, NGOs, and social service agencies can play in recovery. In New Orleans, however, the scale of damage meant that many of these Latino-serving agencies were also displaced and therefore limited in their ability to offer charitable aid. Catholic Charities provided evacuees with "gasoline, food vouchers, cash and emergency services" (Miyashita, 2005, n.p.). Latin American Consulates, notably the Mexican and Honduran Consulates, did some provide outreach to the Latino community. On its website, American Utility Metals noted the difficulties facing the Honduran consulate and "provided office space and facilities to the consulate staff" (American Utility Metals, 2005, n.p.). In Houston, the Resource Center for Central Americans (CARECEN) provided services to evacuees in their areas.

The problems Latinos experienced in securing relief assistance were reflected in other private charitable assistance. For instance, U.S. law (8 U.S.C. § 1611, 1611(b)(1)(A)-(E) and 8 U.S.C. § 1621) allows undocumented persons, (i.e., nonqualified aliens), to receive short-term shelter. Nonetheless, Muñiz (2006) found that the Red Cross made "mistakes" that included "volunteers evicting Latino hurricane victims on the presumption that they were workers and not actual survivors and requesting documentation proving legal status as a condition for receiving assistance" (p. 9). Muñiz also noted that law enforcement promoted disparities in relief assistance because they racially profiled Latinos at ARC shelters and "asked them to leave under the assumption that they were undocumented workers and not hurricane survivors" (p. 13). The role perceptions played in practice were central to the ways Latinos experienced relief services.

The changing political context surrounding DHS, FEMA, and ICE activities and decisions in New Orleans undermined Latinos' recovery. More specifically, the decisions surrounding relief entitlement and immigration enforcement hampered many Latinos' ability and desire to leave the state. These decisions also promoted a context where many Latinos' only alternative was to return to their mold-ridden homes and take up jobs in recovery efforts. The presumption that Latinos were unilaterally "imported workers" who migrated to New Orleans after Hurricane Katrina was not only incorrect, but also ignored the structural disadvantages many Latino evacuees faced. Latino evacuees who lacked financial resources, legal status, and/or social networks became part of the recovery workforce because they faced obstacles in leaving New Orleans, such as checkpoints outside the city, and they had nowhere to go. With limited support from relief agencies, many were easily recruited for dangerous jobs in cleanup and recovery.

Latino evacuees experienced Hurricane Katrina as a racial/ethnic minority. They faced a variety of structural obstacles in accessing relief services, including ineligibility and discrimination. As FEMA officials failed to protect all evacuees equally, irrespective of legal status, many Latinos found themselves in an ironic position. On the one hand, many undocumented Latinos had nowhere to go. The organizations they knew might help them had evacuated the city. Many were afraid of leaving through the checkpoints surrounding the city. Many were also afraid of approaching Red Cross shelters. On the other hand, Latinos were simultaneously being recruited at churches like *Lugar Sanidad* for recovery jobs. In this way, the structures that increased the likelihood Latinos would be negatively affected by Hurricane Katrina were reproduced in the post-impact phase. As evacuees, Latinos' vulnerability was compounded by dangerous jobs that often included crowded and unsafe housing.

Latinos and Disaster

The demographic profile of pre-Katrina Latinos gives us some basis upon which to draw cautious inferences about how Latinos were affected by Hurricane Katrina. For instance, Map 1 below represents Mid-City and specifically 2000 U.S. Census tract 65. Map 2 represents a flood zone map that includes the Mid-City area, which demonstrates that the area received the highest level of flooding that was categorized by the map (4+ feet).[4]

The higher representation of Latinos in New Orleans in Census tract 65 indicates that Latinos in New Orleans were significantly affected by the floods that followed in the wake of Hurricane Katrina (see Figures 9.1 and 9.2).

Speaking with Mid-City residents in early October 2005, I confirmed the existence of an integrated Latino community in the area. Although some respondents had friends, acquaintances, and family members who lived in Kenner and had considered moving there, many older Latinos felt they were being pushed out by both blacks and whites who had recently moved into the area. Unlike other New Orleans residents, Latino residents of Mid-City felt the area had been a Latino community before it had experienced these changes. They pointed to the Latino-owned businesses in the area and emphasized their longstanding relationships to one another. They discussed activities they shared, such as soccer and baseball, as evidence of the community Latinos felt they had established in Mid-City. For Latinos who lived in Mid-City, Hurricane Katrina had disrupted their lives and their community.

Although Latinos may have felt they had established a community in New Orleans prior to the hurricane, disaster responders, politicians and the broader

---

4. Map developed by Jasmine James, Research Associate, LSU GIS Information Clearinghouse: CADGIS Research Lab, Louisiana State University, Baton Rouge, LA. 2005/2006, http://www.katrina.lsu.edu.

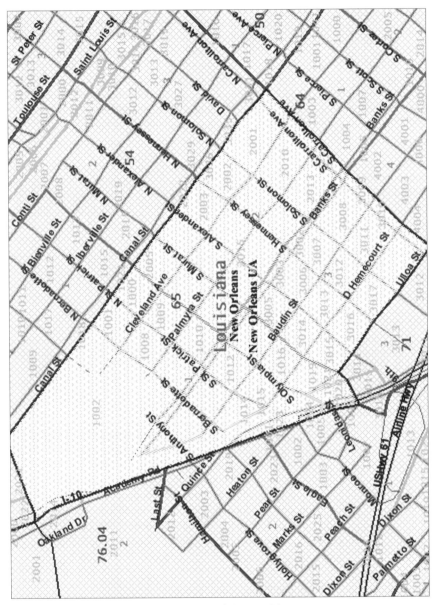

Figure 9.1 Map of Census Tract 65

public generally took another perspective by assuming that the Latino population had not ever formed a significant community within New Orleans. After
the hurricanes, relief officers explained that there was a small Latino commu-

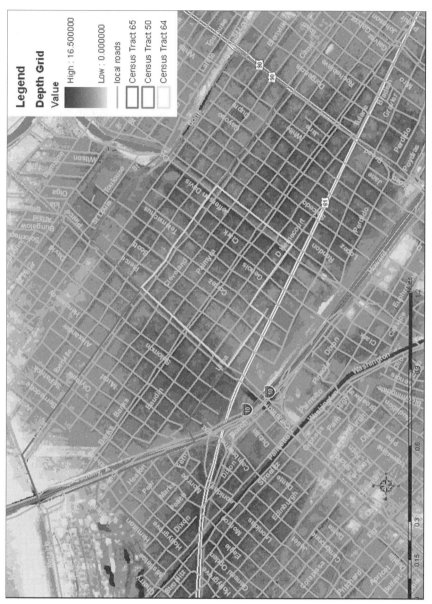

Figure 9.2 Flood Map of Census Tract 65
Census Tracts with Water Depth

nity they could not access, and claimed that this was due in part to the fact that
there was no community infrastructure to guide their efforts. As one officer ex-

plained, "we didn't see any Latinos in the area."[5] Although many businesses and community organizations were closed in the immediate post-impact period, this perception ignored Latinos' long history in the area that included important developments in community infrastructure that could have supported relief efforts. For example, the growth of the Latino population within the Greater New Orleans area was accompanied by businesses that catered to the community. The 2003–2004 Hispanic Directory lists professional, commercial, and social services available to the Spanish-speaking community within Greater New Orleans. Its pages list churches, restaurants, and supermarkets that could have aided in disseminating public announcements. Unfortunately, disaster responders did not develop coordinated efforts to reach a Spanish-speaking population.

Outreach to the Latino community in the U.S. has been a persistent problem in disaster recovery for many years. For instance, Wallrich (1996) argued that "populations that were especially vulnerable to social upheaval due to poverty, lack of English language skills, disability, irregular immigrant status, or other conditions" were not considered in disaster recovery plans (p. 13). Among the Latino-owned businesses listed in the 2003–2004 Hispanic Directory, however, Radio Tropical (1540 AM) took the initiative to publicize evacuation and relief information. Radio Tropical (1540 AM) was an important community institution because it illustrated how the broader lack of a Spanish-language infrastructure and limited public support affected the Latino community in New Orleans. Despite his efforts to have city officials publicize relief information on his station, the owner, Schweikert, noted that this information was often only available in English. (In an interview with a Spanish-speaking FEMA official, "Sofia" contradicted Schweikert's claim by insisting that she had "of her own initiative," provided information on *disaster preparation* and eventually *evacuation instructions* in interviews to Spanish-language television and radio stations that served the New Orleans area.) Schweikert's concerns about the lack of Spanish-language information continued after the hurricanes had passed. His concerns motivated him to return to New Orleans and run the station from electric generators because he realized that the station would be the only accessible source of information for many Latinos in the weeks following Hurricane Katrina. As a result of the lack of systematic outreach from local officials, Radio Tropical took on the role of explaining the forms of public relief available to different Latino communities, including un-

---

5. The problems of coordinating disaster management efforts and outreach pushed me into the role of assisting officials in locating "Latino spaces," such as restaurants, which posed significant ethical problems because this information could have been relayed to Immigration and Customs Enforcement (ICE) officers. For instance, although officials promised confidentiality of information, ICE officers had visited these spaces repeatedly in the following months.

documented immigrants. Despite its initiative, however, the station was a private endeavor with a low wattage that limited its range and audience. Other sources of crisis information for the Latino population were also needed to supplement its efforts.

Other Latino organizations also attempted to substitute for the lack of public outreach to the Latino community. For instance, the Hispanic Apostolate took the initiative to support the predominantly-Latino residents at Redwood Apartments in Kenner. Similarly, *Iglesia Lugar Sanidad* centralized communication between the Mexican and Honduran Consulates and evacuees. It also offered evacuees shelter, food, and relief assistance in the weeks following the hurricanes. Although local churches and church organizations played an important role in supporting evacuees, they could not access many Latino evacuees who lost their belongings and fled to nearby cities like Houston.

When sociologists have paid attention to how disasters affect Latinos, they emphasize Latinos' reliance on private support. For instance, Perry and Mushkatel (1986) found Mexican-Americans relied on social networks to relay warning information more than blacks or whites. Morrow (1997) discovered that Latino families were more likely to receive help in preparing for a disaster from their relatives than whites. Ibanez et al. (2003) found that Mexicans and Mexican-Americans in both Mexico and the United States claimed they received more support from "informal sources (family, neighbors) than formal sources (government)" (p. 1). Peguero (2006) found that Latino homeowners preferred to utilize friends and family as sources of disaster preparation information.

Unfortunately, scholars have also found that Latinos' reliance on private support does not always mitigate their vulnerability to disasters or facilitate their recovery. In particular, Fothergill, Maestas, and Darlington (1999) reviewed a variety of unpublished reports and detailed scholars' findings regarding the role race and ethnicity play during different periods of disaster. They related findings demonstrating that Mexican Americans were less likely to evacuate than whites in crisis situations (Lindell, Perry & Greene, 1980). Latinos were also disadvantaged by incorrect information from Hispanic radio stations, authorities' use of Spanish-language translations that implied Latinos' potential criminality, and Red Cross volunteers' insensitivity to Latinos' cultural needs (Fothergill, Maestas & Darlington, 1999).

The limited scholarship on Latinos and disasters suggests that Latinos' efforts to help each other are influenced by the character of their social networks, their culture, and government inadequacy. Klinenberg (2003) previously found that local ecology, which includes "the material substratum of busy streets, dense residential concentration, proximate family habitation, and booming commerce," may have promoted social interaction and network ties that mediated the impact of a "heat wave" on Latinos (p. 109). Wisner, Blaikie, and Cannon (2003) also found that social networks played an important role in mediating a population's vulnerability amidst disasters. They argued that people rely on support networks because they learn they cannot rely on services authorities provide. These findings suggest that Latinos' efforts to help one another stem from both their recent migration experiences and their presumption that government will not address their unique needs.

The Latino population of New Orleans faced a variety of phenomena that undermined the strength and ability of networks to mediate the impact of Hurricanes Katrina and Rita. It was a growing population with increasing numbers of undocumented immigrants. In turn, the increasing number of undocumented immigrants created new and changing needs that local agencies had only begun to consider and work toward addressing. The growth of the population also meant informal networks were recently developed, which undermined their capacity to compensate for government inadequacy. In other disaster contexts, Latinos benefited from strong institutional infrastructure. For example, in reference to the Loma Prieta earthquake, Wallrich (1996) argued that populations made vulnerable by lacking English skills or regular immigrant status benefited from "a large network of CBOs ... [who] forced reconsideration of policies that denied service to these most vulnerable populations" (p. 13). In New Orleans, however, these CBOs had also been displaced amidst the hurricane's devastation.

Latinos' reliance on informal networks was in part a limited effort to compensate for the devastating impact of exclusive social policies. Latinos could not find support in local or federal government agencies. Public announcements regarding evacuation and reentry were often available only in English or via the Internet in a city with limited access to telephone signals. When I visited New Orleans in October 2005, I could not find evidence of any Spanish-language signage regarding the safety of entering or occupying flooded properties. These information gaps compounded the Latino population's vulnerability.

Conclusion

Latinos' post-disaster experience reflects both their social and political vulnerability and their central role in the affected areas' recovery efforts. Soon after Hurricanes Katrina and Rita had passed, many commentators noted the rapid influx of Latino workers into New Orleans. What many commentators missed was the fact that the alleged "imported workers" included many evacuees struggling to reestablish their lives after the hurricane's devastating impact.

The case of Hurricane Katrina demonstrates important trends in how Latinos experience discrimination and racism in the United States. For example, they found they were discriminated against based on the presumption that

Latinos were not a part of the pre-Katrina population in New Orleans. Federal welfare policy also limited their eligibility for disaster assistance. As many Latinos struggled to recover through immediate or informal networks, they found they were also not protected by federal officials who instead put some evacuees into deportation proceedings. These dynamics demonstrate how many Latinos were excluded from the protection and support that other evacuees enjoyed. Latinos were not recognized as "evacuees" and were instead political scapegoats in the immediate aftermath of the disaster.

The factors involved in Latinos' recovery point to ironic contradictions between economic dynamics and political rhetoric that made Latinos simultaneously vulnerable and central to New Orleans' recovery. On the one hand, in the weeks following Hurricane Katrina, New Orleans Mayor Ray Nagin worried about the role that the influx of Latino workers would have on displacing native-born workers from the city's labor force. He wondered how to prevent New Orleans from being "overrun by Mexican workers" (Roig-Franzia, 2005, p. A03). Nagin's concern reflects broader anxieties about a growing non-white immigrant population in the United States. On the other hand, this political rhetoric ignores the important structural conditions that produce distrust and disasters. As political officials implicitly blamed Latinos' fear for inequitable relief assistance, they ignored the ways their decisions and the dynamics of recovery reproduced Latinos' vulnerability. In essence, many Latinos found disaster management was less about making their "dispensable" labor disappear after the Hurricane than it was about ensuring the reappearance of their vulnerable, low-wage labor.

References

American Community Survey. (2005). Retrieved September 15, 2006 from http://www.census.gov/acs/.

American Utility Metals. (2005, Oct. 11). Katrina aftermath. Retrieved Dec.31, 2006 from http://www.aum1.com/news_detail.cfm?AID=192.

Associated Press. (2005, Sept. 13). Aerolínea Mexicana transportará gratis a víctimas. *La Opinion*. Retrieved August 25, 2006 from http://www.la opinion.com/latinoamerica/?rkey=00050912200915972700.

Bolin, R. & Stanford, L. (1998). *The Northridge earthquake: Vulnerability and disaster*. New York: Routledge.

Campo-Flores, A. (2005, Dec. 5). A new spice in the gumbo: Will Latino day laborers locating in New Orleans change its complexion? *Newsweek*, p. 46.

Cevallos, D. (2005, Sept. 5). Thousands of Latin American immigrants among Katrina's victims. *Inter Press Service News Agency*. Retrieved August 25, 2006 from http://ipsnews.net/interna.asp?idnews=30150.

————. (2005, Sept. 12) Latin American immigrants harmed by Katrina. *The Louisiana* Weekly. Retrieved August 25, 2006 from http://www.louisiana weekly.com/weekly/news/articlegate.pl?20050912j.

————. (2005, Sept. 21). Latin American storm victims adrift. *Inter Press Service News Agency.* Retrieved on August 25, 2006 from http://ipsnews. net/news.asp?idnews=30370.

Chandler, B. & Gamboa, G. (2005). Written testimony: Hurricane Katrina response and immigrants. In *Select Bipartisan Committee to Investigate the Preparation for and Response to Hurricane Katrina*: Retrieved on August 25, 2006 from http://www.oxfamamerica.org/newsandpublications/ publications/research_reports/research_paper.2005-12-06.4237647120.

Ciria-Cruz, R. (2005). Ethnic media keep a worried eye on Katrina's wake. *Pacific News Service.* Retrieved August 26, 2005 from http://news.pacific news.org/news/view_article.html?article_id=3dab39de1628d5f4894e8ddd 1b892681.

Contreras, José. (2005, Sept. 7). Salvaban a blancos; a negros y latinos los dejaban morir, *La Cronica De Hoy*, p. 1.

Dawson, M. C. (2006). After the deluge: Publics and publicity in Katrina's wake. *Du Bois Review*, 3(1), 239–249.

Deggans, E. (2005, Sept. 2). In many ways, journalists struggle to find the story. *St. Petersburg Times online.* Retrieved September 22, 2005 from http://www.sptimes.com/2005/09/02/Worldandnation/In_many_ways__ journal.shtml.

Fix, M. E. & Tumlin, K. (1997). Welfare reform and the devolution of immigrant policy. Urban Institute. Retrieved August 25, 2006 from http://www. urban.org/url.cfm?ID=307045.

Fothergill, A., Maestas, E., & Darlington, J. D. (1999). Race, ethnicity and disasters in the United States: A review of the literature. *Disasters*, 23(2), 156–173.

Giroux, H. A. (2006). Reading Hurricane Katrina: Race, class, and the biopolitics of disposability. *College Literature*, 33(3), 171–96.

Glenn, E. (2000). Citizenship and inequality: Historical and global perspectives. *Social Problems*, 47(1), 1–20.

Huddy, L. & Feldman, S. (2006). Worlds apart: Blacks and whites react to Hurricane Katrina. *Du Bois Review,* 3(1), 97–113.

Ibanez, G. E., Khatchikian, N., Buck, C.A., Weisshaar, D. L., Abush-Kirsh, T., Lavizzo, E.A., & Norris, F.N. (2003). Qualitative analysis of social support and conflict among Mexican and Mexican-American disaster survivors. *Journal of Community Psychology*, 31(1), 1–23.

Klinenberg, E. (2003). *Heat wave: A social autopsy of disaster in Chicago.* Chicago: University of Chicago Press.

Kutz, G. D. (2006). *Expedited assistance for victims of Hurricanes Katrina and Rita: Fema's control weaknesses exposed the government to significant fraud and abuse.* Washington D.C.: General Accountability Office.

Lindell, M. K., R. W. Perry, R. W., & Greene, M. R. (1980). *Race and disaster warning response.* Seattle: Battelle Human Affairs Research Center.

Lovato, R. (2005, Oct. 18). The Latinization of the new New Orleans. *New America Media.* Retrieved Nov. 1, 2005 from http://crm.ncmonline.com/news/view_article.html?article_id=fa92e2c88a63985418da75582292b5c7.

Miyashita, A. M. (2005, Sept. 18). Leaders say aid is too slow in reaching Hispanic evacuees. *Hispanic Link News Service.* Retrieved Aug. 25, 2006 from http://www.hispaniclink.org/newsservice/columns/2005/4124e.htm.

Moore, J. D. (1999, Fall). Who remains eligible for what? *Popular Government,* 22–37.

Morissens, A. N. N., & Sainsbury, D. (2005). Migrants' social rights, ethnicity and welfare regimes. *Journal of Social Policy,* 34(4), 637–660.

Morrow, B.H. (1997). Stretching the bonds: The families of Andrew. In W.G. Peacock, B.H. Morrow, & H, Gladwin (Eds.), *Hurricane Andrew: Ethnicity, gender, and the sociology of disasters* (pp. 141–170). New York: Routledge.

Muniz, B. (2006). *In the eye of the storm: How the government and private response to Hurricane Katrina failed Latinos.* Washington, D.C.: National Council of La Raza.

Peguero, A. A. (2006). Latino disaster vulnerability. *Hispanic Journal of Behavioral Sciences,* 28(1), 5–22.

Perry, R.W. & Mushkatel, A. H. (1986). *Minority citizens in disasters.* Athens, GA: University of Georgia Press.

Raices, Inc. (2003). *Directorio Hispano de Louisiana.* New Orleans: Raices Incorporated.

Roig-Franzia, M. (2005, Dec. 18). In New Orleans, no easy work for willing Latinos. *Washington Post,* p. A03.

Rozemberg, H. (2006, Mar. 19). The changing face of the Gulf Coast work force. *San Antonio Express-News,* p. 1A.

Sainsbury, D. (2006). Immigrants' social rights in comparative perspective: Welfare regimes, forms in immigration and immigration policy regimes. *Journal of European Social Policy,* 16(3), 229–244.

Simmons, A.M. (2005, Sept. 20). Latinos in New Orleans suburb feel slighted. *Los Angeles Times,* p. A12.

Siskin, A.(2002, Feb. 15). *Noncitizen eligibility for disaster-related assistance.* Congressional Research Service. Retrieved September 15, 2005 from http://65.36.162.215/files/nda.pdf.

Stallings, R.A. (2002). Weberian political sociology and sociological disaster studies. *Sociological Forum*, 17(2), 281–305.

Stein, R. S. (1976). *Urban Latins: A fictional community in New Orleans*. Master's thesis. New Orleans: University of New Orleans.

Terhune, C. & Pérez, E. (2005, Oct. 3). Roundup of immigrants in shelter reveals rising tensions. *Wall Street Journal*, p. B1.

U.S. Census Bureau. (2000). Income in 1999 below poverty level: Hispanic or Latino population for whom poverty status is determined" in Census tract 65. Retrieved September 15, 2005 from http://factfinder.census.gov/servlet/DatasetMainPageServlet?_program=DEC&_submenuId=&_lang=en&_ts=.

Wallrich, B. (1996). The evolving role of community based organizations in disaster recovery. *National Hazards Observer*, 21(2), 12–13.

Walsh, B. (2006, Aug. 22). Most Relief Money Still Unspent. *The Times-Picayune*. Retrieved on April 1, 2005 from http://www.nola.com/newslogs/tpupdates/index.ssf?/mtlogs/nola_tpupdates/archives/2006_08_22.html#1 74900.

Wasem, R. E. (2005a). Hurricane Katrina-related immigration issues and legislation. *CRS Report for Congress*. CRS Publication Date: September 9, Doc. No.: RL33091.

Wasem, R. E. (2005b). Hurricane Katrina-related immigration issues and legislation. *CRS Report for Congress*. CRS Publication Date: October 18, Doc. No.: RL33091.

Wisner, B., Blaikie, P., & Cannon, T. (2003). *At risk*. Routledge.

Chapter 10

From Invisibility to Hypervisibility: The Complexity of Race, Survival, and Resiliency for the Vietnamese-American Community in Eastern New Orleans

Karen J. Leong, Christopher Airriess,
Angela Chia-Chen Chen, Verna Keith, Wei Li,
Ying Wang, and Karen Adams

"Invisibility is an unnatural disaster."

—Mitsuye Yamada[1]

Mitsuye Yamada and her family were removed from their home in Seattle, Washington, in 1942 because they were Japanese Americans, and placed in an internment camp in Minidoka, Idaho. She and her brother eventually were able to leave the camp to attend college. A powerful poet, Yamada exposes the invisibility of Japanese Americans in American society in the 1940s, and her own invisibility as an Asian American woman in American society today (Yamada, 1976, 1988). Her words serve a dual purpose in framing this chapter: Hurricane Katrina was a natural disaster—to some extent out of anyone's control. The lack of effective response and the process of rebuilding however, has revealed the invisibility of certain stakeholders to be an unnatural disaster. At

---

1. See Yamada, M. (1983, pp. 36, 38).

the same time, the specificity of Yamada's own experiences also powerfully evoke the experiences of Asian American communities during Hurricane Katrina; the Vietnamese-American community in eastern New Orleans went virtually unmentioned in early media coverage that instead focused on the traditional binary relationships of black and white, underprivileged and affluent.

In the sixteen months since Hurricane Katrina devastated the Central Gulf Coast the Vietnamese-American community in its efforts to rebuild and mobilize for political action has emerged from initial invisibility to a state of what might be called hypervisibility. This trajectory reveals the complex intersections of gender, race, and class in structuring access to visibility, and demonstrates how Asian American communities so often are located as intermediaries within the black and white racial binary that continues to dominate the United States' discourse of race, economic justice, and power.

Poverty, race, and gender work together to render certain people more invisible than others in society. Peter Dreier (2006) notes that 35 percent of African Americans in New Orleans and 15 percent of whites did not own cars. He also cites studies showing that New Orleans is ranked third in the nation among metropolitan areas with the highest concentrations of poverty, and the twelfth poorest city in the nation. Furthermore, Joni Seager (2006) discusses how the intersections of gender, race, and class have been overlooked, rendered invisible, in media coverage of the disaster: 68 percent of the New Orleans population is African American, and 54 percent consists of women. Echoing Yamada's articulation of who is visible and who is not, Seager argues that invisibility is an unnatural status bestowed by social structures that pay attention to certain stakeholders and ignore others. Critical race theorists Mari Matsuda, Kimberle Crenshaw, Richard Delgado, and others similarly have made significant contributions to making visible these intersecting social structures and especially how they become codified in law (Crenshaw, 1994; Delgado, 2001; Matsuda, 1997). For those who are engaged in seeking social justice and human rights for all people, regardless of race, ethnicity, gender, socioeconomic status, sexuality, able-bodiedness, and so on, part of the task—regardless of vocation—is to make these structures, and the people they overlook or ignore, visible.

Mayor Raymond Nagin's "Chocolate City" notwithstanding, the city of New Orleans historically has been an African-American city (Midlo Hall, 1992), from its inception as a French colony in the seventeenth century. Prior to Katrina, African Americans constituted the majority population in New Orleans. Beginning in the 1970s, new immigrants contributed to greater diversity. Louisiana, and especially New Orleans, became home to one of the larger concentrations of Vietnamese Americans outside of California. Approximately 15,000 Vietnamese Americans resided in New Orleans in 2005. The intersections of race and class, so often visible in public discourse about African-

American communities, are apparent in the geographic distribution of Vietnamese Americans: nearly 50%, or 7000, live in neighborhoods that are marked by poverty (Airriess, 2005; U.S. Census Bureau, 2000).

The authors of this chapter received a small grant for exploratory research from the NSF Human and Social Dynamics initiative to conduct a multidisciplinary research project (funded by a National Science Foundation Human and Social Dynamics Division Small Grant for Exploratory Research, #0555135 and 0555086) that analyzed the evacuation and rebuilding processes for the African American and Vietnamese-American residents living in New Orleans East as a result of Hurricane Katrina. The use of surveys, focus group discussions, and in-depth interviews allowed us to examine the different impacts on the social, cultural, political, and geographic lives of Southeast Asian Americans and African Americans who were dislocated by the flooding in New Orleans in the wake of Hurricane Katrina. Our research finds that both communities relied on the media for information about Katrina, and relied upon assistance from community organizations, religious institutions, as well as the federal government. The ongoing rebuilding process demonstrates how certain forms of social capital and inter-group collaborations within and beyond the study area have contributed greatly to community resiliency.

In this article we seek to theorize the absent presence of Vietnamese Americans within the discourse of race, class, and Hurricane Katrina, and to argue that these absent presences must be exposed in order to develop more nuanced analyses of the fissures of race and class in the nation's urban centers that have been exposed through this disaster. Simply analyzing the lack of certain resources among the Vietnamese-American and African-American communities will only contribute to distorted media images of passivity and dependency that have dominated the news media regarding this event and have historically been associated with communities of color and poverty. The efforts of community leaders in the New Orleans Vietnamese community, the National Alliance of Vietnamese Service Agencies (NAVASA), and several other non-profit groups have made visible the needs of the community. In the past eight months, these efforts have been quite successful, resulting in the emergence of the Vietnamese-American Versailles community as a media success story. While ideology of meritocracy in the United States might celebrate the Vietnamese-American community's resilience in eastern New Orleans as a "miracle" or evidence of "model minority" status, we instead examine this success through the lens of a critical race theory framework of community cultural wealth. This framework suggests that marginalized communities often possess distinct forms of capital—linguistic, resistant, aspirational, familial, navigational, and societal—and demands historical specificity when seeking to understand community resiliency.

A Tale of Two Communities

The impact of Hurricane Katrina on the Central Gulf Coast region, especially New Orleans, presented in vivid details the effects of chronic concentrated poverty and the vulnerability of residents that live in such neighborhoods. The city of New Orleans was 67 percent African Americans and about a third lived below the poverty line. Furthermore, the segregation index was .66 overall (Glaeser & Vigdor, 2001) and about .75 for African Americans. Residing in segregated, poor neighborhoods is associated with unequal access to city services and to a host of social ills. City services tend to be of poorer quality but more costly to residents. Graffiti, abandoned buildings, vandalism, poor lighting, fewer recreational and green spaces, and trash and garbage on sidewalks are part of the physical landscape (Aneshensel & Sucoff, 1996; Ross & Mirowsky, 2001) in poor urban neighborhoods owing to a tax base that is insufficient to support services, a lack of responsiveness on the part of elected leaders, and a lack of political organization among residents. Restricted economic opportunities, as well as the physical landscape of neighborhoods, create conditions for numerous social ills including crime and violence. As noted in the extensive media coverage, those residents who were unable to escape the city prior to the hurricane and those trapped after the levee break were disproportionately African American and poor.

At the same time, the media and analysts, in the first two months especially, largely overlooked the Vietnamese-American community that also was located in the eastern New Orleans subdivisions of Versailles and Village d l'Est that boasted an almost equal distribution of ethnic Vietnamese and blacks (Airriess, 2002; Zhou & Bankston, 1994). Residential segregation based on ethnicity is pronounced in the Section 8 apartment complex where African Americans comprise 75.3 percent of the population. In 40 of the 59 blocks groups, Vietnamese are the majority population. There exists a reasonably large ethnic Vietnamese commercial enclave with approximately 93 businesses serving the local-co-ethnic population. There is not a single African-American-owned business. While suburban in residential location, the ethnic Vietnamese population is economically disadvantaged relative to the larger ethnic Vietnamese in the Metropolitan Statistical Area, and even more so when compared to ethnic Vietnamese nationally. Because only 12 percent of those 25 years or older have bachelor's degrees or higher, the working population is relegated to low-wage service, non-skilled manufacturing, and agricultural (fishing) occupations as sources of employment. Only seven percent of the working population is in management, professional and related occupational categories. Poverty rates for Vietnamese Americans in 2000 stood at 31.3 percent, but were substantially lower than poverty rates for African Americans (40.8%) in these neighborhoods.

Clearly, socioeconomic status affected both the location of the community and access to necessary resources during this emergency. Poverty can explain the lack of access to fuel, water, and supplies, the inability to evacuate to a lack of private transportation, and the lack of access to communication. Poverty and race also can explain why existing informal community networks for both Vietnamese and African Americans were neither granted access to institutionalized networks of emergency communications, nor incorporated as resources in the development of emergency evacuation strategies. Yet poverty alone is not sufficient enough an explanation.

In 2000, approximately 36.7 percent of the ethnic-Vietnamese population in the study area was isolated linguistically. Published or broadcast descriptions of the experiences of Vietnamese Americans in the study area during the flooding suggest that language ability was a critical factor in determining access to resources. Although a Vietnamese radio station exists in Louisiana, the lack of electric power rendered this resource unreliable for the community. What we have found is that children and grandchildren stayed behind if the elders were not mobile, and that it was the younger members of the community who provided information about the flooding and emergency efforts. The role of the local Catholic Church, Mary Queen of Vietnam, in Versailles also was critical. The pastor perhaps most effectively raised awareness of the severity of the situation when he announced the need for evacuation during mass.

While African Americans may not have faced linguistic barriers to emergency aid, the reports of African Americans on the far eastern side of the city indicate that cultural and racial barriers may have contributed to the delay in emergency relief efforts. Racial stereotypes of African Americans as violent, combined with the reports of looting and gunshots, may have kept police and emergency relief personnel from entering certain communities. Since the immediate coverage of Hurricane Katrina, there has now been reported a second bridge incident in which parish police prevented people fleeing the flooding based on fears of violence and crime. In addition the lack of political capital associated with poverty (Blank, 2005) has been connected with the lack of institutional response to the needs of African Americans during the flooding.

Beyond a Black and White Analysis of Katrina

A comparative analysis of Vietnamese Americans in addressing the unnatural disasters following Katrina is not simply about New Orleans, but about the larger discourse about race and the need to move beyond perceptions of race relations as more than white and black.

The impact of Hurricane Katrina on the Vietnamese-American community in eastern New Orleans raises key questions about the dominant discourse about race, class, and social justice in the United States. The conspicuous absence of Vietnamese Americans from the discourse of Katrina reflects a continuing racial paradigm in the United States that race is solely black and white. On the one hand, this paradigm suggests that Americans of Asian descent continue to be perceived as not fully American, but as perpetual foreigners and outsiders. While exploring the divergence of immigration and racial discourses in U.S. society is beyond the purview of this chapter, it is not a coincidence that Latinos are omitted as well from this paradigm. American Indians, also affected by the devastation of Katrina, are further obscured by the legacy of colonization.

In moving beyond the racial dichotomy of black and white, discussions of social justice in the aftermath of Hurricane Katrina likewise must shift. In a society that perceives race primarily as black and white, Asian Americans become pivotal. Especially in urban areas since the late 20th century, Asian Americans played a critical role—for example, as the perceived middle men in the LA uprisings in the wake of the Rodney King decision, where the media focused primarily on Korean-Black tensions. As model minorities who, according to the social narrative, work harder and thus are more likely to succeed than other non-white groups, and as immigrant entrepreneurs who are accused of profiting from urban poverty, Asian Americans are rendered visible at specific moments to obscure the system of whiteness, the system of racism at work. Yet when it comes to issues of resources, Asian Americans often are excluded based on their representations as perpetual foreigners who live amongst themselves, or overlooked because the assumption is that they can take care of themselves.

This dynamic itself has contributed to the development over the past two or three decades a strong grassroots infrastructure among the national (and local) Vietnamese community. As with other Asian American groups, the lack of responsiveness by government institutions has led communities to develop their own resources. Ironically, these resources also explain why the community has been so resilient—they have not been able to depend on government institutions in the past, and so they have developed other strategies. One local priest observed,

> When we return, we came to rebuild.... We wonder why the city has not decided anything yet but we have to move on without the government's help. We do as best as we can to re-establish and reclaim our place. They have meetings and meetings and meetings and people show to protest but we can't wait long for the government so we do ourselves for the community we've been building for 30 years.
>
> (Webster, 2006, n.p.)

Imagine how much more effective the community could be in rebuilding their lives in New Orleans had they been informed about the million dollars worth of small business loans from the state, had they been included as stakeholders in the Mayor's commission to rebuild New Orleans. The omission of Vietnamese-

American representation across the board in federal and local government re-building initiatives was yet another unnatural disaster for this community.

Thus, the rebuilding by Vietnamese Americans of their community institutions and neighborhoods has been all the more striking. Indeed, the community has journeyed from a lack of visibility within New Orleans to a hypervisible status as one of the success stories of community resiliency. After the first couple of months, news agencies like MSNBC, NPR, the *New York Times* and *Los Angeles Times*, began to feature human interest stories about Vietnamese immigrants facing their second dislocation, the first fleeing their homeland to rebuild a life on the Central Gulf Coast, and the second their determination to rebuild again. In the past six months, the role of Mary Queen of Vietnam Church in Versailles has received abundant press coverage as the anchor of the community's resiliency.

These national organizations were not solely Vietnamese American either. Pan-ethnic Asian American identification served to mobilize politicians like Japanese American Mike Honda, House Representative (D) from San Jose, California, who counts a large Vietnamese-American community in San Jose among his constituency, to speak out on behalf of the needs of Southeast Asian Americans in rebuilding their businesses and homes. Significantly, he emphasized the linguistic isolation of Southeast Asian immigrant communities in the Gulf regions affected by Katrina,

> Before Katrina, Texas had about 134,000 Vietnamese, a sizable portion of the country's total Vietnamese-American population of more than 1.2 million. Approximately one-half of Louisiana's 30,000 Vietnamese have taken refuge in Houston, a gigantic displacement that is being assisted by the community's established leadership.... As caregivers mobilize to care for victims, I am concerned that many APAs will not get necessary treatment due to long-standing disparities in health care. There is a lack of language access, for example, which underscores a persistent failure of services in this country. Such disparities are very real, and they exist throughout American society. Specific services such as providing linguistic and culturally competent care are essential to addressing all the wide-ranging needs within the various APA communities. Many of the storm-related fatalities will likely result from inadequate medical care.
>
> (Honda, 2006, n.p.)

In order to meet these needs, activism at the local level has been key. Even with federal funding, the ability to identify and assist individuals and families has required local knowledge and existing relationships of trust. In the Versailles neighborhood, the church's leadership thus was instrumental in persuading the Vietnamese-American parishioners to return and make their presence visible to the city government. At the same time, the community also found support from co-ethnic national organizations that sought to make visible the needs of the Vietnamese-American community for financial assistance. Several organizations sent bilingual staff to work in the Katrina-affected areas and to provide translation assistance.

Significantly, the Vietnamese Americans in New Orleans were able to utilize a national network that developed to support Vietnamese immigrant communities that emerged in the aftermath of migration during the 1970s and 1980s. This network includes the development of national radio and television networks, as well as several national Vietnamese-American organizations, some of which developed out of what initially were organizations for refugee assistance. Catholic churches around the nation who served Vietnamese communities as far away as Orange County, California or North Carolina, for example, essentially constituted informal relocation assistance network for evacuees, and opened up churches and members' homes for the dislocated. Boat People SOS, formed as a resource for new Vietnamese immigrants in the 1980s, was awarded a 4.5 million dollar grant specifically to assist those who were affected by Katrina in accessing federal assistance and other services. It is the only organization that works specifically with Southeast Asian immigrants and is a member of the consortium of nonprofit groups that received funds to assist those affected by Katrina in identifying and applying for assistance. NAVASA—the National Alliance of Vietnamese American Service Agencies—announced the Operation Community Building Project in December 2005, which trains high school students to volunteers in the National Dan Than Corps to assist in locating housing and in rebuilding neighborhoods and community resources. In addition, the National Congress of Vietnamese Americans focused its efforts in gathering data that can be used in generating more assistance and informing government policies. One example is *Vietnamese Americans in Hurricane-Impacted Gulf Areas: An Assessment of Housing Needs* that NCVA released in August 2006, which surveyed residents displaced by Katrina throughout Louisiana and provided policy recommendations for the rebuilding of Vietnamese-American communities (Pham, Shull, Tranguyen, & Hoang, 2006). All of these organizations have or had staff on site to assist the community members with accessing necessary resources in order to return to Versailles.

Knowledge about this community's resilience would not have reached the widespread national audience that it did without the galvanizing effect of Mayor Ray Nagin's decision to circumvent zoning rules and to authorize the reopening of the Chef Menteur Landfill site for household hurricane debris. This site is within two miles of Village de l'Est. The city argued that this location would save on dumping costs in landfills located beyond the city; a further incentive was that Waste Management agreed to pay the City of New Orleans 22 percent of the revenues (Myers, 2006).

Concerns about pollutants leeching from the landfill waste entering the water and endangering residents and a nearby wetland preserve resulted in the emergence of a powerful, multi-ethnic coalition of environmental, religious, residential, and other organizations. The pastor of Mary Queen of Vietnam continually pressed the issue of toxins infiltrating the soil where residents planted small gardens. African Americans and Vietnamese Americans, the primary residents of Versailles, further protested being shut out of the process of public input in the mayor's decision. They formed the Coalition for a Strong New Orleans East and forged ties with the Louisiana Environmental Action Network in order to leverage greater visibility and presence in this discussion. Together, these organizations and individuals raised national awareness about environmental racism, pollution, and putting a primarily African-American and Vietnamese-American community at risk with the location of the landfill.

The efforts to protest the landfill also drew upon national networks. Representative Honda, who continued to follow the impact of Katrina upon Asian American communities in the Central Gulf states, issued a statement to the Army Corps of Engineers that "opening Chef Menteur [landfill] would be an unwise decision that trades serious long-term costs for short-term expediency" (Honda, 2006, n.p.). He stated in his letter that the Vietnamese community in Village de l'Est were among the residents who returned to New Orleans the quickest, and that "Placing a landfill that might pose serious health risks in the coming years to the courageous and hopeful residents of Village de l'Est who are leading the way in rebuilding a still ravaged and debilitated city is not an appropriate award." The prolonged demonstrations and public awareness relating to the landfill ultimately forced the Mayor to halt the use of the landfill on August 15, 2006.

The successful organization against the Chef Menteur landfill affirms scholarly literature about environmental racism and community resistance. The research of Mary Pardo (1998) and her work on the Mothers of East Los Angeles and their successful community mobilization in protesting the vulnerability of their neighborhoods to environmental pollutants suggests that immigrant and ethnic minority groups utilize different strategies in order to access political power. Pardo argues that these Mexican American mothers in East Los Angeles—assumed to lack the political engagement of college-educated, white collar residents in more affluent neighborhoods—indeed successfully resisted environmental racism. The role of religious institutions and leadership, the motivation of protecting the community as a whole, and the successful mobilization of existing social networks, were key to the Catholic Mexican American women gaining access to city government decisions. Pardo thus refutes notions that certain immigrant and/or ethnic minority groups are less politically active.

The contestation over Chef Menteur landfill suggests that the City of New Orleans attempted to generate revenues by minimizing neighborhoods that were spatially, socially, and economically marginalized from the city itself. From the time of the landfill's reopening to its closing, Waste Management Resources earned 3.825 million dollars and "donated" 800,000 dollars to the city's coffers (Myers, 2006). Clearly, New Orleans faced a dire lack of resources and the need for funding to restore the civic infrastructure was not insignificant. The local government did not expect to face a campaign of organized resistance that drew upon multiple forms of protest (demonstrations, national media, and a multi-interest, multi-ethnic coalition).

This successful mobilization reflects what environmental scholar Barbara L. Allen (2003) asserted in her study of environmental justice in New Orleans,

> ... the strongest citizens' groups have the following: 1) alliances with well-organized national and multi-national environmental and social justice groups; 2) have enrolled the support of activist and independent scientists and professional experts to work on their behalf, and; 3) are cross-class and multi-ethnic in composition.
>
> (as cited in Allen, 2006, n.p.)

The success in shutting down the landfill revealed the resilience of a community that did not fulfill traditional expectations of active political participants. At the same time, the Vietnamese-American community utilized newer technologies together with traditional community traditions of the Versailles Vietnamese immigrant community in their response to the immediate threats of flooding in their neighborhood.

Community Capital and Social Justice

Analysis of the Vietnamese-American residents' success in reconstituting their community in Village d l'Est suggests that community capital can be just as significant as what is traditionally considered "political capital" — possessing college educations, above median income levels, and living in middle-class or affluent neighborhoods. Lacking political capital and facing linguistic barriers, the Vietnamese nonetheless were able to utilize community networks beyond the city and state in order to save and rescue 300 community members (Elliott, 2005; Lam, 2005). Trang Nguyen, an engineer living in Arlington, Texas was the daughter of residents in Versailles. After learning that many Vietnamese were not able to evacuate and knowing that the flood level was increasing by viewing online maps, Nguyen contacted the church to warn them of the impending threat to those residents who had not evacuated. The church's role as an ethnic community institution allowed the priest to communicate with his parishioners and to alert them to the emergency. He went door-to-door to warn people to move to the church, which was on higher ground. Although this effort allowed over 300 people to escape the floodwaters, repeated calls by Nguyen and others to the Coast Guard and other public safety offices for assistance went unanswered. She began a nationwide e-mail and phone campaign, and was able to engage the NCVA and other community networks for assistance. Many of those who did not evacuate were either elderly and had poor health, or stayed behind to assist these elders. Nguyen then sent e-mails alerting people to the emergency. These e-mails eventually reached the National Congress of Vietnamese Americans, a national network of Vietnamese Americans, which mobilized Vietnamese-American communities in other states, resulting in the private efforts of the Vietnamese community in Houston in hiring three trucks to go to the community secured the safety of these people after five days of isolation without food or water. Here, the woman's ability to access the Internet and ability to access a national network of ethnic Vietnamese allowed her to negotiate the linguistic, political, and socioeconomic limitations of the local community. The evacuation of these 300 individuals demonstrates how new technologies were incorporated into cultural institutions sustained from Vietnam and prior to arrival in the United States.

This particular Vietnamese-American community had an advantage of already operating within a strong organizational structure, due to the fact that a majority of their residents were Catholic. The pastor of the local Catholic church was able to draw upon social networks that already were institutionalized by the Catholic Church in North Vietnam, and brought with the villages fleeing the Communist rule into South Vietnam. "'The majority of the people were Catholics,' he said. 'The whole village migrated, so the priest was the frontier person that was leading the community to a new locale to set up, to build, to establish. It's part of our tradition.'" (Pope, 2006, n.p.). This pre-existing leadership structure was a key resource in rebuilding. The church leadership successfully called its members back to the parish based on the tight social bonds that existed and were institutionalized among the relatively recent immigrant community.

The hypervisibility of the Vietnamese-American success story conversely threatens to render invisible the continuing structural deficiencies for working-class former New Orleans residents who cannot afford to return to the city or for those communities that have not been able to rebuild or mobilize as effectively. Even as this community's accomplishment is celebrated, it is essential that the differential capital between ethnic minority communities as well as the community capital as a result of recent experience be understood.

Deficit thinking assumes that material poverty or marginalized social status reflects a deficit in cultural values or normative skills. During field research in New Orleans in November 2006, we found in informal conversations that the Vietnamese-American community was praised for its organization, hard work, and self-sustainability. Recent Latino immigrants employed by the construction business likewise were perceived as hard working and industrious, even though frequent comments were made about drug trade and crime associated with this community. By far the most disparaging comments, however, were directed at the African-American community, reflecting longstanding racialized assumptions about a lack of work ethic, a reliance on government assistance, and a lack of leadership. These projections of the Vietnamese-American community as a "model minority," a stereotype that has historically been attached to Asian Americans since the 1960s, are particularly troubling. This stereotype assumes that Asian Americans by virtue of their ethnic identity possess a particular cultural capital that is valued in United States society: Asian immigrants are more likely to succeed and advance socioeconomically, due to *inherent* cultural values of hard work, family cohesiveness, and educational attainment. The stereotype affirms that people who work hard will succeed, and that those who do not succeed socioeconomically do not work hard enough. In other words, the "model minority" also posits that other non-white ethnic groups are deficient in this cultural capital, and thus attain lower levels of education, do not enjoy upward mobility, and so on.

The problem with the model minority label is that it is a distorted perception that does not take into account specific historical experiences and realities that may contribute to the ability of the Versailles Vietnamese-American community to rebuild so quickly. Unlike other Asian immigrants since the late 1960s who have entered with significant educational capital including college and post-graduate education, Vietnamese who entered the United States were refugees from political conflict in their homeland. This experience of having to rebuild one's life is relatively recent—less than two generations old. Leaders within the community are themselves quick to point out how their experiences are distinct from other communities who were adversely affected in New Orleans:

> "You have to remember that the experience of this community is very unique," says Father Vien, the community's leader [pastor of Mary Queen of Vietnam Catholic Church]. "The overwhelming majority of these people were forced to migrate to the South in very arduous conditions, risking their lives. They had to walk through the killing fields of Cambodia to Thailand, and wait for years in a dismal environment before finally making it to America. And so—and I say this with all sincerity—Katrina was a minor inconvenience to us."
>
> (Shenker, 2006, n.p.)

So although no one would claim that fleeing political conflict is a privilege, one might draw upon Peggy McIntosh's description of "earned strength" that results when one does not enjoy privilege but must negotiate those structures that limit one's access in society (McIntosh, 1988). This earned strength moreover, was one forged in community networks upon which the refugees relied as they adjusted to U.S. society in the 1970s and 1980s.

These networks, the role of the church in sustaining a community identity, and the knowledge of community resiliency based on experience of survival, constitute examples of what some critical race theorists call "community cultural wealth." More specifically, this wealth consists of different forms of capital, including aspirational, navigational, familial, societal, linguistic, and resistant

(Yosso, 2006). The Vietnamese-American community demonstrates all six forms of capital. Societal capital describes the close Vietnamese-American immigrant and pan-ethnic Asian American networks that exist nationally and locally. Several residents within the Versailles Vietnamese American initially came from the same village, attracted to New Orleans because of friends and family already residing there (Leong, 2006). These pre-existing bonds only contributed to the strong relationships exhibited during evacuation. Familial capital also emphasizes the value of community, which played a key role in the evacuation process. This sense of familial capital was evidenced even nationally by Vietnamese-American communities in other states offering resources and shelter for evacuees. One Vietnamese American who resettled in Houston after Katrina noted that a primary difference between fleeing Vietnam and fleeing Katrina was family support, "It is harder leaving from your culture. Hurricane is nothing. In the hurricane, you have your family with you all the time" (Leong, 2006, n.p.).

This statement also demonstrates the acquisition of resistant capital emerged from the specific history of the Vietnamese immigrants in New Orleans as political refugees who were forced to rebuild their lives in the United States. One community member, the FEMA community liaison, voices this resistance, remarking that, "Thirty years ago we didn't have nothing," and "Do you think that it will be hard for us now?" (Joe, 2005, n.p.). As a story in the *Village Voice* reported,

> The Vietnamese residents of New Orleans East say that it is their shared culture that makes them so steadfast. That history … goes back at least as far as 1954, when the country was partitioned and the residents of three North Vietnamese villages fled to the relative freedom of the South. Leading the migration were Catholic priests. When the south fell in 1975, the parishioners once again fled the communists together, this time to America, most of them by way of refugee camps. They settled in New Orleans at the invitation of the Catholic Church here.
>
> (Shaftel, 2006, n.p.)

Finally, some community members have exhibited navigational capital, or the knowledge and experience required to negotiate social institutions; second-generation children, because of their bilingual ability, out of necessity learned how to navigate bureaucracy related to education, housing, assistance, or and medical care in the United States for themselves and their parents. The second generation's navigational capital has been essential in assisting their family members in registering for government assistance, moving into and out of shelters, and locating housing. These forms of capital, although not material nor economic, nonetheless have tremendous value.

The disaster of Hurricane Katrina offers a basic tenet for future emergency preparedness planning: when technology and political processes break down, it comes down to human relationships. Communities with significant social and familial capital locally *and* nationally were better able to navigate the proportions of this disaster in the face of slow response on the part of local, state, and federal governments. The strong social networks combined with the recent historical memory of rebuilding lives in the United States equipped the Versailles Vietnamese-American community with the invaluable resource of hope that motivated residents' return and commitment to rebuild.

At the same time, one must understand the structural barriers that can prevent the flow and access of this capital. The media have reported that older African Americans may not have enough insurance to rebuild their homes in certain areas. The majority of African Americans in New Orleans were renters, and while these former residents may possess societal capital and the desire to return and rebuild the city, the lack of affordable rental units is a key issue in their return to Versailles and Village d l'Est in eastern New Orleans. Several interviewees said they would not return to New Orleans because they did not have hope for a better future there. Some may interpret this as a lack of fortitude; indeed, the model minority status bestowed upon the Vietnamese-American community could also be used to censure other communities. But just as the Vietnamese-American community's cultural wealth can only be understood within the historical specificity of that community's experiences, a closer focus on other communities will reveal the specific forms of cultural wealth they possess that may or may not prove effective in confronting equally historical societal barriers.

These societal barriers constitute an unnatural disaster, the true disaster that Katrina laid bare. Making visible this unnatural disaster that still divides the national community is essential. As feminist historian Gerda Lerner observed, if we believe patriarchy is the natural state of affairs, we then have no hope to create an alternate system in which women are equal to men (Lerner, 1986). Similarly, we must expose the lie of invisibility, expose these unnatural divisions amongst ourselves that we participate in every day, in order to truly achieve social justice for all.

References

Airriess, C. A. (2002). Creating landscapes and place in a Vietnamese community in New Orleans, Louisiana. In K. Berry and M. Henderson (Eds.) *Geographical identities of ethnic America: Race, place and space* (pp. 228–254). Reno: University of Nevada Press.

———. (2005). Scaling central place of an ethnic-Vietnamese commercial enclave in New Orleans, Louisiana. In D. Kaplan and W. Li (Eds.), *Landscapes of ethnic economies* (pp. 23–46). Lanham, MD: Rowman and Littlefield.

Allen, B.L. (2006). Environmental justice and after-disaster planning. Paper written for New Orleans, the Mississippi Delta, and Katrina—Lessons from the Past, Lessons for the Future conference. Center for Bioenvironmental Research, Tulane University, New Orleans. Retrieved June 7, 2006 from http://newdirections.unt.edu/katrina/meetings/marchpercent20readings/ Allen percent5B1%D.EJ.Disaster.

Aneshensel, C. S. & Sucoff, C.A. (1996). The neighborhood context of adolescent mental health. *Journal of Health and Social Behavior, 37*(2), 293–310.

Blank, R. M. (2005) Poverty, policy and place: How poverty and policies to alleviate poverty are shaped by local characteristics. *International Regional Science Review, 28*(4), 441–464.

Crenshaw, K. (1994). Mapping the margins: intersectionality, identity politics, and violence against women of color. In M. Albertson, Fineman and R. Miykitiuk (Eds.), *The Public Nature of Private Violence* (pp. 93–118), New York: Routledge.

Delgado, R. & Stefancic, J. (2001). *Critical race theory: an introduction.* New York: New York University Press.

Drier, P. (2006). Katrina and power in America. *Urban Affairs Review, 41*(4), 528–549.

Elliott, D. (Host). (2005, September 3). E-mail campaign leads to church rescue. *All Things Considered.* Washington, DC: National Public Radio.

Glaeser, E. L., & Vigdor, J. (2001). Racial segregation in the 2000 census: Promising news. Washington, DC: Center for Urban and Metropolitan Policy, The Brookings Institution.

Honda, M. (2006, May 24). Reps. to army corps of engineers: don't open New Orleans landfill [press release]. Retrieved July 5, 2006 from http://www.house.gov/list/press/ca15_honda/NOLANDFILL.html.

Joe, M. (2005, October 28). Resurrecting the Church after Katrina. *Asian Week.* Retrieved February 24, 2006 from http://news.asianweek.com/news/view_article.html?article_id=387b.

Lam, A. (2005, September 1). Dozens of Vietnamese Americans stranded outside of New Orleans (Trans.), *Saigon Broadcasting Television Network* [online]. Retrieved December 12, 2006 from http://news.Ncm online.com/news/view_article.html?article_id=52bda9eb48677e05a945d227365e6b22.

Leong, K (2006, March 18). Focus group with Vietnamese Americans relocated to Houston from New Orleans. Transcribed by Hanh Nguyen.

Lerner, G. (1986). *The creation of patriarchy.* New York: Oxford University Press.

Matsuda, M. (1997). *Where is your body? And other essays on race, gender, and the law.* Boston: Beacon Press.

McIntosh, P. (1988). *White privilege and male privilege: A personal account of coming to see correspondences through work in women's studies.* Wellesley, MA: Center for Research on Women.

Midlo Hall, G. (1992). The formation of Afro-Creole culture. In A.R. Hirsch & J. Logsdon (Eds.), *Creole New Orleans: Race and Americanization* (pp. 12–57). Baton Rouge, LA: Louisiana State Press.

Myers, L. and NBC Investigative Unit. (2006), September 26). Tossing trash, and taxpayer money, in Big Easy. MSNBC News. Retrieved September 27, 2006 from http://www.msnbc.msn.com/id/15017363/.

Pardo, M. S. (1998). *Mexican American women activists: Identity and resistance in two Los Angeles communities.* Philadelphia, PA: Tempe University Press.

Pham, V., Shull, S., Tranguyen, T. & Hoang, L. (2006, August). *Vietnamese Americans in hurricane-impacted gulf areas.* Washington, DC: National Congress of Vietnamese Americans.

Pope, J. (2006, September 3). East N.O. priest personifies resilience. *New Orleans Times Picayune.* Retrieved January 7, 2007 from http://www.nola.com/news/tp/frontpage/index.ssf?/base/news6/115726414841810.xml&coll=1&thispage=2.

Ross, C. E. & Mirowsky, J. (2001). Neighborhood disadvantage, disorder and health. *Journal of Health and Behavior,* 42(3), 258–276.

Shaftel, D. (2006, February 27). The Ninth Re-Ward. The Vietnamese community in New Orleans East rebuilds after Katrina. *Village Voice.* Retrieved February 10, 2007 fromhttp://www.villagevoice.com/news/0609, shaftel,72328,2.html.

Shenker, J. (2006, October 17). Nothing's simple in the Big Easy. *Spiked.* Retrieved March 21, 2006 from http://www.spiked-online.com/index.php?/site/article/1900/.

Seager, J. (2006). Noticing gender (or not) in disaster. *Geoforum,* 37(1), 2–3.

U.S. Census Bureau. (2000). U.S. Census 2000, Retrieved September 10, 2005 from http://www.census.gov/.

Webster, R. (2006, September 25). Tidal forces Tsunami recovery outpaces Katrina rebuild, N.O. delegates say. *New Orleans City Business.* Retrieved March 21, 2006 from http://www.neworleanscitybusiness.com/viewStory.cfm?recID=16819.

Yamada, M. (1976). *Camp notes and other poems.* San Lorenzo, CA: Shameless Hussy Press.

———. (1983). Invisibility is an unnatural disaster: Reflections of an Asian American woman. In C. Moraga and G. Anzaldúa (Eds.), *This bridge called my back: Writings by radical women of color* (pp. 35–40). New York: Kitchen Table Press.

————. (1988). *Desert run: Poems and stories.* Latham, NY: Women of Color Press.

Yosso, T.J. (2006). Whose culture has capital? A critical race theory discussion of community cultural wealth. *Race, Ethnicity, and Education.* 8(1), 69–91.

Zhou, M. & Bankston, C.L., III. (1994). Social capital and adaptation of the second generation: The case of Vietnamese in New Orleans. *International Migration Review, 28*(4), 821–845.

Chapter 11

Disaster Pornography: Hurricane Katrina, Voyeurism, and the Television Viewer

Benjamin R. Bates and Rukhsana Ahmed

Whenever disaster strikes, the news media seem to be the first to arrive. It seems that pictures of casualties and property loss emerge from the disaster zone before water, food, and emergency shelter go in. In the case of Hurricane Katrina in particular, the news media broadcast the destruction from the moment of landfall, well before the Federal Emergency Management Agency and National Guard were mobilized. Although the media were there first, what did their pictures tell the audience? In the broadcast images, survivors all too often lost their individuality, and the story became removed from the reality of suffering.

In media coverage of disaster, it becomes easy for us to detach ourselves from people whom we did not know. This choice between unification with others or detachment from others is the difference between what Buber (1970) calls an "I-Thou" relation and an "I-It" relation. In an I-Thou relation, we relate ourselves as a subject to other subjects we encounter. In an I-It relation, we instead relate ourselves as a subject to other people as objects. In disaster coverage, we too often enter into an I-It relationship to survivors. Instead of seeking a deep understanding of the other, media coverage allows us to observe the other from afar and keep ourselves out of moments of relationship with them as valued others.

The objectification of the other in images points to the contradictions inherent in reporting on disasters. Although Alexander (2000) asserts that vivid pictures "lend a strong sense of reality to events that otherwise would usually be remote in the minds of the public" (p. 139), the camera may work to bring survivors close to the viewer as objects instead of as subjects. Despite the limitations of media reporting, images of disaster frame public understanding. Because people come to know about "reality" as it is presented to them by media productions, Button (2002) states that the critical observer must note, "the role of framing in reproducing ideologies and reinforcing the privileged positions of authority" (p. 145). Media frames that emphasize an I-It relation can result in the perpetuation of existing inequities.

The need for a fully human portrayal of the other becomes particularly acute when the "visual objects" of the represented other are people who live on the lower rungs of the social ladder. In the case of Katrina, New Orleans was populated by mostly poor and mostly black people. If we consider media framing as "products of culture" (Button, 2002, p. 147) the *othering* of New Orleanians in the wake of Katrina can be looked as the perpetuation of hegemonic power. As such, natural disasters are more than social and physical disorders; they are politically grounded events (Button, 2002).

In this essay, we discuss images of disaster presented by the media in the United States. We begin by outlining the role of media in providing frames for current events. We then define the frame used by CNN and Fox News to report on Katrina in the first 72 hours after landfall, a frame we call "disaster pornography." Using this frame, we discuss the pornographic impulses in media coverage of Katrina. Finally, we offer some implications that disaster pornography has for social justice efforts and future disaster planning.

Media and the Framing of Disaster

Media play a significant role in public perception and public discourse. Media coverage of natural disasters such as Katrina becomes a form of political discourse as media outlets choose how to present information. Button (2002) describes such choices as media's "attempt to control the social production of meaning … to define reality in accordance with a favored political agenda" (p. 146).

Digital advancements have created an information society with implications for the practice of journalism (Herbert, 2000). News coverage now is more immediate, and live broadcasting from any location has become regular (Young, 1992). Because of new technologies, media play a significant role in dealing with crisis situations. Although coverage of crisis situations focuses on anguish and tragedy, the viewer should consider whether images of suffering capture newsworthy moments or serve opportunistic professional values. As argued by Christians, Fackler, Rotzoll, & McKee (2001), the "photographer should consider the moral guideline that suffering individuals are entitled to dignity and respect, despite the fact that events may have made them part of the news" (pp. 124–125).

The dilemmas media professionals face are related to a great extent to the ease by which their equipment can not only capture and transmit images, but can manipulate these images as well. Lester and Ross (2003) trace the problem of media framing at the individual level. They argue, "Journalists employ incomplete and unfair frames and stereotypes because they are people, and people often find it easier and more comfortable *not* to confront their ingrained stereotypes and prejudices" (p. 34). Iyer (2002) claims that there are two ways of regulating the actions of the press: statutory, or legal, regulation and voluntary self-regulation. She concludes that "self-regulation is by no means a guaranteed cure for the ills of bad journalism" (p. 2). Tester (1994), on the other hand, spotlights another form of regulation, regulation by audience members. He claims that "it is through the media that individuals become aware of their obligations and duties as people who uphold the right and who condemn the wrong" (p. 83). He further argues that media shape socio-cultural relationships such that, "media audiences are in the last instance so unconcerned about goodness or badness of what they see, do and like" (pp. 104–105).

To analyze media coverage of Hurricane Katrina, we consider the values employed and the kind of images constructed in this coverage. Rather than fulfilling a significant news function, we contend that media coverage of Hurricane Katrina was "disaster pornography." Moreover, instead of building an I-Thou relation between viewers and victims, this frame allowed viewers to encounter victims in an I-It relation. Although Katrina may have shocked the audience into pity, in the absence of proper information and critical knowledge, chances become slim for transforming that compassion into action for social justice.

Defining Disaster Pornography

Our focus in this essay is on the images in the televised media in the immediate aftermath of Katrina. By foregrounding the image, television introduces new forms of perception and suggests new ways to view society (DeLuca & Peeples, 2002). Presented images, though, are always partial; images are manipulated to tell a particular kind of story (Hariman & Lucaites, 2003). Nevertheless, images take on a sense of being reality and, thereby, affect our beliefs and actions. Moreover, emotionally powerful images—images that tap into basic human drives of fulfilling the desire for food, shelter and sex or of avoiding fear, pain, or death—can have particularly powerful effects (Ewen & Ewen, 1992). When these powerful images have been studied, it has been more popular to study images that appeal to erotic (pleasure/sex) drives than those that appeal to thanatotic (death/destruction) drives. Indeed, one of the most studied image sets is pornography as a representation of the erotic drive. Before we outline the parallels between pornography as an appeal to erotic drives and *disaster pornography* as an appeal to thanatotic drives, we have to first consider pornography.

Potter Stewart once wrote, "I shall not today attempt further to define the kinds of material" that are pornography, "but I know it when I see it" (*Jacobellis v. Ohio*, 1964). This idea that we know pornography when we see it provides an unclear standard for separating art from pornography. Drawing these lines became important in the mid-1900s because many states wanted to ban pornography, but not all depictions of sexuality. Rather than attempting to define pornography, the Supreme Court defined its offensive features. The central feature that could be regulated was *obscenity*. Warren Burger defined materials to be obscene based on three standards:

> (a) whether "the average person, applying contemporary community standards" would find that the work, taken as a whole, appeals to the prurient interest, (b) whether the work depicts or describes, in a patently offensive way, sexual conduct specifically defined by the applicable state law; and (c) whether the work, taken as a whole, lacks serious literary, artistic, political, or scientific value.
>
> (*Miller v. California*, 1973)

If the material is found to appeal to the prurient interest, depicts sexual conduct offensively, and lacks other value, then the material is judged to be pornographic and obscene. If the material does not meet any one of these three standards, then the work is not obscene.

Although many states initially regulated pornography because of concerns about public morality, more recent attempts to regulate have been based on pornography's social effects. Since the Attorney General's investigation of the effects of pornography in 1986, researchers have asked whether viewing pornography increases a man's likelihood to rape women or to accept other men's excuses regarding rape. Social scientific studies provide a mixed research record of the direct effects of pornography (Dines, Jensen, & Russo, 1988; Donnerstein, Linz, & Penrod, 1987; Linz & Malamuth, 1993; Segal, 1993). Although early meta-analyses claimed a clear connection between viewing pornography and these effects (e.g., Russell, 1993; Russell & Trocki, 1993; Silbert & Pines, 1993), later meta-analyses have concluded that there is no direct relationship (e.g., Fithian, 1999; Green, 1999; Simon, 1999).

More interesting may be the cultural effects of pornography. Dines, Jensen, and Russo (1988) argue that, rather than adopting "simplistic notions about how mass communication causes specific behavior," analysts "can think about how pornography cultivates certain views about sexuality" (p. 5). Pornography may not be about the sex, it may be about power (Cole, 1995). And, because most pornography is created by men, the power relationships depicted are ones where men decide when to have sex, what kind to have, and with whom (Clover, 1993; Linz & Malamuth, 1993). Thus, pornography naturalizes the view that men should be empowered and women should be subordinated, and men may hold concordant attitudes, all clear examples of I-It relations (Dworkin, 1989; Itzin, 1992).

Our view of pornography shapes our view of disaster coverage explicitly. We believe that the Katrina coverage is *disaster pornography*. Rewriting the standards from *Miller*, we define obscenity in disaster coverage with three standards: (a) whether the average person would find that the work, taken as a whole, appeals to the thanatotic interest; (b) whether the work depicts or describes, in a patently offensive way, disaster; and (c) whether the work, taken as a whole, lacks serious literary, artistic, political, or scientific value. Based on feminist work on sexual pornography, we define disaster pornography as depictions meeting these elements. Firstly, disaster pornography emphasizes the images of disaster. Such pictures offer sensory impressions and convey emotions that heighten the mediated confrontation with death and destruction. In the Katrina coverage, these images are at best cathartic, in their instantaneous production of emotion, and at worst superficial gloss, as these images require no understanding beyond the impression.

Secondly, we view these images as patently offensive when they are not properly contextualized. Disaster pornography displays the body of the other as an object. Although many people appear in the Katrina coverage, they are rarely engaged as interlocutors. Instead, survivors are displayed as objects—victims, refugees, looters—for the home viewer's consumption. Rather than treating them as humans in a relationship with viewers, viewers are encouraged to relate to the people of Orleans parish as subordinate humans or as "Its."

Thirdly, disaster pornography displays these objectifying images without providing additional literary, artistic, political, or scientific value in the disaster coverage. Throughout the first 72 hours of coverage, reporters referenced the lack of information and the lack of context for the images. By encouraging the viewer to watch the film without linking these images to a larger social setting, the reporting on Katrina obviated questions of social justice.

Finally, we believe that disaster pornography, when habitualized, can have the same kinds of negative effects as sexual pornography. In the case of Katrina, disaster pornography encouraged viewers to see themselves as safe and powerful, even as New Orleanians and others in the southern United States were seen as refugees and victims. The heightened exposure to Katrina did encourage donations to organizations like the Red Cross. This giving, however, was predicated on differences in relative power between the viewer and the victim. In this coverage, the viewer may see the "I" as safe and powerful, while "they" are endangered and weak. Yet, the compassionate response emerges when "they" are placed in greater danger and weakened so that "I" must help. Without disaster pornography's imagery to reproduce these power relationships, we question whether similar giving will occur and whether non-crisis fund-raising efforts will be undermined.

Analysis

In our analysis we focused upon the first 72 hours of Hurricane Katrina coverage as shown on CNN and Fox News. We chose to examine CNN and Fox

News for three reasons. First, although there are many news networks, CNN and Fox News have the largest market share of 24-hour news networks in the United States. The continuous coverage model they employ provides the largest scope of coverage. In addition, both networks have built their reputation on constantly updating their coverage, thus providing more possible variation than the more highly-rated, but less broad, coverage provided by the nightly news reports on ABC, CBS, and NBC. Last, as both CNN and Fox News transcripts were completely archived, the comparison of their framing on a specific topic during a specific period was feasible, whereas other news outlets were less completely archived.

Our analysis was conducted under the principles of frame analysis. News frames select "aspects of a perceived reality and make them more salient in communicating a text, in such a way as to promote a particular problem definition, causal interpretation, moral evaluation, and/or treatment recommendations" (Entman, 1993, p. 52). When a message producer's frames are identified, analysts can better understand how media structures messages and, in turn, can structure people's perceptions of those messages (Miller & Reichert, 2001). Although most frame analysis uses an inductive approach that seeks to identify all possible frames in a message (Gamson, 1992), the inductive approach is designed for description only. Because we viewed our role as critics as intervening in socially unjust situations toward constructing better practices, we employed deductive frame analysis. In a deductive approach, analysts begin by defining a frame (as we have done by defining disaster pornography) and then examine the news for the occurrence of this frame. Although this approach is less "objective" (Tian & Stewart, 2005) than others, it allows analysts to better serve as advocates for improved media practice.

Throughout the coverage of Katrina, loss of contextualization to create offensive portrayals, appeals to the thanatotic interest, and a lack of serious artistic, literary, political, or scientific value were common. Although these themes can be separated to define disaster pornography, they worked together in the coverage to emphasize emotionally intense images over the news functions of television reporting. We examined the language surrounding images of Katrina and closely studied the selected images to demonstrate the pornographic impulses of this coverage.

The emphasis on the images in the Katrina coverage was clear. Many reporters for both CNN and Fox News allowed the pictures to tell the story. Jeanne Meserve on CNN's *Situation Room* outlined the importance of the image in disaster stories. She stated, "I've seen hurricane destruction. I have stopped and said, 'Oh, my gosh, look at that building. We have to get a picture.'" But, during Katrina, there were too many images available. Meserve further stated, "Today, every building looked like that. There were cars smashed to smithereens. There were buildings that had totally collapsed. I have trouble coming up with the words to describe it" (Blitzer, 2005b). Despite

Meserve's difficulty in finding words to articulate the destruction she observed, words were unnecessary; the news stations had pictures. Fox's Molly Henneberg stated, "The pictures kind of tell the story of what happened on Canal [Street]" (Henneberg, 2005). Likewise, CNN's Paula Zahn portrayed the images as the whole story when she told viewers, "These pictures tell you everything you need to know" (Zahn, 2005).

In addition to the use of images as the story, the coverage of Katrina emphasized that the images were a shared experience. John Gibson (2005b) addressed the viewer directly on Fox News and said, "You have probably been seeing these really incredible pictures today." Fox's Sean Hannity and Alan Colmes (2005b) broadened the number of viewers who had seen the images by stating, "The entire world has been watching the dramatic and sad images today." Similarly, an exchange between CNN *Showbiz Tonight* hosts Karyn Bryant and A. J. Hammer (2005a) indicated that the collective experience of the images was one of awe at the power of the hurricane:

> HAMMER: What we are about to show you is so dramatic it's almost hard to believe it's real. We're talking about the frightening images of the aftermath of Hurricane Katrina.
>
> BRYANT: Those images had millions of people watching in absolute amazement today as it all unfolded on TV.

This collective experience was one in which the viewer was expected to have an intense emotional response. Bryant and Hammer (2005b) reported on a web poll about the hurricane coverage. The poll asked viewers "Are the images affecting you?" Hammer stated, "Not surprisingly, 84 percent of you say, yes, the images are affecting you; 16 percent of you somehow say they are not." The implicit judgment was that the majority response was natural and that the minority response—being unaffected—was likely pathological. There was, apparently, a "correct" way to respond to the images of devastation.

The coverage focused on the emotive power of the image. Bill O'Reilly (2005) of Fox News noted that "the thing about television is it captures images that are indelible, and Katrina supplied plenty of those." CNN's Anderson Cooper (2005a) similarly stated, "There have been so many extraordinary images … I wanted to bring you some of the most poignant, the most remarkable, the most dramatic images that we experienced." And, should the viewer not be affected, the reporters ensured that these images would draw on thanatotic drives. Throughout the coverage, newscasters promised the viewers more connections to death and destruction. Eight hours after Katrina made landfall, Soledad O'Brien (2005a) on CNN's *American Morning* stated, "You see those pictures and of course, it [the death toll] will [rise]. Those homes are obliterated. They're blown off the map essentially. I think that that's a very fair guess that we're going to see those numbers rise and maybe even very significantly." Fox News's Greta Van Susteren (2005b) told her viewers, "we see these horrible pictures, and we do know that the death count is going to grow." Even if these images did not affect the viewer, Van Susteren, O'Brien, and others each pointed to the possibility of more death that the viewer could see later.

As if simple death was not enough, the thanatotic drive is heightened by associating these images with other scenes of destruction. Miles O'Brien on *American Morning* was the first to compare Hurricane Katrina to the tsunami of December 2004. He held that the aftermath of Katrina was "truly a dramatic scene. The mayor of Biloxi calling it 'our tsunami.' And when you look at the damage and when you look at those pictures, it does seem apt" (O'Brien, 2005a). Given that both the tsunami and the hurricane were natural disasters, the comparison may have been appropriate. O'Brien, in a later broadcast, claimed that the images of Katrina reminded him "of some of the pictures that you see in the wake of, say, Hiroshima in World War II, devastation. Block after block of home, every single home destroyed" (O'Brien, 2005b). Both the tsunami and Hiroshima were outside of the United States. To bring the hurricane closer to home, Robert Thompson told CNN, "Certainly as a nation, [we] have gotten very used to seeing some really, really disturbing images over the past several years. In real life, September 11th, and as well as in our movies and entertainment." In response, *Showbiz Tonight* host Karyn Bryant noted that "all week long, journalists have been bringing you the surreal images of the devastation and destruction in the wake of Hurricane Katrina" (Bryant & Hammer, 2005b). The real and the surreal are collapsed here; the strangeness and otherness of massive destruction are tied into the collective experience of viewing television.

The difficulty with the images is not that they were shown, but that the images were shown as if they told the complete story. Typical of the emphasis on image over information was an exchange between CNN's *Situation Room* host Wolf Blitzer (2005b) and field reporter Jack Cafferty. Blitzer told his viewers, "I just want to walk over and show our viewers these pictures. These are live pictures coming in from New Orleans, right over there, live pictures of a fire underway in the French Quarter." After Blitzer showed the images, he then asked Cafferty for perspective. Jack Cafferty was unable to provide any context; he stated, "I just keep wondering, Wolf, when we're going to come to work and have a day where we can say, OK. Now we understand how big the story is. I don't think we're there yet. And I don't know when we're going to get there." The magnitude of the story was clear. Just what that story was—that story's significance—was not as clear.

The images took on additional significance in that they displaced the news function of televised media. To use the terms of the theory of uses and gratifications (Smith, Wright, & Ostroff, 1998), the entertainment function of the coverage—i.e., the disaster pornography—overwhelmed the surveillance function—i.e., meaningful information about the hurricane. In the best cases, images were supplemented with information by voiceovers. More commonly, the images of disaster pornography replaced information entirely. CNN's Aaron Brown (2005) introduced a segment by stating, "The first stories will be exactly that, they'll be the first stories. I think we'll get a much better, broader and more relevant picture when we piece together a lot of stories, which we'll do in the next hours and certainly in the next day." Minutes later, Brown said, "Just as we have the last few nights, we want to take a moment to show you some of the more powerful pictures that have emerged from this ever-growing story. The still photos that will be in our minds a long time to come." Brown's words portray the images as complete, but the stories as incomplete.

Images can implicitly substitute for stories and emotive pictures can replace useful information. Indeed, this substitution is made explicit in the post-Katrina coverage. When Fox's John Gibson (2005c) spoke to field reporter Jeff Goldblatt it became clear that field reporters were fulfilling the entertainment function of news, not the surveillance function:

> GIBSON: We have had pictures of them up on that bridge, out in the heat, with no water, no sanitation facilities. Is there any word that they're actually getting some help now?
>
> GOLDBLATT: I'm not sure, because I'm in a communication bubble right here. I have no communication all day. This is my primary means of talking to people.

Although Goldblatt was on the bridge and could have spoken to the people directly, Goldblatt's function was not to obtain information but to obtain images. More disturbing was that the field reporter relied on the New York production studio to obtain information about what was happening on the very bridge upon which he stood. The disinterest in the individuals on the bridge as meaningful informants and the interest in them as objects to show on television indicate the pornographic operation in the Katrina coverage. Moreover, the reporter was able to get to this bridge in the Lower Ninth Ward, but the reporter appears to have provided no assistance. The story in this report is markedly incomplete, and these people are not given the opportunity to tell their story.

The interest in image over information led to an imbalance in the coverage. The newest and most graphic pictures were displayed without interpretation. Indeed, this imbalance was so extreme that, in some cases, information was dismissed when it contradicted the images. An exchange between Sean Hannity of Fox News and Louisiana Attorney General Charles Foti is telling:

> HANNITY: These images of looting have literally shocked a nation. How bad is it?
>
> FOTI: I flew over that area myself today. And there was very few people on the street at the time I flew over. But we will aggressively …

> HANNITY: Can I interrupt you, Charles? You seem to be minimizing it, but the images that we have and that we've been showing, do not really back up what you're saying (Hannity & Colmes, 2005a).

Foti, an eyewitness, reported that there was little looting. Hannity, ensconced in his studio in New York, relied on images. The images may not have been representative. In addition, the same images were shown repeatedly, even though there may not have been additional looting. Foti recognized the limits of his observation, but Hannity did not recognize similar limits. Instead, Hannity claimed that the images were more real than Foti's direct observations.

These images were offered as a way to observe the effects of Katrina. The images not only displaced information, they also sought to encourage reaction to the scenes of destruction. This propensity was addressed by Anderson Cooper (2005b) when he said, "I know it's frustrating, when you're sitting in your home, you see these images, you want to do something. We're putting on the screen now a number of organizations you can contact to help." Similarly, Daryl Kagan (2005) told viewers, "You can read eyewitness accounts of Katrina at cnn.com/hurricane. You can also check out storm images and find a list of aid organizations, whether you're looking for help or looking to help yourself." Viewers were told that, to respond to the images of destruction, they should contribute to aid organizations. Both CNN and Fox News added telephone numbers and websites of aid organizations to their screen crawls and closed nearly every segment of their coverage with this contact information. This naturalization of a response—see destruction, give money—may have allowed these aid organizations to obtain more funds than they would have without the promotion by news organizations.

Giving money was not the only response to the disaster generated by the images shown on the news. Another response was to use laughter as a defense mechanism. A conversation between Andy Serwer and Soledad O'Brien (2005b) shows how images sometimes hindered appropriate responses. Serwer had obtained an image of an oil rig that had washed ashore. Given the disruption of oil supplies by the hurricane, the ability of oil companies to recover equipment was a significant story. Yet, the newscasters' own words indicate that the emotional potential of the image overwhelmed their ability to responsibly report:

> SERWER: No oil company has yet claimed it. We don't know—seriously. No one knows whose rig that is.
>
> O'BRIEN: We're laughing …
>
> SERWER: Truly remarkable.
>
> O'BRIEN: … but that's not—that's not even funny.
>
> SERWER: It's terrible. It's unbelievable what's going on.

The attempt to retain a reportorial stance failed; CNN had to cut to commercial to allow their newscasters to recover. There are several possible responses to any image, but as the thanatotic impulse is heightened without meaningful context or consequential information, a response that makes it unnecessary to see events as real becomes more likely. But, when the only responsible response to the image is to give money, the viewer may see donating to aid organizations much as they do buying a movie ticket. As long as one pays for the image, even images of destruction become mere entertainment.

Concluding Remarks

In this essay, we have problematized the U.S. media portrayal of disaster images in the first 72 hours following Hurricane Katrina. We have defined the frame used by CNN and Fox News to report on Katrina as "disaster pornography." After watching the first 72 hours of news coverage, the viewers could not consider themselves "well-informed." People watched the natural disaster for information *and* entertainment. We believe disaster coverage too often draws on thanatotic drives. As a result, consumers of media content can fall victim to voyeurism. As "visual images are products of our sense of sight, not our cognition" (Lester & Ross, 2003, p. 1), overused and misused visual images can result in short-term and short-sighted reactions to events, instead of creating public memory that could motivate efforts toward social justice.

The voyeuristic potential of watching the hurricane was enhanced by CNN's and Fox News's reliance on the framework of disaster pornography. Moreover, this coverage was obscene under our definition of disaster pornography. The flooded streets, floating corpses, and devastated homes and businesses promoted an interest in death and destruction. This wreckage, in the first 72 hours at least, was shown without reference to a larger context, making these images patently offensive. Moreover, because this lack of context or other added value, the images lacked other merit that would justify the continuous portrayal of fatality and ruin. Finally, the habitualization of these portrayals through their comparison to other images of destruction—the Asian tsunami, the Hiroshima bombing, and the like—may have normalized the thanatotic impulse. When combined, this disaster pornography encouraged seeing New Orleanians and others as "Its" to be watched, rather than "Thous" to be valued.

The barrage of disaster images was disturbing. Yet, this coverage kept the audience detached from the event by highlighting "moving" stories and disregarding survivors' efforts to tell their own stories. We argue that this dehumanizing media coverage denies the dignity of the survivors by their portrayal as "voiceless victims." The more the audience view these disparate images, the more likely viewers are to get locked inside a "fantasy world" with uninterrupted access to media outlets and their seemingly infinite supply of material to feed the viewers' thanatotic drives. Thus, disaster pornography continues to diminish humanity and compassion. Viewers of the Katrina coverage do not need to comprehend the causes and implications of disaster because they become addicted to a perverted form of reality television. The viewer should be wary of these pornographic modes of coverage. Media coverage should alert the world about massive humanitarian disaster. Yes, showing death and casualty are parts of this information. What the media should avoid, however, is voyeurism.

As with any pornography, the "visual" loses his/her humanity and is removed from reality. We argue that disaster pornography has implications for efforts related to social justice and disaster planning. No one can explain the cost of Katrina in three minutes of television, but everyone can relate to powerful images. Nevertheless, the images become problematic when death and casualty become the only way to establish an event's currency. Moreover, charitable trust does not gain from the stream of funds that are released only in the wake of public concern. Pornographic images of Hurricane Katrina do not provoke sustained inquiries into systems that allow disaster to have its maximal impact and that could be reformed to prevent future disasters.

Based on the above arguments, if we acknowledge media's role in forming a global civil society and in communicating messages about social justice, we as conscious audience members have to question how disaster is framed for the home television viewer. As we have discussed, pictures seem to entertain the audience to keep them interested in the "story." Audience members should consider the balance of information and images in disaster coverage, the breadth and depth of disaster coverage, and the ways that disaster coverage shapes their attitudes toward and beliefs about the survivors of disaster. Media professionals should consider whether their reportage encroaches upon the humanity of the survivors, uses the anguish of survivors as entertainment, or sensationalizes the image of disaster. Lastly, media critics should consider how disaster coverage in media aids in raising awareness of disasters and efforts to respond in their immediate aftermath, as well as the ways that disaster coverage undermines survivors' humanity, self-respect, and dignity as a matter of social justice.

References

Alexander, D. (2000). *Confronting catastrophe: New perspectives on natural disasters.*Oxford: Oxford University Press.

Blitzer, W. (Host). (2005a, August 30). *The Situation Room.* Atlanta: Cable News Network.

Blitzer, W. (Host). (2005b, August 31). *The Situation Room.* Atlanta: Cable News Network.

Brown, A. (Host). (2005, August 31). *CNN Newsnight*. Atlanta: Cable News Network.

Bryant, K., & Hammer, A. J. (Hosts). (2005a, August 30). *Showbiz Tonight*. Atlanta: Cable News Network.

Bryant, K., & Hammer, A. J. (Hosts). (2005b, August 31). *Showbiz Tonight*. Atlanta: Cable News Network.

Buber, M. (1970). *I and thou* (W. Kaufmann, Trans.). New York: Touchstone.

Button, G. V. (2002). Popular media reframing of man-made disasters: A cautionary tale. In S. M. Hoffman & A. Oliver-Smith (Eds.), *Catastrophe & culture* (pp. 143–158). Santa Fe, NM: School of American Research Press.

Christians, C.G., Fackler, M., Rotzoll, K. B., & McKee, K. B. (2001). *Media ethics: Cases and moral reasoning* (6th ed.). New York: Longman.

Clover, C. J. (1993). Introduction. In P. C. Gibson & R. Gibson (eds.), *Dirty looks: Women, pornography, power* (pp. 1–4). London: British Film Institute.

Cole, S. G. (1995). *Power surge: Sex, violence & pornography*. Toronto: Second Story.

Cooper, A. (Host). (2005a, August 29). *Anderson Cooper 360*. Atlanta: Cable News Network.

Cooper, A. (Host). (2005b, August 31). *Anderson Cooper 360*. Atlanta: Cable News Network.

DeLuca, K. M., & Peeples, J. (2002). From public sphere to public screen: Democracy, activism, and the "violence" of Seattle. *Critical Studies in Media Communication*, 19, 125–151.

Dines, G., Jensen, R., & Russo, A. (1998). *Pornography: The production and consumption of inequality*. New York: Routledge.

Donnerstein, E., Linz, D., & Penrod, S. (1987). *The question of pornography: Research findings and policy implications*. New York: Free Press.

Dworkin, A. (1989). *Pornography: Men possessing women*. New York: Dutton.

Elliot, D. (2003). Moral responsibilities and the power of pictures. In P. M. Lester & S. D. Ross (Eds.), *Images that injure: Pictorial stereotypes in the media* (pp. 7–14). Westport, CT: Praeger Publishers.

Entman, R. (1993). Framing toward clarification of a fractured paradigm. *Journal of Communication*, 43(4), 51–58.

Ewen, S., & Ewen, E. (1992). *Channels of desire: Mass images and the shaping of American consciousness*. Minneapolis: University of Minnesota Press.

Fithian, M. A. (1999). Importance of knowledge as an expert witness. In J. Elias, V. D. Elias, V. L. Bullough, G. Brewer, J. J. Douglas, & W. Jarvis (Eds.), *Porn 101: Eroticism, pornography, and the First Amendment* (pp. 117–136). Amherst, NY: Prometheus.

Gamson, W. A. (1992). *Talking politics.* New York: Cambridge University Press.

Gibson, J. (Host). (2005b, August 30). *The big story with John Gibson.* New York: Fox News.

Gibson, J. (Host). (2005c, August 31). *The big story with John Gibson.* New York: Fox News.

Green, R. (1999). Pornography: The expert witness. In J. Elias, V. D. Elias, V. L. Bullough, G. Brewer, J. J. Douglas, & W. Jarvis (Eds.), *Porn 101: Eroticism, pornography, and the first amendment* (pp. 105–116). Amherst, NY: Prometheus.

Hannity, S., & Colmes, A. (Hosts). (2005a, August 30). *Fox Hannity & Colmes.* New York: Fox News.

———. (Hosts). (2005b, August 31). *Fox Hannity & Colmes.* New York: Fox News.

Hariman, R., & Lucaites, J. L. (2003). Public identity and collective memory in U.S. iconic photography: The image of "accidental" napalm. *Critical Studies in Media Communication, 20,* 35–66.

Henneberg, M. (Host). (2005, August 29). *Special coverage: Hurricane Katrina pounds New Orleans.* New York: Fox News.

Herbert, J. (2000). *Journalism in the digital age: Theory and practice for broadcast, print and online media.* Oxford: Focal Press.

Itzin, C. (1992). *Pornography: Women, violence, and civil liberties.* Oxford: Oxford University Press.

Iyer, V. (2002). Media ethics: Obedience to the unenforceable. In V. Iyer (Ed.), *Media ethics in Asia: Addressing the dilemmas in the information age* (pp. 1–8). Singapore: AMIC, SCI, NTU.

Jacobellis v. Ohio, 378 U.S. 184 (1964).

Kagan, D. (Host). (2005, August 31). *CNN Live Today.* Atlanta: Cable News Network.

Lester, P. M. & Ross, S. D. (Eds.). (2003). *Images that injure: Pictorial stereotypes in the media.* Westport, CT: Praeger.

Linz, D., & Malamuth, N. (1993). *Pornography.* Newbury Park, CA: Sage.

Miller v. California, 413 U.S. 15 (1973).

Miller, M. M., & Riechert, B. P. (2001). The spiral of opportunity and frame resonance: Mapping the issue cycle in news and public discourse. In S. D. Reese, O. H. Gandy, & A. E. Grant (Eds.), *Framing public life: Perspectives on media and our understanding of the social world* (pp. 107–122). Mahwah, NJ: Lawrence Erlbaum Associates.

O'Brien, S. (Host). (2005a, August 30). *American Morning.* Atlanta: Cable News Network.

O'Brien, S. (Host). (2005b, August 31). *American Morning*. Atlanta: Cable News Network.

O'Reilly, B. (Host). (2005, August 31). *The O'Reilly Factor*. New York: Fox News.

Russell, D. E. H. (1993). Pornography and rape: A causal model. In D. E. H. Russell (Ed.), *Making violence sexy: Feminist views on pornography* (pp. 120–150). New York: Teachers College Press/Columbia University.

Russell, D. E. H., & Trocki, K. (1993). Evidence of harm. In D. E. H. Russell (Ed.), *Making violence sexy: Feminist views on pornography* (pp. 194–216). New York: Teachers College Press/Columbia University.

Segal, L. (1993). Does pornography cause violence? The search for evidence. In P. C. Gibson & R. Gibson (Eds.), *Dirty looks: Women, pornography, power* (pp. 5–21). London: British Film Institute.

Silbert, M. H., & Pines, A. M. (1993). Pornography and sexual abuse of women. In D. E. H. Russell (Ed.), *Making violence sexy: Feminist views on pornography* (pp. 113–119). New York: Teachers College Press/Columbia University.

Simon, W. (1999). The social scientist as expert witness. In J. Elias, V. D. Elias, V. L. Bullough, G. Brewer, J. J. Douglas, & W. Jarvis (Eds.), *Porn 101: Eroticism, pornography, and the first amendment* (pp. 137–144). Amherst, NY: Prometheus.

Smith, F. L., Wright, J. W., & Ostroff, D. H. (1998). *Perspectives on radio and television: Telecommunication in the United States*, 4th ed. Mahwah, NJ: Lawrence Erlbaum.

Tapsall, S. & Varley, C. (2001). *Journalism: Theory in practice*. Melbourne: Oxford University Press.

Tester, K. (1994). *Media, culture and morality*. New York: Routledge.

Tian, Y., & Stewart, C. M. (2005). Framing the SARS crisis: A computer-assisted analysis of CNN and BBC online news reports of SARS. *Asian Journal of Communication, 15*, 289–301.

Van Susteren, G. (Host). (2005a, August 29). *Fox On The Record with Greta Van Susteren*. New York: Fox News.

———. (Host). (2005b, August 30). *Fox On The Record with Greta Van Susteren*. New York: Fox News.

Young, P. (1992). *Defence and the media in time of limited war*. London: Frank Cass.

Zahn, P. (Host). (2005, August 29). *Paula Zahn Now*. Atlanta: Cable News Network.

Chapter 12

Access to Mediated Emergency Messages: Differences in Crisis Knowledge across Age, Race, and Socioeconomic Status

Kenneth Lachlan, Patric R. Spence, and Christine Eith

Introduction

Hurricane Katrina made contact with the Gulf Coast on August 29, 2005, moving across New Orleans and causing arguably the worst natural disaster in United States history. The city's failing levy system was largely to blame for the flooding and damage that ensued (Adams, 2005). By September 12 an estimated 400,000 Katrina evacuees had relocated to shelters, hotels, homes and other housing in 34 states. There were well over 1000 documented fatalities (Kearney, 2006), though the exact death toll may never be calculated. U.S. government estimates concerning the cost of the cleanup and recovery have checked in at around $87 billion (Bazinet, 2006).

A crisis can be defined as "a specific, unexpected, and non-routine event or series of events that create high levels of uncertainty and threaten or are perceived to threaten" high priority goals (Sellnow, Seeger, & Ulmer, 2002, p. 233). These goals may include the protection of life and property, or more general concerns for the preservation of individual and community well-being. Natural disasters have received less attention from those studying crisis messages than other types of crises, such as organizational and political scandals. Likely reasons for their omission include their precipitation by natural processes, their geographically centered nature and their severe impact on large groups of people (which often renders data collection difficult or impossible) (Kreps, 1984; Quarantelli, 1978; Sellnow et al., 2002). Furthermore, all natural disasters do not have the same outcome; some may impact a local community while others will affect a much larger population. How the message is transmitted, and to whom, varies a great deal across disasters. Given the above challenges, scholars have largely ignored the study of crisis messages during natural disasters and instead have focused their efforts on organizational crises, which tend to be more predictable and follow less variable development patterns.

In events such as hurricanes and other natural disasters, issues of crisis communication intersect with those of risk communication. Risk communication can be defined as the exchange of information between interested parties concerning the nature, significance, probability, and possible prevention of a risk (Coombs, 1999; Seeger, Sellnow, & Ulmer, 2003). These messages are disseminated in the time before individuals are likely to be affected by an undesirable event, such as a hurricane or other predictable disaster. This differs from crisis communication in that crisis communication is typically thought of as occurring in the wake of an undesirable event. While crisis communication aims to reduce negative outcomes associated with a crisis, risk communication messages are intended to encourage the receiver to engage in proactive behaviors ahead of time to avoid threats and negative consequences (Seeger et al., 2003).

Of course, crisis and risk communication messages can only effectively meet these high profile goals if they reach their intended audience and effectively inform them. The Knowledge Gap hypothesis (Tichenor, Donohue, & Olien, 1970, p. 159) states that "segments of the population with higher socioeconomic status tend to acquire this information at a faster rate than lower status segments," putting the underprivileged at a disadvantage when information acquisition is critical. Knowledge gaps have been found between the wealthy and the poor in dozens of empirical studies dealing with subject matter as varied as public affairs, science, and health information (Viswaneth & Finnegan, 1995). Of particular note, one study (Kahlor, Dunwoody & Griffin, 2004) examining environmental risk found socioeconomic status to be significantly related to knowledge acquired concerning an outbreak of a water-borne parasite in a local water supply. This particular study suggests that knowledge gaps may exist in public health crises, a proposition with grave consequences in circumstances such as those surrounding Hurricane Katrina.

At no time in recent memory has the plight of the underclass been illustrated as profoundly as it was during Hurricane Katrina. This chapter aims to outline exactly what information was available to those whom found themselves in the midst of Hurricane Katrina—the New Orleans evacuees who were removed from their homes and relocated to other parts of the country. A discussion of crisis communication and the Knowledge Gap hypothesis is offered, followed by an analysis of interview data from Katrina evacuees in the Houston Astrodome and in relief centers in Lansing, Michigan and Cape Cod, Massachusetts. The findings include the importance of information seeking for participants, the type of information they sought out, the ways in which they found out about the evacuation, the perceived adequacy of the information provided through the media and other channels, and preparations taken by Katrina victims before the storm made landfall. The findings are framed as evidence of knowledge gaps among the underprivileged during Katrina and are offered in the hope that they may help us understand ways to avoid a repeat of the massive loss of life and property witnessed during Katrina.

Crisis Communication Basics

A discussion of the role of risk communication practitioners in alleviating fear and providing behavioral advice in the face of Hurricane Katrina must begin with a discussion of the theoretical and definitional criteria surrounding crisis and risk communication. Weick (1995) defines crisis scenarios as "low probability/high consequence events that threaten the most fundamental of goals of the organization. Because of their low probability, these events defy interpretations and impose severe demands on sensemaking" (p. 305). Because crises such as natural disasters are by definition non-routine events, they lead to an increase in uncertainty, fear, and stress among those who stand to be affected.

Research in social psychology posits that individuals are fundamentally motivated to seek resolution, certainty, and the return of predictability to their surroundings (Berlyne, 1960). The need to seek information for the purposes of reducing uncertainty is especially strong during natural disasters, when the potential outcomes of the crisis may be extremely harmful (Heath & Gay, 1997) and almost completely uncontrollable (Miller, 1987). The problem is that information gathering is not equally distributed among the population affected by a crisis.

Historically, crises have been typified as beginning with a clear trigger event indicating the beginning of the crisis. However, in the case of a slowly emerging crisis such as Katrina, a clear and dramatic trigger (such as planes hitting the towers on 9/11) may not be immediately apparent, and realization of the existence of the crisis may evolve over several days as information is accumulated. In the absence of a clear trigger event, the official declaration or general realization of a crisis will typically be interpreted as an indication that events are inconsistent with routine events and procedures and are moving in an unpredictable and threatening direction.

Individuals then tend to seek out information to resolve the uncertainty proposed by the newly identified crisis (Brashears et al., 2000; Lachlan, Spence & Seeger, 2009). Media outlets, such as television and radio, are typically the main source of this information (Murch, 1971), as the news media have long been considered valuable and timely sources of crisis information (Heath, Liao, & Douglas, 1995), particularly at a local level. The fundamental need for information under crisis circumstances requires that related information must be organized, highly specific, and distributed through local news media available to those who need the information most: those directly affected and at risk.

Knowledge Gap Hypothesis

While source considerations are relevant to the construction of effective crisis messages, they may also be a source of message failure if not addressed correctly. In addition, there may be some segments of the population for whom crisis messages meet these goals, and other segments for which they may not. The plausible result amounts to subpopulations who have not received adequate information, have not been appropriately aroused in terms of hazard perceptions and motivation to respond, and/or who may not be aware of pragmatic steps to take to avoid negative consequences.

If there is a traceable relationship between socioeconomic status and those who have not had access to appropriate crisis messages, there may be evidence of a knowledge gap process. The following paragraphs briefly explain the fundamental tenets of knowledge gap, offer potential indicators of knowledge gap in terms of crisis knowledge during Katrina, and pose questions of examining these differences in awareness and response across age, race, and socioeconomic status.

The Knowledge Gap hypothesis was first forwarded by Tichenor, Donohue, and Olien (1970). Examining several sets of longitudinal data, and assuming education level to be an indicator of socioeconomic status, the original research in this area demonstrated differences over time in terms of the amount of knowledge acquired regarding public affairs. Data gathered by the American Institute of Public Opinion revealed that over time, the college-educated acquired more knowledge concerning satellite technology, the NASA lunar program, and the link between smoking and cancer than their less educated contemporaries.

The watershed study on knowledge gaps also offered evidence of knowledge differences occurring at a static time point. Tichenor et al. (1970) offered evidence of this process, using data from a previous study concerning public knowledge of a newspaper strike (Samuelson, 1960). In addition to a difference in knowledge across education levels, a difference emerged between knowledge in a community in which the strike had been publicized and a community in which it had not. In short, the knowledge gap was more pronounced in communities with a high level of media coverage, suggesting that those of higher status and education may have more access to or interest in mediated messages concerning the event.

Tichenor et al. (1970) were quick to offer some potential mediators in this relationship. First, they suggested that communication skills are a critical consideration, as those with better reading ability should be able to access critical information more easily than those with less developed reading skills. Second, they noted that relevant social contact may be important, as those with interpersonal exposure to issue-relevant information may still be able to obtain knowledge. Third, selective exposure is a factor, as attitudinal differences may drive people toward or away from different information sources. Fourth, pre-existing knowledge may be an important consideration. Finally, the nature of the medium may play a role in this process, as the level of detail and intellectual sophistication tends to be much higher in print media than in electronic media. Regardless, they pointed out that all five of these factors, while important moderators, are likely related to socioeconomic status. They offered that those in lower economic strata may have reduced communication and comprehension skills, have fewer social contacts with detailed information, be less interested in news and information, have less pre-existing issue knowledge, and are less likely to pursue intellectual demanding media (e.g., newspapers and magazines) than those in higher economic strata. Based on this and other data, they offer the following formal hypothesis:

> As the infusion of mass media information into a social system increases, segments of the population with higher socioeconomic status tend to acquire this information at a faster rate than the lower status segments, so that the gap in knowledge between these segments tends to increase rather than decrease.

> (Tichenor, Donohue, & Olien, 1970, pp. 159–160)

In the thirty-six years since the Knowledge Gap hypothesis was originally offered, over 70 studies have produced findings that support its contention that there are differences in issue-relevant knowledge between those in the higher and those in the lower socioeconomic strata (Viswaneth & Finnegan, 1996). For the most part, these studies have attempted to identify additional mediating variables in the knowledge gap process, such as personal interest in the subject matter (Bailey, 1971), motivation to seek information on the subject (Ettema & Kline, 1977), level of concern (Lovrich & Pierce, 1984), and training in public affairs (Griffin, 1990). Fewer have attempted to explicate differences in knowledge gap processes across different types of information, such as information about crisis or public health concerns. Of particular note, is a study in which Kahlor, Dunwoody, and Griffin (2004) attempted to explain knowledge gap processes in the midst of a parasitic infestation of the drinking water in Milwaukee, Wisconsin.

Based on open-ended survey data, Kahlor, Dunwoody, and Griffin (2004) attempted to examine differences in knowledge concerning the source of the parasitic outbreak and the effect it had on the body when ingested. Their findings generally supported knowledge gap processes. Those of a high education level reported more acquisition and understanding of information related to what effect the parasite would have on people than did respondents with a limited education. In addition, respondents of a high socioeconomic status were more aware of information concerning how the parasite got into the water in the first place than those respondents of a lower socioeconomic status.

Although Kahlor, Dunwoody, and Griffin (2004) offered limited insight into knowledge gap processes in one highly specified instance, their findings do give us pause when considering potential outcomes of crisis messages during Hurricane Katrina. If knowledge gaps do occur in crisis scenarios, the question then manifests as to what critical information may have been unavailable to the vulnerable and underclass populations. Given the well documented accounts of the vulnerable populations, including the elderly and urban poor, who were killed, injured, relocated, or otherwise adversely affected by the storm, one can only wonder what took place in terms of access to and comprehension of emergency messages.

Based on this supposition, the current chapter offers insight on knowledge gap processes that may have occurred among those victimized by Katrina. Using self-report data (see Spence et al., 2008), it aims to examine differences across age, race, and socioeconomic status in terms of the information-seeking patterns (i.e., types of information that were sought out), primary sources of information, message accuracy, and crisis preparation. The results are then framed with an eye toward improving future risk communication efforts in order to better serve the underprivileged in times of crisis.

Evacuees and Their Experiences

Some, after evacuating the greater New Orleans area for other cities along the Gulf Coast, initially stayed in campgrounds, hotels, or with strangers. Homeless and in need of food, water, and proper shelter, they were relocated en masse to different parts of the country. Following the evacuation, surveys were administered to Katrina evacuees who had been relocated to shelters in Cape Cod, Massachusetts, Lansing, Michigan, and federal aid distribution centers throughout Texas. The participants were 86 percent African American, 6 percent Caucasian, and 8 percent other ethnicity. The sex split was 67 percent female and 33 percent male. Some 68 percent of respondents reported a gross household income of less than $25,000 a year (see Table 12.1). A total of 554 usable surveys were collected. The surveys included items pertaining to information-seeking behaviors, crisis preparation, media identified as primary sources information, and perceived message adequacy.

An important caveat should be made concerning the sample. The nature of a natural disaster prohibits a more rigorous scientific sampling technique to be employed shortly after the event. Although this sample was not random, comparisons to U.S. Census data indicate that the sample was representative of New Orleans. However, even with the similarity between the present sample and census data, the current data may be in danger of over-representing both the poor and individuals that were least prepared for the onset of Hurricane Kat-

Table 12.1 Sample Demographics

Age	Frequency	Valid %	Cumulative %
<25	108	20.1	20.1
26–30	92	17.2	37.3
31–35	75	14.0	51.3
36–40	52	9.7	61.0
41–45	52	9.7	70.7
46–50	61	11.4	82.1
51–55	44	8.2	90.3
56–60	23	4.3	94.6
61–65	12	2.2	96.8
66+	17	3.2	100.00
Missing	18		
Total	554		

Sex	Frequency	Valid %	Cumulative %
Male	178	32.6	32.6
Female	368	67.4	100.00
Missing	8		
Total	554		

Race	Frequency	Valid %	Cumulative %
African-American	468	86.2	86.2
Caucasian	34	6.1	92.4
Other	41	7.4	100.00
Missing	11		
Total	554		

Income	Frequency	Valid %	Cumulative %
<$10,000	171	37.7	37.7
$10–15,000	60	13.2	51.0
$15–20,000	31	6.8	57.8
$20–25,000	48	10.6	68.4
$25–30,000	22	4.9	73.3
$30–35,000	24	5.3	78.6
$35–40,000	28	6.2	84.8
$40–45,000	19	4.2	89.0
$45–50,000	5	1.1	90.1
$50–60,000	19	4.2	94.3
$60–75,000	14	3.1	97.4
$75–100,000	5	1.1	98.5
$100,000+	7	1.5	100.00
Missing	93		
Total	554		

rina. Because the data was collected over a longer period of time, and in diverse geographic locations, it allows for the potential of a more representative sample of evacuees. However, the risk of sampling bias still exists and readers are cautioned concerning the generalizability of the findings to larger populations.

Information Seeking Prior to the Storm

Ten Likert items on the survey addressed information-seeking patterns. Respondents were asked to indicate what types of information were most important to them from among the categories of information related to: the scope of the damage, government responses to the crisis, food and water distribution, evacuation, shelters, rescue operations, the larger impact of the storm, who was affected, friends and family, and where to get healthcare or medication. An index score across all items was also computed by taking the mean score across all ten items, in order to produce a measure of general information seeking (α = .93). This score demonstrates the general importance placed on information seeking across a range of topics.

Primary Information Sources

Respondents were also asked to indicate how they first learned of the evacuation procedures from among ten categories of information sources. These sources included face-to-face interaction with friends/acquaintances, face-to-face interaction with a stranger, a telephone call, written notice, notification by an official (such as a police officer), the radio, the television, newspapers, the Internet, e-mail, or other.

Crisis Preparation

In order to assess possible negative outcomes that would be associated with a knowledge gap process, two items measured the participants' preparations for the storm. The first measured proactive preparations in the home, and asked, "Before the hurricane, did you prepare an emergency kit or emergency supplies?" The second tapped into evacuation plans by asking, "Did you have any escape or preparation plan at all in mind this hurricane season?" Participants were asked to answer yes or no for each question.

Message Adequacy

Respondents' impressions of media message accuracy were measured along a five-point scale ranging from "very adequate" to "very inadequate." The scale

Table 12.2 Linear Regression Analyses

Demographic Predictors of Information Seeking, Perceived Message Adequacy, Understanding, and Perceived Accuracy
Standardized Regression Coefficients for Demographic Predictors

Predictor	Model 1 (Information Seeking)	Model 2 (Message Adequacy)	Model 3 (Understood Message)	Model 4 (Perceived Accuracy)
Age	.033	.017	-.035	.044
Sex	.117**	.036	.123***	-.064
Race	.098*	.088	.093**	.069
Income	.034	.112**	-.046	.087
F	3.26**	3.04**	3.66***	1.54
R^2	.030	.030	.039	.005

* p<.05, ** p<.01, *** p<.001

addressed information concerning subjects such as, the scope of the damage, the government response, and food and water distribution. The mean score across these items was once again calculated as an indicator of general perceived accuracy, $\alpha = .95$. Additional single items addressed whether participants felt they received adequate information from officials and clearly understood what to do.

Analyses

Age, sex, race, and income were entered into a linear regression model aimed at predicting the value for the information-seeking index score in order to explore the demographic differences in information-seeking behavior. Women and African Americans reported slightly higher index scores for aggregate information seeking than other categories of respondents, perhaps indicating that these populations are less likely to seek additional information (see Table 12.2).[1]

A series of one-way ANOVA analyses further examined differences across race in terms of information-seeking patterns. The results reveal significant differences for information about food and water, and information about shelter. African Americans were more likely than subjects who were neither African American nor Caucasian to seek out information concerning food and water,

---

1. The aggregate information seeking index was computed by averaging the individual information-seeking items. These items were reversed scored; thus in the index higher scores equate to less information seeking.

Table 12.3 Oneway ANOVA Analyses

Race Differences in Information Importance

Information Category	African American	Caucasian	Other	F	p<
Scope of damage	1.33	1.24	1.47	.614	n.s.
Government response	1.44	1.65	1.75	2.11	n.s.
Food/water distribution	1.46[a]	1.78	1.86[a]	3.90	.020
Evacuation	1.51	1.84	1.82	2.71	n.s
Shelters	1.57[b]	2.00[b]	1.85	3.19	.040
Rescue operations	1.51	1.46	1.56	.080	n.s.
Larger impact	1.55	1.80	1.54	.856	n.s.
Others affected	1.33	1.50	1.37	.588	n.s.
Friends and family	1.21	1.24	1.42	1.35	n.s.
Healthcare	1.53	1.58	1.51	.038	n.s.

Note: Matched pairs in superscript significantly different at p<.05
Items were reverse scored; lower means indicate greater perceived importance

and were more likely than Caucasians to seek out information about shelter. Again, the implication here is that this information may not have been readily available to African-American hurricane victims, thereby forcing them to actively seek out this information on their own (see Table 12.3). Sex differences across these items were also examined using mean comparisons. Women generally placed greater importance than men on information concerning food and water, evacuation, shelter, rescue efforts, the larger impact of the storm, who else was affected, friends and family, and locating healthcare or medicine (see Table 12.4).

The data in Tables 12.3 and 12.4 provide some initial information on differences in the types of information desired between sex and race. Consistent with past research (Seeger et al., 2002; Spence et al., 2005, 2006) women appear to be more concerned with socially positive responsibilities such as food and water distribution and shelter. Men indicated having the most concern over issues of response and scope of the damage. In regards to race, notable differences emerge in terms of the desire for knowledge concerning food and water distribution and heath care. These results suggest that future research should focus more closely on these differences in the creation of messages. It should also be noted that it may be advantageous to target more pro-social messages about basic needs to women, as there are data to suggest they may be looking for this information which could then reduce the harm and duration of the crisis.

To explore differences in perceptions of message adequacy, a series of regression analyses were performed on the dependent variables perceived adequacy, perceptions of information from officials, and the extent to which re-

Table 12.4 T-Tests for Mean Comparisons

Sex Differences in Information Importance

Information Category	Men	Women	t	p<
Scope of the damage	1.36	1.33	.443	n.s.
Government response	1.66	1.40	2.65	.008
Food/water distribution	1.76	1.41	3.67	.001
Evacuation	1.80	1.45	3.35	.001
Shelters	1.89	1.51	3.61	.001
Rescue operations	1.74	1.40	3.45	.001
Larger impact of storm	1.72	1.49	2.20	.028
Who was affected	1.52	1.26	3.07	.001
Friends and family	1.33	1.17	2.27	.024
Healthcare/medicine	1.68	1.47	2.05	.040
Other	1.55	1.91	1.01	n.s.

Note: Items were reverse scored; lower means indicate greater perceived importance

spondents reported understanding what to do under the circumstances. Independent variables included demographic variables (age, sex, race, and income) and the extent to which participants relied on varying media.

Overall adequacy. For the perceived adequacy index, income predicted general perceptions of message adequacy, with poorer respondents reporting lower levels of perceived adequacy than wealthier respondents (see Table 12.2). Reliance on different media proved not to be an important factor in understanding crisis messages, as only sex and race were detected as significant predictors of understanding. Caucasians and men reported that they had a clearer understanding of what to do than did non-Caucasians and women, again indicating differences across race and sex in the effectiveness of crisis messages.

Crisis preparation. Given the demographic differences in perceived message adequacy, outrage responses, and information-seeking patterns, we conducted a series of logistical regression analyses that explored the possibility that message inadequacy manifested itself in a lack of preparation for the storm (see Table 12.5 for details). Significant results were detected, as age, race, and income were found to predict whether or not a respondent had an emergency kit available. Regression coefficients indicated that older respondents, those in *higher* income brackets, and African Americans were less likely to have such a kit available than other respondents. Additional chi-squared analyses also confirmed the finding that African Americans (43.6 percent) were less likely than Caucasians (57.6 percent) or others (60.0 percent) to have an emergency kit.

Similar analyses were repeated for the presence of a hurricane evacuation plan in case of a hurricane or other emergency. Entering demographic infor-

Table 12.5 Logistical Regression Analyses

Demographic Predictors of Preparations Taken Before the Storm
Exp (B) functions for Demographics

Predictor	Model 1 (emergency kit)	Model 2 (evacuation plan)
Age	.989***	.973***
Sex	.857	1.05
Race	.606**	.776
Income	.935*	.919***
Nagelkerke R^2	.100	.080
χ^2	32.29***	25.05***

* p<.05, ** p<.01, *** p<.001

mation and income into the predictor block produced a significant overall model. The demographic variables of age, and income were found to predict whether or not respondents had a plan in place, as older respondents and those in *higher* income brackets were less likely to have developed an evacuation plan than younger respondents and those in lower income brackets.[2]

Discussion

This study provides insight on the impact that ineffective communication of crisis messages had on victims of Hurricane Katrina. At first glance, the sample of displaced victims tells a particularly important story. Almost 90 percent of the displaced victims were African American, over two-thirds were women, and just over two-thirds reported living around or below the poverty line. When Wilson (1987) spoke of the predominant issues among the "underclass," he was expressly addressing joblessness, low levels of education, and increasing social isolation, all of which are key components of the Knowledge Gap hypothesis. Social isolation is reinforced as neighborhood poverty grows and contact between diverse groups becomes more and more limited, possibly explaining the finding that these subpopulations are less likely to report seeking additional information. When an individual experiences social isolation, the likelihood that s/he has the social ties to seek additional information from a non-media source is low. The underclass is the forgotten population, often in-

---

2. These findings contradict the Knowledge Gap hypothesis and may be related to the fact that our sample consisted solely of people residing in shelters. See the Limitations section for further discussion.

visible to the public and policy makers even during a time of crisis. Further-more, previous research has found that racial and ethnic minorities are less likely to accept a risk or warning message as credible without confirmation of the message from others, causing a delay in response time (Fothergill et al., 1999; Lindell & Perry, 2004; Spence et al., 2007). As the findings of this study suggest, if there is a desire for social justice, government and crisis manage-ment teams should address the method by which crisis information is trans-mitted to the populations in jeopardy.

At the point at which these individuals reached crisis, African Americans were found to be more likely to seek information concerning necessary provi-sions such as food, water and shelter than were others. In the affected areas, African Americans were over-represented in the socially isolated underclass and probably forced to seek out information instead of having the informa-tion provided to them. There are a number of possible explanations for this finding, but the most likely would be that the lack of resources translated into further isolation from society and the mediated message. These members of society do not have the resources to purchase needed provisions for a disaster of this proportion, much less to flee the city and their homes. This suggests that in times of crisis the first wave of emergency responders should focus on those areas inhabited by the underclass. These individuals are not receiving effective messages about the crisis at hand, and are limited in their access to provisions. As witnessed in the Katrina disaster, those in the most need of as-sistance were living in the most vulnerable areas. Perhaps because they be-lieved that the levy breach was not imminent, the scope of the disaster caught emergency professionals off-guard. When the crisis situation emerged the vul-nerable members of society were further isolated from resources, necessities, and communication. They were left alone to experience their outrage and the anomie that ensued was forever captured on the front pages of national news-papers and television.

It was clear that Caucasians and males received the crisis messages in a clear and understandable fashion, while members of minority populations as well as women found the messages to be largely ineffective. The question that remains asks how to best improve crisis and risk communication to ensure that all populations in the area affected by a disaster are addressed. This study provides some insight into the breakdown in communication. It is clear from these findings that emergency communication must be transmit-ted through more than one message and in more than one medium. In a so-ciety where racism and structural inequality is pervasive, it is naïve to assume that one centralized crisis message will be transmitted to an entire popula-tion and effectively inform the actions of the least privileged members of our society.

Conclusion

With crises becoming more common and more severe it is important to learn from the victims of Hurricane Katrina. Effective communication is a key element in understanding how to most appropriately prevent, prepare, respond to, and learn from risks and crises. However, when populations are unable to access information for preparation and prevention message elements become secondary. The relationship between the Knowledge Gap hypothesis and crisis preparation needs further examination. Results clearly support the view that African Americans and the working class and poor were less likely to be prepared and have an evacuation plan or general preparations than others in the affected population, which can be attributed to isolation from information. These results are similar to findings in past studies (Gladwin & Peacock, 1997) and seem to suggest that the issues may go beyond the construction of crisis communication messages and require continued risk campaigns targeting subpopulations.

Current messages (such as those available on http://www.Ready.gov) are very general and appear to be undifferentiated in terms of target audiences. Risk messages are often parts of larger communication campaigns and use combinations of radio, television and print to distribute messages. These campaigns are funded by federal government grants, non-profit organizations or community action groups that have an interest in the goals of the campaign. Often the messages in these campaigns are quite general, focused on reducing a risk behavior in the overall population. Even more specific programs such as D.A.R.E. (Cudill, 1995) or the Social Norms Campaign (Smith, Atkin, Martell, Allen, & Hembroff, 2006) are useful but still have a focus on a broader group (such as teenagers or college students). Campaigns such as these do not examine differences within that population with the goal of tailoring messages based on such differences. Further, differences in audience responses associated with race and socio-economic status are given even less attention.

Future campaigns should focus on providing preparation knowledge before the triggering of a crisis event and further educate subpopulations regarding knowledge acquisition during a crisis event (see Lachlan & Spence, 2007). This requires placing mediated messages in targeted areas. For example, differences exist between African Americans and Caucasians in television viewing habits. One study (Initiative Media, 2003) found that African Americans watched more television at 76.8 hours per week compared to the 53.1 hours per week average of Caucasians. Furthermore, there were differences in programming preference, as 14 of the top 20 top-ranked programs among African Americans did not score in the top 100 shows watched by Caucasians. It is critical that these and other differences in patterns of media use across subpopulations be taken into consideration when designing and implementing risk and crisis communication campaigns. Although the study of media placement alone will not solve larger social issues of inequality, neither will a simple implementation of uniform message campaigns. The findings do, however, provide a place to begin efforts reduce this knowledge gap.

Limitations

While the findings of the current study shed an important light on knowledge gap processes that may have taken place during Katrina, no study is without its limitations. The data was collected over an uneven timeframe; a portion of the participants responded hours after evacuation, others days, and some after weeks. This is a result of the complex and time-consuming process of locating and interviewing hurricane evacuees. Future efforts should seek to obtain audience responses at one time point, and as quickly as possible, in order to reduce the likelihood of hindsight bias and memory distortion in the responses. Although researchers should strive for the most scientific methods of data collection, it is often unrealistic to have the opportunity to obtain IRB approval, test an instrument, and obtain the means to employ a robust sampling plan immediately after a crisis. Further, the current results are useful in application to different types of crisis scenarios and distribution of information; however, caution should be used when making such decisions. The knowledge gap and information needs will likely vary from crisis to crisis, and while the findings of the current study are informative they are by no means definitive of all crisis events.

Three Years Later: Hurricane Ike

Hurricane Ike was the third most destructive hurricane to make landfall in the US.

Ike was a storm of great interest not only because of its size and destructive potential, but because of memories of the devastation associated with Hurricane Katrina two years earlier. In an attempt to explore whether or not things had changed on the ground, the current authors surveyed 691 Houston area residents in the aftermath of the storm (Spence, Lachlan, & Burke, 2009). The results are somewhat mixed. Replicating identical analyses for the impact of socioeconomic status on information seeking or level of preparation failed to reveal differences. Detectable differences were still found for other demographic strata. In fact, further analyses revealed differences between the sexes and between Caucasians and African-Americans in terms of information seeking and specific informational needs, in a pattern almost identical to that indicated in this study. While there was some evidence of a narrowing of a literal knowledge gap, there is still evidence that some communities may be underserved in times of crisis and that the need for differentiated messages must be explored further.

References

Adams, S. (2005). Learning the lessons of Katrina for the unexpected tomorrow. *Risk Management, 52*(12), 24–30.

Bailey, G.A. (1971). The public, the media, and the knowledge gap. *Journal of Environmental Education, 2,* 3–8.

Bazinet, K. (2006, February 3). $18B more sought for Katrina rebuild. *Daily News* (New York), p. 6.

Berlyne, D.E. (1960). *Conflict, arousal, and curiosity.* New York: McGraw-Hill.

Brashears, D. E., Neidig, J. L., Haas, S. M., Dobbs, L.K., Cardillo, L.W., & Russell, J. A. (2000). Communication in the management of uncertainty: The case of persons living with HIV or AIDS. *Communication Monographs, 67*(1), 63–84.

Coombs, W. T. (1999). *Ongoing crisis communication: Planning, managing, and responding.* London: Sage.

Cudill, S. K. (1995). *D.A.R.E.: A success story.* Central, SC: Southern Wesleyan University.

Ettema, J. S. & Kline, F. G. (1977). Deficits, differences and ceilings: Contingent conditions for understanding the knowledge gap. *Communication Research, 4,* 179–202.

Fothergill, A., Maestas, E. G. M., & Darlington, J. D. (1999). Race, ethnicity, and disasters in the United States: A review of the literature. *Disasters, 23*(2), 156–173.

Gladwin, H. & Peacock, W. G. (1997). Warning and evacuation: A night for hard houses. In W. G. Peacock, B. H. Morrow, & H. Gladwin (Eds.) *Hurricane Andrew: Ethnicity, gender and sociology of disasters* (pp. 52–74). London: Routledge.

Griffin, R.J. (1990). Energy in the eighties: Education, communication, and the knowledge gap. *Journalism Quarterly, 67,* 554–566.

Heath, R.L. & Gay, C.D. (1997). Risk communication: Involvement, uncertainty, and control's effect on information scanning and monitoring by expert stakeholders. *Management Communication Quarterly, 10,* 342–72.

Heath, R. L., Liao, S., & Douglas, W. (1995). Effects of perceived economic harms and benefits on issue involvement, information use and action: A study in risk communication. *Journal of Public Relations Research*, 7, 89–109.

Initiative Media. (2003). African American television viewing study. New York: Initiative Worldwide.

Kahlor, L.A., Dunwoody, S., & Griffin, R.J. (2004). Accounting for the complexity of causal explanations in the wake of an environmental risk. *Science Communication*, 26(1), 5–30.

Kearney, S. (2006, January 22). Is it too soon to party? *The Houston Chronicle*, p. 1.

Kreps, G. A. (1984). Sociological inquiry and disaster research. In R. E. Turner & J. F. Short, Jr. (Eds.), *Annual Review of Sociology* (pp. 309–330). Palo Alto, CA: Annual Reviews.

Lachlan, K. A., Spence, P. R., & Seeger, M. W. (2009). Terrorist attacks and uncertainty Reduction: Media use after September 11th. *Behavioral Sciences of Terrorism and Political Aggression*, (1).

Lachlan, K. A., & Spence, P. R. (2007). Hazard and outrage: Developing, validating, and testing a psychometric instrument in the aftermath of Katrina. *Journal of Applied Communication Research*, 35, 109–23.

Lindell, M.K. & Perry, R.W. (2004). *Communicating environmental risk in multiethnic communities*. Thousand Oaks, CA: Sage.

Lovrich, N.P. & Pierce, J.C. (1984). Knowledge gap phenomenon: Effects of situation specific and trans-situational factors. *Communication Research*, 11, 415–434.

Miller, S. M. (1987). Monitoring and blunting: Validation of a questionnaire to assess styles of information seeking under threat. *Journal of Personality and Social Psychology*, 52, 345–353.

Murch, A. W. (1971). Public concern for environmental pollution. *Public Opinion Quarterly*, 35, 100–106.

Perry, R. W. (1985). *Comprehensive emergency management: Evacuating threatened populations*. Greenwich, CT: JAI Press.

Quarantelli, E. L. (1978) *Disasters: Theory and research*. Beverly Hills, CA: Sage.

Samuelson, M. E. (1960). Some news-seeking behavior in a newspaper strike. Unpublished dissertation: Stanford University.

Seeger, M. W., Sellnow, T., & Ulmer, R. R. (2003). *Communication and organizational crisis*. Westport, Connecticut: Praeger.

Seeger, M. W., Vennette, S., Ulmer, R. R., & Sellnow, T. L. (2002). Media use, information seeking and reported needs in post crisis contexts. In B.S. Greenberg (Ed.), *Communication and terrorism* (pp. 53–63). Cresskill, New Jersey: Hampton Press, Inc.

Sellnow, T., M. Seeger & Ulmer, R. R. (2002). Chaos theory, informational needs and the North Dakota floods. *Journal of Applied Communication Research*, 30, 269–292.

Smith, S., Atkin, C., Martell, D., Allen, R., & Hembroff, L. (2006). A social judgment theory approach to conducting formative research in a social norms campaign. *Communication Theory*, 16, 141–152.

Spence, P. R., Lachlan, K. A., & Burke, J. M. (2008). Crisis preparation, media use, and information seeking: Patterns across Katrina evacuees and lessons learned for crisis communication. *Journal of Emergency Management*, 6 (2), 11–23.

Spence, P. R., Lachlan, K. A., & Burke, J. M. (2009). *Differences in crisis knowledge across age, race, and socioeconomic status: Hurricane Ike.* Unpublished manuscript: Calvin College.

Spence, P. R., Lachlan, K. A., & Griffen, D. (2007). Crisis communication, race and natural disasters. *Journal of Black Studies*, 37, 539–554.

Spence, P., Westerman, D., Skalski, P., Seeger, M., Ulmer, R., Venette, S., & Sellnow, T. (2005). Proxemic effects on information seeking following the 9/11 attacks. *Communication Research Reports*, 22, 39–46.

Spence, P., Westerman, D., Skalski, P., Seeger, M., Ulmer, R., & Sellnow, T. (2006). Gender and age effects on information seeking following the 9/11 attacks. *Communication Research Reports*. In Press.

Tichenor, P. J., Donohue, G. A., & Olien, C. N. (1970). Mass media flow and differential growth in knowledge. *Public Opinion Quarterly*, 34, 159–170.

Viswaneth, K. & Finnegan J. R., Jr. (1996). The knowledge gap hypothesis: Twenty-five years later. *Communication Yearbook*, 19, 187–227.

Weick, K. (1995). *Sensemaking in organizations.* Thousand Oaks, CA: Sage.

Wilson, W.J. (1987). *The truly disadvantaged: The inner-city, the underclass, and public policy.* Chicago: University of Chicago Press.

Chapter 13

Discrimination, Segregation, and the Racialized Search for Housing Post-Katrina*

Jeannie Haubert Weil

My own experience as a Katrina evacuee led me into this project so I'll begin this chapter with a short personal story. Before the hurricane, my husband and I were living in a little town on the Mississippi Gulf Coast called Pass Christian. Few people had ever heard of it before the storm, but it has gotten a good bit of attention since as it was one of the coastal towns almost completely wiped off the map. Our house was about 3 blocks from the Gulf before Katrina, and about 3½ blocks from the Gulf after Katrina since the storm surge actually lifted the house off of its foundation and deposited it in a neighboring yard! Upon looking at the ravaged neighborhood, we concluded that the houses on our street and all their contents must have floated around like beach balls until the water retreated. It was an amazing sight with dead fish and demolished houses in the middle of the streets, couches stuck in trees, and dogs wandering around wondering where home was now. Like so many others, we too began wandering, looking for some place to go. We were displaced for about a month and a half until we eventually found rental housing in southern Alabama.

As evacuees, we traveled from Mississippi to northern Louisiana and then over to southern Alabama. People in these areas treated us with overwhelming kindness and generosity. Complete strangers gave us free haircuts, discounted dinners and car repairs, and one exceptional family even gave us a free furnished vacation

*Acknowledgments: I would like to thank my introductory sociology class at Tulane University's Mississippi campus for their substantial contributions to the data collection portion of this project. Not only did the class help with the survey design, but each of the following students also called or e-mailed numerous housing volunteers to interview them and/or conducted content analyses of the advertisements. Many thanks to Juanita Bundy, Michael Carle, David Dale, Gregory Dedeaux, Kristina Hanck, Robert (Ben) Lassiter, Jason Lebeau, Yolanda Martin, Kimberly Matthews, Becky McMillan, Natalia Silver, and Billy Yates.

223

rental apartment for as long as we needed. We found the apartment on an Internet site that offered vacation rentals at a discounted price to Katrina evacuees. All of the individuals we contacted on the site offered us a place to stay at little or no charge. The generosity was truly moving and that one act of kindness gave us time to get ourselves together and develop a plan for moving forward.

Paradoxically, at the same time we were experiencing such generosity, we were also on the receiving end of numerous bigoted and disparaging remarks about evacuees of color, often by the same people who were helping us out. Racist jokes, generalizations about African-American evacuees and crime, and repeated rental agent comments about the racial makeup and the desirability of neighborhoods eventually led us to wonder how much of our speedy recovery was attributable to the privileges and sympathies afforded to us based on our white skin color. If our e-mails inquiring about housing had been signed, "Sincerely, Jamal and Tanisha," would we have had the same experience? Out of curiosity, I began searching around on the Internet, looking at ads placed by everyday individuals offering free or discounted housing for evacuees. I searched their ads for key terms such as white, black, race, and color. To my surprise and horror, I found many housing offers that contained comments such as, "whites only" or "not racist, but my town is all-white." The following is the research project that ensued.

Introduction

Hurricane Katrina was a national crisis of unparalleled proportions that glued people around the world to their television sets to witness firsthand the destruction brought about by one of Mother Nature's most powerful forces. As the hurricane left hundreds of thousands of people without homes, meals, and jobs, thousands more responded with an outpouring of goodwill. In an unprecedented demonstration of generosity, thousands of people from all over the U.S. offered to take complete strangers into their homes until they could get back on their feet; but in some cases, there was a catch. Some housing providers were only willing to house evacuees of a particular race. On an individual level, such discriminatory actions may seem forgivable as many people can empathize with selectivity opening one's home to strangers; however, on a larger level, it *is* highly problematic when race is used as a proxy for whether one is a desirable candidate for charitable giving. Cumulatively such acts reinforce and perpetuate physical and racial segregation resulting in important social inequalities.

A large body of evidence exists that suggests that racial and ethnic housing discrimination is a significant contributor to the high degree of racial residential segregation in the United States. Individual acts of discrimination are detrimental not only for individuals—where they can be psychologically damaging, can affect opportunities to accumulate wealth, and can significantly raise the costs of housing searches—but they are also damaging at the group and societal levels where cumulative acts of housing discrimination contribute to larger systems of social inequality. Numerous sociological studies demonstrate that where one lives affects his/her social networks, role models, educational opportunities, employment opportunities, and propensity for exposure to crime, poverty, and other social ills (see Jargowsky, 1996; Wilson, 1987). Individually, these consequences represent disadvantages, but cumulatively they result in seriously limited life-chances and large racial and ethnic gaps in socioeconomic attainment. In that housing discrimination systematically denies qualified minorities access to housing and high quality neighborhoods, such discrimination is intimately connected to the formation and reproduction of racial stratification in U.S. society. This stratification is not an inherent characteristic of the structure of the housing market; rather it is produced and reproduced on an everyday basis by individual actors.

The driving question for this study is: how do individuals who discriminate on the basis of race account for their actions? This study is focused on post-Katrina housing offers, but may also be useful in understanding the rationales that housing market agents employ in deciding whom to rent to, whom to sell to, and where individuals of various racial and ethnic backgrounds should and should not live. Most importantly, understanding why people say they discriminate is useful in understanding the way race continues to operate as a fundamental axis of differentiation in our society bestowing privileges on some groups while denying those privileges to other groups.

It is important to note that the racially exclusive housing offers examined in this study came from both urban and rural areas in all regions of the country, and that given the total number of housing offers the proportion of blatantly discriminatory ads was relatively small. That does not mean however that only a small proportion of evacuees were discriminated against in the weeks and months after the storm. In fact, using quasi-experimental methods, one study found that *black* Katrina evacuees were discriminated against in 66 percent of their attempts to acquire rental housing in states near the disaster area (NHFA, 2005). Why might many evacuees of color have experienced discrimination while the proportion of discriminatory housing offers was relatively small? This is because overt statements of racial exclusion are unpopular, and therefore, uncommon in the current post-civil rights era. Instead, housing discrimination today usually takes a much more subtle form as when a minority home seeker is very politely lied to and told that an advertised housing unit has already been occupied. While it is important to understand the scope of racial discrimination in housing, the focus of this study is not on what proportion of people discriminate nor on what types of people discriminate; rather it is an examination of *why* people say they discriminate.

To be clear, a majority of the housing ads did not contain discriminatory wording; in fact, many specified in their ads that all races were welcome. Further, many of the discriminatory ads excluded evacuees for reasons other than race (for example, some providers specified religious, familial status, and gender preferences all of which are arguably illegal under the Federal Fair Housing Act). Thus, the following are only a sub-sample of posted housing offers. Nonetheless, we know that race-based discrimination continues to be a problem in the housing market; therefore this is an important project because it provides a unique opportunity for researchers to better understand the rationales behind racially discriminatory behavior.

I began this project as a content analysis of a website wherein everyday individuals could post offers to house Katrina evacuees. Later a group of interviewers followed up with short interviews with some of those housing providers. The following is an analysis of the text of eighty-one discriminatory housing ads and seventeen interviews with the housing providers in the spring of 2006. The analysis produced several important findings, namely that negative media portrayals of *black* evacuees, the perceived intersection of race and class, and current residence in a racially segregated community all contributed to housing providers' decisions to place racially-exclusive housing offers.

Racetalk and Accounts

This examination of how people talk about race is one of several studies of its kind, but it is the first to study rationales for racial discrimination through an analysis of talk. Other studies of what Bonilla-Silva and Forman call "racetalk" included interviews with college students exploring their views on affirmative action and other controversial race topics (Bonilla-Silva & Forman, 2000), and interviews with restaurant servers wherein they discussed stereotypes of good and bad customers (Mallinson & Brewster, 2005).[1] They note that, "Since the civil rights period, it has become common for whites to use phrases such as 'I am not a racist, but ...' as shields to avoid being labeled as racist when expressing racial ideas. These discursive maneuvers or *semantic moves* are usually followed by negative statements on the general character of minorities (e.g., 'they are lazy,' 'they have too many babies')" (Bonilla-Silva & Forman, 2000, p. 50). These authors argued that how people talk about race has shifted from overt expressions of distaste for cer-

---

1. See also Bonilla-Silva, Lewis & Embrick (2004), Eliasoph (1997), and Scott (2000).

tain racial groups to more covert racial arguments that are still rooted in ideologies of racial superiority.

In their study of restaurant servers, Mallinson and Brewster (2005) also examined expectations for interactions with members of other social groups along the lines of race and class. In addition to racetalk they also introduced the concept of "regiontalk" whereby class-based stereotypes of "white-trash" and "hillbillies" become salient in server-client interactions. The data I will present below suggest that in the case of Katrina evacuees, racial *and* regional stereotypes intersect to shape the willingness of housing providers to assist evacuees of color. I use the framework of "accounts," to understand how people excuse and justify excluding groups from their offers on the basis of skin-color.[2]

When there is a mismatch between societal expectations and one's behavior, individuals often give what Scott and Lyman (1968) called "accounts" to rationalize socially deviant behavior. Accounts are similar in nature to explanations; however, accounts are given when the actions are more serious and might damage the reputation of the actor (Scott & Lyman, 1968, p. 47). Individuals give accounts for their behavior in a wide variety of social situations. For example, previous studies of accounts detailed how convicted rapists appeal to forces outside of their control to excuse or justify their deviance (Scully & Marolla, 1984). Others study illicit drug users' accounts for their behavior (Weinstein, 1980). In the context of race in the United States, and especially in the context of charitable giving, the societal expectation is that race should not be a factor in determining who is eligible for housing, nor should it factor into charitable giving. In fact, in the context of housing, stating a racial preference is illegal.[3] Thus, in this study, housing providers gave accounts to explain their racial preferences despite societal expectations that people, especially charitable givers, be colorblind.

There are two distinct categories of account giving, excuses and justifications (Scott & Lyman, 1968). Excuses can be understood as rationalizations in which an individual recognizes that his or her behavior is wrong, but *denies full responsibility* for the act, as with a soldier who admits that killing is wrong, but denies responsibility because he was acting under orders. In contrast, a social actor who gives a justification to explain his or her behavior *accepts responsibility* for the act in question, but *denies that the act is wrong* as with a soldier who

---

2. This is similar and related to C. Wright Mills' idea of *vocabularies of motive* (Mills, 1940).

3. Such acts are illegal according the Fair Housing Act as Amended, 42 U.S.C. §3604(c). Although Fair Housing agencies arguably could have filed complaints against the individuals who placed the ads detailed in this chapter, the agency who did file chose instead to sue the organizations who published the discriminatory housing offers on the internet.

admits to killing, but claims that the act was not immoral because members of the enemy group deserve their fate.

Data and Methods

Using one of the most popular websites that contained housing offers for Katrina victims, I systematically searched for ads containing key words such as: white, race, color, black, African American, Mexican, Hispanic, Asian. Because almost no ads used the terms Mexican, Hispanic, or Asian, the study was necessarily limited to a binary, black/white conception of race. I found nearly three hundred ads that used these terms to convey various racial messages, from inclusion of all groups, to exclusion. A discussion of all ads containing racial messages is beyond the scope of this chapter however and shall be reserved for later analysis.

The research strategy for this project was as follows. First, I searched all of the ads on this particular website for key words relating to race. Second, I selected those ads that contained racially exclusive text for analysis. Third, I selected racially exclusive ads that provided contact information for interviewing.[4] After the various selection and elimination processes, sixty-two housing providers remained in the sample for interviewing.

Students in my introductory sociology class, men and women who lived on the Gulf Coast and had been evacuees, conducted the interviews. Students who did not wish to make phone calls were permitted to survey respondents via e-mail or conduct content analyses. Since recent linguistics research shows that, over the phone, individuals are able to make a positive ethnic identification more than 80 percent of the time simply based on the word "hello" (Purnell, Isardi, & Baugh, 1999), and because the race of the interviewer is likely to affect the responses that the interviewee gives, callers were matched racially to the stated preferences of the housing providers. In other words, I matched white students with housing providers who stated that they preferred whites, and black students with housing providers who stated that they preferred blacks. Because fewer offers stated a preference for blacks, I instructed black students and one student with a discernable foreign accent to use e-mail and a "racially neutral name" to contact the housing providers.

Because the students were evacuees, and because they presented themselves to interviewees as interested in learning more about charitable givers, respon-

---

4. I omitted those ads in which the contact information was listed as "private" indicating that the evacuee could post a response on the website, but not e-mail or call the housing provider directly.

dents generally welcomed their inquiries. In fact, of those respondents that were reached, only four declined to participate in the study. The interviews consisted of six short questions, one of which was the key question of study. After a scripted introduction and a series of "warm up questions" the students were instructed to ask the following question: "A lot of people have preferences for particular types of people that they would like to help. I noticed that you stated that you prefer to house evacuees of a particular race. Can you tell me more about that decision?" They were also instructed to probe for more depth responses once the respondent had completed his or her answer.

While most of the students worked diligently on the project, not all followed through on their assignment. In total, the students attempted to contact forty-nine of the housing providers. Response rates for the interviews were relatively low due mostly to low response rates over e-mail and homes in which there was no answer.[5] For these housing providers who only provided an e-mail contact, the students simply e-mailed the questionnaire along with a short explanation of our study and hoped for a response. E-mail and phone interviews combined, the students collected interview data from seventeen respondents. Thus the interview sample may be somewhat biased in that it contains just over 1/5 of all housing providers who placed racially exclusive ads. However, assuming that more tolerant individuals are more likely to respond to email surveys or complete a phone interview that asks them to explain their racial preferences, that bias is likely in the direction of more, rather than less, racially tolerant views. Importantly though, the accounts of those who were not reached for an interview were not missed altogether. While the number of interviews was limited, many of the housing providers gave excuses and justifications in the text of their ad. Thus, I use quotes from both the seventeen interviews and the eighty-one ads to illustrate accounts for racial biases in charitable housing offers. In the interest of representing the housing providers as accurately as possible, I did not correct any spelling or grammatical errors in the text of the ads.

"I Know It Is Wrong but ...": Excuses for Race-Based Exclusions

Accounts are situated in time and place and when the interactants are of different social statuses, or in the case of our interviewees, strangers whom one would never see or hear from again, the giving of accounts may be viewed as

---

5. The students were instructed to make at least four attempts to reach the housing provider.

unnecessary. In fact a few of the interviewees did not care to elaborate on their racial preferences. One Asian interviewee from Scio, Ohio, said, *"As for why I chose to offer my home to a white American family, that is just my preference. I do not wish to explain or further discuss the subject."* Another man from Shreveport, Louisiana stated in his e-mail, *"I have helped all races with hardships caused by the hurricanes. However I did choose to house someone who was Caucasian. No particular reason and nothing should be read into my answer."* These were the only cases in which the individuals did not feel compelled to explain when questioned about their racial preferences.

The vast majority of individuals felt a strong need to either excuse or justify their behavior to neutralize the act and to maintain their own self-identity as non-racists. In fact, many offered excuses or justifications in the text of their ads. Others elaborated their views in interviews. The vast majority of excuses given can be classified as *scapegoating*. Housing providers scapegoated either the evacuees themselves or the intolerance of other white people in place where the housing provider lived.

Scapegoating

Scapegoating is when an individual alleges that the behavior in question is in response to the anticipated attitudes or behavior of others (Scott & Lyman, 1968, p. 50). In both the text of the ads and the interviews, scapegoating took two forms, one scapegoating the evacuees, and the other scapegoating the intolerant attitudes of the neighborhood, town, or city that the housing unit was located in. Both are related to racial residential segregation in that housing providers thought that black evacuees from a majority black city would not feel comfortable in their majority-white neighborhoods, or that neighbors in these all or majority-white neighborhoods would react negatively to the evacuees. While there are numerous examples of each to choose from, below are a few of the most illustrative.

This woman from Urania, Louisiana, placed the following commentary in her housing offer:

> Due to the town we live in it has to be a white couple or a white single mom with no more than two children. We live near schools and I am also a nurse.

When the interviewer asked her about her racial preferences, she replied, *"Well, we just moved to a small town, and it's really hard to bring in any different type of race of people."* Note that non-white is characterized as "different." This is a prime example of how whiteness in U.S. society is construed as normal or invisible while color such as blackness or brownness is seen as different and visible.

This woman from Jasper, Alabama, placed the following comments in her online ad:

> I would love to house a single mom with one child, not racist, but white only.

When asked about her racial preferences, she provided the following explanation, "The white aspect is because of the town I live in, you know? It's mostly white and I don't want people to start talking, you know? I'm not racist, or nothing, but I just thought it would be best to keep the stress level as low as possible, all things considered." This issue of inter-racial housing causing undue stress was evident in the text and interviews of many of the housing offers and some housing providers who were physically challenged even went so far as to claim that the stress would be detrimental to their already fragile health.

Another woman from Leesville, South Carolina, placed the following comments in her offer:

> I would like to adopt a little girl ages 0–3 and try fostering a little boy ages 9–11. Prefer white. But will consider others.

When asked about her racial preference, she cited that she lives in a racially segregated community and she scapegoated the evacuees, claiming that she was only acting in their best interest. Individuals hoping to adopt were common among those stating a racial preference. Most did not view such a preference as wrong because our society does not stigmatize racial exclusivity in adoption practices and many claimed that it would be easier for children to be with their own race. This was common in non-adoption contexts as well and even in cases involving adults. Her response was typical. *"I felt like it would be hard for the evacuees to fit, if that makes sense. The neighborhood that I live in is predominately white. For a family that had already been through so much, I didn't want them to feel any more pain or exclusion."* It is certainly ironic that so many of the ads excluded people of color in order to protect them from the pain of exclusion in a majority white community. Perhaps for children, such protective instincts could be justified, but for the ads that excluded adults for the same reasons can be viewed as both patronizing and paternalistic.

Defeasibility

Other individuals offering excuses appealed to ignorance or what Scott and Lyman call *defeasibility*. This appeal often went hand-in-hand with scapegoating. Appeals to defeasibility are when an individual claims that he or she was not fully informed, and that had all of the information been available to the actor, his or her behavior would have been different. In this case the information that was missing was first-hand knowledge of the character of the evacuees. It seemed that many of the white housing providers who fell into this category either had little exposure to people of color in general or were concerned that the people of color in the hurricane-affected areas might be different or more dangerous than other people of color they know. These individuals seemed fearful of evacuees of color and claimed that they just did not know what to expect. Had they known them personally or had more information about them, they might have made an exception, but because this information was not available, they were forced to rely on media portrayals and negative stereotypes.

This man from Independence, Missouri, is typical of those who offered the defeasibility excuse. He is unique though in that he combines various excuses and justifications making him a good example of various types of accounts that were evident across ads and interviews. Not only does he appeal to defeasibility, or a lack of full information about the evacuees and their character, but he also tries to justify his behavior by referencing negative racial stereotypes as well as his belief that racial segregation is natural and desirable. All three of those neutralization techniques were evident in other interviews as well. His ad read as follows:

> We are a husband and wife living near Kansas City, Missouri. We do have a 32-foot motor home equipped with all adminities [sic] such as fridge, ac, shower, bathroom one full size bed and two single beds, closet space etc.… We do apologize but we are requesting only white or Chinese families. Sorry. If you have any questions or have a family in mind …

When asked to elaborate on his decision to house evacuees of a particular race, the man gave the following statement:

Uh, I have not been around many black people, but, uh, everything I know about 'em, like I say, from Florida and Georgia, and maybe even Alabama, they seem to be pretty down to earth people. But knowing that people are different everywhere you go, I didn't want to invite the wrong people, because people in New Orleans and the Gulf Coast are different from people from other places, from what I've seen and heard. I know black people in the Northern states, near Kansas City, where I have lived, don't really like white people, because they act like we owe them something. I didn't know if people from the Gulf Coast and New Orleans would be like that, or not. 'Cause I didn't know, and I didn't want to take that chance. I guess it's kinda like dogs ... they're all different. They are all different species, you can't put 'em all together at the same time. It doesn't mean they're all bad or worse than others, it just means that everyone can't live happily together. It's like putting a Rottweiler and a Pit Bull together. They're both mean, but good dogs. They just don't mix. Don't get me wrong, I don't have a problem with black people. If it was a black family I knew already or had the chance to meet beforehand, it would have been no problem. If a black family had called me and I had had the chance to speak with them, I doubt that I would have turned them away. But the closest I've been is Jackson, Mississippi, and things down there are a whole lot different than from where I'm from.

Earlier in his interview, the man noted that he had never been to New Orleans or the Gulf Coast. Still, he expressed a belief that black people in those areas were somehow different from others based on what he has seen and heard. In this circumstance, we might assume that what he has seen and heard are sensationalized media images of African-American criminal activity after the hurricane and widespread poverty. Not only does the man draw the inappropriate parallel between racial difference and different species of dogs to justify his belief in racial segregation, but he also scapegoats the evacuees anticipating that they might have negative attitudes towards him.

The Sad Tale[6]

One man from Staten Island, New York, was unusually candid about his racial biases, and invoked what Scott and Lyman call a *sad tale* to justify his behavior. A sad tale is a particular arrangement of the facts to highlight an ex-

---

6. Scott and Lyman called the sad tale a type of justification. I disagree however in both this circumstance and in the examples that they cite. Because an individual giving the sad tale *does acknowledge wrongdoing* and deflects responsibility away from him/herself by pointing instead to a troubled past, I believe that it falls more accurately in the category of an excuse.

tremely dismal past that explains the individual's current state. The comments in the man's ad read as follows:

> WOULD PEREFER A WHITE FAMLEY BUT WOULD HELP ANY PLEASE EXCUSE MY BIGGORTY

In the interview the man confessed:

I am truly guilty of racial and cultural bias. Although I realize that race does not signify criminal. I would only feel comfortable opening my home to another white person. I have many black friends and we attend social gatherings together, but recognize our cultural differences ... I consider myself a reformed racist. I attended school in the south and pledged a fraternity that was almost as bad as the KKK. Now that I've matured, I have friends of many different races, but I still just don't trust blacks as much as whites.

The man blamed negative socialization and cultural differences between races for his particular biases. Note that he used the term "reformed racist" and had the same remorseful tone as a recovering alcoholic who was still trying to straighten himself out. Also note that he said that he did not *trust* people of color as much as whites. When attempting to explain their racial preferences, several of the interviewees brought up similar issues of trust.

"It's not wrong because ...": Justifications for Race-Based Exclusions

While the previous interviewee seemed to recognize wrongdoing, others denied any wrongdoing. As mentioned previously, many whom were looking to adopt fell into this category. Others believed that racial segregation was simply part of the natural order. Still others believed that their actions were justifiable because evacuees of color were known to not have good moral character.

While examples of individuals who believed that racial segregation is natural and desirable have already been given above, the following is another interesting example of a woman from Harlan, Kentucky who held such beliefs and offered no excuses for her behavior. The comments section of her housing offer read as follows:

> I have wrote twice in the past two weeks I wrote I would keep a little girl around the age of 4, 5 that's white American please contact me on this

In the interview the woman justified her racially exclusive offer by referencing her childhood socialization and citing her belief that racial segregation is natural. Nonetheless, like so many others, she struggled to maintain a non-racist identity in the interaction. *"(name of student omitted), where I come from and how I was raised contributed to my decision. I was taught that people of different races should be with people of their own kind. I am not a racist person. I just believe white with white and black with black and so on."*

Denial of the Victim

In some cases the individual may argue that the act was permissible since the victim deserved the injury that occurred, for example, blaming the victim of a rape for dressing provocatively. Such rationalizations are not uncommon when the victim is a stigmatized racial or ethnic minority (Scott & Lyman, 1968, p. 51).

In his interview, a man from Thomson, Georgia, provided a clear example of denial of the victim. His arguments were not uncommon. His online posting contained the following comments:

> We are a rural family of five and have limited rooms available; however we have a spacious home and could partition off areas. We can provide possible job opportunities and transportation. We would prefer a middle class white family.

When asked if he had ever been to New Orleans or the Gulf Coast the man responded, "TV is my first real exposure ... My heart goes out to all of the people affected by the hurricane, especially the Cajun people. I'm a Christian man and the Cajun people are some of the nicest people I've ever met, and the poor black people. They had it bad...." Notice that the line of questioning was not about race, but the man brought race into the discussion. Then, when the interviewer attempts to ask him about his racial preferences, the man avoids the subject of race and talks instead about class differences and crime. "I wanted someone who was used to the same environment that I live in. There were a lot of poor people affected by the hurricane as well as others. A friend of mine has a boat out at a dock near here and there were a lot of evacuees from New Orleans and the inner city staying at a hotel near the dock. My friend never had a problem with people messing with his boat until the evacuees stayed there. We have crime here, everywhere does, but bad stuff happened once they got into town."

From the text of the ad we can assume that, by environment, he is referring to a white, middle-class neighborhood. The man assumes that the black people who were affected were poor and from the inner city, which as we know only characterizes a portion of the black population affected by the hurricane, but certainly the population that got the most media attention. The term "inner city" is often used by whites to indirectly refer to poor black people, and is a semantic move that draws attention away from the question of race to focus on class and culture. Note also that the man does not have any direct evidence that evacuees committed crimes, but rather relies on circumstantial evidence to justify his belief that poor black evacuees were criminals. He apologizes for his bigotry, but then implies, that he was right to exclude them because they are probably criminals because his friend had problems.

Just as the man above employed a negative racial stereotype associating African Americans with criminal activity, the man below from Shreveport, Louisiana, also makes use of common negative stereotypes of African Americans. The comments in the housing offer read as follows:

> Room available to single white mother with child or younger to middle aged-white couple. Be willing to find employment as soon as possible. Willing to help out the best that I can and get someone back on their feet. God Bless America.

In the interview he says, *"It was a trust issue. I wanted to house people who were about the same age as me and who are self-sufficient. No senior citizens. I wanted people who would be able to take care of themselves and be able to get a job and back on their feet as quickly as possible."* Like the man from Georgia, this man avoided directly addressing the issue of race and he also drew on negative stereotypes of blacks and older people as groups that are not self-sufficient. He also mentioned a tendency to distrust non-whites. Such a justification whereby it is viewed as okay to discriminate against members of particular group because they are not morally worthy of fair treatment was implied if not directly stated in a number of ads and interviews. Unlike the case of the man from

Georgia, here the issue was not crime, but rather self-sufficiency, a trait arguably treated in U.S. society as a sign of morality.

"I Prefer a Black Family": Responses to White Prejudice

Of the ads that specified a racial preference, relatively few expressed a preference for non-whites. Those who preferred to house black individuals cited two justifications, both of which can be viewed as a response to anticipated prejudice on the part of whites. For example, one interracial family worried that white evacuees might not be accepting of her interracial family. The ad from this woman from Dunkirk, New York, who could not be reached for comment read as follows:

> I am white ad my children are blk so it might be better for someone blk to be housed with me in case of prejudice.

Another justification for preferring black evacuees appeared to be an attempt by a white family to combat racism. The family worried that black evacuees might be excluded from many housing offers; therefore, they targeted their offer toward black evacuees in particular. This family from Grayslake, Illinois, posted this ad not only to help those whom they believed to be most in need, but also to promote anti-racist thinking amongst their own children. The comments of their housing offer were as follows:

> We are a white family with 3 kids. 5, 3, and 9mos looking to open our home and our hearts to a black family, any kind, preferably with kids. We want to teach our kids that love is colorblind.

In the interview the woman said, "I did not want to choose a white family with money because they wouldn't need it most. I felt that the hardest impact was on the black race, so I wanted to help someone who was black." The interviewer asked her if the media played any role in her decision. She responded, "In a way it did, however not in a negative way, but in a positive way. The media portrayed all blacks as being horrible as far as stealing items out of the stores. Some people were stealing items that could not be used at that time, but some were actually taking things they could survive from like food." In other words, the woman felt that black folks were being portrayed in an unfair and negative light, thus she implied that part of her decision to house black evacuees rested on her belief that they might be receiving less help from white housing providers, and in response, she employed her own version of affirmative action to correct for anticipated white prejudice.

Discussion and Conclusion

Many scholars have argued that the dominant racial ideology in the U.S. is one of color-blindness in which our society teaches us that we should no longer consider race, but that such an ideology only serves to mask persistent racial inequalities and reinforce hegemonic relations based on race (see Bonilla-Silva & Forman, 2000; Brown et al., 2005). Person to person, as Martin Luther King's "I Have a Dream" speech intended it, such colorblindness is perhaps desirable. At a societal level however, if we hope to alleviate race-based inequalities, it is important that we recognize how race continues to operate in our society as a fundamental axis of social differentiation that bestows power and privileges on some groups while denying power and privileges to other groups (Omi & Winant, 1994). The housing offers cited in this study demonstrate that race does still matter, both in access to housing, and in hurricane recovery. More importantly however, they provide insight into *why* people say that race matters to them. If we as a society hope to move beyond race-based inequalities, we must address the *why*. This study suggests three reasons why race matters to housing providers.

First, the data suggest that media portrayals played an important role in shaping the perceptions of housing providers studied in this project. In general, media portrayals created real sense of cultural difference and distance between white housing providers and black evacuees. The media heightened fears associated with criminal activity and focused incessantly on urban poverty, squalor, and helplessness. This had three effects: one, it created a sense among housing providers that black evacuees would not fit into white suburban neighborhoods and rural areas; two, it exacerbated a fear that black evacuees would not be able to get back on their feet and may become permanently dependent on the person providing free housing; and three, it gave some housing providers the sense that black evacuees would be treated unfairly in the weeks and months after the storm encouraging some to specifically make black evacuees feel included in their offers.

Second, the data suggest that race and the perceived class of evacuees intersected in important ways to influence the actions of housing providers. Although a great many of the white evacuees in the hurricane-affected area were also poor, poor white evacuees were not viewed as threatening in the same way that poor black evacuees were viewed. Additionally, in the case of evacuees, "black" was often taken as a proxy for being a poor inner-city resident systematically excluding middle-class and suburban-dwelling and rural-dwelling black individuals from housing offers as well. In this way we can see an important intersection between "racetalk" and "regiontalk" in which race and region are combined to exacerbate negative stereotypes.

Third, and perhaps most importantly, the data reveal a reciprocal and reinforcing relationship between racial discrimination and racial residential segregation. Most of the people who provided accounts for discrimination blamed the neighborhood, town, or city that they lived in. Whites who lived in segregated communities admitted that they did not have much interaction at all with people of color and that as a result they did not trust them in the same way that they trusted white people. They viewed housing an evacuee of color in a segregated neighborhood as stressful all around, for themselves, for their neighbors, and for the evacuees. Also, some had even become so immersed in the world of racial segregation that they believed it to be natural and integration to be problematic. Many of the housing providers implied that if they lived in more integrated communities, that they would have not have limited their offers to whites only. Yet ironically, race-based discrimination by housing providers is known to be a major contributing factor to racial residential segregation. The effects are reciprocal, trapping the U.S. in an endless cycle of discrimination and segregation.

This study highlights why people say they discriminate, and living in segregated neighborhoods is one of the foremost reasons given. This information is important beyond the context of Katrina in that it is consistent with discrimination literature that focuses on the attitudes of realtors and rental agents who deny housing to qualified applicants. It complicates the problem even further when racial discrimination interacts with regional discrimination to deny needy individuals one of their most basic requirements, shelter. As one Fair Housing advocate put it in his testimony before Congress, "victims of natural disasters shouldn't be forced to forfeit housing opportunities because of the color of their skin" (Perry, 2005, n.p.). Beyond the unfairness of the individual-level however, the cumulative effects of such discrimination can be disastrous in that they perpetuate racial segregation, class differences, and racial and ethnic tensions. Individuals need to be aware, however, that they are not helpless pawns in the social system of racial segregation. They can choose to act to change the system just as they act to reinforce it. If more charitable givers were inclined to "buck the system" as did the family from Grayslake, Illinois, perhaps some of the trust issues and stress could be confronted rather than avoided and perpetuated.

References

Bonilla-Silva, E., A. Lewis, E. A. & Embrick, D. G. (2004). "I did not get that job because of a black man …".": The story lines and testimonies of color-blind racism. *Sociological Forum*, 19(4), 555–581.

Bonilla-Silva, E. & Forman, T. A. (2000). "I am not a racist but ..." mapping White college student's racial ideology in the USA. *Discourse and Society*, 11(1), 50–85.

Brown, M. K., Carnoy, M., Currie, E., Duster, T., Oppenheimer, D. B., Shultz, M.M., & Wellman, D. (2005). *Whitewashing race*. Berkeley: University of California Press.

Eliasoph, N. (1997). "Everyday Racism" in a culture of political avoidance: Civil society, speech, and taboo. *Social Problems*, 46(4), 479–502.

Jargowsky, P.A. (1996). *Poverty and place: Ghettos, barrios and the American city*. New York: Russell Sage.

Mallinson, C. & Brewster, Z.W. (2005). "Blacks and bubbas": Stereotypes, ideology, and categorization processes in restaurant servers' discourse. *Discourse and Society*, 16(6), 787–807.

Mills, C.W. (1940). Situated actions and vocabularies of motive. *American Sociological Review*, 5(6), 904–913.

NHFA (2005). *No home for the holidays: Report on housing discrimination against Hurricane Katrina survivors*. New York. National Fair Housing Alliance.

Omi, M. & Winant, H. (1994). *Racial formation in the United States: From the 1960s to the 1990s*. (2nd ed.) New York: Routledge.

Perry, J. (2005). *Draft Congressional testimony (Housing Subcommittee on Housing and Equal Opportunity)*. Retrieved April 1, 2005 from http://www.gnofairhousing.org.

Purnell, T., Isardi,W., & Baugh, J. (1999). Perceptual and phonetic experiments on American English dialect identification. *Journal of Language and Social Psychology*, 18(1), 10–30.

Scott, E. K. (2000). Everyone against racism: Agency and the production of meaning in the anti-racism practices of two feminist organizations. *Theory and Society*, 29, 785–818.

Scott, M. & Lyman, S. (1968). Accounts. *American Sociological Review*, 33(1), 46–62.

Scully, D. & Marolla, J.(1984). Convicted rapists' vocabulary of motive: Excuses and justifications. *Social Problems*, 31(5), 540–544.

Weinstein, R. (1980). Vocabularies of motive for illicit drug use: And application of the accounts framework. *The Sociological Quarterly*, 21, 577–593.

Wilson, W. J. (1987). *The truly disadvantaged: The inner city, the underclass, and public policy*. Chicago: Chicago University Press.

Chapter 14

Katrina's Indecorous Voices: Ethos, Race, and Survivor Testimonials

Terence Check

On the morning of August 29, 2005, Hurricane Katrina made landfall near the Louisiana-Mississippi border and caused one of the deadliest natural disasters in American history. A torrent of water breached levees in New Orleans, causing a majority of the city to become submerged. Many residents who had not evacuated the city searched for safety in the Superdome and the Convention Center, only to encounter subhuman conditions due to the lack of food, water, electricity, and sewage facilities. The issues of race and class quickly became central to the discussion of the social consequences of Katrina. Television cameras showed the plight of some of the thousands of residents who struggled for survival in the aftermath of the storm, revealing that "the vast majority of those worst affected were black, in numbers disproportionate even to the large percentage of blacks within the city" (Gilman, 2005, p. 1).

The Bush Administration and the Republican majority in Congress were placed on the defensive, needing to explain why the federal government's response to the disaster was so poor given that meteorologists had predicted the force and direction of the storm with uncanny accuracy. Musician Kanye West, during a Katrina fundraiser on live television, offered one explanation when he suggested that, "George Bush doesn't care about black people" (Ollison, 2006, p. 1F). A poll conducted by the *Washington Post*, the Kaiser Family Foundation and Harvard University of randomly selected evacuees from New Orleans, revealed 61 percent thought "government doesn't care" about their plight, and 68 percent of those surveyed believed that the federal government would have responded more quickly to Hurricane Katrina if more of the victims were white (Alpert, 2005, p. 3).

In response to these attitudes, the White House hurried "to quell perceptions that race was a factor in the slow federal response to Katrina and that its policies have contributed to the festering poverty propelled into public view by the disaster" (Fletcher, 2005, p. A02). President George W. Bush, in a speech to the nation from New Orleans on September 15, mentioned "a history of racial discrimination which cut off generations from the opportunity in America" (Cochran, 2005, p. 2). Earlier that same day, the House of Representatives passed a resolution establishing the Select Bipartisan Committee to Investigate the Preparation for and Response to Hurricane Katrina. The Democratic leadership asked its members to boycott the process, as they insisted that an independent, 9/11-type commission was necessary to investigate the government's response to the disaster ("Natural Disasters," 2005, p. 257). The Republican leadership went ahead and created the Select Committee, which held nine hearings over three months. The hearings featured dramatic testimony from former FEMA Director Michael Brown and DHS Secretary Michael Chertoff. Receiving less attention, however, was the hearing on December 6, 2005, on "Hurricane Katrina: Voices From Inside the Storm." During this extraordinary hearing, lawmakers heard emotional testimony from several Katrina survivors and New Orleans evacuees.

Some of those who testified at the hearings compared themselves to victims of genocide and the Holocaust, prompting a rebuke from lawmakers who found the analogy offensive. At one point during the hearings, a lawmaker questioned the truthfulness of some of the testimony. Media response to the hearings—at least from those sources that reported on the testimony—was even more critical. For example, James Gill (2005) of the New Orleans *Times-Picayune* described the witnesses as an "ill-mannered bunch" and the hearings themselves as an "embarrassment" (p. 7). Conservative columnist Mark Goldblatt (2005) of the *American Spectator* wrote that it "was perhaps the most ludicrous performance by a panel of witnesses ever entered into the *Congressional Record*; it made the finger-pointing blather of the baseball steroid hearings seem like a Lincoln-Douglas debate" (p. 1). Although the Select Committee's final report summarized the hearings and included a few scattered quotations from Katrina survivors, it did not address any of the serious allegations regarding racism.

This omission was due to lawmakers' dismissal of claims of racism made by witnesses. As Representative Christopher Shays remarked at one point during the hearings in response to a claim that one of the panelists had witnessed the bombing of a levee in New Orleans, "I can't let that pass. I don't know if that's theater or the truth" (Hearing, 2005, p. 19). It was important symbolically for conservative lawmakers to address the topic of race in the hearings, for at least two reasons. First, it allowed them to frame the hearings as a bipartisan effort, since some Democratic lawmakers were willing to participate if the proceedings addressed this subject. Second, it helped Republicans to deflect criticism of their social agenda, since the poor federal response to Hurricane Katrina created the public impression that conservatives were indifferent to the misery of African-Americans. However, it is quite possible that lawmakers at the hearings had no interest in actually addressing issues of race in a meaningful way. So when Katrina survivors presented the Select Committee with personal testimonials of racist acts they had witnessed or endured, it became necessary for lawmakers to question the credibility of the witnesses' claims as a means to avoid confronting them. While it would be easy to suggest that the witnesses at the hearing failed to establish the credibility necessary to persuade their audience, I argue that lawmakers symbolically defined the witnesses as "indecorous," or acting and speaking in ways that were inappropriate for the congressional setting. Thus, the labeling of the witnesses as "Katrina Konspiracy Kooks" (Lopez-Calderon, 2005, p. 1) and the dismissal of their claims as "loony" (DeBerry, 2005, p. 7) functioned to rhetorically frame survivors' voices as untrustworthy and unfit for the occasion. This essay incorporates rhetorical theory to examine the public arguments made by community activists and Katrina survivors at the House Select Committee hearings on the role of race and class in the government's response to the disaster, as well as the congressional and media reaction to these arguments. It describes the concept of ethos and examines how committee members and the popular press constructed survivor testimony as indecorous, thus discrediting African-American voices.

Ethos and the Art of Persuasion

Since ancient times, theorists have recognized the importance of credibility in advancing persuasive claims. Aristotle noted that speakers employ three main artistic proofs when making an argument: logos, or logical reasoning; pathos, or emotional appeals; and ethos, or the speaker's character. Writing specifically about ethos, Aristotle claimed, "[There is persuasion] through character whenever the speech is spoken in such a way as to make the speaker worthy of credence; for we believe fair-minded people to a greater extent and more quickly [than we do others] on all subjects in general and completely so in cases where there is not exact knowledge but room for doubt" (1991, p. 1356a). Communication scholars have suggested the rhetor's "perceived character is most important in making persuasive discourse" (Truscello, 2001, p. 330). According to Aristotle, a speaker must show "good sense" (*phronesis*, or practical knowledge), display "good moral character" (*arête*, or virtue), and establish "good will" (*eunoia*, or acting in the audience's best interests). In short, the credibility of a persuader is a central feature in that person's ability to convince an audience of his or her arguments.

Scholars have defined ethos in two ways: as a "mode of persuasion that draws upon the prerequisite virtue of the speaker" (Johnson, 1995, p. 243), that is, whether audiences view the rhetor as credible prior to the rhetorical act, and as "self-presentation in response to specific rhetorical situations" (Harrison, 2003, p. 246). Because rhetoric involves employing the available means of persuasion to sway audiences at given moments, an audience "must often rely on its impression of the trustworthiness of the speaker" (Wisse, 1989, p. 247), and ethos "may therefore be defined as the element of a speech that presents the speaker as trustworthy"(Wisse, 1989, p. 33). Studies in the 1960s showed that factors such as expertness, trustworthiness, dynamism, competence, objectivity and intention were key aspects of a speaker's credibility (McCroskey, 1966; McCroskey & Young, 1981; Whitehead, 1968) and since then critics have further expanded on the importance of ethos (Baumlin, 1994; Corder, 1977; Corts, 1968; Oft-Rose, 1989) and looked for these features when evaluating the success or failures of major public addresses (Ross, 1980).

Beason's (1991) research on "signalled ethos" is especially relevant to the testimony at the Select Committee on Katrina, given that the witnesses were ordinary citizens who needed to establish credibility in the oral testimony itself. "With signalled ethos," Beason contended, "the communicator's persona is moved toward the forefront of the message, offering what is likely the conspicuous opportunity—whether intended or not—for an audience to focus on what the text suggests about the communicator as a person" (p. 328). In other words, a speaker may employ language about experiences and their own understanding of events in a manner that bolsters an audience's confidence in their credibility. Beason identified several major ways this is done: 1) through similitude, or a shared identification between speaker and audience; 2) expertise, the reputation of the rhetor; 3) self-criticism, a humble presentation of the claims; and 4) deference, a presentation style that emphasizes courteous and respectful appreciation of the audience's authority. Although Beason applied these standards to a set of business and professional speeches, his overall point was that "self-referential language carries with it the potential for audiences to discern something about a communicator's persona and be influenced by it" (pp. 328–329), so its application seems especially useful in those circumstances when a speaker is unknown to an audience and must establish credibility in the presentation of the arguments.

But a significant flaw with such conventional approaches to ethos is the assumption that speakers generate credibility only when they conform to rhetorical situations. Such an approach discredits rhetors that fail to respect the "decorum" of the moment. As Cox (1999) argued in his study of public participation by low-income communities in environmental decision-making, the labeling of discordant voices as "indecorous" functions rhetorically to construct publics as emotional, ignorant, or as having a personal agenda. As a result, the decorum takes on "a much more constraining role," as it dismisses as inappropriate the arguments and experiences of disadvantaged Publics (p. 22). Such was the case in the Select Committee hearings on the role of race and class in the government's response to Hurricane Katrina, because members of the committee did not believe the narratives the witnesses presented, thus diminishing the credibility of the survivors' arguments.

A Voice to the People: Congressional Hearings on Race and Katrina

Although the Select Committee consisted only of appointed Republican members, several Democrats participated in the investigation "in defiance of their leadership's decision not to appoint members officially to the panel" (Select Bipartisan Committee, 2006, p. 10). One of them was Representative Cynthia A. McKinney of Georgia, who "chose to get my foot in the door on this Committee because I knew that time was urgent for the hurricane survivors, who needed our help and our answers, and who needed to connect with Congress" (McKinney, 2006, p. 4). McKinney participated as a "guest" on the Select Committee and requested a special hearing focusing on whether race and class may have played a role in the federal government's poor response to the flooding in New Orleans following Hurricane Katrina. Virginia Republican Representative Tom Davis, the chair of the House committee, likely agreed to hold this hearing to offset perceptions that Republicans were indifferent and unresponsive to the plight of Katrina victims.

The testimony offered an extraordinary snapshot into the travails of Katrina victims, many of whom felt that government had abandoned them. According to Representative William J. Jefferson of Louisiana, another Democrat who participated in the hearings, the December 6, 2005, hearing "was designed to give a voice to the people who felt race was an impediment to the government's response" (2005, p. 6). Referencing President Bush's televised speech on Katrina, Representative Tom Davis opened the hearings by claiming poverty has "roots in the history of racial discrimination" and suggested that it was important to hear from citizens who had direct experience with the storm (Hearing, 2005, pp. 1–3).

After opening statements from lawmakers, five New Orleans citizens delivered prepared testimony. Terrol Williams began by describing what happened to him as he stayed in his home while the storm passed. He recalled traveling to his mother's house after the storm and rescuing her with a raft. He described the actions of law enforcements officers who pointed guns at teenage boys but acknowledged, "I understand why they did what they did," given the need to evacuate the city (Hearing, 2005, p. 5). Doreen Keeler, who recounted how she evacuated to another state to avoid the storm, discussed the difficulties in working with government agencies to secure housing and schooling for her family. Then the most spirited testimony came from the next three witnesses. Patricia Thompson stated that she and her extended family used a variety of shelters and made the dramatic claim that her family "slept next to dead bodies. We slept on streets at least four times next to human feces and urine.

There was garbage everywhere in the city. Panic and fear had taken over" (Hearing, 2005, p. 8). She also asserted that armed police forced evacuees— even young children—to "sit on the ground with their hands in the air" (Hearing, 2005, p. 8). Leah Hodges followed and immediately criticized the government's response to the disaster. She used dramatic language to refer to abusive treatment suffered by evacuees in what she dubbed, the "Causeway Concentration Camp," an area under Interstate 10 at the "causeway" exit where folks waited to be evacuated. "People were allowed to die," she lamented, referring to evacuees as "prisoners of war" (Hearing, 2005, p. 11) who had survived an "act of genocide and of ethnic cleansing" (Hearing, 2005, p. 9). She concluded her testimony by admitting "some people are shocked to hear me say a concentration camp. But if you have ever seen footage of the Hitler concentration camps of World War II, I assure you that is what happened to us at the very lowest level all the way up to the level of some people dying and pregnant women losing babies" (Hearing, 2005, p. 11). The last resident to testify was Dyan French, who made a variety of points in a loosely structured address.

Representative Davis began the question-and-answer session with a question about the role of race and class in the government's poor response to the storm. All but one of the witnesses thought race was a significant reason that evacuees did not receive help sooner, with Patricia Thompson proclaiming, "No one is going to tell me it wasn't a race issue. Yes, it was an issue of race, because they knew one thing. When the city had pretty much been evacuated, the people that were left there mostly was black" (Hearing, 2005, p. 16). Leah Hodges noted rescuers had saved some animals before they had evacuated people and suggested, "Race had everything to do with the ethnic cleansing and the massacre of predominantly African-American people being blamed on Hurricane Katrina" (Hearing, 2005, p. 17). This was followed later by two noteworthy exchanges that received the most media coverage. Representative Shays challenged the believability of some of the claims and tried to extract a precise answer from Dyan French about her location to the levee, as a way of undermining her claim that she witnessed or heard explosions that caused one of the breaches. Additionally, Representative Jeff Miller challenged the appropriateness of the concentration camp metaphor that Hodges had used, prompting a sharp exchange between them. Near the end of the hearings, with some members of Congress and some of the evacuees left exasperated by the verbal exchanges, French commented, "My problem with all of this—and I said this. I said this in September. I said, nobody is going to believe us. This is an unbelievable story" (Hearing, 2005, p. 27).

The participants in the hearings provided shocking examples of the treatment of African-Americans at the hands of the authorities. However, while committee members allowed the victims the opportunity to talk, some lawmakers were openly skeptical of the claims that the witnesses made. This stemmed in part from the inability of many of the witnesses to conform to societal conventions of credibility and authority. An examination of how witnesses at the hearings failed to employ similitude, expertise, self-criticism and deference helps to explain why some lawmakers did not view their testimony favorably.

According to Beason (1991), an important type of signaled ethos results when speakers "point out similarities between themselves and their audiences" because, "such commonality gives the impression that communicator and audience share backgrounds, goals, and values" (p. 331). Such identification between speaker and audience stresses shared values of unity and loyalty, of commonality in seeking shared solutions to common problems. The persuasive presentation should always emphasize commonality, rather than differences. Literary critic Kenneth Burke (1969), whose concept of "identification" best summarizes this process, wrote "You persuade a man only insofar as you can talk his language by speech, gesture, tonality, order, image, attitude, idea, *identifying* your ways with his" (p. 55).

In his opening remarks to start the December 6 hearing, Select Committee chair Tom Davis noted that a CNN Gallop poll reported that 60 percent of African-Americans but only 12 percent of whites believed race was a factor in the slow response to Katrina. By highlighting this difference in racial views, Davis was most likely trying to establish its significance as a topic worthy of the committee's investigation, as he acknowledged that issues of race and class warranted further discussion, "especially within the context of understanding the experiences of those quite inside the storm" (Hearing, 2005, p. 2). Still, the reference to the polls reinforced differences between the members of the committee and the African-American witnesses. In their study of the racial differences of rumor, Fine and Turner (2001) argued that Whites often see the African-American community as predisposed to paranoia, while African-Americans are often suspicious of the motives of government. The difference in the poll numbers cited by Davis is an indication that whites and blacks define racism differently. For whites, racism is often equated with racial prejudice (Gilman, 2005). Most whites acknowledged that the federal government bungled the response to Hurricane Katrina, but fewer felt that this failure was a result of bigotry. On the other hand, a high proportion of blacks felt that government's response to Katrina revealed racial inequality (Pew Research Center, 2005).

The witnesses who appeared before the Select Committee faced a rhetorical dilemma, since any argument about racial discrimination would emphasize difference, whereas the goal of identification and similitude is to eliminate or reduce those differences. In her testimony before the committee, Leah Hodges linked the failed response after Katrina to a history of indifference on the part of the federal government to the plight of black people:

These and all other violations both expressed and implied arise directly from the failure of the United States' government to eliminate apartheid practices and all other forms of oppressive government practices against poor and working poor citizens of the United States who are mostly African-Americans or otherwise people of color. These violations are historical and continuing.

(Hearing, 2005, p. 11)

While the members of the Select Committee were not involved directly in the decisions about the government's immediate response to the storm, they represented a political party that was implicated and that had strained relations with the African-American community even before the disaster (Dyson, 2006). In offering suggestions for change, New Orleans resident Patricia Thompson said, "In order to rebuild New Orleans I think every elected official should be replaced, starting with the President" (Hearing, 2005, p. 8). Unfortunately for Thompson and the other witnesses, these statements reinforced difference rather than commonality. As pointed out by Enos (1990), effective argument "arises from the union of speaker and listener, writer and reader; the opening up of a world holding within it values that both participants adhere to underlies the whole concept of ethos" (p. 101). In promoting this sense of similitude, speakers can stress shared group membership, similarity in background, common experiences, and shared cultural values and goals. In this case, the credibility of the witnesses in the eyes of the committee members may have been diminished as a result of the very charge—racism—that was the subject of the hearings.

In addition to similitude, communication scholars agree that expertise is an important feature of ethos. "Good sense is a cluster of characteristics made up of several components," wrote Jaffe (1995). "One aspect is intelligence. You demonstrate your intelligence by showing that you are knowledgeable" (p. 107). In general, a speaker's credibility "is enhanced if he or she has conducted extensive research and marshals an impressive amount of diverse evidence ... uses reasoning that meets the tests of logical validity, and displays 'common sense'" (Samovar & Mills, 1995, p. 303). Summarizing the consensus of scholarship on this topic, Grice and Skinner (1995) contended, "Communication theorists agree that speakers who appear competent, trustworthy, and dynamic are viewed as credible speakers" (p. 329).

During the hearings, participants sought to enhance their ethos by referring to their experiences in a variety of ways, both before and after the storm. Terrol Williams opened his statement by noting he had "finished paying for my house three years ago and had started my own construction company" and had worked as a federal employee for 18 years prior to that (Hearing, 2005, p. 5). In her testimony, Doreen Keeler mentioned that she was a mother who was struggling to keep her daughter in school, despite the dislocation caused by the storm. Patricia Thompson identified herself as a lifelong resident of New Orleans who did part-time work through her church and once had a job as a "career development specialist" who was "used to sending people out to go to work, used to helping people get bills paid" (Hearing, 2005, p. 8). Leah Hodges noted that prior to Katrina, she had taken time off from pursuing a law degree to care for her sick grandfather, and now she was worried that she lost a brother in the storm who she was unable to contact. Finally, Dyan French was introduced as a "New Orleans community leader who did not evacuate and has opened her home as a makeshift shelter" (Hearing, 2005, p. 5). She identified herself as a former government employee: "I'm eight years sanitation, five years Department of Transportation" (Hearing, 2005, p. 12).

As eyewitnesses to the storm and its aftermath, the evacuees should have attained credibility—at least initially—because they had first-hand experience with what had happened. Furthermore, their personal narratives affirmed American values of individualism and selflessness. Williams paid for his own home and Hodges pursued an advanced degree, contrary to harmful stereotypes suggesting that poor Southern blacks are "backward, belligerently opposed to enlightenment, and tethered to self-defeating cultural habits that undermine their upward thrust from a life of penury and ignorance" (Dyson, 2006, p. 21). Contrary to the vicious stereotype that African-Americans exploit government services, these witnesses were self-motivated and some even had been government employees whose work helped get "bills paid." The witnesses presented themselves as loving family members who struggled to protect their children and grandchildren during and after the storm. Finally, the witnesses were hailed as community leaders, allowing audience members to infer that the reason that some of them stayed in the city was because they selflessly refused to leave their neighbors behind. It would appear, at first glance, that the witnesses established the expertise necessary to advance their claims. And yet, by the start of the question-and-answer session, it was apparent that some of the witnesses lost credibility, as lawmakers openly challenged their claims. In large part, this had to do with the presentation of assertions that lawmakers found dubious or inappropriate.

Zarefsky (1996) wrote, "But in any speech, to a greater or lesser degree, audiences will make inferences from your credibility to the truth or falsity of the claims you advance" (p. 211). The reverse is also true. That is, audiences who find a claim preposterous may distrust the person who delivers it. During the hearings, this was probably most evident when Hodges presented the "concentration camp" analogy. Claiming that evacuees endured "harsh military treatment and the tensioned fascist style" of police and National Guard troops, Hodges went on to claim that she and others were "tortured" by military officers who were "full of hatred, and pointing guns at us and treating us worse than prisoners of war" (Hearing, 2005, p. 11). Lawmakers bristled at the comparison, and one of them, Representative Jeff Miller of Florida, asked Hodges to refrain from referring to the causeway area as a concentration camp. Hodges refused, saying, "I'm going to call it what it is. If I put a dress on a pig, a pig is still a pig" (Hearing, 2005, p. 26).

When a persuader reasons by analogy, he or she compares two situations that "have the same essential characteristics and reason that a specific characteristic found in one situation also exists in the analogous situation" (Rieke & Sillars, 2001, p. 122). Argumentation scholars have long asserted that, far from being an ornamental device a speaker adopts merely to make his or her language more poetic, analogies function as persuasion (Juthe, 2005; Whaley, 1997; Whaley & Holloway, 1997). Winston Churchill once said, "apt analogies are among the most formidable weapons of the rhetorician" (as cited in Gross, 1983, p. 38). One can only speculate about Hodges's motives for using the "concentration camp" analogy, but it is reasonable to assume that she used it to impart significance to her claims and to call attention to the suffering that her and other evacuees endured after the storm. It is important to remember that her audience consisted of mainly conservative lawmakers who represented a party that had long ignored African-American voices and more recently had failed to provide New Orleans residents with immediate assistance despite pleas of help scrawled or sprayed on the rooftops of flooded houses and displayed on national television. Furthermore, Hodges delivered her testimony in a cultural context in which the Holocaust "has emerged—in the Western World—as probably the most talked about and oft-represented event of the twentieth century" (Cole, 1999, p. 3). For better or worse, Holocaust imagery has become ubiquitous in Western culture, as evidenced by its widespread use among both liberal and conservative politicians and its prominence in popular culture.

However, the Holocaust is a highly contested symbol, and its frequent use invites widespread rebuke (Leibovich, 2005). As part of this historical narrative, Americans perceive themselves as liberators of the Nazi concentration camps. Any use of the analogy to suggest that our own troops use methods comparable to fascists is sure to draw considerable criticism, as Senator Richard Durbin learned in another context when he compared the alleged mistreatment of prisoners at Guantanamo Bay, Cuba, to the tactics of the Nazis (Leibovich, 2005). By invoking a concentration camp analogy, Hodges undermined the credibility of the rest of her claims, even if the harrowing treatment she experienced was truthful. After questioning Hodges's familiarity with history, Representative Miller flatly stated, "Not a single person was marched into a gas chamber and killed" (Hearing, 2005, p. 26).

While it is important to establish the authority of one's claims, speakers also establish effective credibility through the use of "self-criticism." Here, speakers persuade audiences of the truthfulness of their claims by admitting their shortcomings; they "engage in a brand of self-criticism demonstrating trustworthiness, frankness, and honesty" (Beason, 1991, p. 335). Kearney and Plax (1996) wrote, "It turns out that audiences appreciate forthright, honest, and open speakers" (p. 393). This process tends to be subtle, since a speaker does not want to diminish the force of his or her argument by admitting to its faults. Still, by admitting to some limitations in their expertise or experience, speakers can bolster their overall claims, since they will appear to be open and self-reflective of their positions. However, in the Select Committee hearings, Katrina evacuees stood firm on some claims that lawmakers openly questioned. For example, Patricia Thompson claimed that her young granddaughter was "sitting on the ground with her hands in the air with a beam pointed between her eyes, saying, Mummy, am I doing it right because I'm scared they're going to shoot me—5 years old. My grand baby is going to be traumatized" (Hearing, 2005, p. 17).

Claims that seem far-reaching can have damaging effects on a speaker's overall credibility. Samovar and Mills (1995) stated, "Although enthusiasm and commitment are admirable traits, most people are fearful of an extremist. Hence, moderation should be your guide. People tend to be wary of those who indulge in overstatement, in personal abuse, or in unseemly emotional displays" (p. 304). Believability and trustworthiness are important features of a speaker's ethos. But lawmakers questioned the accuracy and truthfulness of some of the witnesses during the hearings. In the question-and-answer session following the prepared testimony, Representative Christopher Shays reminded witnesses that they were "under oath, every one of you, you're before a hearing of Congress," implying that some of the testimony had not been truthful. Shays explained, "When I hear that a beam, the impression is of a laser beam on your 5-year-old daughter's forehead, I just don't frankly believe it. But I'm just being honest with you" (Hearing, 2005, p. 19). Additionally, lawmakers questioned the assertion that someone had bombed the levee, a conspiracy argument that reinforces white perceptions that blacks harbor irrational paranoia toward authorities (Fine & Turner, 2001). When French presented the bombing hypothesis, Shays responded, "When I hear that you were on your porch and you saw that the levee was blown up and bombed, I can't let that pass" (Hearing, 2005, p. 19). When he tried to get French to pinpoint specifically where her house was in relation to the levee, French avoided providing the details, causing Shays to exclaim, "So far I've asked you two questions and you've been very unresponsive" (Hearing, 2005, p. 20). At the end of the exchange, French says, "I have no reason to lie to you. Who are you, Mr. Shays? What have you done for me?" (Hearing, 2005, p. 20). These appeals, like those that invoked Holocaust imagery, worked to undermine the witnesses' credibility, at least from the perspective of lawmakers.

Persuaders looking to win the adherence of their audience also show deference, or the "ability to show courteous regard for their audiences by not being presumptuous or brusque" (Beason, 1991, p. 333). To conform to this component of ethos, speakers must be respectful and polite when presenting their claims and show an appreciation of the opportunity to present their views before the audience. Furthermore, according to those who promote this view of ethos, speakers should adopt an inoffensive tone when making their arguments so that audiences can make up their own minds about the validity of the claims. "Conversation, and most other talk, is a collaborative activity that can be successful only if the speaker respects, or takes into account, the rights, capabilities, propensities, and feelings of the other parties" (Levelt, 1989, as cited in Beason, 1991, p. 335). This seems especially relevant at congressional hearings, since witnesses testify under oath in a formal hearing. Furthermore, the visual structure of the hearings reinforces this hierarchy, as lawmakers are seated in rows that are elevated, while witnesses sit at a single table and look up at the questioners, signifying subordination to them.

Given the harrowing experiences of some of the witnesses in the aftermath of Katrina, it is understandable why many of them would express anger and frustration at the hearings, rather than the politeness and deference that Beason claims is important in establishing ethos in a presentation. When one lawmaker signaled to Dyan French that she was running out of time in her speech, she replied, "You know what, baby, I'm from the sixties. Call the police. I'm going to stop talking when I finish with my messages from my community. That's the only reason why I'm here. I didn't come to represent me" (Hearing, 2005, p. 13). A video of the hearings reveals several moments when participants raised their voices to be heard or to emphasize a point (Hurricane Katrina Evacuees, 2005). Additionally, there are several moments during the question-and-answer session when some of the witnesses spoke simultaneously. This ran counter to established rules and procedures of the Senate and conveyed potential disregard for the format of the hearings.

Representative Steve Buyer of Indiana lauded the least vocal witness at the hearings, Terrol Williams, for "a very good job" in his written testimony, but Williams was also the only witness to downplay the importance of race as a factor in the government's response to the storm. On the contrary, lawmakers admonished the other witnesses. "This is a big deal," said Shays to the witnesses as he reminded them they were under oath at a congressional hearing and bound to tell the truth. When he became impatient with French's responses to his questions, Shays insisted, "Don't interrupt me now please. I listened to your presentation. I didn't interrupt you" (Hearing, 2005, p. 21). Offended by Shays' line of questioning, French angrily retorted, "Damn, now we're going to play with people's intelligence?" (Hearing, 2005, p. 21). Hodges said she was "appalled" that lawmakers were accusing evacuees of "lying," while Thompson said, "I don't mean any insult, but when you walk a mile in my shoes, tell me what you believe then" (Hearing, 2005, p. 22).

Decades of research have reinforced the importance of source credibility. A review of this work has concluded, "Few areas of research ... have produced results as consistent as the findings that sources high in expertise and/or trust-

worthiness are more persuasive than those low in these qualities" (Inch & Warnick, 1998, p. 76). While some audiences assign credibility to speakers based
on their prior reputation, it is "what you do to prepare and present your arguments" that "has a strong impact on whether your audience will perceive you as
credible" (Rybacki & Rybacki, 1996, p. 230). The evacuees who testified before
the Select Committee on December 6, 2005, failed to establish identification
with lawmakers, undermined their expertise by advancing claims that some
lawmakers found unbelievable, failed to qualify the most sensational claims,
and lacked the deference that some lawmakers thought was needed in the proceedings. This led some of the lawmakers to discount claims of racism and resulted in frustration among some of the witnesses. "You know, it's just unfortunate that … I would waste my time to come before you all," lamented
Hodges (Hearing, 2005, p. 22).

Listening to Indecorous Voices

The *San Francisco Chronicle* suggested "the image of impoverished hurricane
victims waiting in vain for government help" forced "a national conversation on
race and urban poverty" (Sandalow, 2005, p. A13). The Select Committee decided to take up the topic of race in its December 6, 2005, hearings on the federal
government's response to Hurricane Katrina. Several witnesses testified they experienced racist treatment at the hands of white authorities, while others spoke
of desperate conditions after the storm that they felt they would not have endured had they been white. Cynthia McKinney, the Georgia Democrat who requested the hearings, called the personal testimonials of the witnesses "shocking
and disturbing" (McKinney, 2006, p. 4). While Katrina represented "a watershed
moment" because it "forced Americans to confront the taboo on discussions of
race and poverty at home," McKinney was disappointed when the Select Committee's final report "elected not to tangle with these issues in any depth" (p. 8).

From the perspective of the lawmakers who presided over the hearings and
many of the media sources that covered the event, the Katrina evacuees who
delivered testimony at the hearings lacked the ethos necessary to persuade their
audience. As James Gill (2005) wrote in the New Orleans *Times-Picayune*, "to
invoke the Gestapo is to forfeit all credibility" (p. 7). Jarvis DeBerry (2005)
lamented on the same editorial page, "there have got to be others who can testify to our pain in a way that doesn't encourage the world to tune us out" (p.
7). Such perspectives blamed the victims for their rhetorical incompetence—
that is, the lack of skills necessary to convince audiences. My argument, however, is that lawmakers undermined the standing of the storm survivors by
symbolically framing them as indecorous. This maneuver allowed lawmakers
to avoid addressing complex issues of race and social justice. As Marable

(2006) pointed out, "'racism' can only be rationalized and justified through the suppression of Black accounts or evidence that challenges society's understanding about itself and its own past" (p. 6). Thus, to avoid addressing larger questions of race, White conservative lawmakers diverted the discussion to other issues. The dismissal of evacuees' experience as irrational or unbelievable maintained an order that failed to address systemic racial issues. Standards of ethos that required speakers to conform to established patterns of identification, expertise, humility, and deference functioned to valorize those who are already in power and discredited voices that are not in the mainstream. Minority voices, in particular, became silenced.

This is not to say that one should accept—without question—all of the claims made by participants in the hearings. But to dismiss their testimony as "mostly nonsense" (Lopez-Calderon, 2005, p. 2) and the witnesses themselves as "a few hysterics telling fairy stories" (Gill, 2005, p. 7) is itself a convenient way to avoid addressing larger questions of race that Hurricane Katrina brought to the surface. In their final report, the Select Committee acknowledged that there was "little question that Katrina had sparked renewed debate about race, class, and institutional approaches toward vulnerable population groups in the United States" (Select Bipartisan Committee, 2006, p. 19). However, the final report failed to describe the experiences of the witnesses or delve into the race issue specifically. In fact, the report mentioned that a majority of the Select Committee's members did not believe charges of racism were well founded (Select Bipartisan Committee, 2006, p. 20). The report cited several polls showing evacuees thought race was a factor in the government's poor response to Katrina, but this only functioned to reinforce the skepticism of committee members, as it implicitly suggested that racism was a mere perception among African-Americans, but not grounded in reality. The polls showing black criticism of the government's response became justification for holding the hearings (as a means of signaling "concern" over the issue) but those same polls also became a justification for inaction (based on white skepticism that such claims had merit).

The Select Committee's final report quoted President Bush's September 15 address where he famously admitted, "poverty has roots in a history of racial discrimination" but it followed this with references to other claims about race, such as Jesse Jackson's analogy that shelters resembled slave ships and Louis Farrakhan's speculation that someone intentionally bombed levees to flood African-American neighborhoods. The final report then admitted race "warranted further discussion" but also noted some of the commentary about race had not been "constructive, substantiated, or fair" (p. 19). Rhetorically, this characterization had three main effects. First, it marginalized African-American criticism of the government as radical and extremist. By juxtaposing Bush's remarks with those of Jackson and Farrakhan, the Select Committee identified with the more "reasonable" approach of the President and dismissed the witnesses' testimony, as it was implicitly linked to the "unfair" and "unsubstanti-ated" claims of Jackson and Farrakhan. Second, the attention placed on histor-ical analogies (to the Holocaust or to slavery) and the bombing conspiracy ar-gument functioned as a straw man argument that diverted attention from the witnesses' thesis that they endured extreme hardship made worse by an inat-tentive government. Disproving the conspiracy claim—an easier task than de-fending the government's response to the storm—became a means to discredit or ignore all of the other testimony related to racism.

Finally, the dismissal of witness testimony as fantasy ignored the historical narrative of institutional racism. Even the most far-reaching claim the wit-nesses presented at the hearing—that someone bombed the levee—had some grounding in real suspicion. The water flow at both the 17th Street Canal and the Industrial Canal breaches were directed toward African-American commu-nities. Given that local parish governments maintained each levee, the wealth-ier neighborhoods had the resources to invest in safer structures (McKinney, 2006). Additionally, "the noise of the breach would have sounded like a huge explosion" (McKinney, 2006, p. 32) which explains why some residents thought they heard a bomb. The possibility that the levees were bombed would have coincided with historical experience. There is evidence that on two occa-sions—the Great Mississippi Flood of 1927 and Hurricane Betsy in 1965—of-ficials breached levees intentionally as a means of saving affluent communities. "Since the flood of 1927 was a turning point for many black families in the south, the bitterness of those experiences are no doubt still associated with the flood," wrote Representative Cynthia McKinney in her supplementary report to the findings of the Select Committee, "and the flood as we know is associated with the blowing of the levees" (McKinney, 2006, pp. 31–32).

Understood in this context, one can better evaluate the outrage of the wit-nesses at the congressional hearings. By the time Congress convened the De-cember 6, 2005, hearing, it was already apparent that some officials had treated evacuees poorly. In one famous incident, police turned back evacuees crossing the Crescent City Connection Bridge into Gretna (Simmons, 2005). Yet, law-makers at the Select Committee hearings remained skeptical of the claims of New Orleans residents who asserted they had witnessed similar racism. They questioned the credibility of the witnesses and their stories as a way of deflect-ing attention from systemic issues related to race. Standards of ethos enhance-ment, such as identification, expertise, humility, and deference, worked against witnesses who questioned the authority of lawmakers to render judg-ments about their experiences. If persuaders need to adopt the prejudices of their audience, then ethos will always be "a rather conservative approach to rhetorical character" (Baumlin, 2001, p. 266). Instead, critics need to under-stand that social activists may have legitimate grievances that they need to voice outside the conventions of accepted rhetorical practice.

References

Alpert, B. (2005, December 7). Racism cost lives, N.O. evacuees say; bitter exchanges erupt as they testify in D.C. *Times-Picayune*, p. 3. Retrieved December 10, 2005 from LexisNexis.

Aristotle. (1991). *On rhetoric: A theory of civic discourse* (G. A. Kennedy, Trans.). New York: Oxford UP.

Baumlin, J.S. (Ed.) (1994). *Ethos: New essays in rhetorical and critical theory.* Dallas: Southern Methodist UP.

Baumlin, J.S. (2001). Ethos. In T.O. Sloane (Ed.), *Encyclopedia of rhetoric* (pp. 263–277). New York: Oxford UP.

Beason, L. (1991). Strategies for establishing an effective persona: An analysis of appeals to ethos in business speeches. *The Journal of Business Communication*, 28, 326–346.

Burke, K. (1969). A rhetoric of motives. *Berkeley: University of California Press.*

Cochran, J. (2005, September 19). The race issue confronts GOP. *CQ Weekly*, p. 2486.

Cole, T. (1999). *Selling the Holocaust: From Auschwitz to Schindler, how history is bought, packaged, and sold.* New York: Routledge.

Corder, J.W. (1977). Efficient ethos in Shane, with a proposal for discriminating among kinds of ethos. *Communication Quarterly*, 25, 28–31.

Corts, T.E. (1968). Special report: The derivation of ethos. Speech Monographs, 35, 201–202.

Cox, J.R. (1999). Reclaiming the "indecorous" voice: Public participation by low-income communities in environmental decision-making. In C. B. Short & D. Hardy-Short (Eds.), *Proceedings of the Fifth Biennial Conference on Communication and Environment* (pp. 21–31). Flagstaff, AZ: Northern Arizona University, School of Communication.

DeBerry, J. (2005, December 9). Sane witnesses abound, but not in D.C. *Times-Picayune*, Metro p. 7. Retrieved December 10, 2005 from LexisNexis.

Dyson, M.E. (2006). *Come hell or high water: Hurricane Katrina and the color of disaster.* New York: Basic Books.

Enos, T. (1990). "An eternal golden braid": Rhetor as audience, audience as rhetor. In G. Kirsh & D.H. Roen (Eds.), *A sense of audience in written communication* (99–114). Newbury Park: Sage.

Fine, G.A., & Turner, P.A. (2001). *Whispers on the color line: Rumor and race in America.* Berkeley: University of California Press.

Fletcher, M.A. (2005, September 12). Katrina pushes issues of race and poverty at Bush. *Washington Post*, p. A02. Retrieved April 21, 2006 from LexisNexis.

Gill, J. (2005, December 9). Lunatic fringe hijacks the spotlight. *Times-Picayue*, Metro p. 7. Retrieved December 10, 2005 from LexisNexis.

Gilman, N. (2005, September 14). What Katrina teaches about the meaning of racism. *Understanding Katrina: Perspectives from the social sciences*. Retrieved January 14, 2006 from http://understandingkatrina.ssrc.org/Gilman/pf/.

Goldblatt, M. (2005, December 22). Race, reason, and reaching out. *The American Spectator*. Retrieved January 14, 2006 from http://www.spectator.org/ util/print.asp?art_id=9183.

Grice, G.L., & Skinner, J.F. (1995). *Mastering public speaking* (2nd ed.). Boston: Allyn and Bacon.

Gross, A.G. (1983). Analogy and intersubjectivity: Political oratory, scholarly argument and scientific reports. *Quarterly Journal of Speech, 69*, 37–46.

Harrison, K. (2003). Rhetorical rehearsals: The construction of ethos in confederate women's civil war diaries. *Rhetoric Review, 22*, 243–263.

Hearing of the Select Bipartisan Committee to Investigate the Preparation for and Response to Hurricane Katrina. (2005, December 6). Hurricane Katrina: Voices from inside the storm. *Federal News Service*. Retrieved December 15, 2005 from LexisNexis.

Hurricane Katrina evacuees: Experience. (2005, December 6). *Hearing of the Select Bipartisan Committee to Investigate the Preparation for and Response to Hurricane Katrina* [Videocassette]. West Lafayette, IN: C-SPAN Archives.

Inch, E.S., & Warnick, B. (1998). *Critical thinking and communication: The use of reason in argument* (3rd ed.). Boston: Allyn and Bacon.

Jaffe, C. (1995). *Public speaking: A cultural perspective*. New York: Wadsworth.

Jefferson, W.J. (2005, December 14). Congress has a duty to hear from everyone. *Times-Picayune*, Metro-editorial, p. 6. Retrieved December 15, 2005 from LexisNexis.

Johnson, N. (1995). Ethos. In T. Enos (Ed.), *Encyclopedia of rhetoric and composition: Communication from ancient times to the information age* (pp. 243–245). New York: Garland.

Juthe, A. (2005). Argument by analogy. *Argumentation, 19*, 1–27.

Kearney, P., & T.G. Plax. (1996). *Public speaking in a diverse society*. Mountain View, CA: Mayfield.

Leibovich, M. (2005, June 25). The comparison that ends the conversation: Senator is latest to regret Nazi analogy. *Washington Post*, p. C01. Retrieved 10 July 2006 from http://www.washingtonpost.com/wpdyn/content/article/2005/06/21/AR2005062101753_pf.html.

Lopez-Calderon, M. (2005, December 9). Katrina "konspiracy" kooks. *The American Thinker*. Retrieved January 14, 2006 from http://www.american thinker.com/articles_print.php?article_id=5060.

Marable, M. (2006). Katrina's unnatural disaster: A tragedy of black suffering and white denial. *Souls*, 8, 1–8.

McCroskey, J.C. (1966). Scales for the measurement of ethos. *Speech Monographs*, 33, 65–72.

McCroskey, J.C., & Young, T.J. (1981). Ethos and credibility: The construct and its measurement after three decades. *Central States Speech Journal*, 32, 24–34.

McKinney. C.A. (2006, February 6). *Supplementary report to the findings of the select bipartisan committee to investigate the preparation for and response to hurricane Katrina*. Washington: GPO.

Natural disasters: The federal response. (2005, November). *Congressional Digest*, 257.

Oft-Rose, N. (1989). The importance of ethos. *Argumentation and Advocacy*, 25, 197–199.

Ollison, R.O. (2006, January 29). Savior self: Kanye West and his God complex. *Baltimore Sun*, 1F. Retrieved February 12, 2006 from LexisNexis.

The Pew Research Center for the People and the Press. (2005, October 31). The black and white of public opinion: Did the racial divide in attitudes about Katrina mislead us? The Pew Research Center for the People and the Press Commentary. Retrieved January 14, 2006 from http://peopleress. org/commentary/display.php3?AnalysisID=121.

Rieke, R.D., & Sillars, M.O. (2001). *Argumentation and critical decision making* (5th ed.). New York: Longman.

Ross, D. (1980). The projection of credibility as a rhetorical strategy in Anwar el-Sadat's address to the Israeli parliament. *The Western Journal of Speech Communication*, 44, 74–80.

Rybacki, K.C., & Rybacki, D. J. (1996). *Advocacy and opposition: An introduction to argumentation* (3rd ed.). Boston: Allyn and Bacon.

Samovar, L.A., & Mills, J. (1995). *Oral communication: Speaking across cultures* (9th ed.). Madison: Brown and Benchmark.

Sandalow, M. (2005, September 23). Katrina thrusts race and poverty onto national stage. *San Francisco Chronicle*, p. A13. Retrieved December 10, 2005 from LexisNexis.

Select Bipartisan Committee to Investigate the Preparation for and Response to Hurricane Katrina. (2006). *A failure of initiative: The final report of the select bipartisan committee to investigate the preparation for and response to hurricane Katrina*. Washington: GPO.

Simmons, A.M. (2005, November 8). The nation; Protesters make a stand on bridge that was blocked; Three days after Katrina pounded New Orleans, police in nearby Gretna refused to let evacuees enter. Marchers say it was an act of racism. *Los Angeles Times*, p. A10. Retrieved December 10, 2005 from LexisNexis.

Truscello, M. (2001). The clothing of the American mind: The construction of scientific ethos in the science wars. *Rhetoric Review*, 20, 329–350.

Whaley, B.B. (1997). Perceptions of rebuttal analogy: Politeness and implications for persuasion. *Argumentation & Advocacy*, 33(4), 161–169. Retrieved February 20, 2006 from Communication & Mass Media Complete.

Whaley, B.B., & Holloway, R.L. (1997). Rebuttal analogy in political communication: Argument and attack in sound bite. *Political Communication*, 14, 293–305.

Whitehead, J.L. (1968). Factors of source credibility. *Quarterly Journal of Speech*, 54, 59–63.

Wisse, J. (1989). *Ethos and pathos from Aristotle to Cicero*. Amsterdam: Adolf M. Hakkert.

Zarefsky, D. (1996). *Public speaking: Strategies for success*. Boston: Allyn and Bacon.

Section Three

Images of the Future:
Policy, Activism, and Justice

Chapter 15

George Bush Does Not Care about Black People: Hip-Hop and the Struggle for Katrina Justice[1]

David J. Leonard

Introduction

On Monday, January 16, 2006, Bill O'Reilly interviewed conservative author John McWhorter and Clarence Jones, a former speechwriter for Martin Luther King, Jr. Using the King Holiday as an opportunity to denounce "black leaders," O'Reilly stated that the two most pressing issues facing the black community, which in his estimation were being ignored by black leaders, were out-of-wedlock births and rap (hip-hop) culture (O'Reilly, 2006). Beyond reflecting the nature of contemporary racial discourse that erases racism, instead demonizing black women and youth as sources of problems, his comments, which were endorsed by both his guests, embody the very narrow vision of hip-hop and the ease in which American social ills are readily displaced onto black bodies. His comments, while nothing new given his longstanding war on hip-hop as a threat to American children, seemed especially powerful in wake of Katrina.

Yet, the demonization of hip-hop on the *O'Reilly Factor*, on Fox News, and within much of conservative America fits with the continued demonization of black youth, the urban poor, and those left behind in a post-civil rights America. The media coverage that surrounded Hurricane Katrina was but one ex-

---

1. I would like to dedicate this piece to those who died or lost their livelihoods during Hurricane Katrina as well as those who have used their voice, energy, and creative, political, and activist spirits to help rebuild New Orleans. I would also like to dedicate this to Sophie Nicole Leonard, whose death taught me what is important in life.

ample in this regard. Whether watching Fox News, MSNBC, or CNN, or reading any number of newspapers, the media coverage was clear: the storm, governmental failures, and American racism was not as significant as lawlessness, looters, ignorant (black) residents who refused to evacuate, murder, mayhem, and savagery. Bill O'Reilly blamed "wild gangs" and an "urban menace" (who probably listen to hip-hop) for slow search-and-rescue efforts and the dangers facing many residents (Cunningham, 2005). The stories of survivors, perseverance, rescue, and recovery found little attention within America's fourth branch of government. Questions about racism and the failures of American policy and the Bush administration were even less common,

> The celebration of the media during Katrina is perhaps ultimately ironic since it is the media that has largely been responsible for communicating the culture's spleenful bigotry toward the black poor. To be championed as the defenders of the very population that media has harmed so much, whether intending to or not, should provide more than one occasion of intense discomfort and squirming for journalists.

> (Dyson, 2006, p. 176)

Interestingly, it was not the media pundits, Anderson Cooper, Geraldo Rivera, Bill O'Reilly or any number of folks, who fully reported the devastation of Hurricane Katrina; it was not the mainstream media that gave voice to the pain and suffering, to the efforts of people to survive in spite of a government and nation that had left them behind. It was hip-hop; it was hip-hop that offered counter narratives and provided a vehicle of collective anger and outrage. It was hip-hop that offered an alterative frame or lens to examine the devastation, the governmental response, and the context that allowed for this injustice. It was hip-hop that called for action and demanded accountability. It was artists and practitioners, fans, and the entire hip-hop community that in the face of crisis offered hope of a brighter day.

The reaction of the hip-hop community in wake of Hurricane Katrina offered a reminder of the history, power, and potential of hip-hop as a source of commentary, unity, and empowerment. "Since that first era of the conscious rapper, many have invested in the idea of hip-hop as the likely incubator for a cross-racial progressive political movement" (Neal, 2004, n.p.). Yet, though many artists have followed in this tradition, "very little has ever translated into concrete political action (n.p.). Jay Woodson (2006), a cultural critic and activist, beautifully described hip-hop as "a virtual place which we identify and validate ourselves." In his estimation, "Hip Hop is a social construct and has political implications. Talking about Hip Hop is a conversation about social issues and politics. Hip Hop has always been a hyper verbal; it is a space to express thoughts, feelings, dreams, inspiration and teach lessons" (n.p.). The efforts of artists to give voice, to counter narratives, provide hope, and demand action in the days and months after Hurricane Katrina demonstrated the truth in Woodson's analysis and the truth that is hip-hop. Often silenced by machinations both internal and external—the unquestioning pursuit of bling and Fox News' character assassinations—the political potential of hip-hop is unmatched in the current historical moment. The voice of now two generations, hip-hop reaches audiences from New York to Los Angeles, Seattle to Miami, Minneapolis to Dallas; it is continually inspiring and electrifying, prompting praise and condemnation. In the case of Hurricane Katrina and its aftermath, hip-hop is, once again, a force to be reckoned with.

Within this context, this chapter examines the controversial comments of Kanye West as part of a larger collective response to the racism and poverty that penetrated American discourses in the days following Hurricane Katrina. It looks at his comments and the widespread support as evidence of a political potential in the hip-hop generation, arguing that the aftermath of Katrina represented a profound moment for the hip-hop movement in its struggle to secure social justice. Discussing the response of the hip-hop community to Hurricane Katrina (in statements, in artistry, and in organizational action), this chapter chronicles the struggle over the political and cultural place of hip-hop in the struggle for justice following Hurricane Katrina. It brings to light the political potential of the hip-hop lyric, as well as the power in numbers that the hip-hop community can affect, demonstrated by the massive organizing and fundraising efforts undertaken by hip-hop players, big and small, in the wake of Hurricane Katrina.

George Bush Doesn't Care about Black People: So Says Kanye West

On September 2, 2005, in the aftermath of Hurricane Katrina and several days of twenty-four-hour-a-day news coverage, hip-hop artist Kanye West appeared on a one hour fundraiser for the American Red Cross on NBC. Deviating from his script, West took the opportunity to voice his outrage toward the Bush administration, the media, and the state of American poverty:

I hate the way they portray us in the media. You see a black family, it says, "They're looting." You see a white family, it says, "They're looking for food." And, you know, it's been five days [waiting for federal help] because most of the people are black. And even for me to complain about it, I would be a hypocrite because I've tried to turn away from the TV because it's too hard to watch. I've even been shopping before even giving a donation, so now I'm calling my business manager right now to see what is the biggest amount I can give, and just to imagine if I was down there, and those are my people down there. So anybody out there that wants to do anything that we can help—with the way America is set up to help the poor, the black people, the less

well-off, as slow as possible. I mean, the Red Cross is doing everything they can. We already realize a lot of people that could help are at
war right now, fighting another way—and they've given them permission to go down and shoot us! George Bush doesn't care about
black people!

(as cited in De Moraes, 2005, n.p.)

Before West had uttered his final words, the controversy surrounding
"Kanye's controversial comments" had exploded on the Internet, on the air-
waves, in newspapers, and within every political circle. Throughout the media,
commentators denounced West as misguided, inappropriate, and typical of the
hip-hop generation's willingness to "play the race card" in almost every instance. Bill O'Reilly (2005) of Fox News, chastised West for his comments,
which he stated were part of a larger cultural problem within hip-hop, "And
the remarks are simply nutty. I mean, come on, West is saying authorities want
to shoot blacks? It doesn't get more irresponsible than that. But what do you
expect from an ideologically-driven newspaper industry and the world of rap,
where anything goes? What do you expect?" (n.p.). O'Reilly was not alone, with
commentators, bloggers, and others taking ample shots at West for his critiques of the president and his efforts to use his platform as an artist to advocate for social justice in the wake of Hurricane Katrina. Laura Bush described
West's comments about her husband as "disgusting" during an interview on the
American Urban Radio Network, "I mean I am the person who lives with him.
I know what he is like, and I know what he thinks, and I know he cares about
people" ("First Lady," 2005, n.p.). On *Larry King Live*, President George H.W.
Bush similarly came to the aid of his son, expressing his outrage against the
"particularly vicious comment that the president didn't care, was insensitive on
ethnicity.... Insensitive about race. Now that one hurt because I know this
president and I know he does care ... that's what in his heart" ("Interview,"
2005, n.p.). Interestingly, none of Bush's defenders engaged the questions
raised about governmental failure, media racism, American racism, and the
failures of a nation, all of which would be prominent ones for hip-hop artists.

While much of the post-fundraiser commentary denounced West for his
comments, erasing his rightful protests against this injustice and challenges to
American racism and turning them into a personal attack against a single person, many inside the hip-hop community came to his aid, not only offering
support for his right of free speech, but celebrating his courageous statement
as reflective of the vast majority of voiceless and powerless African Americans
and youth of color. Throughout the Internet, websites, blogs, and chatrooms
sprung up to support his comments, and to create a call for action. In communities throughout the country, fans donned "Kanye Was Right," "Vote for
Kanye," and "George Bush Does Hate Black People" t-shirts to voice their support for West and their collective outrage toward the Bush administration and

its inaction following Katrina. The support for West was not limited to fans, as others also came to the aid of the beleaguered star, focusing not just on his right of free speech but on the truth of his statements. Jay-Z, P-Diddy, David Banner, and others called West a hero, thanking him for giving voice to the frustration of many within the African-American community.

The counter narratives and the efforts to give voice to the powerless were not limited to rap artists, who in both performance and in public statements offered scathing critiques of both America and its government, but were forwarded by spoken word artists as well. Following Kanye West's statements on NBC, Etan Thomas offered public support for West, using the moment as an opportunity to further protest the mistreatment of the African-American community in New Orleans. "Had this been a rich, lily-white suburban area that got hit, you think they would have had to wait five days to get food or water? When the hurricane hit in Florida, Bush made sure people got the help the next day," reminded Thomas. "But now, when you are dealing with a majority poorer class of black people, it takes five days? Then you still don't send help instead sending the National Guard to 'maintain order?' Are you kidding me?" (Zirin, 2005, n.p.). Young City, a New Orleans rapper, defending West for his comments, took this a step further, arguing that the resources of the Bush administration were tied up in Iraq, focused on making millions for those living in America's lily white suburbs. "I just think that it's real crazy that our government ain't kicking in to send something to New Orleans. He's [President Bush] talking about how we need to help people in Iraq but he isn't even concerned with people in our own country" (Hamilton, Williams, & Strong, 2005, n.p.). Thus, not only did West's comments prompt widespread support within the hip-hop community, who defended his comments and anger, but they also drew attention to the issue of national defense as a means of further protesting the failures of the Bush administration.

The aftermath of Katrina and Kanye West's comments was marked by the hip-hop community demanding justice, accountability, and answers, and also by artists challenging the black community and hip-hop itself for its own failures, which had deadly consequences in August and September of 2005. Michael Eric Dyson (2006) reflected on this important and often overlooked dimension of West's comments, and how his challenge of the president served as a reminder of the courage needed by hip-hop in this moment of crisis, "Not only did West redeem the sometimes sorry state of a hip-hop world careening on gaudy trinkets of its own success—booze, broads, and bling—but his gesture signaled a political courage on the part of the black blessed that is today all too rare" (p. 154). His words served as a denunciation of the Bush administration and American racism; his actions served as source of critique of hip-hop and inspiration for the hip-hop community.

Southern Rapper T.I. blasted hip-hop for aiding and abetting the government, for its own selfishness and disregard for the poor: "I called everybody's bluff who is talking all that ballin' shit," stated T.I. "Popping all them bottles in the club … talking about how much girls and jewelry and cars they got. Let's see how much money they've got for a good cause. Basically, I told everybody to put their money where their mouths are, and if you ain't got no money to give to the cause, I don't want to hear that shit no more" ("T.I, David Banner," 2005, n.p.). Twista, a Chicago-based rapper, agreed, arguing that it was a given that the government and the vast majority of America would show little concern for the despair of America's underclass, particularly those who are black and brown, and demonstrating the necessity of the intervention of the hip-hop and the black community as a whole through action and art: "They've been bogus, so what is everybody so shocked about.… I feel the response was real slow, but I look at my own harder than I look at them" ("T.I, David Banner," 2005, n.p.). West's comments created a space for critique of hip-hop. Artists, who heeded his courage and his denunciations of the Bush administration, both challenged America's claims of shock and made clear the truth of West's comments, and took the opportunity to blast hip-hop and the black community for joining the Bush administration and white America in leaving behind the residents of New Orleans and ghettos throughout America. His stand was not only significant because of his refusal to be silent, but because of his efforts to create a space of dissent, opposition and action,

> Kanye West's words and those of the figures who supported him suggest that not nearly enough of us are invested in consistently raising our voice for the voiceless.… Too many of us are safe until all black people are safe, Kanye West saw his identity tied to the identity of the poor, and realized that the people were drowning were "my people".… If Bush and black elites had forgotten the poor, black artists from the Delta have remembered their peers with eloquence.
>
> (Dyson, 2006, p. 157)

In fact, artists and activists that embodied the hip-hop generation took the challenges set forth by West and the failures of a nation, by protesting against injustice, and bringing to voice the experiences of those that had been erased within the mainstream media.

Hip-Hop to the Rescue: Mainstream Rappers and Hurricane Katrina

Juvenile, a rapper from New Orleans whose career embodies the "sometimes sorry state of a hip-hop world careening on gaudy trinkets of its own success—booze, broads, and bling," (see Dyson, 2006, p. 154) offered some of the most damning criticisms of American poverty and the complicity of all levels of government in leaving people to die after the hurricane:

All we lost was our home. A lot of people lost their lives. But we lost beyond a house or a door. We lost an environment. So we lost everybody. Everybody lost. We lost the spirit.... There ain't nothing like New Orleans. We got spirit. We the smallest city; the highest poverty. We was the lowest in the education system. We was just about to go on strike with the teachers. The school board system was corrupt. Our police system is corrupt. Our judicial system is corrupt.

(as cited in Satten, 2005, pp. 112–114).

He, like so many others, was unwilling to let Bush off the hook, seizing the opportunity emblazoned by West's comments to question the priorities of the president and to give voice to the dissatisfaction of many within the black community; to him, the government, military, and communal focus on Iraq and Afghanistan had diverted attention and resources away from the Gulf Coast, further illustrating the misplaced priorities of the Bush administration: "If we [as the United States] could put a million people, a million soldiers in Afghanistan and Iraq, we can definitely put the same effort towards New Orleans, and Mississippi. They have the ability to fly down and save people" (as cited in Hamilton, Williams, & Strong, 2005, n.p.). Yet, for Juvenile, Katrina had the potential to inspire a remedy for the many ills facing New Orleans and its residents. In the days after Katrina hit, he hoped that it would bring resources and change; it had already brought attention and national concern for problems that had otherwise been off the American radar, notwithstanding the efforts of hip-hop artists and activists. For Juvenile, the potential change, attention, and allocation of resources may have been the silver lining of all of Katrina's despair and destruction: "It didn't take a hurricane for me to do nothing for New Orleans, cause like Chris Rock said we was fucked up before the hurricane hit. Y'all should've been sending us ... FEMA. We've been fucked up. For a lot that shit was a blessing" (as cited in Satten, 2005, pp. 112–114). In other words, he noted that the pain, death, and poverty evident in the days predating Katrina, had the potential to generate concern and resources. His optimism, however, only proved to be false, given the lack of national and governmental attention given to the aftermath of the crisis, a fact not lost on Juvenile. Almost a year after Katrina, the national discussions about America's underclass, inequality, poverty, and the racial divide have once again been muted; the rebuilding process has been painfully slow, and the future of the victims of Katrina remains nebulous at best. In "Get Ya Hustle On," Juvenile (2006a) rapped about these frustrations and the persistent neglect of the government in a song that does not comment directly on Katrina, but on the state of black America and the difficulties of survival. In this context, he powerfully commented on the failure of the federal government during and after Katrina as yet another example of state violence, which in his estimation contributed to the necessity of hustling, because "I lost it all in Ka-trina (damn)" (n.p.).

The importance of Katrina and its aftermath to "Get Ya Hustle On," was clarified in its video (Juvenile, 2006b), which began with somber music play-ing as he dedicated the song and the video to those who lost their lives during Hurricane Katrina and those who continue to struggle to rebuild their lives. Using a quick-shot montage of a destroyed New Orleans, the anger expressed in the song was amplified by images of lost lives, ruined houses, bleak futures, and abandoned neighborhoods. The sight of an Escalade (a symbol of the American Dream within the hip-hop community) pulled by two horses, a man holding a sign that read "Still Here," and two other signs that stated "1905 or 2005?" and "You already forgot," offered a powerful narrative that not only brought to life the injustices Juvenile rapped about, but countered the fears ex-pressed in the song: that we have forgotten the injustices, America's failures, and the lost lives of black residents of New Orleans. Equally powerful, the video left its viewers with a simple conclusion: the conditions that pre-existed and resulted from Katrina, alongside a neglectful government and inept media, mandates survival by any means necessary, including "getting your hustle on."

Juvenile was not the only mainstream, or popular, rapper who recorded a song about Hurricane Katrina. Not surprisingly, Public Enemy,[2] with assistance from Paris, who have long stood at the forefront of the conscious rap, or politi-cally progressive rap activist movement, began working on a song shortly after Hurricane Katrina hit New Orleans. The start of "Hell No (We Ain't Alright)," with the sounds of a raging storm in the background, captured its anger and its message: that as devastating and destructive as Hurricane Katrina was to New Orleans and to the black underclass who resided there, the policies of the Bush administration, the erasure of those left behind from the national consciousness, and the lack of concern and action on the part of the American people had been equally, if not more, devastating (Chuck D, 2005; Public Enemy, 2006). In other words, the United States, and particularly a United States led by the Bush ad-ministration, did not abandon its poor, the black underclass, on rooftops and in attics following the storm and the destruction of the levees, because it had al-ready left them behind to starve, struggle, and live in poverty and despair.

Mos Def, recorded a song in early September 2005 that was "leaked to mix-tape DJs and to the Internet shortly thereafter" (Patel & Reid, 2005, n.p.).[3] He started his Katrina tribute song, entitled "Dollar Day for New Orleans (Katrina Klap)," in a similar way, reminding listeners that to understand Hurricane Kat-

---

2. It should be noted that a version of the song, in what appears to be a spoken word piece, was published on http://www.counterpoint.com on September 6, 2005.

3. It, however, would eventually be released at the end of 2006 as part of his *True Magic* album; the title of this song is "Dollar Day."

rina and to begin to think about available avenues of secured justice necessitates an examination of history; it requires a recognition that it was not just a Category 5 hurricane, weak levees, or even an incompetent government response that resulted in so much despair, but years of neglect, state violence, and lack of care from the government. He dedicated the song to the people and the community devastated by "a storm called, America" (Mos Def, 2005, 2006, n.p.). Both songs attributed the injustices of Hurricane Katrina to the failures of the Bush administration. As with West's comments, much of the post-Katrina hip-hop focused on the failures of the Bush administration and its complicity in the suffering of the black residents of New Orleans. The focus, however, was not on incompetence, but rather on the manner in which "the government had callously broken its compact with its poor black citizens and that it had forgotten them because it had not taken them seriously" (Dyson, 2006, p. 28). Likewise, both "Hell No," and "Katrina Klap," like the polemic offered by West, were not concerned with Bush as an individual, or his personal beliefs, but "Bush as the face of the government," (Dyson, 2006, p. 28), and as a representative for failed American democracy and policy. Mos Def (2005) offered the following assessment of the Bush administration, who in his belief was more concerned with gas prices, profit margins, and even taking out the trash than with the people of New Orleans: "And if you poor you black…,/You betta off on crack, dead or in jail, or with a gun in Iraq (a aq) …" (n.p.; also cited in Patel & Reid, 2005, n.p.).

Public Enemy (2006) took similar aim at the Bush administration, arguing that it seems only concerned with black America when it comes to incarceration and finding someone to send to war. Katrina resulted not from a natural weather phenomenon but from neglect, from a Bush administration that was more focused on oil and Halliburton contracts, that was more dedicated to overseas wars and tax cuts for the rich than protecting and serving the black community, particularly poor black communities like those in New Orleans. In its focus on padding the pockets of Halliburton, and global imperialism, the Bush Administration (and its predecessors) had left black America behind, so much so that even as evacuees they were not afforded basic human necessities.

Jay-Z (2006) criticized the Bush administration not only for its failures during Katrina, but for neglecting America's poor, and for confining and inflicting violence on black communities inside America long before Katrina, ("People was poor before the hurricane came") (n.p.). The title of his song, "The Minority Report," clearly marked it as a report on the state of black America and other communities of color, a report that revealed anger, pain, devastation, and the unacceptability of current affairs. Similarly, another hip-hop artist, Lil-Wayne, in a song entitled "Georgia … Bush," which masterfully samples Ray Charles' "Georgia," chastised Bush for his ineptitude during Katrina, linking his blasé attitude to his whiteness and his privileged position, (he dedicates the song to the person with "white skin and his eyes bright blue"), ultimately asking if it might be more appropriate if the disaster were renamed, "Hurricane Bush" (Lil' Wayne, 2006, n.p.).

These songs elucidated the failures of the media, focusing specifically on their neglect (and demonization) of the black community prior to Hurricane Katrina. Each took aim at the media's coverage of Katrina, making clear that their racism, bias, and continued demonization of the black poor not only affects public opinion and policy, but makes hip-hop important as a teller of truth; Katrina demonstrated that hip-hop must continue to be the CNN of Black America. Focusing on the ways the media demonized blacks during Hurricane Katrina and the aftereffects of a societal practice of demonizing blacks, who in this case were said to be looting while whites were merely trying to survive under awful conditions, Public Enemy gave voice to the belief that the media, military, and police demonized blacks resulting in harassment and violence, "Racism in the news ... Saying whites find food ... Cause them blacks loot" (Chuck D, 2005, n.p.). Echoing West's anger about the media's racially charged coverage of New Orleans and focus on black looting (news reports tended to use the same three shots of looting as part of its many stories) rather than black suffering or even whites looting, Chuck D, who ultimately teamed up with the rest of Public Enemy to produce the song, saw this coverage as just more of the same from the racist American media.

These songs challenged dominant media and political discourses that scoffed and denied the implications of race in the aftermath of Katrina. Kanye West stated that George Bush hated "black people," not poor people; others, like Etan Thomas and P-Diddy made clear that had Katrina hit a predominantly white community the response from the government and the nation as a whole would have been significantly different. Likewise, given the realities of racism and the state of black America, race matters because the devastation of the disaster reflected the legacies and effects of American racism. To Mos Def, George Bush was guilty of having treated African Americans as "worse than trash," (Mos Def, 2005, n.p.). Public Enemy (2006; Chuck D, 2005) also made clear that Hurricane Katrina and the lack of response was racist given its effects on the black community; racism left the levees susceptible, it contributed to people being unable to evacuate, it affected societal and governmental responses, and impacted the lack of concern America had for the impoverished and the destitute populations of New Orleans. In their estimation, the failed response of the government and the nation revealed that the pain and suffering of black Americans didn't warrant action or inspire despair. In other words, the sight of dead black bodies, or suffering black children did not warrant national outrage or action, even if it was clearly visible to Public Enemy and much of black America.

What is most striking about both songs, as well as "Get Ya' Hustle On," is that they all seemed to represent a call to action. The songs themselves were a response to the failures of the Bush administration and the media in particular.

More importantly, Public Enemy and Mos Def used their songs to remind their listeners that Hurricane Katrina was proof that the government, the media, and even those outside the black community could not be relied on for saving New Orleans. Mos Def described the purpose of "Katrina Klap" as less about raising consciousness and more about raising money: "My real aim with 'Dollar Day' is, God willing, to raise $250 million independently, to help adjust the means of the poorest and the weakest, in not just New Orleans but all throughout the Delta region" (as cited in Jeremy K, 2005, n.p.). On August 31, 2006, when holding an impromptu concert in front of MTV's Video Music Awards, which resulted in his arrest for disorderly conduct, Mos Def attempted to counteract the persistent failures to help the victims of Hurricane Katrina. According to Carlene Donovan, his publicist, the performance reflected his desire "to heighten the awareness of a serious situation that still exists in our country. He does not want people to forget that although it's one year later, the people and cities hit by the hurricane still need the help of the American people" ("Mos Def Arrested after VMAs 2006," 2006, n.p.). His effort to use hip-hop as a space of consciousness-raising and fundraising was clear through the song itself, and was especially evident in its powerful hook, which asks for 1 dollar, and reminds the listeners that freedom costs and that everyone and anyone needs to dig into their pockets to help pay for it (Mos Def, 2005).

The message of the song was further emphasized by the comments that followed Mos Def's arrest outside the VMAs and in the video for the song (Skjodt, 2005). As with several other videos, the video for "Katrina Klap" powerfully linked the lyrics with the devastating images of Katrina and the government destruction of those black communities in New Orleans. Yet, in line with the song itself, the video provided a space to encourage viewers to donate money, along with providing specific information as to where and how people could give back, with at least one dollar, as an ultimate Klap for Katrina.

Public Enemy (2006) took this a step further lyrically, not only calling for action, for folks to give financially and spiritually to the rebirth of New Orleans, but demanding a change from hip-hop, from its fans, and from the entire community in terms of priorities. While the failures of the government were obvious and while racism resulted in much devastation and black people became "refugees" in the imagination of many, it was still time for people of color and America as a whole, and particularly the hip-hop generation, to look themselves in the mirror. It was a time to trade in a culture of bling-bling for a culture of compassion; if anything was learned from Katrina, it should be that pimped-out-rides, "keepin' it real," and the popularity and visibility of black entertainers did not save the victims of Hurricane Katrina.

Public Enemy stated that Hurricane Katrina was not simply a manifestation of governmental failures or American racism, but a result of the selfishness of hip-hop, the neglect by those who have secured a part of the "American

Dream," and those who have accepted injustice. They called upon listeners to check themselves, and to hold their elected officials accountable; they called upon listeners to demand and take the fight to the streets; to use the Millions More Movement and this injustice as the "inspiration" for a challenge to the too-long accepted injustices in America. As the government and the mainstream America have shown little concern and care for saving its most impoverished and most disenfranchised "citizens" (or evacuees), it is incumbent upon hip-hop and black America to fight for justice. Flavor Flav, who seems to only have a platform when appearing on VH-1 as a clown, reminded listeners of the stakes and who bears responsibility at the conclusion of "Hell No," by urging listeners to not simply listen to music, but to give in the form of money, food, resources, and compassion. His message was especially powerful because it was clearly directed at all black Americans (see Chuck D, 2005; Public Enemy, 2006).

The outrage felt towards the federal government for perceived neglect, before, during, and after Katrina, and for its efforts to provide democracy elsewhere, whether it be in Connecticut or Baghdad, dominated the efforts of mainstream hip-hop artists. Yet, the lyrical protests were not reserved for popular artists, as underground artists used the space of hip-hop as a site of protest and collective memory, the subversive potential of art in the underground opened up a whole new level of resistance of which musicians, in the disaster's aftermath, tenaciously took advantage.

Underground Hip-Hop: The Internet and the Struggle for Justice

Like Mos Def and Public Enemy, numerous underground rappers used their artistry and their lyrical genius in the weeks after Katrina to give voice to communal outrage, and to call upon folks to demand action and accountability. In 2005, rappers like The Legendary KO ("George Bush Doesn't Care about Black People"),[4] Skillbill ("Blue Monday"), Hollowman and Nickels[5] ("New Orleans Tribute Song"), The Militant Advocates ("Tribute to the Hurricane"), and Christy B, O'Neal, Top Cat, Mack Larry, and D-Texas of On a Mission Records in Dallas, Texas ("Gulf Coast: 5:45")[6] utilized the Internet and local venues to

---

4. For additional information on this artist, see http://www.myspace.com/georgebush doesntcareaboutblackpeople.

5. For additional information on this artist, see http://www.myspace.com/nickelz music.

6. For additional information on this artist, see http://www.onamissionrecords.com/index.htm.

deliver in-the-moment commentaries that sought to educate and inspire action (in the form of contributions). The use of the Internet and other noncommercial avenues after Katrina demonstrated the immense possibilities for hip-hop working toward social justice: it allowed for immediate statements on social injustice, it avoided the monopoly of a record industry most concerned with making money and promulgating dominant ideologies, and it provided a vehicle of reflection and teaching that reached across country, class, and geographic lines and other boundaries with great ease. This power and potential was on full display with the Notorious KO's "George Bush Doesn't Care about Black People."

Paying tribute to Kanye West for his statements in title and by sampling (although without permission) West's "Goldigger," the Legendary KO, two rappers—Randle and Nickerson from Houston, who have been at the forefront of conscious Internet/underground rap, echoed the anger and analysis of many within the hip-hop community. Four days after West "pulled off that bit of historical graffiti" (Scholtes, 2005, n.p.), the group, which was somewhat surprised by West's comments in that particular setting, but not their substance, completed its tribute to West and its effort to speak to the homelessness of many victims of Hurricane Katrina. "Not till you see these people face to face and talk to them can you appreciate the level of hopelessness," said Randle, who by day works as a financial adviser at a Houston bank. "The one common feeling was that they felt abandoned, on their own little island" (as cited in Scholtes, 2005, n.p.). On the first day that the song was posted, the song was downloaded 10,000 times, offering a powerful denunciation of the injustices perpetuated by the Bush administration and a song that captured the anger and hopelessness of the thousands who were now the rappers' neighbors in Houston.

The song's hook, which was prominent throughout the song, reminded listeners of the big picture, making clear that the failed response was a matter of race, politics, and class divisions in America,

I ain't saying he's a goldigger,

but he ain't messing with no broke niggas

(Legendary KO, 2005)

As with West, KO wasn't reducing policy decisions and the lack of emergency response to the personal feelings of Bush, but rather to the absence of political capital and social significance of the black underclass within the American consciousness. In fact, throughout the song, KO blasted Bush as the face and symbol of the presidency, of the government, and the nation as a whole. The group angrily protested claims that Katrina wasn't that bad and the conditions in the days after Katrina looked worse on television because, "Nigga's been use to dying!" (Legendary KO, 2006). They rapped about starvation, death, and destruction, and about being stranded, while the president was on vacation and promises of a rescue proved elusive at best. They denounced the media representations of the victims of Hurricane Katrina as criminals and looters, those who despite searching for food and merely trying to survive were subjected to the violence of the news and the police ("police shot a black man trying to loot"), making clear who they thought were the true criminals of the situation: a government that supposedly exists to serve and protect the people, which instead focused its energy and resources on protecting the pocketbook of its wealthiest citizens and corporations (Legendary KO, 2005).

Not surprisingly, the online video for "George Bush Doesn't Care About Black People," which was produced and created by Franklin Lopez, the Black Lantern, and the Legendary KO (2005), focused viewers' attention upon the anger and despair of Katrina's (and the state's) victims and the failures of George Bush and his administration. With shots of Bush fishing, golfing, giving press conferences, staring into space, and attending fundraisers for the rich, its message, like that of the song, was that the black community of New Orleans and people of color throughout the nation (as is evidenced by rising prison populations, increased poverty/ unemployment rates, the Iraq war, attacks on social services, and inaction on the Darfur genocide) were betrayed by a racist incompetent by the name of George W. Bush. As to emphasize this point, the video ended with a picture of President Bush in a Klan costume and a call for action through protests and his removal from office.

All of the underground/Internet hip-hop did not necessarily follow formula, tending to focus more on Katrina as a national failure, the struggles of its victims, and the necessity for action. The Militant Advocates, an underground hip-hop group composed of four high school students from Baltimore—Chris Goodman, Xzavier Cheaton, Wayne Washington and Bryant Muldrew—offered one of the most powerful songs on Hurricane Katrina. The group, who is mentored by Bob Moses, one of the principle organizers of Freedom Summer and current head of the Algebra Project in New York City, created "Tribute to the Hurricane," a song that powerfully illustrated the racial dimensions of the disaster. The song vividly captured the misery and despair experienced before, during, and after Hurricane Katrina. More than this, it demonstrated the power and possibility of hip-hop as a source of collective memory. For many people, a vast majority who were black, their "hopes," life aspirations, and "love" were lost because of Katrina and because of this national failure (as cited in Dyson, 2006, pp. 162–163). The Militant Advocates used their art form as a means to make sure we never forget their pain and suffering, as well as our collective failures and inadequate responses.

What is evident here is that conscious rap, that which is political or activist-oriented, is not merely a vehicle for denunciations of the government, white America, or the Bush administration, but is a means of giving voice to the destruction and despair of New Orleans. As was evident in the Militant Advocates' song, and with several other songs (e.g., "Gulf Coast 5:45" & "New Orleans Tribute Song"), the focus was less on cause (that seems to be a given and already accepted as part of communal memory) and more on effects and steps needed for redemption, empowerment, and a brighter day. "Tribute to the Hurricane" was a song of hope as much as it was one of pain and suffering. Yet, the Militant Advocates made clear that this pain and suffering, and the necessity of the community to provide for the basic necessities of its people, was a result of the neglect and the failures of the government, as well as the persistence of racism and social injustice in America. New Orleans could have just as easily been Los Angeles, Detroit, New York, Baltimore, or any other number of communities with sizable black populations, whose blackness continues to impact policy throughout the United States. Moreover, despite the hurricane being a clear catastrophe, a moment where financial and spiritual support were most needed, those with resources and power were, for the most part, missing in action. In Verse 4 of "Tribute to the Hurricane," Chris, a.k.a., CMG, made this clear:

Where's the help the A.I.D …

Didn't you see the eyes that cried for help?

(as cited in Dyson, 2006, p. 162)

Vigorously reminding listeners that the neglect and racism that allowed for Katrina to happen existed throughout the country, the Militant Advocates offered a counter narrative concerning a post-civil rights United States, "framing for their generation the racial consequences of a natural and economic disaster" (Dyson, 2006, p. 164). The Militant Advocates, much like the other hip-hop artists discussed herein, worked to call not just their peers, but also their audience into account for the injustices perpetrated through the institutional and media response to Hurricane Katrina. Making clear that Katrina is not an isolated incident but another entry on a timeline of hundreds of years that define U.S. racism, the Militant Advocates and their comrades in the hip-hop industry have worked to draw much-needed attention not only to Katrina survivors, but also to the desperate state of American race and class relations.

Hip-Hop and a Social Justice Imagination

The response of the hip-hop generation, the generation so often disparaged and demonized within American cultural discourse, was significant in the days and months following Hurricane Katrina. More specifically, black hip-hop artists and those activists, who saw hip-hop as a basis of collective identity and struggle, reacted to the injustices evident during and in the aftermath of Hurricane Katrina. Kanye West refused to remain silent just because he was on NBC, just because he was loved by white America, and called out George Bush as a racist failure who had literally and figuratively left the vast majority of New Orleans residents on their rooftops to die. Supporters of West not only spoke about his right to publicly state his opinion within a democracy, but offered support for his analysis during interviews and within Katrina protest songs. Using the Internet, hip-hop artists offered in-the-moment commentaries, challenging mainstream reporting and dominant discourses, and providing pointed analysis about Katrina, American racism, and widespread state violence. This fight was not waged purely through artistry, as hip-hop came together to raise money and attention for the victims of Hurricane Katrina. P-Diddy and Jay-Z each donated one million dollars to the American Red Cross, and also provided clothes from their clothing companies (Sean John and Rocawear respectively) for those displaced by the hurricane. Others not only donated funds, but also organized and participated in fundraisers. Master P, David Banner, Common, Juvenile, and Omarion appeared on a telethon on Black Entertainment Television, which was sponsored by the National Urban League and Russell Simmons' Hip-Hop Action Network. Similar events took place throughout the nation and continue today. For example, as late as the summer of 2006, individuals and organizations, from Kevin Powell to Common Ground Network, were still engaging in events that raised awareness of the continued issues facing Katrina victims, while additionally trying to raise funds.

What was most striking about hip-hop's response was that the efforts of artists and activists did not merely serve as a space of opposition and counter narratives, but as a vehicle of continued struggle for social justice. They elucidated the power of hip-hop by allowing it to serve as a political linchpin of a larger movement. While artists certainly have had a political role, as is evident with the songs discussed in this chapter, in providing context and pushing discussions, hip-hop, in terms of its artistry has not yet reached its full potential in terms of inspiring social change. In times past, Mahalia Jackson and Nina Simone provided a soundtrack for struggles in 1960s Mississippi, and James Brown and Sly and Family Stone gave lyrical voice to the issues and political ideologies of the Black Panthers, yet none of these artists worked in isolation from organizers, organizations, or others agents of social change. Just as television and artists of the 1960s sought to make sure that America did not forget about Emmett Till, Fannie Lou Hamer, police brutality, and poverty by using its artistry to push the U.S. to a moral crossroad, hip-hop can and has begun to serve in a similar vein, working to make sure that we don't forget about Katrina, its victims, the failures of the Bush administration, and most of all those who face the brutal effects of post-industrial global capitalism; it has the potential to give voice to our generation's Bull Connor and police dogs (George Bush and Fox News), yet without activists and organizers who heed this call, hip-hop holds the potential to provide a context for only limited action. Young people thus far have heeded the calls toward action, participating in the National Hip Hop Political Convention (NHHPC), which has been at the forefront of relief work, and the Hip Hop Caucus. Founded in December 2004 by Jeff Johnson and Reverend Lennox Yearwood, the Hip Hop Caucus has emerged as a powerful voice of civil rights. Since Hurricane Katrina, they have been working with the Congressional Black Caucus to increase social activism around racial and economic injustice. "Katrina is our lunch counter moment," says Reverend Yearwood (Woodson, 2006, n.p.). Assisting in relief efforts and working with survivors, the Hip Hop Caucus has been instrumental in demanding action from the federal government, in terms of health care and housing for those displaced by the Katrina and demanding substantive changes toward securing justice for America's underclass. Together, artists and activists have taken the lead in challenging the injustices evident during and after Katrina, jointly dreaming and demanding an alternative and equitable American reality.

As to make clear that this process is ongoing and requires all within the hip-hop generation, from artists and activists, to teachers and students, to never forget Katrina and never forget the consequences of neglect, American racism, and silence, I would like to end this chapter by including a piece written by myself and one of my students, Fresh 1 (a.k.a., Cameron Sparks),[7] who like so many hip-hop artists reminded me not just of the power of voice and hip-hop, but its necessity.[8]

"George Bush Doesn't Care about Black People: Does America?"

Please have a moment of silence for those that lost their lives in the devastation of the hurricane and its aftermath.... you may not be known but you will truly be remembered!

Listen gas is 4 bucks a gallon, then they blame it on those in new Orleans, instead of cabinet fiends, big oil business steady stackin that green, what's the terror alert level now green?, tell me what does all this mean, they standin on the freeway while he's flying, came 2 days late wasn't through golfing, everybody I know felt a lil something, Marbury ballin not bush crying, can't tell me he was hurt I just seen his demeanor, when the people of my color was hit by Katrina, don't worry bush had bigger issues 2 handle, like if his gloves look right on the handle, watched empty buses drive away by the handful, turned away from the astrodome when the room left was ample, they scarin the shit out em talkin bout disease, wait they couldn't hear it they ain't have TVs, but on every channel they talkin bout loot-ing, "its wrong to take diapers" while they kids peeing, but don't pee in the water contaminating, white people walk in it too don't be so mean, what you

7. For additional information on this artist, see http://www.myspace.com/freshone 206.

8. I want to thank Paula Groves Price, Sanford Richmond, Kristal Moore, Kim Christen, Carmen Lugo-Lugo, Lisa Guerrero and the many others whose insight and knowledge contributed to this piece; much respect to Kristin Bates and Richelle Swan for their tireless effort and support. Most importantly, I would like to thank those artists who have shined a spotlight on the travesty and tragedy that is Hurricane Katrina.

want em to do them stores is ruined, can't get rain boots all cuz of insurance?, worried bout the dome and the holes that gape, instead of lil girls leavin bathrooms raped, everybody downin em because they stayed, couldn't make it til the 1st fast winds don't wait, its good 2 know our poor people in bush's sure hands, dropped the ball in Iraq and been chasin it ever since, he's all about the money don't make no since, wasn't enough that he stole the presidence, cy (see) good thing he did away with welfare, you see it was in the best interest of our welfare, add a lil money and the levees would stand there, dept. of defense wouldn't lend a hand there, unless its to shoot those who loot, I'm glad in God they trust cuz we can't trust you! I'm glad in God they trust cuz we can't trust you! I'm glad in God they trust cuz we can't trust you!

Listen gas is 6 bucks a gallon, then they blame it on those in New Orleans, instead of cabinet fiends, big oil business steady stackin that green, what's the terror alert level now green?, tell me what does all this mean, they standin on the freeway while he's flying, came 2 days late wasn't through golfing, how far along bush is bush now in all his schemes?, to keep us believ-ing, he gotta blow off a lil Afghanistan, Iraq had weapons or so it seems, instead he wanted oil so sent those with dreams, took away some futures sent our 18s, leave entire families at night on their knees, on top of that he couldn't find bin ladeeen, must've been a lil bit frustrat-ing, 49% of people don't want hiiiim, Ohio the new florida fucked up vot-ing, I said Ohio's new Florida fucked up vot-ing, how do you steal from half of America, by takin office but punish those looting?, or not care about those who we don't know their hereabouts, but continue to still look for Bin Ladeen?, sumthin ain't right or so it seems, that we hear less from you than football teams, I got family that lost they houses, but you still blame it on those that lost they houses, husbands and wives can't find they spouses, and you was on vacation in Texas loungin?, how could you do a job that God damn lousy?, they didn't have cars what'd you want em 2 do?, bad educations cuz of guess who?, I'm glad in God they trust cuz we can't trust you!, I can only take this 4 a few more bars, instead of puttin us behind bars, Bush if we can spend billions to create a war, we show could take that same money and fix up New Orleans

And the worst part is I don't even study this shit, so this stuff is blatantly obvious, I mean right in our face, the balls on this guy, its a damn shame ... tell em Dave

125
MPH Winds
Not what destroyed New Orleans, that left the lives of so many in

ruins
Facing an uncertain future already uncertain within Bush's America

71.2
Million Dollars
Sliced from the Budget of the Army Corp of Engineers
Leaving the levees and water pumping system unable to save New
Orleans

33.8
Billion Dollars
Allocated to the Department of Homeland Security
Protecting who from what, just not Hurricanes or poverty

67
Percent
Of New Orleans is African American
Surviving race riots, Jim Crow, deindustrialization and an unavail-
able American Dream

30
Percent
Of New Orleans lives below the poverty line
Astounding to some, but the end result of Hurricane free market

120,000
People
Without Cars, and thousands more without options
Media blaming them for their stubbornness, for choosing not to leave

5
Days
People desperate to survive, to hug and feel their loved ones again
Waiting for food, water, transportation and security

90
Percent
Of those stranded on I-10, without food, water or the spoils of
America were black and poor
Demonstrating that American continues not to be America for much
of America

100s
Of questions
To victims of American Racism, of poverty, of another hurricane
Wondering why they didn't just leave, work harder, and pull them-
selves up by their bootstraps

1000s
Of Images

Those looters who take food, bread, shoes and televisions
Stealing from the hand that feeds them no water, food, or Future

2
Comments
From Bill O'Reilly, that unfair and unbalanced media hack
Calling them, the victims, those black victims, a urban menace that deserves to be shot

SHUT UP!

1000s
Of comments
On the Internet, in the street, and behind closed doors
Blaming the victims, those black victims, referring to them as animals and savages

SHUT UP!

1
Image
That of Mardi Gras, beads, flaming desserts, and parties
Denying the reality of New Orleans, of America, one of poverty, inequality and despair

SHUT UP!

George Bush, T.D Jakes, Michael Brown, Bill O'Reilly, that asshole at Nuevo, Barbara Bush, skinheads, haters and those who tell Kanye to sit down, who deny race, who laugh at the death, who make jokes, who don't give, who live in their bubble.... Shut up and Listen and Learn

40
Percent
Illiterate

50
Percent
Of Children Living in Poverty

50
Percent
Drop Out Rate

$4,724
Spent Per Child

48th
In Teacher Salaries

60
Students Drop out each day

50,000 students
Absent each Day from School

No Child Left Behind??
No Child Left Behind
Left Behind in Angola State Prison

Number 1
Factor
Being Race in the geographic organization of communities
Leaving people of color in the worst, most vulnerable places

10,000
Dead
Mostly African American men, women and children
Dying not from a natural disaster, but from racism, from neglect
from the violence of America

100,000s
Dead
Mostly men, women and Children of color
Dying not from natural causes, but from greed, from capitalism,
from violence

Hurricane Katrina
A Natural Disaster
If only poverty, police brutality, structural adjustment, the prison industrial complex, environmental racism, neglect, ignorance, and
white supremacy were natural

References

Chuck D (2006, September 6). *"This Ain't No TV Show"* Hell No We Ain't Alright. Retrieved March 13, 2007 from http://www.counterpunch.org/
chuckd09062005.html.

Cunningham, D. (2005, September 7). Media hurricane is spinning out of
control. *The Louisiana Weekly.* Retrieved March 13, 2007 from https://ns1.
louisianaweekly.com/weekly/news/articlegate.pl?20050907b.

de Moraes, L. (2005, September 3). Kanye West's torrent of criticism, live on
NBC. *Washington Post.* Retrieved July 18, 2006 from http://www. washing-
tonpost.com/wpdyn/content/article/2005/09/03/AR2005090300165.html.

Dyson, M.E. (2006). *Come hell or high water: Hurricane Katrina and the color
of disaster.* New York: Basic Books.

First lady: Charges racism slowed aid "disgusting." (2005, September 9). CNN.com. Retrieved May 15, 2006 from http://www.cnn.com/2005/ POLITICS/09/08/katrina.laurabush.

Hamilton, T., Williams, H. & Strong, N. (2005, September). Katrina: Hip-hop reacts and responds. *AllHip-Hop.Com.* Retrieved May 15, 2005 from http://www.allhiphop.com/features/?ID=1170.

Interview with George H.W. Bush, Barbara Bush. (2005, September 5). *Larry King Live.* CNN.

Jay Z, featuring Ne-Yo (2006, November 21). "Minority Report." *Kingdom Come.* New York: Atlantic.

Jeremy K. (11, October 2005). The Katrina klap. Retrieved May 27, 2006 from http://www.guerrillanews.com/articles/1755/The_Katrina_Klap.

Juvenile (2006, March 7a). Get ya' hustle on. *Reality Check.* New York: Atlantic.

Juvenile (2006b). Get ya' hustle on/What's Happening (Music Video). *Reality Check.* New York: Atlantic. Retrieved from http://www.mtv.com/over drive/?vid=76618.

Legendary KO (2005). George Bush doesn't care about black people. C.I.G.A.C Mix, http://www.k-otix.com/.

Lil Wayne, et al. (2006) Georgia … Bush. Lil Wayne DJ Drama Dedication 2 (Mixtape) CD Gangsta Grillz.

Lopez, Franklin, The Black Lantern, and Legendary KO. (2005). George Bush doesn't care about black people. Retrieved March 13, 2007 from http://www.myspace.com/georgebushdoesntcareaboutblackpeople.

Militant Advocates (2005). Tribute to the hurricane. In Dyson, M.E. (2006) *Come Hell or High Water: Hurricane Katrina and the Color of Disaster* (pp. 162–163). New York: Basic Books.

Mos Def Arrested After Video Music Awards (2006). *Sfgate.com,* Retrieved March 12, 2007 from http://www.sfgate.com/cgi-bin/blogs/sfgate/detail? blogid=7&entry_id=8499.

Mos Def (2006, December 29). Dollar Day. *True Magic.* Geffen Records.

Mos Def (2005). Dollar day for New Orleans (Katrina klap). Retrieved March 13, 2007 from http://www.guerrillanews.com/articles/1755/The_ Katrina_Klap.

Neal, M.A. (2004, July 16). Taking on politics, leadership and Hip-Hop culture. *SeeingBlack.Com.* Retrieved February 25, 2006 from http://www. seeingblack.com/2004/x071604/stand_deliver.shtml.

O'Reilly, B. (2005, September 5). Keeping the record straight on the Katrina story. *Fox News.* Retrieved May 15, 2005 from http://www.foxnews.com/ story/0,2933,168552,00.html.

O'Reilly, B. (2006, January 16). Personal story segment 20th anniversary of MLK, Jr. Day. *The O'Reilly Factor*, Fox News.

Patel, J., and Reid, S. (2005, September 9). Mos Def Among Those Quick with Music Inspired by Katrina. MTV.com. Retrieved March 13, 2007 from http://www.mtv.com/news/articles/1509274/20050909/mos_def.jhtml?head lines=true.

Public Enemy featuring Paris. (2006, March 7). Hell no (We ain't alright). *Rebirth of A Nation. Guerrilla Funk*. Retrieved August 15, 2006 from http://www.guerrillafunk.com/publicenemy/rebirthofanation/index.htm.

Public Enemy relevant again. *City Pages*. Retrieved May 15, 2006 from http://citypages.com/databank/26/1300/article13839.asp.

Satten, V. (2005, December). Still lives through. *XXL*, 112–114.

Scholtes, P. (2005, November 11). Welcome to the Superdome: How Hurricane Katrina Made Public Enemy Relevant Again. *Citypages*. Retrieved May 15, 2006 from http://citypages.com/databank/26/1300/article13839. asp.

T.I, David Banner get behind Bush's comments. (2005, September 6). MTVNEWS.Com. Retrieved May 15, 2006 from http://mtv.com/news/articles/1509000/20050906/story.jhtml.

Skjodt, Christian, Jeremy K, and Mos Def (2005b). Dollar day for New Orleans (Katrina Klap). Retrieved March 17, 2007 from http://www.guerrillanews.com/articles/1755/The_Katrina_Klap.

Woodson, J. (2006, June 1). Hip Hop's black political activism. *ZNet*. Retrieved May 25, 2006 from http://www.zmag.org/content/showarticle.cfm?ItemID=10365.

Zirin, D. (2005, September 28). Etan Thomas rises to the occasion. *The Nation*. Retrieved May 15, 2006 from http://www.thenation.com/20050926/zirin.

Chapter 16

Ordinary Struggle and the "Public Good": Navigating Vernacular Voices, State Power, and the Public Sphere in Quests for Social Justice

Lisa R. Foster

In the days immediately following Hurricane Katrina, American mass media outlets were glued to the events in New Orleans and the Gulf Coast. Major U.S. networks held hours-long broadcasts, focusing on the mass numbers of displaced people, insurmountable living conditions, and tragic loss of human life. News anchors, once administration-friendly, began critically questioning President Bush and FEMA's actions. Public discussions from online blogs to congressional hearings levied condemnation of a great American failing to help those within our own country at a time when they needed it most.

The disaster of Hurricane Katrina was an important moment for the potential of social justice deliberations as ordinary struggle became public concern. Images compelled people to think outside the individualistic framework that often isolates citizens into private households. Americans grieved for New Orleans; rushed to aid New Orleans and Gulf Coast residents when the government did not, and put charitable contribution campaigns into action moments after the levees broke. But the devastating effects of Hurricane Katrina, though notably the worst mass displacement of persons since the Great Depression, are arguably no graver in scope than the burdens of mass displacement from public housing closures and the signing of "The Personal Responsibility and Work Reconciliation Act of 1996." In stark contrast, these displaced citizens have gone unwelcomed and without national empathy.

The question of this chapter, then, is why did the public entertain deliberations on social justice in the wake of natural disaster but not in the aftermath of public policy reforms? If housing closures and hurricanes have a similar effect, why do we fail to see social justice as a civic responsibility only in the case of the latter? Many people may suggest that this comparison is unfair, that there is an immense difference between those displaced by natural disaster and those displaced by economic hardship and public policy. However, we know historically that natural disaster devastates those who have the least and social injustice is as likely to result through politics as it is through storms. Both groups of displaced citizens shared striking similarities. Of the near 500,000 residents from the great city of New Orleans, 1 in 4 (over 120,000) lived below the national poverty line, making less than $15,000 per year to support a family of three. Two-thirds of those people were single mothers with young children who were left without an accessible extended family network to help ease the cost of childcare. Another two-thirds of the people were black, and over half of the impoverished held full-time jobs (Urban Institute, 2005).

These statistics of race and poverty mirror the composite citizenry displaced by welfare and public housing reform in the late 1990s. However, the case of welfare reform yields recognizable differences in public sphere deliberations. Regular citizens rarely engaged in critical public discussions of social injustice and mass media outlets work descriptively rather than argumentatively in chronicling the relationship of the displaced to the U.S. administration. Jamie Daniel (2000) chronicles the discursive rituals of disqualification used in the mainstream media to discount the 42,000 residents (all poor and mostly black) who were displaced in 1998 by the Chicago Housing Authority. Rather than fostering aid for residents, the media linked those soon to be displaced to, "histories of spontaneous anti-social and/or criminal behavior," and as "a volatile threat to the 'public good,' rather than an important member of 'the public'" (p. 64).

In this chapter, I will examine the relationship between the public and the displaced in media coverage of Hurricane Katrina and the closing of the public housing units in Chicago to better understand our potential to enact civic deliberations in a continued quest for social justice. In the case of Katrina, rhetorics of displacement will be shown to violate collective ideologies of the public good, suggesting social justice deliberations become necessary not only for the aiding of those displaced but for saving our collective self. In the displacement of public housing residents, however, vernacular voices are shown as violating the individual American values of the good life, thereby limiting the potential for public deliberation by casting those displaced as antithetical to the public. From these texts, I will argue that spaces for civic deliberation and social justice are greatest when vernacular voices are present as an essential part of the public whose interests are in alignment with the good of the public over the good of the state.

Locating Rhetoric in Relation to Social Justice

Rhetorical inquiry is a process of interrogating all the means of persuasion that may be part of any moment of public address. Thus, in looking at the media coverage surrounding Katrina and public housing displacement, it is important to recognize media as a kind of contemporary public address or speech that shapes audience response in instrumental and constitutive ways. The rhetorics surrounding U.S. welfare reform and Hurricane Katrina not only describe how events unfold but constitute avenues for civic deliberation and discussion of those events. The rhetorics from both events of displacement point to very different processes of citizenship. Before moving to the analysis of media texts, I want to suggest two important theoretical concepts central to the role of rhetoric in relation to social justice: the public sphere and vernacular rhetoric. The first concept, the public sphere is a theoretical construct that describes the democratic space of civic engagement necessary for social justice. The second, vernacular rhetoric, refers to the voices of ordinary citizens often left out of a dominant public sphere, in this case those displaced by Katrina and housing reform.

The value of the public sphere to questions of social justice is immense as the public sphere is a site of civic participation, deliberation, and social change. Habermas (1989) has been credited with introducing the conception of the public sphere to critical theories that seek to understand social justice and the creation of egalitarian societies. His construct of the public sphere maintains the possibility for egalitarian citizenship as citizens engage in rational-critical debate in a realm outside the state. However, Habermas has been widely criticized for elevating the role of rational debate above relations of power in discussing the democratic public sphere. His preliminary theories fail to take into consideration aspects of marginalization that may prevent all people from participating in the utopic deliberative ideal. Not only does his theoretical public sphere leave out the voices of the marginalized, it also fails to recognize the economic barriers that might inhibit or change who might get to engage in that deliberative process (Negt & Kluge, 1993).

Nancy Fraser (1997) speaks against the homogenous portrait of Habermas' public by articulating the notion of "subaltern counterpublics" in which members of subordinated social groups form oppositional public spheres via deliberation and dialogue (p. 122). Asen and Brouwer (2001) further argue that Habermas' elite character of the public sphere, "engendered a shared vision of the good that blocked potential topics of deliberation, the arrangements that sustained actual exclusions from the public sphere" (p. 5). Thus, the public sphere is simultaneously a space for deliberations on social justice and one steeped with exclusions that may continue injustice. While offering the potential for civic engagement, the requirements for participation in a dominant public sphere may also function ideologically to limit topics of debate and the social actors welcome in those debates.

To understand how the public sphere makes room for ordinary people's voices requires scholars to examine the relationship between the public and vernacular discourse. Many critical rhetorical scholars have stressed the significance of examining these non-dominant voices. Ono and Sloop (1995) propose studies of the vernacular as necessary ways of "understanding the voices of those historically oppressed" (p. 27). Vernacular voices must become a primary source of investigation for the enactment of social justice in a dominant public sphere because, "without an examination of rhetoric of those struggling to survive, no significant social statements can be made about political, social, and cultural liberation" (Ono & Sloop, 1995, p. 39). Similarly, in *Vernacular Voices*, Hauser (1999) argues for the prioritization of ordinary people's rhetoric, which he sees as generative of important issues for public deliberation. To attain a thriving democratic public sphere, he posits that we, "must widen the discursive arena to include vernacular exchanges, in addition to those of institutional actors" (p. 89).

Thus, while scholars and citizens often come to understand the enactment of social justice through official discourses, presidential rhetoric, legal rhetoric, and even mediated rhetoric, social justice requires the inclusion of vernacular rhetorics. Following these theorists, I will examine the presence of vernacular voices in a dominant public sphere via media coverage of human displacement during Hurricane Katrina and public housing reform. Specifically, I will consider who is a part of the public sphere espoused in media coverage by asking what vernacular voices and counterpublics are present and what avenues for participation are available to those ordinary citizens. In locating the relationship between the displaced and the dominant public, we can understand how citizens felt compelled to question policy after Katrina, but not during public housing displacements.

Textual Analysis

The texts to be discussed in the following pages have been selected from a broad range of media ownership (both private and public), media formats (television, print, radio), and media content (editorial, news, talk). This decision was based upon an effort to let the argument work from media accounts rather than to have it be about media accounts themselves. In addition, the breadth of my sample was designed to account for questions concerning media bias.

I narrowed the media texts for analysis to those that discussed each displacement with some reference to the relationship between ordinary people, the state, and the public. Final textual selections represented the breadth of coverage regarding ownership, format, and content, while yielding a coherent and insightful narrative on the relationship between vernacular voices and the public in each instance of displacement. The texts selected also represented media venues traditionally considered valued sources for information in times of national crisis and controversy: major network newscasts (*ABC World News*), National Public Radio programming (*Talk of the Nation and All Things Considered*), and a nationally syndicated press with a local presence (*the Chicago Sun Times*).

Ideological criticism was employed to analyze the chosen texts. A critique of ideology is a rhetorical method closely connected to a quest in Marxist thought to analyze social texts not only for their surface meaning, but for the ways in which they organize power relations in society. The critic of ideology examines, "the interplay of meaning and power" (Thompson, 1990, p. 9) in a given text by mapping "the relation of an utterance to its social context" (Eagleton, 1991, p. 9). Beyond its obvious benefits for theorizing power in relation to social justice, ideological criticism is particularly useful when examining mass communication as media outlets routinely, "reinforce the ideological thrust of a particular world view" (Hardt, 2004, p. 27). In this study, I examined ideologies concerning American values (e.g., nationalism, liberalism, and the public good) that influenced the relationship between vernacular voices, the state, and the public sphere.

Displacement as Public Responsibility or Public Threat

Hurricane Katrina is a significant event on many different levels, but especially in terms of its consequences for the enactment of a dissenting and deliberative mass media as part of a healthy public sphere. While reporting on Katrina was at times problematic,[1] it was the first moment in five years of Bush Administration policy that mass media outlets became critical of the state in the interest of its citizens. Citizens left to weather the storm were depicted as "abandoned" by the state. These images, juxtaposed against the president's rhetoric, became a key element of dissonant civic critique in the mass media. Consider the opening of *ABC's World News Tonight*, seven days after the storm:

---

1. By no means should one take this argument as portraying the mass media without genuine and significant faults. Coverage of aftermath was plagued with clear institutional racism that constructed black residents as looters and white residents as people struggling to survive. However, it was an exigence in which mass media aided participation in a public sphere by making space for civic dissent and civic social action. As such, it is a significant moment for locating possibilities for social change in a system that often perpetuates the status quo.

(Charles Gibson) On World News Tonight, boots on the ground, *finally* making a difference in the hurricane zone (pictures of rescue workers with stretcher/children). Though some complain they're still looking for leadership after the storm (picture of George Bush sitting and talking with black male/female couple).

(white male) We've helped every other country in the God-damned world, ya know. I hope we can help the state of Louisiana.[2]

(President Bush) So long as any life is in danger, we got work to do. (September 5, 2005; emphasis added)

Though the language choices here are subtle, they signal an important relationship between hurricane victims and the public very early in the controversy of Katrina. Victims are a part of rather than a hindrance to civic conceptualizations of the national public. Ordinary people's voices are represented alongside the president's, and those criticisms are a key component of opening news events. Notice even the use of "we" here works to include displaced hurricane victims as a part of the nation that has, by most criticisms, abandoned them. Victims of the hurricane are seen as having weathered both natural disaster and the failings of their government.

Accordingly, displaced victims of the hurricane were greeted by the public in communities across the nation; "Houston and other cities in Texas *welcomed* survivors, and the rest scattered across the country to Atlanta, Memphis, Chicago, New York, Los Angeles, even Anchorage (*Talk of the Nation*, 2005, emphasis added). And when the government began to run out of room for Katrina evacuees, ordinary citizens began making room for victims in their own homes:

> Bob Woodruff, reporting from a flooded New Orleans: An official State of Emergency now exists in 13 different states and in many places it has been declared by states so that they can get federal money to deal with the *influx* of people from the hurricane area. But it's becoming quickly evident that *the government cannot handle* all of the people that are coming from the hurricane. So Nancy Weiner tonight, on the people *all across the country*, opening up their *private* doors.

> Nancy Weiner: With 230,000 people now staying in shelters, this tragedy has spawned a variation of the foster home. (Byline: Helping Hands, crowded shelters) In Baton Rouge, 11 members of the Raine family, including 4 children, a great grandmother and twins on the way, are out of the shelter and in the home of a woman they just met, Shandra Earle. (Visual: images of people living together, washing dishes, cooking, talking)

---

2. Later in broadcast it becomes clear that this man is the Sheriff of St. Bernard Parish.

Martha Raine, evacuee: She said, "Baby, you don't know why I'm here?" I said, "No Ma'am." She said, "I come here to get a family." I said, "You come here to get a family?" She said, "Baby, get your family and I'm going to take you to my home."

Weiner: This *is not* a wealthy neighborhood. (Visual: track houses, littered lawns, older model cars, graffitied mailbox, with a black man pulling two young black children in an old red wagon down the street) and Miss Earle *is not* a wealthy woman but she is sharing her space, her food, her washer and dryer (Visual: Earle's home).

Earle: A foster parent is a person that uhm ... takes care of people who have no place to go (shaking her head). That's it. They help them. They just take them in. (Nods head).

Wiener: (off camera): And is that you?

Earle: (Laughing) I guess.

Weiner: In Atlanta Walter Tardiff (ph[3]) is putting up 33 relatives in his three bedroom house. (Visual: children and filled house) Tardiff: They're here until they get back on their feet....

San Diego Businessman David Perez (ph) chartered a 737 to take 87 flood victims to California, where he is setting them up with *homes, schools, and jobs.* (Visual: loaded plane, families hugging Perez)

Many displaced families would like to find a place to rent. They have the means to rent, but they can't find anything. Alex Lewis (ph) manages 10 apartment complexes in Baton Rouge. (Visual: Lewis walking through apartment complex)

Lewis: We've got no vacancy signs up, but people are still stopping'.

Weiner: Since word got out about Miss Earle's generosity her phone has been ringing off the hook.

Earle: And how many babies you need pampers for? (Visual: on the phone taking notes)

Weiner: It may not be home, but it's a home. Nancy Weiner, Baton Rouge. (Visual: child eating a grape to Earle and the 11 Raines, smiling, outside her home) (*ABC World News Tonight*, 9/5/2005)

Because the state has been unable to care for its citizens, ordinary people begin to step in where the government cannot. Notice the repetition in both language and image of ordinary people helping those displaced to gain access to the basic building blocks of American life (i.e., food, family, homes, schools, jobs). In this instance, the mass public comes to identify with the plight of oppressed people over the interests of the state. Not only does the re-

---

3. The use of the (ph) throughout the paper refers to the phonetic spelling of names.

port foster identification with the concerns of those displaced, it also suggests a public that is taking action, attempting to remedy public problems through private means. Although the action is not deliberative, it does signal a collective responsibility to aid those individuals displaced by the storms. Katrina evacuees again, are a part of "the public" to be helped, cared for, and aided by ordinary citizens when the government fails them.

Private homes and family members often bear the cost of political policies and economic hardships that displace people. However, in the case of Katrina, this private burden becomes a public responsibility. The private response of ordinary people to aid citizens where the government fails is significant for two reasons. First, the response shows us a public collectively interested in the needs of displaced people. Second, the mediated response works as a criticism of a state that has failed to adequately care for its citizens. This is not the case when people struggle to maintain the same basic tenets of American life after losing their homes to the closing of federal public housing. Consider this report from a suburb of Chicago following the closing of Cabrini Green residences:

> The Chicago Housing Authority is in a period of transition. For decades, low-income residents were crowded into high-rise public housing. Over the years, the buildings have become squalid and riddled with crime. The project will take 10 years. In the meantime, tenants are getting vouchers to help pay their rent, and many of them are finding new homes in predominantly black suburbs south of Chicago. But as NPR's, David Welna reports, the mayor of one of these suburbs says he wants no more refugees from public housing.
>
> Mayor NICHOLAS GRAVES (Harvey, Illinois): This city was the greatest city south of the loop of Chicago at one time in industry, in work, in schools and everything. I'm sure people sat there at that time and didn't think this would ever happen, but it did.
>
> WELNA (reporting): What happened to this blue-collar city of 30,000 was that the steel mills that provided most of its jobs closed down, property values plunged. A virtually all-white suburb became nearly all black, as residents fled further south and African-Americans from Chicago moved in. Some came with housing vouchers. Congress approved these Section 8 vouchers to help poor people rent privately owned housing rather than live in ghettos of public housing. Harvey, with depressed rents and a growing black population, attracted more Section 8 voucher holders than any other Chicago suburb. Mayor Graves points to where some of those voucher holders moved in. It's a block full of two-story brick buildings with most of their windows boarded up.
>
> Mayor GRAVES: Right now it *looks like a bombed-out city*. I mean, it's just terrible. *You shouldn't even have to look at something like this, much less people live next door to it.*

WELNA: Graves, who's a white former police chief, defeated Harvey's first black mayor five years ago with *promises to discourage the influx of welfare renters*. He's tripled his housing inspectors, and he's taken a wrecking ball to some 200 abandoned properties. *It's gone over well with voters.* Graves was re-elected this year. And he says Harvey is in much better shape today than when he took office. But he called a news conference this week *to warn that Harvey faces a new wave of public housing refugees* as Chicago steps up the demolition of its high-rises.

Mayor GRAVES: These *unfortunate people* have to go someplace. Everyone knows where they will go. They will go to the south suburban communities.

WELNA: Graves wants the U.S. Department of Housing and Urban Development to stop issuing housing vouchers in Chicago until there's a better plan for relocating displaced public housing tenants. Right now, he suspects the Chicago Housing Authority is steering people to his town because it's affordable and mostly black. But CHA spokesman Francisco Arcaute(ph) says that's nonsense.

WELNA: But most of the mayors in the south suburbs favor a moratorium on new Section 8 vouchers. Joe Martin(ph) heads an effort funded by those mayors called Diversity Inc., which aims to stem white flight from the region. He says it's not fair that so many Section 8 recipients are concentrated in one area.

Mr. JOE MARTIN (Diversity Inc.): And so it's not a matter of, "Well, not in my backyard." It's a matter of this is the responsibility of all of the communities throughout the metropolitan area to provide housing opportunities in the areas where there are good schools, low crime rates, high rate of job growth and economic development.

WELNA: Rolf Pendall of Cornell University says the "not in my backyard" attitude is typical of suburbs all around the country also faced with Section 8 recipients. *Wealthy suburbs have effectively kept them out* by having few affordable apartments.

Mr. ROLF PENDALL (Cornell University): That's why in a lot of metro areas the recipients of vouchers are returning their housing vouchers because they can't find a place to live within the stipulated time period, which I believe is 120 days. (*All Things Considered*, 8/10/2000, emphasis added)

There is a stark contrast in these passages between the public responsibilities to displaced Katrina victims and displaced residents from closures of public housing. Although both groups of citizens seek the same material ends—schools, jobs, and safe places to live—residents from public housing neighborhoods are not seen as a valued part of the public. Displaced residents have not been welcomed; in fact, they are so unwelcome that Harvey's mayor is elected on a platform to "discourage the influx of welfare renters." Notice the same language here is used to denote the state of these residents and the state of Katrina evacuees. They are *an influx, refugees* of public policy rather than a natural storm. Yet in this instance, welfare renters are seen as a *problem* of the public instead of an integral part of it. The displaced become almost plague-like: they are the reason for Harvey looking like "*a bombed-out* city," the state *warns* local residents that more may be coming, and they threaten the public way of life. Where government policies have been enacted to provide assistance to displaced residents (by means of Section 8 vouchers) local officials have organized to *ban* the acceptance of those policies. The social injustice here is framed not in terms of those victims of public housing reform but of the residents of suburban areas where they may move. "*It's not fair*" states one official, "that so many Section 8 recipients are concentrated in one area." Diversity is reclaimed in the interests of an elite public seeking to save the whiteness of Harvey.

Whereas portrayals of Katrina victims elicit identification and civic empathy, the plight of residents displaced from public housing is never articulated in a manner identifiable to the public. No mention is made of the literal destruction of their homes that has left residents with few places to turn. No voices of the displaced are present. The report does signal the real location of injustice for Harvey, the massive drop in property values from the closing of corporate steel mills, but this does not speak to the injustice of displaced residents. Welna also points to the growing inability of welfare recipients to use Section 8 vouchers, and in this way, the text opens up the possibility for broader social justice deliberations. The problem, however, is that the locus of social injustice is negotiable. The text does not clearly engender identification with the oppressed, over the state, as seen in the Katrina reporting.

Displacement as a Public Loss or Public Gain

In addition to whether displaced peoples are seen as part of the public, the value placed on that belonging serves as a basis for broader concerns of social justice. Though the composite of citizens stranded in New Orleans after Katrina practically mirrored that of individuals displaced by public housing reforms, Katrina evacuees were more likely to be seen as part of valuable communities with rich cultural heritages. On National Public Radio's *Talk of the Nation*, listeners were given the opportunity to call in and engage deliberations concerning the value of some of New Orleans' poorest residential neighborhoods to the nation as a whole. The broadcast opened with the following segment:

> Residents of New Orleans are gradually being allowed back into that city, and as the city assesses the damage left by Hurricane Katrina, the people who live there and city leaders face the daunting task of re-

building. The higher parts of New Orleans, which include the well-known French Quarter, escaped with minor damage. But the city's Lower Ninth Ward was hit hard ... Of the 20,000 or so mostly African-Americans who lived in the Lower Ninth, a third lived below the poverty line. About half of the residential housing was rental property and crime was rampant.

This past weekend, firefighters put red tags on thousands of homes thought to be unsafe, and last week Housing and Urban Development Secretary Alphonso Jackson advised Mayor Ray Nagin against rebuilding the Lower Ninth Ward. But advocates for the Lower Ninth point out that it had one of the highest homeownership rates in the city. Its shotgun and camelback houses reflect a rich architectural heritage. Desire, the street made famous in the Tennessee Williams play, runs through the Ward, which was home to many artists and musicians. And generations of families and neighbors have been woven together in a close-knit community separated from the glitz and revelry of the nearby French Quarter.

Today on our program, we examine what should become of the Lower Ninth Ward. Should it be bulldozed and its residents transplanted or can it be recreated in a new form?

The introduction of the broadcast is central to understanding the credibility lent to vernacular voices and vernacular culture from the region. It makes a solid distinction between the "generations of families and neighbors ... woven together in a close-knit community" and the "glitz and revelry" of the French Quarter. The introduction places value in the vernacular and sets the tone of the controversy as contrary to the state. Also significant in this broadcast is the manner in which local problems become part of the conversation about the larger national public good. Couple this segment with the following conversation with a Ninth Ward community advocate:

NEARY: This is TALK OF THE NATION. I'm Lynn Neary in Washington, sitting in for Neal Conan. We're talking about the future of New Orleans' Lower Ninth Ward and how best to rebuild it after the floods of Hurricane Katrina. And we'd like to hear from residents of the Ninth Ward as well as business owners. *What do you think is needed to rebuild your community?....* And my guest is Pam Dashiell. She's the president of the Holy Cross Neighborhood Association in the Lower Ninth Ward. And, Ms. Dashiell, tell us about something about the Holy Cross Neighborhood. *I understand it's a very historical area.* What's it like?

Ms. DASHIELL: Well, it is on the National Register of Historic Districts, *both local and national.* It's a wonderful place. It's got an eclectic mix of styles, of architectural styles. The homes range from, oh, about, I don't know, 40 or 50 years old to 150 years old. And it's got a very country feel. It's right on the levee of the Mississippi River and the Industrial Canal. And *it's the kind of place where people play all day.* People run and walk and bicycle and there are children out there kite-flying and it's extremely well-used.

NEARY: *And you said there's a very strong sense of community, of connectedness there among the people.*

Ms. DASHIELL: Oh, absolutely. The area has had some problems in the past with people leaving and with abandoned houses and *crime and all the problems that really beset any urban area. But the people in the Ninth Ward, people in Lower Nine and Holy Cross, have been working furiously to make those problems—to make them go away.* There are all kinds of organizations. There *are almost a hundred churches just in Lower Nine,* and many of them have community development corporations. The Holy Cross Neighborhood Association with the Preservation Resource Center has had rebuilding projects and programs and helping the elderly to repair their homes. There are all kinds of initiatives. There was all kind of activity. People love—loved the neighborhood.

(*Talk of the Nation*, Oct. 4, 2005, emphasis added)

For a student of social justice deliberations, this is an incredibly significant moment. Here, public mass media open air time for the purpose of deliberations on the social value of rebuilding an urban community. The broadcast privileges vernacular voices over state recommendations as residential advocate, Ms. Dashiell, is given platform over the "expert" endorsements from HUD secretary Alphonso Johnson. Local problems are given national significance as local residents become a community that is an integral part of the American public good. The people who resided in the Lower Ninth Ward are regarded as active, church-going citizens who love their neighborhood. They are constructed as a community working against crime, rather than criminals to be removed from the public.

This image contrasts stridently with a similar meeting between vernacular voices and the state—a meeting between advocates from Cabrini Green public housing towers and Chicago city officials. In the following passage from *The Chicago Sun Times*, residents are portrayed as barriers to social justice instead of necessary voices in community deliberations. While the initial image that accompanies the article portrays a woman in prayer, beginning to march to the meeting, the depiction of the public housing community as a whole is exceedingly different from the portrayal of "community" in New Orleans' Lower Ninth Ward:

The concept for a new Cabrini-Green neighborhood with as many as 2,300 new town houses, duplexes and six-story mid-rises was presented to Near North Side residents Saturday, *but a dispute over how many will be available to the poor created a melee.*

"We want changes but we want changes for us and not for them to ex-port the rich in," *some* Cabrini residents *screamed at officials who were prevented for 40 minutes from calling the meeting at Metro High School to order.*

More than 400 residents of both Cabrini-Green and its surrounding area filled an auditorium to overflowing to hear details of the $ 315 million redevelopment plan *for the beleaguered neighborhood.*

It was the first time the plan was unveiled to residents *who have been* complaining *they were left out of the plan's formulation.*

"Every great plan has to start somewhere," said Dave Tkac, special as-sistant to the mayor. *"After the starting point, you have community input and we are using that as a basis for moving forward."*

City officials said the redevelopment, covering an area bounded by North Avenue on the north, Chicago Avenue on the south, the Chicago River on the west and Wells Street on the east, is *targeted for completion* in 2006.

The plan calls for a new state-of-the-art public library, a new park, and a new elementary and high school. *Current schools would be torn down.*

It also calls for a new "Town Center"—a commercial district with a grocery store and small mall. Out of the redevelopment, about 2,500 construction jobs and 900 permanent jobs are expected to be created, city officials said.

A new police station would be built in the heart of the neighborhood, along with a new community center providing a range of services for area residents.

Some 1,324 units of public housing would be demolished.

Of 2,000 to 2,300 new housing units planned, *650 to 700 are reserved for Cabrini residents*, in keeping with the desired mixed-income ratio of 30 percent public housing residents, 20 percent working poor, and 50 percent home sales, city officials said.

Some residents who formed a group called the Coalition to Protect Public Housing argued that income requirements for the new hous-ing would preclude many of the poorest families. Before the meeting, the group marched in the development, chanting, "Fix it. Don't tear it down!"

According to the public housing group's calculations, only 350 units will be available for them, with a net loss of 1,000 units of low-income housing.

"The residents of Cabrini are not opposed to redevelopment. We are opposed to the displacement of families when there is no plan to relo-cate them," said the group's spokeswoman, Carol Steele.

> At one point, some *Cabrini residents stormed out of the meeting. An altercation ensued. Three people were arrested, and extra police were called.*
>
> Some area residents, however, were pleased with the plan. "*They don't speak for everyone*," said Greta Bowe, who lives near Cabrini.
>
> (Wu, 1997, p. 18).

Whereas the NPR broadcast welcomed and invited Ninth Ward resident comments and concerns, this report suggests that Cabrini residents a) were to be heard only after those in power had made initial and important decisions regarding the fate of the community, b) were not valued voices of a rich historical culture but a blight to the Chicago public, and most importantly, c) were not unified nor credible sources on the subject of their own housing fate.

The deliberations here are not in the same open, pre-planning, moment that awaits the fate of the lower Ninth Ward. As such, this forum seems less democratic deliberation and more after-the-fact political protocol. This meeting was a forum for "hearing" concerns rather than engaging them. Consider the irony in the assistant's statements, "'Every great plan has to start somewhere ... *After the starting point, you have community input* and *we are using that as a basis for moving forward*.' City officials said the redevelopment ... is *targeted for completion in 2006*." Interestingly, the statements from the mayor's office confirm the false premise of the forum. The meeting is being held so that plans can move forward, not so that they can change or even speak to the concerns of the community. Even the byline suggests a verb tense that puts the plan already into action, "which *will replace* 1324 units of public housing." The plan has a projected completion date, presenting an enormously different context for hearing resident concerns than is the pre-planning moment that awaits the displaced residents of New Orleans' Lower Ninth Ward.

Another significant difference between the New Orleans' and Chicago examples lies in the value attributed to the preservation of current residential homes. In the case of Katrina, the Lower Ninth Ward is portrayed as a place of rich cultural heritage. Listeners of NPR are led to feel as though the public would suffer a great cultural loss should that community not re-emerge. Early in the *Chicago Sun Times'* article, however, we are made very aware that this is not the case for the area surrounding Cabrini. This area is a historically "beleaguered neighborhood." The reporting very much privileges the plans for the creation of new over the old, reporting the city's redevelopment plans for a "*new* state-of-the-art public library," "*new* park," "*new* elementary and high school," "*new* "Town Center," "*new* police station" and "*new* community center."

The problem, of course, is that the future recipients of this "newness" are especially unclear. The new depends upon the destruction of the old, which currently belongs to the poor. The article does chronicle that, "Current schools would be torn down" and "1,324 units of public housing would be demolished" but these phrases are secondary to the constant reiteration of "newness" awaiting the area. This imbalance of the new, coupled with continual news framing of the area as a public blight rather than a public value, leaves very little room for Cabrini residents' concerns to impact policy. These concerns are further discredited as having emerged not from a valuable community but from a disruptive and fragmented counterpublic.

Residents' voices are written as if they are impeding the orderly and timely progression of the meeting. Cabrini neighborhood advocates are not granted the credibility afforded to Katrina victims. The text discounts residents and relies on negative language to describe legitimate concerns over who will be benefiting from all the "newness" and rebirth the plan affords. Phrases "dispute ... *created a melee,*" "*complaining,*" and "*some* residents" all work to disrupt the legitimacy of social justice arguments and counterpublic solidarity. Identification to the state is fostered over vernacular counterpublics as details from altercations and arrests work to criminalize any who may have disputed the city's plans. In portraying advocates for public housing as antithetical to readers' conceptions of a well-functioning public, necessary deliberation on the social justice of housing reform is lost.

Conclusion

In spite of mass media's many faults during the crisis of Hurricane Katrina, their emphasis on the plight of ordinary people over the interests of the state helped to create critical space for deliberations on social justice. Displaced residents were portrayed as an integral part of the American public, their aid portrayed as a collective rather than an individual responsibility, and their survival noted as crucial to the overall public good. In comparison, space for social justice deliberations on human displacement from public housing policies was gravely slim. In each testament of the public housing crisis, the interests of the state trumped the interests of policy victims, leaving audiences to identify with the plight of institutional actors rather than the plight of actual people. The public sphere becomes aligned with the interests of the state over those oppressed as vernacular voices are absent or discounted as detrimental to the public good.

Thus, potential deliberations on social justice require marginalized vernacular voices to be seen as 1) legitimate social actors in a public sphere, 2) integral and necessary aspects of the public good, 3) the responsibility of the social collective rather than individual circumstance, and 4) having interests in alignment with the people over the state. The importance of listening to the plight of ordinary citizens, as well as recognizing that plight as part of the public, are essential to the enactment of social justice. While the media itself will never stand in for those vernacular voices, it serves as a critical barometer for the state of social justice in a public sphere.

In this way, the unfolding rhetorics of displacement from Hurricane Katrina and public housing reform have immense significance not only for how social justice deliberations have unfolded to date, but how the enactment of social justice will evolve for decades. Displacement is not a momentary humanitarian crisis, it is an ongoing struggle. Chicago's public housing reforms of the last decade largely impacted residents who ended up there as the result of years of migration on the part of black and poor Americans seeking to escape the racism and poverty of the Mississippi River Delta. Ironically, Chicago once welcomed those very people who today are forced to leave it. The same fate is likely in the case of those displaced by Hurricane Katrina if we are not vigilant about incorporating the interests of those oppressed over the interests of the state. In Houston alone, rhetorics that criminalize those displaced by Katrina as a growing threat to the public good are on the rise, and continuing conversations on the state of New Orleans include fewer and fewer vernacular voices and a growing number of institutional voices. A continued commitment to seeking out and listening to vernacular voices will be fundamental to the evolution of the struggle for social justice in the aftermath of Hurricane Katrina.

References

ABC World News Tonight. (2005, September 5). Katrina: State of emergency. New York: American Broadcasting Company.

All Things Considered. (2000, August 10). Reconcentration of Chicago's public housing residents into black suburbs surrounding Chicago. Washington, D.C.: National Public Radio.

Asen, R. and Brouwer, D.C. (2001). Introduction. In Robert Asen & Daniel C. Brouwer (Eds.), *Counterpublics and the state* (pp. 1–34). Albany; University of New York Press.

Daniel, J. (2000). Rituals of disqualification: Competing publics and public housing in contemporary Chicago. In Mike Hill & Warren Montag (Eds.), *Masses, Classes, and the Public Sphere* (pp. 62–82). New York, NY: Verso.

Eagleton, T. (1991). *Ideology.* New York: Verso.

Fraser, N. (1997). Rethinking the public sphere: A contribution to the critique of actually existing democracy. In C. Calhoun (Ed.), *Habermas and the Public Sphere* (pp. 109–143). London, England: Cambridge University Press.

Habermas, J. (1989). *The structural transformation of the public sphere.* Cambridge, MA: MIT Press.

Hardt, H. (2004). *Myths for the masses.* Malden, MA: Blackwell Publishing.

Hauser, G. (1999). *Vernacular voices: The rhetoric of publics and public spheres.* Columbia, SC: University of South Carolina Press.

Negt, O. and Kluge, A. (1993). *Public sphere and experience: Toward an analysis of the bourgeois and proletarian public sphere.* Minneapolis: University of Minnesota Press.

Ono, K. and Sloop, J. (1995). The critique of vernacular discourse. *Communication Monographs,* 62, pp. 19–46.

Talk of the Nation. (2005, October 4). Trouble and desire: Rebuilding the Ninth Ward. *Talk of the Nation.* Washington, D.C.: National Public Radio.

Thompson, J.B. (1990). *Ideology and modern culture.* Stanford, CA: Stanford University Press.

Urban Institute. (2005). Katrina: Demographics of a disaster. Retrieved September 12, 2005 from http://www.urban.org/url.cfm?ID=900835.

Wu, Olivia. (1997, February 23). Residents say redevelopment will displace poor; Cabrini plan disputed. [Sunday News]. *Chicago Sun Times,* p. 18.

Chapter 17

Human Rights in Disaster Policy: Improving the Federal Response to Natural Disasters, Disease Pandemics, and Terrorist Attacks

Hannibal Travis

Introduction

Megadisasters such as 9/11, Hurricane Katrina, and existing and emerging pandemics such as HIV/AIDS and bird flu are likely to outdo even those scourges of the twentieth century, war and economic collapse, in destroying American lives and undermining the democratic constitution of the U.S. In a matter of days, these events claimed more fatalities than months of intense warfare or unremitting poverty (see Rao, 1973; Specter, 2004). Given that the September 11th World Trade Center attack triggered a recession, a hurricane strike on New York or bird flu pandemic could put enough people and infrastructure out of commission that another Great Depression could ensue (Crouch, 2006).

Twenty-first century national emergencies in the U.S. also aggravate long-standing human rights crises involving racial, ethnic and class-based disparities. America's urban centers are at gravest risk for such global threats as terrorism, mass casualty earthquakes and the flooding of coastal cities, heat waves, and pandemics of infectious disease spread via international travel and shipping (Lies, 2005; Schmid, 2005). These urban centers, in turn, are inhabited by some of the nation's least powerful residents, including racial and ethnic minorities and recent immigrants, the unemployed residents of our deindustrialized inner-city neighborhoods, single mothers and their children, and the elderly struggling to survive on fixed incomes (U.S. Census Bureau, 2005;

Williams, 2001; Wilson, 1996). Minority communities in particular tend to suffer disproportionately from disasters because their financial reserves are frequently insufficient to ride out displacement or job losses, their housing is less resilient, their neighborhoods more exposed to storms or flooding, and government and private assistance are slower arriving in their areas (Salmon, 2005).

This chapter will present a legal and legislative policy framework to promote human rights during responses to natural and human-made disasters such as hurricanes, earthquakes, disease pandemics, and terrorist attacks. Its thesis is that federal action may avert human rights catastrophes that might otherwise result from breakdowns in essential infrastructure during a crisis. This will require reforming the legal traditions and principles that operate in the U.S. to frustrate an effective national response to contemporary megadisasters. First, we must clarify that the authority of the federal government under the U.S. Constitution and laws amply justifies a unified national response to emergencies. Second, all levels of government must better prioritize resources toward evacuations and post-disaster housing and health care for the neediest children and families displaced by disasters. Third, disparities in access to essential services that contribute to both chronic and sudden disasters should be eliminated. Finally, deficiencies in the generation, release, and distribution of disaster threat and preparedness information must be remedied by a comprehensive public information campaign.

Human Rights Implications of Natural and Human-Made Disasters

Sound policies can vindicate the human rights of people caught up in disasters, including "the right to food, the right to education, the right to adequate housing and the right to the highest attainable standard of health" (International Commission of Jurists, 2003). The U.S. led the process of drafting and adopting codes of human rights in the Universal Declaration of Human Rights, the International Covenant on Civil and Political Rights, and the International Covenant on Economic, Social and Cultural Rights (Glendon, 2001; Keller, 2001). As binding international law (Glendon, 2001), these documents prohibit denying any member of a society "the right to a standard of living adequate for the health and well-being of himself and of his family, including food, clothing, housing and medical care and necessary social services, and the right to security in the event of unemployment, sickness, disability, widowhood, old age or other lack of livelihood in circumstances beyond his control" (U.N. General Assembly, 1948, Art. 25(1)). The right to health is "fundamental" and should be protected against poverty and discrimination using the "maximum available resources" of the government (Hunt, 2006).

International human rights law requires the federal government "to ensure that each person within its jurisdiction is afforded the opportunity to obtain basic need satisfaction, as recognised in human rights instruments, which cannot be secured through personal efforts" (International Commission of Jurists, 2003). This implies a duty to provide basic need satisfaction "when no other possibility exists, due to e.g., unemployment, disadvantage or age, sudden crisis/disaster, or marginalisation" (International Commission of Jurists, 2003). Nations also have the obligation not to engage in unnecessary "forced evictions," and particularly not in a manner that results in homelessness due to the absence of "adequate alternative housing, resettlement or access to productive land" (International Commission of Jurists, 2003).

The Lessons of 9/11: Heeding Warnings, Sharing Information, Evacuating Victims

Global economic activity may be increasing the frequency and severity of natural disasters by emitting carbons into the atmosphere, which trigger global warming trends that may intensify hurricanes and other extreme weather phenomena (Hayden, 2006; Schmid, 2006). Similarly, global trade and travel may be quickening the pace of mutation and infection during epidemics of communicable disease, and global financial, military, and telecommunications links may be enhancing the sophistication of international terrorist groups (Bostrom, 2002; Meyer, 2003; National Commission on Terrorist Attacks Upon the United States, 2004; Richens, 2006).

Despite the acceleration of international catastrophes brought on by globalization, emergency planning in the U.S. is premised upon outmoded notions of federalism and states' rights. Federal law currently relegates national health and emergency management officials to a secondary support role, whereby they subsidize, coordinate planning, and disseminate information regarding state and local disaster response practices and procedures. The federal government has construed these principles to require the states to take primary responsibility for hurricane evacuations and influenza quarantines, despite their manifest incapacity to do a thorough job on such matters (Homeland Security Council, 2006). As the National Commission on Terrorist Attacks Upon the United States (the 9/11 Commission) concluded (2004), 9/11 "overwhelmed the response capacity of most of the local jurisdictions where the hijacked airliners crashed" (p. 397).

Almost four years prior to Katrina's strike on the Gulf Coast, New York City police and fire departments became the primary agencies responding to the events of September 11, 2001. The White House and U.S. Department of Defense did not coordinate an effective response to the attacks, despite their hundreds of billions of dollars in budgetary authority to do so. The U.S. North

American Aerospace Defense Command (NORAD) could not intercept any hijacked flights, despite the fact that its mission is "aerospace control" for North America, including "warning of attack against North America whether by aircraft, missiles, or space vehicles" (9/11 Commission, 2004, p. 457). The Federal Aviation Administration (FAA) and the Federal Emergency Management Agency (FEMA) did not help much until after the disaster was already over, despite their jurisdiction over aviation and emergencies, respectively.

Warnings That Were Not Passed on to the Public or First Responders

Long before September 11th, the White House Presidential Daily Brief had documented a severe risk of hijackings of U.S. aircraft by terrorist allies of Osama bin Laden (9/11 Commission, 2004). The CIA Director, FBI agents, and foreign intelligence services, had all warned and shared information with U.S. authorities about the pending attack, but the American public was not warned (9/11 Commission, 2004; Coll, 2004; Fainaru & Grimaldi, 2001; Landay, Strobel & Walcott, 2006; Shenon, 2001; U.S. Senate, 2004). The FAA in particular possessed intelligence "that associates with Usama Bin Ladin in the 1990s were interested in hijackings and the use of an aircraft as a weapon," but told airlines and airports in early 2001 that "we have no indication that any group is currently thinking in that direction" (9/11 Commission, Staff Statement No. 3, 2004, p. 3). Measures such as reinforcing aircraft cockpit doors with bulletproof material, as had been proposed on multiple occasions to prevent "skyjacking" as early as 1967, were never implemented (Pasternak, 2001).

Starting at 8:13 a.m. on September 11th, American Airlines Flight 11 was not responding to FAA air traffic controllers, who sent a notification of an in-progress hijacking through the system at 8:25 a.m. (Levitas, Lee, & Schlein, 2002; 9/11 Commission, 2004). A flight attendant had informed American Airlines of the attack by 8:19 a.m. FAA controllers realized that a hijacking was in progress by 8:24 a.m., and FAA headquarters was notified by 8:32 a.m. (9/11 Commission, 2004).

At 8:37 a.m., fifteen to twenty minutes after being notified that an American Airlines flight had been hijacked, the FAA notified NORAD (NORAD, 2001). This was insufficient time to get fighter jets into the air, locate the hijacked plane, ascertain its trajectory, and intercept it (9/11 Commission, 2004). At 8:46 a.m., Flight 11 crashed into the World Trade Center's North Tower, exploding up to 3,000 gallons of jet fuel with the force of 480,000 pounds of dynamite and sparking a fire that generated up to five times as much energy as a nuclear power plant (Levitas et al., 2002).

Similarly, the FAA did not inform NORAD of the hijacking of United Airlines Flight 175 until eleven minutes after it occurred, too late to prevent Flight 175's impact into the South Tower. NORAD fighters had been airborne nearly

10 minutes before the second impact, but without a flight number or further tracking information from the FAA they could not intercept Flight 175. The White House and Department of Defense never even learned of the hijacking of either of the planes that hit the World Trade Center until after they had made impact, so that NORAD was not authorized to intercept hijacked aircraft by force until all had already crashed. (9/11 Commission, 2004).

FAA air traffic controllers in Boston urged that the FAA order all commercial aircraft threatened with hijacking to secure their cockpit doors, but this was not done. The failure to issue such a warning may have contributed to the hijacking starting at 8:51–8:54 a.m. of American Airlines Flight 77, which terrorists crashed into the Pentagon at 9:38 a.m, and to the hijacking starting at 9:28 a.m. of American Airlines Flight 93, which terrorists crashed into the ground at 10:02 a.m. after a passenger revolt (9/11 Commission, 2004). Even after witnessing a second aircraft explode into the World Trade Center, FAA officials and airline officials did not warn other aircraft pilots about the danger. One senior FAA air traffic control manager said that it was simply not the FAA's place to order the airlines what to tell their pilots (9/11 Commission, 2004). In actuality, federal law gave the head of the FAA, and any employee to whom he or she delegated the task, the authority to issue emergency regulations and take other measures to protect air passengers and persons on the ground threatened by air crashes (U.S. Code, 2000b).

Later, Senator Mark Dayton, a member of the Senate Armed Services Committee, charged the FAA with "unbelievable negligence" in not issuing a system-wide warning in time for the pilots of the remaining planes to lock their cockpit doors, and not notifying NORAD of developments in time to intercept the hijacked planes (Gordon, 2004). Senator Dayton also criticized the FAA for misinforming NORAD that a plane that had already hit the World Trade Center was headed for Washington, and noted that the FAA lacked the capacity to track the hijacked planes using radar once the onboard communications equipment had been disabled (Dayton, 2004).

Victims Who Were Not Evacuated

Not only did the federal government fail to prevent the impact of either plane upon the World Trade Center, it also did not materially aid in evacuating New Yorkers from the burning and collapsing buildings. Instead, first responders from the Fire Department of New York, New York Police Department (NYPD), and Port Authority Police Department (PAPD) helped thousands of civilians evacuate the area (9/11 Commission, 2004). With only about one-twentieth of deaths occurring below the impact zone of the two planes, "the evacuation was a success for civilians below the impact zone" (p. 316).

Although the self-sacrifice of these government employees was heroic, the flawed planning and leadership of the Mayor's Office and its non-uniformed employees may have contributed to the toll of nearly 2,000 dead civilians at or above the impact zone (9/11 Commission, 2004). To start with, the Port Authority of New York and New Jersey, which organized evacuation planning after the 1993 attempt to topple the World Trade Center towers using a truck bomb, established grossly inadequate procedures and gave bad advice to those trapped in the buildings (Garcia, 2003; 9/11 Commission, 2004). The 9/11 Commission found: that the Port Authority "had no protocol for rescuing people trapped above a fire in the towers," conducted "[n]either full nor partial evacuation drills," told World Trade Center workers simply "to await the instructions that would be provided at the time of an emergency," and did not instruct them to use the stairwells (pp. 280–281). On 9/11, Port Authority security officials told some civilians to "stand by for further instructions," while others were told to evacuate. The public address system and security personnel in the South Tower told civilians that despite the enormous explosion in the skyscraper next door, "their building was safe and that they should remain on or return to their offices or floors" (pp. 287–289). "As a result of the announcement, many civilians remained on their floors. Others reversed their evacuation and went back up" (p. 289). The civilians in the South Tower who did try to evacuate tried to squeeze into the elevators, and when many failed to fit, they were killed or injured upon the impact of the second plane.

The Port Authority was not alone in making questionable decisions that day. New York City's emergency telephone 911 operators told civilians both above and below the impact zone in both the North and South Towers to "stay low, remain where they are, and wait for emergency personnel to reach them" (9/11 Commission, 2004, pp. 286–287). The operators struggled under "rigid standard operating procedures" that resulted in some evacuees being placed on hold several times as the building burned around them (p. 295). One group trapped on the 83rd floor "pleaded repeatedly to know whether the fire was above or below them, … [but was] transferred back and forth several times and advised to stay put. Evidence suggests that these callers died" (p. 296).

The 9/11 Commission (2004) noted multiple failures by the Mayor's Office on September 11th. Firefighters died unnecessarily when the order for the FDNY to evacuate the North Tower was issued because some had not been issued radios and others had not been given training on the use of different channels to avoid interference. Fewer FDNY fatalities might have resulted had the Mayor's Office better coordinated its efforts with those of the NYPD and PAPD, so that "redundant searches of specific floors and areas" did not have to be performed (p. 321). The Mayor's Office did not implement the "integrated communications and unified command" between police and fire rescue services that its own emergency management planning indicated would be essential. Among other things, the FDNY lacked adequate communications equipment, clear radio frequency assignments, and the leadership and "information sharing" that the Mayor's Office of Emergency Management (OEM) was supposed to assure.

The OEM should have had "a crucial role in managing the city's overall response," but it was established in 7 World Trade Center, mere yards from a prime terrorist target, and without a backup location (pp. 283). The mayor, OEM personnel, and a "big portion of city government" had to be evacuated themselves to avoid the collapse of the building (Giuliani, 2002, pp. 21).

Civilians Whose Health and Safety Were Not Protected

At 11 a.m., New York City Mayor Rudolph Giuliani ordered an evacuation of Manhattan south of Canal Street, but did not provide significant aid in transporting or salvaging the personal effects of evacuees who had not been in or who had left the World Trade Center towers (Levitas et al., 2002). The absence of governmental assistance forced thousands of civilians to walk home over the bridges connecting Manhattan to Brooklyn, Queens, and New Jersey, many across long distances, a scenario that would be repeated during the 2003 North American blackout (Julavitz, 2003; Levitas et al., 2002).

Photographs from September 12, 2001 show Mayor Giuliani, New York State Governor George Pataki, and New York Senators Hillary Clinton and Charles Schumer conducting a tour of a street outside the World Trade Center site, clutching or strapping respiratory masks close to their faces (Levitas et al., 2002). Photographs taken the very next day and over the course of the next month, however, show firefighters climbing on top of the smoldering rubble, most of them not wearing respiratory masks over their mouths, and some wearing merely paper masks, although some workers wore full gas masks (Levitas et al., 2002). The vast majority of firefighters, transit workers, and steel workers had little or no respiratory protection (Chen, 2005). "We had no protection at all," said one FDNY firefighter suffering from asthma and other respiratory ailments after working at Ground Zero until 2002 (Francescani, 2006, n.p.).

About 300 firefighters had to go on leave for respiratory problems by January 2002, due to inhalation of toxic dust and fumes from the disaster (Levitas et al., 2002). A study released by Mount Sinai Medical Center near the fifth anniversary of 9/11 revealed that of firefighters, police, and emergency personnel "who had no health symptoms before the attacks, 61 percent developed lung symptoms while working on the toxic pile" (Westfeldt, 2006). Rescue and recovery personnel who did substantial work at the World Trade Center site are at "great risk" because the collapse of its 110 stories released tremendous amounts of asbestos, and asbestos-related cancers can develop after a few weeks of exposure (Baard, 2001). In spite of this fact, billionaire Mayor Michael Bloomberg opposed an effort by the New York State legislature to expand care for sick and disabled first responders (Westfeldt, 2006). Instead, the FDNY bureaucracy has slashed benefits for ailing firefighters by imposing artificial testing requirements (Francescani, 2006).

Many government employees and civilians living or working in the area of the toxic dust cloud suffered unnecessarily because New York City's Department of Environmental Protection allowed landlords to remove toxic materials at their discretion without legal guidance (Barry, 2006). Latina/o and Polish immigrants who cleaned office buildings around the World Trade Center had scarred lungs from the particles of lead, mercury, arsenic, asbestos, concrete, glass, and dioxin they inhaled; as a result, many lost their health, jobs, and homes (Barry, 2006; Chayes, 2006). After their parents "were encouraged to clean up the contaminated World Trade Center dust in their homes themselves, with wet mops and rags," asthmatic children in Chinatown "had significantly more asthma-related clinic visits for symptoms and also required greater use of asthma medication during the year after the attack" (Sierra Club, 2004, n.p.). Representative Carolyn B. Maloney called the "shockingly high levels of respiratory illness and other emerging sickness" among civilians and government employees near Ground Zero "a national health emergency," to which "the federal response has been tragically inadequate" (Chen, 2005, n.p.). A federal judge ultimately dismissed a negligence and wrongful death lawsuit brought by thousands of injured workers against the corporations that stood to profit from a fast and unsafe cleanup of World Trade Center site, but allowed their claims against the Port Authority and the City of New York to proceed. (*In re World Trade Center* Disaster Site Litigation, 2006).

In addition to well over 2,500 people and several major skyscrapers, New York lost more than 80 billion dollars and about 1.6 million jobs due to the September 11th attack and response (Levitas et al., 2002). But even close to three years after 9/11, New York City lacked an emergency management plan that unified and coordinated the FDNY's and NYPD's activities to "deploy and monitor all first responder resources from one overall command post" (9/11 Commission, 2004, p. 322). Instead, Mayors Giuliani and Bloomberg and Governor Pataki proposed lavishing $800 million or more on subsidies and tax breaks to replace the Yankees' and Mets' stadiums. (Carolan & Keating, 2002; deMause, 2005).

Hurricane Katrina: Ignored Warnings, Withheld Information, and a Delayed Evacuation

Federal officials confronting the human rights crisis that was the flooding of New Orleans faltered on many of the same points that impeded disaster response on 9/11. Specifically, they responded in a lackluster fashion to urgent calls to action. Moreover, they initially deferred to state and local efforts to evacuate the local population, which once again failed due to poor planning, personnel constraints, and underinvestment. Finally, post-disaster relief ef-

forts too often suffered from inequitable and positively harmful policies, prof-
iteering, waste, and failures to allocate charitable funds to some of the neediest persons.

The Warnings: Visions of Nightmares

In August 2001, FEMA ranked "a super-strength hurricane hitting New Orleans" as second only to a terrorist attack on New York as the greatest disaster
threat facing the U.S. (Chong & Becerra, 2005). In 2002, *The Times-Picayune*
of New Orleans published a five-part series devoted to warning residents and
government officials that "[e]ventually a major hurricane will hit New Orleans
head on." The series noted that a string of hurricanes had killed thousands of
Louisiana residents, including storms in 1893 (2,000 people), 1900 (8,000
people in nearby Galveston, Texas), 1909 (353 people), 1915 (275 people),
1947 (51 people and inundation of most of New Orleans), 1957 (526 people
at the Louisiana-Texas border), 1965 (81 people and "worst flooding in
decades"), and 1969 (262 people in Louisiana and Mississippi) (McQuaid &
Schleifstein, 2002). An accompanying graphic warned that storm surges and
waters from Lakes Pontchartrain and Borgne could "flood populated areas"
(Mayer, 2002, n.p.).

On Friday evening, August 26, 2005, the National Weather Service "projected that Katrina would make landfall as a category 4 storm ... 65 miles
south-southeast of New Orleans" (U.S. House of Representatives, Select Bipartisan Committee, 2006, p. 70). But the Director of the National Hurricane
Center did not call state officials in Louisiana, Mississippi, and Alabama to
communicate the storm's likely intensity and catastrophic impact until late Saturday evening He did call New Orleans Mayor Ray Nagin, but did not advise
him to "immediately order a mandatory evacuation," instead vaguely hinting
that the nature of the storm would make "very difficult decisions" necessary.
Sometime on Saturday, New Orleans refused an offer by Amtrak to carry hundreds of evacuees out of the path of the hurricane (Dyson, 2006, p. 58).

The storm reached Category 5 status on Sunday morning, with winds of
161 miles per hour (Dyson, 2006, p. 59). Late on Sunday afternoon, the National Weather Service issued predictions of a storm surge of 18 to 28 feet, with
" 'large and battering' waves on top of the surge," so that " 'some levees in the
greater New Orleans area could be overtopped' " (Dyson, 2006, p. 59). That
day, U.S. President George W. Bush "was warned ... [by] federal staff and experts" that Hurricane Katrina would not merely overtop but "breach levees in
New Orleans, putting lives at risk ..." (Associated Press, 2006a, n.p.). At that
meeting, FEMA director Michael Brown noted with "concern that hospitals
were not being evacuated" and evacuees being sent to the Superdome might
not be "safe" or "have adequate medical care" (Associated Press, 2006a, n.p.).

The Evacuations: A Deadly Delay

Prior to Hurricane Katrina, federal law and policy gave the U.S. Department of Homeland Security (DHS) abundant power to evacuate and provide relief to persons at risk from the storm. DHS told the public that it would "assume primary responsibility on March 1st [2005] for ensuring that emergency response professionals are prepared for any situation," including by "providing a coordinated, comprehensive federal response to any large-scale crisis and mounting a swift and effective recovery effort" after a "terrorist attack, natural disaster or other large-scale emergency ..." (U.S. Department of Homeland Security, 2005, n.p.). Under federal law, DHS was the "focal point regarding natural and manmade crises and emergency planning" (U.S. Code, 2004, n.p.).

The U.S. Department of Homeland Security National Response Plan (2004) designated the U.S. Department of Health and Human Services and Department of Defense to coordinate "[t]ransportation to provide support for the evacuation of seriously ill or injured patients to locations where hospital care or outpatient services are available." (p. ESF #8–9) This plan, which the President ordered the Secretary of Homeland Security to prepare in February 2003, minimized the role of the National Guard, "our greatest single National resource for responding to major catastrophes" (U.S. House of Representatives, House Committee on Science, Democratic Staff, 2005). Over 30,000 Army National Guard members had been activated for combat operations in Iraq by that time, a number that would rise to over 40,000 in a few months and to 80,000 by late 2003 (U.S. General Accounting Office, 2004).

FEMA's role is to "reduce the loss of life and property and protect the Nation from all hazards" by "evacuating potential victims"; "providing food, water, shelter, and medical care to those in need"; "restoring critical public services"; and "rebuilding communities so individuals" can "return to normal life, and protect against future hazards" (U.S. Code, 2004, n.p.). From 2001 to 2004, however, FEMA had "slashed" "key federal disaster mitigation programs," with "[f]ederal funding of post-disaster mitigation efforts designed to protect people and property from the next disaster ... cut in half" (Elliston, 2004, n.p.). FEMA director Joe Allbaugh told a Senate appropriations subcommittee in May 2001 that "federal disaster assistance may have evolved into both an oversized entitlement program and a disincentive to effective state and local risk management," so "[e]xpectations of when the federal government should be involved and the degree of involvement" in disasters would need to be reduced (Ellison, 2004, n.p.). By 2005, a senior FEMA official told *The Washington Post* that FEMA's personnel were capable of "so much less than what we were in 2000," before 9/11 (Elliston, 2005, n.p.). FEMA's funding was doubled after 9/11, but its Hazard Mitigation Grant Program was halved in 2003 (Elliston, 2004).

New outsourcing requirements and a push for privatization delegated disaster preparedness and response to outside contractors. State governments warned that these new policies "would cost the government more because many communities will be unable to afford preventative measures and as a result will require more relief money when disasters strike ..." (Elliston, 2004, n.p.). In June 2004, a "Baton Rouge-based emergency management and homeland security consultant" known as IEM, Inc., announced that it had secured a $500,000 contract with FEMA to "lead the development of a catastrophic hurricane disaster plan for Southeast Louisiana and the City of New Orleans" (IEM, 2004, n.p.). IEM noted that given New Orleans' "vulnerability, unique geographic location and elevation, and troubled escape routes, a plan that facilitates a rapid and effective hurricane response and recovery is critical ..." (IEM, 2004, n.p.).

IEM's plan assumed that over 100,000 New Orleans residents would not be able to evacuate the city by car and would need to be bused, but failed to recommend that any agency in particular take "responsibility for identifying and arranging for this transportation armada" (U.S. House of Representatives, House Committee on Science, Democratic Staff, 2005). The 2000 Census revealed that "52 percent of poor blacks lacked car access," and that New Orleans residents had less access to cars than in any metropolitan area except the New York area, where subways and commuter trains abound (Berube & Raphael, 2005, pp. 1–2; Dyson, 2006).

On Saturday, August 27, 2005, Louisiana Governor Kathleen Blanco provided official notification to the president pursuant to the Stafford Act that Hurricane Katrina would be "of such severity and magnitude that effective response is beyond the capabilities of the State and affected local governments, and that supplementary Federal assistance is necessary to save lives, protect property, public health, and safety ..." President Bush declared an emergency in the state of Louisiana and authorized FEMA to coordinate disaster relief in the area (U.S. House of Representatives, House Committee on Science, Democratic Staff, 2005, n.p.). The Louisiana National Guard, Louisiana Emergency Operations Center, Louisiana Department of Transportation and Development, and the Louisiana State Police began implementing an evacuation plan pursuant to which 1.2 million Louisiana residents fled their homes in private cars and trucks (U.S. House of Representatives, Select Bipartisan Committee, 2006).

A mandatory evacuation was not ordered until the Sunday morning of August 28th (U.S. House of Representatives, Select Bipartisan Committee, 2006). Although buses were the "obvious linchpin for evacuating a city where nearly 100,000 people had no cars, ... federal, state and local officials ... had failed to round up [enough] buses in advance ..." (Lipton, Drew, Shane & Rohde, 2005, n.p.). New Orleans expected help in evacuating residents from the Louisiana Department of Transportation, Louisiana National Guard, U.S. Coast Guard, and Amtrak The Mayor and the Governor "did not implement evacuation procedures for all of the citizens of New Orleans that reflected the seriousness of the threat." They failed to order a mandatory evacuation until Sunday, and even that order simply " 'ask[ed]' people who had not evacuated to go to checkpoints for bus service" and then transported "people only as far as the Superdome." This led to many deaths and injuries as "more than 70,000 people remained in the City to be rescued after the storm" (U.S. House of Representatives, Select Bipartisan Committee, 2006, pp. 111, 359).

The Louisiana National Guard "was not available to drive buses," so "hundreds of city buses and school buses that could have been used for evacuation sat useless, flooded or without drivers" (U.S. House of Representatives, Select Bipartisan Committee, 2006, p. 119). "In Louisiana, [Governor] Blanco asked for the immediate return of Louisiana National Guard troops from Iraq" (U.S. House of Representatives, Select Bipartisan Committee, 2006, p. 228), but the Department of Defense insisted that Louisiana already had enough troops despite having 3,500 fewer on hand than Alabama and 1,700 fewer than Florida (Associated Press, 2005a; Dyson, 2006). The National Guard Bureau refused "to extract Louisiana troops from combat operations in Iraq" (U.S. House of Representatives, Select Bipartisan Committee, 2006, p. 228). Up to 40 percent of the Louisiana National Guard may have been deployed to Iraq when Katrina hit (Dyson, 2006).

In New Orleans, a loose barge caused the breach of the Industrial Canal floodwall adjoining the Lower Ninth Ward neighborhood, and a mysterious "bulldozer"-like breach 300 feet wide was somehow torn in the 17th Street Canal floodwall (Dyson, 2006; McQuaid, 2005;). Hundreds of residents died "as floodwaters enveloped low lying neighborhoods in waters above the roof lines" (U.S. House of Representatives, Select Bipartisan Committee, 2006, p. 115). In a nearby parish where the sheriff implemented a mandatory evacuation on Saturday, 97% or more of residents evacuated, and far fewer people died—about three. Preliminary data from the Louisiana Department of Health and Hospitals indicated that 588 people died in neighborhoods that should have remained dry if the levees had worked properly (U.S. House of Representatives, Select Bipartisan Committee, 2006).

Poor planning and execution of disaster prevention and relief programs led to deterioration in the human rights situation of the poor in particular. Only about 80 percent of New Orleans residents were evacuated, leaving over 16,000 women, children, and elderly people in the Superdome, along with 8,000 men (Lipton, Dre, Shane & Rohde, 2005). By the time the post-hurricane evacuation was completed, 10 people had died in the Superdome, and "some children were so dehydrated that guardsmen had to carry them out" (Lipton, Dre, Shane & Rohde, 2005, n.p.). In the New Orleans Convention Center, on higher ground to which 19,000 residents had fled for shelter after the flooding of the city, there was "no ... security on hand, no weapon screening, no food[,] no water, ... no electrical power, no lighting, no air conditioning, and no functioning toilets" (U.S. House of Representatives, 2006, p. 118). Residents fleeing to higher ground on highway overpasses and levees also lacked "food, water, or medical treatment" (U.S. House of Representatives, 2006, p. 119). FEMA refused offers of help and supplies from Germany and several other countries, the Coast Guard, the City of Chicago, a Virginia city, Wal-Mart, other American cities, and private entities (Dyson, 2006).

As residents became increasingly hungry and dehydrated, Governor Kathleen Blanco ordered the Louisiana National Guard to shoot to kill residents appropriating food or water from abandoned stores (Chamberlain, 2005; CNN, 2006). Governor Blanco warned that "troops fresh back from Iraq" had M-16s and were "battle-tested" for deployment in New Orleans (Dyson, 2006, p. 114). A grandfather and a mentally retarded man were reportedly shot to death by New Orleans police, who claimed to be reacting to gunshots in the area and who were trained to shoot to kill rather than wound as a matter of official policy (CNN, 2005b; CNN, 2006).

The poor and elderly who utilized Louisiana's charity hospitals suffered disproportionately from Hurricane Katrina's flooding and blackouts. Dozens of patients died in the overheated beds of Memorial Medical Center, as the electricity was knocked out, generator capacity was insufficient, medicines were depleted, and at least one doctor reportedly administered lethal doses of morphine to kill suffering patients (Drew & Dewan, 2006).

The Relief and Reconstruction Effort:
A Mammoth Effort, but Slow Improvement

The situation in New Orleans only began to improve with robust federal action. The National Guard rescued more than 25,000 people and evacuated 70,000 in all, the U.S. Coast Guard rescued more than 33,000 residents, the U.S. Air Force rescued more than 4,000, and the U.S. Army's Third Brigade 82nd Airborne and U.S. Navy rescued more than 11,000 (along with the private Bear Search & Rescue Foundation) (Bear Search & Rescue Foundation, 2006; Cope, 2005; Hart, 2006; Urban, 2005; U.S. House of Representatives, Select Bipartisan Committee, 2006). The Department of Health and Human Services "delivered 27 pallets of medical supplies from [its] stockpiles ... includ[ing] bandages, suture kits, stethoscopes and portable oxygen tanks ... used to set up a mobile hospital ... in Baton Rouge" (Stevenson, 2005, p. A21). The Department of Homeland Security and Department of Transportation "shipped 13.4 million liters of water, 10,000 tarps, 5.4 million meals, 3.4 million pounds of ice, 144 generators and 135,000 blankets, among other essential supplies" (Stevenson, 2005, p. A21). FEMA eventually provided more than 170,000 trailers for displaced Gulf Coast residents (Glaser, 2006; Joyner, 2006). It denied housing aid to 11,000 more families, however, until a federal judge ordered it to provide aid and help the families procure emergency shelter, on the basis that FEMA violated the families' constitutional rights by acting arbitrarily (*ACORN v. FEMA*, 2006).

After New Orleans Mayor Ray Nagin ordered everyone remaining in the city to leave, a week after the hurricane and apparently regardless of how dry or safe their houses were (BBC, 2005), it took billions of dollars in federal aid to subsidize hotel rooms, trailers, rented apartments, mortgage assistance and foreclosure relief for tens of thousands of residents (U.S. Department of Housing and Urban Development, 2006). Congress passed legislation that earmarked $11.5 billion for programs such as those in Louisiana and Mississippi to "make one-time grants of up to $150,000 to aid households whose primary residences were ... destroyed or severely damaged [in Louisiana] following Hurricanes Katrina and Rita" (U.S. Department of Housing and Urban Development, 2006). As an apparent sop to the insurance industry, these grants were not available to the neediest families whose houses were located inside designated flood zones (U.S. Department of Housing and Urban Development, 2006). These grants were also moot for many homeowners affected by Mayor Nagin's policy of seizing and destroying up to half of the 125,000 homes that were damaged by Hurricanes Katrina and Rita because they were not fully cleaned and repaired by a premature deadline of August 2006 (Associated Press, 2006d; Eggler, 2006a; Eggler, 2006b). As this deadline came and went, New Orleans residents who failed to pay thousands of dollars to gut and rebuild their homes faced seizure of the property as "blighted" (Ross, 2006).

One million people were homeless at the height of the crisis (Chamberlain, 2005). Racial and ethnic minorities complained of inadequate housing in the immediate aftermath of the hurricane, as the Red Cross set up most shelters in locations far from minority communities (Salmon, 2005). City and state officials, instead of expanding public housing to replace the 100,000 submerged and polluted homes in New Orleans, began demolishing public housing units that had suffered little damage (Dyson, 2006; Saulny, 2006; Warrick & Grunwald, 2005). Local officials made clear that they "do not want a return to the intense concentrations of" poor people who lived in public housing, and one expert noted that officials leading the recovery process "never wanted poor people to return ... in the first place" (Saulny, 2006, p. A19).

Delayed cleanup and repairs of essential infrastructure frustrated many residents' ability to return to their homes and rebuild. A month after Katrina, two-thirds of New Orleans had no electricity, all of the hospitals were still closed, the sewage system was "iffy," less than a tenth of zip codes received their mail, and the "city [was] an environmental hazard, with toxic mold ... [and] 22 million tons of contaminated solid waste ..." (CNN, 2005a, n.p.). The EPA warned that it would be "very dangerous" for residents to return "without protection" (CNN, 2005a, n.p.).

Two-thirds of the 450,000 people living in New Orleans had fled the storm and related events by January 2006 (Whoriskey, 2006a). One year after Katrina's impact, the New Orleans population was still half of its pre-storm amount, and the number of jobs in the city had declined by 70 percent (Whoriskey, 2006b). Two-thirds of hospitals remained closed and almost 60 percent of damaged homes and businesses had no electricity or heating gas (Callimachi, 2006).

Louisiana's children, many of whom lived in poverty prior to the storm, suffered disruption to their educations and social networks (Dyson, 2006). The public schools in New Orleans "collapse[d]" and "ha[d] not even begun to bounce back" by the next summer (Saulny, 2006). Less than half of them enrolled any students for the 2006–2007 school year (Callimachi, 2006). In 2008, the student population remained at half its pre-storm level, but spending per student had reached twice the national average due to federal and state aid, including a $685 school rebuilding plan paid for largely by FEMA (Toppo, 2008). New Orleans schools require $1.7 billion in repairs, and serve a population of extremely poor children by national standards.

Emerging Threats: Bird Flu, Earthquakes, Tsunamis, and Nuclear Terrorism

The next major disaster in the U.S. may be an outbreak of a deadly flu strain that crosses over into humans from bird populations. Although fewer than 200 people have died from bird flu worldwide, there are over 36,000 influenza deaths each year in the U.S. (Associated Press, 2006c; Baker, 2006). The last major bird flu pandemic killed 500,000 Americans and 50 million people worldwide in 1918 and 1919, and reduced the life expectancy of Americans by 13 years (McKay, 2005; Parks, 2006; Trafford, 2005;). The 1918 flu killed more people than World War I (Jervey, 1917; McKay, 2005;). The flu pandemic also may have contributed to the outbreak of World War II by sickening President Woodrow Wilson during the critical negotiations over German disarmament via the Treaty of Versailles (Parks, 2006).

Bird flu is already widespread in bird populations throughout Africa and is the subject of continued outbreaks of human infection in China and Indonesia (Associated Press, 2006b). Mutations in the bird flu virus currently spreading throughout the Eastern Hemisphere indicate that it is following a similar path as the 1918 virus (McKay, 2005). The virus is continuing to evolve into "a potential global pandemic" (Associated Press, 2006b, n.p.). The bird flu is not the only virus undergoing potentially catastrophic mutations; scientists are currently experimenting with genetic engineering of the smallpox virus, which caused 300 million deaths in the twentieth century alone (Connor, 2005; Preston, 1999).

In 2009, the mutation of the bird flu into the swine flu captured headlines and struck fear into many affected populations. Influenza virus A, subtype H1N1 is a mutated combination of bird flu, human flu, and two variants of swine flu (North American and Asian/European (MacKenzie, 2009). A U.N. report leaked in September 2009 indicated that millions of people could die around the world from the virus and its devastation of economic activity (Syal, 2009). Some models of a flu pandemic prepared as part of the U.S. Pandemic Preparedness Initiative indicated that 2.2 million Americans may die and 90 million may fall ill if the 1918 flu pandemic is repeated in 2009–2010 (Trust for America's Health, 2007). This would require a severe adverse mutation of the H1N1 virus, which is currently forecast to kill tens of thousands of Americans in the winter of 2009–2010, far short of what the events of 1918 would suggest (Fox, 2009). Some federal estimates of the death toll, however, reach 90,000 (CBS, 2009). Earthquakes remain a serious threat to 75 million Americans in most U.S. states, with faults not simply in California but in the Midwest, South, and in places along the East Coast (Redlener, 2006). Should history repeat itself along the San Andreas Fault and a 7.9 magnitude earthquake hit San Francisco as occurred in 1906, estimates are that 5,000 people would die (Reuters, 2006). It is estimated that an earthquake of 7.5 magnitude along a fault in Los Angeles would kill 18,000, leave 300,000 homeless, and trigger economic losses of $250 billion (U.S. House of Representatives, Select Bipartisan Committee, 2006). Local police in the U.S. are hard pressed to direct traffic during an electrical blackout unaccompanied by mass casualties, let alone do that and "assist the injured, secure facilities that are critical…, [and] prevent disorder," all at once (Bernstein, 2005, n.p.).

Another potentially devastating event would be a tsunami along the east or west coast of the U.S., triggered by an earthquake or asteroid impact. Many of us watched in horror and amazement as the Indian Ocean tsunami swept away tens of thousands of people with barely any warning, resulting in a death toll that will never be fully known or appreciated, and leaving millions homeless and bereft of family members (Jordans, 2006). An earthquake along the U.S. west coast could trigger a tsunami just as destructive as the one in 2004, with 15 feet of water surging across a city at 50 miles per hour, carrying with it boats, gasoline, and other debris and hazardous materials (Redlener, 2006).

Astronomers have warned that the solar system is filled with asteroids that, like the one that hit Siberia around the turn of the twentieth century, may plow into the earth at more than seven miles per second, impacting with the force of 100 nuclear bombs and leaving a blast crater 100 miles in diameter. Were such an asteroid to plummet into the Pacific Ocean, it would cause a tsunami up to 55 feet high to flow across the California coast for up to three hours (PBS Nova scienceNOW, 2006). In order to avoid sharing the fate of the hundreds of thousands who died in the Indian Ocean tsunami, governments must prepare coastal dwellers to seek higher ground in the event of a strong earthquake or recession of the sea (Jordans, 2006).

Finally, a variety of authorities have declared that international terrorists may someday have the capability to detonate a nuclear bomb in an American city (Redlener, 2006; Weimann, 2004). In the 1990s, Russian generals and environmental activists reported that dozens or even hundreds of tactical nuclear weapons had gone missing, and could have been transferred to separatist groups or international terrorists (Center for Nonproliferation Studies, 2002). The former head of British intelligence warned in 2005 that a nuclear attack on a major city cannot be "ruled out" (Rozenberg, 2005). Such an event would kill hundreds of thousands of people in a city like New York or Chicago, inflict major injuries on about as many, and render the area's hospitals, communications, and transportation infrastructure useless (Redlener, 2006).

Toward Comprehensive and Forward-Looking National Disaster Policies

Nationalizing Responses to Inherently Interstate and Global Disasters

We should discard the outdated notion that states and localities that struggle to provide even basic services must have the main responsibility for protecting the health and safety of Americans in an emergency. Hurricanes, disease epidemics, and terrorist attacks have inherently interstate and international origins and effects that fall well within the Constitution's grant of federal powers. Comprehensive national disaster planning and relief efforts claim constitutional and legal legitimacy from the federal government's authority to provide for the "common defence" by raising and deploying armies and militia forces, regulating interstate and foreign commerce, and promoting the "general welfare" of the American people (U.S. Constitution, 1787).

Congress and the President should recognize the importance of the military, especially the National Guard, in aiding victims and protecting human rights through the planning and carrying out timely evacuations. They should prepare and execute a national strategy for evacuating those American cities under the most imminent threat of disaster without delay, and without regard to the eccentricities of local officials. Cities and states lack the financial strength, intelligence-gathering capacity, and technological expertise that are required to anticipate and respond to 21st century megadisasters. The confusion and disarray of state and local officials in large American cities is palpable during terrorist alerts, hurricane warnings, pandemic scares, and other catastrophes.

State and local leaders fritter away billions of dollars on entertainment and sports complexes while failing to provide basic transportation and health care in emergencies. New York City spent hundreds of millions on stadiums, and comparatively little on preventing cancer and respiratory diseases at Ground Zero. The State of Louisiana has agreed to pay up to $186.5 million in subsidies on the Superdome by 2011, while leaving New Orleans' levees vulnerable to a Category 4 hurricane (Duncan, 2006; Tanneeru, 2006). When U.S. cities were surveyed in 2006, nearly half said that they had failed to create or update evacuation plans in light of Hurricane Katrina and its aftermath and three-quarters admitted to being unprepared to respond to a bird flu pandemic (Hall, 2006b).

While the Constitution plays an important role in preventing the militarization of American society, it is being misapplied when underfunded states and localities are expected to respond to internationally propagated and technologically complex threats. The Department of Defense should no longer regard internal disasters as FEMA's primary responsibility, or its role in disaster response as a "last resort" (U.S. House of Representatives, Select Bipartisan Committee, 2006, p. 39). Only the federal government has the personnel and equipment to evacuate hundreds or thousands of square kilometers of radioactive territory in the vicinity of a nuclear explosion, transport large numbers of infected patients out of medically overwhelmed areas during a pandemic, or plan and carry out a national strategy for vertical evacuations to high ground or man-made structures from areas threatened with tsunamis (Homeland Security Council, 2006; Speed & May, 2005; Western States Seismic Policy Council, 2005). At the same time, there is no need to repeal the 1878 Posse Comitatus Act or the ban on military cooptation of civilian law enforcement authority that it represents. Civil liberties may be preserved without implementing overly broad bans on a military role in rescuing injured, diseased, or drowning people (Redlener, 2006). The military should confine its role to preparing and executing voluntary evacuations of Americans from disaster-affected areas, instead of the more predictable role of social control to which it sometimes reverts. Proposals such as those of the Homeland Security Council (2006) to use the Department of Defense to assign "military personnel [to] perform[] law enforcement functions" are contrary to the vision of the Framers of the Constitution that the federal "army [should] never be formidable to the liberties of the people" (Hamilton, Jay, & Madison, 1788). A middle ground between full federalization of disaster response including law enforcement, and the present system of relying on local officials to perform many logistical tasks that are way beyond their capabilities, will best preserve American lives and liberties.

A pandemic, earthquake, tsunami, or large-scale terrorist attack would rapidly overwhelm state and local officials in a way that would make the near-collapse of New Orleans' city services after Hurricane Katrina seem like a model of resilience. Millions of Americans may require evacuation from radioactive or flu-stricken communities in a matter of days or even minutes. If thousands of families are left to fend for themselves as during Hurricane Katrina and its immediate aftermath, the result may be wave upon wave of preventable deaths.

Redirecting Disaster Dollars Based on Need

Our nation's planning for major disasters should consciously account for human rights in developing plans and programs to evacuate, compensate, and reintegrate disaster victims. The U.S. military, the Department of Homeland Security, and relevant state agencies should redirect their spending toward those urban areas at greatest risk for megadisasters. Policymakers may limit harmful effects of disasters by prioritizing the post-disaster relief of those least able to help themselves. They should ensure that relief aid does not miss its neediest potential beneficiaries as a result of allocation principally on the basis of prior income or property holdings. Similarly, they should refrain whenever possible from excluding small and minority-owned businesses from reconstruction contracts.

After Hurricane Katrina many evacuees reported having received little or no assistance with housing, employment, or health care from governmental agencies allocated billions of dollars by Congress for the relief effort, most notably FEMA (Dyson, 2006; Redlener, 2006). Nearly ten thousand campers and mobile homes FEMA had acquired for hurricane survivors went unused for close to a year, as 7,500 families in the New Orleans metropolitan area lacked trailers to live in (Lipton, 2006; Strom, 2005; U.S. House of Representatives Minority Leader, 2006). In late 2007, the Government Accountability Office reported that FEMA was wasting tens of millions of dollars, including half of the money on contracts for temporary housing in trailers in Mississippi. The agency had awarded four no-bid contracts, contributing to a situation in which $229,000 was spent per trailer, more than the value of a home (Hsu, 2007). The Department of Homeland Security later validated the complaints of many Katrina evacuees by reporting that FEMA failed to remedy dangerous levels of formaldehyde found in over 50,000 of the 203,000 trailers, mobile homes, and other housing units (Associated Press, 2009).

Katrina survivors also had serious difficulties in rebuilding their finances due to unhelpful bankruptcy and small-business policies. A new bankruptcy law that entered into force about a month and a half after Katrina hit imposed paperwork hurdles (including a requirement to document six months' worth of income and expenses) that denied many storm victims the ability to recover from crushing disaster-related debts (Bosworth, 2005; Mayer, 2005; *The Los Angeles Times*, 2005). A month after Katrina, the Small Business Administration (SBA), with over 3,000 employees, had approved only 76 out of 12,000 applications for emergency assistance by small businesses devastated by the storm (*The New Republic*, 2005). By March 2006, the paperwork for about $6 billion in SBA loans had been approved, but less than a tenth of that amount had actually been loaned out (*The New Republic*, 2006).

FEMA helped award hundreds of millions of dollars in relief and reconstruction contracts to large, wealthy firms such as Carnival Cruise Lines and Fluor Corporation, often on a no-bid basis, so that smaller companies owned by African-Americans, Latina/os and other minorities were locked out of 98.5% of $1.6 billion in FEMA relief and reconstruction contracts (Dyson, 2006; FEMA, 2006; McCoy, 2005; Weisman, 2005; Witte & Hsu, 2006).

The inequalities in aid to New Orleans and the Gulf Coast of Mississippi are glaring. The affected areas of Louisiana had a 50% higher poverty rate than the Mississippi Gulf Coast (Congressional Research Service, 2005), and three times as many homes destroyed as that state, and yet less rebuilding occurred in Louisiana than in Mississippi, where reconstruction proceeded much faster (Copeland, 2006). Mississippi's Republican governor and two Republican Senators had more leverage in Washington than Louisiana, with a Democratic governor and one Democratic Senator (Copeland, 2006). In New Orleans, as a result, the "economy was rebounding less rapidly, a much higher percentage of hospitals and school remain[ed] closed, and disputes over where to put storm debris [was] slowing its removal ..." (Copeland, 2006, n.p.).

Likewise, the September 11 Victim Compensation Fund, under the leadership of Special Master Kenneth Feinberg, failed to award compensation evenhandedly or based on economic need, instead skewing its allocation of funds to families who could prove high incomes prior to the attack. The fund could have awarded $1.6 million to each family to compensate them for the loss of the affection, parenting, and economic potential of their loved ones (Weinbaum & Page, 2002). Instead, it awarded some families as little as $250,000, valuing those person's contributions to family life very parsimoniously, while giving other families several million dollars, based principally on their value in the labor market but with little regard for social mobility (Dixon & Stern, 2004; Weinbaum & Page, 2002). While victims' families had to waive their right to sue airlines or state or local governments for negligence contributing to wrongful death, the typical award for "noneconomic damages [was] substantially lower than those from a sample of aviation wrongful death cases from the mid-1990s ..." (Dixon & Stern, 2004). These inequities were magnified by the fact that undocumented immigrant families of victims were "effectively excluded from the compensation fund" because they were understandably reluctant to provide extensive personal information to an agency overseen by the U.S. Department of Justice, which also conducts deportation proceedings, without some guarantee of confidentiality or non-prosecution (New York State Attorney General, 2002). Meanwhile, hundreds of millions of dollars out of the federal government's more than $20 billion in post-9/11 aid were wasted by state and local officials on "old-fashioned pork-barrel spending" and payoffs to cronies that "had nothing to do with 9/11" (Buettner, 2005). Recent scandals have brought to light how the American Red Cross provided many of the disadvantaged victims of September 11, the Indian Ocean Tsunami, and Hurricane Katrina with insufficient aid to rebuild their lives, despite raising billions of dollars by exploiting media reports of these disasters and enjoying a privileged legal status among American disaster assistance organizations (see U.S. Code, 2000a). For months after 9/11, charities failed to disburse hundreds of millions of dollars donated to help victims and their families, and some even stopped soliciting or even accepting contributions (Katz, 2003). By March of 2002, the Red Cross had only paid out $558 million of $930 million in 9/11 aid that had been donated to it (Levitas et al., 2002). More than 70 percent of funds raised by the Red Cross for tsunami relief remained unspent two years later (Westhead, 2006). Finally, the International Committee for the Red Cross criticized the American Red Cross for "responding too slowly [to Katrina], neglecting some areas and treating minorities with insensitivity" after having "collected more than $2 billion in donations for the disaster" (Salmon, 2006, p. A14). Litigation, like that threatened by the Attorney General of the State of New York over unspent 9/11 aid, seems to be the only remedy when charities like the Red Cross are accused of misleading donors about whom their contributions would help (Katz, 2003).

Removing the Underlying Barriers to Self-Protection

Many Americans would be able to better protect themselves from disasters if legislative reform removed the barriers to their obtaining reasonably priced health care, housing, and property insurance. More than 46.6 million Americans went without health insurance in 2005, including about 8 million children, as premium hikes raced past increases in wages and overall inflation (Urban Institute, 2006; Toner & Stolberg, 2002). Hundreds of billions of dollars, more than 30% of health care spending in the United States, are consumed by inflated administrative costs and excessive paperwork, physician malpractice and medication errors, monopolization, health maintenance organization (HMO) profits and overhead, subsidies for private companies, fraud and overbilling, and out-of-control executive compensation exceeding a billion dollars for some HMO executives (HealthGrades, 2004; Krauskopf, 2006; Physicians for a National Health Program, 2003; Woolhandler & Himmelstein, 2002).

Improving our health care system could save countless lives and vindicate the human right to health both during and between major disasters (Redlener, 2006). In 2003, two former U.S. surgeons-general and more than 7,000 other physicians criticized the U.S. health care system for being "unable to ensure basics like prenatal care and immunizations, [so] we trail most of the developed world on such indicators as infant mortality and life expectancy ..." (Fox,

2003). Due to disparities in access to health insurance, 4,700 more African-American babies than non-Hispanic white babies die before their first birthday, an unnecessary result in the "world's richest health care system" (Fox, 2003). Overall, American babies are two to three times as likely to die in their first year of life compared to those in Scandinavia or Japan, which offer free health services for infants and pregnant women (Green, 2006).

Remedying inequities in access to housing and property insurance would also improve the human rights climate in the United States. Disparities in access to housing left millions of Americans homeless, including up to 1.3 million children, for at least a significant period of time in 2002 (Egan, 2002). Improving the minimum wage could alleviate some of these disparities, as its buying power is at a 51-year low and market rents for one-bedroom apartments range from one and a half to three times as high as the minimum wage (Center for Budget and Policy Priorities, 2006; The National Low Income Housing Coalition, 2004). In the New Orleans area, half of residents that did have access to housing did not appreciate the need for, or could not afford, flood insurance (Drew & Treaster, 2006). Many only found after Hurricane Katrina had destroyed their homes that the reassuring words of the local insurance agent that they would be covered in a hurricane were worthless when it came to the damage inflicted by storm surges that flooded their homes with ocean, lake, or canal waters (Treaster, 2006). Reforming the national flood insurance program to expand coverage and reduce premiums paid by the poor for flood and windstorm insurance would help remedy these failures in the markets for hurricane and other disaster insurance (Melancon, 2006).

Even those New Orleans homeowners or renters with property insurance have struggled to persuade their carriers to pay their Katrina claims, as only about 58% of $25 billion in claims filed had actually been paid by insurers a year after the storm. More than 8,000 Louisiana residents filed complaints with the Louisiana Department of Insurance over companies that paid out far less than the cost of repairing the damage to homes. African-American homeowners, however, have sought state government assistance with their insurance claims only a third as often as non-Hispanic white homeowners. (Callimachi & Bass, 2006).

Providing Better Access to Knowledge in the Service of Human Rights

Finally, public education regarding emergency preparedness and evacuation procedures needs to be transformed into much more detailed instructions, presented in a more compelling way, for immediate evacuation in the event of an emergency with the help of ample federal assistance. Unwillingness to evacuate is rampant, and is likely tied to inadequate warnings and state and local ineffectiveness in facilitating transportation and shelter for evacuees (U.S. House of Representatives, Select Bipartisan Committee, 2006).

Critical warnings issued to and within the U.S. government about the risk of airplanes being crashed into buildings by terrorists or mentally disturbed Americans were never conveyed to the public (Fainaru and Grimaldi, 2001; Pasternak, 2001; Wastell and Jacobson, 2001). *Newsweek* reported:

> [T]he state of alert had been high during the past two weeks, and a particularly urgent warning may have been received the night before the attacks, causing some top Pentagon brass to cancel a trip. Why that same information was not available to the 266 people who died aboard the four hijacked commercial aircraft may become a hot topic on [Capitol] Hill (Hirsh, 2001).

Similarly, the urgent warnings about imminent levee breaches that were circulating in Washington, DC prior to Katrina's landfall seem not to have been shared with New Orleans residents struggling to decide whether to stay home or risk crowded roads or the long lines at the Superdome (Associated Press, 2006a). Perhaps as a result, "thousands of people in New Orleans did not obey the mandatory evacuation order" (U.S. House of Representatives, Select Bipartisan Committee, 2006, p. 312).

To remedy this situation, disaster forecasting and response planning should be open to public examination and modification before the fact, and not simply made available for postmortem analysis. The excessive secrecy that shrouds disaster response shields incompetent officials from effective democratic oversight, and maintains public ignorance. The Freedom of Information Act and its state law counterparts should no longer be interpreted to deny ordinary citizens access to critical facts regarding disaster threats and responses (Citizens for Responsibility and Ethics in Washington, 2006; Smith, 2005). Official inquiries into failures of disaster response should be independent, nonpartisan, and fully empowered to investigate negligence and wrongdoing, regardless of political damage (Associated Press, 2005b; U.S. House of Representatives, Minority Leader, 2006). The federal government should formulate a nationwide public education program to inform all Americans about the dangers they face in a natural disaster, infectious disease epidemic, or armed conflict, and to give them concrete steps to take in the event that disaster strikes (Redlener, 2006).

Conclusion

Protecting the health and human rights of disaster victims is neither easy nor inexpensive, but it is an obligation of governments to achieve using their maximum available resources. This chapter has analyzed several legal reforms that may facilitate compliance with these international legal norms by the United States. Specifically, the federal government should ensure a minimally effective response, across state and local lines, to disasters that implicate Americans' human rights to food, housing, health care, and education. This chapter has identified several legal mechanisms by which these rights may be vindicated before and during a crisis, including:

- consistent and robust federal evacuation policies and procedures, including guarantees that persons finding themselves in buildings or neighborhoods affected by disasters have adequate and timely transportation out of the area;
- reform of federal administrative agencies to speed the delivery of federal resources like FEMA trailers and Small Business Administration loans to disaster-stricken communities;
- improved generation and dissemination of early warnings concerning potential hurricanes, pandemics, tsunamis, and terrorist attacks;
- affordable health insurance and free medical services to reduce the effects of disasters, and of racial and ethnic disparities, on life expectancy and child mortality;
- disaster victims' compensation laws that account for the interpersonal value of lost lives rather than simply foregone earning power or damaged property;
- federal or state enforcement of laws governing the solicitation and disbursement of charitable funds to effectuate donors' intent and meet victims' needs;
- environmental and city planning initiatives that place a priority on human health and shelter rather than landlord discretion and developer largesse;
- rebuilding and reconstruction efforts that are equitable across political constituencies and racial and ethnic groups, and that do not expropriate disaster victims' properties unfairly as in New Orleans; and
- laws guaranteeing wider and more equitable access to information regarding federal and state disaster planning.

References

ACORN v. FEMA. (2006, Nov. 29). Civil Case No. 06cv1521 (RJL), 2006 U.S. Dist. LEXIS 86048 (United States District Court for the District of Columbia).

Arana-Barradas, L.A. (2005, Sept. 8). Air Force rescues top 4000 mark. *Air Force Print News*. Retrieved on October 16, 2006 from http://www.af.mil/news/story.asp?id=123011679.

Associated Press. (2005, Aug. 30). Federal agencies dispatch help. *St. Petersburg Times*. Retrieved October 16, 2006 from http://www.sptimes.com/

2005/08/30/Worldandnation/Federal_agencies_disp.shtml.http://www.sp
times.com/2005/08/30/Worldandnation/Federal_agencies_disp. shtml.

———. (2005, Sept. 7). Senate kills bid for Katrina commission. *USA Today.*
Retrieved on October 16, 2006 from http://www.usatoday.com/news/
washington/2005-09-14-katrina-probe_x.htm.

———. (2006, Mar. 2). Video shows Bush being warned over Katrina.
Guardian Unlimited (United Kingdom). Retrieved on October 16, 2006
from http://www.guardian.co.uk/katrina/story/0,,1721895,00.html.

———. (2006, Sept. 18). U.N. experts Say Africa, east Asia are key risk
zones for bird flu. *WSJ.com.* Retrieved on October 16, 2006 from
http://online.wsj.com/article/SB115847387699965565.html?mod=2_117
7_1.

———. (2006, Oct. 6). FDA approves 5th vaccine for flu season. *USA Today,*
p. 5A.

———. (2006, Oct. 12). Think tank says Orleans gutting deadline may be getting
results. *The Times-Picayune (New Orleans).* Retrieved on October 16, 2006
from http://www.floodinfo.lsu.edu/downloads/oct_news1/10_12_06.pdf.

———. (2009, July 24). Report Criticizes FEMA Response on Trailers. *The*
New York Times, http://www.nytimes.com/2009/07/24/us/24fema.htm.

Baard, E. (2001, Sept. 26–Oct. 2). The dust may never settle: how dangerous
was that dark cloud hanging over Manhattan? *The Village Voice.* Retrieved
on October 16, 2006 from http://www.villagevoice.com/news/0139,baard,
28488,6.html.

Baker, M.L. (2006, May 4). Facing off a flu pandemic with IT. *Ziff Davis Inter-*
net. Retrieved on October 16, 2006 from http://www.eweek.com/article
2/0,1895,1957931,00.asp.

Bankrupting the victims. (2005, Sept. 9). *The Los Angeles Times,* p. B10.

Barry, E. (2006, Oct. 14). Lost in the dust of 9/11. *The Los Angeles Times.* Retrieved on October 16, 2006 from http://www.latimes.com/ news/nation-
world/nation/la-na-cleaners14oct14,0,3275974.story?coll=la-home-head-
lines.

BBC. (2005, Sept. 7). Police told to clear New Orleans. *BBC News.com.* Retrieved on October 16, 2006 from http://news.bbc.co.uk/2/hi/
americas/4221310. stm.

Bernstein, S. (2005, Sept. 17). Southland not ready for disaster. *Los Angeles*
Times. Retrieved on October 16, 2006 from http://democrats.assembly.
ca.gov/members/a48/hurricane/press/h482005021.htm.

Berube, A. & Raphael, S. (2005, Sept. 15). Access to cars in New Orleans. *The*
Brookings Institution. Retrieved on October 16, 2006 from http://www.
brook.edu/metro/20050915_katrinacarstables.pdf.

Bostrom, N. (2002). Analyzing human extinction scenarios and related hazards. *Journal of Evolution and Technology* 9. Retrieved on October 16, 2006 from http://www.jetpress.org/volume9/risks.html.

Buettner, R., Evans, H., Gearty, R., Kates, B., Smith G.B., & Pienciak, R.T. (2005, Dec. 3). 4-year scandal of the 9/11 billions. *Newsday (New York).* Retrieved on October 16, 2006 from http://www.nydailynews.com/front/story/371524p-315959c.html.

Callimachi. R. (2006, Aug. 24). New Orleans revival: A city fights to be reborn. *Associated Press / The Fayetteville (North Carolina) Observer.* Retrieved on October 16, 2006 from http://72.14.209.104/search?q=cache:eXW96i YIk-FkJ:www.fayettevillenc.com/article%3Fid%3D240348+%22will+enroll+students+this+fall%22&hl=en&gl=us&ct=clnk&cd=1.

Callimachi, R. & Bass, F. (2006, Oct. 24). Whites appealed Katrina insurance more. *Associated Press / washingtonpost.com.* Retrieved on November 20, 2006 from http://www.washingtonpost.com/wp-dyn/content/article/2006/10/24/AR2006102400392_pf.html.

Carolan, M. & Keating, R. (2002, Jan. 1). Giuliani stadium deal is corporate welfare. *Newsday (New York).* Retrieved on October 16, 2006 from http://www.commondreams.org/views02/0101-03.htm.

CBS (2009, Aug. 24). Report: H1N1 'Poses Serious Threat' to Nation. *WCBS TV.* Retrieved on August 5, 2009 from http://wcbstv.com/health/h1n1.swine.flu.2.1142469.html.

Center for Budget and Policy Priorities. (2006, June 6). Buying power of minimum wage at 51 year low: Congress could break record for longest period without an increase. Retrieved on October 16, 2006 from http://www.cbpp.org/6-20-06mw.htm.

Center for Nonproliferation Studies. (2002, Sept. 23). "Suitcase Nukes": A reassessment. Retrieved on October 16, 2006 from http://cns.miis.edu/pubs/week/020923.htm.

Chamberlain, G. (2005, Sept. 3). Hungry, thirsty and scared—hurricane victims blame Bush. *The Scotsman (United Kingdom).* Retrieved on October 16, 2006 from http://news.scotsman.com/index.cfm?id=188 4012005.

Chayes, M. (2006, Sept. 7). Ground Zero workers rally to demand reparations for medical care. *The New York Sun.* Retrieved on October 16, 2006 from http://www.nysun.com/article/39270.

Chen, M. (2005, Jan. 24). Ground Zero: The most dangerous workplace. *The New Standard.* Retrieved on October 16, 2006 from http://newstandardnews.net/content/index.cfm/items/1402.

Chong J.-R. & Becerra, H. (2005, Sept. 10). California earthquake could be the next Katrina. *The Los Angeles Times.* Retrieved on October 16, 2006 from   http://www.latimes.com/news/local/la-earthquake08sep08,1,2126 004.story?coll=la-util-news-local.

Choo, K. (2005, Nov.). The Avian Flu time bomb. 91 *ABA Journal*. Retrieved on October 16, 2006 from http://www.cphp.pitt.edu/PDF/THE%20 AVIAN%20FLU%20TIME%20BOMB.pdf.

Citizens for Responsibility and Ethics in Washington. (2006, Jan. 30). CREW sues DHS over continuing Katrina cover-up. Retrieved on October 16, 2006 from http://www.citizensforethics.org/activities/campaign.php?view=95.

CNN. (2005, Oct. 3). Transcripts: Lou Dobbs tonight. Retrieved on October 16, 2006 from http://transcripts.cnn.com/TRANSCRIPTS/0510/03/ldt.01.html.

————. (2005, Dec. 28). New Orleans chief defends fatal shooting. *CNN.com*. Retrieved on October 16, 2006 from http://www.cnn.com/ 2005/US/12/28/nola.shooting/index.html?eref=sitesearch.

————. (2006, Oct. 12). Transcripts: CNN presents: Shoot to kill. Retrieved on October 16, 2006 from http://transcripts.cnn.com/TRANSCRIPTS/ 0610/14/cp.02.html.

Coll, S. (2004). *Ghost wars: The secret history of the CIA, Afghanistan, and bin Laden, from the Soviet invasion to September 11, 2001*. New York, NY: The Penguin Press.

Connor, S. (2005, Jan. 22). Outcry over creation of GM smallpox virus. *The Independent (United Kingdom)*. Retrieved on October 16, 2006 from http://www.findarticles.com/p/articles/mi_qn4158/is_20050122/ai_n 9692912.

Conyers, Jr. (2005, Sept. 08). Statement of introduction of the Hurricane Katrina Bankruptcy Relief and Community Protection Act of 2005. E1803.

Cope, J. (2006, Apr. 4). NAS JRB, NSA receive 'Extraordinary Service' award. *Navy Newsstand*. Retrieved on October 16, 2006 from http://www.news. navy.mil/search/display.asp?story_id=22981.

Copeland, L. (2006, July 25). In Mississippi, Katrina recovery gaining steam. *USA Today*, pp. 1A, 2A.

Crouch, B. (2006, Apr. 9). Bird flu and what you should know. *Sunday Mail (South Australia)*, p. 76.

Davis, M. (2006). *The monster at our door: The global threat of the avian flu*. New York: Owl Books / Henry Holt.

Dayton, M. (2004, Aug. 13). On the recommendations of The 9/11 Commission. Retrieved on October 16, 2006 from http://dayton.senate.gov/news/ details.cfm?id=228409&&.

DeMause, N. (2005, Nov. 14). Bloomberg's gift horse. *Village Voice*. Retrieved on October 16, 2006 from http://www.villagevoice.com/news/ 0546demause,70002,5.html.

Dixon, L. & Stern, R.K. (2004). Compensation for losses from the 9/11 attacks. *Rand Corp.* Retrieved on October 16, 2006 from http://www.rand.org/pubs/monographs/2004/RAND_MG264.sum.pdf.

Drew, C., & Dewan, S. (2006, July 20). Accused doctor was said to face chaos at New Orleans hospital. *The New York Times*, p. A18.

Drew, C., & Treaster, J. (2006, May 15). Politics stalls plan to bolster flood insurance. *The New York Times*. Retrieved on October 16, 2006 from http://www.nytimes.com/2006/05/15/us/15flood.html?ex=1305345600%26en=e2cb7d7a3adb31e6%26ei=5088%26partner=rssnyt%26emc=rss.

Duncan, J. (2006, Sept. 24). Trio keeps low profile despite huge contribution. *The Times-Picayune (New Orleans)*. Retrieved on October 16, 2006 from http://www.nola.com/printer/printer.ssf?/base/sports-25/1159086828317680.xml&coll=1.

Dyson, M.E. (2006). *Come hell or high water: Hurricane Katrina and the color of disaster*. New York: Basic Civitas Books.

Egan, J. (2002, Mar. 24). The hidden lives of homeless children. *The New York Times Magazine*, pp. 32–35.

Eggler, B. (2006, June 27). Lawsuits expected in N.O. gutting law. *The Times-Picayune (New Orleans)*. Retrieved on October 16, 2006 from http://www.nola.com/news/t-p/frontpage/index.ssf?/base/news-6/1151389725142370.xml&coll=1.

———. (2006, Aug. 18). Ease gutting deadline, activists urge. *The Times-Picayune (New Orleans)*. Retrieved on October 16, 2006 from http://www.nola.com/news/t-p/metro/index.ssf?/base/news-16/115588091877510.xml&coll=1.

Elliston, J. (2004, Sept. 22). Disaster in the making. *The Independent (North Carolina)*. Retrieved on October 16, 2006 from http://www.indyweek.com/gyrobase/Content?oid=oid%3A22664.

———. (2005, Sept. 7). The disaster that shouldn't have been. *The Independent (North Carolina)*. Retrieved on October 16, 2006 from http://www.indyweek.com/gyrobase/Content?oid=oid%3A25117.

Fainaru, S. and Grimaldi, J.V. (2001, Sept. 23). FBI knew terrorists were using flight schools. *The Washington Post*. Retrieved on October 16, 2006, from http://www.washingtonpost.com/ac2/wp-dyn?pagename=article&node=&contentId=A10840-2001Sep22.

Francescani, C. (2006, Sept. 8). Firefighters went from 'heroes to zeroes.' *ABC News*. Retrieved on October 16, 2006, at http://abcnews.go.com/ US/story?id=2407850&page=1.

Fox, M. (2003, Aug. 12). Doctors call for universal health insurance. *Reuters*. Retrieved on October 16, 2006, from http://www.defeatdiabetes.org/Articles/insurance030814.htm.

Fox, N. (2009, Sept. 16). Swine Flu Death Rate Similar to Seasonal Flu: Expert. *Reuters/ABC News*. Retrieved on August 5, 2009 from http://abcnews.go. com/Health/WireStory?id=8590433&page=2.

Gabe, T., Falk, G., McCarty, M. & Mason, V.W. (2005, Nov. 4). Hurricane Katrina: Social-demographic characteristics of impacted areas. *Congressional Research Service*. Retrieved on October 16, 2006, from http://www.gnocdc. org/reports/crsrept.pdf.

Garcia, M.J. (2003, June 5). Statement of Nominee for Assistant Secretary, Bureau of Immigration and Customs Enforcement, U.S. Department of Homeland Security, to Committee on Homeland Security and Governmental Affairs. Retrieved on October 16, 2006, from http:// www. senate.gov/~govt-aff/060503garcia.pdf.

Gellman, B. (2002, Mar. 3). Fears prompt U.S. to beef up nuclear terror detection. *The Washington Post*, p. A01.

Giuliani, R. (2002). *Leadership*. New York: Miramax Books / Hyperion.

Glaser, B. (2006, Oct. 16). Fire safety in small spaces. *KPLC-TV*. Retrieved on October 16, 2006, from http://www.kplctv.com/Global/story.asp?S= 5542660&nav=0nqx.

Glendon, M.A. (2001). *A world made new: Eleanor Roosevelt and the Universal Declaration of Human Rights*. New York: Random House.

Gonzalez, J. (2004, Aug. 19). Dust must clear on veil of deceit. *The New York Daily News*. Retrieved on October 16, 2006, at http://www.nydailynews. com/news/story/223498p-192024c.html.

Gordon, G. (2004, July 31). Dayton: FAA, NORAD hid 9/11 failures. *The Minneapolis Star Tribune*. Retrieved on October 16, 2006 from http:// www.freerepublic.com/focus/f-news/1694347/posts.

Hall, M. (2006, July 25). FEMA reduces initial disaster aid after fraud. *USA Today*, p. 3A.

———. (2006, July 26). Cities' disaster plans lacking. *USA Today*, p. 1A.

Hamilton, A., Jay, J., & Madison, J. (1787–88). *The Federalist papers*. Champaign, IL: Project Gutenberg. Retrieved on October 16, 2006, from http://www.gutenberg.org/dirs/etext98/feder10a.txt.

Hart, D. (2006, Aug. 29). Katrina allows Airmen to help in new way. *Moody Air Force Base*. Retrieved on October 16, 2006, from http://www.moody. af.mil/news/story.asp?id=123026124.

Hayden, T. (2006, Aug.). Super storms. *National Geographic* 210(2): 66–77.

HealthGrades. (2004, July). Patient safety in American hospitals. Retrieved on October 16, 2006 from http://www.healthgrades.com/media/english/ pdf/HG_Patient_Safety_Study_Final.pdf.

Henderson, M. (2006, Feb. 21). Deadly viruses mutating to infect humans at rate never seen before. *The Times (United Kingdom)*. Retrieved on October 16, 2006 from http://www.timesonline.co.uk/article/0,,3-2049697,00.html.

Henson, A. (2006, Jan. 13). Senator unhappy about Citizens program. *Key West Citizen*. Retrieved on October 16, 2006, from http://www.fldfs.com/pressoffice/Documents/Senator%20unhappy%20about%20Citizens%20program06.htm.

Hirsh, M. (2001, Sept. 13). We've hit the targets. *Newsweek*. Retrieved on October 16, 2006 from http://www.msnbc.msn.com/id/14738274/site/newsweek.

Homeland Security Council. (2006). *National strategy for pandemic influenza: Implementation plan*. Washington, D.C.: The White House. Retrieved on October 14, 2006 from http://www.whitehouse.gov/home land/nspi.pdf.

Hsu, Spencer S. (2007, Nov. 16). FEMA Accused of Wasting More Katrina Funding; $30 Million Misspent Last Year On Trailers in Miss., GAO Says. *The Washington Post*, Retrieved on August 5, 2009 from http://www.washingtonpost.com/wp-dyn/content/article/2007/11/15/AR2007111502311.html.

Hunt, P. (2006, Mar. 3). Report of the Special Rapporteur on the right of everyone to the enjoyment of the highest attainable standards of physical and mental health. E/CN.4/2006/48. Retrieved on October 16, 2006 from http://daccessdds.un.org/doc/UNDOC/GEN/G06/114/69/PDF/G0611469.pdf?OpenElement.

IEM, Inc. (2004, June 3). IEM Team to develop catastrophic hurricane disaster plan for New Orleans & Southeast Louisiana. Retrieved on October 16, 2006 from http://web.archive.org/web/20041126062052/http://www.ieminc.com/Whats_New/Press_Releases/pressrelease060304_Catastrophic.htm.

In re World Trade Ctr. Disaster Site Litig. (2006, Oct. 17). Case No. 21 MC 100 (AKH), 03 Civ. 00007 et al. (AKH) (United States District Court for the Southern District of New York). International Commission of Jurists. (2003, June 1). Responses to States' concerns with regard to the International Covenant on Economic Social and Cultural Rights and the proposed Optional Protocol. Retrieved on October 16, 2006 from http://www.icj.org/news.php3?id_article=2753&lang=en.

Jervey, T. D. (1917). *The Great War: The causes and the waging of it*. Columbia, S.C.: The State Company, Printers. Retrieved on October 16, 2006 from http://books.google.com/books?vid=OCLC06050034&id=G5TIlvKXo84C&printsec=titlepage.

Johnson, N. (2005, Apr. 3). Many in area ignored hurricane evacuation—Study jolts emergency officials. *Tampa Tribune*, p. 1.

Jordans, F. (2006, Sept. 8). Tsunami could hit the Med-scientist. *Independent Online (South Africa)*. Retrieved on October 16, 2006, from http://www.int.iol.co.za/index.php?set_id=14&click_id=143&art_id=qw1157680083799B245.

Joyner, C. (2006, Oct. 15). 92,000 still live in campers. *Jackson Clarion Ledger*. Retrieved on October 16, 2006 from http://www.clarionledger.com/apps/pbcs.dll/article?AID=/20061015/NEWS/610150388/1001/news.

Julavits, R. (2003, Aug. 27–Sept. 2). Point of collapse. *Village Voice*. Retrieved on October 16, 2006 from http://villagevoice.com/news/0335,julavits,46559,1.html.

Katz, R.A. (2003). A pig in a python: How the charitable response to September 11 overwhelmed the law of disaster relief. *Indiana Law Review*, 36: 251–316.

Keller, L.M. (2001, July). The indivisibility of economic and political rights. *Human Rights & Human Welfare* 1: 9. Retrieved on October 16, 2006, from http://www.du.edu/gsis/hrhw/volumes/2001/1-3/Keller-Sen.pdf.

Krauskopf, L. (2006, Oct 15). UnitedHealth CEO to leave amid options probe. *Reuters*. Retrieved on October 16, 2006, from http://money.cnn.com/2006/10/16/news/united_health.reut/index.htm.

Levitas, M., Lee, N., & Schlein, L., Eds. (2002). *A nation challenged: A visual history of 9/11 and its aftermath*. The New York Times / Callaway.

Lies, E. (2005, Jan. 18). Disaster looms for megacities, UN official says. *Reuters*. Retrieved on October 16, 2006, from http://www.enn.com/today.html?id=6955.

Lipton, E. (2006, June 27). 'Breathtaking' waste and fraud in hurricane aid. *The New York Times*. Retrieved on October 16, 2006 from http://www.nytimes.com/2006/06/27/washington/27katrina.html?ex=1309060800&en=1683e5fa71ecfb90&ei=5090&am.

Lipton, E., Drew, C., Shane, S., & Rohde, D. (2005, Sept. 12). The path from storm to anarchy. *The New York Times*. Retrieved on October 16, 2006, from http://www.iht.com/articles/2005/09/11/news/response.php.

MacKenzie, D. (2009, Apr. 26). Deadly New Flu Virus in US and Mexico May Go Pandemic. *New Scientist,*. Retrieved on Aug. 5, 2009 from http://www.newscientist.com/article/dn17025-deadly-new-flu-virus-in-us-and-mexico-may-go-pandemic.html.

Mayer, C. (2005, Sept. 7). Looming bankruptcy law may hurt victims of hurricane. *The Washington Post*, p. D06.

Mayer III, E. (2002, June 23). Last line of defense: Hoping the levees hold. *The Times-Picayune (New Orleans)*. Retrieved on October 16, 2006, from http://www.nola.com/hurricane/popup/nolalevees_jpg.html.

McCoy, K. (2005, Sept. 14). Contracts for recovery work raise controversy. *USA Today*. Retrieved on October 16, 2006, from http://www.usatoday.com/money/companies/2005-09-14-katrina-contracts_x.htm.

McKay, B. (2005, Oct. 6). Avian virus caused the 1918 pandemic, new studies show. *The Wall Street Journal*. Retrieved on October 16, 2006, from http://online.wsj.com/article/SB112850011860760437.html?mod=2_1177_1.

McQuaid, J. & Schleifstein, M. (2002, June 24). Washing away: The Big One. *The Times-Picayune (New Orleans)*. Retrieved on October 16, 2006 from http://www.nola.com/hurricane/?/washingaway/part2.html; http://www.nola.com/hurricane/index.ssf?/washingaway/threat_1.html; http://www.nola.com/hurricane/?/washingaway/part5.html.

McQuaid, J. (2005, Sept. 13). Mystery surrounds floodwall breaches: Could a structural flaw be to blame? *The Times-Picayune (New Orleans)*. Retrieved on October 16, 2006 from http://www.nola.com/newslogs/tporleans/index.ssf?/mtlogs/nola_tporleans/archives/2005_09_13.html#079207.

Melancon, C. (2006, June 27). Melancon supports Flood Insurance Solvency and Accountability Bill. Retrieved on October 16, 2006, from http://www.melancon.house.gov/news.asp?ARTICLE3337=5414.

Meyer, J. (2003, Aug. 2). Report links Saudi government to 9/11 hijackers, sources say. *Los Angeles Times*.

Morello-Frosch1, R., & Jesdale, B. (2006, Mar.). Separate and unequal: Residential segregation and estimated cancer risks associated with ambient air toxics in U.S. metropolitan areas. *Environmental Health Perspectives*, 114(3): 386–393.

Office of the New York State Attorney General. (2002, Jan. 23). Gov, AG object to 9/11 compensation fund rules. Retrieved on October 16, 2006, from http://www.oag.state.ny.us/press/2002/jan/jan23c_02.html.

Oberg, A. (2006, July 25). The real first responder in a storm? You. *USA Today*, p. 13A.

Parks, C. (2006, Oct. 12). Your health matters. *Union Sentinel (Georgia)*. Retrieved on October 16, 2006, from http://www.unionsentinel.com/news/2006/1012/Arts_Leisure/033.html.

Pasternak, J. (2001, Oct. 6). FAA, airlines stalled major security plans. *Los Angeles Times*.

PBS NOVA scienceNOW. (2006, Oct. 3). Transcript. *PBS.org*. Retrieved on October 16, 2006 from http://www.pbs.org/wgbh/nova/transcripts/3313_sciencen.html; http://www.pbs.org/wgbh/nova/sciencenow/video/3313/w01-220.html.

Piposzar, J.D. (2005). Preparing for an influenza pandemic: Lessons from the "Spanish Flu" of 1918. *University of Pittsburgh, Graduate School of Public*

Health, Center for Public Health Preparedness. Retrieved on October 16, 2006 from http://www.cphp.pitt.edu/upcphp/ppt/PandemicFlu1918.pps.

Preston, R. (1999, July 12). The demon in the freezer. *The New Yorker*, pp. 44–61.

Physicians for a National Health Program. (2003, Aug. 20). Administrative costs in market-driven U.S. health care system far higher than in Canada's single-payer system, new research shows. Retrieved on October 16, 2006 from http://www.pnhp.org/news/2003/august/ administrative_costs.php.

Rao, S.L.N. (1973). On long-term mortality trends in the United States, 1850–1968. *Demography*, 10(3): 408–10.

Rashid, A. (2001, Sept. 23). How a holy war against the Soviets turned on U.S. *The Pittsburgh Post-Gazette.*

Redlener, I. (2006). *Americans at risk: Why we are not prepared for Megadisasters and what we can do now.* New York: Knopf.

Richens, J. (2006, May–July). Sexually transmitted infections and HIV among travellers: a review. *Travel Med Infect Diseases*, 4(3–4), 184–95.

Ross, J. (2006, Oct. 21). No gutting, no glory *The Times-Picayune (New Orleans).* Retrieved on October 16, 2006, from http://www.nola.com/ search/index.ssf?/base/living-1/1161409830142190. xml?LHGIO&coll=1.

Rozenberg, J. (2005, Nov. 3). UK 'cannot rule out nuclear attack by terrorists.' *The Daily Telegraph (United Kingdom).* Retrieved on October 16, 2006, from http://www.telegraph.co.uk.

Salmon, J.L. (2005, Dec. 5). Red Cross bolstering minority outreach: recruitment a priority after storms expose sensitivity gaps. *The Washington Post*, p. A01.

———. (2006, Apr. 5). Counterparts excoriate Red Cross Katrina effort. *The Washington Post*, p. A14.

Saulny, S. (2006, June 13). U.S. gives charter schools a big push in New Orleans. *The New York Times*, p. A19.

Schmid, R. (2005, March 1). Disaster worries grow as more Americans live near coasts. *Associated Press.* Retrieved on October 16, 2006, from http://www.livescience.com/forcesofnature/ap_050301_coastal_pop.html.

———. (2006, Sept. 26). White House said to bar hurricane report. *ABC News.* Retrieved on October 16, 2006 from http://abcnews.go.com/ Technology/wireStory?id=2494368.

Shenon, P. (2001, Dec. 22). FBI ignored attack warning: Flight instructor told agency of terror suspect's plan. *San Francisco Chronicle.*

Sierra Club. (2004, Sept. 1). Final Day of Sierra Club Ground Zero Community Vigil During Republican Convention Focuses on Children. Retrieved on October 16, 2006, from http://www.commondreams.org/news2004/0901-14.htm.

Smith, J. (2005, May 11). Cox Newspapers Prez Smith discusses need for FOIA reform. *Sunshine Week.* Retrieved on October 16, 2006 from http://www.sunshineweek.org/sunshineweek/smithtestimony.

Specter, M. (2004, Oct. 11). The devastation. *The New Yorker*, p. 58.

Speed, R. & May, M. (2005, Mar./Apr.). Dangerous doctrine. *Bulletin of the Atomic Scientists*, 61(2), 38–49. Retrieved on October 16, 2006 from http://www.thebulletin.org/article.php?art_ofn=ma05speed.

St. Onge, J., & Epstein, V. (2006, April 1). Ex-chief says FEMA readiness even worse. *Boston Globe.* Retrieved on October 16, 2006,from http://www.boston.com/news/nation/washington/articles/2006/04/01/ex_chief_says_fema_readiness_even_worse.

Stevenson, R.W. (2005, Sept. 1). Hurricane Katrina: Federal response. *The New York Times*, p. A21. Retrieved on October 16, 2006 from http://query.nytimes.com/gst/fullpage.html?res=9C0CEFDB1731F932A3575AC0A9639C8B63&sec=travel&pagewanted=print.

Strom, J. (2005, Oct. 19). Going south. *The Independent (North Carolina).* Retrieved on October 16, 2006 from http://www.indyweek.com/gyrobase/Content?oid=oid%3A25398.

Syal, R. (2009, Sept. 20). Swine Flu 'Could Kill Millions unless Rich Nations Give £900m'. *The Observer.* Retrieved on September 23, 2009 from http://www.guardian.co.uk/world/2009/sep/20/swine-flu-costs-un-report.

Tanneeru, M. (2006, May 22). Is New Orleans ready for another Katrina? *CNN.com.* Retrieved on October 16, 2006 at http://www.cnn.com/2006/US/05/22/louisiana.preps.

The City of New York, Independent Budget Office. (2006, Apr. 10). Financing plans for the New Yankee Stadium. Retrieved on October 16, 2006 from http://www.ibo.nyc.ny.us/iboreports/yankstadiumtestimony.pdf.

The City of New York, Independent Budget Office. (2006, Apr. 21). Financing plan for the proposed stadium for the Mets. Retrieved on October 16, 2006 from http://www.ibo.nyc.ny.us/iboreports/Metsanalysis.pdf.

Toner, R. & Stolberg, S.G. (2002, Aug. 11). Decade after health care crisis, soaring costs bring new strains. *New York Times*, p. A1.

Treaster, J. (2006, Aug. 16). Judge rules for insurers in Katrina. *The New York Times.* Retrieved on October 16, 2006 from http://www.nytimes.com/2006/08/16/business/16insure.html?ex=1313380800&en=ee5920c47ca6894c&ei=5088&partner=rssnyt&emc=rss.

The National Commission on Terrorists Attacks Upon the United States. (2004). *The 9/11 Commission Report: Final report of the National Commission on Terrorist Attacks Upon the United States*. New York: W.W. Norton.

The National Commission on Terrorists Attacks Upon the United States, Staff. (2004, Jan. 27). *Staff Statement No. 3: The Aviation security system and the 9/11 attacks*. Retrieved on October 16, 2006 from http://www.9-11commission.gov/staff_statements/staff_statement_3.pdf.

The National Low Income Housing Coalition, (2004). Out of reach 2004. Retrieved on October 16, 2006, from http://www.nlihc.org/oor2004/data.php?state%5B%5D=_all.

The New Republic. (2005, Oct. 17). Welcome to the hackocracy. *The New Republic*, p. 21.

———. (2006, Oct. 30). Where are they now? Hacks 2006. *The New Republic*. Retrieved on October 16, 2006 from http://www.tnr.com/user/nregi.mhtml?i=20061030&s=hacks103006.

Toppo, G.(2008, Aug. 27). Superintendent of New Orleans Watched by Other City Schools. *USA Today*, http://www.usatoday.com/news/education/2008-08-26-new-orleans-superintendent_N.htm.

Trafford, A. (2005, Nov. 8). It's deja flu all over again. *The Washington Post*, p. HE01. Retrieved on October 16, 2006 from http://www.washingtonpost.com/wp-dyn/content/article/2005/11/04/AR2005110402194.html.

Trust for America's Health (2007, Mar. 22). Severe Pandemic Flu Outbreak Could Lead to Major Recession in Vermont, According to New Report. Retrieved on September 23, 2009,from http:// www.healthyamericans.org/reports/flurecession/releases/VT.pdf.

United Nations General Assembly. (1948). General Assembly Resolution 217A. U.N. GAOR 1, p. 71. U.N. Doc. A/810 (1948).

Urban, P. (2005, Sept. 11). "It was just something pretty surreal." *The Connecticut Post*. Retrieved on October 16, 2006, from http://msnbc.msn.com/id/9311507.

Urban Institute. (2006). Health insurance trends. Retrieved on October 16, 2006, from http://www.urban.org/toolkit/issues/healthinsurance.cfm.

U.S. Code, Title 6, Chapter, 1. Department of Homeland Security. (2004). Retrieved on October 16, 2006 from http://web.archive.org/web/20041113172631/www.law.cornell.edu/uscode/html/uscode06/usc_sec_06_00000111——000-.html.

U.S. Code. Title 36, Subtitle III, Chapter 3001. American National Red Cross. (2000). Retrieved on October 16, 2006 from fttp://frwebgate.access.gpo.gov/cgi-bin/getdoc.cgi?dbname=browse_usc&docid=Cite:+36USC300101.

U.S. Code. Title 49. Federal Aviation Administration. (2000). Retrieved on October 16, 2006 from http://frwebgate4.access.gpo.gov/cgi-bin/waisgate.cgi?WAISdocID=8608242806+3+0+0&WAISaction=retrieve.

U.S. Constitution. (1787). Retrieved on October 16, 2006 from http://memory.loc.gov/service/rbc/bdsdcc/c0801/0001.jpg and http://memory.loc.gov/service/rbc/bdsdcc/c0801/0002.jpg.

U.S. Department of Health & Human Services. (2006). The Great Pandemic of 1918: State by state. Washington, D.C. Retrieved on October 14, 2006 from http://www.pandemicflu.gov/general/greatpandemic.html.

U.S. Department of Homeland Security. (2004). National Response Plan. Washington, D.C. Retrieved on October 14, 2006 from http://www.dhs.gov/interweb/assetlibrary/NRP_FullText.pdf.

———. (2005). Emergencies and disasters. Washington, D.C. Retrieved on October 14, 2006 from http://web.archive.org/web/20050204043722/http://www.dhs.gov/dhspublic/theme_home2.jsp.

U.S. Department of Housing and Urban Development. (2006, Sept. 6). HUD Katrina accomplishments—One year later. Retrieved on October 16, 2006 from http://www.hud.gov/news/katrina05response.cfm.

U.S. Federal Emergency Management Agency. (2006, Feb. 24). Cruise ships leaving New Orleans March 1. Retrieved on October 14, 2006 from http://www.fema.gov/news/newsrelease.fema?id=23839.

U.S. General Accounting Office. (2004, Apr. 29). Reserve forces: Observations on recent National Guard use in overseas and homeland missions and future challenges. Retrieved on October 14, 2006 from http://www.gao.gov/new.items/d04670t.pdf.

U.S. House of Representatives, House Committee on Interstate and Foreign Commerce. (1968, Mar. 26). Aviation safety: Hearings before the Subcommittee on Aviation. Retrieved on October 16, 2006 from http://books.google.com/books?vid=0UlefSA40Gp2yWe2pG2bss-&id=vfVocvph8RUC&q=%22aviation+safety%22+%22cockpit+doors%22&dq=%22aviation+safety%22+%22cockpit+doors%22&pgis=1.

U.S. House of Representatives, House Committee on Science, Democratic Staff. (2005, Oct. 20). Failing to protect and defend: the Federal emergency response to Hurricane Katrina. Retrieved on October 14, 2006 from http://democrats.science.house.gov/Media/File/Reports/katrina_response_26sep05.pdf.

U.S. House of Representatives, Minority Leader. (2006, Aug. 23). Broken promises: The Republican response to Katrina. Retrieved on October 16, 2006 from http://www.democraticleader.house.gov/pdf/Katrina1Year.pdf.

U.S. House of Representatives, Select Bipartisan Committee to Investigate the Preparation for and Response to Hurricane Katrina. (2006 Feb. 15). *A*

Failure of initiative: The final report of the Select Bipartisan Committee to investigate the preparation for and response to Hurricane Katrina. Washington, D.C. Retrieved on October 14, 2006 from http://katrina.house.gov/full_katrina_report.htm.

U.S. North American Aerospace Defense Command & U.S. Northern Command. (2001, Sept. 18). NORAD'S response times, Sept. 11, 2001. Retrieved on October 14, 2006 from http://www.google.com/search?q =cache:WGWDXavXqtcJ:www.norad.mil/index.cfm%3Ffuseaction%3Dh ome.news_rel_09_18_01.

U.S. Senate, Select Committee on Intelligence (2004). *Joint inquiry into intelligence community activities before and after the terrorist attacks of September 11, 2001*. Washington, D.C. Retrieved on October 14, 2006 from http://a257.g.akamaitech.net/7/257/2422/24jul20031400/www.gpoaccess.gov/serial set/creports/pdf/fullreport_errata.pdf.

U.S. v. Lopez. (1995). *U.S. Reports* 514, p. 549. Retrieved on October 14, 2006 from http://www.law.cornell.edu/supct/html/93-1260.ZO.html.

Warrick, J. & Grunwald, M. (2005, Oct. 24). Investigators link levee failures to design flaws. *The Washington Post*, p. A01.

Weimann, G. (2004, June 14). *The sum of all fears?* Washington, D.C.: United States Institute of Peace.

Weisman, J. (2005, Sept. 28). $236 million cruise ship deal criticized. *The Washington Post*, p. A01. Retrieved on October 14, 2006 from http://www.washingtonpost.com/wp-dyn/content/article/2005/09/27/AR200509270 1960_pf.html.

Western States Seismic Policy Council. (2005, Sept. 14). WSSPC policy recommendation 05-1: Improving tsunami warning, preparedness, and mitigation procedures for distant and local sources. Retrieved on October 14, 2006 from http://www.wsspc.org/PublicPolicy/PolicyRecs/2005/policy 051.html.

Westfeldt, A. (2006, Sept. 5). Lung problems rife among WTC responders. *Associated Press*. Retrieved on October 14, 2006 from http://www.breitbart.com/news/2006/09/05/D8JUP5V00.html.

Westhead, R. (2006, Dec. 26). Tsunami millions unspent. *The Toronto Star*. Retrieved on October 14, 2006, from http://www.tamilcanadian.com/page.php?cat=488&id=4688.

Whoriskey, P. (2006, June 7). Katrina displaced 400,000, study says: New Orleans becomes whiter, Mississippi coast more diverse. *The Washington Post*, p. A12.

Whoriskey, P. (2006, Aug. 27). Silence after the storm: life has yet to return to much of a city haunted by Katrina. *The Washington Post*, p. A01.

Williams, D. R., & Collins, C. (2001). Racial residential segregation: a fundamental cause of racial disparities in health. *Public Health Reporter*, 116: 404–416.

Wilson, W. J. (1996). *When work disappears: The world of the new urban poor.* New York: Alfred A. Knopf.

Witte, G. & Hsu, S.S. (2006, Aug. 10). Big Katrina contractors win more FEMA work. *The Washington Post,* p. D01. Retrieved on October 14, 2006 from http://www.washingtonpost.com/wp-dyn/content/article/2006/08/09/AR2006080901931.html.

Woolhandler, S. & Himmelstein, D.U. (2002, Jul.–Aug.). Paying for national health insurance—and not getting it. *Health Affairs* 21(4): 88–98. Retrieved on October 14, 2006 from http://content.healthaffairs.org/cgi/reprint/21/4/88.

Chapter 18

Hurricane Katrina and the Nation's Obligation to Black Colleges

Marybeth Gasman and Noah D. Drezner

"The shock and hurt on campus were deafening. It was as though everyone had lost a close member of the family."

— Norman Francis, President, Xavier University

In spite of all its furious destruction, Hurricane Katrina may be remembered more for tearing down the myth of American racial equality than for tearing down homes and businesses. For too long, Americans, mostly of the racial majority, believed that Martin Luther King, Jr.'s dream had been realized. Yet, Hurricane Katrina demonstrated the fact that there is a long road ahead of us to achieve the civil rights leader's dream that "one day this Nation will rise up and live out the true meaning of its creed: 'We hold these truths to be self-evident: that all men are created equal'" (King Jr., 1963). And, while there has already been debate over how to rebuild the physical structures lost to the storm, there has been little mainstream discussion about how to bridge that racial rift. One of the most effective and least costly ways to rectify racial injustices is to support our nation's black colleges financially. Giving to black colleges now will help repair not only the physical damage done by the hurricane but also the historical damage inflicted over the past century.

The purpose of this chapter is to examine the black colleges ravaged by Hurricane Katrina, exploring their contributions to both black higher education and American society. In addition, we discuss the past discrimination that led to the current situation for New Orleans' black colleges. Lastly, we examine the giving to black colleges that has come from the black community, the Foundation community and the giving that could potentially come from American citizens overall.

Background on New Orleans' Black Colleges

There are three black colleges in New Orleans: Xavier University of Louisiana, Dillard University, and Southern University of New Orleans. Xavier University, established in 1915, is the nation's only historically black and Catholic institution. Using money from her inheritance, Katherine Drexel (along with the Sisters of the Blessed Sacrament) founded the institution, as a teachers college. Specifically, Sister Katherine wanted to educate black and Native American students. The college is also set apart from other institutions by its leadership. Xavier's president Norman C. Francis has been at the helm for over three decades, far longer than the average college presidency, lending stability to the small university. In addition to tripling the endowment to $54 million (still meager in comparison to its predominantly white counterparts, but larger than that of most black colleges), Francis has shaped the institution into a place that nurtures students in the sciences. According to the American Medical Association, Xavier University is responsible for placing more blacks in medical school than any other institution in America. And, even more importantly, 92 percent of these students complete medical school and pass board exams. With an enrollment of only 4,000, the university awards more undergraduate degrees in biology and the life sciences to blacks than any other college or university. Moreover, since 1927, Xavier has graduated over 25 percent of the 6,500 black pharmacists in the United States, many of whom are committed to working in low-income neighborhoods. Xavier's work is even more impressive when considering that other institutions might not consider its incoming students desirable. The institution's 1991 incoming cohort had a meager average score of 464 on the quantitative portion of the Scholastic Assessment Test (SAT) (Mitchell, 1993). However, Xavier empowers and educates its students far beyond what their original standardized test scores suggest. In the words of Xavier's president, the institution is "a model for destroying the myth that young people and minorities can't succeed in science" (Mangan, 2006b, p. A48).

Dillard University was formed by the merger of Straight College and New Orleans College in 1930. Straight and New Orleans Colleges were founded in 1869 by the American Missionary Association and the Freedmen's Aid Society of the Methodist Episcopal Church to provide teacher training in elementary education. Eventually, Dillard University grew to include an emphasis on instruction in secondary and collegiate education as well. Prior to Hurricane Katrina, the Dillard campus was lush, with two rows of ancient trees lining the "Avenue of the Oaks" and leading to the heart of the campus. Students took immense pride in the appearance of their university. According to Dillard graduate and Brown University president Ruth Simmons, the university "has for so long been the route many of us have taken to middle class that for students from disadvantaged backgrounds, the beauty of the site is a way of orienting them toward making a life for themselves that would include the beauty" (Hoover, 2005, p. 21). Currently, the institution provides a large percentage of New Orleans' nurses, focusing on both the professions and the liberal arts. Moreover, Dillard, ranked among the top 25 Southern comprehensive colleges by *U.S. News and World Report*. Compared to its historically black contemporaries, Dillard too has a strong endowment of $47.6 million.

Southern University, a publicly funded institution, originally established as an extension of Southern University and Agricultural and Mechanical College in 1956, is now an open admission institution, serving low-income students determined to move themselves out of poverty. The first graduating class received bachelor's degrees in 1963 under the university's new name, Southern University of New Orleans. If not for the university, many of these students would not be able to afford to attend college. Prior to the hurricane, the institution enrolled 3,600 students, most of them over 25. Southern has a profound commitment to community service and places its graduates in social service positions throughout the U.S. and abroad. The institution is ranked 45th in its production of all black baccalaureate degrees overall, 11th in its production of science baccalaureates, and 15th in its production of math baccalaureates out of all four-year institutions in the United States (2,466).

Starting from Disadvantage

Although founded and funded on an unequal basis, black colleges have shown remarkable resilience, continuing to enroll a substantial share of blacks who receive a college education. In most cities across the country, black colleges were sited on undesirable land—a situation amply demonstrated in New Orleans, where Xavier, Dillard, and Southern universities were built on the lowest ground, thereby suffering the greatest damage when the levees broke. Dillard is under a mile from the London Avenue Canal that breached in four places, flooding the campus with 8 feet of water destroying the institution's prided "Avenue of the Oaks" and causing $400 million of damage. Southern University sits just south of Lake Pontchartrain and west of the Inner Harbor Navigation Canal that connects the lake to the Mississippi River. There were five breaches along the Canal, causing $350 million of damage to the public institution. And, Xavier, although a fair distance from the lake, is in the downtown business district near the Washington Avenue Canal. Most of the time, the Canal contains barely any water but during the aftermath of Hurricane Katrina, the Canal became a lake, flooding the campus and causing $100 million in damage. On the other hand, Tulane University and Loyola University of New Orleans are located in New Orleans' well manicured Garden District on much higher ground.

According to Michael Eric Dyson (2006), the "concentrated poverty [in New Orleans] is the product of decades of public policies and political measures that isolate black households in neighborhoods plagued by severe segregation and economic hardship" (p. 7). This type of systematic inequity has been in existence since the founding of the United States. The Constitution, in Article I, Section 2, from its ratification in 1789 to the adoption of the 13th Amendment adoption in 1865, counted blacks as 3/5 (0.6) of a white person for purposes of representation and taxation. According to the National Urban League's 2006 Equality Index, blacks are still far from being on an equal playing field with whites in the United States. Using current data the Equality Index compares conditions between blacks and whites on health, education, economics, social justice, and civic engagement indices. The study found that in 2006 the black index value is 0.73, where white Americans are the control and therefore are valued at an index of 1.0 (Thompson & Parker, 2006).

Like black individuals and families, black colleges, over the course of their existence, have had fewer resources than their historically white counterparts. For example, many white philanthropists and state governments historically have given less to black education, believing black colleges cost less to maintain than their white counterparts. Due to discriminatory employment practices, black alumni had little access to wealth and therefore, less disposable income to contribute to their *alma mater*. As a result, black colleges have smaller endowments and less access to discretionary funds. In the words of Xavier president Norman C. Francis, "We don't have large endowments like our counterparts in the major institutions. The income that some of the other institutions get from their endowments is twice as much as our endowments themselves. And so we can't use endowment money to the extent that they can" (Gordon, 2005, p. 3). Despite these circumstances, black colleges, especially those in New Orleans, have educated a distinguished slate of elected leaders, doctors, lawyers, judges, teachers, and college professors.

Damage Done

Not only were the three historically black colleges hit the hardest in terms of physical damages, but fewer of their students returned when classes reopened, in January 2006, after a semester hiatus. Tulane, a predominantly white university announced that 88 percent of its students returned compared to 75 percent at Xavier. In fact, just recently, Tulane was cited as making the fastest recovery of any college hurt by Hurricane Katrina. Dillard and Southern were able to retain 50 percent and 44 percent of their students respectively. In addition, for Dillard the problem was exacerbated by the fact that the institution was unable to open its campus, instead the institution taught from a hotel.

In addition, none of the black colleges have endowments that come anywhere near Tulane's $850 million. Moreover, Xavier University faces a public perception that because it is a Catholic college, it receives support from the

Church. Its president is crisscrossing the country, trying to dispel this myth (Goodman, 2005). In order to make ends meet, all three institutions had to terminate employees, even tenured faculty members, a fact that received far less press than the proposed termination of Tulane faculty.

In the post-Katrina period, Southern has adopted an on-line format for most of its classes as most of its campus was destroyed. Traditional classes are being held in 400 trailers, located north of the main campus. Southern University's eleven academic buildings have yet to be gutted and decontaminated; these are on a list of over a 1000 public buildings in need of work. In all likelihood, these structures will not be repaired soon, making the institution the only college in New Orleans that will not be operating on its own campus in the fall of 2006. Faced with vast damage and a meager endowment of only $2 million, the institution had no choice but to scale down its services. However, some members of Southern University's administration feel that the state board of overseers' decision to cut 19 academic fields after Katrina, including math, English, and physics, went too far. According to Joe Omojola, the former dean of the College of Science, "It is wrong to use the devastation of Hurricane Katrina as a cover to attack an institution at its most vulnerable state" (Mangan, 2006c, p. A31). Omojola is referring to the state's efforts, prior to Katrina, to close Southern in the past due to low graduation rates. The university's transient commuter student population translates into less than desirable graduation rates and these graduation rates lead to questions of accountability.[1] Regardless, Southern University is still offering low-income students a chance for education and producing informed citizens who strengthen the city of New Orleans and beyond.

Given the contributions of these three institutions, it is not sound to abandon them during this time of need. If these black colleges are to survive, they need deeper pockets. In January 2006, President Bush announced a $200 million relief package for institutions of higher education affected by Hurricane Katrina in Louisiana and Mississippi. After a $10 million allocation to the Department of Education to support colleges throughout the country that accepted displaced students, the remaining $190 million was split evenly between the two states, regardless of the fact that Louisiana sustained greater damage and had more institutions affected by the storm (Brainard, Burd, Field, & Selingo, 2006). The federal government allowed each state to distribute its share of the higher education allocation. Of the $95 million distributed to Louisiana, $75 million will be distributed to both public and private institutions based on full-time enrollment, lost tuition revenue, and the size of their

---

1. Many of the Southern University students stop in and stop out of the institution, taking classes for professional development or taking a leave until they have additional funds to pay for college.

financial aid budgets. Additionally, $8.5 million is set aside for incentives to encourage students to return to Louisiana institutions (Mangan, 2006a). In the decision on how to allocate the funds, physical damage incurred by the institution was not considered (Mangan, 2006a).

This distribution, while important to New Orleans's black colleges, is not enough to meet the recovery costs. Black colleges, particularly Xavier and Dillard, are hard pressed to find the money needed to rebuild. In the year 2000, Congress, through the Disaster Mitigation Act, excluded private colleges from FEMA's flood aid program. That decision has left Xavier and Dillard (both private universities), who with tight operational budgets were not able to full insure their campuses, with little to no support for rebuilding infrastructure after Katrina. Other private colleges, such as Tulane, with larger operational budgets and endowments are not affected as much by the Disaster Mitigation Act since they had the resources available to properly insure their campuses.

Are Blacks Helping Their Own?

Some Americans may wonder whether blacks are themselves helping black colleges. The answer is a resounding yes! Although conventional wisdom says that blacks don't give, statistics show that they do and often more generously than whites to the church, education, and health-related programs (Gasman, 2006). According to a recent survey conducted by *The Chronicle of Philanthropy*, blacks give 25 percent more of their discretionary income to charity than does the general population. In the case of Hurricane Katrina relief, according to a poll by the Pew Research Center for the People and the Press (2006), blacks are twice as likely as their white counterparts to be related to or know someone directly affected by Hurricane Katrina. As a result, black giving of time and money has been taking place at an unprecedented rate. Blacks have been opening their homes, donating clothes and food, baby supplies, books to restock libraries, and adopting churches (Perry, 2005). Individual blacks are also giving to mainstream charities such as the American Red Cross.

Many prominent celebrities have been prompted to help as well. Through his foundation, Tom Joyner, gave $1 million to scholarships for students attending the New Orleans' black colleges. Even rap celebrities such as Ludacris and P. Diddy, traditionally apolitical, have given time and money to Hurricane Katrina victims. Likewise, the Twenty-First Century Foundation, a leading black philanthropy, gave $200,000 to higher education in New Orleans. Of most significance is the $2.8 million dollars raised by the United Negro College Fund, specifically for Xavier and Dillard Universities. These funds were garnered through a combination of individual donations and corporate sponsorships.

Lastly, both Howard and Texas Southern Universities, each designated as Historically Black Colleges and Universities (HBCUs), provided a broad range of services to Katrina-displaced students. These institutions offered medical, legal, psychological, and religious support. Both institutions took in great numbers of students, providing a hospitable learning environment to those who had been displaced by the storm.

Who Else Is Giving to New Orleans' Black Colleges?

Many mainstream foundations have given to those HBCUs destroyed by Hurricane Katrina. The Bush Foundation, endowed by 3M Corporation executive Archibald G. Bush, donated $4 million to Dillard and Xavier and an additional $1 million to Tougaloo College in Jackson, Mississippi (Bush Foundation, 2006). The Andrew Mellon Foundation gave $2.8 million through the Southern Education Foundation to Serve Historically Black Colleges and Universities to support private black colleges that absorbed students displaced by the storm. The money was distributed directly to the institutions to help defray the cost of enrolling the additional students (Foundation Center, 2006). In addition to the Mellon Foundation gift, the Charles Stewart Mott Foundation donated $1 million of its total $1.6 million hurricane relief grants to the Southern Education Foundation to establish a Presidential Leadership Fund for Dillard and Xavier universities. The Fund supports salaries for central administrators, faculty, and staff as well as consulting costs related to the rebuilding each of the devastated campuses (Mott Foundation, 2006). Beyond private foundations, former Presidents George H. W. Bush and William J. Clinton established a joint fund with the United Negro College Fund, Black Entertainment Television (BET), and Jet magazine to support both Dillard and Xavier universities. Presidents Bush and Clinton also announced a grant of $30 million to all higher education institutions affected by Hurricane Katrina. Xavier, Dillard, and Southern University are likely to receive some of largest grants of the 30 institutions selected because of a distribution formula that takes into account the extent of damages on each campus.

Perhaps the most interesting and least expected donor to a historically black college is the nation of Qatar. The Muslim monarchy has given $60 million to Katrina-affected organizations, including a $17.5 million gift to Xavier. The majority of the gift ($12.5 million) is to add 60,000 square feet to College of Pharmacy to increase enrollment, with the remaining $5 million going to scholarships for students affected by Katrina. Qatar decided to give the money directly to organizations rather than through the United States State Department, as it is traditional for foreign governments to do, in order to ensure that the most affected people benefited (Strom, 2006).

The Individual Responsibility of Americans

While there are numerous structural changes that are required in order to fully support black colleges, we offer suggestions for immediate individual-level action. The simple fact is that the majority of the wealth in the United States is controlled by whites. As mentioned earlier, if black colleges typically have small endowments, it is because their alumni do not have the same access to wealth as the white middle class. According to the National Black United Fund, the median income in 2002 for black Americans was $31,778 compared to $51,244 for white Americans. Even more importantly, the median net worth (i.e., savings and capital assets) in 2002 for black households was $5,988. For whites, that figure was $88,651, almost 15 times higher (NBUF, n.d.). Quite simply, this means that black families alone lack the means to put these black colleges on stable financial footing. Black colleges need the assistance of whites in order to flourish, and all Americans have an obligation to support them.

The United States benefits from black colleges. These institutions have not only produced individuals who have excelled in the arts, sciences, law, medicine, music, and sports, but they continue to graduate educated citizens who contribute to our economy and to the fundamental values of our nation (see Appendix). For centuries, blacks have served the country, providing both paid and unpaid labor. It is time for the United States to pay back our debt to blacks and we can do so, in part, by supporting black colleges, those ravaged by Hurricane Katrina and those in our own state and local communities. How? We suggest several ways:

1. Give to the United Negro College Fund (UNCF). This organization was created by blacks to support black higher education. Since 1944, the UNCF has provided scholarships and operating funds for black colleges.

2. Give to the Thurgood Marshall Fund. This organization supports the nation's public black colleges—Southern University included. It acts in much the same way the UNCF does—providing scholarships and funding to member colleges.

3. Give to the individual colleges affected by Hurricane Katrina. All of these institutions are in great need and make it easy to give to their institutions via the Internet.

4. Give to your local private and public black colleges. There are 103 historically black colleges in the United States, most are located in Southern and border states. Giving to these institutions will help to stabilize them, helping them to be prepared when faced with disasters such as Hurricane Katrina.

References

Brainard, J., Burd, S., Field, K., & Selingo, J. (2006, January 6). Congress adopts austere budget for research and student aid. *The Chronicle of Higher Education*, 52(18), p. A35.

Bush Foundation (2005). Bush foundation donates $5 million to storm ravaged historically black colleges and universities in New Orleans and Jackson, MS. Retrieved May 15, 2006 from http://www.bushfoundation.org.

Dyson, M.E. (2006). *Come Hell or high water: Hurricane Katrina and the color of disaster*. New York: Basic Civitas Books.

Foundation Center (2006). Hurricane relief efforts in the Southeast. Retrieved March 1, 2006 from http://www.fdncenter.org/atlanta/at_katrina.html.

Gasman, M. (2006, March 3). Trends in African American philanthropy. *On Philanthropy*. Retrieved March 3, 2006 from http://www.onphilanthropy.com.

Goodman, A. (2005, September 27). Has the government abandoned New Orleans' top black colleges? Retrieved October 10, 2005 from http://www.democracynow.org.

Gordon, E. (2005, September 8). Roundtable: Black colleges and Katrina. *News & Notes with Ed Gordon*, National Public Radio (transcript). Retrieved October 10, 2005 from http://www.npr.org.

Hoover, E. (2005, September 16). A beloved black university fights to survive. *The Chronicle of Higher Education*, 21–22.

King, Jr., M. L. (1963, August 28). I have a dream. Washington, D.C.

Mangan, K. (2006a, February 9). Louisiana colleges get their share of $95-million in hurricane relief. *The Chronicle of Higher Education*. Retrieved March 17, 2006 from http://www.chronicle.com.

Mangan, K. (2006b, February 10). At Xavier U. of Louisiana, an "indefatigable fighter." *The Chronicle of Higher Education*, p. A48.

Mangan, K. (2006c, May 26). Still without a campus, Southern U. at New Orleans struggles to stay in business. *The Chronicle of Higher Education*, p. A31.

Mitchell, R. (1993). *The multicultural student's guide to colleges: What every African-American, Asian-American, Hispanic, and Native American applicant needs to know about America's top schools*. New York: Noonday Press.

Mott Foundation (2006). Mott foundation funds long-term hurricane relief efforts. Retrieved April 5, 2006 from http://www.mott.org.

National Black United Fund. (n.d.) Retrieved May 12, 2006 from http://www.nbuf.org.

Perry, S. (2005). "Shell-shocked into action" black groups, critical of slow response to Katrina, vow to strengthen their own charitable efforts. *The Chronicle of Philanthropy*, 10, 22.

Strom, S. (2006, May 2). Qatar grants millions in aid to New Orleans. *The New York Times*. Retrieved May 5, 2006 from http://www.nytimes.com.

Thompson, R. & Parker, S. (2006). The National Urban League equality index. *The state of black America 2006*. New York: National Urban League.

Appendix

Prominent Graduates of Xavier, Dillard and Southern

Xavier University of Louisiana

Bernard Randolph, four-star general, U.S. Air Force

Alexis Herman, U.S. Secretary of Labor

Regina Benjamin, first African-American woman named to the American Medical Association's Board of Trustees

Dillard University

Ruth Simmons, President of Brown University and first African-American president of an Ivy League institution

Ellis Marsalis, Jazz musician

Billy Ray Hobley, Harlem Globetrotter

Bishop Alfred Norris, United Methodist Church

Andrew Young, Jr., Civil rights activist and politician, former mayor of Atlanta, first African-American U.S. ambassador to the United Nations

Southern University at New Orleans

Michael Bruno, owner, largest black-owned CPA firm

Elton Lawson, obstetrician and gynecologist

Chapter 19

Social Justice after Katrina: The Need for a Revitalized Public Sphere

Peter G. Stillman and Adelaide H. Villmoare

Disaster Relief in the United States

As *A Prairie Home Companion* nostalgically commemorates, there has always been a tradition of people helping each other in the United States, whether with local barn-raisings or volunteer fire departments; and local disaster relief, organized by neighbors, towns, churches, and other organizations was common.[1] Only gradually and haltingly did the federal government become involved with disaster relief and mitigation. In the late nineteenth century, Grover Cleveland vetoed a bill to grant federal aid to farmers suffering a serious drought on the grounds that individuals and locales were responsible for taking care of themselves:

> I can find no warrant for such an appropriation in the Constitution; and I do not believe that the power and duty of the General Government ought to be extended to the relief of individual suffering.... Federal aid in [cases of misfortune] encourages the expectation of paternal care on the part of the Government and weakens the sturdiness of our national character, while it prevents the indulgence among our people of that kindly sentiment and conduct which strengthens the bonds of a common brotherhood.

> (as cited in Moss, 2002, pp. 254–255)

Shortly after Cleveland's words the federal government established the American Red Cross as the national agency for disaster relief. With close ties to the

---

1. In the nineteenth century disaster relief, whether private or city government-generated, was overlaid with a resistance to aid because of concerns about self-reliance (Steinberg, 2000, p. 17).

federal government, but not a part of the executive branch and with most of its funding from private sources, the Red Cross took primary responsibility for disaster relief. But additional catastrophes—such as the 1927 Mississippi River flood that overtaxed the Red Cross—and changing political attitudes provided impetus for further federal involvement in disaster mitigation and relief.

Ad hoc assistance to state and local governments was regularized only with the 1950 Disaster Relief Act, which institutionalized presidential disaster declarations to help repair state and local governmental infrastructures. Even then the Red Cross kept responsibility for aiding individuals; not until after Hurricane Camille (1969) was federal government assistance extended to victims of disaster (Hoover, 2005; Steinberg, 2000). In 1979 under President Carter the Federal Emergency Management Agency (FEMA) was created to provide structured federal action in disasters.

Under President Reagan (1980–1988), FEMA's chief responsibilities were for civil defense and preparation for future disasters related to nuclear arms. The obligation of the federal government to assume a key role in natural disaster policy remained undeveloped in part because the Reagan (1980–1988) and Bush (1988–1992) presidencies believed that the federal government was not capable of doing many of the tasks that it had gradually accrued over the course of the twentieth century. With the Clinton (1992–2000) administration, which saw a constructive role for government, FEMA turned to forward-looking, professional planning for natural disasters. Although FEMA's budget continued to be modest, its role matured into one where the federal government worked to mitigate disasters as well as respond more fully to them after the event. They began to aid not only government agencies but individuals as well. By the end of President Clinton's administration, there was an ethos, a skilled agency, and a tradition of federal governmental intervention in disaster prevention, mitigation, and relief. Residents came to expect that the federal government, usually in conjunction with the Red Cross, would assist those affected by the disaster. This assistance and the expectation of it were on top of the traditional reliance on friends and neighbors, local groups, and local, county, and state governments to aid with disasters. In terms of both ideology and policy, disaster relief had developed to a point where the federal government clearly had an established obligation, all levels of government worked together, and semi-public non-governmental organizations (NGOs) like the Red Cross contributed their expertise and resources.

As with the Reagan and Bush administrations, the George W. Bush administration (2000–2008) doubted the efficacy of federal government agencies and strived to lessen the direct federal role in disaster relief and to replace federal agents and agencies with private organizations contracted by the government. In Bush's conservative perspective, individuals should be held accountable for their lives, including their lives under disaster circumstances, and the private sector can do tasks better than government at any level, especially the federal government. Indeed President Bush's first FEMA Director, Joe Allbaugh, echoed Cleveland's words when he told Congress on May 16, 2001 (as cited in Hurricane Katrina, 2005), "Many are concerned that federal disaster assistance may have evolved into both an oversized entitlement program and a disincentive to effective state and local risk management. Expectations of when the federal government should be involved and the degree of involvement may have ballooned beyond what is an appropriate level" (n.p.).

The devastation produced by Hurricane Katrina on the Gulf Coast and especially in New Orleans put into sharp focus these political arguments about the role of government, particularly the federal government, in disaster relief and mitigation. The catastrophe in New Orleans unquestionably was a failure of government at every level and in many ways. The full brunt of the hurricane missed New Orleans, but in the aftermath the levees were breached, flooding much of the city infrastructure and knocking out public services. Roads, including interstates, were under water; telephones and cell phones did not work; and even those in dry areas lacked electricity and water. Many people were trapped in their flooding homes or in two overcrowded and understaffed facilities—the Convention Center and the Superdome—that were not intended to be used as shelters and that lacked food, running water, working toilets, and other basic necessities. Were the lessons of these dire circumstances that government is incapable of preparing for and responding to disasters, and thus they should be handled by the private sector?

Or were the lessons that the government and the public sphere were obliged under the democratic expectation of the people to do much better? The failures of Katrina argue for reimagined and reinvigorated public dedication to and federal involvement with disaster mitigation and relief. And the nature of this public action must move away from the emphasis on maintaining order through the exercise of force that New Orleans experienced to instituting substantial mitigation and relief policies, as well as responding to the inequities apparent in the aftermath of disasters. Prevention of the worst consequences of disaster and efficient care work in the face of massive destruction of communities are public obligations and required by social justice. Certainly responses to disaster may be carried through private means as well, but the primary obligation is public and must be openly embraced as such by the federal government.

The Public Sphere

The public sphere differs from the private sphere of private corporations and business guided by the pursuit of economic self-interest and values of individualism and the private sphere of independent individuals, following their self-interest and acting freely. The public sphere involves values that move beyond individual self-interest and entail more wide-ranging responsibilities and connections, a sense of community both large and small. This is not to deny that politics, as one segment of the public sphere, is driven in part by economic self-interests or that private groups may volunteer out of concern for community. Indeed, the line between public and private cannot be drawn unambiguously or permanently (Wolfe, 2006), they interact with each other and they overlap (Bailey, 2002). But the distinctions are worth drawing because politics and the public require a consideration of social, common, and national interests. And it is only through the public sphere that the moral and political obligations required of democratic politics can gain full articulation and support.

In general, in a democracy the concept of the public involves a web of meanings and practices that center around publicity, transparency, and accountability to the larger community. The public carries a sense of responsibility for all members of society. It also requires public voice and participation: democratic discourse, open to all, inclusive of different perspectives, where each person counts equally. Democratic politics should mean that all sectors of society, the dispossessed and the powerful, as Boggs (2000) puts it, "come together, interact, make decisions, forge citizen bonds, carry out imperatives of social change, and ultimately search for the good society" (p. 7). The public entails civil society and government working for democratic purposes of social justice.

Civil society, which Bailey (2002) characterizes as "those collective public activities that are independent of the state's regulating, controlling, and shaping activities," (p. 21) is certainly crucial to the ways in which the governmental public sphere operates in a democracy. Media and political discourse constitute a significant part of civil society, as do the various ways in which people come together to "do" politics. Protest against public policy is as much a part of the public sphere as the policy itself. Social justice and democracy require not only open, responsible, and equitable governance, but awareness and participation on the part of those not in the government. An inert civil society diminishes the value of the public.

Values of equity, fairness, and social justice have more ideological purchase in the public sphere than in the private. Private decisions frequently can be made by a few and kept secret; they are not subject to public or governmental oversight and usually include no expectation of equality or fairness. While many public policies support profoundly inequitable results (e.g., the war on drugs), in public there is at least a chance of engagement—of open information and debate—with the unjust consequences of such policies.

From the perspective of the public sphere, the key questions about the catastrophe in New Orleans following Katrina are those of social justice: What was and is owed to the people of New Orleans, especially those who were trapped by the flooding or those damaged by the catastrophe? What is owed in the future to other Americans in similar circumstances?

Public Discussion of Order

Media reports and pundit comments reflect important myths or assumptions about Americans in times of crisis. When the police are not around, one myth goes, individuals will do whatever they wish (including rampant, random, and purposeless looting), lawlessness will flourish, and order can be reestablished only by force.[2] Indeed, the initial public response to Katrina in New Orleans emphasized individual criminality and called for force. Building on rumors, the first news reports and pundits created a frenzy about lawlessness, particularly among African Americans. Peggy Noonan remarked: "As for the tragic piggism that is taking place on the streets of New Orleans, it is not unbelievable but it is unforgivable, and I hope the looters are shot" (Voices in the Storm, 2005). According to one study of reporting on Katrina, the panicky coverage even supplanted images of disorder and crime with those of a "war zone" (Tierney, Bevc & Kuligowski, 2006, pp. 63, 72). The hype about looting and "thuggism" played over and over in the media. The message was that individuals, notably African-American individuals, were simply out for themselves; they were taking advantage of a bad situation.[3]

Most of those stranded in New Orleans were African American; most of the identified looters were African American.[4] Two well publicized AP photos and captions that circulated the Internet framed the racialized talk about

---

2. This view represents a kind of racist Hobbesianism: when there is no force powerful enough to overawe us then we will descend into a state of war of all against all, where laws are flouted, everything is permissible, and force and fraud are common—and urban African Americans will most quickly enter the state of war, perhaps because their lives so closely approximate it already (Hobbes, 1651).

3. Alongside these media portrayals were others that evinced anger at the abandonment of mostly African-American New Orleans by the government (Purdum, 2005).

4. Michael Lewis (2005) writes brilliantly about the rumors: "... here is what I knew, or thought I knew: Orleans Parish Prison had been seized by the inmates, who also controlled the armory. Prisoners in their orange uniforms had been spotted outside, roaming around the tilapia ponds—there's a fish farm next to the prison—and whatever that meant, it sounded ominous: I mean, if they were getting into the tilapias, who knew what else they might do? Gangs of young black men were raging through the Garden District, moving toward my parents' house, shooting white people. Armed young black men, on Wednesday, had taken over Uptown Children's Hospital, just six blocks away, and shot patients and doctors. Others had stolen a forklift and carted out the entire contents of a Rite Aid and then removed the whole front of an Ace Hardware store farther uptown, on Oak Street. Most shocking of all, because of its incongruity, was the news that looters had broken into Perlis, the Uptown New Orleans clothing store, and picked the place clean of

looting and law and order. In each photo people were shown with bags and soda; the one of a black person referred to "looting" and the one of a white person referred to "finding" bread and soda (Dyson, 2006, p. 164). Those who were "looting" and were labeled as "thugs" were black, and those, like the doctors who were said to have "commandeered" drugs, were white. Dyson (2006) observes that, "Even those critics who were sympathetic to the urgent conditions of the abandoned blacks felt pressured to embrace the frame of reference of black criminality before otherwise defending poor blacks" (pp. 166–167). This frame of reference and the law-and-order rhetoric associated with it played out the myth that individuals are to be held fully accountable for their actions and that African Americans and whites are to be held accountable in different ways. Looters were to be policed and incarcerated because the first priority of government was seen as order; one of the first governmental institutions re-established after the storm was a temporary jail at the bus station.

Gradually, the media acknowledged that most reports of disorder and criminality were wrong. According to *A Failure of Initiative* (2006), the U.S. House of Representative's Report by the Select Bipartisan Committee to Investigate the Preparation for and Response to Hurricane Katrina:

> Throughout the early days of the response, media reports from New Orleans featured rampant looting, gunfire, crime, and lawlessness, including murders, and alleged sexual assaults at the Superdome and Convention Center. Few of these reports were substantiated, and those that were—such as gunfire—were later understood to be actually coming from individuals trapped and trying to attract the attention of rescuers in helicopters. (p. 169)

Violence, including sexual violence, did occur. But in the well-off and white uptown areas, "houses may have been violated by trees but not by looters, despite how easily they could have been entered" (Lewis, 2005, p. 46). As Louisiana National Guard Colonel Thomas Beron explained, at the Superdome "bad things happened, but I didn't see any killing and raping and cutting of throats or anything.... Ninety-nine percent of the people in the Dome were very well-behaved" (Brinkley, 2006, p. 193).

That other public responses—of care and rapid assistance rather than policing—might do more to counteract disorder did enter the public dialogue as journalists became outraged at the inadequacy of rescue efforts. Media attention shifted from a focus on the city as a war zone overrun by looters to coverage that reflected the conditions of suffering and surviving in New Orleans. The reality of much "looting" became clear to those observing events and a

---

alligator belts, polo shirts with little crawfish on them and tuxedos most often rented by white kids for debutante parties and the Squires Ball" (p. 48).

counter-story developed: that many people were taking what they need to survive and cope with their destitute circumstances. The "Robin Hood Looters" scavenged for food to help those stranded (Rodriguez, Trainor, & Quarantelli, 2006). Two African-American men were sighted carrying supplies from Rite Aid and later distributing them to elderly people left behind in a high-rise (Brinkley, 2006). As their perceptions of the facts changed, the media were willing to change their story—and to shift their ideological rhetoric. Newspapers and television reporters were shocked and then outraged at government's failures to provide the most basic care for its people, at the social injustices they witnessed. One part of the public sphere, the media, was holding another part of the public, the government, accountable.

Policing and Order

The government is supposed to maintain order. In the heat of the moment, this task is often interpreted primarily as the imposition of deadly force to protect property and impose peace. In New Orleans from the beginning official responses to "black criminality" and disorder were almost universal: to employ armed police, authorized to shoot. According to Senator Vitter, Governor Barbour of Mississippi "made it clear that looters would be shot" (Brinkley, 2006, p. 363). Mayor Nagin declared martial law and at one point ordered the police to stop rescuing people and to arrest looters instead (Brinkley, 2006). The publicly stated priority on policing over rescue was made clear.

Two related governmental responses also surfaced, both based on the assumption of unrestrained violence in New Orleans. One response was to secure the perimeter of New Orleans, keeping African Americans and disorder in, and keeping aid out. The sheriff of mostly white Gretna, Louisiana used drawn and pointed guns to stop a mostly African-American group of people from crossing a bridge out of New Orleans into his town (Riccardi, 2005). FEMA prevented aid (including Red Cross aid) from entering the city until FEMA declared the city safe. The second, related governmental response was the framing of New Orleans as a war zone or an ungoverned territory of violent anarchy. Brigadier General Jones of the Louisiana National Guard said: "This place is going to look like Little Somalia. We're going to go out and take this city back. This will be a combat operation to get this city under control" (Voices in the Storm, 2005). The military was deployed in record numbers,[5]

---

5. Tierney et al. (2006) write: "By the fifth day after the hurricane's landfall in the Gulf region, the number of National Guard and active military deployed in Hurricane Katrina had tripled the number deployed within the same period following Hurricane Andrew in 1992" (p. 70).

and their high-powered weaponry reinforced the definition of the city as a war zone rather than a site of human need, even though the many police could have assisted people with obtaining food and water.

Policing may have been intended to secure social order, but the weaponry, the paramilitary and military character of those patrolling, the lack of law, and the commitment to protecting the client and his property[6] were a recipe for further violence and abuse of the disempowered. As Lewis (2005) describes the situation, "Pretty quickly, it became clear that there were more than a few people left in the city and that they fell broadly into two categories: extremely well armed white men prepared to do battle and a ragtag collection of irregulars, black and white, who had no idea there was anyone to do battle with" (p. 49). The militarized forces of order were looking for a war rather than seeking to assist the abandoned. The private, armed guards and few homeowners remaining uptown believed the rumors of African-American people with automatic weapons hunting white people (Lewis, 2005). They prepared for armed battle between whites and blacks. There was little public constraint on racism, unfounded rumors, or the ability to use force and violence for private purposes. It is as if the Civil War, emancipation, the civil rights movement, and the election of African-American officials had not taken place, and a war of an old order was being undertaken.

In a city with an infestation of guns, sharp economic and racial inequalities, and devastating flooding paralyzing the city's work forces, and with the media's inevitable tendency to generate "disaster myths" about looting (Tierney et al., 2006, pp. 60–61), the American recipe for law-and-order panic was in place. That panic created the agenda and tone of the initial responses, in which policing overwhelmed alternative priorities. Responding to disorder, rather than to stranded and vulnerable people, meant that policing— public and private—was the first priority. Social justice had little place in this activity.

Care, Assistance, and Social Justice

When the police use force to try to establish "law and order" to protect property rights, they are performing a role. But trying to create order by force, that is, by using violence to perform the repressive functions of the state, is only one role. The public and their agents—including the police—are also charged with

---

6. Private security employees poured into New Orleans immediately after the hurricane. Blackwater, Instinctive Shooting International, and other groups were for the most part hired to protect private property, although Blackwater did claim to be operating under contract with the Department of Homeland Security (Scahill, 2005).

promoting the general welfare. In cases of catastrophic devastation like Katrina the need to protect all citizens from danger, to care for them, to secure their well-being, and to assure social justice becomes desperately apparent.

The victims of Katrina in New Orleans were victims of environmental and social injustice, specifically the unequal distribution of environmental and social burdens. Those who had means and money to leave had, by and large, already done so. Those who remained in New Orleans were in many instances those who had no means to leave: they did not own cars, they had little savings or credit for a motel room, their family and friends lived in flooded New Orleans, or they had pets who were their close companions and who were excluded from Red Cross shelters (Fussell, 2005). They could not turn to government: neither city nor state had made plans to evacuate the car-less or the frail (Shane & Lipton, 2005).

Those who became refugees on rooftops, in the shelters, or in the water were those who had been flooded because the levees did not hold. They were victims of the politically created vulnerabilities of New Orleans. Repairs for the levees had been underfunded for years, even though it had long been known that a strong hurricane—a Category 4 hurricane or stronger—would overtop the levees and flood the city; the *New Orleans Times-Picayune* had published a series of articles on such a hurricane in June 2002 (Washing Away, 2002), and city, state, and federal officials had run simulations, complete with flooding and evacuations, in 2000 ("Hurricane Zebra") and 2004 ("Hurricane Pam") (Shane & Lipton, 2005).

Once the extensive flooding occurred many in New Orleans no longer had a home or any familiar safe place where they could stay. The power was off, and with it went modern forms of communication. If a store was open, there was no way to buy anything except with cash; ATMs and credit card charge devices did not work. But most stores were not open; the owners or managers had locked the doors and fled the town. So many residents of flooded New Orleans who needed necessities like water, food, prescriptions, or baby formula had no way to buy them. The normal economic arrangements had collapsed. Moreover, early in the storm FEMA did not allow aid agencies into the city. For many there was no way to eat or drink except to break into stores. Stories told by the looters reflected these circumstances.

> One woman outside a Sav-a-Center on Tchoupitoulas Street was loading food, soda, water, bread, peanut butter and canned food into the trunk of a gray Oldsmobile. "Yes, in a sense it's wrong, but survival is the name of the game," said the woman, who declined to identify herself. "I've got six grandchildren. We didn't know this was going to happen. The water is off. We're trying to get supplies we need."
>
> (as cited in Barringer & Longman, 2005, p. A16).

Although their comments had to be circumspect, even government officials and police recognized the motives behind some of the looting. Cynthia Hedge-Morrell, Vice President of the New Orleans City Council, said:

> When there's no food, no water, no sanitation, who can say what you'd do? People were trying to protect their children. I don't condone lawlessness, but this doesn't represent the generous people of New Orleans.
>
> (as cited in Barringer & Longman, 2005, p. A16)

As some officials and many looters recognized, the looters were not criminals engaged in breaking the law so much as they were people in dire need trying to survive in a catastrophe where the normal means of obtaining necessities had been withdrawn and where government for the most part had failed to help people sustain life.

Relief aid would have decreased the need for looting. But all too often in New Orleans, the government forgot its role of taking care of the people.[7] FEMA has come under for much justified criticism for its failures to act. Too often, FEMA seemed either too distant to have a sense of what was going on in New Orleans, too concerned about controlling the population, or too involved in making sure that all the paperwork was in place, with the result that FEMA lost its focus on its role as disaster relief—its role as the agency to coordinate care for those who were victims of circumstances beyond their control.

FEMA's disengagement from events was most striking when Director Michael Brown told network television interviewers on Thursday, September 1 that federal officials had learned just that day that there were evacuees at the Convention Center. Ted Koppel on *Nightline* asked him, "Don't you guys watch television? Our reporters have been reporting about it for more than just today" (Treaster, 2005, p. A12). The most notorious instance of FEMA's failure to care for people occurred when FEMA denied the Red Cross entry into New Orleans when the organization wanted to distribute food and water to those in need at the Superdome, Convention Center, and other places. There is no doubt that the need was great: "Some people there [in the convention center] have not eaten or drunk water for three or four days, which is inexcusable," acknowledged Joseph W. Matthews, the director of the city's Office of Emergency

---

7. Such behavior by FEMA had happened before, in the pre-Clinton era, when FEMA was a low priority of the first Bush administration. The mayor of Charleston, S.C., Joseph P. Riley, Jr., noted that in 1989 "With the eye of [Hurricane] Hugo over my City Hall, literally, I said to a FEMA official, 'What's the main bit of advice you can give me?' and he said, 'You need to make sure you're accounting for all your expenses.'" (Purdum, 2005, p. A17).

Preparedness (Treaster & Sontag, 2005, p. A1). Despite the hunger and thirst of thousands of people, FEMA claimed two reasons for keeping the Red Cross out. One was that New Orleans was not safe—even though, of course, the Red Cross is no stranger to dangerous places. The other is that FEMA wanted to evacuate people from the city and was worried that the availability of food and water at the shelters in the city would prevent people from evacuating (Brinkley, 2006; Dyson, 2006)—even though FEMA did not have the means to evacuate refugees from those overcrowded, fetid shelters.

Throughout the catastrophe FEMA adhered rigidly to rules and procedures designed by bureaucrats in air-conditioned offices. FEMA halted trucks carrying thousands of bottles of water because they lacked "tasker numbers," sent firefighters to Atlanta for training in community relations and sexual harassment, insisted on security searches for evacuees boarding planes, and prevented planes from carrying out evacuees unless air marshals were aboard (Lukes, 2005). MREs (meals ready to eat) were confiscated because they were metal containers. Without functioning fax machines, FEMA could not receive requests for aid in the proper form. Volunteer physicians were prohibited by FEMA from helping because they were not licensed in the state (Perrow, 2005). FEMA not only failed to help those in desperate need, it profoundly hindered rescue efforts and contributed to inhumane and unjust treatment of hurricane survivors.

FEMA's questionable behavior continued after the immediate crisis of Katrina. Questioning Michael Brown before Congress on February 9, 2006, Senator Lautenberg complained:

> Nearly six months after two hurricanes ripped apart communities across the Gulf Coast, tens of thousands of residents remain without trailers promised by the federal government for use as temporary shelters while they rebuild.... I spoke to the people, and what I got was, "Please, give use a place to cover our heads with, a place that we can lie down and go to sleep."
>
> (Senate Hearing, 2006, n.p.)

Articles in *The New York Times* and elsewhere indicated that FEMA's performance at giving aid had not yet improved, and (as of late June 2006) Congress was still looking into how to improve FEMA (The Aftermath, 2006).

Public Service as Social Justice

Despite the well-documented, well-known, and ongoing problems with FEMA many bright spots of public action, at all levels of government and civil society, occurred during and after Katrina. The Louisiana Department of Wildlife and Fisheries (LDWF), for example, knew the terrain, had many flat-bottomed boats, worked tirelessly, and saved 10,000 people by September 3 (Brinkley, 2006, p. 297). This group operated on its own terms, sidestepping FEMA and often the New Orleans Police Department. By all accounts it was efficient and dedicated. Members of the city's Sewerage and Water Board (S&WB) stayed on the job throughout the crisis, especially trying to assure that the flooded city could be pumped out properly. And their work meant that the city drained much more quickly than observers thought possible.[8] The U.S. Coast Guard rescued more than 33,000 people (U.S. House of Representatives, 2006). States offered all kinds of immediate and long-term assistance ([Illinois] Governor's Office, 2005). Texas Governor Rick Perry, for instance, established shelters in Houston and said that school-age children of the evacuees would be promptly admitted to Texas public schools and given textbooks, lunches, and transportation. "In the face of such tragic circumstances," Governor Perry commented, "we know we're neighbors and we're going to pull together so that these families can find as much normalcy as they can. We realize that by the grace of God we could be the ones that have this extraordinary need" (McFadden & Blumenthal, 2005, p. A17).

Many people were safely evacuated. Deputy Director of Louisiana's Homeland Security, Jeff Smith, asserted: "We estimate that over 1 million people, or approximately 90 percent of the affected parishes' populations, evacuate[d] in about a 40-hour period. I don't know of any other evacuation that has occurred with that many people under these circumstances with that high of percentage of people being evacuated in that short of a time period" (U.S. House of Representatives, 2006, p. 102). The Red Cross prepared and organized for relief efforts even though it was not allowed in New Orleans. Private companies, especially Wal-Mart, opened their doors to give needed supplies and offered their resources. The public, semi-public, and private spheres took up a call for public service and care.

People and institutions eagerly engaged in a spirit of public service. They acknowledged that individuals are not totally responsible for their fates and

---

8. In an interview (2009) Reverend Robert and Grisela Jackson explained how important this dedication was, even though it was below most media and politicians' radar. As the S&WB's Director of Intergovernmental Relations, he was one of those determined to do their critical work during and after the storm. A recruitment website for an S&WB position (2009) notes: "With total power loss, submerged pumps, and fleeing populations, the Army Corps of Engineers direly predicted that it would take several months to pump the water out of the city. The staff of S&WB, heroically maintaining their posts during Katrina, had restarted most of their 24 pumping stations within a few days. The water began to recede and within about three weeks, the city was mostly pumped out and prepared to enter the next phase of a monumental recovery."

that social responsibility the idea that individuals are responsible for the fate of other individuals and the greater collective—required organized action. In one working class neighborhood of New Orleans, for instance, a group of people gathered their neighbors in a local school with supplies they needed to weather the storm (Rodriguez et al., 2006). Volunteers quickly formed the "Cajun Navy" with boats to work with the LDWF (Brinkley, 2006). Camp Edwards Base on Cape Cod served as a shelter for evacuees. Enormous amounts of money were raised to help survivors.[9] Katrina made manifest a passionate public dedication to those harmed by the hurricane.

Krause (2005) argues, "... this disaster has produced its own public; that is, it fostered a shared experience that made social contexts visible, articulated interests and led to collective debates about social justice" (n.p.). This public was concerned with issues that went beyond the self-interest of each individual and that reached out to others dedicated to social justice. Those who gave money to aid the survivors recognized that there were those in need because of circumstances beyond their control. Some may wish to think about these gifts as individual charity, but the gifts—which were given not to individual sufferers per se but to funds that support the survivors as a group—may also be a reflection of the donors' attempts to right the wrongs of racism and environmental and social injustice.

Although the U. S. media are notable for their short attention span, there was, as of June 2006,[10] an ongoing discussion about the meaning and impact of Katrina through articles in *The New York Times*, reports on NBC, articles in news magazines and journals, and *A Failure of Initiative*, the U.S. House of Representatives' report on Katrina. One focus of the conversation was on social justice: how the impact of the hurricane fell disproportionately on the most vulnerable members of society and how the city, state, and country could do right by the inhabitants of New Orleans and other affected regions, especially those who were uprooted, whose homes were destroyed, and who were trying to put their lives back together.

Some aspects of the discussion moved along only in fits and starts. Before Katrina the limits of the levees were known; during Katrina, they proved themselves more vulnerable than thought. But repair and reconstruction have been slow, and many levees have been rebuilt to inadequate pre-Katrina standards and have left those who rebuild their homes inside the repaired levees unable to obtain flood insurance (Crenson, 2006). Also at issue is how to restore and make resilient a Louisiana coastline that has eroded over the years as

---

9. Gifts after Katrina outpaced "anything we have had," including the 9-11 donations, according to Ryland Dodge, spokesman with the American Red Cross. Wal-Mart and the Walton Family Foundation contributed about $32 million in the first week for disaster relief (Updates, n.d.).

10. For the issues of public space, inclusion and exclusion, political discussion, and planning in New Orleans through 2009, see Villmoare and Stillman (2010).

the current channel and its delta have been dredged farther into the Gulf of Mexico, allowing rich silt to be wasted miles offshore. To address levee reconstruction and hurricane mitigation seriously requires a wide discussion in which many actors—and many members of the public—are and should be participating.

Equally vital discussion occurred about how to rebuild New Orleans. Here it was desperately important to make sure that the discussion was democratic and included as broad a public as possible to make sure that those whose homes were damaged or destroyed, for instance, had a serious voice and a fair chance to take part in the policy debates about the ultimate fate of the properties where they have lived their lives. Because of the number of citizens' groups that sprung up eager to work discussion also needed to occur about who was to do the reconstruction work. A group called "Community Labor United," for instance, argued that much of the reconstruction work should be done by local groups and local labor (Klein, 2005). There has been a danger that too many citizens were being closed out of the discussion and out of the rebuilding and that the operative definition of the public will be truncated in New Orleans.

Public and open discussion, debate, and decision-making—with a concern for democratic values including social justice—need also to be part of the re-evaluation of governmental response to catastrophe. Here the complex issue of how to assure and organize the federal government response is important. One absolutely critical reform should occur. FEMA as an agency needs to be regarded, as it was under the Clinton administration, as a significant agency with an important public responsibility for the mitigation of and response to natural disasters. The militarization of federal government agencies since the September 11, 2001 terrorist attacks led to dismissing FEMA's role in disasters. FEMA needs an esprit de corps, with thoughtful, educated, and competent leaders and administrators who are experts on disasters and see FEMA as a significant public resource responsible for people. FEMA needs to be prepared for catastrophes and, importantly, to recognize that catastrophes involve unexpected events; no matter how well planned and positioned the response, the plan will have to be modified, policies changed, and new initiatives taken to fit the circumstances of the particular set of events. In such circumstances a top-down hierarchical system is bound to meet serious failures, when the plans cannot be implemented as planned, when communications are awry, and when the planners do not know what is happening (e.g., at the Convention Center). As the Coast Guard, the S&WB, and many private citizens showed, a lot of good work can be done by those in the field acting on their own sense of what should be done, co-operating with others when possible, innovating responses, and sharing knowledge and action. Rather than stress command-and-control, the emphasis needs to be on social responsibility so that information can be obtained, relief distributed, and those in need discovered and assisted.

Beyond internal changes to FEMA (and to equivalent state and local agencies), disaster response requires public discussion and a concern with social justice, a key element of which is the relation between the right to property and the right to life. The experience of Katrina suggests that the fear of looting was magnified way out of proportion and that policing was given a narrow goal of enforcing order defined as the protection of private property. Shifting the NOPD to "law and order" and telling the National Guard to "shoot to kill" both reflected a narrow sense of justice as property rights that often works in racist ways. Those who study disasters and the media know that the media present much more looting, mayhem, and disorder during a crisis than actually occur (Tierney et al., 2006). Exaggerated reports in part caused Mayor Nagin, not a disaster expert, to shift the function of the New Orleans Police Department (NOPD) from rescue to "law and order" on the third day and led FEMA to keep Red Cross aid out of the city. Neither criminal disorder nor murderous violence was common in New Orleans and so the governmental responses based on those reports were misguided, unnecessary, and in most cases counterproductive to helping people.

The sight of well-fed, mostly white National Guardsmen with guns and canteens driving by without stopping did not help generate order, peace, and contentment among mostly African-American residents. A social justice approach suggests that order and peaceable behavior would have been better served by National Guardsmen or Red Cross employees and volunteers bringing in and sharing food and water. The disaster experts should be able to counter the patterns of media coverage, and public discussion should center on the issue of how to help a city full of traumatized, thirsty, and starving people, a city where in the face of catastrophic flooding people do and should matter more than property. Thinking of disaster relief in terms of the public requirement of social justice allows politicians, administrators, and citizens to see that the right to well-being is paramount.

The public might have an enhanced role in disasters. Despite the difficulties during Katrina and after, the public in many forms—the outpouring of public activity and of successful government groups (like the LDWF)—has much potential for effective action to alleviate suffering and attend to the welfare of the people. One important implication is that in a disaster people—citizens, government officials, and business owners—can be active and helpful. Their contributions are important in themselves, and highlight the many sources of mutual aid among the citizens of New Orleans. Working with competent and imaginative government agencies, a vigorous public sphere, responsive to shifting conditions during a catastrophe, concerned with protecting life and advancing the general welfare, engaging citizens at all levels of activity, and committed to planning and reconstruction through open debate, can respond to the requirements of social justice.

References

The Aftermath of Hurricane Katrina. (2006). Retrieved October 25, 2006 from http://www.nytimes.com/pages/national/nationalspecial/index.html.

Bailey, J. (2002). From public to private, *Social Research*, 69, 15–31.

Barringer, F., & Longman, J.(2005, September 1). Owners take up arms as looters press their advantage, *The New York Times*, p. A16.

Boggs, C. (2000). *The end of politics.* New York: The Guilford Press.

Brinkley, D. (2006). *The great deluge.* New York: William Morrow.

Crenson, M. (2006, May 22). Levee rebuilding may not be enough. *Cleveland Plain Dealer*, p. A1.

Dyson, M. (2006). *Come hell or high water.* New York: Basic Books.

Fussell, E. (2005). Leaving New Orleans: Social stratification, networks, and hurricane evacuation. Retrieved October 24, 2006 from http://understandingkatrina.ssrc.org/Fussell.

Hobbes, T. (1651). *The leviathan.* London: Andrew Crooke.

Hoover, M. (2005). Rowboat federalism: The politics of U.S. disaster relief. Retrieved October 24, 2006 from http://mrzine.monthlyreview.org/hoover 281105.

Hurricane Katrina. (2005). Retrieved October 24, 2006 from http://cooperativeresearch.org/timeline.jsp?katrina_statements=katrina_state mentsMitigation&timeline=hurricane_katrina.

[Illinois] Governor's Office Press Release. (2005, September 3). Retrieved October 24, 2006 from http://www.illinois.gov/PressReleases/ShowPress Release.cfm? SubjectID=3&RecNum=4283.

Interview with Reverend Robert and Grisela Jackson by Peter G. Stillman and Adelaide H. Villmoare. (2009).

Klein, N. (2005, September 26). Let the people rebuild New Orleans, *The Nation*. Retrieved October 24, 2006 from http://www.thenation.com/doc/20050926/klein.

Krause, M. (2005). New Orleans: The public sphere of the disaster. Retrieved July 2, 2006 from http://understandingkatrina.ssrc.org/Krause.

Lewis, M. (2005, October 9). Wading toward home. *The New York Times Magazine*. Retrieved July 2, 2006 from http://select.nytimes.com/search/restricted/article?res=F60911F63B540C7A8CDDA90994DD404482.

Lukes, S. (2005). Questions about power: Lessons from Hurricane Katrina. Retrieved July 2, 2006 from http://understandingkatrina.ssrc.org/Lukes.

McFadden, R. and Blumenthal, R. (2005, September 1). Bush sees long recovery for New Orleans; 30,000 troops in largest U.S. relief effort. *The New York Times*, pp. A1, A17.

Moss, D. (2002). *When all else fails*. Cambridge: Harvard University Press.

Perrow, C. (2005). Using organizations: The case of FEMA. Retrieved July 2, 2006 from http://understandingkatrina.ssrc.org/Perrow.

Purdum, T. (2005, September 3). Across U.S., outrage at response. *New York Times*, pp. A1, A17.

Recruitment Website for a Sewerage and Water Board Position. (2009). Retrieved 11 April 2009 from http://www.boulwareinc.com/index.php?option=com_content&view=article&id=40%3Adeputy-general-superintendent&catid=2%3Acurrent-searches&Itemid=16.

Riccardi, N. (2005, September 16). After blocking the bridge, Gretna circles the wagons. *The Los Angeles Times*, p. A1.

Rodriguez, H., Trainor, J., and Quarantelli, E. (2006). Rising to the challenges of a catastrophe: The emergent and prosocial behavior following Hurricane Katrina. *The Annals of the American Academy of Political and Social Science*, 604 (March), 82–101.

Sayre, A. (2005, August 21). Murder on the rise in the ill-equipped Big Easy. *Pittsburgh Post-Gazette*. Retrieved July 2, 2006 from http://www.postgazette.com/pg/05233/556827.stm.

Scahill, J. (2005, October 10). Blackwater down. *The Nation*. Retrieved October 25, 2006 from http://www.thenation.com/doc/20051010/scahill.

Senate Hearing on Government's Response to Hurricane Katrina.(2006). Retrieved July 2, 2006 from http://www.nytimes.com/2006/02/10/national/nationalspecial/10katrina-transcript.html?ex=1161921600&en=82386fe2c0ba56d7&ei=5070.

Shane, S., and Lipton, E. (2005, September 3). Government saw flood risk but not levee failure. *The New York Times*, pp. A1, A16.

Sklansky, D. (2006). Private police and democracy. *The American Criminal Law Review*, 43(1), 89–105.

Steinberg, T. (2000). *Acts of God*. New York: Oxford University Press.

Tierney, K., Bevc, C., and Kuligowski, E. (2006). Metaphors matter: Disaster myths, media frames, and their consequences in Hurricane Katrina. *The Annals of the American Academy of Political and Social Science*, 604 (March), 57–81.

Treaster, J. (2005, August 31). Life-or-death words of the day in a battered city: "I Had to Get Out." *The New York Times*, p. A12.

Treaster, J., and Sontag, D. (2005, September 2). Despair and lawlessness grip New Orleans as thousands remain stranded in squalor, *The New York Times*, p. A1.

U.S. House of Representatives. (2006). *A failure of initiative. A final report of the Select Bipartisan Committee to Investigate the Preparation for and Response to Hurricane Katrina.* (H.R. Report 109-377). Washington, D.C.: U.S. Government Printing Office.

Updates as they come in on Katrina. Retrieved October 24, 2006 from http://www.wwltv.com/local/stories/WWLBLOG.ac3fcea.html.

Villmoare, A. & Stillman, P. (2010, forthcoming). Civic culture and the politics of planning for neighborhoods and housing in post-Katrina New Orleans. In Hackler, M., (Ed.) *Culterin the Wake: Rhetoric and Reinvention on the Gulf Coast.* Jackson: University of Mississippi Press.

Voices in the storm. (2005, September 9). *The Nation.* Retrieved October 24, 2006 from http://www.thenation.com/doc/20050926/chronicle.

Washing away. (2002, June 23–27). *New Orleans Times-Picayune.* Retrieved September 17, 2005 from http://www.nola.com/hurricane/?/washing away/.

Wolfe, Alan. (2006). Why conservatives can't govern. Retrieved July 2, 2006 from http://www.washingtonmonthly.com/features/2006/0607.wolfe.html.

Chapter 20

Whose City Is It?
Public Housing, Public
Sociology, and the Struggle for
Social Justice in New Orleans
before and after Katrina

John D. Arena

We finally cleaned up public housing in New Orleans. We couldn't do it, but God did.

> —Congressman Richard Baker, on
> Hurricane Katrina's "silver lining"
> (as cited in Babington, 2005, p. 4)

We're warriors. We're strong and we're going to fight until the end, until we get back our homes and our neighborhood.

> —Sharon Jasper, St. Bernard public housing
> development resident (personal interview,
> New Orleans, June 2006)

Sociology will continue to matter little politically if we accept this status quo, if we do not seek to reach beyond the shrinking circles of interested publics, and if we do not grow beyond our narrow academic roles as writers and teachers to also become shapers of the societies we study.

> —Paul Lachelier (2003, p. 5)

The impact of Hurricane Katrina on New Orleans has been a contradictory affair. On one level, for the city's working-class, overwhelmingly black, majority, the natural disaster has been turned into a human tragedy. The lack of any serious evacuation and emergency preparedness plans, by any level of government, meant the poorest and most vulnerable segments of the New

Orleans community were abandoned to horrendous conditions in the Super-dome and Convention Center, left to die in their homes, or drown in flood waters. If it had not been for the many initiatives that people took on their own to save and assist those in need, the death toll of over 1,500 in New Orleans and Louisiana would have been much higher. These numerous courageous acts included the ingenuity of young men in New Orleans' St. Bernard public housing development who commandeered fishing boats to ferry people from the development to the nearby interstate overpass (Irving, personal interview, 2006; Jasper, personal interview, 2006). Not only residents, but people from the surrounding neighborhoods sought refuge in the "bricks," the sturdy 1940s built development, which withstood the storm and provided shelter for many people. Ironically, these and other "anachronistic," "dysfunctional," public housing developments that stood out as life preservers for people abandoned by the government's non-existent "homeland security," are now scheduled for demolition by the federal government's Department of Housing and Urban Development.

Federal, state, and local officials not only provided very little help for residents, but *they actually blocked attempts to bring aid into the city in the immediate aftermath of the hurricane.* As Ryland Dodge of the Red Cross acknowledged on September 3, five days after the storm hit, "We are not in New Orleans ... The federal Department of Homeland Security has basically told us they don't want us, our Red Cross folks, in New Orleans because our presence would keep people from evacuating" (Geller, 2005, p. 1). Indeed, National Guard troops and New Orleans police worked to enforce this edict, by blocking aid from arriving, including a caravan of buses organized by Houston school district bus drivers (Bayer, 2005; Red Cross, 2005). In addition, police and sheriffs from neighboring Jefferson Parish set up a roadblock on the Mississippi River Bridge and fired upon evacuees, mainly black New Orleans residents, seeking an escape route through the unflooded "West Bank" of the metropolitan area (Bradshaw & Slonsky, 2005; Brown, 2006).

When the Department of Homeland Security (DHS), and its ineffectual Federal Emergency Management Agency (FEMA) finally responded with buses for evacuation, they further added to the trauma people had faced by splitting families up and treating them as criminals. Local activist Malcolm Suber (2005) recounted the harrowing experience people faced at the convention center and Superdome when help finally arrived:

> Men and women, husbands and wives, mothers and children, brothers and sisters, were split up. When you got on the bus, you didn't know where you were going. They had officers with guns and soldiers with guns on the bus. They wouldn't let you get off the bus. If you said, "my child is out there," they wouldn't let you get off the bus. And you thought, "at least they're in the bus behind me, they'll meet me at

the next city." But when those busses left New Orleans they went in every direction. Our people are split up all over this country. (p. 1)

For those who remained in the city, officials tried to make life unbearable. The police and military, as mentioned, blocked aid from reaching the city. By September 2, and especially with the mandatory evacuation order *by force* signed by Mayor Nagin on September 6, the police (with local forces now strengthened by police units from around the country) and military began threatening and forcing residents out of the city, especially the poor (Howells, personal interview, 2005). As New Orleans 9th Ward resident Wallace Shelton explained, "They forced us out by gunpoint,"

> They took us to the airport by gunpoint on a bus. At the airport they put us on a plane for Knoxville. They did not say where we were going, only knew when we landed and saw the signs at the airport. Sometimes the National Guard would give you water, but even they were told to not give us water. The out of town cops terrorized us. They just assumed that if you were in town you were a looter.

(Personal interview, 2005)

Now, one year after the storm, over half of New Orleans' pre-Katrina population of 460,000, 70 percent of whom were African American, remains in exile (Quigley, 2006). The fact that a large portion of the city has not returned does not seem to be a problem for the city's political and economic leadership, who are not experiencing the trauma of being "internally displaced persons"—the official term used under international law. Authorities are not putting out a welcome mat for the poor and working class, particularly the black working-class people, who called the city home and provided New Orleans with its unique character and culture. Indeed, in the aftermath of the hurricane, ruling elites in New Orleans, Baton Rouge and Washington have seized upon the hurricane to undertake a systematic dismantling and privatization of public services, from housing to schools, and from hospitals to city government, to ensure that the black working-class majority does not return. Furthermore, this remaking of New Orleans along orthodox, neoliberal lines, that is, the lifting of all control over private profit making and protections for the working class, is seen as a model that can be exported to promote such "reform" in the rest of the country. Thus, what happens to New Orleans has enormous implications for people across the country.

This opportunity to remake New Orleans is the "silver lining" that many politicians, think tanks, and real estate and other corporate interests, are referring to when they talk about Katrina. As the former director of the city's planning department explained, Katrina was "... horrible because of the destruction ... and the lives that are being blasted apart. *But it also offers a chance to think about things that in the past were unthinkable*" (as cited in Carr & Meitrodt, 2005, p. 1). James Reiss, a leader of the New Orleans Business Council, elaborated to a Wall Street Journal reporter—only a week after the storm, and before floodwaters had even receded—on what the "unthinkable" meant:

> Those who want to see this city rebuilt want to see it done in a completely different way: demographically, geographically and politically. I'm not just speaking for myself here [but other powerful interests].

(as cited in Cooper, 2005, p. 5)

Purging the city of the poor, turning former working class neighborhoods into "green spaces," privatizing public services and breaking public sector unions are the demographic, geographic, and political changes to which Cooper was referring. Louisiana's Republican U.S. Senator, David Vitter, outlined the benefits that could be accrued from the disaster with regard to health care.

> Ironically, we have a unique opportunity because of the enormity of the destruction, the enormity of the loss ... to discard the creaky New Deal era medicine [in Louisiana] that should long ago have been discarded.

(as cited in Varney, 2006, p. 7)

Douglas J. Besharov, a researcher at the right-wing American Enterprise Institute, went beyond Reiss' and Vitter's visions, and saw national implications: "If there is a silver lining in this tragedy it is that it is creating an atmosphere to try new approaches to ending long-term poverty" (as cited in Editorial Board, 2005, p. 1). In translation, this means Katrina has created an opportunity for the government to address poverty by eliminating programs that serve the poor and working-class people, while privatizing public services ranging from schools to hospitals. These "opportunities" have not only been identified by right-wing think tanks, such as the Heritage Foundation and the Cato Institute; liberals have also joined the chorus. For example Bruce Katz of the Brookings Institute's metropolitan division, along with a list of prominent liberal academics, particularly sociologists, including William Julius Wilson, Todd Gitlin, Alejandro Portes, and Herbert Gans, among others, have called on the government to use reconstruction as a way to break up concentrated poverty. This, as we will see, was the same rationale given for the federal government's HOPE VI reform of public housing that drove thousands of, mostly black, families from valuable central cities properties across the country. This same canard of attacking poverty is being used to justify permanently closing the city's public housing developments, and keeping the poor from to returning to the city.[1]

In the face of the elite agenda, a grassroots struggle, of which public housing residents have been central, has emerged in New Orleans to promote a popular, anti-racist, anti-neoliberal, pro-working-class reconstruction effort.

---

1. For an excellent critique of the pernicious role of liberal academicians in legitimating the destruction of public housing, see Reed & Steinberg's (2006) article, "Liberal bad faith in the wake of Hurricane Katrina."

The focus of this paper is documenting, in part, this movement, and my own role, as a sociologist. That is, from this concrete case, I identify, within a geographic and historical context, the obstacles and possibilities of using sociology to promote social justice. In this paper I analyze a multiracial, grass roots movement that emerged prior to Katrina to challenge a key component of the local neoliberal agenda—the privatization of the Iberville public housing development. In this analysis I highlight my own involvement in the struggle for the city to identify ways sociologists and other academic workers can link research and activism. I situate this discussion within the theory and practice of "public sociology" (Burawoy, 2005) or what others call "liberation sociology" (Feagin & Vera, 2001). I draw on my own experience in this movement to highlight the possibilities, and obstacles, of using sociological knowledge, and "organic sociology," to promote racial and economic justice. I conclude the section and paper by highlighting the insights this case provides on the possibilities for pursuing social justice through sociology and, more generally, the larger anti-racist, social justice issues that are at stake in the reconstruction of New Orleans.

What Is Public Sociology?

U.S. sociology, over the last few years, has had an extensive debate over what "public sociology" is and whether it should be a part of the discipline.[2] During their terms as presidents of the American Sociological Association, in 2000 and 2004, prominent sociologists Joe Feagin and Michael Burawoy both used their positions of power to promote this debate and advocate in favor of a *public* sociology—one that plays an active role in identifying, addressing, and taking action to address social injustices and problems faced by oppressed peoples. Feagin (2001), in his presidential address, emphasized the legitimacy of a public, social justice-oriented sociology, by placing the discussion in a historical context. He argued that the linking of social justice and sociology is what animated the early founders of American sociology in the 19th and early 20th century. W.E.B. DuBois, Jane Addams, Albion Small, Charlotte Perkins Gilman, and Ida Wells-Barnett, and other early sociologists employed innova-

---

2. The journals *Social Problems* (February 2004), *Social Forces* (June 2004), *Critical Sociology* (Summer 2005), *The American Sociologist* (Fall/Winter 2005), and the *British Journal of Sociology* (September 2005) dedicated issues to the discussion and debates surrounding public sociology. In addition, *Footnotes*, the newsletter of the American Sociological Association developed a column on public sociology. Further underscoring its importance, increasingly sociology departments, as reflected in the job descriptions posted on the ASA job bank website, are requesting job candidates with expertise in this area.

tive sociological research methods, while, at the same time, undertaking studies with the aim of "significantly reducing or eliminating societal injustice … such as the oppression of women, black Americans, the poor, and immigrants" (Feagin, 2001, p. 6). Yet, by the 1920s and 1930s, this activist sociology was being marginalized by a self-proclaimed "value-free," detached variety. In practice this really meant that sociology and sociologists became "increasingly linked [to] the interests of certain corporate-capitalist elites, such as those represented by the Rockefeller foundation" (Feagin, 2001, p. 8). Yet, it is important to emphasize that although supporters and practitioners of critical, public, sociology have historically faced many obstacles, they have, nonetheless, periodically challenged the hegemony of the corporate-oriented, state-serving, practice of sociology.

The early and mid 2000s seems to be another period when corporate sociology is being challenged. Indeed, while it has its detractors (see Nielsen, 2004; Pock, 2000; Tucker, 1999) many sociologists and departments profess their support of public sociology and identify it as part of their mission and work. Nonetheless, there are still differences over what it encompasses and how it should be practiced. Burawoy (2005), in his elaboration of public sociology, argued there are two types. One is what he called "traditional public sociology" (p. 7), which involves sociologists who write opinion papers for newspapers on matters of public importance. Another variety is that of the "organic public sociologist" who collaborates with local labor, neighborhood, immigrant rights, or other grass root organizations in support of agendas developed through "dialogue, a process of mutual education" (p. 8). The two types are not antagonistic, but, ideally, compliment one another. For example, traditional public sociology can play an important role, Burawoy argued, in helping inform and frame a sociologist's collaboration with a grass roots group, while the organic variety can help to contribute, deepen and inform the traditional. The ultimate goal is to bring theory and practice together.

While a strong advocate of public sociology, Burawoy was also diplomatic. He did not see it as the only form of sociological labor, nor should or can it be, from his perspective, for the discipline to flourish. The other necessary components of his Durkheimian "division of sociological labor" are the policy, professional and critical components. Each has its own audience and knowledge—that is, like public sociology, they address the questions of knowledge for *whom* and *what*. Policy sociology involves sociologists providing solutions to problems defined by a client, while the professional variety, directed to those in the discipline, encompasses the development of various research programs. Finally, critical sociology, as he defined it, involves the critique of the research foundations of professional sociology. A famous example of this was C. Wright Mills' 1959 critique of the meaningless, ahistorical, decontextualized, "abstracted empiricism" practiced by much of professional sociology (as cited in, Burawoy, 2005, pp. 9–11).

While recognizing the usefulness of his analysis, some have criticized Buraway for developing a functional, division of labor that does not recognize the contradictions and conflicts between these various forms of sociology. Baiocchi (2005), for example, argued that we need to draw a clearer line between what he calls "critical-public sociology" and other forms of engagement with communities outside the university. He argued there is a long tradition of universities having apolitical, technocratic, "public missions" in the service of applying "scholarly expertise to community problems" (p. 343). In contrast to this type of engagement that is palatable to mainstream liberals and conservatives, he advocated for a critical-public sociology that engages and fosters various publics of oppressed and exploited groups in civil society, not to control them, but in support of their self-determination. While universities often support "civic engagement" with the community, they are increasingly hostile, as the corporatization of the university deepens, to academic workers forging critical connections with groups engaged in ongoing struggles against oppression and exploitation.

Katz-Fishman and Scott (2005) were even clearer about one, the distinctions and contradictions between public and professional sociology, rather than their functional compatibility; two, the constraints placed by the university on practicing public sociology; and three, the need for aspiring public sociologists to "immerse themselves and their analysis in a social practice that embraces struggles and movements" (p. 373). These scholar activists were clear that their "public" was the working class, and their agenda or goal was democratic socialism. This approach contrasted with what Bonilla-Silva (2001, p. 16) called liberal academics, who direct their counsel to the state and corporations to address social problems, in an effort to legitimate, and/or manage the excesses of capitalism. The letter by academics directed to state policy makers in the aftermath of Hurricane Katrina, criticized by Reed and Steinberg (2006) above, would be a good example of this type of liberal academic work. Instead, the public sociology advocated by Katz-Fishman and Scott grounds itself within, and speaks to, the social struggles for fundamental and systemic change. This is the form of public sociology that informed my work around public housing in New Orleans.

Combining Sociology and Social Justice: Research and the Pre-Katrina C3/Hands Off Iberville Campaign

During the 1990s and into the 2000s, then New Orleans Mayor Marc Morial, who now presides as president of the National Urban League, oversaw the destruction of approximately half of New Orleans stock of 14,000 public housing apartments. In the mid 1980s the city's public housing, which encompassed ten conventional developments (mostly two and three-story rowhouses, not high-rises) and collections of smaller apartments, known as "scattered sites," had been home to over 60,000 people, almost all African Americans, comprising approximately 20 percent of the city's black population. In the face of resident calls for improved public housing, job opportunities, and an end to police brutality, the city, working closely with the Clinton administration, responded with demolition and dispersal. Developers, who coveted the valuable property occupied by many public housing developments, lauded this approach. They identified these black public housing communities—that along with other black working class communities, create the culture New Orleans is famous for—as obstacles to expanding tourism.

A case in point is the former St. Thomas public housing development, which had been led by the most combative, and well organized, tenant council in the city. Located along the New Orleans riverfront, and considered an impediment to the expanding tourist industry, the city and local housing authority, using the Clinton administration's ironically entitled HOPE VI grant program, "revitalized" the development by reducing the number of public housing units from 1,500 to under 200. Adding to the misery, biased entrance criteria have made it very difficult for many former residents to return to the limited number of units available. In place of the development, expensive condos and high-end rentals, out of reach for many black working-class residents, were built as part of the redevelopment effort. As in the crushing of a city workers' union drive in 1998, the black political leadership relied on community activists and non-profits to gain the consent of tenant leaders and help sell the downsizing (Arena, 2003). While hundreds of poor black families lost homes and were removed from the center of the city, white developers reaped tens of millions in profits, and government subsidies, from the class and ethnic cleansing of the St. Thomas (Arena, forthcoming).

Academic, or what Burawoy (2005) would call "policy" sociology, had a central part to play in this tragedy, not only in New Orleans, but all across the U.S., from Chicago, to Washington to Miami, where HOPE VI was used to push out long-established black and Latino communities from public housing. The Clinton administration, and local authorities, invoked the work of renowned sociologist, and former American Sociological Association president, William Julius Wilson, to justify the HOPE VI, public housing reform initiative, as an antipoverty one. Below Adolph Reed (2002) provided a trenchant criticism of how Wilson's work, which was invoked by many other sociologists in support of downsizing public housing, was used to legitimate a new round of 1990s, post-civil rights era "Negro removal,"

> In fact, the HOPE VI program, the main vehicle that Clinton's Department of Housing and Urban Development used to displace poor people from inner-city locations attractive to developers, has drawn its perverse legitimation as an antipoverty strategy largely from Wil-

son's [work] … *The Chicago Housing Authority explicitly cited Wilson as justification for its plan to displace residents from the Cabrini-Green low-income housing project and raze the site for construction of upscale housing. Other housing authorities, and even private developers, evoke his formulations in their proposals.* Just as "blight" and "slum clearance" sanitized the destruction of poor people's housing as humane social policy under urban renewal a half-century earlier, Wilson's "concentrated poverty" and "isolation effects" now provide similar rhetorical lubricant for a yet more concerted and more surgically extensive effort to remove poor people from desirable central city locations and to replace them with upper-income occupancies. (p. 170, emphasis added)

I chose the HOPE VI-funded "redevelopment" of the St. Thomas public housing development as my dissertation topic to, in part, draw greater public attention to what I saw as a huge racial and class injustice. In addition, I wanted to identify insights from this case to improve the political practice of grass roots social movements opposing modern forms of racial and class cleansing. Sooner than I thought, an opportunity to apply my knowledge presented itself.

As I conducted my doctoral research and writing on St. Thomas, I began to notice how the same social forces, tactics, and legitimation used to destroy the development were also being employed to "redevelop" another strategically placed public housing community: the 850 apartments of the Iberville public housing development, which sit next to the historic French Quarter. Iberville had been the location of the famous Storyville red light district, and in the early 1940s the area was condemned and converted to a segregated, white-designated, public housing development. It was de-segregated beginning in 1965. With the raging real estate market, condominium conversion of the surrounding area, and the continued expansion of tourism, developers were openly stating their plans to "redevelop" this black community of almost 2000 people in 2004 and 2005 (Eggler, 2004; Thomas, 2004, 2005).

I faced a dilemma. I needed to finish my dissertation, but I clearly saw that the knowledge and insights I had garnered from my study of the St. Thomas could be useful in forging an effective opposition to the destruction of the Iberville development. This was an opportunity to, as sociologist Paul Lachelier (2003) stated above, go beyond my narrow academic role to use my knowledge to become a "shaper of society." The case also underscored the political decisions that are embedded in every step of the research process. From the questions that scholars ask, to the concepts, theories and methods we employ, to the funding we receive, to, importantly, how our knowledge is—or is not—applied, involves political choices and implications (Becker & Horowitz, 1972, pp. 51, 63). In this case, not doing anything was with my knowledge also political. I decided to act.

My sociologically informed political intervention began by engaging the local anti-war group in New Orleans, C3—Community, Concern, Compassion— which emerged in the aftermath of September 11 attacks to oppose any attack on Afghanistan, and later became the leading group in the city organizing protests against intervention in Iraq. In January 2005, in collaboration with another local activist, Mike Howells, I made an argument, at the regular C3 weekly meeting, to build an alliance with Iberville residents to oppose the destruction of their community. Drawing from critiques of new social movement theory that sociologists have made, I argued that conceiving of our movement as simply a post-materialist peace movement was wrong and limited our growth. I argued the war, and the movement against it, was part of a deeply racialized class struggle, on various levels—including how it dealt with allocations of the federal budget. Furthermore, in a majority black city, with enormous racial injustice, it was absurd not to have a predominately white peace group address the racist war that was also going on in our very own community. The attempt to take the land and homes of the Iberville community was a prime example, and indeed, paralleled what the U.S. imperialist state was doing in Iraq. We had to reframe our movement, and make a concrete connection between the war abroad and at home. Some were unhappy with the transformation, and stopped attending, but, as I will discuss, our movement, unlike many other anti-war groups at the time, actually grew and became more racially diverse, and working class.

Drawing from my research on the St. Thomas case, I knew we could not simply meet with the Iberville tenant council to propose an alliance. Locally and nationally developers, housing authorities, and HUD have co-opted official tenant councils, and non-profit organizations and leaders, to sign off on HOPE VI and other redevelopments to consensually introduce downsizing and privatization. Underscoring this role, the president of the Iberville tenant council, as our movement developed, actually monitored the residents entering the building where our meetings were held! To get around the obstacle of the official representation structure we used leafleting to contact and work with residents who were unhappy and wanted to fight back. We were able to acquire use of a community center a few blocks from the development for our meetings, which made it convenient for residents. Our organizing efforts were facilitated by the fact that residents lived in one location—indeed, this is one of the agendas behind breaking up public housing, to destroy a structure that facilitates political mobilization.

At the first meeting we decided on a new name—C3/Hands Off Iberville. This was chosen for two reasons. First, it expressed our theoretical outlook, which argued for a connection between the two fronts of the war—at home and abroad. Second, the confrontational name—*Hands Off* Iberville—drew from the lessons of St. Thomas. The key to a politically successful privatization was to suppress the real class and racial power lines and interests that were involved in redevelopment. The white corporate leaders, and the black political functionaries, of the local black urban regime, who were pushing for Iberville's excision, wanted to mask the real issues at stake. The name we forged was a pre-emptive strike at this effort; to forge a racialized class justice polarization model, rather than one of collaboration. Thus, in a collective effort, we attempted what Burawoy (2005, p. 8) saw as a key part of public sociology—to define the "publics" that public sociology seeks to address. In opposition to both the narrow white peace movement, and the equally narrow exponents of identity politics that advocate for oppressed groups to organize separately, we defined our movement and public as those committed to an anti-racist, anti-imperialist, inter-racial, working class movement.

Our first public demonstration was on February 12, 2005, just after Mardi Gras, when political activity again became possible in the city. The action was held at the edge of the development, and was aimed at breaking down the deeply racialized barrier, the "wall" as Mike Howells called it, between the Iberville and other segments of the working class. Incessant media coverage of violence and danger when referring to Iberville and other developments, of hailing one police "strike force" after another and harassing residents, was part of the strategy to demonize and destroy the community. Our racially integrated protest, held at the development, was about reversing that image and constructing new space—one of solidarity. While reaffirming this black working class community, and their control of the land, we also showed, by our presence, that the community was not isolated either. The event, which was the top story on all the local television stations, allowed us to deliver a clear message that we wanted to maintain Iberville as a public housing development and oppose the loss of even one apartment. In fact we called for rebuilding the 7,000 public housing apartments lost over the previous ten years. A indication of the action's impact was that a local black newsweekly emblazoned the front page of their issue following the protest with the headline, which took up the whole page, "*Hands Off Iberville, The Community Strikes Back*" (Haddad, 2005). Through this action we effectively broke through the ruling class' framing of public housing reform, peddled by leading sociologists, that it must be redeveloped into "mixed income" communities—that is, the new post-civil rights code language for class and ethnic cleansing (Bonilla-Silva, 2001).

Following our initial protest we continued our aggressive actions, and weekly meetings, whose attendance was significantly larger than when we dealt only with anti-war issues. We achieved our first concrete victory at the end of June 2005, less than two months before Katrina, when, at the public hearing on the Housing Authority of New Orleans' (HANO) annual plan, we successfully defeated a HOPE VI redevelopment application for Iberville. We began preparing for the event weeks earlier after we obtained a report that the housing authority had released to the city in October 2004, which proposed downsizing the development from 850 to only 200 public housing apartments

(HANO, 2004). This occurred in a city with a waiting list of 14,000 families for public housing, and one where black working class families were increasingly being driven from the city center (Filosa, 2005a). The downsizing was to be part of creating a new "mixed-income" development, in a purported effort to replace "concentrated poverty." C3/Hands Off Iberville mobilized for the June 30 hearing, where we denounced the plans. Consistent with our agenda of unmasking the real power relationships of the city, we showed how HANO's "scheme"—the term we employed—mirrored those presented by a wealthy developer, and his chief lobbyist, former Mayor Barthelemy, to city officials the year before. I helped obtained the minutes of this meeting through a public records request, a process I learned about while collecting data for my dissertation. HANO later revoked its plans, with the agency's HUD overseer, Carmen Valenti, apologizing, saying it was an error to include Iberville as a HOPE VI candidate, adding, "… it should never have been include in the agency's plans. It caused some embarrassment" (Filosa, 2005b, p. 1).

Katrina: The Empire Strikes Back; Movements Respond

The hurricane, and the state's response to it, not only disrupted communities, but also disrupted pre-existing social movements. Indeed, the state's seemingly inept response can be seen, drawing from social movement theory, as a social control response to undermine social movements and working class power, and clear the way for its political, economic, social and spatial reorganization plans. Soon after the hurricane, as the Wall Street Journal reported, the ruling elite were taking advantage of the opportunities mass expulsion provided to hatch and implement far reaching restructuring plans (Cooper, 2005). With regard to Iberville, developer Pres Kabacoff, who led the St. Thomas privatization, was already floating plans for the development before the floodwaters had even receded (Branston, 2006).

C3/Hands Off Iberville opposed the implementation of these blueprints but we had faced a setback since so many public housing residents, and supporters, had been displaced. Although apartments in the Iberville had not been flooded, everyone, due to lack of support from authorities, was forced out. Also, almost all our non-public housing members, except Mike Howells who lived in the French Quarter and was one of the successful, non-uptown elite "holdouts," were now part of the New Orleans diaspora. Yet, by the end of September, when some—not the Lower 9th Ward nor public housing—residents were officially allowed back in to their homes, C3/Hands Off Iberville was preparing a response to what was clearly, even early on, an attempt to use the hurricane to destroy public housing and permanently expel residents.

Our response was a two-pronged, strategic one. First, we—myself and other C3 members—attempted to contact residents to get them back into the area, anyway we could, and re-build the movement, while using various venues to denounce, expose and oppose what was happening. Second, movement activists worked to inform progressive forces nationally and globally about what was happening in New Orleans and build solidarity with our struggle. On the ground, locally, as part of this response, the first action we took was to counter the claims that the Iberville and the other public housing developments had, as HANO claimed, and *Times Picayune* writers repeated, been "ruined" (Filosa & Russell, 2005, p. 1). We took pictures to show that floodwaters had not entered the Iberville and very little flooding had affected the nearby Lafitte projects. Furthermore, we documented how other developments such as the St. Bernard, C.J. Peete, and B.W. Cooper, which encompassed over 3,000 badly needed, rent-controlled units, faced only flooding on their first floors and were in much better condition than most of the city's private housing stock, of which approximately 110,000, out of 180,000 units, were seriously flooded (Bullard & Harden, 2005). At the first post-Katrina HANO board meeting in October, we presented evidence to show that most units had not been damaged and, in other cases, were not beyond repair. Speakers at the hearing denounced, as examples of racial/ethnic and class cleansing, and violations of international law, attempts to use the hurricane as a pretext to destroy public housing.

While making these public attacks, C3/Hands Off Iberville activists also began trying to contact residents, by telephone calls, and Internet postings. In fact, many Iberville residents, despite HANO's official policy of keeping their homes off limits, took direct action and returned to their homes, even though they were without electricity. In December C3/Hands Off Iberville, along with a broader coalition, NO-HEAT, which the aid group Common Ground participated in, organized a protest at the development to demand that it be re-opened. I, along with other leading activists, also wrote extensively—a form of traditional public sociology—to national and local audiences, about this struggle and its political significance, to garner support. The local indymedia site, Z-Net, and various email listservs, were used to inform people about what was happening, to invite us to speak, and to encourage activists to come to New Orleans, not to aid in the gutting of homes, but to help build a movement. This focus, on building a political response, differentiated us from other groups, such as ACORN and even Common Ground, who focused on self-help initiatives, such as repairing homes. In contrast, we argued it was the U.S. state's responsibility to rebuild the city and the whole Gulf Coast. In a piece I wrote for *Z-Net*, the *War at Home*, which was part of a national call to attend the annual Martin Luther King March in the city beginning in the traditional starting point of the devastated Lower 9th Ward that the mayor abandoned, I made an argument which outlined our program. The article included a call for a massive, democratically controlled public works program to rebuild the whole Gulf, and the U.S., arguing that the same social and physical decay the storm exposed in New Orleans actually exists across the country and needs to be addressed. We proposed financing this program by means of ending the war in Iraq and imposing $1 tax on oil companies for every $1 increase in the price of gas or home heating oil that had occurred since the run-up to the Iraq war in 2002.

Even as we built our forces, the ruling class was moving quickly to advance their plans. The state of Louisiana-run Charity Hospital in New Orleans, the largest public hospital in the state with 2,700 beds and a hospital that cared for 90 percent of those without medical insurance in the metro area, was ordered closed, and was declared by Director Don Smithburg to be "beyond repair." He took this action in September when medical staff, with the help of German engineers, and dozens of military personnel, were successfully pumping out water and cleaning the hospital, which was not badly damaged. Smithburg was surprisingly honest about his goal of using the hurricane to close the hospital, opened in 1939, and the key part of the Charity hospital system created by populist Governor Huey Long in the late 1920s, to privatize healthcare, "We need a new model, less reliant on public dollars, with a new mission—one serving both private and indigent patients. This storm has told us you can't rely on government resources" (as cited in Nossiter, 2005, p. 16).

Next on the hit list were public schools, where the school board fired 7,500 employees in January and summarily broke their union contract. The state of Louisiana then took over 107 of the city's 126 schools; of the 57 being re-opened for the fall 2006, most are being run as privatized charter schools (Ritea, 2006). The Recovery School District that the state has set up to administer these schools is almost all white, has only a ten person staff for some 30,000 students, and as of August 1, 2006 had only hired ten teachers (Hill, 2006)! The public bus service has been restructured, which means that staff were reduced from 1,357 workers to 479 workers, and public transportation is being eliminated in large parts of the city, further guaranteeing that many working-class flooded neighborhoods will not come back. (Regional Transit Authority, 2006).

Public housing was not exempted from, but rather faced the brunt of this attack. Alphonse Jackson, the black secretary of HUD, remarked after the hurricane that New Orleans "was not going to be as black as it was for a long time, if ever again" (as cited in Davis, 2005, n.p.). The policies he has instituted have guaranteed his prophecy would become a reality. He made it clear that the storm would be used to break up the failed policies of "concentrating poverty" in New Orleans' public housing. If they would be rebuilt at all, "St. Thomas would be the model" according to Jackson, which was a guarantee that many poor people would not be able to return home. Mayor Nagin concurred, saying he wanted it "dedensified" along the lines of St. Thomas (Filosa & Russell, 2005). Right-wing forces, unsurprisingly, cheered the reforms. The chancellor of University of New Orleans, Tim Ryan, who for decades has put out position papers backing every and any position of local industry, including opposition to a minimum wage referendum, advised taking "Iberville and make it a retirement community ... [it] has retarded French Quarter growth for 30 years" (as cited in Warner, 2005, p. 1). One unidentified person established a website to collect signatures supporting the closing of all public housing. S/he was joined by leading black politicians and administrators, such as councilman Oliver Thomas who, after residents of the St. Bernard development caravanned in February from Houston to demand their homes be reopened, stated, in reference to black public housing residents, "We don't need soap opera watchers right now ... at some point there has to be a whole new level of motivation, and people have got to stop blaming the government for something they ought to do" (as cited in Varney, 2006, p. 1).

Taking care of a home, in addition to the low-paid jobs that many residents had, did not seem to count for Thomas. Nadine Jarmon, whose consulting company had a generous contract to oversee HANO, chimed in that, "Sometimes you have to not do what's politically correct; you have to do what's right" (as cited in Varney, 2006, p. 5). This advocation of political incorrectness is also a violation of international law, which makes it duty for the government to facilitate the return of displaced residents:

> Competent authorities have the primary duty and responsibility to establish *as well as provide the means*, which allow internally displaced persons to return voluntarily in safety and dignity, to their homes or places of habitual residence, or to resettle voluntarily in another part of the country. *Such authorities shall make efforts to facilitate the reintegration of returned or resettled displaced persons.*
>
> (United Nations, 1998, n.p.)

It was clear that the political leadership, at the behest of powerful economic interests, locally and nationally, would do what it would take, including breaking international law, to prevent the return of public housing residents. Our focus, therefore, by the spring of 2006, was to bring people, many who were displaced in Houston, as well as other cities, including Memphis, Atlanta and Baton Rouge, to protest in the city, and, if they were willing, to re-occupy their homes. Movement activists recognized the need to make transparent the contradiction between the claims of authorities that everyone was welcomed back, and their actions that were blocking former residents' return; between the internal pain people were facing, and the way that exile hid it from public view. In February (2006) we began this effort with a protest at the St. Bernard development, where, in contrast to the media's message, residents made it clear they wanted to come home. An inspiring message by anti-war activist Cindy Sheehan, who attended the event, helped to drive home our message about the two fronts of the war. On April 4, the anniversary of Martin Luther King's assassination, with longtime community activist Endesha Juakali now actively involved, the stakes were raised as residents and activists barged en masse past a police blockade to get into the St. Bernard development and apartments. We were led by a 70-year-old grandmother in her wheelchair, Gloria Irving, who exclaimed, underscoring the dedication of residents, and their attachment to place and community, "I want to come home ... if I have to die, let me die in New Orleans" (Personal Interview, 2006). This event was followed up with a larger rally, on June 3 that led to the emergence of a tent city in front of the development, which garnered national attention while we intensified efforts to re-open all of the apartments at Iberville (Saulny, 2006). Our movement had by then expanded, and C3/Hands Off Iberville was now part of the larger United Front for Affordable Housing.

HUD responded with a tougher line. On June 14 HUD secretary Jackson announced that four developments, that is approximately 5,000 of the city's 7,000 public housing units, would be demolished (NOLAC, 2006). The movement has refused to accept this. The challenge, in the summer of 2006, as we approach the one-year anniversary of the hurricane, is for the movement to make a qualitative advance and be able to re-occupy the apartments designated for demolition. We must make the broader links between the brutal neglect carried out in New Orleans, with most of the city still in ruins, while the imperialist U.S. state spends billions to destroy Iraq. Although the public housing movement has filed a lawsuit to prevent demolition and force reopening, the power of our lawyers will only be as strong as the movement we can build on the streets. We encourage those that want to build what Feagin and Vera (2001) called a "sociology of liberation" to support us in these efforts. Yet, as Howard Zinn (1982) argued, this will involve confronting the controls of the academy.

> There is a form of control operating in the university which is more insidious than governmental control. I am speaking of self-censorship, self-control, where the interests of the state, of the great corporations are internalized by the academy itself: its administration, its faculty, its students. That is the most effective form of control, because it takes on the appearance of freedom, even self-determination. (p. 14)

In the neoliberal era, when the university is increasingly being harnessed to support the needs of capitalism, including the dismantling of social services, the controls that Zinn identified are even stronger. Clearly the U.S. ruling class, although embarrassed internationally by its state's incompetence in the face of this disaster, is nonetheless using the disaster to deepen racist attacks on working people. New Orleans is being used as social laboratory whose "successes" will be exported across the country. The university, as it was before the hurricane, is deeply involved in these attacks. Thus, I would argue, drawing from my experience, that key to building the social justice sociology some in the discipline advocate is for sociologists, as Katz-Fishman and Scott (2005) argued, to immerse themselves in grass roots struggles, particularly those in their communities. We need to engage and participate in, not simply lecture to, the ongoing struggles of the working class. As the late Italian revolutionary Antonio Gramsci (1971) stated, this is part of becoming a true intellectual:

> The intellectual's error consists in believing that one can know without understanding and even more without feeling and being impassioned (not only for knowledge in itself but also for the object of knowledge): in other words that the intellectual can be an intellectual (and not a pure pedant) if distinct and separate from the people-nation, that is without feeling the elementary passions of the people, understanding them and therefore explaining and justifying them in the particular historical situation and connecting them dialectically to the laws of history and to a superior conception of the world, scientifically and coherently elaborated ... (p. 418)

References

Arena, J. (2003). Race and hegemony: The neoliberal transformation of the black urban regime and working class resistance. *American Behavioral Scientist*, 47(3), 352–380.

————. (Forthcoming). *Bringing the black working class into urban change: Race, Class, and Neoliberalism.* Ph.D. Dissertation. New Orleans: Tulane University.

Babington, C. (2005, September 10). Some GOP legislators hit jarring notes in addressing Katrina. *Washington Post*, p. A4.

Baiocchi, G. (2005). Interrogating connections: From public criticism to critical publics in Burawoy's public sociology. *Critical Sociology*, 31(3), 339–352.

Bayer, A. (2005, October 22). Bush administration blocks arrival of buses to New Orleans. Speech Delivered at *Commission of Inquiry on Crimes Against Humanity Committed by the Bush Administration*, New York City. Retrieved December 10, 2006 from http://www.freespeech.org/videodb/index.php?action=detail&video_id=10456&browse=1.

Becker, H, & Horowitz, I. (1972). Radical politics and sociological research: Observations on methodology and ideology. *American Journal of Sociology*, 78, 48–66.

Bonilla-Silva, E. (2001). *White supremacy & racism in the post civil rights era.* Boulder: Lynne Reinner.

Bradshaw, L. & Slonsky, L. (2005, September 5). Trapped in New Orleans. *Counterpunch.* Retrieved August 8, 2006 from http://www.counterpunch.org/bradshaw09062005.html.

Branston, J. (2006, May 10). Under development: Eight months after Katrina, big problems—and a few opportunities—confront the Gulf Coast and New Orleans. *Memphis Flyer Online*. Retrieved August 8, 2006 from http://www.memphisflyer.com/memphis/Content?oid=oid%3A15616.

Brown, M. (2006, August 5). Bridge blockade goes to grand jury. *Times Picayune*, p. A1.

Bullard, R. & Harden, M. (2005, November 10). *Will "greening" the Gulf Coast after Katrina hurt or help blacks?* Retrieved December 10, 2006 from http://www.ejrc.cau.edu/greeningafterkatrina.html.

Burawoy, M. (2005). Presidential address: For public sociology. *American Sociological Review*, 70(1), 1–28.

Carr, M. & Meitrodt, J. (2005, December 25). What will New Orleans look like five years from now? *Times Picayune*, p. A1.

Cooper, C. (2005, September 8). Old-line families plot the future. *Wall Street Journal*, p. A1.

Davis, M. (2005, October 25) Gentrifying disaster: New Orleans: Ethnic cleansing, GOP style. *Mother Jones*. Retrieved December 10, 2006 from http://www.motherjones.com/commentary/columns/2005/10/gentrifying_disaster.html.

Editorial Board. (2005, September 19). Tax cuts to continue, social programs to be slashed in wake of Hurricane Katrina. World Socialist Web Site. Retrieved September 19, 2005 from http://www.wsws.org/articles/2005/sep 2005/hurr-s19.shtml.

Eggler, B. (2004, March 1). Sweeping overhaul outlined for Canal. *Times Picayune*, p. B1.

Feagin, J. (2001). Social justice and sociology: Agendas for the twenty-first century. *America Sociological Review*, 66(1), 1–20.

Feagin, J. & Vera, H. (2001). *Liberation sociology*. Cambridge: Westview Press.

Filosa, G. (2005a, July 1). HANO says it has no plans to demolish the Iberville complex. *Times Picayune*, p. B1.

———. (2005b, July 28). Iberville stays, HANO chief says. *Times Picayune*, p. B1.

Filosa, G. F. & Russell, G. (2005, October 9). Faltering safety net. *Times Picayune*, p. B1.

Geller, A. (2005, September 3). Katrina donations top $200 million. Semissourian.com. Retrieved August 5, 2006 from http://www.semissourian.com/story/1116552.html.

Gramsci, A. (1971). *Selections from the prison notebooks*. New York: International Publishers.

Haddad, J. (2005, March 12). Hands off Iberville. *Data*, p. 1.

Hill, L. (2006, July 31). Ten staff for 30,000 students in New Orleans. *Hill listserv update on educational justice in New Orleans.* In possession of author.

Howells, M.(2005). Personal Interview.

Housing Authority of New Orleans. (2004, October). *2005–2012 Long range plan for renovation and redevelopment.* New Orleans: Housing Authority of New Orleans.

Irving, G. (2006, April 2). Personal Interview.

Jasper, S. (2006, April 1). Personal Interview.

Katz-Fishman, W. & Scott, J. (2005). Comments on Burawoy: A view from the bottom-up. *Critical Sociology*, 31(3), 371–374.

Lachelier, P. (2003). On the modern division of labor. *From the Left, The Marxist Sociology Newsletter of the American Sociological Association*, 24(2), 7–9.

Nielsen, F. (2004). The vacant "we": Remarks on public sociology. Social Forces, 82(4), 1603–1618.

New Orleans Legal Assistance Corporation (NOLAC). (2006, June 28). *Public housing issues facing New Orleans.* New Orleans: New Orleans Legal Assistance Corporation.

Nossiter, A. (2005, December 17). Dispute over historic hospital for the poor pits doctors against the state. *New York Times*, p. A16.

Pock, J. (2000, February). No ASA in 2000. Footnotes. Retrieved January 30, 2007 from http://www2.asanet.org/footnotes/feb00/pf.html.

Quigley, B. (2006). Trying to make it home: New Orleans one year after Katrina. *Common Dreams.* Retrieved January 10, 2006 from http://www.commondreams.org/views06/0822-31.htm.

Red Cross. (2005, September 2). *Hurricane Katrina: Why the Red Cross is not in New Orleans.* Retrieved March 15, 2006 from http://www.redcross.org/faq/0,1096,0_682_4524,00.html.

Reed, A.(2002). America becoming—what exactly?: Social policy research as the fruit of Bill Clinton's race initiative. *New Politics*, 8(4), 165–173.

Reed, A. & Steinberg, S. (2006, May 4). Liberal bad faith in the wake of Hurricane Katrina. Retrieved December 16, 2006 from http://www.zmag.org/content/showarticle.cfm?ItemID=10205.

Regional Transit Authority. (2006, July 27). *Restructuring the RTA.* New Orleans: Regional Transit Authority.

Ritea, S. (2006, August 5). Schools to help confused parents. *Times Picayune*, p. B1.

Saulny, S. (2006, June 6). Residents clamoring to come home to projects in New Orleans. *New York Times*, p. A14.

Shelton, W. (2005, October 1). Personal Interview.

Suber, M. (2005, October 10). Text of speech given at New York conference. *Workers World*. Retrieved March 15, 2006 from http://www.workers.org/ 2005/us/wwp-forum-1103.

Thomas, G. (2004, November 19). Local developer floats plan to redo Iberville complex. *Times Picayune*, p. A1.

———. (2005, March 16). Big changes in store. *Times Picayune*, p. C1.

Tucker, J. (1999, November). Politics and the ASA. *Footnotes*, p. 5.

United Nations. (1998). *U.N. guiding principles on internal displacement, Section V, Principle 28*. Retrieved January 17, 2007 from http://www.brook. edu/fp/projects/idp/gp_page.htm.

Varney, J. (2006, February 21). HANO only wants working tenants. *Times-Picayune*, p. A1.

Warner, C. (2005, November 3). UNO moves to revive campus. *Times-Picayune*, p. B1.

Zinn, H. (1982). *Academic freedom: Collaboration and resistance*. Cape Town: University of Cape Town.

Chapter 21

Redistribution of Responsibility: The Gendered Division of Labor and Politics of a Post-Disaster Clean-Up Project

Emmanuel David

Introduction

In the years since Hurricane Katrina, there has been a great deal of social science research and critical commentary on the racial and class-based inequalities made visible at each stage of the social catastrophe. There also has been a small but critical mass of feminist activists and gender scholars who have argued that Katrina was undeniably a gendered event in ways inseparable from race and class (Enarson, 2005; Gault, Hartmann, De-Weever, Werschkul, & Williams, 2005; Ransby, 2006; Ross, 2005; Seager, 2005).

After nearly two decades of research on the gendered dimensions of disaster, it is no surprise that Hurricane Katrina, like most disasters, was not gender neutral. In the emerging interdisciplinary literature on gender and Hurricane Katrina, scholars have begun to examine women's lived experiences of vulnerability and resilience at various stages of the catastrophe as well as the many structural inequalities based on race, gender, and class that were firmly in place across the U.S. Gulf Coast long before the 2005 storm. Researchers have found that before, during, and after Hurricane Katrina, these pre-existing social conditions made some women (but not all) more vulnerable than men to downward economic mobility, inadequate health care, psychological trauma, strains on parenting responsibilities, sexual and domestic violence, and challenges securing safe and affordable housing (Belkhir & Charlemaine, 2007; Bergin, 2008; Davis & Land, 2007; DeWeever, 2008; DeWeever & Hartmann, 2006; Gault et al., 2005; Jenkins & Phillips, 2008a, 2008b; Laska, Morrow, Willinger,

& Mock, 2008; Litt, 2008; Luft & Griffin, 2008; Mock, 2008; Overstreet & Burch, 2008; Peek & Fothergill, 2008; Willinger & Gerson, 2008).

Some important themes related to women's vulnerability have emerged from this research. For example, the economic consequences were gendered. Prior to Katrina, the women of New Orleans had strong attachments to the full-time labor force, participating at roughly the same rate as women across the nation though earning less (DeWeever & Hartmann, 2006). But following Katrina the earnings and employment opportunities of New Orleans women worsened (Willinger, 2008a), and men's earnings rose while women's fell (Williams et al., 2005). In addition, both gender violence during and after Hurricane Katrina, including domestic violence and rape, and strain experienced by social service providers such as battered women's shelters have been documented (see Brown, 2009; Jenkins & Phillips, 2008a, 2008b; Thornton & Voigt, 2007). Social justice organizations and progressive recovery movements have faced challenges integrating race, class, and gender relations. For example, as documented by Luft (2008), there were difficulties in addressing racism and sexism following reported sexual assaults in a radical community of activists and volunteers.

While these studies point to the many challenges and burdens placed on women, especially low-income women and women of color following Hurricane Katrina, there were signs of hope amidst the widespread devastation. Researchers have also documented women's resilience, capacity building, and socio-political, environmental, and cultural activism (David, 2008; Ransby, 2006; Tyler, 2007; Vaill, 2006; Willinger, 2008b). These studies demonstrate the ways in which women have been, as one scholar predicted, "at the heart of this great city's rebirth and the emotional center of gravity for others on the long road to the 'new normal'" (Enarson, 2005, p. E1). Women's resilience often took shape in a social group context and centered around a group-based politics of collective recovery.

In the storm's aftermath, New Orleans in particular witnessed the rapid and widespread formation of women-led and women-organized groups, which typically drew upon existing social networks and often attempted to cross lines of social difference in pursuit of social, political, and environmental justice (David, 2008; Tyler, 2007). Core concerns of these women's groups during immediate and long-term recovery addressed broad and far-reaching social change efforts, including political reform, environmental justice, women's health and safety, and securing federal appropriations for recovery efforts. All of these efforts reflected women's leadership, creativity, and persistence in responding to structural crises in and around post-Katrina New Orleans.

These interrelated processes—vulnerability and resilience—have become necessary starting points in many scholarly analyses of gender and disaster. Academics and practitioners have made concerted efforts to reframe the "women as victims" image by focusing on women's capacities, strengths, and resources in order to convince decision makers to tap their knowledge and experience.

This process, called gender mainstreaming, ensures that women are full participants in planning for, responding to, and recovering from disaster, and refutes
the popular discourses that portray women as dependent on men and men's
activities during disaster. Yet, this approach to addressing gender inequalities,
while a useful starting point, continues to treat resilience as an end in itself,
while rarely asking what this resilience means for women's lived experiences.
By tapping women's resources, or this reserve army of labor, these efforts may
potentially add to the heavy burden that many women already carry in both
routine and non-routine times. As such, participatory disaster recovery efforts,
which often rely on community-driven projects and engage NGOs and community groups where there is often a high concentration of women, have the
potential to actually increase, rather than relieve, the pressures on women.

As scholars interested in issues of social justice and gender justice, it is necessary that we engage in more nuanced discussions about the multiple and
contradictory functions of women's active participation—of these moments of
resilience—following disaster and the ways in which these activities are linked
to other large scale social forces, market economies, and governance. To do
this, and to do this seriously, we must begin to ask tough questions: Who and
what gets left off the hook when women step in, "resiliently," to pick up the
pieces following disaster? Who absorbs the work and under what conditions?

This chapter is guided by two main goals. First, through a close examination of one women-led emergent group known as Katrina Krewe, which took
to the streets of post-Katrina New Orleans to clear litter, refuse, and storm debris, I add to the gender and disaster archive by providing case-study evidence
of women's active participation in disaster-related activities. By focusing on the
group's collective activities, I demonstrate that women, rather than being pas-
sive or helpless victims fraught with emotion and requiring men's help and
protection, are important agents of social change (Enarson & Morrow, 1998).
In the latter part of the chapter, I use the case of Katrina Krewe as a point of
departure to investigate one example of the gendered division of labor in recovery efforts as well as more general concerns surrounding the catastrophe. I
argue that the conditions that gave rise to the group in the first place are symptomatic of broader social and political processes that have mobilized social justice movements across the globe. These processes include privatization, state
restructuring, and neo-liberal reform projects, all of which have become no-
ticeable components of the social catastrophe known as Hurricane Katrina. I
conclude that these processes rely on the tendency of non-profit groups to ab-
sorb important social and public services, and that this has important material
consequences for women in disaster-stricken areas.

Data on Katrina Krewe are drawn from a variety of sources, including documentary sources and in-depth qualitative fieldwork in New Orleans in the
months following Hurricane Katrina. Twelve interviews were conducted with

members of Katrina Krewe as part of a larger research project on women's participation in Hurricane Katrina recovery efforts. Interviewees were originally selected based on their participation with and/or ties to another women's group, Women of the Storm (see David, 2008, 2009). All of the people in this sub-sample were interviewed in spring of 2006 in the New Orleans metropolitan area, and at the time each interviewee held a position on the Katrina Krewe's Board of Directors or its organizing committee.

The demographics of the interview sample reveal important information about the composition of the group's leadership. With the exception of one woman in her early 50s and another woman in her early 40s, all women in the interview sample were between 37 and 40 years old. The women came from upper-middle class and upper-class backgrounds and all self-identified as white or Caucasian. With the exception of one woman, all were mothers. All had completed college and over half in the sample had completed a master's degree or equivalent. In terms of work, three-fourths reported their primary occupation to be homemakers and housewives, though some were trained in professional fields, law, or academia. The remaining quarter worked as bankers, freelance writers, consultants, administrators, and special projects coordinators. Finally, and especially relevant to this collection on disaster, most women in this sample lived in areas that escaped major flooding during and after Katrina. Together, these factors helped shape the women's goals, activities, and reflections, and are essential for understanding their participation in Katrina recovery efforts.

Unless otherwise noted, all quotations in this chapter are drawn from these interviews, which were digitally recorded and transcribed in their entirety. During my fieldwork, I engaged in several Katrina Krewe cleanups. Thus, my analysis is also informed by participant observation and fieldwork on group activities.

Katrina Krewe: Trash Issues, Street Sweeps, and Debris Clean-Ups

> "You may have heard of them. The Katrina Krewe is a bunch of women — most of whom fall under the newly pejorative category of "Uptown ladies" — who have realized, like we all have, that no one is ever going to clean up this city. Ever. So they decided they will."
>
> — Chris Rose, Columnist, The Times-Picayune
> (January 31, 2006, Living p. 7)

New Orleans had a trash problem before Hurricane Katrina; in a Times-Picayune article after the storm about his confrontation with a litterbug in a convenience store parking lot, columnist Chris Rose reflected on the widespread practice of littering that had plagued the city for decades, "It's almost like litter is part of our heritage." After the hurricane, trash pick-up and removal issues became a central focus of the recovery effort. Contractors and subcontractors swarmed the streets and leaders of the U.S. Army Corps of Engineers described the work as "their mission" (Varney & Moller, 2005, p. A1). Hurricane Katrina left in its wake an estimated 22 million tons of debris in southeast Louisiana, with almost half of that in and around 160,000 damaged or destroyed homes in the New Orleans metropolitan area. The unprecedented quantity of waste, not including 350,000 vehicles and 35,000 fishing boats destroyed by floodwaters, amounted to over three decades worth of trash produced in normal times (Hamilton, 2005). Because many services were spread thin in those early months after the storm, trash collection in post-Katrina New Orleans was sporadic at best. Duties held by trash-removal companies before the storm were taken over by the U.S. Army Corp of Engineers, which awarded multi-million dollar contracts to three or four prime contractors, who in turn distributed the work to 23,000 subcontractors (Hamilton, 2005; Varney & Moller, 2005). Rows upon rows of duct-taped refrigerators waited on the streets to be picked up, rats and flies flourished, and pets and stray animals that died in the flood were deposited in public spaces or remained on roadsides for weeks and sometimes months. A stench permeated the city as decaying food, spoiled meat, and rotting refuse piled up on the curbs and "neutral grounds" (the New Orleans terms for medians), next to and sometimes under mountains of storm debris.

In late November 2005, over two-and-a-half long months after Hurricane Katrina, New Orleans native Becky Zaheri, a 38-year-old white woman and self-identified mother of two by occupation, became frustrated by the mountains of debris that lined the streets of the once-flooded city. Just before the storm, she and her husband had evacuated to Baton Rouge with their children and promptly enrolled them in school there until their New Orleans school re-opened. On the weekends, they would return to New Orleans to check on their home and on the progress of the city's recovery. Zaheri was repeatedly disheartened by the heaps of trash that filled the city. She was not alone in her feelings of frustration with the lack of progress and the minimal social services; in fact, the local newspaper published numerous editorials and letters to the editor about the burgeoning trash problem, and other informal groups were beginning to conduct self-organized trash and debris cleanups, with volunteers ranging in numbers from two dozen to three hundred (Bickford, 2005; Duncan, 2005; Friedman, 2005; Rose, 2005; *The Times-Picayune*, 2005, 2006; Young, 2005).

Zaheri considered not coming back and entertained the idea of permanently moving her family away from New Orleans. It was during a drive back to Baton Rouge that she decided to contact her friends, requesting to meet for a few hours to clean a particularly debris-ridden and litter-scattered street. On November 14, 2005, Zaheri emailed contacts in her address book and asked if they would participate. Both women and men were invited, but it was 15 women who showed up that first day to clean the block in front of one woman's Uptown home, which had received six feet of floodwater. After a few hours, the women were tired and dirty, but nonetheless inspired by their accomplishments. The group agreed to meet again the following week for a similar undertaking in another location, and they decided they would work a few hours every Wednesday morning while their children were in school.

But Zaheri and a few others in the group soon realized that their hard work might be futile. Observing the gradual homecoming of evacuated residents, the members realized that returning neighbors would begin the same process of pitching and dumping the contents of their homes on the curbside. It was at that point that the group, or at least Zaheri, decided that they would focus their next efforts on major thoroughfares connecting neighborhoods across the city to ensure the group's long-term effectiveness. As a result of lessons learned from the inaugural gathering, the second cleanup took place along a well-traveled street just off a major highway. Located on Carrolton Avenue, near the exit ramp from the I-10, one of the major highways that cut through the city, the particular stretch of road was one of the first signs of abandonment and neglect that many residents and visitors witnessed upon reentering New Orleans. In an effort to make the routine returns to the devastated city easier for herself and for other residents and to "lift people's spirits and to give people a sense of hope" in those trying times, the group cleared a section of the major thoroughfare under the I-10 highway and its adjacent streets.

Soon after, the group began meeting twice a week, including a Saturday morning shift for those who couldn't make the cleanups on Wednesdays. By mid-December, the women had recruited others in their social networks, announcements were made on local radio stations, and local press picked up their activities. Strangers began to show up at the cleanups and the group began developing a more formal organizational structure to manage the swell of volunteers. Week after week, the cleanups continued every Wednesday and Saturday from 9:00am to noon.

The group soon took the name, Katrina Krewe (Krewe Aiding in the Trash Removal In the New Orleans Area), filed for 501(c3) status in order to make donations tax exempt (Tyler, 2007), and received sponsorship and donations from companies and organizations like Glad Products, Home Depot, the New Orleans Saints, ESPN, First Bank and Trust, and The Garden Club of Junior League New Orleans.

Soon after its inception, the group began to receive nationwide media attention, including television coverage on CBS, NBC, CNN, print recognition in the Chicago Tribune, Washington Times, and the Los Angeles Times, as well as several appearances on *The Ellen Degeneres Show*. With an organizational structure in place, the group helped manage thousands of volunteers, both

women and men, who converged on the city from across the nation to participate in disaster recovery efforts. Inspired by the group from afar, some came to
New Orleans to work specifically with Katrina Krewe. Others, already in New
Orleans, located the group through its announcements in local media. International donations helped fund these activities, which had previously been
provided out-of-pocket by group members. According to the group's website
(http://www.cleanno.org), over 10,000 volunteers from the city, around the nation, and from the international community participated in Katrina Krewe's
cleanups. In all, volunteers bagged and removed an estimated 250,000 tons of
Katrina storm and flood debris. Zaheri told reporters, "Whatever floated in
those waters and wherever it landed, we were picking it up" (Ritea, 2006, p.
Metro 1). This is a successful case of resilience in disaster, and of both men and
women working under the leadership of strong women.

The group moved outward to various neighborhoods across the city, some
of which experienced more severe flooding and storm damage than others.
This process helped expose workers to the geography of the devastation, especially in the low-income areas. Though it initially formed to take on the monumental task of clearing the streets of storm debris left when floodwaters from
Hurricane Katrina receded, the group had the latent effect of transforming the
women's lives. Some were propelled into leadership positions and gained experience managing large groups of volunteers; one participant composed a
point-of-view article, which was published in the local paper (Downing, 2006)
The work itself was difficult but emotionally rewarding, and the experience of
sifting through debris, through the destroyed remains of those who went
through the disaster, left a lasting impression on the women:

> At the beginning it was like a passion. I couldn't wait. I lived for
> Wednesdays. It felt so good. And it was hard work. In the beginning, I
> would take an Advil before I went. And I exercise. I'm not bench-
> pressing or anything like that, but I'm an active person, and it was
> muscles I really hadn't used before, and you're dragging heavy things.
> Sometimes it's the contents of people homes, sometimes it's just—I
> mean, the first couple days we were finding shoes. Some of it was just
> stuff that had been carried along by the flood. It was before that many
> people had come and starting gutting their homes.

The participant continued to discuss the paradoxes of the work: "It was disgusting stuff. It was stinky and gross, and we loved it." For many participants,
the work was rewarding, in part, because it humanized the disaster and served
as a therapeutic mechanism to deal with the overwhelming sense of collective
loss. On several occasions, participants encountered artifacts that painfully reminded them of the struggles that others endured to survive the flood:

> We found a raft. This was when we did Carrollton. It was right by the
> interstate. It was a raft made out of wood. It had one of those blow-

up mattresses on top of it. It was electrical wire that they had tied onto this wood and they had pulled it, but it was just heart-wrenching that someone was on this raft. We put it against the—(long pause)— hoping it would get picked up, and for a while it didn't. It was just this constant reminder up against there.

Participants were overwhelmed with the collective witnessing of the destruction, and their efforts served to establish a sense of social cohesion. In some circles around the city, they were even dubbed the "Katrina Warriors." One reveled in the newly earned title, "I'm a homemaker-slash-warrior."

Despite feelings of increased solidarity and connection to those who experienced loss, the women felt the work was never-ending and they began to envision a long-term solution to the litter problem. The cycle of accumulation and removal of trash seemed unending and the patchwork gutting of homes meant that cleared streets were soon trashed again; as the debris was hauled away, a new trash pile would inevitably appear on the recently manicured roadways with each newly gutted home. In just a few months, core participants realized that the group's efforts were not sustainable, especially as the early recovery efforts shifted to long-term rebuilding and reconstruction.

The group slowed its cleanups during mid-May 2006 through summer 2006, and Katrina Krewe conducted its final cleanup on August 26, 2006, just days before the first anniversary of the storm. During this period of phasing out the cleanups, Katrina Krewe began to read up on the "broken windows theory," an approach to addressing urban disorder and crime, which has become popular among neighborhood groups nationwide, and it shifted its collective efforts to more long-term anti-litter campaigns targeting youth through school programs and public service announcements. Persuaded by the theory that neighborhood decay (i.e., broken windows) would result in increased criminal activity and social disorder and the eventual abandonment of the community, the women sought to "'clean-up' minor disorder" such as graffiti and litter with the aim of reestablishing a sense of social cohesion and security for returning residents. Attempting to establish a greater sense of security and stability through clean-up projects along major thoroughfares, the group partnered with local law enforcement to promote citywide awareness and enforcement of litter ordinances, activities reminiscent of anti-vice campaigns and social reform movements. For example, the group purchased "No Dumping/Littering" aluminum signs, hanging them in "targeted" areas throughout the city.

Few interviewees, if any, reflected on the ways in which these clean-up efforts could be used to socially control communities based on race and class. Instead, the women saw their activities as part of a larger social reform and renewal movement, which reflected their classed interests and social location in the New Orleans community. One participant put it this way:

So part of the Katrina Krewe frustrations, and one of the reasons that Becky moved to being a nonprofit organization and having a philosophy and a movement where we educate people and we go into schools and let them know that you need to be responsible for your own trash is that there's a much bigger problem here. Katrina Krewe is not there to keep picking up everybody's trash forever, you know?

Similarly, in a *The Times-Picayune* article on Katrina Krewe's final cleanup (Ritea, 2006, p. A1), Zaheri, the group's founder, discussed the transformation of the group's focus from collectively organized labor to the promotion of personal responsibility for keeping New Orleans clean and litter free. Zaheri said, "Now it's up to you and you and you to keep it clean and maintain your area. Mama's not going to be there to pick up after you every time."

Disaster Recovery and the Gendered Division of Labor

While the case of Katrina Krewe is yet another example in the growing literature on women's resilience to disaster, focusing only on resilience without any further critique is misleading and overly simplistic. Such literature could be used in unfortunate ways to inform responses to future disasters and place additional burdens on the women who are likely to take on this labor. The gendered dimensions of Zaheri's comments about the final cleanup are in need of further examination. In a telling way, her words reveal the centrality of the gendered division of labor in disaster (Enarson, 2001) as well as in Hurricane Katrina recovery efforts, privatization, and the restructuring of responsibility for the public good. Elsewhere, Zaheri made similar remarks, "Our goal was to provide immediate relief to what resulted from Hurricane Katrina, not to become the indefinite garbage men and women of the city."[1] For several months after the storm, the group had assumed a fair amount of this responsibility, and the names of the board of directors and committee members reveal the gendered organizational structure of the group. The upper echelons of the group were all women, and the labor itself was feminized. A participant reflected on one of her first cleanups:

There was probably about eight people. What I think is so neat about it, and I don't think there's been much mention of it, but we were all housewives. A lot of these people, like, they're people who go out to

---

1. Quoted in "Storming Back: Our Annual Female Achievers—The Post-Katrina Revival Class." *New Orleans Magazine*, July 2006.

lunch with friends. I don't want to call them, like, 'ladies who lunch' and make it sound like they don't do anything. But these are not— these are people who go and get manicures and pedicures and live a very good life. And they were out there pickin' up trash. Those are the people that started the group and were out there in their grubby clothes, and we were bringin' our own garbage bags and gloves and rakes and shovels.

The interview data are revealing because they are evidence of a self-reflexive analysis of the women's social standing within the New Orleans community. The words also show that there were role shifts that took place during the clean-ups. However temporary these transformation may have been, the clean-up activities were a departure from the women's pre-storm lives. The narrative also explains that the early clean-ups were self-funded with the participants absorbing the cost of supplies. Prior to receiving sizeable donations from local businesses and national corporations, participants spent considerable amounts of their own money on supplies, including the expensive industrial strength contractor bags that were durable enough to hold the storm debris. As one participant told me, "I was probably about $4000 into my husband's pockets."[2]

In addition to being largely self-funded, at least at the group's inception, it is striking that Katrina Krewe's localized recovery work in the immediate post-impact area of New Orleans was an unpaid, volunteer effort. This conjures arguments made by generations of Marxist feminists about the sexual division of labor within the household, the bifurcation of labor and value in the domestic and public realms, and the devaluation of women's waged and community work. Certainly, this raises concerns about the prevalence of women's unpaid labor associated with the tedious chore of picking up trash and storm debris in public places as a result of the near absence and slow return of state services. My claims only refer to the observable gendered labor of one women-led group. I can only speculate about the gendered division of emotional labor that has been occurring within countless households, social service agencies, and support groups across the region as thousands of affected residents try to rebuild their lives.

At the same time that the group absorbed tasks historically carried out by state bodies, discourses of individualism and personal responsibility emerged as integral to the ongoing Katrina recovery. And these tasks were part of juggling other parts of everyday life. Like Enarson (2001) and Fothergill (2004), who found that women experienced role accumulation, role strain, and role

---

2. In a study of the same group, Tyler (2007) cites a dollar amount ($2000) half of that reported to me. Tyler's interview was conducted four months after mine in 2006.

conflict in managing community, family, and work following the Grand Forks flood of 1997, many Katrina Krewe participants were torn between competing obligations and responsibilities. Describing the ways in which many group members not only participated in Katrina Krewe, but in other recovery groups as well, one woman felt that she was being spread thin between these organizations and other responsibilities; she said, "And a lot of us are doing all of it. […] A lot of us are doing double, triple, quadruple duty, and that's without the Brownie troop and soccer and our own homes being taken apart and put back together."

The historical record provides points of comparison that help shed additional light on the gendering of labor conditions during recovery and reconstruction activities. For example, privileged white women helped bring about structural reform following the devastating 1990 hurricane in Galveston (Turner, 1997). Another scholar compared Katrina Krewe's clean-up efforts to progressive-era reform movements in New Orleans specifically (Tyler, 1996, 2007). In a global context, Katrina Krewe bears striking similarities to the women that cleared debris in post-war Germany, and reconstruction activities following war and political violence provide important windows into the gendered organization of recovery activities.[3] For years after 1945, for example, "Rubble Women" cleared debris from the streets of war-torn German cities as part of massive post-war reconstruction projects (see Heineman, 1996, pp. 374–80; Koshar, 2000, pp. 221–22; Schofield, 1994). Engaging in what disaster scholars would today consider recovery-related activities, the women participated in extensive physical labor sorting reusable bricks and building materials, not for petty monetary compensations, but for "better ration cards they received as heavy laborers" (Heineman, 1996, p. 375). Elizabeth Heineman (1996, p. 375) has written of the Rubble Women, "However mixed their motivations for taking on this chore, women set to the tedious, heavy work of moving, cleaning and sorting building material for reuse—the first step of Germany's physical reconstruction." In these massive postwar projects, the labor was paid.

Like the "Rubble Women" engaged in Germany's post-war reconstruction efforts, Katrina Krewe in post-Katrina New Orleans organized mass clean-ups, which were characterized by incredibly demanding physical labor. In both reconstruction projects, gender was an important organizing principle. There were several differences. The work done by Katrina Krewe was linked to debris removal, refuse disposal, and waste management rather than the sorting of

---

3. For another comparison in a quite different context, see the 9/11 documentary, "9/12: From Chaos to Community," in which one female first responder reports male colleagues giving her a three-pronged gardening tool to sift through debris at Ground Zero in New York City.

reusable materials. A more important difference, however, is that Katrina Krewe's work was a volunteer-based activity that was never compensated, except in the currency of increased social status in the community.[4] Decades of Marxist and socialist feminist work has encouraged critical debate about the sexual division of labor, and in the context of post-Katrina New Orleans, the widespread presence of unpaid or undervalued labor operated within an ethos of volunteerism and charity, which itself was supported by an ethic of personal responsibility and giving.

This analysis is by no means a criticism of Katrina Krewe. In fact, the women who organized these efforts deserve praise for cleaning up the city when others did not. Nor am I suggesting that the women themselves did not find these activities meaningful. In fact, these clean-ups served an important social function beyond the original goals and the material tasks at hand, and most women interviewed reported that they found the clean-up work to be highly therapeutic and an important means for recharging a sense of community, restoring social bonds, and enhancing a sense of social solidarity.

While the case presented in this chapter focuses on one women-centered group, there are broader issues at stake here in understanding disaster volunteerism in general under particular historical conditions, notably issues related to the social organization of responsibility and the collective caring for others that is displaced onto "third sector groups" that are "located between the market and state" (Jessop, 2002, p. 463). The quiet restructuring of the state and market relies on and promotes non-profit groups, social justice organizations, care-giving groups, and social service agencies, which are likely to survive on shoestring budgets and volunteer labor. Taken together, these issues take on particular importance in a volume on social justice in the United States. Any discussion of social justice following Hurricane Katrina must consider uncomfortable questions about how social movement organizations, relief groups, activists, and community-based organizations potentially strengthen the state-apparatus and systems of capital accumulation by relieving pressures on governments bodies to provide services (supply distribution, gutting of homes, debris removal) to the public at large.

---

4. In February 2006, during the first Mardi Gras following Hurricane Katrina, Zaheri was selected to ride atop the most prestigious parade float in the Krewe of Muses, an all-women carnival organization. The float is designed in the shape of a single red shoe, and many women covet the chance of being selected for this honor. One participant explained, "I was like, 'Oh, my gosh, she's on the shoe!' That's huge. That's a big deal. She was just a rider, like me. We've always been on the same float. This year she got to be on the shoe because she was an honoree, basically, and because she had started this group. And it's usually the bigwigs in muses, and she was asked to be on it." The Krewe of Muses made headlines when it donated $50,000 to help defray city expenses related to police overtime during Carnival celebrations in 2006 (see Finch, 2006, p. Metro 1).

Privatization, State Restructuring, and the Redistribution of Responsibility

In the remaining section of this chapter, I would like to link the case of Katrina Krewe to issues that have taken central importance in the social catastrophe: privatization, restructuring, and the redistribution of resources and responsibility. Long before Hurricane Katrina, New Orleans erupted in battles over the privatization of many sectors of social life, including public housing, education, sewage and water services, and the criminal justice system and the for-profit prison industry (Agid, 2007; Arena, 2007). Following Katrina, conflict over privatization remained central to discussions of short-term and long-term recovery. One might be asking how these explicitly political confrontations are related, if at all, to Katrina Krewe's widespread volunteer work across New Orleans. I argue that this volunteerism is actually linked to broader shifts in modes of social and economic relations under neoliberal political projects that have come to characterize the Katrina moment in U.S history. In making this link, I would like to show how Katrina Krewe's clean-up effort has much in common with the social justice battles over the privatization of public goods and services.

As a newly formed non-profit organization, the group's efforts were measures that confirmed the logic of volunteerism and supported in many ways what INCITE! Women of Color Against Violence (2007) has called the "non-profit industrial complex." As Jessop (2002, p. 455) observes, neoliberalism, in part, "tends to promote 'community' (or a plurality of self-organizing communities) as a flanking, compensatory mechanism for the inadequacies of the market mechanism." Put another way, responsibilities for the public good tend to shift to community groups and groups in the health and human services sectors, and these are locations where women are often concentrated as both users and providers (see also Enarson [2001] for a typology of women's flood work in the 1997 Grand Forks Flood and her examination of social visibility and waged status of women's work). Similarly, in a note to a theoretical investigation of privatization and the politics of social reproduction in the Hurricane Katrina catastrophe, geographer Katz (2008) noted:

> … the contradictions raised when grassroots organizations, individuals, and other community groups cover for the state and capital in the myriad tasks and social formations of relief, recovery and reconstruction. In certain ways their-our-stepping into the breach confirms the neoliberal ethos of privatization, in other ways it reminds us of the radical imperatives of moving beyond the state in accomplishing and altering social reproduction, and in still other ways it lets the government and corporations off the hook they should be skewered on. (p. 27)

Katrina Krewe stepped in to provide essential social services through the collective exertion of volunteer labor, which was couched in discourses of social cohesion and economic recovery. Katrina Krewe, like countless other groups across the region, let the "government and corporations off the hook," despite partnerships with local law enforcement, coordination with waste management agencies, and corporate sponsorships. It is telling that connections were made with state and private sectors, which curiously provided enough resources to keep the group going in the months after the storm, but not enough to fully replenish its efforts and energy. In the end, the group transitioned out of those responsibilities when its members realized that they might become the "indefinite garbage men and women" of the city.

In light of Katz's critique, it is all the more significant that one woman in my study reported that the Gulf Coast recovery was a "citizen-led recovery." This narrative of recovery as being driven from the "bottom up" obscures important large-scale social processes at play. Rather than attributing any great progress with the Gulf Coast recovery to the triumph of civil society over the state or over the corrosive character of capital, I assert that the issues raised in this chapter surrounding labor and disaster recovery work are symptomatic of a larger restructuring of state services in an era of neo-liberal reform, in which public services, responsibilities for social welfare, and provisions of public goods have been increasingly privatized or displaced onto the nonprofit sector or what some have called the "shadow state" (Mitchell, 2001; Wolch, 1990).

As New Orleans prepared for its annual carnival celebration, the "city's beleaguered sanitation staff has sought help from all corners in the massive clean-up effort. From supplemental labor pools to grass-roots groups to neighborhood associations, hundreds are rolling up their sleeves to pitch in" (Duncan, 2006, p. Metro 1). In February 2006, for the first time in its 150 year history in New Orleans, the city's Carnival celebrations had a corporate sponsor: Glad Products, the same corporation that donated trash bags to Katrina Krewe's efforts. Glad contributed an "un-specified six figure sum to the city to help pay for public safety and sanitation expenses," and donated 100,000 trash bags for the post-Carnival clean-up (Mowbray, 2006, p. National 1). Hundreds of volunteers helped city sanitation staff with the massive clean-up efforts. Among them was Eli Manning, a National Football League quarterback and New Orleans native, who said, "I want to encourage this effort to not stop after Mardi Gras. This needs to continue because the city is going to need it" (Duncan, 2006, p. Metro 1).

The displacement of clean-up responsibilities onto volunteer groups had another very prominent supporter: President Bush, who in spring 2006 encouraged the nation to visit New Orleans and volunteer, specifically highlighted Katrina Krewe's efforts in a speech on the one-year anniversary of Katrina:

> Of course, government has a part, but the truth of the matter is a lot
> of the effort, a lot of the success, and a lot of results were achieved be-

cause of faith-based and community groups. Groups like Katrina Krewe have mobilized thousands of volunteers, ranging from students on spring break to moms and retirees. Isn't it interesting to have a country where people are willing to show up to help clean out houses and remove debris for someone they didn't even know? It's a spectacular nation, isn't it, when compassion overflows to overwhelming? (http://georgewbush-whitehouse.archives.gov/news/releases/2006/08/20060829-2.html)

Bush's speech continued, "That's the spirit that we're trying to capture." One year later, on the second anniversary of Hurricane Katrina, former President Bush and First Lady Laura Bush attended a dinner honoring community and cultural leaders at the famous Dookie Chase restaurant. Katrina Krewe founder and president Zaheri also attended this dinner (Hammer, 2006). Set against Bush's shameful absence during the Katrina crisis, the glorification of this volunteer labor as compassion supports all too well the main points in this chapter: the notion that the state is transferring work and responsibility to women's unpaid labor (see Glazer, 1993 for a discussion of "work transfer").

The conditions that made Katrina Krewe so incredibly popular among locals and visitors are an extension of many of the same processes, namely state devolution and privatization, which figured so prominently in the social crisis that we now know as Hurricane Katrina. The process of devolution involves the displacement of responsibility and resources, but significantly not regulation or oversight, onto local and "small" governments, corporations, nonprofits and individuals. Cope (1997, pp. 184–85) refers to processes of state devolution as involving the "flexible dispersion of labor" with "the goal of spatially dispersing and politically diluting labor in order to get an upper hand for capital accumulation processes." She continues with several useful interpretations of the "flexibility" of accumulation and "dispersion":

> In the flexible *accumulation* of capital, small-scale business operations are increasingly depended on to rationalize and absorb the demands and contradictions of large-scale economic forces. Similarly, in flexible *dispersion* of labor, smaller scale social welfare operations and individuals are called on to rationalize to and absorb the demands and contradictions of large-scale economic forces." (p. 185)

The case of Katrina Krewe helps reveal the state's shifting relationship to labor, production, and social reproduction at a critical juncture for U.S. society. In many ways, the women's volunteer work is part of the same set of conditions as many social justice projects that are taking form in various communities across the U.S. and around the globe. I argue that the state is operating through a set of practices, carried out by "non-state" actors or third-sector groups in the form of volunteer and community work, which simultaneously masks and obscures the structural displacement of responsibility for larger public goods onto the activities of civil society groups, corporations, non-profit organizations, and women.

Conclusion

As revealed in this chapter's case study of Katrina Krewe, restructuring tied to privatization, state devolution, and the redistribution of responsibility and resources has taken specifically gendered forms, and in Katrina's wake it was often women and women's organizations that assumed responsibility for these difficult tasks. While "women's labor can provide a key asset for recovery [from Hurricane Katrina], whether in their temporary communities or in their old or new homes" (Williams, Sorokina, DeWeever, & Hartmann, 2006, p. 1), critical scholars of gender inequalities must always be mindful of the ways in which the state's relationship to organized work operates through (women's) unpaid labor and draws crucial support and validation through mainstream, gendered discourses of volunteerism, service to the community, and the ethos of personal responsibility. Non-profit organizations as well as justice movements in the United States must be prepared to reflect on their multifaceted relationships with the state, capital, and the reproduction of inequalities. As such, any opposition to government power or state regulation, on the one hand, or praise and celebration of civil group activities, on the other, must consider the discomfiting, but likely, possibility that their efforts might actually strengthen the current modes of operation in eras of the state's supposed decline.

The women negotiated physical and emotional labor, unpaid work, and family obligations while maintaining a public commitment to community level recovery efforts. At the same time, the latent function of volunteer efforts relieved pressures and demands put on the state, and to some degree the private sector, to provide essential public services in times of crisis. The city's sanitation department was relieved to let the women-organized group take on the tasks. To the extent that the burden and responsibility unevenly fell on women's shoulders, the emergence of post-Katrina clean-up crews suggests a need to critically analyze the privatization of disaster recovery efforts. Rather than illustrating a creative partnership, gender, community, and unpaid work are in a complex tension with the state and for-profit contractor work in the private sector. Because the women's unpaid work was not sustainable as a semi-permanent compensatory measure for the slow restoration of state public services, the life-course of the group reflects this dilemma. Signaling an embrace of a personalized politics, the group's focus shifted from recovery activities to longer-term educational measures that integrate new lifestyle discourses of personal responsibility into public institutions and social practices. If the state apparatus should fail again in future disasters, should we count on women's emergent organizations and civil society groups to bear the responsibility to take on disaster-related tasks through unpaid labor in the name of community?

Feminist analyses of gendered division of labor and the social reproduction of gender norms in disaster would suggest that, despite active participation in the recovery efforts as evidence that signals women's resiliency and agency, as well as physical and emotional strength, these post-Katrina recovery activities were not adequately or fairly compensated and thus reinforce an asymmetrical gendered division of labor at the community level. This observation consequently signals a structural inequality that reinforces both disaster capitalism and gender inequality. While volunteerism has served the function of stepping-in to fill the void where the state or private sectors have failed or simply refused, the response by civil society groups, in this case a women-centered group, to engage in unpaid labor (and care work for individuals and whole neighborhoods) is one of the major challenges of post-Katrina volunteer movements, especially to the extent that women's unpaid labor is systematically used to promote discourses of community and social cohesion.

References

Agid, S. (2007). Locked and loaded: The prison industrial complex and the response to Hurricane Katrina. In Bates, K. A., & Swan, R.S. (Eds.). *Through the eye of Katrina: Social justice in the United States* (pp. 55–76). Durham, North Carolina: Carolina Academic Press.

Arena, J. (2007). Whose city is it? Public housing, public sociology, and the struggle for social justice in New Orleans before and after Katrina. In Bates, K.A., & Swan, R.S. (Eds.). *Through the eye of Katrina: Social justice in the United States* (pp. 367–386). Durham, North Carolina: Carolina Academic Press.

Belkhir, J.A. & Charlemaine, C. (2007). Race, gender and class lessons from Hurricane Katrina. *Race, Gender, and Class*, 14(1), 120–152.

Bergin, K.A. (2008). Witness: The racialized gender implications of Katrina. In Marable, M. & Clarke, K. (Eds.). *Seeking higher ground: The Hurricane Katrina crisis, race, and public policy reader* (pp. 173–190). New York: Palgrave Macmillan.

Bickford, S.R. (2005, October 19). Uptowners tiring of the trash. *The Times-Picayune*, p. Metro 6.

Brown, B. (2009). *Organizational response and recovery of domestic violence shelters in the aftermath of disaster.* PhD dissertation, Department of Sociology and Criminal Justice, University of Delaware, Newark, DE.

Cope, M. (1997). Responsibility, regulation, and retrenchment: The end of welfare? In L.A. Staeheli, L.A., Kondras, J.E. & Flint, C. (Eds.). *State devolution in America: Implications for a diverse society* (pp. 181–205). Thousand Oaks, CA: Sage Publications.

David, E. (2008). Cultural trauma, memory, and gendered collective action: The case of Women of the Storm following Hurricane Katrina. *National Women's Studies Association Journal*, 20(3), 138–162.

———. (2009). *Women of the Storm: An ethnography of gender, culture, and social movements following Hurricane Katrina*. PhD Dissertation. Department of Sociology, University of Colorado at Boulder.

Davis, O.A. and Land, M. (2007). Southern women survivors speak about Hurricane Katrina, the children and what needs to happen next. *Race, Gender, and Class*, 14(1), 69–86.

DeWeever, A.J. (2008). *Women in the wake of the storm: Examining the post-Katrina realities of the women of New Orleans and the Gulf Coast*. Washington, DC: Institute for Women's Policy Research. Retrieved on March 2, 2009 from http://www.iwpr.org/pdf/D481.pdf.

DeWeever, A.J. and Hartmann, H. (2006). Abandoned before the storms: The glaring disaster of gender, race, and class disparities in the Gulf. In Hartman, C. & Squires, G. D. (Eds.). *There is no such thing as a natural disaster* (pp. 85–101). New York: Routledge.

Downing, V. (2006, February 27). Imagine our favorite city, litter-free. *The Times-Picayune*, p. Metro 5.

Duncan, J. (2005, October 6). Piles of rotting garbage raise their own stink; Nauseated neighbors try to tackle problem. *The Times-Picayune*, p. National A16.

———. (2006, February 24.) Clean-up challenge; Big mess expected after Carnival to pose test for Big Easy; Hobbled city counts of fresh strategies. *The Times-Picayune*, p. Metro 1.

Enarson, E. (2001). What women do: Gendered labor in the Red River Valley flood. *Environmental Hazards*, 3, 1–18.

———. (2005, September 25). Women hard-hit by Hurricane Katrina disaster. *The Denver Post*, p. E1.

Enarson, E. & Morrow, B.H. (1998). Women will rebuild Miami: A case study of feminist response to disaster. In Enarson, E. & Morrow, B. H. (Eds.). *The gendered terrain of disaster: Through women's eyes* (pp. 185–199). Westport, CT: Greenwood.

Finch, S. (2005, February 9). Kicking in for Carnival: Muses donates $50,000 to help pay police overtime. *The Times-Picayune*, p. Metro 1.

Friedman, B. (2005, November 6). Group takes clean-up into their own hands; Debris is eyesore to local residents. *The Times-Picayune*, p. Algiers 1.

Gault, B., Hartmann, H., DeWeever, A.J., Werschkul, M. & Williams, E. (2005). *The women of New Orleans and the Gulf Coast: Multiple disadvantages and key assets for recovery. Part 1. Poverty, race, gender, and class.* Washington, DC: Institute for Women's Policy Research. Retrieved on March 3, 2009 from http://www.iwpr.org/pdf/D464.pdf.

Glazer, N. (1993). *Women's paid and unpaid labor: The work transfer in health care and retailing.* Philadelphia: Temple University Press.

Hamilton, B. (2005, November 16). Three decades worth of trash; New Orleans area struggles with what Katrina left behind. *The Times-Picayune*, p. National 1.

Hammer, D. (2007, August 29). Bush shares gumbo with Brees, Nagin; Meal at Dooky Chase's welcomes president to town. *The Times-Picayune*, p. National 15.

Heineman, E. (1996). The hour of the women: Memories of Germany's 'crisis years' and West German national identity. *American Historical Review*, 101(2), 354–395.

INCITE! Women of Color Against Violence. (Eds.) (2007). *The revolution will not be funded: Beyond the non-profit industrial complex.* Cambridge, MA: South End Press.

Jenkins, P. & Phillips, B. (2008a). Domestic violence and disaster. In Willinger, B. (Ed.), *Katrina and the women of New Orleans* (pp. 65–69). Newcomb College Center for Research on Women. New Orleans: Tulane University.

———. (2008b). Battered women, catastrophe, and the context of safety after Hurricane Katrina. *National Women's Studies Association Journal*, 20(3), 49–68.

Jessop, B. (2002). Liberalism, neoliberalism, and urban governance: A state-theoretical perspective. *Antipode*, 34(3), 452–472.

Katz, C. (2008). Bad elements: Katrina and the scoured landscape of social reproduction. *Gender, Place & Culture*, 15(1), 15–29.

Koshar, R. (2000). *From monuments to traces: Artifacts of German memory, 1870–1990.* Berkeley: University of California Press.

Laska, S., Morrow, B.H., Willinger, B. & Mock, M. (2008). Gender and disasters: Theoretical considerations. In Willinger, B. (Ed.). *Katrina and the women of New Orleans* (pp. 11–20). Newcomb College Center for Research on Women. New Orleans: Tulane University.

Luft, R. (2008). Looking for common ground: Relief work in post-Katrina New Orleans as an American parable of race and gender violence. *National Women's Studies Association Journal*, 20(3), 5–31.

Luft, R. & Griffin, S. (2008). A status report on housing in New Orleans after Katrina: An intersectional analysis. In Willinger, B. (Ed.). *Katrina and the women of New Orleans* (pp. 50–53). Newcomb College Center for Research on Women. New Orleans: Tulane University.

Mitchell, K. (2001). Transnationalism, neo-liberalism, and the rise of the shadow state. *Economy and Society*, 30(2), 165–189.

Mock, N. (2008). Health and health care. In Willinger, B. (Ed.), *Katrina and the women of New Orleans* (pp. 54–58). Newcomb College Center for Research on Women. New Orleans: Tulane University.

Mowbray, R. (2006, February 7). Glad Products to back, and bag, Carnival in N.O.; But with time winding down, there's no "presenting sponsor." *The Times-Picayune*, p. National 1.

Overstreet, S. & Burch, B. (2008). Mental health status of women and children following Hurricane Katrina. In Willinger, B. (Ed.), *Katrina and the women of New Orleans* (pp. 59–65). Newcomb College Center for Research on Women. New Orleans: Tulane University.

Peek, L. & Fothergill, A. (2008). Displacement, gender, and the challenges of parenting after Hurricane Katrina. *National Women's Studies Association Journal*, 20(3), 69–105.

Ransby, B. (2006). Katrina, black women, and the deadly discourse on black poverty in America. *Du Bois Review: Social Science Research on Race*, 3(1), 215–222.

Ritea, S. (2006, August 25). Katrina Krewe calls it a day; Thousands helped clean city after storm. *The Times-Picayune*, p. Metro 1.

Rose, C. (2005, October 7). Sense and the city; Sight and sound are improving, but the smell has a long way to go. *The Times-Picayune*, p. Living 7.

Ross, L. (2005, October 10). A feminist perspective on Katrina. Z-Net: The Spirit of Resistance Lives. Retrieved on March 3, 2009 from http://www.zmag.org/znet/viewArticlePrint/5233.

Schofield, M.A. (1994). "Rubble women": The clean-up crew of World War II. *The American Journal of Semiotics*, 11(1–2), 129–149.

Seager, J. (2005). Noticing gender (or not) in disasters. *Social Policy*, 36(2), 29–30.

The Times-Picayune. (2005, October 7). Garbage in, garbage out. *The Times-Picayune*, editorial, p. Metro 10.

————. (2006, January 22). A flood of volunteers; Hundreds help scrub the streets of New Orleans clean of hurricane debris. *The Times-Picayune*, p. Metro 1.

Thornton, W.E. and Voigt, L. (2007). Disaster rape: Vulnerability of women to sexual assaults during Hurricane Katrina. *Journal of Public Management and Social Policy*, 13(2), 23–49.

Turner, E.H. (1997). *Women, culture, and community: Religion and reform in Galveston, 1880–1920.* New York: Oxford University Press.

Tyler, P. (1996). *Silk stockings & ballot boxes: Women & politics in New Orleans, 1920–1963.* Athens: University of Georgia Press.

———. (2007). The post-Katrina, semiseparate world of gender politics. *Journal of American History*, 94, 780–788.

Vaill, S. (2006). *The calm in the storm: Women leaders in Gulf Coast recovery.* San Francisco: Women's Funding Network and New York: Ms. Foundation for Women. Retrieved on March 11, 2009 from http://www.wfnet.org/documents/publications/katrina_report_082706.pdf.

Varney, J. & Moller, J. (2005, September 30). Clean-up could take at least a year; More than half La. debris is in N.O. *The Times-Picayune*, p. A1.

Willinger, B. (2008a). The effects of Katrina on the employment and earnings of New Orleans women. In B. Willinger, (Ed.), *Katrina and the women of New Orleans* (pp. 32–49). Newcomb College Center for Research on Women. New Orleans: Tulane University.

———. (2008b). The power to influence. In Willinger, B. (Ed.). *Katrina and the women of New Orleans* (pp. 73–75). Newcomb College Center for Research on Women. New Orleans: Tulane University.

Willinger, B. & Gerson, J. (2008). Demographic and socioeconomic change in relation to gender and Katrina. In Willinger, B. (Ed.). *Katrina and the women of New Orleans* (pp. 25–31). Newcomb College Center for Research on Women. New Orleans: Tulane University.

Wolch, J.R. (1990). *The shadow state: Government and voluntary sector in transition.* New York: Foundation Center.

Young, T. (2005, October 16). Clean sweep. *The Times-Picayune*, p. Metro 1.

Chapter 22

The Disappearing Neighborhood: An Urban Planner's Tour of New Orleans

Kim Knowles-Yánez

Introduction

I visited New Orleans in late May-early June 2007, one year and nine months after Hurricane Katrina landed on August 29, 2005. I knew that I would see areas in need of reconstruction, but I was unprepared for the magnitude of destruction and inaction that still dominates so much of the city. I was in New Orleans for the annual Planners Network conference, which is held at a different site each year. This year the conference was in New Orleans in order to shine a light on the state of the city. The conference's theme was "Race, Class and Community Recovery: From the Neighborhood to the Nation and Beyond." Planners Network is an organization for progressive planners (academics, students, practitioners) who are interested in using planning to promote social justice. I had expected to see at least some level of redevelopment projects everywhere in New Orleans. Instead I was struck by how little redevelopment has been attempted, how many places have yet to even be cleaned up, and how deserted some parts of the city still are. It is difficult to explain just how damaged New Orleans is to people who have not been there since the storm hit. I know because before I went I read many articles, saw hours of TV, grieved for the lost, and watched Spike Lee's amazing *When the Levees Broke* before my visit and still, I was unprepared for the extent of the damage and lack of cleanup I saw, 21 months after the storm hit.

On my drive from New Orleans' Louis Armstrong airport into the city and the French Quarter, where my hotel and almost all of the other tourist hotels are located, I did not see much evidence of the storm. From the freeway, I noticed just one burned-out apartment complex, which I guessed could have also just been a "regular" fire and not one of the apocalyptic post-Katrina days fires.

That evening in our hotel, I was falsely lulled into thinking things were not as bad as I had feared. This comfort would become fiercely unwound on the following day.

On the second day of the conference, I took what is called a "mobile workshop" at planning conferences. These kinds of day-long workshops, in which local planners show visiting planners projects in the area, are typical of and an important part of planning conferences. After all, planners are first and foremost interested in how people use land in their communities, and nothing beats going out and seeing in person how people have developed their communities. My mobile workshop was sponsored by the Association of Community Organizations for Reform Now (ACORN) and their university partners, University of Illinois at Urbana-Champaign, Cornell University, and Columbia University. Teaching and research faculty and students from each university accompanied us and talked about their community planning efforts with ACORN. About 25 of us boarded the bus for the tour.

The Disappearing Neighborhood

The theme for our mobile tour became readily apparent, though no one named it as such. At each place we stopped, we heard descriptions of what had been lost in Katrina and evidence of what is disappearing as a result. At each of the fairly deserted neighborhood places we visited in the Bywater and Lower 9th Planning Districts, we couldn't help but see that neighborhoods are disappearing in New Orleans or are already lost and may not return. A planner worries about neighborhoods and is keenly aware of the elements which make a strong one; grocery stores, housing, and schools are very high on the list of vital elements. When these things have disappeared, what are the chances for the return of the neighborhood?

The Disappearance of the Grocery Store: Lack of Access to Healthy Food

First we visited the historic St. Roch Market in the city's Bywater Planning District. The market was damaged by Katrina and is now boarded up, as are all of the large grocery stores in this part of New Orleans—some because of Katrina, but some also because they were not deemed economically viable by their corporate owners. Of course, the market was never a "grocery" store, but it was one of the places where people in the neighborhood could buy fresh vegetables and other foods. Now the neighborhood has no market or grocery stores. It only has expensive corner/convenience stores, which do not have much of a selection of healthy foods. The distance to grocery stores and markets in other parts of the city makes it very difficult for Bywater residents without cars to buy their groceries. As we stood by the market, umbrellas up in the rain, several moms pushing strollers carried plastic bags of pre-packaged foods. During the course of the day, we found that this is true for many of New Orleans' poor neighborhoods. They have been forsaken by big box corporate grocery chains and thus struggle to find reasonably priced, healthy food. The Bywater neighborhood is working with students and faculty at Cornell to revitalize the market, and via the market, the whole neighborhood. It's a quality of life issue that planners care a lot about—would you want to live in a neighborhood where you cannot find reasonably priced, healthy food? Planners want to make this kind of convenience happen for people in their lives, thus the focus of the Cornell students work with the neighborhood post-Katrina is on revitalizing their market.

At the St. Roch Market, Stephen Bradberry, the lead organizer of ACORN New Orleans, boarded our tour bus to talk to us about community organizing and planning efforts post-Katrina. Bradberry is the 2005 winner of the Robert F. Kennedy Human Rights Award for his work post-Katrina—he is also the first African American to win this prize. He told us how ACORN became involved in the post-disaster efforts. This national organization, which supports and works for social justice for low and moderate income families across the United States, already had a strong presence and members in some neighborhoods in New Orleans before Katrina. During the storm, ACORN members outside of New Orleans worked to locate displaced New Orleans members via text messaging in order to direct them to shelter and other resources. National ACORN leaders came to New Orleans just as soon as they were allowed or could sneak into the city. In the nearly two years since the hurricane, ACORN volunteers have worked steadily to gut houses and work on planning with neighborhoods and preparing them for habitation again. They have also worked with neighborhood organizations and university partners in crafting an approach to rebuilding. You can look at their report, "Rebuilding After Hurricane Katrina: ACORN Planning Principles," at http://acornlaw.org/fileadmin/KatrinaRelief/report/Planning_Principles.pdf.

The Disappearance of Housing

Planning in New Orleans has taken many twists and turns post-Katrina in that there have been several state and city-wide attempts that have met varying degrees of acceptance and rejection. So far, no one planning approach has been accepted and virtually nothing has been funded. We heard this several times during our trip, that the money allocated to planning and rebuilding is just sitting under wraps until officials can agree what to do with it. Meanwhile, according to Bradberry and others we spoke with, neighborhoods are doing their own planning, and in some cases have presented the city with their plan in hopes of support for rebuilding. Still, the city and other officials have not been able to release money for these efforts. And at an individual level, money for rebuilding is also very hard to come by. During the day, we heard many references to the charmingly named "Road Home" funds, which only a few people have been awarded, but which thousands are awaiting in order to begin their journey home.

In the next neighborhood we visited, this lack of support for local level and individual efforts was echoed. In the Desire neighborhood of the Upper 9th Ward in the Bywater District, we met in a community gym with a Baptist preacher/community activist who said that his congregation was doing everything they could to help themselves and others, including those outside of their faith, but that they needed help from the government and were not receiving anything at all. He felt like they were being steamrolled. They are part of an organization called "Churches United for Revitalization and Evangelism" or CURE. He made it clear that one of the reasons he took time out of his day to meet with us was because he wanted to tell as many people as possible about his community's needs so that they will not be forgotten. The gym we were in still smelled from the days and days of flooding in the surrounding neighborhood. He thanked us for visiting and urged us not to forget his people. I was filled with admiration for the role he has had to fill—to minister to his people, and to help keep their faith afloat in front of circumstances that could be read to tell them at every turn that nobody cares. He said that many in his congregation were fighting depression and that the only thing they knew they have is each other, given the indifference of governmental authorities to his people's suffering.

He described how rebuilding efforts were hampered by property title issues. Many families had not kept title to their properties in order as property was passed down through the generations. Now hundreds of condemned properties are without a transferable title. CURE wants to take control of some of these properties and rebuild so that people can come home to New Orleans with a place to live. However, because of intricacies in the title process, the city cannot figure out how to legally turn them over. Thus the boarded-up properties blight the neighborhood.

This blight truly has to be seen to be believed. As we drove through Desire and the adjacent Florida neighborhood (all still in the Bywater District), I had my first impression of what hundreds of boarded-up houses for miles and miles looks like. The occasional occupied home looks lonely. In fact, I saw several old men and children come out of their houses to watch our tour bus go by. This gave me an awkward exploitative feeling because I both wanted to leave them to their privacy and to stop the bus immediately and sit down and hear the stories of the tragedy they inevitably had on their minds. I wondered if coming out of their houses to watch the tour bus go by was from a feeling of weariness with their spectacle and exploitation and tragedy or if they were eager that we were there to bear witness, in the spirit of the Baptist preacher we talked to. Or were they just plain lonely and eager for distraction?

During the visit to Desire, I saw my first FEMA trailer, and saw many more for the rest of that and following days. They are small, white boxes with PVC piping coming out of them for water and sewage and are planted in the owner's front, side, or back yard or in other vacant lots. Many people waited months to get their trailers because electricity and sewage had to be reinstalled in the neighborhood before FEMA would release a trailer and allow it to be hooked up in the neighborhood. I wondered how long the trailers had been there and how people were feeling living in them almost two years after the storm. Living in a small, temporary trailer is bad enough, but the trailer's location next to a boarded-up home awaiting gutting, demolishing or rebuilding has to be dispiriting. And as I've stated, it's not just one boarded-up home; it's hundreds of them for seeming miles and miles.

One beacon of hope we saw in this area—by now we were driving through the Upper 9th Ward (which, in fact, is still the Bywater District)—was the Musicians' Village built by Habitat for Humanity and conceived by Harry Connick, Jr. and Branford Marsalis. The houses are delightful looking pastel concoctions, very neighborly, lovingly occupied, and filling several city blocks. While every little bit of housing built helps all New Orleans residents, where rents and housing prices are sky high due to scarcity, we couldn't help but comment on the fact that famous names had to be attached to the project in order for it to move forward. Planning and reconstruction clearly move at a much slower pace for regular folk in New Orleans.

Still these glimpses in the Upper 9th did not prepare me for the next neighborhood we visited, the Lower 9th Ward, which is both the name of the neighborhood and the city planning district. As we drove in the neighborhood, our hosts reminded us that this was one of the neighborhoods with the greatest loss of life. Again, we saw block after block, mile after mile of boarded-up, spray painted, and destroyed housing and virtually no rebuilding or evidence of current habitation in huge chunks of the neighborhood. Our tour bus drove down to the restored levee. We got out of the bus to walk around the area where the Industrial Canal Levee broke (and remember this was only one of many levee breaks in New Orleans during Katrina). The area was an open field, knee-high in weeds, which only somewhat disguised the housing foundations and pipes that are the only remnants of the hundreds of houses which stood pre-Katrina in that now open field. Surrounding the field were houses that had not yet been demolished, some on their sides, others merely boarded up. Some bore signs of their owners impending return, stating, "We will return!," "Do Not Bulldoze!". Down the road, we saw some bulldozers working to raze one home. On the far edge of the field, Common Ground, a grassroots organization that organizes volunteer rebuilding efforts had set up shop in a tent-like structure. College students and volunteers from all over the country had come to the city to help gut, tear down, and rebuild houses.

Some of the faculty with us who had been working in the neighborhood described how the levee broke and the effect of the barge that came through the breach. The barge floated over the houses (that's how high the water was) ripping off their tops, and as the water receded, ground what was left of the houses into the mud. It was quite something to stand next to the levee and imagine many feet of water above my head.

We heard about the sentiment of residents in the Lower 9th who are convinced that the city and developers want to use the destruction of Katrina for their own means. The Lower 9th contains one of the highest rates of home ownership in the city, though the face of that homeownership is poor and black. Right after Katrina, city officials made comments which convinced these poor homeowners that they would not be welcomed back to the city. Another caveat to think about here is that in relative terms, the Lower 9th is not as dangerous as other parts of New Orleans because it is only 2–3 feet below sea level, while wealthier parts of the city are further below sea level. The reason that the Lower 9th is the most damaged part of the city is not because it is the lowest part of the city; rather it is the most damaged because the levees protecting it failed—catastrophically. If better levees are in place, the Lower 9th is in fact safer than lower parts of the city. Therein lies the rub for homeowners in the Lower 9th, many of whom are convinced the city wants to take their desirable, safer land and redevelop it as fancy waterfront (the irony should not be lost here) development—hotels, offices, and shopping centers.

Thus these residents, with the help of ACORN and other grassroots organizations, have waged an epic battle since Katrina. They have asserted their right to return to their neighborhoods, in the face of politicians and developers who have said outright that they should not return and who have put many financial and practical roadblocks in the way of their return. It is not hard to imagine all of the ways in which progressive-minded planners could be helpful in the right of return movement—all the way from validating residents' concerns by listening to them, to collecting data and writing plans with residents, to working to implement the plans once they are finalized.

Next we drove from the "waterfront" by the Industrial Canal levee breach to the only place in the Lower 9th where any housing has been restored. Tanya Harris, an ACORN activist who you might recall from "When the Levees Broke," proudly recounted the rebuilding of her grandmother's and aunt's houses, as we stood in front of the houses. The two houses are bright and cheery and a beacon in the surrounding desolation. How brave these two women must be to return to this neighborhood, virtually alone. Surrounding the two houses are boarded-up houses and empty fields. Harris pointed to the fields and said that's where her friends and neighbors lived and that the neighborhood now looks nothing like the tight-knit bustling neighborhood of her childhood. Yet she beamed enthusiasm for the rebuilding efforts and exhibited pure faith that the people would prevail and be allowed to return and rebuild. Her demeanor was inspiring, like that of the other ACORN and CURE officials we talked to. This is how New Orleans will restore itself—by the sheer grit and determination of a people who will not back down and be told they cannot come back to their city, despite the bumbling and posturing of government and elected officials. The gumption of seemingly disempowered residents is slowly trumping powerful business and financial interests. Can it be that there is yet a chance for grassroots social justice practice to triumph in New Orleans? Again, planners can play a vital role in this process in their work of putting residents' aspirations into action.

The Disappearance of Schools

Concern for kids and schools loomed large in what we were hearing from ACORN and other locals we spoke to. Planners are acutely aware of the interdependence of schools and neighborhoods. "Good" neighborhoods have desirable schools and "bad" neighborhoods tend to have undesirable schools. Before this trip to New Orleans, I had never thought about what it means if there are no public schools in a neighborhood. The New Orleans School District was shut down after Katrina and is being replaced with charter schools. One of the ACORN representatives told us they shut down the schools, which could have been repaired, in order to break the teachers' union. All of the teachers were fired right after Katrina. We heard that many families are not returning to New Orleans because of the uncertainty surrounding New Orleans schools. They have their kids settled in at schools in Houston and other places and do not want to disrupt their children's lives anymore by bringing them back to New Orleans and trying to figure out which charter or private school to send them to. We also heard that some kids just have not been back to school since Katrina, or that they lost their 2005–2006 school year and have fallen so far behind that they are starting to be talked about as the "lost generation."

Planners, and real estate professionals and landlords for that matter, know there is no reason for families to return to their old neighborhoods if there are no schools for their children. I found myself wondering if the lack of public schools is a tool being used to keep poor people from returning to New Orleans neighborhoods. If the poor and working class cannot afford private school and the new charter school is untested and perhaps far from their neighborhood, wouldn't individuals find it in their best interest not to return with their children to the neighborhood? And then, do these individual decisions lead to what some civic leaders called for in the immediate aftermath of

Katrina—a new New Orleans, bereft of its minority working poor? This example underscores how policy decisions involving issues of social justice come to shape our neighborhoods and citizenry. Would you want to live in a neighborhood that does not have schools for your children?

Final Thoughts

Planners everywhere deal with the problem of policy and governmental failure thwarting the quality of life and goals of social justice for residents. Planners know how important our role can be in bridging the divide between the powerful economic forces of our society and a better quality of life for all. We understand the practice of listening to residents, helping them put their ideas and aspirations on paper, helping residents present these ideas to other city officials and people in power, and, finally, persevering with these plans until residents are able to realize their dreams for their neighborhoods. At the Planners Network conference, we examined the colossal failure of the government at so many levels to help most of the people it serves, such that New Orleanians are still fighting for the right to return to their city. The conference statement said that the conference would "confront issues of race, class, injustice and the failures of planning, while seeking to learn from the work of community-based organizations, local planners, and individuals impacted by Katrina" (http://www.pn2007.org/). The conference did just that, and the planners who attended walked away inspired to apply the lessons of Katrina to our own cities as we listen closely to and advocate for the economic and politically marginalized members of our communities.

The intricacies of the different plans and government inaction in New Orleans are monumental and overwhelming. Each neighborhood and its planners will face their own unique sets of challenges and goals. I left overwhelmed and inspired by how much individuals and neighborhoods are trying to do at the individual and grassroots level, but equally underwhelmed by official planning and rebuilding efforts. There has not been a lack of planning for the recovery. Many neighborhood plans have been completed. However, there has been very little implementation of any plan because there is so little governmental support at any level. Without a doubt, the current state of New Orleans throws into relief the question: Who is the city for? Those who lived there before and may even own the property their damaged or razed home sits on, or the developers and politicians who are trying to exert their own power and influence in the breach of Katrina? At the macro social justice level, progressive planners would want the people of New Orleans to come back and assert their rights to their neighborhoods, but I am not naïve to the tremendous personal toll this will take. In the face of the disappearance of vital neighborhood elements such as schools, grocery stores, and housing, what are residents to do? Return to their neighborhoods by sheer will and determination to tough out the forces working against their return, all in hopes of being able to maintain the patience and diligence required to restore the neighborhood over the coming years ... or resign themselves to their individual best interests, stay where they have been relocated, and maintain only memories of their New Orleans that once was?

Chapter 23

Social Justice, Planning, and Opportunity Post-Katrina

Kim Knowles-Yánez

Introduction

Paradoxically, the tragedy of Hurricane Katrina provided a remarkable opportunity for universities, and non-profit organizations to engage in social justice-oriented planning. In my chapter for the first edition of this book I discussed how residents' hopes to return to New Orleans, and in particular, the Lower Ninth Ward, were thwarted by the disappearance of their neighborhoods, schools, and grocery stores (Knowles-Yánez, 2007). Again, I return to these residents and the problems of planning when the residents' neighborhoods have been destroyed. This chapter steps back from the on-the-ground focus of the original chapter and provides a broader review of the state of planning and social justice post-Katrina. This chapter is based on a review of the literature written about planning in New Orleans post-Katrina. Because this literature is largely written by academic planners the point of view of academics is well-represented, but the point of view of other collaborators in the planning process is not. Where appropriate I point this out to the reader below.

Planning processes are concerned with the distribution and use of land and other resources in a community. In the United States, there are as many variations of planning practices as there are political and administrative structures. Many municipalities, large and small, such as those that I live near in Southern California—San Diego, San Marcos, Escondido, practice developer-driven planning, where market forces and tax revenue generation play a strong role in shaping community land use and where cities like San Marcos and Escondido might compete to be the location for the next Wal-Mart, desiring its tax revenues, but might be less enthused about planning for affordable housing.

Some cities have strong citizen participation facets of their planning. There are many variations between economic development and community participation oriented planning; less practiced are participation planning techniques which hold as their goal social justice. Land use planners and theorists have long struggled with applications of justice. From advocacy planning, in which planners are charged with working to empower the disempowered in their communities, to equity planning, where issues of fairness among residents and other interests are of utmost consideration, to environmental justice planning, where communities weigh the effects of often unwanted toxins and environmental damage in their local environments, to New Urbanism planning, which brings together creative ideas for the functionality of the built environment with emphasis on livability and walkability, there is a rich legacy of thought about the role of land use planning in addressing justice. Some theorists challenge planners to advocate for and create participatory structures which lead to a more just distribution of resources—a more bottom up/ activist approach to practice than what is typically taken by most cities (see Davidoff, 1965; Forester, 2008). There is a schism between planning theories and practice in that most local practice is, in spite of theorizing in the literature, largely developer oriented and controlled.

According to Olshansky (2006), the extreme circumstance of New Orleans post-Katrina meant that "environmental justice, racial equity, restoration of natural systems, repairing levees and other public works, relocations, environmental cleanup, cultural heritage, hazard mitigation, economic development, and urban redevelopment" (p. 147) all competed for the attention of planners, government officials and residents. Planning processes sprung up which focused on any one, two, or more of these activities. Perhaps surprisingly then, given the general developer-oriented leaning of most planning practice and the profound concerns in many different realms post-disaster New Orleans, what could have been more traditional practices were countered by many attempts at social justice-oriented planning after Hurricane Katrina.

The aftermath of the Hurricane Katrina disaster created an opportunity to implement practices and processes that were not likely to have been put in place before the disaster. A remarkable opportunity to pursue social justice through planning was recognized by universities and non-profits. In the first and second years after the storm, and in the absence of definitive action by governmental authorities in planning and redevelopment, other organizations, including non-profits and universities, stepped into the role of planning.[1] I am using a broad interpretation of social justice in planning. A central component of humanity is home and neighborhood; when this

---

1. Not all post-hurricane planning efforts are social justice-oriented in methods or in expected outcomes. Richardson's (2008) book contains many chapters on rebuilding post-Katrina, and these efforts are based on more traditional policy, economic, engineering, or risk analysis. Indeed the introduction allows for a New Orleans that will be much "smaller than before. Many of the former residents will not come back, and there is little point (given the risks) in attracting new residents" (p. 1).

component becomes a barrier to a healthy life and other opportunities it should be addressed by those most affected and those willing to help. I call any process that helps give voice to residents who want to participate in planning and decision making for their own communities social justice-oriented planning. This includes those who call their planning processes variously: empowerment planning and participatory planning (Evans-Cowley & Zimmerman Gough, 2008) advocacy planning (Wagner, Frisch, & Fields, 2008), advocacy and equity planning (Reardon, Ionescu-Heroiu, & Rumbach, 2008), and environmental justice planning. The entrenched, urbanized poverty of New Orleans is a significant challenge on many, many levels, not the least of which is planning with and for residents who have been completely disempowered by the circumstances of their neighborhoods. Yet, it is these very circumstances of poverty and disempowerment that draw those interested in the aims of social justice to New Orleans.

Poverty and the Return to Neighborhoods

According to Logan (2008), there is still a barrier to return to New Orleans if you are poor; the majority of New Orleans's "population is still living elsewhere … the largest share is living outside the state, and black residents (especially poor black residents) are disproportionately found at the greatest distance from their prior homes" (p. 282). Poverty limits the ability of former residents to return. Policies that eliminated much of the damaged public housing post-Katrina meant that there were few public resources to enable poor people's return to the city. "… in the context of a zero-vacancy rental market at any price, the decision to press ahead with public housing demolition means that few displaced low-income families will have any opportunity to live in New Orleans in the future" (Logan, 2008, pp. 287–288). And poor, former residents are assured virtually no political power in their absence and thus will be largely unable to lobby for policies that might help them return. How do displaced residents lobby for support to return while simultaneously engaging in keeping their new life and family afloat wherever they have been displaced? They cannot because they must use their meager resources to try to survive.

Green, Bates, and Smyth (2007) note that damage from flooding was not the only impediment to residents rebuilding in the Lower Ninth Ward. They found the following factors that impeded recovery:

- labor, teacher and rental housing shortages
- uncertainties regarding levee reconstruction
- high flood insurance premiums
- scarcities in service sectors (including schools, stores, restaurants, police, fire, garbage collection, postal)

- lack of "access to rebuilding capital" (p. 326),
- public perception overstated heavy structural damage, in part due to intense media scrutiny of the most devastated areas,
- many people assumed it would be impossible to rebuild the neighborhoods,
- rebuilding infrastructure was slowed by these perceptions
- and that "pre-existing social and economic marginalization" (p. 329) limited governmental response to neighborhoods

Media portrayals created an image of the Lower Ninth Ward as being destroyed. The apocryphal image perpetuated by the media called into question whether or not the area should be repaired and redeveloped. These portrayals reached displaced residents in their new locations, and fed hesitation about returning. Surveys found that "Low-income residents of the Upper and Lower Ninth Ward wanted to return, but were wary about committing resources to repairing homes that may later be bulldozed, or about returning to neighbourhoods that might never regain municipal services" (Green, Bates, & Smyth, 2007, p. 325). Furthermore, the poorest evacuees were often those displaced the greatest distance from New Orleans, which made it even harder to actively participate in repairing, rebuilding and planning for their neighborhoods. Even a year later, some areas in the Ninth Ward did not have municipal services such as running water restored, which meant that residents were not able to place a FEMA trailer on their property. That so much of the Ninth Ward remains to be rebuilt should not be taken as a measure of residents' preferences regarding rebuilding, where poverty and other impediments to rebuilding remain (Green, Bates, & Smyth, 2007).

Historic Distrust

According to the Brookings Institution, the economic segregation of New Orleans neighborhoods "did not appear by accident. (Segregation) emerged in part due to decades of policies that confined poor households, especially poor black ones to these economically isolated areas" (Berube & Katz, 2005, p. 1). They note that "... extremely poor neighborhoods serve to limit the life chances and quality of life for poor families that live in their midst, above and beyond the barriers imposed by their own personal circumstances" (Berube & Katz, 2005, p. 2).

The relationship between New Orleans' government and poor residents was difficult even before Katrina. Historic environmental injustices have shaped current day mistrust of government in New Orleans. In 1927, federal authorities, holding local business interests above those of indigenous people's livelihoods, "dynamite(d) a hole in the levee below the city" (Colten, 2007, p. 175), thereby allowing flood water to flow through the city more quickly, even though the downstream result was devastation to wildlife and indigenous culture. The distrust caused by this incident led to the urban myth that levee flood gates in the Ninth Ward were opened during Hurricane Betsy in 1965 and again in August 2005. According to Colten, "The flooding was real in both instances, and the causation myth had its roots in a decision that many considered an environmental injustice in 1927" (p. 175). Previous governmental actions seasoned New Orleans residents to distrust authorities; in addition to all of the physical damage still unrepaired, mistrust of government is also key to understanding how difficult the situation is for displaced residents. If residents don't trust leaders, why will they participate in planning processes? In return, if residents don't participate, then it will be impossible to include them in discussions of their own needs.

Allen (2007) outlines impediments to the implementation of environmental justice post-Katrina, including the contrast between local and outside knowledge. For example, some historic structures were considered unsalvageable by outsiders who came to New Orleans to help assess storm damage. Since they lacked local knowledge about building construction and materials used historically to deal with flooding, they did not understand what they were seeing and tore down historic buildings that, according to local knowledge and customs, were actually salvageable. Activities such as these hinder recovery because they engender and perpetuate mistrust between residents and policy makers.

There are many more examples of the lack of trust between poor New Orleans residents and officials. For example, three years after Katrina, *The Nation* published an exposé of vigilante attacks by white people in Algiers Point against African-American males who entered the white neighborhoods on their way to somewhere else in the mass confusion immediately following the hurricane (Thompson, 2009). The fact that this story was exposed so long after it occurred underscores the difficulty of imagining justice for the poor of New Orleans. If justice for people shot by vigilantes may never be attained, why then hope that justice will be attained for neighborhoods and housing? Still, and in spite of the evidence that might draw people away from trying to plan in a socially just manner for New Orleans and the Gulf Coast in the aftermath of Katrina, attempts to apply social justice in planning have been notable for their creativity, inclusiveness, and sheer determination. The following is a review of some of these notable attempts by universities and non-profit organizations (including those guided by celebrities).

University Collaborations

Faculty at several universities organized opportunities for students to engage in planning in New Orleans and the Gulf Coast areas post-Katrina. The disaster created an opportunity to try practices that were not likely to have been put in place before the disaster. Students participated in learning opportunities they would not have had otherwise. The uniqueness of this situation is underscored by two 2008 publications: 1) the dedication of a large section of one of the most prestigious planning scholarly journals, *Planning Theory and Practice*, to a series of articles about Cornell University, Columbia University, and the University of Illinois at Urbana-Champaign's collaboration on the "New Orleans Planning Initiative (NOPI)" (Forester, 2008) [NOPI later came to be known as the Association of Community Organizations for Reform Now (ACORN) Housing University Collaborative (AHUC)] and 2) a special issue of Housing and Urban Development's (HUD) *Cityscape: A Journal of Policy Development and Research* titled "Design and Disaster: Higher Education Responds to Hurricane Katrina," which further describes the collaboration noted above, as well as post-hurricane work by researchers and students at Ohio State University, University of Missouri-Kansas City, Louisiana State University, University of Virginia, Mississippi State University, Tulane University, University of Kansas, and University of Nebraska-Lincoln (Dorgan, Monti, & Wright, 2008). In 2009, Reardon, Green, Bates, & Kiely published a follow-up article summing up lessons from AHUC's experiences. I take care in identifying these sources for this section because it is here where we see the academic planners' point of view so well represented in the literature. ACORN and other community residents were very active in these processes, but because the story is told through the filter of the academic planners, we know less about how it was experienced from the perspective of other community collaborators.

These authors of these articles discuss their respective projects in great detail, as if in deference to the historical importance of the rare opportunity presented by the situation. HUD's Office of University Partnerships created a grant program called Gulf Coast Universities Rebuilding America Partnership post-Hurricanes Katrina and Rita (Wagner, Frisch, & Fields, 2008). Because many universities in the Gulf Coast were shut down for the semester or quarter immediately following Hurricane Katrina, and their faculty and students were so affected by the hurricane that they were less able to reach out and work within their own communities, universities as far away as Ohio, Missouri, and New York were among the first to step in and connect students to local post-Hurricane projects. Social justice is embedded in many of these projects. The stories below are from these journal articles.

ACORN, a community non-profit organization, contacted Cornell and other universities for help in planning for the return of residents to their neighborhoods, which eventually led to Cornell focusing its efforts on the Ninth Ward (Reardon, 2008). ACORN organized community collaboration meetings and Cornell faculty began working with faculty at Columbia University and University of Illinois. These universities are widely recognized for their participatory planning legacies. This collaboration came to be known as AHUC (Reardon, Green, Bates, & Kiely, 2009). Cornell faculty were able to respond quickly and refocused several planning and design classes that semester and subsequent semesters on Katrina-specific issues. They also began working on a comprehensive planning effort for the City of New Orleans. The AHUC process was unique because of the fact that it linked a strong community collaborator, ACORN, and outside university resources. And it was highly social justice-oriented in that the faculty and staff interview data collection recognized and validated the role of everyday people's knowledge in understanding their communities. The university faculty and students' early focus was deep public participation; however ACORN began to put up barriers because they were unused to public participation efforts that extended beyond members of ACORN (Reardon, 2008). Indeed, how difficult it was to work with ACORN from the academic planners' perspective was underscored by another faculty member from the Massachusetts Institute of Technology who was also called in to New Orleans; Thompson (2009) elected early on not to work with ACORN because he saw that they could be divisive and were not aligned with smaller black organizations in the community.

Members of ACORN working within AHUC were politically minded; Steve Bradberry, one of the ACORN leaders said, "Had we not been [political] as well as [doing] that plan, we would not be where we are today. This was not a normal circumstance under which planning takes place. It was a hostile environment particularly for the Ninth Ward" (in Reardon, Green, Bates, & Kiely, 2009, p. 396). The hostility was coming from the larger community's resistance to rebuilding the Ninth Ward and also from tensions within AHUC. ACORN organizers were uncomfortable with the White university students' ability to represent their interests. Bradberry (quoted in Reardon, Green, Bates, & Kiely, 2009) notes:

... the Lower Ninth is used to light skinned blacks coming in to take over. It is a very politicized neighborhood and their understanding of power is very, very keen.

In the beginning, ACORN members were very happy about [student-facilitated planning activities] but when they found out meetings were happening [without them] they were upset. They thought "Are you representing me?" [The students believed] that everything is equal and everybody's trying to just "do a good job." But almost nobody is just trying to do a good job. Everyone is trying to get what their piece is.... What you may think is fair and balanced on the outside will probably be weighted in a direction that is not in favor of lower income communities. (p. 397)

Internal tension within AHUC was not the only barrier the universities faced when they tried to practice inclusion; local, state, and federal officials were mismanaging the overall recovery process. Officials were not distributing rebuilding resources equitably or in a timely manner. Additionally, officials were not providing the right kinds of expertise to weary residents. This situation was exacerbated by the fact that so many residents were no longer physically in New Orleans and were easily left out of rebuilding and planning processes. Reardon (2008) underscores the social justice orientation of the Cornell faculty and students: "Here we were trying to develop a comprehensive plan to help people in the poorest census tracks (sic) in the city to return home—and they are waiting again, like they were waiting on the rooftops to be rescued and we really felt there was a moral and ethical and professional responsibility to give voice to the aspirations of these people" (p. 525).

AHUC faculty and students continued in their efforts through sheer grit and determination, and in the face of dwindling internal support from ACORN. What kept them going was realization that their data on the quality of the remaining housing stock belied the notion that rehabilitation would take extraordinary amounts of money. According to Green et al., the university collaborative's on-the-ground survey of the neighborhoods demonstrated that damage to structures in the Ninth Ward was not as widespread as what was depicted in the media, and "Throughout the Upper and Lower Ninth Ward, 75 per cent (sic) of the existing structures surveyed in October 2006 had either no or minor structural damage" (p. 317). The community was eminently more repairable than presumed by the media. AHUC was determined to take advantage of the actual viability of saving the neighborhood rather than giving in to the perceived lack of viability created by the media and given credence by officials.

In the end, the AHUC plan resonated and achieved buy-in with residents and their internal collaborator ACORN because of the depth of community input, which is a tribute to its attempts to plan in a socially just manner (Reardon, 2008). Specific ways in which community residents collaborated with AHUC faculty and students included participating in the process which selected AHUC to lead the planning process, letting AHUC faculty and students come to know them and their neighborhoods in a personal way, and participating in interviews, surveys, and focus groups on the status of their neighborhoods conducted by AHUC students and faculty. Residents also provided feedback as reports were being written. The full title of their plan is suggestive of its social justice ambitions: *The People's Plan for Overcoming the Hurricane Katrina Blues: A Comprehensive Strategy for Promoting a More Vibrant, Sustainable, and Equitable 9th Ward.* This kind of planning takes its direction from the seminal social justice-oriented planner, Paul Davidoff (Reardon, Ionescu-Heroiu,

& Rumbach, 2008). Davidoff (1965) is known for advocacy planning, which includes roles for everyday people, especially the most impoverished and un-empowered, in planning processes. In fact, Rubin (2009) notes that AHUC's work was an intensive test of the concepts underlying advocacy planning's call for giving voice to low-income people's concerns.

Students working on this process saw it as a referendum on their times: "Many students viewed the question of the nation's willingness to rebuild New Orleans and its poorest neighborhoods as a litmus test of society's commitment to racial justice and equality" (Reardon, Ionescu-Heroiu, & Rumbach, 2008, p. 66) and were upset by the thin response of local and national authorities. This provided for very profound learning experiences. A Cornell undergraduate student describes how the leadership of ACORN challenged his expectations of how a community organization should operate. He notes that, "My understanding of planning meant you left no one behind. As a community planner, you plan for everyone" (Bycer, 2008, p. 553), yet ACORN was willing to leave out partici-pants and other community organizations who were not members of ACORN. Bycer's writing about his experiences in New Orleans typifies how many social justice oriented planners-in-training feel about their work. Examining the young life of privilege that brought him to being an undergraduate student at Cornell in light of the political disempowerment he saw affecting working class residents, he writes, "We have an obligation as privileged, well-educated, and re-spected citizens to use this power for the people who need it most" (Bycer, 2008, p. 556). He felt the need to fight with the people of New Orleans, to be strong, and not to give into the emotionally draining aspect of this particular process.

A Cornell graduate student thoughtfully explains the charged atmosphere going into New Orleans in January 2006. The physical environment was devas-tated, yet the situation felt inspiring and full of opportunity. He explains that in the early stages of the project, helping to tear down houses was "enormously satisfying" (Rumbach, 2008, p. 542). Yet when his group began to apply typical pre-planning visioning techniques in order to understand what residents wanted out of the process, ".... well-intentioned planners, especially those from outside New Orleans, were shouted down with people's immediate, pressing concerns. One Lower Ninth Ward mother all too poignantly shouted: 'We've been planned to death!'" (p. 543). This student explained the pressure that many of the students felt to justify the importance of rebuilding the Ninth Ward in the face of developers who questioned the ability of the area to be saved. This dedication remained even during a period of time in which AHUC was fired from working on planning for the Ninth Ward, for internal and ex-ternal city-based political and organization reasons [in particular ACORN was accused of unethically trying to act as both planner and developer, by planning to buy tax delinquent properties for the neighborhood, though in reality they had yet to buy anything (Reardon, Green, Bates, & Kiely, 2009)], from the city's planning effort in Fall 2006. AHUC university partners remained dedicated and defiant in the face of their firing and continued their data analysis, interviewing, and report preparation. Finally, ACORN used their political organizing skills to bring important political players to a January 2007 meeting publicizing AHUC's efforts. This led to the "People's Plan" being officially adopted in February 2007 by the City Council, a complete turnaround for the previously fired planning team (Rumbach, 2008). AHUC was instrumental in changing the long-term situation for the Lower Ninth Ward in that the city has now recognized it as a ReBuild Zone, where previously the initial city planning efforts post-Katrina advised against redeveloping the area. "AHUC's participants felt that they had contributed, in a modest way, to one of the most important planning efforts recently undertaken by our profession" (Reardon et al., 2009, p. 399). And the members of AHUC came to realize that they could not have done it without each other, as one of the leaders of ACORN, Wade Rathke, notes in Reardon, Green, Bates, & Kiely (2009):

> I do honestly believe that if we had not been able to get the support from our friends in the university community, it would have been a much different fight. The collaboration helped our members, leaders and staff to step back and to see that this was the right thing to do, that it was possible, and that it could be done. (p. 398)

Other universities were also engaged in social justice-oriented planning in New Orleans. Cuddeback & Bosworth detail their students' collaboration on the construction of the first two houses in the Lower Ninth Ward that I wrote about in the first edition of this book. The constuction sites and houses themselves became learning laboratories for Louisiana State University students. In their journals students wrote of the isolation and desolation of the neighborhood. They also "witnessed first-hand the effect that two small houses had on the psyche of the neighborhood and the effect these houses has in influencing a renewed commitment of neighbors to rebuild and return" (Cuddeback & Bosworth, 2008, p. 93). Another group of students learned about the importance of preserving the cultural fabric of damaged communities. University of Kansas students worked with residents of New Orleans' Seventh Ward in creating community structures designed to preserve the cultural heritage of the neighborhood and strengthen community cohesiveness. They worked with residents to create a community garden and tool shed, a mobile stage, an outdoor classroom, and community notice boards (Corser & Gore, 2008).

Finally, other universities were at work in other areas of the Gulf Coast. Evans-Cowley & Zimmerman Gough (2008) report on a process they refer to as both empowerment planning and participatory planning in Harrison County, Mississippi. Their primary goal "was to create a citizen-engagement process that increased community capacity to implement the plans" (p. 22).

The faculty took students in a studio class at Ohio State University to work with residents. Students expected to be able to call, make appointments with, and interview residents, but found that local residents were not used to returning calls from strangers, nor were they used to the idea of planning. When they planned town hall meetings in order to gain the community's trust, "the first citizen who arrived immediately got on his cell phone and started calling everyone he knew, telling them to get down here because there were folks from up north here and that could only be bad news" (p. 27). Indeed, in an interview with the county zoning administrator, they found out that little planning had gone on in the communities prior to the hurricane, that residents did not think positively of planning, and, indeed, they likened planning to communism (Bonck, 2005 as cited in Evans-Cowley & Zimmerman Gough, 2008). Students found that they had to first make personal connections with established community members, who could then help them make connections to more residents and so on. The students had a learning curve of their own as they had to negotiate the residents' fears of communism and distrust of planning. They learned to explain planning processes on citizens' own terms. The faculty note, "To gain the community's trust, the team avoided using planning terms and instead used the citizen's own words.... The team would make statements such as, 'you told us that you wanted to make sure that the community maintains its farming areas'" (p. 32).

Social justice planning is not merely collaborating with local and interested participants, but being aware of how different communication patterns and norms can intimidate and strike fear as even well-meaning outsiders step into unfamiliar communities. Even the very presence of outsiders who use technical planning terms like "agricultural zoning" and "density per unit" can thwart social justice-oriented planning. In this case, students made progress in understanding how to work with locals, and locals gained an understanding of the outsiders as students who they were educating about working with local communities. As Evans-Cowley & Zimmerman Gough (2008) note,

> In reviewing the students' journals, instructors found that their attitudes toward citizen engagement had clearly changed. Although at the beginning of the course students viewed citizen participation as an important part of planning, by the end of the process they understood how engaged citizens could result in a truly positive transformation for a community. (p. 31)

In a sign of their long-term commitment to working with these communities, they have laid groundwork for future students in the form of a "Mississippi Survivor's Guide," which advises students "on how to work with teammates, the community, officials, stress, and the culture of the coast" (p. 34).

Celebrity Non-Profits and Planning

As I noted with a tinge of planning envy in my chapter in the first edition of this book:

> One beacon of hope we saw in this area—by now we were driving through the Upper 9th Ward (which, in fact, is still the Bywater District)—was the Musicians' Village built by Habitat for Humanity and conceived by Harry Connick, Jr. and Branford Marsalis. The houses are delightful looking pastel concoctions, very neighborly, lovingly occupied, and filling several city blocks. While every little bit of housing built helps all New Orleans residents, where rents and housing prices are sky high due to scarcity, we couldn't help but comment on the fact that famous names had to be attached to the project in order for it to move forward. Planning and reconstruction clearly move at a much slower pace for regular folk in New Orleans.
>
> (Knowles-Yánez, 2007, p. 391)

Envy aside, it is impossible to deny the social justice-orientation of this kind of planning. Harry Connick Jr. and Branford Marsalis realized that a certain group, low-income musicians, would likely be left out of rebuilding and took it upon themselves to take care of their own by enlisting the help of Habitat for Humanity. According to the New Orleans Area Habitat for Humanity "Construction began in March 2006 and as of March 2009, 70 homes are complete and another 12 homes are under construction!" (http://www.habitat-nola. org/projects/musicians_village.php), Habitat for Humanity volunteers, many of whom come from other parts of the country, work with future homeowners in constructing homes. Future homeowners must invest at least 350 hours of "sweat equity" in their homes or by working on other homes in the program. They are then able to buy the homes for no-interest loans.

Since this effort, an even more ambitious celebrity planning process has taken on long-term efforts to rebuild housing in the Ninth Ward. Brad Pitt is among the most prominent of a group who have formed an organization called "Make it Right" to build new housing and which advocates a "cradle to cradle" design philosophy, in which materials can be recycled and are energy efficient (Clarke, 2009). As with the university collaborations, this is an example of an approach that would likely not be tried in other places or in New Orleans if not for Hurricane Katrina. The recognition of this nexus of opportunity and the desire to pursue social justice is summed up by Pitt in an article in *Architectural Digest* in which he speaks about the architects his organization invited to New Orleans: "… they offered their brain power, their expertise and their time. They also felt this was a place of injustice—but also a place of opportunity" (Clarke, 2009, p. 67).

Conclusion

As of August 2009, four years after Hurricane Katrina, the Lower Ninth Ward is still a cause of grave concern at the national level. CNN notes that there is some rebuilding and most debris has been removed but that the neighborhood is still an "abandoned wasteland" (King, 2009). The neighborhood trails New Orleans in terms of rebuilding and in return of the population. For New Orleans as a whole, 75% of the population has returned since Katrina struck, whereas only 19% of the population has returned to the Lower Ninth Ward. Those who have returned and rebuilt face sparsely populated neighborhoods and scarce community services. There is still only one school in the ward (King, 2009). Clearly the promise of social justice is still only a promise as the years move on and the condition of the neighborhood improves at a very slow pace. Larger societal forces of racism, classism, and historical distrust may prevent justice ever being served for former residents of the Lower Ninth forever unable to return.

Talen (2008), a leading New Urbanist scholar, indicates how implementing social justice policy via planning is historically problematic in that designer/planner's "social equity goals," balancing resource distribution, are often not backed up by policy created by planners or others. She cautions that those who try to use the opportunities for planning created by Hurricane Katrina for advancement of social equity goals will be impeded by the lack of concomitant social equity policy. A design-based approached in the absence of a parallel policy-based approach will create tension, which may doom social equity efforts. Indeed, she finds that Gulf Coast rebuilding efforts have not met New Urbanist social equity goals and that neighborhood planning has been a significant disappointment. She writes, "Greatly needed are the merger of design, policy, and program and the integration of a more complete participatory approach" (p. 291). This is a cautionary tale for the post-Katrina social justice-oriented planning efforts, for without a governmental policy orientation toward the same goals, efforts may be short-lived.

Achieving social justice-oriented planning is an ongoing challenge given the lack of concomitant social justice policy and the developer-oriented nature of most planning in the United States. Yet, the depth of the tragedy in New Orleans was so great that it inspired people across the country to collaborate with the people of New Orleans in rebuilding their communities. Many academic and celebrity planners wholeheartedly embraced this opportunity. The celebrity planning efforts have been relatively small in scope and quite successful. On the other hand, academic advocacy planners who came to work with community organizers and residents on large-scale planning efforts have been met with considerable outside and internal collaborative challenges and barriers. As the AHUC collaboration demonstrates, in spite of the difficulties in such a large planning process, there are successes in fits and starts.

Perhaps one of the most tangible results for social justice in this quagmire is that hundreds of students engaged in community organizing and planning in New Orleans and the Gulf Coast areas in the years following Katrina. Faculty brought their students to these devastated areas so that they could learn on the ground what would be largely unavailable to them in the classroom. The tragedy of New Orleans occasioned the training of many more planners in social-justice oriented planning than might have occurred otherwise.

Out of these fits and starts and paradoxical opportunities arise insights into new ways of conducting business as usual, including those which take into account the voices of the all affected by any given planning process. For those unable to return to New Orleans, certainly nothing can justify their displacement and inability to return to their beloved neighborhoods. But, for the profession of planning, perhaps there is a stronger sense of the profession's ability to address social justice issues and a strengthening of its capacity to do as students graduate and take their experiences to their new jobs.

However, social justice-oriented planning is still not widespread in New Orleans or the Gulf Coast or anywhere else in the United States, nor is it ever likely to be given current planning structures that favor tax revenue generation. It will take the dedication of individual residents to advocate for their own interests, and those planners trained to allow this to happen, to bear the task of standing up to power structures in their given community. This is the eternal struggle of all humans and communities: to assert their rights to socially just outcomes, and in the case of New Orleans and the Gulf Coast, to take advantage of these paradoxical opportunities created by major upheaval and disaster to argue for something that did not exist before, to replace the old way of doing business with structures that take into consideration interests of all people, especially the most disempowered.

References

Allen, B.L. (2007). Environmental justice, local knowledge, and after-disaster planning in New Orleans. *Technology in Society, 29*, 153–159.

Berube, A., & Katz, B. (2005). *Katrina's window: Confronting concentrated poverty across America.* Washington, D.C.: The Brookings Institution Metropolitan Policy Program.

Bonck, P. (2005, November 7). Harrison County zoning administrator. (J. S. Evans-Cowley, & M. Zimmerman Gough, Interviewers).

Bycer, E. (2008). Politics, inspiration and vocation: An education in New Orleans. *Planning Theory and Practice, 9*(4), 552–558.

Clarke, G. (2009). Brad Pitt makes it right in New Orleans. *Architectural Digest, 66*(1), 60–72.

Colten, C.E. (2007). Environmental justice in a landscape of tragedy. *Technology in Society, 29,* 173–179.

Corser, R., & Gore, N. (2008). Rebuilding for the Seventh Ward's cultural life. *Cityscape: A Journal of Policy Development and Research, 10*(3), 159–166.

Cuddeback, M.R., & Bosworth, F.M. (2008). Rebuilding community block by block. *Cityscape: A Journal of Policy Development and Research, 10*(3), 77–99.

Davidoff, P. (1965). Advocacy and pluralism in planning. *Journal of the American Institute of Planners, 31*(4), 331–338.

Dorgan, K., Monti, M., & Wright, K.D. (2008). Guest editor's introduction. *Cityscape: A Journal of Policy Development and Research, 10*(3), 1–8.

Evans-Cowley, J.S., & Zimmerman Gough, M. (2008). Citizen engagement in Post-Hurricane Katrina: Planning in Harrison County, Mississippi. *Cityscape: A Journal of Policy Development and Research, 10*(3), 21–37.

Forester, J. (2008). Interface, Introduction: Making a difference in response to Hurricane Katrina. *Planning Theory and Practice, 9*(4), 517–518.

Green, R., Bates, L.K., & Smyth, A. (2007). Impediments to recovery in New Orleans' Upper and Lower Ninth Ward: One year after Hurricane Katrina. *Disasters, 31* (4), 311–335.

King, J. (2009, March 22). King: Lower Ninth Ward trails in New Orleans 'new normal.' Retrieved on May 8, 2009 from http://www.cnn.com/2009/POLITICS/03/19/sou.la.ninth.ward/index.htm.

Knowles-Yanez, K. (2007). The disappearing neighborhood: An urban planner's tour of New Orleans. In K. A. Bates, & R. S. Swan (Eds.), *Through the eye of Katrina: Social justice in the United States* (pp. 387–395). Durham, North Carolina: Carolina Academic Press.

Logan, J.R. (2008). Unnatural disaster: social impacts and policy choices after Katrina. In H. W. Richardson, *Natural Disaster Analysis After Hurricane Katrina* (pp. 279–297). Cheltenham, UK: Edward Elgar.

New Orleans Area Habitat for Humanity. (n.d.). Retrieved June 9, 2009 from http://www.habitat-nola.org.

Olshansky, R.B. (2006). Planning after Hurricane Katrina. *Journal of the American Planning Association, 72*(2), 147–153.

Reardon, K.M., Green, R., Bates, L.K., & Kiely, R.C. (2009). Overcoming the challenges of post-diaster planning in New Orleans: Lessons from the ACORN Housing/University Collaborative. *Journal of Planning Education and Research, 28,* 391–400.

Reardon, K.M., Ionescu-Heroiu, M., & Rumbach, A. J. (2008). Equity planning in post-Hurricane Katrina New Orleans: Lessons from the Ninth Ward. *Cityscape: A Journal of Policy Development and Research, 10*(3), 57–76.

Reardon, K. (2008). Planning, hope, and struggle in the wake of Katrina: Ken Reardon on the New Orleans Planning Initiative. *Planning Theory and Practice, 9*(4), 518–540.

Richardson, H.W., Gordon, P.I., & Moore, J.E. (Eds.) (2008). *Natural disaster analysis after Hurricane Katrina: Risk assessment, economic impacts and social implications.* Cheltenham, UK: Edward Elgar.

Rubin, V. (2009). Response to "Post-disaster planning in New Orleans": Necessary conditions for community partnerships. *Journal of Planning Education of Research, 28,* 401–402.

Rumbach, A. (2008). Challenges of disaster response, or what the textbooks don't teach us. *Planning Theory and Practice, 9* (4), 540–551.

Talen, E. (2008). New urbanism, social equity, and the challenge of post-Katrina rebuilding in Mississippi. *Journal of Planning Education and Research, 27,* 277–293.

Thompson, A.C. (2009, January 5). Katrina's hidden race war. *The Nation.*

Thomson, J.P. (2009). Response to "Post-disaster planning in New Orleans." *Journal of Planning Education and Research, 28,* 403–404.

Wagner, J., Frisch, M., & Fields, B. (2008). Building local capacity: Planning for local culture and neighborhood recovery in New Orleans. *Cityscape: A Journal of Policy Development and Research,10*(3), 39–56.

Chapter 24

You CAN Get There from Here, But the Road Is Long and Hard: The Role of Public, Private and Activist Organizations in the Search for Social Justice

Kristin A. Bates and Richelle S. Swan

One of the things we have learned while engaged in this project is that the struggle for social justice will not end anytime soon. As the first section of the book, *Images from the Past: Social Justice and Hurricane Katrina in Context*, emphasizes, and the second section of the book, *Images of the Disaster: Reactions to Hurricane Katrina* similarly demonstrates, many of the problems that were highlighted by the events after Hurricane Katrina have been decades, even centuries, in the making. This means that solving the problems that have arisen from Hurricane Katrina necessitates a broader effort than just focusing on the devastation from the storm. As the chapters of this volume discuss, the social disaster exposed after Hurricane Katrina is enmeshed in issues of disenfranchisement, poverty, public housing, politics, racial and ethnic conflict, and unjust criminal justice policies, all of which existed in the United States long before August 29, 2005.

Specifically, we have learned from this book that the quest for social justice is never finished. We must take from this book that racism still exists and has a long history (Miller & Rivera, Chapter 2)—that it is enacted at the individual level as Weil (Chapter 13), Doane (Chapter 7), and Moon and Hurst (Chapter 8) document and at the group/institutional level as Check (Chapter 14) shows. Racism is also institutionalized in policies that were meant to avert injustice (Inderbitzen, Fawcett, Uggen, & Bates, Chapter 3; Trujillo-Pagán, Chapter 9). We also need to recognize that our policies to address poverty have been woefully inadequate (Keyssar, Chapter 6) and in many instances work against the poor (Arena, Chapter 20; and Foster, Chapter 16; Knowles-Yánez).

Although this book highlights the fact that the road to social justice is a long and hard one, contributions to the volume also point out fruitful ways of traveling down the winding path to a more socially just society. We have learned that we need to listen to and learn from multiple perspectives if we are to create just solutions (Knowles-Yánez, Chapter 22; and Leong et al., Chapter 10), that we not subvert social justice to politics or the law (Travis, Chapter 17); to a neoliberal agenda (David, Chapter 21) or to the many industrial complexes—prison, military, consumer—that exist today (Agid, Chapter 4), and that advocating and agitating for a just outcome can often lead to change (Swan, Chapter 5; Leong et al., Chapter 10; Leonard, Chapter 15; and Arena, Chapter 20).

In the rest of this chapter we want to highlight some of the cultural, social, and political decisions that have been made in the recent past that make the quest for social justice so necessary.

From the Welfare State to Neoliberalism: Does This Road Go Anywhere?

Between the first edition and second edition of this book the house of cards known as the global economy officially came tumbling down. For many, the fall was not a surprise—they had been living on the edge long enough to know that a large-scale financial catastrophe was in the making even before officials declared it to be so. The reasons for this financial meltdown and its related injustices are many and would fill several books of their own, however, many of the same social philosophies and policies that were prevalent during prologue to and the aftermath of Hurricane Katrina also contributed to our present situation. While it is easy to lament the injustice(s) that occurred throughout the Hurricane Katrina-ravaged areas of the South in 2005 (and that are still occurring) it would be naïve to have expected anything else. The social disaster that formed around Hurricane Katrina should not have been a surprise to anyone following the political, economic, and social trajectories of the United States.

The Welfare State

As Keyssar (Chapter 6) aptly described, the United States experienced what one might call a welfare state for much of the middle of the twentieth century. While the American welfare state was not cut from the same cloth as its more generous European counterparts, it did spring from similar beliefs in the importance of ensuring social justice, providing a safety net for those who slipped through the cracks, and eliminating poverty. The philosophy behind the welfare state is this: the welfare or social well-being of individuals in the nation is the collective responsibility of all citizens. Instead of focusing on individual merit and deservedness, the focus of the welfare state is on national, state responsibility for providing a minimum standard of living that keeps individuals out of poverty, healthy, educated, and free from hunger.

While there were attempts in the United States to put some welfare policies in place in the late 1800s and early 1900s, the first sweeping policies that took hold were during the Great Depression in the mid-1930s, followed by policies during the "war on poverty" in the 1960s. A third period of sweeping reform concerning welfare happened in the 1990s under President Clinton with the ushering in of workfare and the ushering out of welfare (Bensonsmith, 2009). We argue that this move is not an example of the welfare state, but instead is an example of neoliberalism taking hold in social policy.

Much research has examined the effectiveness of the welfare state. From a social justice perspective, the most important of the research findings that have come out of this body of work are those that consider whether the welfare state has furthered the cause of social justice. This research demonstrates that welfare policy has been shaped by cultural definitions of worth (see Katz, 1986; Steensland, 2006). In other words, the likelihood of finding oneself "saved" has been based on one's worthiness in the eyes of those shaping policy. It has been these judgments of worthiness and unworthiness that have perpetuated social and economic injustices even in a system designed to eliminate them. The group who was the most often targeted as the "undesirable poor," and subsequently, the most controlled and least helped during the height of the welfare state was black women (Bensonsmith, 2009).

Neoliberalism

The onslaught of neoliberalism in the United States came over the course of about 25 years. Its first roots were hatched in the 1970s when stagflation defied the Keynsian understanding that government spending could help a recessionary economy (Mudge, 2008). While this was not the official start of neoliberalism, it offered an opportunity to question the existing welfare state philosophy and gave a space for free-market enthusiasts to offer an alternative. The Reagan Era brought neoliberalism to the forefront of American political thought, and it was solidified during the Clinton administration. Thus, neoliberalism is not linked to any specific political party in the United States, but instead transcends political parties (Mudge, 2008).

The term neoliberalism refers to a political, economic, and social ideology that argues that low government intervention, a privatization of services that in the past have predominately been the domain of government, an adherence to a free-market philosophy, and an emphasis on deregulation (Frericks, Maier, & de Graaf, 2009) constitute "the source and arbiter of human freedoms" (Mudge, 2008, p. 704). What may be one of the most important aspects of neoliberalism from the standpoint of those focused on social justice, is this link between the free markets and morality. While free markets have proven time and again to place the utmost emphasis on the profit motive (because this is what the free market is: an adherence to the notion of supply and demand)—this connection between free markets and "freedom" seems to intrinsically suggest that free markets, and therefore, neoliberalism, have individual well-being as their focus. In addition, it suggests that the free market will allow for the moral, or deserving, person to navigate it successfully.

However, individual well-being in the form of a guarantee that individuals will have access to the basic human needs of shelter, food, clothing, good health care, and safety from harm is not always produced by two of the most central components of neoliberalism—privatization and deregulation. In some ways, privatization and deregulation are opposite sides of the same coin. Privatization means the "opening up of the market" and the loosening of the rules (regulations) that are often the purview of the government. But privatization, at its core, is also the introduction of the profit motive into services that, at *their* core, are about protecting the human condition. A reliance on a neoliberal philosophy and free market economy means that we begin to evaluate everything through the lens of profit and cost-benefit analyses. We abdicate the responsibility of the state to private companies and then feign surprise when those companies defer to the profit motive instead of social justice concerns. In addition to the increased preference for free-markets and profits, privatization both reduces state responsibility for the care of its citizens and masks inability of the government to care for its citizens that quickly develops (Mitchell, 2001).

Roadblocks, Roadblocks Everywhere: Shifting Risk and Responsibility as an Impediment to Social Justice

The Trend from "Social Spending" to "Punitive Spending"

During this shift from the welfare state to a neoliberal state there has been a concurrent build up in the prison industrial complex that has culminated in mass imprisonment, prison overcrowding, and budgets paralyzed by "punitive spending." The Tough on Crime movement represented by the Rockefeller drug laws, truth in sentencing, the War on Drugs, and Three Strikes and You're

Out policies has led us to a point of no return in many states, reflective of the pattern currently evident in California:

> ... from the recently repealed Rockefeller drug laws through the expansion of the prison systems in Texas and Florida, onto the increasingly punitive response to poverty in the Clinton years, and the continuing disparity in sentencing laws, states and the federal government have chosen the Iron State over the Golden State. And whatever arguments there may be about the relative effectiveness of imprisonment in affecting crime rates (a topic of great controversy amongst scholars and analysts), one thing seems certain: a policy that exacerbates the brutalization of society is not one that will make us safer. Investing in prisons means investing in institutions that produce neither goods nor new opportunities (aside from the limited jobs available for prison employees and the one-time opportunities in construction); money spent on imprisonment is money taken from rebuilding our worn out infrastructure, our schools, our communities, and our economic future. Insofar as corrections remains at the heart of our social policy— rather than as a supplemental or marginal support as it was throughout most of United States history—it is the Iron State stealing from the future of the Golden State.

> (Meranze, 2009, n.p.)

This argument that state and federal "punitive spending" have taken precedence over "social spending" has significant implications for social justice and not only how we respond in times of crisis, such as Hurricane Katrina, but whether we are capable of responding at all. Many chapters in this book have documented the type of responses that were employed after Hurricane Katrina. Agid (Chapter 4) made a compelling argument that the onslaught of the prison industrial complex meant that the only response the government was prepared to make after Hurricane Katrina was one of social control. Social control was swiftly and efficiently put in place, and a more humane response focused on viewing individuals affected by the storm as victims instead of offenders was almost completely missing. This makes sense in a society that has experienced this unprecedented surge in "punitive spending" at the expense of "social spending" such as education, health services, and aid programs.

Risky Shifts from the Collective to the Individual

Only days before this massive financial crisis came to a head there were many who still claimed that the economy was in fine shape. However, some of this difference of opinion about the strength of the economy can be attributed to what Jacob Hacker (2006) refers to as a shift in risk and an increase in volatility for U.S. workers. This means that even when the economy may be doing well overall, segments in society that used to be secure have to deal with more risk and volatility than in the past. This fundamental shift has meant that while federal public policy used to spread extreme financial risk across all of society (thus ensuring that the burden was not carried by individuals), since the 1980s this risk has been transferred to individuals (Bernstein, 2006; Gragg, 2007; Hacker, 2006). This shift from public, societal, governmental responsibility to individual responsibility was first introduced within the most vulnerable segment of the population—the poor, through changes in General Assistance and AFDC programs; however, this philosophy is now being applied to programs that affect middle-class concerns too (Gragg, 2007). "Proposals that offer health care savings accounts or tax credits in the place of Medicare or Medicaid are risk shift proposals, Social Security privatization, the shift from defined benefit pension programs ... to defined contribution pensions ..." (Gragg, 2007, n.p.) are all proposals that shift extreme financial risk from a societal responsibility to an individual responsibility. This shift benefits corporations that no longer have to deal with the rising costs of health care or pension programs. It does not hurt the upper class much because they arguably can weather the storm of a personal financial crisis, such as one related to a long-term illness, or rising health care costs after retirement, but the shift strongly affects the middle class and working poor who do not have the personal wealth to weather such storms. In both the short and long runs, it makes it the responsibility of the middle class and working poor to shoulder upheavals in the volatile U.S. economy, while leaving corporations and the upper class in the position to enjoy the upturns without having to take any responsibility for the downturns.

This same philosophy of moving the responsibility of risk from society to the individual permeates many of the analyses of Hurricane Katrina furthered by people in power. One example of this is the argument that the number of Latinos in New Orleans was too low to justify offering hurricane information directed specifically at their community, which has made individuals in this community bear the brunt of the burden related to this lack of information (Trujillo-Pagán, Chapter 9). Similarly, arguments justifying the weakening of FEMA responsibilities and the shift of these responsibilities to local government and individuals support a generalized risk shift. Ironically, when individuals did shoulder responsibility and in the days following the hurricane provided for their families, oftentimes in the only manner available to them, they were labeled as looters and thugs (Bates & Ahmed, Chapter 11).

From Roadblocks to the Expressway: Moving Down the Road to Substantive Change

Many of the experiences described and analyzed in this book may lead some to question the likelihood that social justice can ever be achieved in the United States. We certainly do not want to leave you with the feeling that working toward social justice is ever futile and we offer both suggestions for starting your own path to social justice and specific examples of collective activism that have sprung up after Hurricane Katrina.

Connecting Your Path to the Collective Road: Suggestions for Social Justice

1. Believe that one person can make a difference.

Some of the most impressive social movements started with the ideas and actions of individuals. For example the Sit-In Movement was successfully kicked off by four black college students. While other sit-in movements to protest whites-only lunch counters had existed, the sit-in that took hold was started by four black college students who had very little structured plan besides going to the Woolworths lunch counter and respectfully engaging in a "sit-down protest" (Branch, 1988, p. 271). While collective action take place for most social justice movements to become successful, that collective action often starts with one or two committed individuals who don't give up.

2. Don't give up.

Especially in a society in which social policy has been subverted to the neoliberal belief that the free market solves all problems, making substantive change toward a more just society is no easy task. This change comes in fits and starts, sometimes it ebbs backwards, as we see with the experience of disenfranchisement after Hurricane Katrina (Chapter 3), but we can point to examples of change and those examples tell us not to give up.

3. Do not let your attention be diverted.

Turk (1976) argues that one of the best ways for those in power to remain in power is to be able to engage in diversionary power, the power to capture the attention of individuals and divert it away from issues that may be important or threatening to society. We see this diversionary tactic used consistently and successfully to discourage social justice. For example, one of the best diversionary tactics is to discredit the very people who are the most socially vulnerable. We saw this throughout the discourse surrounding Hurricane Katrina. Doane (Chapter 7) and Moon and Hurst (Chapter 8) critiqued this tactic in their chapters, describing various examples including painting victims as looters and dangerous. Check (Chapter 14) analyzed the Congressional testimony of victims of Hurricane Katrina and the subsequent discourse of Congressional members who called these victims ill-mannered, delusional, and dishonest.

4. Agitate for the state to be responsible to its citizens.

We should expect much more from our elected officials, our social policies, our government than we receive. It is inexcusable that the only strong, organized, efficient response to Hurricane Katrina was a response based in social control that prioritized personal property over individual well-being, and that mobilized to create an on-site jail, but couldn't effectively evacuate the city. Sometimes the only way to get what we expect is to engage in social disapproval.

5. Recognize that social disapproval is useful.

Social disapproval kept both Eisenhower and Nixon from dropping the bomb (Kauzlarich & Kramer, 1998). Social disapproval desegregated lunch counters. Social disapproval brought attention to the plight of thousands of hurricane victims (Leonard, Chapter 15). At the time, social disapproval may look like it is having no effect, but we can never know how bad it might have gotten had we not been protesting.

6. Look to the future.

Achieving social justice will not happen overnight. Perhaps true social justice will not happen in our lifetimes. Does this mean we should assume it is futile to try to achieve it? The worst thing we can do is to assume that the problem is too big for us to fix.

Collective Movement and Hurricane Katrina: Activism and Agitation

In a post-Katrina U.S., residents of the Gulf Coast region are constantly reminded of the ways in which the cumulative effects of racism and classism have intersected to perpetuate disaster. This volume has clearly demonstrated that the hurricanes that struck the southern United States bore down upon communities that were especially socially vulnerable, a concept defined in Chapter 2 and substantiated by numerous additional chapters, and as such their chances of withstanding the physical and social pressures wrought by the hurricanes in the region were diminished significantly. Nevertheless, this is not only a story of pain, it is also one of resilience, as community members have come together in an effort to create changes that will do more than merely exert additional social control on their communities, but will generate changes of a more meaningful sort. The work of these organizations points to the *social* element of social justice efforts that some individuals in the United States are loathe to recognize because of the widespread emphasis on individualism and the myth of a neutral meritocracy that permeates mainstream thought. These community collectives are bringing people together to recognize their common experiences, and to make a connection between individual pain and socially structured outcomes. In many cases, these groups consist of people whose lives exist at both the figurative and literal crossroads of where physical and social disasters have intersected. They assert their voices in an effort to open up the public dialogue—to insert their vernacular voices as Foster described it in Chapter 16 so to speak—so that change can be organically generated by the communities most impacted by longstanding injustices.

As outlined in the third section of this book, *Images of the Future: Policy, Activism, and Justice,* a wide range of social activist groups are moving forward and attempting to create a new world out of the debris of the disaster. These activists come from all walks of life and range from hip-hop enthusiasts, to public housing advocates, to education experts, and in all cases they have lit the spark of creativity and imagination in order to create positive change. This is the core element of *activism*, the simple act of taking a stance in the name of change. These groups are reinvigorating longstanding social justice movements—the civil rights movement, the labor movement, and the environmental justice movements, to name a few (Swan, Chapter 5)—and have inspired many who are not from the affected region to contribute to their causes.

The Backbeat Fund, S.O.S. (Saving Ourselves), the Southern Empowerment Project, Community Labor United (CLU), the Federation of Southern Land Cooperatives, the Louisiana Environmental Network, the Louisiana Welfare Rights Organization, and the Malcolm X Grassroots Movement are but some of the many organizations that have been working to draw attention to the complexities of the current injustices being experienced in the Gulf Coast region (see May First Foundation, 2005; Ms. Foundation for Women, 2006). One such activist group in New Orleans, known as Common Ground, is an example of a community group that has been successful in its attempts to gain such attention. Their mission, embodied by the statement, "Solidarity, not charity," is geared at addressing the immediate survival needs of the community in the aftermath of crisis, as well as its long-term needs. In the years following Hurricane Katrina, Common Ground members have committed themselves to helping residents of the most marginalized areas of New Orleans try to bounce back from the hurricane and they stand fast as a group against racism, sexism, and all forms of oppression (Common Ground Collective, 2007). Activist projects sponsored by the collective range from a campaign for clean water in communities such as the Lower Ninth Ward, assistance in the gutting of homes, bioremediation projects geared at cleaning up the toxins in the environment in a healthy way, and the creation of health clinics, a free legal clinic, and a women's shelter (Common Ground Collective, 2009).

Conclusion

Although the work of community activists provides much evidence for hope that the lessons of Katrina will not be forgotten, this volume has pointed out that long-term, sustained involvement by the public sector is vital to a recovery of the affected region and prevention of future disaster situations. In order to both effectively communicate crisis and risk messages (Lachlan et al., Chapter 12) and to garner sufficient monetary resources to martial against other sorts of predicted and unpredicted disasters, the public sector must be fully engaged in the process (Stillman & Villmoare, Chapter 19). Prevention of social disasters in the future requires the United States government to develop and implement sound environmental and social policies.

The next hurricane WILL happen and the question is: what will we as a community have done to prepare ourselves for that disaster? Will we have embraced privatization as the answer, leaving the state or public sphere bearing none of the responsibility for the good of the group? Will we continue to propagate "punishment spending" at the expense of "social spending," leaving us with only one response to these disasters—to treat everything as an issue of social control?

Or will we recognize that social justice is the touchstone of a civil society and that "responsibility" should be shared by individuals and the state alike? We believe one of the responsibilities of individuals is to advocate for a government that does not shift the risk of disaster to individuals, but instead, plans and prepares for the inevitability of the next disaster with collective responsibility as its core philosophy. If we are to pay heed to the voices and experiences of those affected by the hurricane, we must realize that justice efforts must demand the sustained involvement of the entire society in order for them to have true staying power; to do otherwise is to contribute to the perpetuation of social injustice and social disasters.

References

Bensonsmith, D. (2009). *Lacking legitimacy: Race, gender and the social construction of African American women in welfare policy 1935–2006*. Dissertation Abstracts International, A: The Humanities and Social Sciences, 69(8), 3297.

Bernstein, J. (2006). *All together now: Common sense for a fair economy*. San Francisco: Berrett-Koehler Publishers, Inc.

Branch, T. (1988). *Parting the waters: America in the King years 1954–1963*. Simon & Schuster Adult Publishing Group.

Common Ground Collective. (2007). Website. Retrieved February 20, 2007 from http://www.commongroundrelief.org/.

Common Ground Collective. (2009). History. Retrieved September 11, 2009 from http://www. commongroundrelief.org/?q=node/25.

Frericks, P., Maier, R., & de Graaf, W. (2009). Toward a neoliberal Europe? Pension reforms and transformed citizenship. *Administration & Society,* 41, 135–157.

Gragg, R. (2007, Feb. 22). Personal correspondence with Federal Policy Director of the Workforce Alliance.

Hacker, J. (2006). *The great risk shift: The assault on American jobs, families, health care, and retirement—and how you can fight back*. Oxford: Oxford University Press.

Katz, M. (1986.) *In the shadow of the poorhouse: A social history of welfare in America*. New York: Basic Books.

Kauzlarich, R., & Kramer, R. (1998). *Crimes of the American nuclear state: At home and abroad.* Boston: Northeastern University Press.

May First Foundation. (2005, Nov. 17). Grassroots/low-income/people of color-led Hurricane Katrina relief. Retrieved on February 10, 2007 from http://katrina.mayfirst.org.

Meranze, M. (2009, Aug. 24). California's crisis: Coming to a neighborhood near you. *The Huffington Post.* Retrieved Sept 15, 2009 from http://www. huffingtonpost.com/michael-meranze/californias-crisis-coming_b_267461.html.

Mitchell, K. (2001). Transnationalism, neo-liberalism, and the rise of the shadow state. *Economy and Society,* 30(2), 165–189.

Ms. Foundation for Women. (2006, Aug. 28). Our work: Stories of women's hope, activism and leadership across the Gulf Coast. Retrieved Feb. 20, 2007 from http://www.ms.foundation.org/wmspage.cfm?parm1=375.

Mudge, S. (2008). The state of the art: What is neo-liberalism? *Socio-Economic Review,* 6, 703–731.

Steensland, B. (2006). Cultural categories and the American welfare state: The case of guaranteed income policy. *American Journal of Sociology,* 111 (5), 1273–1326.

Turk, A. (1976). Law as a weapon in social conflict. *Social Problems,* 23 (3), 276–291.

About the Authors

Karen Adams is Professor of English and former director of the Program for Southeast Asian Studies at Arizona State University. Her research focuses on language planning and language rights; she also has a long-term interest in the linguistic construction of opposition. She has written several books and articles about language rights and discourse strategies in politics and popular culture.

Shana Agid is a visual artist, activist, and cultural critic. He holds an MFA in Printmaking and an MA in Visual Criticism, from California College of the Arts. Her work challenges ideas of race, gender, and sexuality in the post-Civil Rights Era United States, and reflects an investment in building new language to address new ideas and possibilities for undoing relationships of power in the 21st century. Shana's visual art has been shown at The New York Center for Book Arts and Southern Exposure and he has been published in FLOW (flowtv.org) and Clamor Magazine. She has given talks on transgender representation and deconstructing "hate crime" in queer politics at the Center for Lesbian and Gay Studies at the City University of New York, Yale University, and Oberlin College. Shana is also a long-time member of Critical Resistance, a grassroots organization fighting the use of the prison industrial complex to address social problems.

Rukhsana Ahmed is an Assistant Professor in the Department of International Relations at the University of Dhaka, Bangladesh. She is currently on leave completing her Ph.D. in Communication Studies at Ohio University. Her work has appeared in such outlets as *BIISS Journal, Journal of International Relations*, and *Identity, Culture and Politics*. She is currently exploring the relationships between and among culture and health.

Christopher Airriess received his Ph.D. in Geography from the University of Kentucky in 1989 and is currently Professor of Geography at Ball State University. His research interests include Asian American ethnic geographies and the development geographies of East and Southeast Asia. Chris has conducted research in the New Orleans Vietnamese American community since the early 1990s.

John Arena earned his Ph.D. in the Department of Sociology at Tulane University. His dissertation, entitled, *Bringing the Black Working Class Into Urban Change: Race, Class and Gendered Challenges to Neoliberalism*, is a historical, in-depth case study of the racialized and gendered class struggle over New Orleans' St. Thomas public housing development. John is also a long time community and labor activist in New Orleans. He is currently an active member in the anti-war/pro-public housing group C3/Hands Off Iberville, which is currently organizing for an economically and racially just reconstruction of New Orleans.

Benjamin R. Bates (Ph.D., University of Georgia) is an Associate Professor in the School of Communication Studies at Ohio University. His work has appeared in such outlets as Quarterly Journal of Speech, Social Science & Medicine, and Public Understanding of Science. He is working on several initiatives to expand health access and health awareness in underserved communities in Appalachia.

Kristin A. Bates is an Associate Professor of Sociology and Criminology & Justice Studies at California State University, San Marcos. She earned her Ph.D. and MA in Sociology from the University of Washington and a B.A. in Sociology and Economics from Pacific Lutheran University. Her research interests are the experiences of racial and ethnic minorities in systems of social control, social justice and pedagogy, and technology and pedagogy.

Terence Check is an Associate Professor of Communication at St. John's University and the College of St. Benedict in Minnesota. Dr. Check has presented scholarship on rhetoric and public address to the National Communication Association, the Alta Conference on Argumentation, and the Conference on Communication and the Environment.

Angela Chia-Chen Chen is a trilingual psychiatric/mental health nurse practitioner and researcher. Dr. Chen's research interests primarily focus on mental health and behavioral issues of vulnerable populations, particularly immigrants and ethnic minority youth. Dr. Chen is currently a principal investigator of three extramural funded studies.

Emmanuel David received his Ph.D. in Sociology from the University of Colorado at Boulder. His research and teaching interests include the sociology of gender, culture, and inequality. He is an Assistant Professor of Sociology at Villanova University and has conducted ethnographic fieldwork on gender, culture, and postcolonial identity formation.

Ashley ("Woody") Doane is Associate Dean for Academic Administration, Chair of the Department of Social Sciences, and Professor of Sociology at the University of Hartford. He has taught courses on race and ethnic relations for over 15 years. Woody is co-editor (with Eduardo Bonilla-Silva) of *White Out: The Continuing Significance of Racism* (Routledge, 2003) and has written numerous articles and book chapters about whiteness, dominant group ethnicity, and public dialogues on race. One of his most recent publication is "The Changing Politics of Color-Blind Racism" (*Research in Race and Ethnic Relations*, Volume 14, 2007). Woody is a past president of the Association for Humanist Sociology and is past Chair of the American Sociological Association's Section on Racial and Ethnic Minorities.

Noah D. Drezner is an Assistant Professor of Higher Education at the University of Maryland. He earned his Ph.D. in Higher Education in the Policy, Management, and Evaluation Division at the University of Pennsylvania Graduate School of Education in Philadelphia, Pennsylvania. He also holds degrees from the University of Rochester (B.S.) and the University of Pennsylvania (M.S.Ed.). His research interests include philanthropy within minority and special serving institutions and the exploration of how minority-serving institutions add to the civic literacy of the nation. Recently, Mr. Drezner published "Thurgood Marshall: A study of philanthropy through racial uplift" in an edited volume *Uplifting a People: African American Philanthropy and Education* by Marybeth Gasman and Katherine V. Sedgwick (Peter Lang, 2005; winner of the Association for Fundraising Professional's Skystone Ryan Prize for Research on Fundraising and Philanthropy) and "Advancing Gallaudet: Alumni Support for the Nation's University for the Deaf and Hard-of-Hearing and its Similarities to Black Colleges and Universities" in the *International Journal of Educational Advancement*.

Christine Eith (Ph.D., University of Delaware, 2003) is an Assistant Professor in the Department of Sociology, Anthropology, & Criminal Justice at Towson University. Her research interests include juvenile delinquency, race and school bonding, and adolescent drug and alcohol abuse. She recently published the text *Delinquency, Schools, and the Social Bond*.

Kelly Fawcett graduated *magna cum laude* from Oregon State University and is currently a graduate student at Washington State University where she is studying inequality and environmental sociology.

Lisa Foster (Ph.D. 2006, University of Texas, Austin) is an Assistant Professor of Mass and Political Communication in the Department of Communication Studies at the University of Oklahoma. Her research investigates moments of civic deliberation and dissent in popular culture, focusing on rhetorics of nationalism, argumentation, and theories of the public sphere.

Marybeth Gasman (Ph.D., Indiana University) is an Associate Professor of Higher Education at the University of Pennsylvania. Her work explores issues pertaining to the history of philanthropy and historically black colleges, black leadership, contemporary fundraising issues at black colleges, and African-American giving. Dr. Gasman's has published several books, including *Charles S. Johnson: Leadership beyond the Veil in the Age of Jim Crow*, *Supporting Alma Mater: Successful Strategies for Securing Funds from Black College Alumni*, and *Uplifting a People: African American Philanthropy and Education*. In addition to these works, Dr. Gasman recently finished a book entitled *Envisioning Black Colleges: A History of the United Negro College Fund*. She is also currently co-editing a book entitled *Understanding Minority Serving Institutions*.

Anthony Hurst earned a Ph.D. in Communication from the University of Iowa, an M.A. in Communication from the University of Montana, and a B.A. in Public Relations from Northern Iowa. The relationship between communication and image, as well as the examination of the development and maintenance of cultural health beliefs and practices in the United States, constitute two topics of his research that fall under the general umbrella of audience/lay interpretations and understandings of public discourse.

Michelle Inderbitzin received her Ph.D. from the University of Washington and is currently an Associate Professor in the Department of Sociology at Oregon State University. Her current research focuses on juvenile corrections, prison culture, and inmates' transitions into and out of institutions, including efforts at reintegration into the community.

Verna M. Keith is Professor of Sociology at Florida State University. Dr. Keith is a medical sociologist with additional training in public health. A major part of her research focuses on how race/ethnicity, social class, and gender stratification are related to mental health and access to health care. She has authored and co-authored articles and book chapters on gender differences in the effects of chronic stressors on depressive symptoms; racism and psychological distress; the effects of skin tone on status attainment and self concept among African Americans.

Alexander Keyssar is the Stirling Professor of History and Social Policy at the Kennedy School of Government at Harvard University. He received his Ph.D. in the History of American Civilization at Harvard and has also taught at Brandeis University, Duke University, and the Massachusetts Institute of Technology. His 1986 book, *Out of Work: the First Century of Unemployment in Massachusetts*, was awarded several scholarly prizes, including the Frederick Jackson Turner Award of the Organization of American Historians; it was also named a Notable Book of the Year by the New York Times. In 2000, he published *The Right to Vote: the Contested History of Democracy in the United States*, which received the Beveridge Prize from the American Historical Association and was a finalist for the Pulitzer Prize, the LA Times Book Award, and the Francis Parkman Prize. He is a co-author of *Inventing America: A History of the United States* and has written widely on public policy issues in the popular press.

Kim Knowles-Yánez is Associate Professor of Urban and Regional Planning in the Liberal Studies Department at California State University San Marcos. Her research focuses on community planning and participation. She is currently at work on several research projects: one examines the implementation of community action research with children and another examines anti-immigrant city policies.

Kenneth Lachlan (Ph.D., Michigan State University, 2003) is an Associate Professor of Communication and Director of the Communication Studies Program at the University of Massachusetts Boston. His research interests include the psychological processing of both linear and interactive media, crisis communication, and media effects. Recent research has been published in *American Journal of Public Health, Journal of Broadcasting and Electronic Media, Human Communication Research,* and *Journal of Applied Communication Research.*

David J. Leonard is an Associate Professor in the Department of Comparative Ethnic Studies at Washington State University. He has written on sports, video games, film, and social movements, appearing in both popular and academic mediums. He has recently completed an edited volume on sports films, set to be published in 2006 from Peter Lang Publishers, with another examining race and the NBA scheduled for early 2007 (SUNY Press). His work has appeared in *Journal of Sport and Social Issues, Cultural Studies: Critical Methodologies, Game and Culture,* as well as several anthologies including *Handbook of Sports and Media and Capitalizing on Sport: America, Democracy and Everyday Life.*

Karen Leong currently is an Associate Professor of Women and Gender Studies and Asian Pacific American Studies at Arizona State University. Her research addresses the intersections of race, gender, and class in the United States. Her publications focus on the experiences of Asian American individuals and communities, and how these experiences are shaped by U.S.-Asia relations, cultural productions, and national ideologies.

Wei Li received her Ph.D. in geography, and currently is an Associate Professor in the Arizona State University. Her research foci are immigration and integration, and financial sector and community development. She coined the term "ethnoburb" to describe some contemporary suburban minority and immigrant settlements, and conducts empirical studies in the Pacific Rim.

DeMond S. Miller, Ph.D. is a Professor of Sociology and director of the Liberal Arts and Sciences Institute for Research and Community Service at Rowan University (Glassboro, New Jersey). He has worked as an evaluator for alcohol and tobacco social norms projects and as principal investigator to facilitate research projects involving: environmental issues and community satisfaction. His primary area of specialization is environmental sociology, disaster studies, the study of the social construction of place, community development, and social impact assessment. Dr. Miller has presented and published several professional papers; recent examples of such work can be found in: *The Researcher, The Qualitative Report, The Journal of Emotional Abuse, Space and Culture: An International Journal of Social Spaces, International Journal of the Humanities, Journal of Black Studies, The Journal for the Study of Radicalism, The Journal of Public Management and Social Policy,* and *The Southeastern Sociological Review.*

Dreama Moon is a Professor of Communication at California State University San Marcos. She holds a Ph.D. in Communication from Arizona State University, an M.A. in Human Relations and Organizational Development, and a B.A. in Criminal Justice. In her scholarly work, she is interested in the social construction of domination and the ways in which both dominant and non-dominant group members negotiate, acquiesce to, and oppose domination. Her research broadly focuses on how ideologies of domination, such as white supremacy, classism, and sexism, are reproduced in and by communication as well as how they are contested, disrupted, and resisted.

Jason David Rivera earned a Master's in Public Administration from Rutgers University. He has recently worked on research dealing with public policy in reference to disaster mitigation and relief, social justice in the face of disasters, the reconfiguration of landscapes and their affect on local and global politics, as well as research pertaining to improving university and community relations. Examples of Jason's research can be found in *The Journal of Public Management and Social Policy, Space and Culture: An International Journal of Social Spaces, Journal of Black Studies, The Journal for the Study of Radicalism,* and *International Journal of the Humanities.*

Patric R. Spence (Ph.D, Wayne State University, 2005) is Assistant Professor in the School of Communication at Western Michigan University. His research focuses on crisis, risk and health communication, in addition to research methods. His work has appeared in the *Journal of Applied Communication Research, Communication Research Reports* and the *Journal of Modern Applied Statistical Methods.*

Peter G. Stillman, Professor of Political Science at Vassar College, teaches modern political theory from the Renaissance through the present. He has also taught in the Environmental Studies Program and the American Culture Program. In his research he pursues especially issues of freedom, justice, and the relation of the individual to the community in Hegel's political philosophy, Marx's political theory, utopian thought, and environmental issues.

Richelle S. Swan (Ph.D. University of California, Irvine) is Associate Professor of Sociology and Criminology & Justice Studies at California State University, San Marcos. Her research interests include the topics of social justice movements, restorative and transformative justice, and critical socio-legal studies. Her recent work has examined issues of framing and collective identification in the restorative justice movement, the development of problem-solving courts in the United States, and the development of welfare fraud diversion programs aimed at reducing the criminalization of low-income and working-class women.

Hannibal Travis teaches and researches in the fields of human rights law, technology law, and legal theory. He graduated *summa cum laude* in philosophy from Washington University, where he was named to Phi Beta Kappa. He graduated *magna cum laude* from Harvard Law School. His published works include law review articles in the areas of human rights, freedom of speech, and intellectual property, including "'Native Christians Massacred': The Ottoman Genocide of the Assyrians During World War I," *Genocide Studies and Prevention: An International Journal* 1(3) (2006), "Google Book Search and Fair Use:

iTunes for Authors, or Napster for Books?," *Miami Law Review* 33 (2006), and "Freedom or Theocracy? Constitutionalism in Afghanistan and Iraq," *Northwestern University Journal of International Human Rights* 3(4) (2005).

Nicole Trujillo-Pagán, Ph.D., is a second-generation Puerto Rican-Mexican immigrant. She has over ten years experience researching Latino/a health in the United States in both academic and not-for-profit research settings. She earned her Ph.D. in sociology from the University of Michigan-Ann Arbor. Her research interests include race, work, and health. Her current research focuses on occupational risk among Latino/a immigrants and race relations between Latino/as and African Americans. She is currently an Assistant Professor in the Center for Chicano-Boricua Studies and the Department of Sociology at Wayne State University.

Christopher Uggen is Distinguished McKnight Professor and Chair of Sociology at the University of Minnesota. He studies crime, law, and deviance, especially how former prisoners manage to put their lives back together. With Jeff Manza, he is the author of *Locked Out: Felon Disenfranchisement and American Democracy* (2006, Oxford University Press). His other research, teaching, and advising interests include crime and drug use, discrimination and inequality, and sexual harassment. Chris is currently executive secretary of the American Society of Criminology, chair of his department, and co-editor of *Contexts* magazine.

Adelaide H. Villmoare, Professor of Political Science at Vassar College, teaches about U.S. politics with a particular interest in citizenship and democracy, the politics of public and private, law, justice and politics, and media and politics. She has taught in the American Culture Program at Vassar on trials, culture and killing, and meanings of citizenship. Her research addresses the politics of rights, feminism and rights, the death penalty, and public and private policing.

Ying Wang received her M.P.P. in Public Policy at Arizona State University in 2006. She has written several reports on health policy in China.

Jeannie Haubert Weil is an Assistant Professor of Sociology at Winthrop University. She earned her Ph.D. in Sociology from Tulane University. She studies racial and ethnic relations, social stratification and inequality, and immigration. Her most recent research involves an analysis of attitudes towards immigrants published in the fall 2006 issue of *International Migration Review*, an analysis of neoliberalism and revitalization in Louisiana published in the 2007 volume, *Urban Communication: Production, Text and Context,* and an ongoing study of Latino migrants and housing on the Mississippi Gulf Coast.

Index